June 12, 2009

SKIDMARKS

Along the Highway of Life

BY HOMER J. OLSEN

TABLE OF CONTENTS

Foreword *1*

1. The Early Years 3

2. The Depression Years. 29

3. The World War II Years 109

4. The College Years 203

5. The Kiewit Years 253

6. The HJO Years. 367

7. The Retirement Years. 485

Just a Few Ole, Lena and Lars Jokes 524

Cover design by Vanessa Perez
Interior design by Vanessa Perez

ISBN 978-0-7998946-1-4

Printed in Canada

Published by Curtis Intl/Books Beyond Borders
P.O. Box 18696, South Lake Tahoe, CA 96151
info@1BestTTT.com

FOREWORD

These Memoirs and Autobiography of and by an inexperienced author were written with the hope they will be of interest to everyone who reads them, but were written mainly for the enjoyment and entertainment of my own family. It is because of their love and encouragement, and as a gift to them, I promised to take on the monumental task of recording the history of my life, as I remember it. Over the years I have often commented to my own children how sorry I was that my parents, and particularly my grandparents, never recorded their own life stories as they were told to me when I was a child. I know I will always cherish those wonderful "Fishing on the North Sea" stories, and others my Norwegian grandfather told me during my most formative *wonder years* growing up on their farm. As I enter my eighties with the knowledge I now have emphysema and glaucoma, it is time I stop procrastinating and live up to the promise I made to my family to record these memories of the wonderful life I have experienced. Readers are advised the memories recorded here, beginning with my own childhood on through my senior years, are through my eyes and my ears only, and may or may not agree in total with the memories others may have of the same occurrence.

I wish to thank and dedicate these memoirs to my wonderful wife, Alice Joyce Deyoe-Olsen, and to my two beautiful daughters, Mary Elizabeth Olsen-Kelly and Barbara Jean Olsen-Curtis, and to my son, Robert Kevin Olsen, for their loving support and patience, and invaluable advice, during my apprenticeship as an author. It was their love and encouragement during the writing of these memoirs that gave me '*the strength to carry on*' I needed to record the history of my life as I remember it. I also wish to thank my good friend and noted author, my WW II Army buddy, retired Colonel Dean E. Smith, not only for his professional editing review and advice, but for his timely support and encouragement to honor my commitment and finish writing the book I promised my family.

ANCESTORS OF
HOMER JUNIOR OLSEN

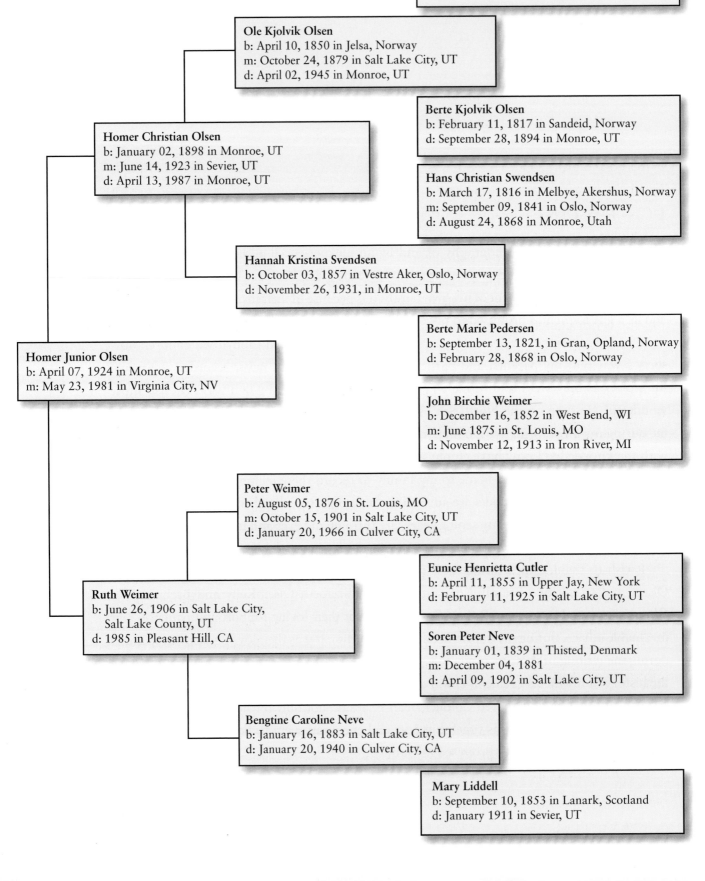

Ole Olsen
b: March 04, 1815 in Vikedal, Norway
m: November 01, 1844 in Jelsa, Norway
d: May 4, 1873 in Vintrevigen Kjolvik, Norway

Ole Kjolvik Olsen
b: April 10, 1850 in Jelsa, Norway
m: October 24, 1879 in Salt Lake City, UT
d: April 02, 1945 in Monroe, UT

Berte Kjolvik Olsen
b: February 11, 1817 in Sandeid, Norway
d: September 28, 1894 in Monroe, UT

Homer Christian Olsen
b: January 02, 1898 in Monroe, UT
m: June 14, 1923 in Sevier, UT
d: April 13, 1987 in Monroe, UT

Hans Christian Swendsen
b: March 17, 1816 in Melbye, Akershus, Norway
m: September 09, 1841 in Oslo, Norway
d: August 24, 1868 in Monroe, Utah

Hannah Kristina Svendsen
b: October 03, 1857 in Vestre Aker, Oslo, Norway
d: November 26, 1931, in Monroe, UT

Berte Marie Pedersen
b: September 13, 1821, in Gran, Opland, Norway
d: February 28, 1868 in Oslo, Norway

Homer Junior Olsen
b: April 07, 1924 in Monroe, UT
m: May 23, 1981 in Virginia City, NV

John Birchie Weimer
b: December 16, 1852 in West Bend, WI
m: June 1875 in St. Louis, MO
d: November 12, 1913 in Iron River, MI

Peter Weimer
b: August 05, 1876 in St. Louis, MO
m: October 15, 1901 in Salt Lake City, UT
d: January 20, 1966 in Culver City, CA

Eunice Henrietta Cutler
b: April 11, 1855 in Upper Jay, New York
d: February 11, 1925 in Salt Lake City, UT

Ruth Weimer
b: June 26, 1906 in Salt Lake City,
   Salt Lake County, UT
d: 1985 in Pleasant Hill, CA

Soren Peter Neve
b: January 01, 1839 in Thisted, Denmark
m: December 04, 1881
d: April 09, 1902 in Salt Lake City, UT

Bengtine Caroline Neve
b: January 16, 1883 in Salt Lake City, UT
d: January 20, 1940 in Culver City, CA

Mary Liddell
b: September 10, 1853 in Lanark, Scotland
d: January 1911 in Sevier, UT

THE EARLY YEARS

I was born April 7, 1924 in Monroe, Sevier County, Utah at a home owned by Randle Nielsen that my parents were renting at the time. My dad told me Dr. Hanks drove over for the occasion from Richfield in his Model "T" Ford to help my mother deliver me and that Grandma Olsen was the one who insisted I be named after my dad, namely Homer Christian Olsen Jr. My mother told me years later she always wanted to name me Robert Christian Olsen because she never liked the name, Homer, but Grandma had insisted on that name for me. Unfortunately, Dr. Hanks forgot my name after his return trip to Richfield and days later registered me as Homer Junior Olsen on my birth certificate at the County Court House. Needless to say, having a middle name like "Junior" from then on has been a source of great hilarity among all my friends and business associates ever since, but as my dad used to say, "If a man wants his son to be a fighter, he should

Homer J. Olsen - 1924

name him Sue, or better yet, *Junior*." My mother, Ruth Weimer, was two months shy of her eighteenth birthday when I was born, and my dad, Homer Christian Olsen, was eight years older than my mother

Mom & Dad - 1923

When Dad and my mother were first married, Dad was working as a cow hand for his older brother, Orson B. Olsen, on his cattle ranch near Marysvale, Utah. According to my dad, he thought everything was going along fine, but my mother felt his job had no future and besides, they should not live so close to Grandma Olsen, her mother-in-law, because of her constant meddling in their affairs. As her youngest son, Grandma Olsen was against my dad marrying my mother from the very beginning, or anyone else for that matter, because in the old country (Norway) the youngest son always had the responsibility of caring for their parents when they got old. From Grandma Olsen's point of view, my mother had ruined her retirement plan by marrying my dad and it had created an awkward situation for all concerned. So, to keep peace in the family, Dad quit his job on his brother's ranch and moved his little family (I was a year old at the time) to Magill, Nevada, where he got a job working in the mill for the Kennecott Copper Company. Dad told me everything began to look up for them right away because the company offered him the swing shift foreman's job shortly after he started and that meant a considerable raise in pay. From Dad's point of view, it was a blessing for a young couple starting out. The bad news was the job required he work a six day afternoon to midnight swing shift which, as it turned out, contributed greatly to the "beginning of the end" of my parents marriage.

My Mother, Ruth Weimer - 1929

My thoughts and comments on what might have occurred that brought about my parents divorce are based somewhat on speculation, but mostly on comments made to me over the years by my dad. My mother never talked much about what happened except to *cuss-out* my dad when the subject came up, so I never really heard her side of the story. All I know is, they were both extremely hurt and bitter towards each other for many years afterwards. Dad told me he received a party line telephone call at work late one night from their neighbor lady saying she had just found a year and a half old baby, complete with sleepers, loaded diaper and all, dragging a Teddy Bear by one leg and crying it's eyes out in front of her house. When she brought the baby into her home and recognized it was me, and found no one at

Homer J. Olsen - 1925

the home my parents were renting, she called my dad at work. Dad said I had apparently found a way to climb out of my crib and opened the front door somehow, and had waddled outside looking for my mother in the middle of the night.

Rodger Dean Sorensen Sr. - 1926

I've always felt my mother at seventeen was way too young and immature in many ways to have married my dad in the first place, and was still too immature at nineteen to be married when they lived in Nevada. I'm happy they did get married or I wouldn't be here now to tell my story of an "American Dream" fulfilled, but I can still visualize her becoming increasingly bored while cooped up at home alone, night after night while Dad was at work, with nothing more exciting to do than baby-sit a squalling brat. I think she finally reached the point where she questioned her marriage to Dad in the first place, and especially so after she met an exciting young cowboy bronco-buster from Idaho named R. D. Sorensen. She told me years later she never really loved my dad in the first place and only married him to get away from her parents. At any rate the facts are, she decided to start over again and abandoned both my dad and me, and ran off with this "Dashing Rodeo Bronco Buster from Idaho." No one I've ever talked to seems to remember when or where they first met.

Homer C. & Homer J. - 1927

Dad said he waited up for my mother that same night the neighbor lady found me, and when she finally staggered home he asked her, "Is this what you really want? When she answered "Yes, and I want out of our marriage", he quit his job, packed me and all our worldly possessions into his old car, and moved the two of us back to the family farm in Monroe, Utah. Several months later, my mother left her dashing wife beating cowboy, and came back to Monroe, badly beaten, battered and pregnant, begging Dad to take her back, but he refused. When Grandma Weimer, who was horrified and still angry with her daughter for what she had done, told the presiding judge she felt my mother was unfit to be a parent and the court awarded custody of me to my dad until I was twelve years old and I would decide which parent I would live with.

My mother was married and divorced a total of nine times (three times to the same man)

MAJOR NEWS RELEASE

June 28, 1919 Germany signs the Treaty of Versailles and in September, Adolph Hitler joins the German Workers Party. In 1920 the German Workers Party renames itself National Socialist German Workers Party, or NSDAP known to the World as the **Nazi Party**.

during her lifetime that I know of, although my dad claims it was more like thirteen times. My mother told me many years later, the only man she really loved of all her husbands, was R. D. Sorensen, but she couldn't take his beatings any longer, and left him. Looking back now at the way my younger half brother Rodger (R.D. Sorensen's son) was raised by my mother and all the problems he had growing up while living with her, that decision by the court to award custody of me to my dad (and my Norwegian immigrant grandparents), was the luckiest break I have ever had during my lifetime.

Homer C. Homer J. Olsen 1927

Although I have only slight recollections before the age of four, looking back now at those early years known as *The Roaring Twenties* is kind of interesting from a historical point of view. The Census Bureau lists the population of the United States as 105,710,620 people in 1920 that increased to 122,775,046 by 1930. In 1924, the year I was born, the average annual per capita income was $2,196, a new car cost $265, a loaf of bread was 9 cents, a gallon of gas cost 11 cents (and was still 11 cents in 1936), life expectancy was only 54 years and you could buy a new home for $7,720. Calvin Coolidge was our country's president for the most part during that period. "Cool Cal", as my dad called him, was sworn in as president in 1923 after President Warren G. Harding died and later was elected president with Charles Dawes as his vice president for the 1924 – 1928 term of office. It was in 1924 that J. Edgar Hoover became the first director of the newly organized FBI, our native-born Indians were granted full citizenship and a right to vote, a product called *Kleenex* was introduced, diesel electric locomotives went into service, a company called IBM was organized and a popular comic strip called *Little Orphan Annie* was first published.

NEWS RELEASE

November 9, 1923, In the Beer Hall Putsch, the Nazi Party attempts to take over the government of Bavaria. Hitler is arrested and sentenced to five years in jail. He only serves eight months during which he writes "Mien Kampf." In 1926, Hirohito takes the Japanese throne.

It was in 1926 that Henry Ford announced the unheard of 8-hour day, 5-day work week, slide fasteners called *Zippers* were marketed for the first time, Gene Tunney whipped Jack Dempsey and Rudolph Valentino, the heart throb of all the women then, died. In 1927 Henry Ford introduced his first Model "A" Ford after turning out fifteen million versions of the Model "T" and Babe Ruth hit his 60th home run in 154 games. On the minus side, gangland murders in Chicago connected with bootleg liquor trafficking and crime in general, was escalating at an alarming rate and in 1925 Al Capone took over as boss of the Chicago bootleggers. By 1926 the prohibition laws had single handedly created a $3.6 billion illegal liquor business. Lucky Strike and Chesterfield also began their ad campaign that same year to encourage women the *in thing* was to smoke cigarettes, and as we know now it was a very successful advertising campaign and the women fell for it like a hog for slop.

Jr, Rodger, GW & Ted - 1928

I dimly recall only one exciting event before I was five, and that was when I was four years old and my dad made me really mad by laughing at Santa Claus when he made his entrance at a children's Christmas party at the church, and I waded into him with fists flying to teach him a lesson. As I recall the city of Monroe had a portly banker named Grant Ridd who volunteered to be Santa Claus that year because everyone thought he looked a lot like Santa. Well, believe it or not, Grant agreed to make a spectacular *rope slide entry* from the church steeple's belfry tower carrying a full bag of toys, figuring he could easily grip-brake to a soft stage landing below with the

"Yunior", Betty and Rodger - 1929

rope. You guessed it, he unfortunately made an error in calculating his own strength to weight ratio and soon discovered his own weight, plus the weight of a full bag of toys, was just too much for his banker hands to grip-brake his descent successfully. Oooh boy, I'll kid you not from any way you looked at it, his over confident entrance coupled with the earth shattering landing that followed was unforgettable. When Grant made his church belfry entrance **Ho Ho Hoing** loudly and began waving to his young appreciative audience below, we kids, unaware we were about to witness history in the making, began screaming hysterically while watching him sashay confidently over to grasp the bell rope. Whooee, you guessed it again. Grant step launched into space and immediately hurtled towards earth like a burning meteorite and made the most fantastic crippling crash landing ever witnessed by man and/or child. He not only burned the hide off both his hands in a frantic attempt to slow his descent, but painfully sprained both his ankles when he crashed into the stage deck below. To make matters even worse, instead of trying to help poor Santa lying painfully flat on his back *ho ho hoing* weakly, my dad

Yunior & the Green Hornet - 1929

busted out laughing so hard he couldn't move when I thought he should be showing some class and helping poor Santa deliver his toys. Like anyone else would have done, I blew my stack over his embarrassing shenanigans and waded into him with fists flying like a buzz saw, to teach him a lesson. But, as Dad used to say, "All that may be true, but on the other hand she had warts". So in retrospect, when you think about it hard enough from his point of view, it was kind of funny.

In 1928, Dad and I were living with Grandpa and Grandma Olsen on their farm named *Gravelbed*, that was located about three miles west of Monroe in a dairy farming area called Brooklyn. My dad and my grandparents had given me a pretty green pedal car for a combination Xmas and birthday present that year and I still remember trying to protect it from being smashed to smithereens with a sledge hammer by my jealous cousin, Neil Olsen. He was one of Uncle Joe's ten children that was jealous of me because I was my dad's only rotten spoiled brat and I had a pedal car and he didn't, resulting in my first fistfight. Neil was two years older and bigger than I was so I lost the fight, but the good news was, I saved my car.

During those early years, I still remember following my dad around like a pup, except when he was on the high mountain summer range above Marysvale or on the desert winter range near Pine Valley, Nevada, with the sheep. When that happened, I would shadow Grandpa Olsen around everywhere he went, constantly asking questions while helping him with his chores and his maintenance jobs in the blacksmith shop. According to my dad, I nearly drove him nuts with my constant questioning about anything and everything, and his favorite reply when I suspect he really didn't know the answer was, "I'm busy; go ask your Grandma and Grandpa." I remember I asked Grandpa Olsen one time, "Why is the sky blue, Grandpa?" He said he asked his own Far Far (Grandfather) that same question when he was a little boy in Norway, and his Far Far's *obviously correct* answer was, "It is just a reflection of the blue water North Sea, up in the sky." I will never forget the stunned look on his face when I said, "But Grandpa, we live in the Rocky Mountains." I remember he picked up a stick and sat down quietly on the bench outside his blacksmith's shop, and began whittling on it with his pocket knife. Finally he looked over at me and said. "Jeg tink jeg vill have to study some more on that vestchon."

Ole K. & Hannah K. Olsen - 1879

Grandma Olsen 1875, age 18

My memories of the few short years I knew Grandma Olsen (Hannah Kristina Swensen – Olsen) were very happy ones. I think she was typical of the pioneer women of her day in that she was a kind, generous and loving human being, but she was also a no nonsense person and a pillar of strength when it came to important matters. From my point of view, she was the heart and soul of our family because she was the only mother I knew for the first seven and most formative years of my life. I remember she was desperately afraid a minor cold might turn into pneumonia if left unattended because she had suffered the loss of two of her daughters when they were nine and eighteen years old, from that dreaded sickness. I remember every time I caught a cold, she would sit up with me all night, wrapping warm woolen stockings soaked in Vick's Vapo-Rub around my neck, putting mustard plasters on my chest and giving me spoonfuls of hot toddy and cough medicine, until I was well again. It was during that terrible drought year and cold winter of 1931; she caught pneumonia herself, and passed away shortly after we had celebrated her 74th Birthday on the first of October.

Jr. in Far Mor's homemade suit - 1928

Before Grandma died, my job assignments were to keep the wood box on the back porch full, help her gather eggs and feed the chickens and turkeys, and help her weed and take care of her vegetable and flower gardens. Later on, I was also given the responsibility of feeding the calves and lambs for Grandpa and herding the milk cows on the ditch bank along the county road. Once a week I got to ride to town with Grandma in her one-horse buggy, to trade her chicken eggs for groceries. On those fun trips, she always gave me two eggs to hold and trade for one candy "all-day sucker" because we traded our eggs for six cents a dozen, and an all-day sucker cost one cent. I still remember wishing the price of eggs would go up to a penny apiece someday so I wouldn't have to worry so much about breaking one of my eggs before they were traded.

Jr, Tex & little Spun - 1928

Grandma never wore glasses, but I discovered her eyesight wasn't up to par when I climbed a tree near the farmhouse one time, and was perched on a limb eating a green apple while she was walking around underneath calling me to come for our noon "dinner." I kept repeating, "Here I am, Grandma, up here" and finally, squinting up at me, she said in her Norwegian accent, "Oh for heavens sake, I thought you were a turkey roosting up there." She scolded me to not climb trees anymore and told Grandpa at dinner, who looked over at me and winked, to spank me if I did. I remember my cousin, Wayne Olsen, recalled in a letter to me from England during WWII of when we were kids and Grandma Olsen chased us down the county road swatting our

Spun, Tex & Yunior - 1928

behinds with a sunflower stalk for climbing her cherry tree. I still remember climbing that same tree to reach some ripe cherries another time, and the limb suddenly snapped, but luckily I landed on top of the limb when it hit the ground and wasn't hurt. When Grandma heard the crash, she ran out of her kitchen to where I was laying on the tree branch and, Oooh boy, I knew I was in for a spanking for climbing that tree, so I pretended I was *knocked out*. Grandma must have thought I was badly hurt when she first saw me because she screamed, picked my limp little body up in her arms, and began to cry. Wow, if they had given Academy Awards for *child acting* in those days, I

"Yunger" on Tex's Trycycle - 1929

know I would have won first prize. To maximize the impact of my act like the movies, I slowly came to from my comatose act and, as an added touch of class, threw in a Clara Bow movie close-up *fluttering eyelids* recovery. Grandma was so impressed, surprised, relieved, and amused by my latest act, she even forgot to tell Grandpa to give me a spanking.

"Yunior" and Rodger - 1929

Later that same year, I pulled the same Clara Bow *fluttering eyelids* act on my dad when we were on the summer mountain range herding sheep, but Oooh boy, this time it didn't work for sour owl you know what. Dad had a Winchester lever action 32-20 caliber rifle he always carried in his saddle scabbard for protection while riding his horse, and sometimes he even wore a really swell looking cartridge belt with a six-shooter on his hip like a real gun slinging cowboy. I remember thinking at the time, Wow, what a good idea to have a rifle and six-shooter that would fire the same 32-20 cartridge. I asked my dad one time if I could shoot his six-shooter and you guessed it, he gave me strict orders, *"Don't you ever, and I mean ever, even think about touching that gun."*

I remember Dad rode off on his horse to check the sheep herd without his six-shooter one time while I was in camp alone, and for no other reason than curiosity and orneriness, I pulled that huge six gun out of its holster (it took both hands to lift it), aimed at a chipmunk, and fired. I missed the chipmunk a mile, but Oooh boy, the gun shot sound from that six-shooter traveled up and down the canyon like a thunderclap and when Dad came racing back on his horse to check what happened, I pulled my famous *pretend to be dead,* followed by my famous Clara Bow *coming to with the fluttering eyelids,* act on him. You guessed it, my act didn't work this time either and Whooee, how it didn't work. I'll kid you not, all hell suddenly

Nephi, Oluf, Orson, Bertha, Joseph, Homer
Ole K. and Hannah K. Olsen 1917

broke loose around there and to this day I still remember the blistering spanking my dad gave me for firing that six-shooter. I figured right then and there, now was a good time to get out of the acting business, once and for all, and start minding my dad (and grandparents) from then on.

Grandma Olsen was a wonderful cook. Our big meal for the day was always at noon and she would always go all out with her hot homemade bread and home churned butter and either pot roast, roast chicken or a pork roast, and some boiled potatoes you mashed with your fork and added milk gravy on top, a home bottled vegetable of some kind, and usually a home bottled fruit with her cake for dessert. Sometimes for our Sunday dinner, we would have her wonderful cake with home made hand cranked ice cream for dessert, that is, until the 4th of July and the north bend canal ice we buried the previous spring in our saw dust pile hadn't melted. Every once in awhile when she baked her homemade bread in her huge wood burning kitchen stove, Grandma would call me and my cousin Tex, or Ted or Wayne, or whoever else was over to play, into the kitchen and cut us crusts of bread the long way of the loaf, then put a thick layer of cream and brown sugar on it for us. I'll tell you, we kids thought we were in heaven, and I still *slobberate* when I think about how wonderful her treats were. Grandma never wasted anything, and she would always save any stale bread to make her wonderful bread pudding later.

Gravelbed Farm House - 1903

I also remember those exciting times when Billy Olson, the thresher man, would come to our farm with his crew and his huge iron tired tractor and machinery to thresh Grandpa's wheat. It was the custom in those days for the farmer's wife to feed the thresher crew their noon meal while they were working on their farm and I always helped Grandma set up the plank tables outdoors underneath the shade trees for the occasion. She would always prepare a wonderful meal for the men and this time for dessert, she made a frosted flat pan cake that she put at the end of the table for later serving. Wouldn't you know it, when it came time to pass the cake around for their dessert, the pan was empty. Well, as it turned out, and you can believe this or not, but one of the men in the crew my dad said was named Dick Barney, was sitting next to the cake and was either too bashful to ask for the other food

Haying Time - 1934

to be passed, or thought the cake was his dinner, and had eaten the whole thing by himself. When Grandma scolded Dick for eating everyone's dessert, he said, "Golly, Mrs. Olsen, I thought it was *sody bread*." I will never forget the shocked look on Grandma's face.

Grandma Olsen was the only one in our family who hung onto the *old country* ways. She would always sing those little Norwegian songs for me that I thought were so pretty, and having a real Norwegian Christmas every year was very important to her. I still fondly remember the Christmas porridge she called "Yule Grout" she prepared every Christmas Eve for everyone that was made from cooked rice with real cream and sprinkled with sugar and cinnamon on top. She would even decorate the Christmas tree in a special way by stringing red and green paper ropes all around it and hang candy canes and different sized red paper accordion bell shapes that unfolded into real looking Christmas bells. She even made mutton tallow candles to place in tree limb candle holders attached to the branches, that is until Grandpa finally convinced her they were fire hazards. We would then all hold hands and she and Grandpa and Dad would sing all those wonderful little *old country* songs in Norwegian, while we all danced around the tree. I remember Grandma insisted we all pray together before the evening meal to give thanks for our many blessings and the good fortune we enjoyed by living in this great land of freedom, the United States of America. She would have us turn our kitchen chairs around so the seats were facing towards us, then we would kneel on the hard kitchen floor with our hands clasped under our chins and elbows on the chair seats, while Grandma prayed in Norwegian. Unfortunately, I never learned to speak or read Norwegian then (or now) so to me it seemed like Grandma droned on and on and on for what seemed like hours until all I could think about was how badly my knees hurt kneeling on that hard kitchen floor and wondering if she would ever finish her prayer. I guess Grandpa (far far) and my dad (far) understood everything she said because when I would peek up at them to see if their knees hurt too, they never moved a muscle until Grandma finished her prayer.

I don't think Grandma ever approved of any of the *new fangled* gadgets that were being introduced commercially around that time because to her, things like indoor plumbing, electric lights and automobiles bordered on a waste of hard earned money. She still had her mother's spinning wheel sitting in the front room, but I never saw her use it because she finally, and reluctantly, decided buying knitting yarn from the store was much more practical than spinning the yarn herself, but maybe her failing eyesight was the main reason. I still remember to this day her refusing to ever ride in Dad's old chevy ever again after Elmer Wynn ran into us during a snowstorm and spun our car completely around while we driving home from church. Fortunately no one was hurt, but from then on Grandma only used her dependable *and much safer* one horse buggy for shopping errands to and from town.

I was raised exactly the same way my dad was raised during the early 1900's by his parents and I lived exactly the same way he did and my Grandpa and Grandma lived during the 1880's and 90's when they were first married. It wasn't until 1937 when I left Utah for good and moved to Nevada and then to California in 1942 to join the Army, my life changed. It was interesting to me that my own children couldn't believe I grew up in a home where we read by *coal-oil* (kerosene) lamps, hauled our drinking water from a neighbor's well in ten gallon milk cans, cooked our meals on a wood burning kitchen stove, used a wooden ice box as a refrigerator if ice was still available, and used Morgan work horses named old Ted and Patty to power all our farm equipment. They seemed shocked to learn our bathroom consisted of only an outdoor privy called a *"two holer"* and we only bathed once a week in a tin wash tub placed near the kitchen stove every Saturday, whether we needed to or not. To this day, I will never forget the stunned looks on my daughter's faces and the shocked remark they made when they first saw my *early years* home and corrals, *"Oh Dad, you were so poor."*

I knew we didn't have any money, but I never thought of us as *poor*. We survived the same way all the early pioneers did when they first settled in the western states, and like them we were not afraid of the hard work it would require to survive. In those *good old days* we were self-sufficient and everything we *really needed* to survive was hunted, handmade and homegrown.

Farm Field Work – 1937

While Grandma Olsen was still alive she made sure everything on the Gravelbed farm was in shipshape condition. Her home was always clean as a whistle and was never in need of paint, inside or out. Her vegetable and flower gardens wouldn't dare grow a weed, and she insisted Grandpa keep his corrals, milking shed, granary, horse stables, wagon shed, blacksmith shop, chicken and turkey coops, fruit orchard, and all his farm equipment in a well maintained condition. She also insisted the wire fences on the farm were kept in ship-shape condition to prevent their milk cows and sheep from breaking through and bloating in the alfalfa fields. All in all, Grandma would have been a fantastic top sergeant in the Army because none of us men, Grandpa, Dad or I, ever had

any spare time to waste and there was always something on her *honey do* list that needed our attention. The one luxury she always wanted and never had was a clean fresh water well near her home with a hand pump on her kitchen sink. I remember Grandpa hired a well digger by the name of, Doad Farmer to dig Grandma her well, but all old Doad found, stick witching and all, was damp sand after digging down 80 feet.

Grandma always bought her cough medicines, aspirin, mentholatum, castoria, castor oil, (oh, how I hated having to take a daily tablespoon of that nasty stuff) and

Grandma Olsen's Egg Money Bowl - 1890 to 1931

Grandpa's peppermints, from a traveling peddler called the *Raleigh Man*. Every month, the Raleigh Man would drive his coal black closed in one-horse buggy to the various farms in the valley to make sales and exchange gossip with all the farmer's wives. When he stopped at a farmhouse, the sides of his buggy would hinge up to expose a shelved, well stocked drug store, but later on he bought a black 1929 Model "A" Ford van (an early version SUV) that was equipped much like his buggy with the same hinged side display panels, but carried more supplies. I remember Grandma had a small blue and white glass bowl that had a lid on it shaped like a chicken sitting on a nest, where she kept all her "egg money" to buy things from the Raleigh Man. That same little bowl was willed to me by my dad's second wife, Ercel, after she passed away some sixty years later, and for some unknown reason that little treasure has a *time-tunneling* effect on me. Every time I look at that little egg-money bowl, I'm carried back to those same happy 1926 to 1932 years and my earliest recollections of my wonderful life on the

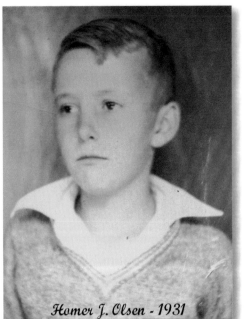

Homer J. Olsen - 1931

Gravelbed farm with my dad and my grandma and grandpa Olsen. It was while staring at that little egg-money bowl, I recalled most of these wonderful boyhood memories.

I was there visiting with Grandma Olsen the day before she passed away. I remember her being very sick with pneumonia and Aunt Bertha, her oldest and the only daughter still living of her three girls, was staying there with her. Grandma was sitting in her rocking chair in the living room by the big pot bellied wood burning stove, gently rocking on the rug with a big St Bernard dog woven in it, and Aunt Bertha was combing out her long black hair. I also remember being startled at the time by her long waist length black hair because I always saw her wearing it in a bun on the back of her head. She told me she felt a lot better that day and thought she would be up and around real soon, and then she gave me a big hug while telling me what a good little boy she thought I was. Then Aunt Bertha came over and shooed me out of the room saying she didn't want me to catch Grandma's cold, but she promised I could talk to my Grandma (meg far mor) again in the morning. That night, November 26, 1931, the

only mother I ever knew for my first seven and most formative years of my life, passed away quietly in her sleep. She was 74 years old.

My Dad was on the winter desert range between Milford and Garrison, Utah with the sheep herd at the time, so the next day I rode out to the range with Uncle Orson and one of Uncle Oluf's sons (I think it was Byron) to bring Dad back for Grandma's funeral. It took all day to drive over that bumpy dirt road in Uncle Orson's old car (a two hour drive today) so we stayed overnight in the sheep wagon that bitter cold night. The next day, the three of us drove back to Monroe, leaving Byron to tend the sheep. Grandma's passing was a devastating blow for everyone in the family, but Grandpa took it the hardest and was

Grandpa Ole Kjolvick Olsen @ age 90

both devastated and heartbroken. Grandma was not only the love of his life and the mother of their eight children, but was also his right arm, his business partner, and his best friend. She was always there to give him the support and the strength he needed to carry on. I don't think

Grandpa ever did anything without first discussing and agreeing on a course of action, with Grandma, and I'm sure he would have lost his will to live at his age of 81, if he hadn't felt his son, Homer C, and his grandson, Homer J., needing him now more than ever. He was right.

As with Grandma, I have so many happy memories of Grandpa Olsen. He was such a kind, generous, easy going old man with a wonderful sense of humor and was the perfect storybook Grandfather for a little boy. He always had the time, or took the time, to listen and talk about anything and everything I wanted to talk about, without being short or condescending. He would always go on with whatever he was doing while listening to me, but interestingly, would also ask me to help him with something while we talked. When he was fixing a wagon or making horseshoes or sharpening mower blades in his blacksmith shop, I would pump the forge blower to keep the coals red hot, or peddle his huge stone-sharpening-wheel while he sharpened mower blades and anything else that needed a sharp edge. There was never any free time on his stock-farm and Grandpa knew the only way a small farmer and stock rancher like himself, could make a go of it was by constantly working and maintaining his land, his livestock and his equipment. There was no doubt about it. *Gravelbed* was truly a working farm.

Vintravigen, Norway - 1973

Grandpa converted from the Lutheran Church to the Latter-Day Saints in Norway, and he and his mother and two sisters were sponsored to America by the Mormon Church in 1874. He said he sold *Vintravigen* (the family farm in Norway) for $200, which paid for his mother's and two sister's passage over, and he worked for his own passage as part of the ship's crew. I'm sure Grandpa felt he paid the church back for sponsoring all of them to America when he volunteered over a year's free labor to help build the Manti Temple for the Latter-

Ola Olsen - 1869

Day Saints. Grandpa was an master journeyman stonemason, blacksmith and carpenter, besides being a fisherman-farmer in Norway, so he did make a major contribution towards the building of the Manti temple. He told my dad one time when I was listening that he almost *seen the light* while working on the Manti temple because the building site was crawling with rattlesnakes the entire time they were working on the temple. In his Norwegian-accent he said, "Not one man working on that temple was ever bitten by a rattlesnake the whole time we were there."

When I took my stepmother, Ercel and my dad on our *100th year anniversary trip* in 1973, to visit Grandpa's *Vintravigen* (winter cove) farm in Norway, I learned for the first time that Grandpa's motivation to come to America was not only for opportunity and freedom, but also to find a man named

Lars Larsen who had gotten his older sister Marta pregnant and snuck off to America to keep from marrying her. Grandpa was determined to find Lars (Dad said his name was Lars; but my cousin, Halvor Olsen, insisted his real name was Ole) and force him, if necessary, to marry Marta

Grandpa Olsen - 1938

come hell or high water, and make Marta an honest woman. I'm also sure Grandpa's motivation and determination to find Lars (Ole) Larsen, came largely from the knowledge his own father was an illegitimate child, and having witnessed first hand all the shame and suffering his father went through, was reason enough to nail Lars. Grandpa's father (Ola Olsen) died at the age of 56 from a heart attack (although his genealogy said it was pneumonia) around the same time Marta announced she was pregnant out of wedlock. Although Grandpa was convinced Marta's shocking news contributed to his own father's death from a heart attack, my dad for some unknown reason, was not. The Mormon missionaries in Norway told Grandpa that Lars had suddenly "seen the light" and joined the LDS church when Marta coincidentally announced her pregnancy and was now living somewhere in northern Utah. So, when the missionaries offered to sponsor Grandpa and his mother, and two sisters to America, (who had joined the LDS Church

earlier according to Halvor) Grandpa suddenly seen a golden opportunity to find Lars and re-seen the light himself to become an even more dedicated Latter Day Saint. It was on our 1973 Norway trip that Dad finally admitted knowing all along (after our relatives told me this story) about this terrible family scandal and told me Grandpa did finally find Lars (Ole) Larsen holed up in Cache Valley, Utah, and sponsored a formal shotgun wedding (where everyone carried white shotguns) for the happy couple's wedding. He said Lars and Marta's little son named, Oluf was four years old at the time and was the ring bearer for his parents wedding.

I'm sure Grandpa was relieved to have the problem behind him and his sister was now an honest woman, and I'm sure Grandpa thought he was doing the right thing at the time. It's still interesting to me however, that Marta never forgave Grandpa for forcing her to marry Lars, even though she and Lars had five more children together after they were married. I remember Dad telling me he and Grandpa drove to northern Utah in Dad's old Essex to visit Marta in 1936, some sixty years after her shotgun wedding to Lars, to try and mend fences with her. Unbelievably, even though Lars was no longer living and Marta was in her ninety's at the time, she still wouldn't speak or even let Grandpa and my dad into her home. Marta went to her grave hating Grandpa for forcing her to marry someone she hadn't *chosen* herself, and in her mind, Grandpa ruined her life. She also stubbornly refused to ever join the Latter-Day Saints church and, as far as I know, was the only immigrant from Norway in our Olsen family who remained a Lutheran all her life.

I've often wondered since then if Grandpa at the age of 23 when he immigrated to America, would have left the Lutheran Church in the first place, and/or joined the Mormon Church in order to come to America, or would have even left Norway in the first place, if it had not been for Marta's pregnancy and his father's fatal heart attack. I also wonder where all of us would be now if he hadn't immigrated to America, and how little dramas of life like this can indirectly impact so many other lives later on, as we travel down our separate highways of life. To this day, over 135 years later, our relatives in Norway are still angry that Grandpa and his family left the Lutheran Church to join the Latter-Day Saints. Their attitude in 1973 when we were there was the same as many other churches. If you are born a Lutheran, you die a Lutheran.

Ole K. Olsen - 1938

I don't recall ever seeing Grandpa Olsen lose his temper except for four times, and two of those times were with two of his ornery old Holstein milk cows. As I recall, the first cow's name was *Tina*, and to this day I still remember seeing her kick Grandpa and his half filled milk bucket head over heels to land flat on his back, while he was sitting there milking her on his one legged stool. I'll kid you not, Grandpa really came unglued. He got up muttering a stream of well chosen Norwegian cuss words, brushed off his bib overalls, and stiff upper lip and all, quietly sat back down on his stool to stubbornly finish milking his cow named Tina. No one I've told this story believes what happened next, but when he finished milking, he stood up nonchalant like while eying the other suspiciously, *sashayed* up to Tina's head end and ---*poured the whole bucket of milk over her horns and face,* just to teach her a thing or two (his words), and stomped up to the farmhouse with his empty bucket. When Grandma saw him sitting in his kitchen chair near the wood stove still muttering to himself while sipping his boiled strong coffee, she asked, "What is it that's troubling you Ole?" Grandpa looked up at her like a dying duck in a snowstorm during it's last gasp of a misspent life, and sadly sighed, "Jeg yust kald a ku." (I just killed a cow).

Grandpa's second milk cow tantrum occurred when he bent under the tail of our best and most productive milk cow named *Old Bluee*, to put on a pair of hobbles for me to milk her. It so happened *Old Bluee,* bless her heart, had been feeding in a green clover pasture all that day and as fate and coincidence will combine sometimes, at the exact moment Grandpa put on her hobbles, old Bluee felt the *spirit* suddenly appear unto her and believe it or not, plopped a pyramid shaped pile of wet cow manure smack dab center on the back of Grandpa's head. I'll tell you, the *you know what,* really hit the fan again and Grandpa really came unglued this time. He began cussing and yelling in every language he knew, (100% Norwegian, 75% Danish, 50% Swedish and 25% English) for someone to bring him a gunny (burlap) sack to *wipe off with.* When my dad saw what had happened, you guessed it, he doubled up laughing so hard his sides hurt and he couldn't move to help Grandpa, (Again!!!) so I ran to the granary for gunny sacks to hand to him. Grandma happened to be gathering eggs in the chicken coop nearby and when she saw what happened, she also began laughing hysterically, but to her credit bless her heart, she managed between guffaws, to help grandpa *clean up somewhat* with wash rags and cold water. Oooh boy, Grandpa might have thrown a s—t fit, but when you think about that historical family story hard enough, it really was kind of funny

When I was a child, Grandpa used to bounce me on his knee and like Grandma, would sing a little Norwegian "ahteetot" tune that sounded a lot like an old Irish jig called, "*The Irish washer women.*" Then he would tell me stories of when he was fourteen years old how he went to sea as a fisherman-sailor on a two master square rigged sailing ship on the North Sea, to fish for herring and salmon. Grandpa really loved the sea and he always ended his sea stories the same way, *They were the happiest days of my life.* I have often wondered since then, what a shame it was that Grandpa couldn't have settled in the Pacific Northwest when he came to America instead of in that Godforsaken high desert country of central Utah. He would have been so much happier living and working near the sea in an area resembling western Norway, the land he loved. But, there I go again wondering again where we would all be now if he had settled in this beautiful western Washington country along Puget Sound where Joyce and I are living now enjoying our retirement years.

When Grandma wasn't listening, Grandpa Olsen would always tell me the story of his first drink of whisky when he was a fisherman-sailor on the two master square rigged sailing ship. He said he was only fifteen years old at the time (1865), but he was one of the few sailors on the ship with enough upper body strength to climb a rope hand over hand. He said a huge storm hit their ship one time and the waves were crashing over the first yardarm when the captain ordered him to climb up and re-tie a loosened sail on the yardarm. He said he was nearly washed overboard several times, but fortunately was able to finish his job without incident. When he reported back to the captain, soaking wet and shivering from the cold ocean water, the captain said, "Did you get vet Ole?" and Grandpa answered, "Yah Yah, Jeg got vet", so the captain handed him a towel to dry himself, and then a flask of whisky, saying, "Drink this Ole, so you von't catch cold." After a pause to cut another plug of chewing tobacco and refill his coffee cup, and to see if I was paying attention, Grandpa would say, "And you know, Jeg never caught a cold."

I asked him one time if he would build me a model of the sailing ship he sailed on during his fishing days and he promised he would if he could find the time. One day, I noticed a block of poplar tree wood he kept whittling on during his *snoose* breaks was slowly beginning to resemble a sailing ship's hull, and I became more and more excited it might be my ship model. Finally Grandpa confessed it was my model of his ship and he began putting it higher and higher out of my reach on the top shelf in the blacksmith's shop. He made me promise never to even think about touching that boat until it was finished, so I crossed my heart and hoped to die if I did until it was ready to launch. I also agreed to pump the forge and pedal the sharpening wheel a lot faster and longer than usual so he could finish his blacksmith work sooner. Well, for some unknown reason all his whittling and carving seemed to go on and on and on forever until the day my cousin Wayne Olsen came over to play. Grandpa and Grandma were in town with the one horse buggy and Dad was busy somewhere; so on our own we decided a quick flight test in the irrigation ditch wouldn't hurt anything.

Well you guessed it. By combining my rationalizing with my cousin Wayne's encouragement, I broke my solemn *cross my heart and hope to die* promise to my wonderful Far Far, and like two lousy crooks, we *stole* that beautiful unfinished ship's hull from the top shelf of Grandpa's blacksmiths shop and sailed it in the full irrigation ditch. Grandpa never had the time to work on my model ship for a week or so afterwards, so he never noticed what we had done, but Oooh boy, when he did, it was the third time I really saw him angry. That unsealed model ship's perfectly carved wooden hull had become water logged and had *swelled* somewhat,, then had *shrunk* while it was drying causing the hull to *split from expansion and shrinkage secondary stresses*. I was devastated because all of Grandpa's hard work was now ruined, but I was really sorry and hurt because Grandpa would never trust me ever again for breaking my solemn promise. He angrily looked at me and said, "That did it, Jeg von't have the time to ever build you another ship model." And he never did.

During the 1880's and 1890's, Grandpa hauled freight by horse and wagon teams from Monroe, Utah through Clear Creek Canyon to Cove Fort and on to Ely and Pioche, and even as far as Eureka, Nevada. He told me the trips to Pioche and Ely took roughly two weeks each round trip, but their most profitable freight haul was to the gold miners in Eureka, Nevada, that took three weeks because of the longer and more difficult route through the mountains. He said on that longer trip they had to dismantle their wagons and lower the wheels, cargo, and wagon frames separately down the cliffs and steep grades using block and tackle and their horses. They would then put their wagons back together and continue their haul until they reached their next steep mountain canyon *take apart* until they finally reached Eureka. I'll tell you, in my opinion, they earned every dime they made. Every time I've driven that same Eureka route in my car on the now paved highway, I've marveled at how those hardy mountain men and their horses were able to make those wagon train trip through such rough mountainous country, long before any roads were built. Nowadays, with our good roads and all, you can drive from Monroe, Utah to Eureka, Nevada and back again in less than 12 hrs, and still have time for lunch at Baker on the Utah-Nevada border.

One of the freight hauling stories Grandpa always loved to tell was one he called "*The Saga of Hans Guldbransen.*" Apparently when Grandpa and his crew parked their wagons for the night, one of the men in their crew named, Hans Guldbransen, (who later married Grandpa's younger sister Olena, by the way) would always go over to his bed role and turn in after he finished his supper, leaving the rest of them sitting around the campfire drinking coffee, telling stories and laughing, without him. After awhile, they all got a little disgusted with Hans and his unsocial behavior so the next time they made camp, Grandpa ran a hose they used to siphon water for their barrels all the way from their campfire to Hans's bedroll, and covered it with dirt with one end under Han's saddle that he used for a pillow. When Hans turned in early for the night and began dozing off, in a slow shaky authoritative tone of voice, Grandpa picked up his end of the hose and said, *Hans, Jeg have come for thee.* Grandpa said they all watched out of the corner of their eye as Hans slowly rose up on one elbow to look around and then over at them as they continued talking calmly by the fire, then shrugged and lay back down. A little while later as he began to snore, Grandpa would repeat, only louder this time, **Hans, *Jeg have come for thee.***

More nervously this time, Hans would quickly repeat his *look around* and then lay back down again, but when Grandpa loudly repeated his "**Hans, *Jeg have come for thee***" the third time, a now frightened Hans Guldbransen hurriedly crawled out of his bedroll, pulled on his britches and boots back on and saunter over to the camp fire to be with the rest of the crew. Grandpa said Hans looked scared with his two silver dollar sized eye balls and all, but he never said *boo* to anybody and just sat down there on a rock and stared silently into the campfire the remainder of the evening, until everyone decided to turn in. As always, whenever Grandpa told a story, he would pause just before the punch line to cut another plug of chewing tobacco and freshen up his coffee, but mostly I think, to make sure anyone with a short attention span was paying attention. Then he would say, "And you know, Hans never went to bed early after that."

If you're not too tired of these stories, another one of Grandpa's favorites he loved to tell was about "Alvey Nay and the Bear" that supposedly occurred shortly after World War I when there were still black bear and a few grizzlies roaming the Central Utah Rockies. For some unknown reason after Grandpa passed away, my dad changed the main character in this story from *Alvey Nay* to *Bud Rich*, but anyway, Grandpa's version was about Alvey Nay herding sheep on the high mountain summer range alone while his camp jack was down in the valley buying more grub. And it was while his side kick was gone Alvey decided to move a side of mutton he had hanging on a tree limb outside his tent, and re-hang it on the ridgepole inside to keep blowflies and yellow jackets away.

Well, you can believe this story or not, your choice, but during that same night after Alvey moved his side of mutton inside the tent and had gone to bed; a hungry black bear wandered in and began pawing at the mutton hanging on the tents ridge pole. Well, when that happened, Grandpa said Alvey's sheep dog cams racing into the dark tent snarling and snapping at the bear with its back fur standing straight up, and Oooh boy, all hell suddenly broke lose between the dog and the bear. The bear began roaring and slashing at both the dog and the mutton, and when the roaring bear backed the snarling dog up on Alvey's chest, it woke him up out of his sound sleep, and how it woke him up. According to Grandpa, "Alvey's eyes suddenly got bigger than two silver dollars" (I remember wondering at the time how Grandpa knew that) and a trembling terrified Alvey Nay began sliding sideways very slowly an inch at a time, patting and feeling around his bed roll in the dark for his gun, or anything to defend himself. Well, he patted something alright, but unfortunately it was only a pencil and a pad of paper and feeling himself slipping into unconsciousness, he hurriedly scribbled something down on his writing pad and fainted dead away.

The next morning when Alvey *came to*, everything was quite again. The sun was shining brightly and the birds were singing, but the mutton was gone, the bear was gone, and his sheepdog had run away. His tent, his camp stove, bedroll and all his canned goods were scattered along side the mountain, but feeling fortunate to still be alive, Alvey began cleaning up the mess. Whooee and Lo and behold, he suddenly found the same piece of paper he had scribbled something on before he passed out, and he picked it up to see what he had written. You guessed it, Grandpa paused once again to recharge his *chaw* with a new plug of tobacco and freshen up his coffee, then pretending to read something in his hand, he said it read, *Alvey Nay, killed by a Bear*. Wow, I thought to myself, Alvey had written his own epitaph.

Homer C. Olsen - 1940

Grandpa said Alvey Nay also had the reputation of being a sleepwalker, and he would actually *act out* his dreams while he was still sound asleep. He said, Alvey woke the whole town up one night by riding a big white horse bare-back, hell bent for election in only his night shirt, right down Main Street in Monroe in the middle of the night, screaming, "The Indians are coming, the Indians are coming." I guess he was dreaming he was Paul Revere or somebody. Another time Grandpa said, in his Norwegian brogue, "You can believe this story or not, your choice, but another time Alvey got out of bed in the middle of the night while he was still sound asleep and harnessed up his team of horses to his hay wagon, drove his team and wagon out to the hayfield and pitched on a full load of hay before he woke up."

My dad loved to tell "Barney Boy" stories, and there were dozens of them. To get the full impact of a *Barney Boy* story, they had to be told in a unique local dialect and accent called, *"The Utah Twang"*, which my dad had down to a tee. For some unknown reason, Grandpa's Norwegian brogue spoiled them somewhat when he told them, but they were still funny to me, no matter who told them. I still have to laugh over the one Dad told about Dick Barney delivering a wagon load of supplies up to the sheepherders on Monroe Mountain. The wagon roads up the mountains at that time (and even now) were nothing more than widened pack horse trails notched into the cliffs that occasionally had very steep grades. For safety reasons, Dick always had two other men helping him on his trips and whenever they would pull up the steeper grades and had to rest the team, Dick and one of the other men, I believe Dad said his name was Siraldo Nielsen, would walk alongside the back wheels of the wagon while the third man drove the horse team from the wagon seat. I interrupted Dad with, "How come one of the men was given a funny name like Siraldo?" and Dad answered with a grin, "When he was born, his mother's favorite song was "Little Siraldo, How Do You Do, You Who, You Who."

Anyway, when the horses give out and needed a rest, Dick would prop the toe of his boot against the iron tire of his rear wheel to hold the wagon with his foot while Siraldo put a rock under the iron tire on his side to keep the wagon from rolling backwards. Well, as you've already guessed, this usually worked out fine, except for this one time. Dick propped his boot toe against the tire wheel on his side, but the wagon kept inching back and inching back until finally, it inched up on Dick's boot toe and, Oooh boy, I'll tell you, his foot really began to smart. Dick looked frantically over at Siraldo, who was just standing there quietly hand rolling himself a Bull Durham cigarette, and said as calmly as he could through his clenched teeth, "Siraldo, you don't have to hurry rolling that Bull Durham if you don't want to; my foot's already mashed." This story always tickled me because after everyone had stopped laughing at the punch line, Dad would always add, -"And that's a true story."

Berta Kjolvick Olsen - 1880

Another story Dad loved to tell was about Dick Barney gathering eggs in Grandma's chicken house that was originally Grandpa and Grandma's first log cabin home when they were first married in 1879 and had built on their *Gravelbed* farm. I'll tell you, that original log cabin was about as primitive as they could be built in those days with only tree limbs as roof joists and straw and dirt for roofing. Grandpa also told me the log building we were using then as a granary was originally his mother Berta's (Berta Kjolvick Olsen) home where she lived and

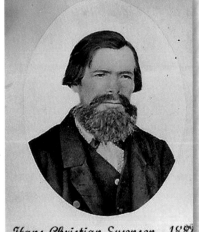

Hans Christian Swensen - 1880

spun wool into yarn with her spinning wheel until she died at the age 77 in 1894. He even told me the little log cabin near the milking shed inside the corral that was currently used as a calf pen, was originally the log cabin home of Great Grandpa Hans Christian Swensen (Grandma Olsen's father), who made shoes and did carpentry work for a living until he died in 1892 at the age of 76. Great Grandpa Swensen was a master carpenter from Christiana, (called Oslo today) Norway, who came to America alone in 1873 after his wife died to earn passage for his three children to join him later in America. When he contacted his three children two years later to join him, his two sons decided to stay in Norway, but Grandma Olsen, at the age of 18, came to America, all the way to Utah by herself, to be with her father in 1875. Grandma Olsen said she worked for another Utah family as a combination nanny-housekeeper until she met (and stole Grandpa Olsen's heart) at a square dance in Kooshurm, Utah. Her father, my Great Grandpa Swensen, helped build several new homes in the Sevier River valley during his life in America, including the large shiplap covered log farm house on the *Gravelbed* farm for his daughter and his new son-in-law, Ole Kjolvick Olsen. Dad willed me Far Far Far Swensen's double barreled percussion muzzle loader shotgun he used to shoot chicken hawks and coyotes, and two of his wooden block planes he made and used in his carpenter shop. I still have those three items proudly displayed in my basement toy building shop of our Gig Harbor retirement home, for all to see and admire.

Anyway, to get back to Dad's story, Dick Barney was a pretty tall guy for a hair lip, so he had to stoop real low in order to enter that pitch dark log cabin hen house, only to be greeted by a flock of angry squawking setting hens that were in no mood to be disturbed. When Dick felt under one of the hens to gather her eggs, that ornery old hen let out a loud squawk and pecked him on the hand, causing him to jerk his head back sharply and nearly cold cock himself on a protruding roof log knot. Somehow, while staggering around inside the hen house in the dark with a splitting headache and deafening hen clucks, he was still able to stumble outside into the bright sunlight and pull off his coat for a *best man wins*, fist fight. While he listened to that ornery old setting hen *cuss clucking* at him from inside, Dick angrily assumed John L. Sullivan's famous boxing position to prepare for their fight to the death. Dad said when he arrived to referee the match, Dick Barney was vigorously sparing around and loudly cuss fighting back, 'Set there and c1uck you brown speckled old biddy, get up and fight like a man.'

It was my dad who told me the story of "The Last Grizzly Bear" on the central Utah Rocky Mountains. Apparently all this occurred around the same time Alvey Nay's black bear story, shortly after World War I ended and the sheep and cattle men were determined to rid the area of their stock predators. Unlike other animals that will kill only enough prey to satisfy their appetites, a grizzly like man himself, will kill many more than are needed for food, just for the sport of it. Dad told me a grizzly bear will wade through a herd of sheep swinging its front paws like a crazed boxer, and litterly bat a swath of forty or fifty head of sheep to death, at a time. Then they will drag off only one of them to eat and leave the rest of their kill for the mountain lions, coyotes and buzzards. A bounty of $1000 was raised by the local stockmen for the head and hide of that last known grizzly in the area and a bear hunter from Montana took them up on it. He arrived with his bear traps and his 50 caliber Sharps rifle, set his traps out and waited. A short time later two cowhands on horses ran across the grizzly in a forest clearing with one of its back feet caught in one of his traps that was tied to a fallen log. They told the Montana trapper the grizzly charged them, and they each fired five 30-30 bullets into the bear with their Winchesters, but it didn't seem to faze him other than make him angrier. When the trapper checked the area their sighting was made and found both the bear and the log the trap was tied were gone, he began following their trail through the trees. That wounded grizzly, using it's fantastic super strength, had dragged that huge log through the forest for nearly a mile to the lake's edge, pulled the log into the water and had swam with it chained to it's back foot, another quarter of a mile to the other side of the lake. When the trapper finally found the wounded and utterly exhausted grizzly bear, it was lying near death among the trees, so he put it out of its misery with his 50 caliber rifle. In the end, the log had become wedged among the lake shore trees and when the bear could no longer move with it chained to its foot, it had lost its will to live. When Dad finished telling me that bedtime story, I remember feeling very sad at the time and sorry for the bear.

Old Bob & Grandpa Olsen - 1940

Even at that young age, I got a big kick out of Grandpa bringing the cows up from the lower pasture to the milk shed for their evening milking. At least half of the calves in the dairy herd had been raised as pets by Grandpa and they would follow him everywhere, even after they became milk cows. He would walk with his Border Collie dog named, *Naddie*, and later *Old Bob*, right in the middle of all those cows, rather than herding them from behind, and it didn't seem to make any difference where Grandpa was in the corral, he was always surrounded by his pets. He even had names for every cow, calf, pig, lamb and horse in and around the corral, and best of all, he always had sugar cubes or rabbit alfalfa pellets in his pocket for each of them when they came for their pat. As a little surprise for us kids, he even had another side pocket with peppermints for us when we gathered around to hear his stories. When it came time to slaughter his pets for food, Grandpa and I, and even my dad, couldn't bring ourselves to kill our pets so Dad would hire a local butcher by the name of Max Andersen (who I thought was a murderer), to do the dirty work while the three of us hid out somewhere. Once that was done, to my amazement, Grandpa and Dad seemed comfortable skinning and butchering the animals for the various meat cuts Grandma wanted and/or needed for her cooking and winter bottling.

I still remember the time Grandpa's pet dog *Naddie* had a batch of pups that I wanted to keep as pets, but Dad said we already had too many dogs on the farm and told me to give them away. When I tried and my friend's parents said they couldn't have anymore dogs as pets either, Grandpa just shrugged and walked away, but Dad ordered me to shoot them. He handed me his single shot bolt action 22 rifle that he gave to me a few years later for my tenth birthday, (which I still have) with a handful of cartridges and some binder twine, and walked away. Fighting back tears, I tied the binder string around each of those little puppy's necks and, sobbing all the way, led them all up on the bench to tearfully tie all those whimpering little puppies along the fence. I tried aiming the gun at each of them, but I would only begin to cry, then I would try aiming again, and I would cry some more, until finally I couldn't even think of shooting any of those little puppies without crying.

Sobbing all the way back down the hill, I led all of those little border collie dogs back down to the corrals and told my dad, "I can't do it, Dad; I just can't shoot these little puppies." Dad angrily said, "Give me that damn gun, I'll show you how it's done", and stormed back up the hill, pulling and jerking and dragging all those little whimpering pups behind him. I remember listening for rifle shots and sniffling, then I would sniffle some more and listened some more, but I never heard any shots being fired. Finally, in what seemed like hours, my dad, with tears streaming down his face, straggled back down the hill blowing his nose, dragging that long line of whimpering puppies behind him, and handed them back to me. He pulled out a handkerchief to wipe his eyes, blew his nose, and while slowly turning away, said hoarsely, "See if you can give them away, only try harder this time", and sauntering off towards the house sniffling, wiping, and coughing, all the way.

Pvt. Ole Hjolvick Olsen, Norwegian Army - 1876

As far as I know, we never had any wild deer or elk meat on our dinner table that actually was hunted and/or shot by my dad or my grandpa. As I recall, whatever wild game we did have for our dinner was given to us by friends and neighbors. We had pheasant occasionally, but even they weren't hunted by Dad or Grandpa and usually resulted from mower accidents in the hay fields. In fact, I don't recall Grandpa ever deer or pheasant hunting during any of those good old days I knew him, but maybe it was because he was getting older (after all, he was 74 when I was born), and I really don't think he enjoyed hunting very much anyway. When I asked him why he stopped hunting for deer, he told me he was getting too old and feeble to gut them out and drag them home anymore, and besides he said, he was too busy on the farm to waste the time. I went along one time to hold the horses for Dad when he went deer hunting with his buddies, and I soon discovered he couldn't shoot those beautiful animals either. He always said as an excuse when he missed, "The sights on this gun need adjusting", which I thought was interesting because he could pick off a coyote fifty yards away from his horse with his Winchester. Anyway, now you know, all three of Grandma Olsen's men (Dad, Grandpa and me) were just soft hearted sissies when it came to messing around with Mother Nature's beautiful wild animals.

Thinking back now, Grandpa really had only one prejudice that I'm aware of. I remember a *hobo* came to our farmhouse door one time during the depression to ask if he could do some work for something to eat (**hobos** *always worked for their handouts while* **tramps** *begged for theirs*) so Grandpa showed him the woodpile and said if he would split some kindling for our stove, he would fix him something to eat. Later when the hobo came into the kitchen for his meal, Grandpa sat down with him and asked his name and where he was from and, as it turned out, he had just come over from the *old country* and his last name was Olson. Well as you can imagine, Grandpa got all excited thinking he might have some news of his relatives, or we might even be related, but first he asked him how he spelled Olsen, with an *"en"* or an *"on."* I remember when the man answered *"on"*, Grandpa's face fell a foot and he said, "Oh, deg var sin, (Oh, that's too bad), Jeg vas hopin vee could be friends" and you can believe this or not, he stood up and walked out of the room. That's when I discovered for the first time how much that proud Old Norwegian disliked Swedes, although he loved the Danes in the neighboring dairy and flour milling town of Ellsinore, which interestingly, had the largest settlements of Danish immigrants in the United States at that time.

I suppose, when you think about it hard enough, Grandpa's prejudice might have been fostered by the way the Swedish and European royalties, who all seemed to be related, played their war and economic games without any regard, concern or conscience how their actions might effect their constituents and/or their countries economies. Grandpa told me he served two years in the Norwegian Army between his 18th and 20th birthdays, fighting the Swedes for Norway's independence before he came to America in 1874 with his mother and his two sisters. As we all know, Norway never were granted their independence from Sweden and become an independent nation, until 1905.

In my opinion, Grandpa's only fault was his attitude towards higher education. He honestly felt high school, and even college educations for the most part, was a waste of time for 99% of our young people, and with the dummying down and the brainwashing going on in our educational system since the 1960's, I'm about ready to agree with him. He told his own children, "Eighth grade is all the education you will ever need. Yust learn to read, write and cipher and jeg vill teach you everything else you need to know." Wow, Grandpa believed in *Home Schooling* even before it became popular. My dad was the only one of Grandpa's eight children to ever graduate from high school and he even got an opportunity to attend Utah State for a year to try and become a *horse doctor*. Not one of Grandpa's other children ever went beyond the eighth grade in a public school as far as I know, but Grandma apparently convinced Grandpa they needed a veterinarian in the family for their livestock, so Dad, as their youngest son, was given that honor. When Grandpa discovered that Utah State didn't have a veterinarian school after all and he had been tricked by Grandma, he jerked my dad out of College after one year, and made him the family's animal doctor anyway. I remember watching my dad stitch badly cut up sheep that had been injured by wool shearers, and watching him dock lambs and deliver many difficult farm animal births. Dad learned his veterinarian trade secrets while attending the "Ole K. Olsen's, Home School of Hard Knocks" on the Gravelbed farm.

Grandpa was probably right about higher education during the early agricultural economy years, but America's economy was changing rapidly during the late 1800's and early 1900's towards an industrial society. The general publics feelings about a higher education were also changing towards "the more technical education a person had, the better his/her chances were of succeeding in the real world of work." Grandpa unfortunately had grown up under an old country philosophy, the lower the class level you were unluckily and unfortunately born in, the less education you needed. I still believe it was that *discrimination* my Norwegian family and German family endured, along with their sharecroppers *no futures* coupled with Europe's economic depression at the time, that all culminated by Marta's illegitimate pregnancy and my Great Grandpa Olsen's untimely death, were the real reasons Grandpa and his family immigrated to this great land of freedom and opportunity, the United States of America. The Latter Day Saints were certainly right about one thing, Grandpa's family, like nearly all the American immigrants, "seen the light" and moved to America for freedom and opportunity, and a chance to escape their locked in poverty cycles.

Despite all the problems we had, I look back now on those early depression years growing up on that old Gravelbed farm with my dad and my Grandpa and Grandma Olsen, as the happiest days in my life. I knew we were thought of as "very poor" then, and nowadays we would have been classified as "poverty stricken" by our government. I knew we didn't have any money, but I never thought of us as poor, maybe it was because misery loves company and our friends and neighbors were in the same boat. One thing for sure, if our net worth had been measured in the love and the respect we had for each other instead of in dollars, we would have been very wealthy.

I will never forget my wonderful Grandma and Grandpa Olsen and my wonderful Dad, as long as I live, and I will always be grateful to them for sharing that part of their lives with me when I needed their love and parenting the most. Grandma Olsen was the only mother I knew for the first seven and most formative years of my life, and Grandpa and my dad were my dual fathers for my first twelve years. It was Grandma and Grandpa Olsen and my dad, who taught me the power of positive thinking, and that anything can be achieved in this wonderful land of freedom and opportunity, *by combining motivation and a good work ethic with a meaningful education.* They taught me to live by the Golden Rule, "do unto others as you would have them do unto you", and I learned from them the true meaning of the words, responsibility and respect, honesty and integrity, kindness and generosity, and the importance of having an optimistic attitude about life and a good sense of humor. I thank you Dad and Grandma and Grandpa Olsen, from the bottom of my heart, for sharing that part of your life with me when I needed you the most

THE GREAT DEPRESSION YEARS

MAJOR NEWS RELEASE

News Release: October 24, 1929, Black Thursday: After the New York Times Industrial Index rises 85% in twenty months, Terror-stricken buyers unload huge amounts of stock. On Black Tuesday, October 29, 1929, the New York Times Industrial Average of selected stocks plummeted from 452 to 38 and 75% of the value of all securities suddenly vanishes.

Black Tuesday, October 29, 1929, marked the beginning of a worldwide depression that became known as "The Great Depression" from 1930 until 1942. Less important headline events that same year were, the first Academy Awards were presented, the Workers Party (also known as the Wobblies), changed their name to what they really were, the Communist Party of the United States, Richard E. Byrd flies over the South Pole and *Happy Days are Here Again,* becomes the song of the year. All I can recall now that happened was, I started first grade in 1929

Dad & me – 1928

and I couldn't go on the summer mountain range with my dad to herd sheep that year. I also remember having my tonsils removed during the summer of 1929 and meeting my mother, Ruth Weimer, for the first time when she visited me at the hospital in Salina, Utah. She and Philip Brim, her third husband, brought me an ice cream cone and we all rode home from the hospital together in Dad's 1927 Chevy coupe with my mother and me in the rumble seat. I also remember thinking when I first saw my mother, "Wow, what a pretty lady."

In 1930, the year following the market crash, 4.5 million people became unemployed and 1300 banks failed nationwide. The average yearly farm income per family fell to $400 and many like my dad and my grandparents, became bare subsistence farmers. The trickle down effect of the stock market crash combined with the *dust bowl drought* of the 1930's, struck with a vengeance throughout the United States for twelve long years from 1930 until 1942.

In 1931 the depression combined with a nationwide drought and high tariffs caused foreign nations to retaliate in kind, resulted in another 2300 banks closing and panic spreads throughout the country as 20,000 people commit suicide. The nation's manufacturing industries began mirroring the Ford Motor Company's experience that employed 128,000 in 1929 and by 1931, only employed 37,000. Congress, in its misguided wisdom, frantically raises the top income tax rate from 25% to 63 %, thereby freezing any future business investment and the unemployment rate by 1932 jumps to an unprecedented 25% nationwide, escalating the failing economy into a free falling economy, and our nation settles into its worst depression in history.

My Mother, Ruth Weimer - 1929

By early 1933, nearly every bank in the country is threatened with bankruptcy and stops paying depositors. The new Democrat Congress in their unlimited stupidity, pass another misguided *wealth tax* bill raising the tax rate from 63% to 75% and by 1935, the unemployment rate in our country reaches 34%, the highest in history. The Great Depression of the 1930's negatively impacts every man, women and child in the United States and it's stagnant economy never improves until after the Japanese sneak attack on Pearl Harbor on December 7, 1941 and America shifts into an all out war economy. The Dow Jones Industrial Average slowly and finally begins to inch upward in 1942 to mark the end of the historic Great Depression.

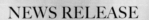
That bitter cold winter and drought of 1931 when Grandma Olsen passed away from pneumonia, was the same miserably cold winter my dad and my uncle Oluf had 750 head of their sheep freeze to death over night on the desert range in Pine Valley, Nevada, during a freezing winter blizzard. They mortgaged everything they had the previous summer to buy 1,000 additional sheep for their herd and that 750 head loss completely wiped them out financially. The bankers had insisted Grandpa Olsen at age 81, also put his farm up as collateral so his two sons could buy their sheep, and that bank

note on the farm was not paid back in full until 1949, eighteen years later and four years after Grandpa passed away. Dad finally *seen the light* and sold *Gravelbed* to pay off the mortgage to net out only $3,000, and began peddling insurance for a living. To this day, I'm still amazed by their stubborn Norwegian bone headed determination to hang in there come hell or high water, because it was the only thing that kept them from losing their stock farming operation when most of the other farms had already been taken over by the banks. At least Grandpa Weimer, my mother's father, had enough Oklahoma "Okie" intestinal fortitude to pickup and leave for California to try something else for a living. Grandpa Weimer immediately got a job as a janitor with the MGM Studios and by the time he reached retirement age he had worked up to *Chief Grip* (General Foreman) building stages for their movies.

I remember in August of 1929, Dad was given a little border collie pup he named "Bob" because of its short bobbed tail, and how hurt I was when he took that little pup on the

Sheep Camp — 1930's

summer mountain range with him instead of me. I remember being so envious (and jealous) of that little dog, all because I had to start first grade and that little pup didn't. To this day I still remember how painful it was standing there beside Grandma and Grandpa waving goodbye to my dad as he rode off on his horse, pulling *Old Jack*, that razor back mule loaded with supplies, carrying that little puppy on his arm. I found out later that *Bob* the dog was just as jealous of me as I was of him because whenever I tried to stand next to my dad, that lousy dog would deliberately nuzzle between us so he could stand closer to my dad than me. I don't think we ever warmed up to each other, but eventually we developed a mutual admiration society and learned to accept each other's right to exist. Bob was by far the smartest dog Dad ever had because a year later, I remember marveling at the way Dad and that wonderful Border Collie dog would work the sheep together. Dad would whistle and wave his arm a certain way, and Bob would disappear over the horizon to bring 2000 head of sheep back, right to the spot Dad wanted them. My dad was so proud of that wonderful dog he gave him a well earned promotion, and from then on "Bob" was known as "Old Bob" and I was heartbroken. I knew right then my dad loved *Old Bob* more than me because he never promoted or even called me, "Old Junior."

I always looked forward to going on that beautiful summer mountain range to look after the sheep with my dad because it was a fascinating wilderness area and such a wonderful experience for a little kid. We lived in a canvas tent, slept on a pine bough mattress bed, and cooked our meals with a small tin tent stove that even had a one-loaf oven for baking sourdough bread. I remember we guarded that old crock (jug) that held our *sourdough start* like it was gold, so we could have our daily loaf of that delicious sourdough bread. Our *breakfast* usually consisted of bacon and eggs, boiled coffee, called *Mormon tea* in my case (half coffee and half canned milk, plus two sugar cubes – called *Latte coffee* today)

Leland Olsen

and sourdough bread. That would be followed by our *dinner* meal at noon of canned soup, canned pork and beans, more boiled coffee, and sourdough bread with peanut butter and Grandma Olsen's home made goose berry jelly. For *supper* we usually had fried potatoes, more pork and beans, fried mutton, canned cream corn, sourdough bread and boiled coffee. All in all, I thought Dad was a pretty fair cook because occasionally he would even prepare a gourmet dish called macaroni and cheese. Unfortunately, his particular dish always came out of the little red hot tin tent stove, *burned on the outside and raw in the middle*, Dad always said, *Just the way I like it.* Then he and my cousin, Leland Olsen, would pretend how much they enjoyed that disgusting mess, by choking it down with buckets of strong boiled black coffee and sourdough bread. All in all, I think my dad had single handedly ruined my taste for macaroni and cheese for life, that is until my second wife Joyce, showed me what it would really taste like if it was properly prepared. Believe it or not, it's not too bad and even better when mixed with peas and a little ham.

Whenever Dad and I were on the mountain range, he would always make me ride that ornery old razor back pack mule named, *Old Jack*, because mules were supposed to be surer footed than a horse and he didn't want me getting hurt. I might have been jealous of *Old Bob*, but I'll tell you, I hated that lousy mule and *Old Jack* hated me. Whenever I rode somewhere on that no good stubborn mule, *Old Jack* would always try to scrub me off by rubbing against every tree we passed. In fact it got so every time I rode that knot headed mule, I spent nearly all my time and energy, swinging my legs from one side of the pack saddle to the other trying to keep from becoming a cripple. My cousin

Leland, one of Uncle Oluf's sons, spent a lot of his time herding sheep with Dad and was his camp jack every time I was on the summer mountain range. He was also the one who told me I wasn't using the right psychology on *Old Jack* and that I should spend more time getting better acquainted with him to gain his confidence and respect. I took Leland's advice seriously and you can believe this or not, but I really tried hard to make friends with *Old Jack* by patting him on the nose and talking to him *man to man* at every opportunity. I even put extra servings of oats in his feed bucket every so often as a token of friendship, but *Old Jack* just eyed me suspiciously. Finally, I felt we were friends and confident we were buddies so I told Dad and Leland to watch us jump over a fallen tree near our tent while riding him bareback with only a rope loop half hitched around his nose for a bridle. They laughed, "Now *that* should be interesting" and Dad picked me up and set me on that bareback razor back mule to taxi down to the starting gate. I was confident *Old Jack* knew how to jump logs because I had seen him do it by himself many times, so I just kicked him into a lope, hung on and hoped for the best.

Well, thinking back about that little drama of life now, I'm more convinced than ever that mules really are the four legged version of Norwegians because they never forget and they never forgive and Oooh boy, are they stubborn. That dirty rotten no good lousy mule galloped right up to the edge of that fallen tree and *just stopped*. Well you guessed it, that quaint little stunt not only caused me to immediately rocket slide all along his razor sharp back and over his neck mane to a crashing stop against his long ears, but to make things worse, he suddenly changed his mind and decided to *jump the log*. Oooh boy, that impromptu little stunt then caused me to immediately reverse my *rocket slide* back along his neck and razor back, but even faster towards his aferendum end for a spectacular *grand finale roll off flip flop landing* and a thundering ovation from my appreciative audience. Dad and Leland (and *Old Jack)*, were holding their sides *hee-hawing,* but for some unknown reason I didn't see one damn thing funny about any of it. I'll say one thing

Leland & Spun — 1941

for my dad though, bless his heart. He went out of his way to comfort me because between guffaws he said, "I'm really proud of you Son, you just won the Academy Award."

Another time, I was following Dad down the mountain trail riding that ornery old stubborn razor back mule doing my side to side leg survival act, when all of a sudden I heard Dad groan and begin swaying dizzily in his saddle. He reined up his horse and slowly got off to stagger over to lean against a *snapping asp* (quaking aspen) tree. Then, facing skyward and moaning like a coyote, he slowly slid down the tree trunk until he was sitting with both knees beside his ears, and launched into a knee jerking St Vitas type dance, much like a Russian dancer. I'll kid you not; I was really scared and I jumped off my mule to run over thinking he might be having a heart attack or something, and. shouted, "Dad, Dad, what happened?" He gasped and wheezed several times and croaked something that sounded like, "I never figured my life would end like this, but this is it son, I'm a goner." and began whispering hoarsely, "I must have picked up a stray 30-30 bullet, I've been shot." I screamed, "Oh my God Dad, where did the bullet hit you?" In a wheezing gasping voice he said, "I want you to listen carefully son because this is my last will and testament." and pausing again to gasp for more air and jerk kick his legs, he squeezed my hand tightly and wheezed "Son, I want you to take Grandpa and the cows and head west" to which I tearfully repeated, "Dad, please tell me, where did the bullet hit you?" With fluttering eyelids he slowly opened his crossed blood shot blue eyes and looking up at me sadly, hoarsely whispered, *"Right between the eyes."*

In shock, I gently tipped Dad's Stetson westerner hat back on his forehead to look at his bullet wound and sighing with relief, reached for my handkerchief to wipe off the splattered remains, and you won't believe this, of a *yellow jacket bee* that had hit him like a 30-30 bullet, right between the eyes. I shook my head in both relief and in disbelief, and slowly showed Dad my handkerchief with the splattered bee, and asked, "Is this your 30-30 bullet Dad?" To this day I've never seen a more stunned look on anyone's face than on my dad's face that day at that moment when he saw that bee. I'll tell you, he suddenly whispered, "Well I'll be damned", and made the most miraculous recovery ever made by man or beast. His leg jerking stopped, his eyes suddenly uncrossed and his dying duck in a snow storm award winning act instantly subsided. After shaking his head from side to side while staring in disbelief at my handkerchief a moment longer, he got up nonchalantly while saying, "I'll be damned", and climbed back on his horse to continue riding his horse down the trail like nothing had happened.

My dad can always tell a good story, but it's nothing compared to the fantastic act's he can put on when he feels the urge. If you've even read this book this far, you know now that neither my dad nor I exaggerate when we tell a story, but when my dad acts out the part in a story, he really knows how to do it *professionally*. To this day, I still think my wonderful dad missed his calling because I have never seen a better *dying duck* act done anywhere that was better than the one he put on that day with the bee for me. I think my dad's even better than Hoot Gibson or Tom Mix ever thought of being. I remember trying really hard not to *snicker* when we were riding along after his *bee act*, but finally I couldn't stand it any longer and busted out laughing so hard my sides began to hurt. Dad just turned around in his saddle to glare at me for a moment and said, "I don't see one damn thing funny about any of it", to which I answered, "I'm proud of you Dad, you just won the Academy Award."

Tex and I always had our birthday parties together at Aunt Maude's (his mother's house) every year because we were only one year and one day apart, and I will never forget my 8th birthday party on April 7, 1932 at his house. After we had eaten all the cake and ice cream and the party came to an end and I went home, my dad called me over to congratulated me on becoming a man by saying, "You're a man now that you're eight years old Son, so I think it's high time you started carrying your own weight around here." Then he added some additional chores to my list like milking *Old Bluee* and feeding the cows and horses, plus some additional field duties like tromping hay on the wagon and driving the derrick horse to unload hay. I told him, "OK Dad, now that I'm a man, I want to be on the payroll and be paid like Grant Barney", his hired hand that was paid one dollar a day. That set him back a little I think, but he said, "OK, your wages including board and room from now on will be fifty cents for a full

days work in the fields because you're only half a man in height, and I'll pay you in cash and/or livestock, your choice." He also said my regular chores were *pro bono* and didn't count and I would still be expected to buy all my own clothes from my wages. We shook hands on it, and as he walked away he reminded me that even though I was only drawing half pay, I was still his son and he didn't want me embarrassing him by not keeping up with the rest of the crew.

Grant Barney overheard all this, and after Dad left he suggested we celebrate my new high paying job by getting plastered on Dad's homemade beer in the *root cellar still*. For the life of me, I don't remember ever being sicker than I was that day after drinking Dad's home made beer, before or since, and I don't remember my dad ever being angrier than he was when he found me lying on the ground retching in front of the wagon shed with the dry heaves. He fired Grant Barney on the spot for getting a little kid drunk (Oooh boy, did I ever un-grow up in a hurry) and he and Grandpa had to do all my scheduled chores for the next few days until I recovered. But, all in all, I had to give Dad credit for sticking to our employment contract despite my screw up. He never fired me

Tex, me and Spun about 1929

from my first high paying job and he only added one additional clause to my employment contract called, *"substance abuse."*

When my mother heard that Grandma Olsen had passed away, she started plotting to get me away from my dad, up to and including kidnapping. I never really knew my mother,

Homer J. Olsen - 1932

having only seen her once before when she came to see me after my tonsils were removed in 1929 at the Salina Hospital. The next time I saw her was three years later in August of 1932, nine months after Grandma Olsen had died, when she drove out to the Gravelbed farm in her cream colored Chevy sedan with my little half brother Rodger in the back seat. I didn't know who Rodger was having never seen him before, so she opened the back door of the car and told me to get inside to meet my little brother, then slammed and locked the door. My dad came running out of the farmhouse shouting, so my mother took off her spiked high-heeled shoe and struck Dad on the head, jumped back in the car and drove off with the two of us screaming bloody murder. I still remember

blood was spurting from my dad's head as we left and both Rodger and I were scared to death. She drove the 180 miles north to Salt Lake City as fast as her old car would go and then dumped the two of us off at a boarding house run by a Mrs. Jorgensen. I remember, she paid Mrs. Jorgensen thirty dollars to cover our first month's room and board, told her not to tell anyone about us, and drove on west to Elko, then south to Ely, Nevada, by herself. Mrs. Jorgensen registered us in a big scary city school with the new names of Rodger and Junior Brim, with Rodger in the first grade and me in the third grade. I still remember being completely traumatized from fear and homesickness during the whole time we were living at Mrs. Jorgensen's boarding house. My teacher even kept sending notes home with me, asking my parents to come see her about my lack of attention in her class and my apparent lack of interest to even learn, but I was afraid to tell her I didn't have any parents. I remember crying myself to sleep nearly every night and I kept praying that my dad and my grandpa would find me somehow someway. I found out later they were frantically chasing down every lead they were given, looking for the two of us.

I wrote the following letter two months after I was kidnapped to my new step father, Philip Brim, on October 1, 1932 while Rodger and I were living at Mrs. Jorgensen's Rooming House on 2160 Lake Street, Salt Lake City, Utah. This is the first letter I've ever written to anyone and apparently was written to practice writing my new last name. I had been given strict orders by my mother to not write to anyone in Monroe, and especially not to my dad, and to change my name from "Olsen" to "Brim." I'll tell you, I was one scared 8 year old.

October 1, 1932

Dear Philip,

I am in the third grade. My teacher's name is Miss Mitchell, I like her. The School I go to is the Forest School. I guess I better quit and go to bed. Write soon. PS Roger is a pig. He needs a trough. A pig is like Roger.

Love from, Junior Brim
Homer Junior Brim

Ferd Ericksen was still the Sevier County judge when I was kidnapped, so he issued an all points bulletins in three states (Utah, Nevada and California) for my mother's arrest. Dad told me he even hired a private investigator to help find me, and that he and Uncle Orson had spent weeks chasing down every rumor and lead they uncovered. Unfortunately, they were on the wrong track because everyone thought my mother would have driven south to Las Vegas, Nevada and/or Los Angeles, but instead, she had driven north to Salt Lake City. It wasn't until December of 1932, five months later, when Philip Brim and my mother had a terrible argument over what she was doing with Rodger and me, and after she stomped out and divorced him, he called my dad to tell him where he could find me.

After Philip and my mother parted ways over my kidnapping, my mother ran off with a knot headed con-artist magician named William (Doc) H. Staley to be his stage assistant, and later married "Doc" when her divorce from Philip was finalized. When Philip Brim called my dad to pick me up in Salt Lake and said he would pick up Rodger, they apparently met separately with Della Pendleton, the Forest School principal, to explain the situation. I found in Dad's things he willed to me when he passed away, my "Card of Transfer" to Monroe grade school for a change of residence dated, December 22, 1932, that was given to my dad by Mrs. Pendleton for the transfer of Junior "Olsen", not Junior "Brim." Rodger kept the name of Brim because he was moving back to Nevada to live with Philip, who was working on Boulder Dam at the time as a highscaler, and living in a construction workers shanty town near Boulder City, called McKeeversville. To this day when I read about a missing child, or see a missing child's picture on a milk carton, my heart goes out to them because I know exactly what they are going through. I was convinced my mother's only motivation for kidnapping me was not because she loved or even wanted me. It was because she wanted to hurt my dad, and that she did. Dad was terribly hurt, but he never pressed charges against my mother and the case was dropped.

Philip and Rodger 1930 and McGill, Nevada

Interestingly, Mrs. Jorgensen made out like a bandit on Rodger's and my kidnapping. Before Dad could take me home, he had to pay her 30 dollars for back room and board as ransom for Rodger and me. Dad told me he was so broke when he finally found me; he was forced to pay my ransom out of my $32 savings account at the Monroe City Bank that I had earned with my lamb and calf sales and jobs. I told Dad he needn't bother paying me back because I was the one that was kidnapped, and therefore should be the one to pay Mrs. Jorgensen her ransom, not him. A week later, when Philip Brim came to pickup Rodger, he also had to pay Mrs. Jorgensen another 30 dollars "back room and board" ransom for Rodger and me. Years later my mother told me, she always kept our room and board "paid in advance" and she knew it was paid up when she and Philip broke up and we were picked up. But like they say, "Crooks always profit when an opportunity presents itself."

Little Rodger begged my dad to let him stay with his big brother and Dad told me it was the hardest decision he ever made, but he just couldn't take little Rodger home with him. Dad had been hurt so badly by my mother he couldn't bring himself up to raising a lousy home breaking bronc buster's kid. I guess that stubborn Norwegian pride to never forget, never forgive, just wouldn't allow him to raise that innocent little child. Philip Brim loved little Rodger like his own son from the time Rodger was six months old and he married my mother to raise little Rodger in the first place. Philip was the only father little Rodger ever knew and when he picked him up at Mrs. Jorgensen's boarding house that day, he thought he would be able to adopt Rodger as his own son.

I will always be grateful to Dora Brown, my third grade teacher at the Monroe grade school, for spending so much extra time with me to bring me back up to third grade level. After my kidnapping, I hadn't learned one thing in the Salt Lake City school system during that first semester and all my third grade work had to be *re-done* during the remaining five months of the 1932 school year. It was Miss Brown who made it possible for me to barely graduate (on condition) with my regular class to the fourth grade in May of 1933. Interestingly, my first grade teacher, Miss Jenny Reynolds,

> ## NEWS RELEASE
>
> *From January through March 1933, Adolph Hitler becomes chancellor of the German Republic, the Nazi Party gains 43% of the German vote and a small majority in the Reichstag. March 4, 1933, in his inaugural address FDR asserts that the only thing we have to fear is fear itself.*

and my second grade teacher, Miss Crawford, had both told my dad they thought I was doing so well in school I could skip third grade and go directly on to the fourth grade, but that was before I was kidnapped.

When Dad first brought me home from Salt Lake City, I was having such terrible nightmares I was even afraid of my own shadow, so Dad and Grandpa, and Aunt Maude and Uncle Orson, thought it best I move in with Uncle Orson's family until my dad, if and when, remarried. I lived with Aunt Maude and Uncle Orson and their four sons (and Muriel) for the next two and a half years, and I thought of Tex, Spun, Stan and baby Sterling, as my younger brothers and Muriel Olsen, my uncle Nephi's illegitimate child, as my older sister. As double cousins, their four boys and I were closely related enough to almost be brothers anyway, because my mother and Aunt Maude were sisters, and my dad and my uncle Orson were brothers. I considered Tex, who was the oldest and only one year and one day younger than I was, my best friend then, and I still consider him one of my best friends now. The four of

Aunt Maud, Uncle Orson, Tex, Nolan, Stanlley

us plus two of my other cousins, Ted Tuft and Wayne Olsen, had wonderful times together dreaming up mischief to get into, including building model airplanes (we all belonged to the Junior Birdmen of America), going pheasant and jack rabbit hunting and swimming and rafting in the South Bend Canal. Looking back now at some of the close scrapes we were in, it was a wonder we survived our childhood.

I thought my height and weight measurements recorded on October 9, 1932 on my third grade report card by my Salt Lake school teacher, Miss Mitchell, was interesting. It states

I was 4 feet 4 1/2 inches tall at that time and I weighed 52 3/4 pounds. For an eight and a half year old boy that tall, the school chart showed I was 25% underweight and I should weigh at least 66 pounds. Apparently, I was under-weight and under-nourished during that great depression period after Grandma Olsen died. In fact, I feel now this may have been the reason my mother, who had letters from her sister (my Aunt Maude) concerning my under nourished condition, decided to kidnap me in the first place. I remember I was so skinny at that time my shoulder blades stuck out like wings and when the other kids teased me about it, I told them they really were wings and I was a boy angel.

Aunt Maud suggested I write a letter to my mother after I moved in with them to forgive her for kidnapping me and tell her I was living with Uncle Orson's family and was gaining weight. The following letter from my Mother, now Mrs. Wm. H. Staley, is in answer to my letter. She mailed her letter from 9434 National Blvd, Palms Station, Los Angeles, California, on April 24, 1933, shortly after Tex and I celebrated my ninth birthday and his eighth on April 8, 1933. This letter is my first contact with her after my kidnapping since she no longer needed to lay low from the law. My dad had dropped the charges against her and the judge had withdrawn his arrest warrant.

April 24, 1933

Dear little Junior,

I just finished reading your letter and I feel a lot better now that I've heard from you and know you are happy. And honey, I'm proud of you for passing your grade in school and getting promoted to the 4th grade. Your skipping right along fast aren't you?

I just got back from the hospital from seeing Staley and he said when I wrote to you to tell you 'Hello' for him. He is so awfully sick right now (from bleeding ulcers) that I spend most of my time up there with him. There is no news to tell you, but honey, write to me right away again won't you? I worry about you when I don't hear from you. I can hardly realize your nine years old. You'll be grown up before I know it almost.

Tell Aunt Maud 'Hello'. I would write only there's nothing to tell her and I've got to be back up to the Hospital at 7 PM and it's six now so 'bye for now honey and remember to write right away again. I'm enclosing a stamped self addressed envelope so you can answer real soon. Remember that I love you and think of you always.

love and kisses,
Fr. Mother.

Uncle Orson was undoubtedly the most successful business entrepreneur and did the best financially of all Grandpa's children. My dad told me his older brother Orson quit school after

he graduated from the eighth grade and began herding sheep in 1905 when he was fourteen years old. He took half his pay in cash and the other half in lambs, to begin building his own herd and by the time he and Ferd Ericksen enlisted in the Army in 1916 during World War I he was well off financially and owned over a thousand head of sheep and cattle. I remember Grandpa Olsen telling me how proud he was of Orson for what he had accomplished, and for enlisting in the Army during World War I to help save democracy for the world. He said the whole town of Monroe turned out to honor Orson and Ferd when they enlisted and they had a big brass band parade all the way from Monroe to the train station in Ellsinore over five miles

Orson B. Olsen — 1934

away, to see their favorite sons off to war. As it turned out, Ferd Ericksen saw action in France and came back from the war in 1919 with a battlefield commission and rank of first lieutenant. Uncle Orson served in England as an aircraft mechanic on *SPAD* fighter planes and returned from the war a corporal. Uncle Nephi, the only other one of Grandpa's sons in the service during World War I, enlisted in the army in 1917 to keep from marrying Maude Barney, the mother of his *out of wedlock* daughter named Muriel Olsen. Dad told me, Uncle Nephi only served in British Columbia, Canada, as a soldier-logger harvesting trees to build Army barracks in the United States, and that Grandpa had to pay old man Barney $500 as a penalty and damages for what Nephi had caused by not marrying his daughter, Maude (Barney). Uncle Orson and Aunt Maude (Weimer) then ended up raising Nephi's daughter, Muriel, who was living with Uncle Orson's family when I moved in with them after my kidnapping.

When Uncle Orson returned from England and was discharged in 1919, he married a beautiful girl from Monroe named Verna Ericksen. They lived happily together for the first two years of their marriage until tragically Verna died in 1921 from complications during the birth of their first child, a little girl named Peggy. I remember Dad telling me Uncle Orson was completely devastated and heartbroken over Verna's death, and in his daughter's best interests turned the responsibility of raising little Peggy over to Verna's parents. Dad was working for Uncle Orson as a ranch hand at the time and three years later in 1924, Uncle Orson married my mother's older sister, Maude Weimer.

Aunt Maude was a Godsend and the perfect wife for Uncle Orson and she was the perfect mother for their four boys and the strays they took in, like Muriel and me. Aunt Maude inherited

Aunt Maude — 1934

from her mother, Tina Weimer, (who was of half Scotch and half Danish decent) the art of good

old fashioned German-Danish cooking and to this day she still deserves first prize (next to her daughter, my Aunt Maude) for being the *best cook* in our family. Grandpa Peter Weimer (her husband who was100% German) used to tell us kids on the sly that Grandma Weimer couldn't boil water when they were first married, and he *learned* her all she knew about cooking. Aunt Maud also inherited the exact opposite personality of her hot tempered, chain smoking, coffee swilling younger sister named Ruth, who was my mother. She had a wonderful, easy going, loving way about her that my mother lacked, and I don't remember her ever being rattled by any of the close calls and near disasters her four boys had. She always treated Muriel and me exactly the same way she treated and loved her own children.

I remember one time, she made a beautiful German chocolate cake with a half inch of chocolate fudge icing on top as frosting that I would have died and gone to heaven for. Dad always told me to be polite and try not to appear overly anxious when asked if I would like a piece of her cake or anything else she had for desert, and the first time it's offered just say, "Oh, I better not." Then when she answered, "Oh come now, try one iddy bitty teeny piece", I was supposed to politely say, "OK, if you insist" followed by a heartfelt "Thank you, it was absolutely delicious" when finished. Well, you guessed it, after Aunt Maude offered me a piece of her wonderful German chocolate cake and I *cued her in* with my, "Oh, thank you, but I better not", and surprisingly, she never said her next line to *coax me*. To this day I still remember standing there watching in torturous silence as my four double cousins sat there gobbling down those huge beautiful slices of that wonderful German chocolate cake with thick layers of chocolate fudge frosting, like four slobbering disgusting pigs at a hog trough, and not one of them even offered me a teeny weensy taste.

Aunt Maude — 1935

Tex and I found some black powder in Uncle Orson's granary one time that he used for stump removals when clearing land, so we decided to set some off by the wood pile to see what would happen. To be on the safe side, we ran a long *powder fuse* trail over to the wood pile to a large coffee can we had filled with black powder, and lit the fuse. Well, you guessed it, the fuse worked fine right up to the edge of the coffee can, but for some unknown reason, fizzled out. After waiting a minute or two, Tex said he should check it out and even though I cautioned him to wait a little longer, he insisted he would be careful and proceeded to crawl over to the coffee can on his hands and knees. Well wouldn't you know it, as luck would have it just as he peeked over the top edge of that coffee can, *Whoosh*, all that black powder suddenly exploded and to this day, I still remember that tremendous "*Whooshing Sound*" followed by a huge mushroom cloud of black smoke billowing skyward with what looked like my best friends arms and legs sticking out every so often. When the *whooshing* finally subsided and the black cloud began to clear, lo and behold, there kneeled old Tex on one knee, stunned but staring straight at me with both arms outstretched and screaming bloody murder. His face was black from the blast soot and his hair had singed off to look like a GI haircut. In fact, he looked so much like Al Johlson kneeling on one knee with his arms outstretched singing "*Mammy*", I busted out laughing, and continued laughing so hard my sides hurt. I knew my best friend Tex was in pain and might even be badly hurt, but for the life of me, I couldn't stop laughing. Well you guessed it, he suddenly stopped hollering and just glared at me for at least a minute, then he yelled, "Set there and laugh while I'm dying will you, I'll kill you" and the race was on. He chased me for nearly an hour, back and forth through that old grove of trees behind the corrals, bawling and cussing and throwing rocks and sticks at me, while I dodged and laughed until I ached all over. Fortunately, he had instinctively closed his eyes before the blast so he saved his eyes and his skin was only slightly burned under all that soot so all in all, aside from his hurt feelings, he was fine. There was no doubt about it, Tex was one very lucky boy that day to have escaped serious injury.

Another time, Tex and Ted Tuft and I discovered someone had forgotten to lock up the old sugar factory (sugar beet processing plant) located on the county road between Hy Madsen's and Lily Winget's farms. We decided to play *hide and seek* inside because it was so dark and spooky and it had numerous ladders and walkways and tanks to hide behind. I remember, I was voted '*it*' to start things while Tex and Ted ran off to hide, but before I even had time to count to *fifty*, we heard Tex screaming bloody murder and Ted and I started running around that dark plant looking for him. His screams kept getting more and more hysterical before we found where he had hidden and wouldn't you know it, the dark empty container tank he had jumped in to hide was a 500 gallon tank nearly full of a highly viscous molasses syrup, and he had already started sinking slowly like he was in quicksand. I remember he was already up to his waist by the time we found him, but fortunately, by working together as a team we finally managed to pull him out. It was while walking Tex home down the recently *chipped with pea gravel* county road, Ted and I thought it was hysterically funny the way the legs of Tex's bib overalls were so sticky even walking straddle legged, he couldn't walk without getting his legs stuck together,. Well, as the say, *necessity is the mother of inventions*, we decided to roll him on the road chips to un-stick him, and it worked. To this day I will never forget Tex *waddling* home covered to his waist in *rock armor*, disguised as the "*Rock Man Monster*", while Ted and I held our sides laughing at the way he waddled home to scare his mother. To this day I still remember Aunt Maude's only comment when she saw the rock monster was, "Oh Tecky, what have you done?"

Uncle Orson had some really mean livestock on his farm too. He had a mean Holstein bull, a mean ram (buck sheep), and one mean old black cow that was rightfully named *Old Meany* when she had a calf. That mean old cow would never let us kids short cut across any field she was in, especially when her calf was with her, and often trapped us on the hay wagon in the middle of the pasture she was grazing in. All we could do then was *Yell* at the top of our lungs for someone to rescue us while that mean old cow pranced around the wagon glaring at us.

Tex's little brother "Spun" (his real name was Nolan Olsen) had a good friend everyone called "Zoney" (his real name was Laurence Nazier) who claimed he wasn't afraid of anything or anybody, so Spun showed him his dad's mean old ram sheep. When he told Zoney, "Whatever you do, don't ever, *and I mean ever*, kick that buck in the face", you guessed it, that good advice only challenged Zoney further. Well, while Zonie was swaggering over to kick the ram that was grazing peacefully in the pasture, the rest of us high-tailed it to the farmhouse. Oooh boy, I'll tell you the minute Zoney kicked that buck in the face just below its huge curled rack of horns; the chase was on, while we watched safely from inside the farmhouse. As I recall, that old farmhouse had steps up to a hand railed porch with a screened front door and a large picture window, so when Zoney raced towards the house with the buck right on his heals, we casually locked the front door and watched this little drama of life unfold from behind the porch window.

Zoney hit that front door wide open on a dead run, but unfortunately was only able to scream, "Open the door" as the buck reached butting range. He would then run to the end of the porch, vault over the handrail and race around the house for another try at the front door. The buck, unable to vault the handrail at the end of the porch, would have to run back down the porch steps to resume the chase around the house. That maneuver caused the buck to lose a few steps, but by the time they both reached the front porch steps again after chasing around the house, the buck had regained lost time and Zoney would only have time to scream again, "Open the door", and repeat the rail vaulting maneuver over again, and again, and again, and so it went. To add insult to injury, as they kept passing wide open by our front row window seats, Spun would yell, "I told you and told you Zoney, *DON'T* kick that buck in the face." Finally, many laps later, an exhausted, deflated, and a rapidly approaching hysteria, a very humble Zoney Nazier was allowed to slip through the front porch door a mille-second ahead of the inspired buck sheep that knew the kill was near.

I used to have nightmares over Uncle Orson's mean old Holstein bull, and even more so after Tex's little two year old brother, Sterling, wandered into the bull pen and was nearly killed. Sterling wasn't more than a baby at the time he and his six year older brother "Spun" were playing in the corral, while their dad was feeding the cows. Like all young children when you take your eyes off them for only a second, Sterling suddenly disappeared by crawling under the slotted fence into that mean bull's pen, before anyone missed him. The bull began snorting and pawing dirt over its back and readying itself to gore little Sterling, just seconds before Uncle Orson noticed Sterling was missing and in the pen. He immediately jumped the fence into the bullpen with his pitch fork and was able to jab the bull away from Sterling until his big brother, six year old "Spun", heroically rescued his little brother. To this day, Sterling still has a scar on his forehead from the '*nick*' made by that bull's horn.

I remember Uncle Orson hired a seventy year old neighbor everyone called, "Old man Crawford", to put in a barbwire fence across the pasture where that same mean Holstein bull was quietly feeding. Apparently the bull took offense to having its property fenced and suddenly charged the old man while he was working alone setting cedar fence posts. When old man Crawford saw the bull rumbling towards him like a freight train, he calmly put a fence post on his shoulder like a baseball player, and just as the bull thundered by, he stepped aside like a matador and swung his bat. As luck would have it, he hit the bull smack dab center on his nose-ring with his bat and, Oooh boy, it must have really smart because the bull stopped and began roaring and pawing dirt over its back. When that happened, old man Crawford calmly moseyed back across the pasture with his shovel on his shoulder, towards the ranch house and calmly poured himself a cup of coffee. He told all us kids who had been watching and marveling his courage, "*Never let a mean animal know you're afraid of them because if you do, they will kill you.*"

My dad told me the same thing after he finished his own mean bull story. He said he rode his horse into the pasture one time to cut John Hansen's Holstein bull out of our herd of love sick milk cows, and the bull wasn't about to leave peacefully. He said the bull angrily turned on his horse and somehow got its horns under Dad's horses belly and butted them over. Dad's horse immediately got up and ran off the field leaving Dad alone with only his riding quirt to defend himself. Luckily, Winifred's little terrier dog she called, *Puppy*, was with my dad at the time and began barking and nipping at the bull's heels, causing the bull to spin in a circle to gore the dog, while Dad sauntered slowly off the pasture towards the corrals. When he reached the corral fence, little Puppy ran to him ahead of the bull and leaped into his arms, tail wagging and all.

NEWS RELEASE

March 23, 1933 the German Reichstag passes the Enabling Act, which gives Hitler special powers and the first concentration Camp is established near Munich at Dachau.

Freddie, Tony & Puppy - 1941

There was no doubt in my dad's mind that little terrier dog saved his life that day, but he also said, "If I hadn't just moseyed off the field to show the bull I wasn't afraid of him, he would have ignored *Puppy* and gored me to death." From then on, Dad thought almost as much of "Little Puppy" as he did of "*Old Bob*", but not quite. How did I know that? He never promoted or gave Freddie's little dog the title, "*Old Puppy.*"

Tex and I designed and built a glider out of some old weathered fence siding one time, and decided to test launch it from the top of Uncle Orson's concrete corn silage silo. By combining block and tackle with a lot of rope and hard work, believe it or not we were able to pull our glider up to the top of that silo and aim it at a haystack fifty feet or so away. After considerable discussion while surveying the situation from the silo top, Tex and I decided we were obviously too heavy to pilot the glider ourselves on its maiden flight, so we sweet talked "Spun", who was smaller, lighter, and two years younger than Tex, into being our test pilot. In retrospect, it was lucky Uncle Orson was keeping a watchful eye on our project because as we were about to tighten Spun's safety belt for take off, Uncle Orson had climbed the silo ladder to our launch site and said, "Just what in the 'double-h-keerist' do you kids think you're doing?" After a long and technical explanation, he still wasn't convinced that we needed a live pilot to test our glider and insisted we test it without a pilot to check the gliders *aerodynamics* first. We reluctantly agreed with his analysis and launched our brilliantly engineered glider from the top rim of the silo without a pilot as he suggested, and you guessed it, the glider dropped like a rock, straight down, disintegrating on impact.

I remember another time, Uncle Orson bought a slightly used 1929 Buick, and Tex and I decided to play service station and give it full station service. We washed the car and all the windows with soap and water from a garden hose connected to the front yard tap, and we even checked the radiator and gas tank levels and found them both low, so we filled them with our garden hose. All in all, we were pretty proud of our accomplishments, and even more so when Uncle Orson gave us each a nickel for washing his car. A little while later, Uncle Nephi (my Cousin Wayne Olsen's dad and Uncle Orson's older brother) stopped by to check out the new used car and Uncle Orson gave him the keys to take her out for a spin. Well you guessed it, an hour later here came Uncle Nephi walking back saying the motor had quit on him. I think Uncle Orson instinctively knew what was wrong, because he picked up his toolbox and a gallon can of gasoline from his fuel barrel by the wagon shed, and walked the two miles back to the car with Uncle Nephi. When they arrived, he unscrewed the car's gas line from the carburetor and began draining the contaminated gasoline from the cars gas tank on to the road shoulder.

Well, the car happened to be parked on the side of the graveled county road on that sloping shoulder, so while the gas and water mixture was draining from the car on to the shoulder and on down into the adjacent borrow pit, Uncle Orson was tinkering with the engines carburetor. All the while this was going on, Uncle Nephi, trying to be helpful, lit a match and nonchalantly threw it into the borrow pit to burn off the fumes, not realizing the "gas-water" trail from the car to the borrow pit would act like a fuse. Oooh boy, you guessed it, that car became engulfed in flames only seconds after the borrow pit was lit and was completely destroyed by the fire shortly afterwards. Even more amazing, Uncle Orson never blew his stack, or even said boo to Uncle Nephi, or to either one of us kids, for what we had done. I will always remember standing there the next day with my best friend Tex, watching that car's smoldering remains, while our inner conscience kept telling us, we were the two incompetent people that were really responsible for that car burning up, not Uncle Nephi.

I don't think time will ever change the fact that little boys will always try to imitate their role models. In the case of Tex and Ted and I, our dads were our role models. My dad's ability to roll a Bull Durham cigarette with one hand while he was riding his horse, proved to me he was a real cowboy, and the sack of Bull Durham he carried in his left front shirt pocket with the string and round tag showing, seemed to me to be the badge of manhood. Ted Tuft's dad, Uncle Elve, was a real man too because he would break a raw egg in his full glass of beer, and it was fascinating to watch him "chug-a-lug" the whole thing down without even taking a breath. He was tall and thin and even looked like Gary Cooper in his cowboy hat. We thought Uncle Orson, Tex's dad, was a real man's man because he not only smoked long expensive cigars, but he wore a Stetson business-rancher's hat called "The Westerner" and owned a big herd of cattle and sheep, and even had a fast race horse he named "Frenchy.".

I will also never forget the time Uncle Orson caught the three of us kids in his horse barn smoking home made cigars that we had made from dry horse manure rolled in newspapers. He said, "Well men, why don't we go into my den together and smoke some real cigars like real men do and talk business?" I remember we jumped at his invitation and immediately threw our cigars away because Uncle Orson's den was an inner sanctum and only men (never any women or kids) were allowed in there. I remember he had two trophy heads, a deer and an antelope, plus a cougar hide and several Charlie Russell type cowboy paintings, all mounted on the walls. He also had a huge hardwood desk and a big leather chair where he did all his paperwork and business reading, and he had a huge couch with two side chairs, all upholstered in real cowhide. Best of all, the room smelled from the aroma of real fine cigars, so there was no doubt in any of our minds; Uncle Orson was a real man's man and his den was a real man's den.

I remember he sat the three of us down together on the cowhide couch and picked out four big long cigars from a large beautifully finished hardwood humidor, and gave each of us a tall glass of water, and lit our three cigars and one for himself. He then sat down in his big leather chair and we all began discussing the lousy wool market, the terribly low cattle and sheep prices, and the terrible national economy in general. We even cussed out Roosevelt together and discussed how all the dumb New Deal Democrats were ruining our country, and all the while Uncle Orson kept insisting we keep puffing on our cigars to keep them lit, and take swigs from the water glasses he had given us. At first, the room just turned a little blue from the smoke, but pretty soon all four walls, and the ceiling, began to slowly spin, and we began to turn a little green. I remember, we had smoked our cigars down about halfway before we began to turn a bright green color, and all of a sudden after that last swig of water, in unison, we asked to be excused. To this day, I will never forget the three of us racing to the backyard with our hands over our mouths, and spending the rest of that afternoon hanging over a ditch bank, retching from the dry heaves, and hoping the good lord would take us and put an end to our suffering. My two cousins, Tex and Ted, never smoked again after that experience, and I never started smoking cigars again until I was nearly thirty years old. One thing still bothers me though. Uncle Orson must have spiked our water glasses with something to accelerate our seasickness, but what was it? (Note to file; Tex solved the mystery while proof reading these stories, he said his dad had put *"Kaopectate"* in our water glasses to speed up our learning experience).

I remember Uncle Orson's wonderful fortieth birthday party, when all five of us kids pooled our pennies and bought him a big long expensive cigar as a gift, and loaded it with explosive cigarette joke sticks. Since it was so big and long, we quadrupled the number of stick charges ordinarily used to explode a cigarette and wrapped it as our extra special, life begins at forty, birthday gift. It was a wonderful party with cake and home made hand cranked ice cream and all, and Uncle Orson was really touched by our gift. In fact, while we were standing around watching in hypnotic anticipation for him to light it, he went out of his way to thank all of us for that wonderful luxurious cigar, and all the sacrifices we had to have made to buy it with our own hard earned money. Finally, with a swooping flourish, he struck a wooden match across the seat of his britches like a real cowboy, and lit his birthday cigar. Oooh boy, I'll tell you, after he took a few puffs to blow a few big smoke rings for our benefit, that cigar suddenly exploded with a spectacular *"Kaboom"* that literally disintegrated the outer one half of that long cigar, and caught Uncle Orson completely off guard by surprise. When he recovered from the shock of that loud explosion, and realized what we had done, it was the first time I ever saw Uncle Orson really angry, and all five of us kids took off wide open on a dead run to hide. Fortunately he wasn't injured except for his feelings, but for awhile, all we heard from under the bed where we were hiding was, Uncle Orson loudly cussing and Aunt Maude howling with laughter.

Around that same time, my cousin Ted Tuft and I, decided to organize a *Safari* business as partners to catch and sell *Magpies* at a profit and retire early as millionaires, because a friend of ours named, Cal Bates, had told us it was possible to teach that particular bird to talk like a parrot, if you split its tongue. We knew there were *jillions* of magpies flying around the Sevier River near Charlie Nielsen's farm called *Jericho*, so we figured we had an unlimited supply for our lucrative business. A rather serious problem arose however, while we were walking across the Sevier River Railroad Bridge to check out our bird supply on the other side. As we approached the middle of the river walking the tracks over the bridge, the rails suddenly began vibrating from a freight train called the "Sevier Valley Creeper" that was rapidly approaching. Well for some unknown reason, but most likely *just for the hell of it*, we decided to climb over the side of that old steel girder bridge and sit on a *pile cap* in the center of the river. We figured it would be fun to find out what it really felt like when that steam engine and its long train of freight cars passed over us on that pile cap. Whoooee, I'll tell you, I will never forget the exhilaration, and the excitement we felt from

that shaking, quivering, vibrating bridge, along with the creaking and groaning and swaying and all that hot steam hissing around us, when the engine, and that long train line of freight cars passed over. It was the most exciting experience either one of us ever had in our whole lives and I couldn't wait to tell my dad and my grandpa about it. Unfortunately, and amazingly to me, neither one of them appreciated what we did one iota and instead, my dad literally came unglued. He grabbed me by the bib of my overalls, turned me over his knees, and between bottom swats kept shouting, "Don't ever let me hear of you doing such a stupid thing like that again." After I finally quit bawling,

Ted Tuft - 1935

he said, "I hope you learned a lesson from that spanking." When between sobs I said, "I sure did Dad", he asked, "What was the lesson you learned?" I said, "Never tell your Dad everything you do from now on."

I don't remember ever doing many chores while I was living with Uncle Orson's family, mostly because there were more kids to spread the work to I guess. There was always plenty of work to do on his farm, but Uncle Orson could afford plenty of hired help in those days, so when our share of the chores where divided five ways, they were minor compared to what I had to do for Dad and Grandpa all by myself. I don't remember having any guilt feelings about not being at Gravelbed to help Dad and Grandpa, although I guess I should have. Tex and I visited them often, and I still remember the time Grandpa was trying to explain to Niels Higgins, his neighbor, what grades we were both in at school that year and Tex and I would crack up laughing when, in his Norwegian brogue, he said, "Yuniors in det fart grade, and Teckees in det turd." Tex and I knew Grandpa loved fish, so we caught him a big carp in an irrigation ditch one time one time and he made such a big fuss over it and how pleased he was with what we had done, then he proceeded to cook and eat it with relish. Oooh boy, was he ever sick afterwards over that fish and from then on he turned down all the suckers and carp we brought to him, but said he would appreciate any trout we caught.

While I was living with Aunt Maude and Uncle Orson's family, Dad and Grandpa were living in absolute poverty on their farm. Roosevelt had already raised the income tax from 25% to 63% in 1933, and again in 1935 to 75%, thereby guaranteeing the economy would stay in a deep long depression for many more years. The first of the "Save the Environment" laws (the Taylor Grazing Act) was passed by the misguided New Deal Congress in 1934 to prevent further live stock permit grazing on federal mountain property and desert range lands. With one stroke of a pen, that new environmental law was the final blow for my dad and my uncle Oluf's sheep and wool business. The drought and the terribly cold winters, plus the loss of 750 head of sheep freezing to death during a freak blizzard on the Pine Valley desert range, coupled with this new grazing law, was the last straw. The good news was, they were completely wiped out financially so they never had to worry about paying any taxes.

I remember my dad telling me about a knot-headed socialist politician named, Henry Wallace that Roosevelt had appointed as his first Secretary of Agriculture. Henry Wallace had unilaterally ordered all the ranchers and farmers in central Utah to destroy half their livestock to improve the price structure, under some screwball supply and demand theory he dreamed up. Dad said the ranchers told Wallace after he had offered them $1 a head to get rid of half their

Farm Husen — 1933

livestock, they would give their animals to the government for nothing if they would pay for shipping them down to the American cities as food for their long soup lines. Henry Wallace refused their offer and the animals were ordered destroyed to end up rotting as coyote and buzzard feed on the hillsides. I remember the City of Monroe had what they called "Lamb Day" barbecues at the city park, so people could enjoy all they could eat before the remaining animals were slaughtered and left to rot on the bench. In the end, the price adjustment plan Wallace envisioned was a complete failure and had no effect whatsoever on any of the livestock pricing.

Dad and Grandpa's morale was so low after that ridiculous dictatorial livestock reduction plan of the New Deal bureaucracy, they gave up all hope of any recovery, and no maintenance whatsoever was done on any of their farm buildings, corrals, fences, farm equipment or anything else, and everything began to rapidly decay. Their bank loan payments were so high; they were forced to sell off shares of their precious irrigation water just to pay interest and major portions of their farmland returned to dust. The few water shares left for the few acres remaining were used to grow only feed for their few milk cows remaining, as they watched helplessly as their neighbor's farms were being taken over by the banks. How Dad and Grandpa were able to hang on to that old farm, I'll never know, but one thing for sure, neither one of them ever voted for another Democrat afterwards. Dad told me, "*Mark my words son; these knot headed New Deal Democrats will break this country some day.*"

Grandpa Olsen used to tell me, "You come from good stock son, be proud of it" and it was his and my dad's stubborn Norwegian pride, coupled with their optimism and wonderful sense of humor, that saved them. Dad and Grandpa had too much pride to ever accept any charity and they ridiculed anyone who accepted relief or WPA help. To this day, I still remember there were many times when our only meal of the day was "milk and bread" and "clabber and bread" when the milk soured. Dad would always crack some kind of a joke and laughingly say how lucky we were to even have that much, but to me it was depressing that anyone should have to live like that. Sometimes, when I was staying with them, Grandpa would be so down in the dumps Dad would pull him out of his chair by the wood stove and they would "Auteetot" (polka) around the room singing some tune, and soon Grandpa would be laughing again. By the same token when Dad was depressed, Grandpa would be reminded of one of his funny stories with a positive point, and Dad would soon begin laughing again.

They both used to tell hysterically funny stories about Uncle Joe, my dad's older brother who was famous for his terribly hot temper. Dad said whenever Uncle Joe would accidentally hit his thumb with a hammer he would throw it as far as he could to teach it a lesson, and Dad, who was working nearby, would run over and pick up the hammer and throw it even further away while Uncle Joe watched in amazement. Finally he would ask Dad, "Just why in Hell's name did you do that?", and Dad would say, "I'm helping you." Another time Joe got mad at his horse and started beating it with a riding quirt, and Dad, feeling sorry for the horse, would grab a stick and started beating his horse on the other side. Joe would then stop whipping his horse and watch Dad for a few seconds and then ask real disgusted like, "Just what in Keerist's name do you think your doing?" When Dad would say, "I'm helping you", Uncle Joe would turn his anger on Dad instead of the horse and start chasing him around the corrals, screaming, "Hit my horse, will you; I'll show you."

The best hot temper story about Uncle Joe and his hot temper was when he was hand cranking his Model "T" Ford to get it started and suddenly it backfired causing the crank to give him a really mean *kick back whack* on his elbow. Whoooee, it must have really smart because Uncle Joe literally flipped his lid, and to teach his Model "T" a lesson it wouldn't forget, he picked up a double tree from the wagon next to his car, and caved in the radiator. When Dad came over to see what had happened saying, "Oooh boy, now what are you going to do?" Uncle Joe just shrugged his shoulders and answered real sarcastic like, "Well, I'll just hitch up the team and drag this damn car over to Cy Bell's garage and get it fixed, that's what I'll do." So, Dad and Uncle Joe harnessed up the team and pulled his Model "T" the three miles into town to the garage and when Cy Bell finished surveying the damage, he said while shaking his head, "Just park the car inside the garage for now and I'll work on it tomorrow." Well, you can believe this or not, your choice, but as bad luck will continue when you need it the least, that night Cy Bell's garage accidentally caught on fire and burned to the ground with Uncle Joes uninsured Model "T" Ford inside. I'll tell you, Uncle Joe was devastated by the loss of his car, but Grandpa wasn't one bit sympathetic with Joe's whining and moaning about his rotten luck. He told Uncle Joe, "Yust let that be a gud lesson to yew for being so hot headed."

Another time Uncle Joe left his horse with Dad and Grandpa to *look after*, and told Dad to ride his horse anytime he felt like it because it needed exercising every so often. My cousin Ted Tuft's parents, my Aunt Bertha and Uncle Elve, always sold a substantial number of turkeys to "Dolly's Mercantile and Meat Market" in Monroe around Thanksgiving every year and they had asked Dad and me to give them a hand plucking feathers. Well, we decided to ride horses up to their farm for some exercise so I picked Uncle Joe's horse that was still a little skittish while Dad rode his own fast little quarter horse. Dad told me, "If Uncle Joe's horse gets too ornery for you, don't worry about it because I can always catch up with you on my fast horse and rescue you right out of the saddle just like Tom Mix does in the movies." Aside from a little raring and prancing around, everything went fine all the way up to the Tuft's farm, and we really put in a good day's work plucking turkey feathers before we headed back home to do chores.

Unfortunately, a problem arose because Uncle Joe's horse apparently decided while he was waiting, no little kid was going to slow him down going home. I no sooner got in the saddle and that ornery horse took off on a dead run, wide open down the county road and, try as I might, I couldn't slow him down. Luckily, I was able to stay in the saddle the first couple of miles, so he decided to stop and put on a little rodeo bucking show in front of Lily Winget's farm house to show Lily how he could buck me off. Well, at first I thought his bucking around was fun while I was waiting for Dad to catch-up on his fast (?) little horse, but unfortunately it ended up with me bouncing off, head down-face first, to a crash landing on the graveled county road. Uncle Joe's horse then loped off "hee-hawing" without me, just as Dad skidded up on his fast horse to rescue me, saying "Whooee, Uncle Joe's horse is faster than I thought." Except for some bruises and gravel scratches on my face, I wasn't hurt, but Oooh boy, was I mad. I said, "That might be a faster horse to you Dad, but by damn, it's going to be a dead horse when I get home."

Dad, Grandpa & "Yunior" - 1934

The interesting thing to me about that little drama of life was, my dad didn't try once to discourage me from shooting that lousy horse when we got home. He agreed with my ranting and raving all the way back to Gravelbed about, "That no good lousy horse deserves to die." When we got home, he even went into the house and brought out his 32-20 Winchester rifle and two cartridges for me to shoot him in case I missed the first time. Grandpa had already unsaddled and unbridled Uncle Joe's horse and had fed him, so he was an easy shot just standing there eating his supper. The problem was, *I wasn't mad any more*. After a few aims to check the sights, I told Dad, "It just doesn't seem right to shoot a horse while he's eating his supper, what do you think?" Dad nodded saying, "Yah, I think you're right about that", and began rolling a Bull Durham cigarette. We then sat down together leaning against the corral fence to study on it some more and let Dad finish his smoke, then I said, "And besides that Dad, it's Uncle Joe's horse, so I really don't think I should be shooting his horse without his OK, do you?" Dad just shrugged his shoulders, and said, "Well, you know you're Uncle Joe and his hot temper as well as I do." That's when I handed the Winchester rifle back to him and said, "I sure do, and I think we should put this whole thing behind us until I have a chance to talk to Uncle Joe about it", and stood up to mosey towards the farmhouse. For some unknown reason, I felt I had just passed another one of Dad's character tests, because when I walked passed him towards the farm house, he had another one of those, *you done the right thing,* looks all over his face.

I'll say this for Uncle Joe, he was a real artist when it came to whittling things with his pocket knife. He would make us kids the best whistles out of green willows, better than anyone else I've ever known including Grandpa. In fact he even whittled Grandma Olsen something that looked like a church steeple with five dowel sized columns holding an inch and a half diameter perfectly whittled spherical ball inside that rolled back and forth, all whittled from one single block of wood without using any glue. There was no doubt in anyone mind; it was truly a work of art. My cousin Halvor told me his dad (Uncle Joe) used to whittle all sorts of toys with his pocket knife for his brothers and sisters that were so much better than anything you could buy in a store. Come to think of it, all ten of Uncle Joe's children were talented in so many different ways, and especially in music. Halvor's older sister Dorothy was so talented she really missed her calling and could have been a concert pianist.

NEWS RELEASE

July through September 1934, Austrian Nazi's assassinate Chancellor Engelbert Dollfuss and German President Paul Von Hindenburg dies mysteriously. Adolph Hitler becomes both head of government and head of state and the Soviet Union joins the League of Nations.

I will always be grateful to my Aunt Maude and my Uncle Orson for taking me under their wing and sharing their happy home and wonderful family life with me on their well run farm. I was a basket case when they adopted me for the two and a half years after that kidnapping experience, and if it hadn't been for their love, support, patience and guidance after that terrible experience, I don't know where I would be now. I am also grateful for my wonderful double cousins who shared their lives with me when I needed their brotherly love the most and grateful to my relatives in the Ole K. Olsen and Peter Weimer families for their support and advice in choosing *the right lane and direction* to travel, along the highway of life.

Dad and Ercel were officially married on November 30, 1934 (although Dad said they were secretly married in November of 1933) and I moved back to Gravelbed from Uncle Orson and Aunt Maude's farm to live with Grandpa, Dad and Ercel, and a brand new six year old step sister named Marilyn (Ercel's daughter from a previous marriage). When Ercel May Allred accepted my dad's proposal and agreed to marry him, it was without question the best thing that ever happened to Dad and Grandpa after Grandma Olsen died. Without a doubt, everything began to change for the better the minute she and Marilyn walked into that old farmhouse. I remember Ercel telling me years later when she first stepped into the kitchen, how shocked she was to see there was absolutely no food in the house except a half empty jar of peanut butter on the shelf. I had forgotten how empty the cupboards were during the great depression, but I do remember Grandpa always having his two gallon coffee pot, brim full of hot strong boiled coffee, day and night.

When Ercel moved in two things happened that really disturbed Grandpa, and it was the fourth and last time I saw him really *blow his stack* angry. Ercel dragged Grandpa's old two gallon coffee pot that he loved so much out into the back forty and cruelly dumped all it's aged coffee grounds, and skowered that old pot clean with *lye soap*. In one fell swoop she had ruined forever that old coffee pot's ability to ever make good strong Norwegian coffee again, and Grandpa was furious, and I mean *really* furious. He tried making coffee in the pot later, but finally gave up because the coffee tasted (he said) like *lye soap*. Grandpa and Dad were also still chewing plugs of tobacco and dipping Copenhagen *snooze*, so Ercel told them in no if ands or buts she would not put up with their tobacco habits and/or Grandpa using the coal bucket by the stove as a spittoon any longer. After Grandpa had finally simmered down from his tirade over the coffee pot and tobacco matter, he reluctantly agreed his failing eyesight was probably causing him to miss the coal bucket occasionally and that Ercel might have a point so in the end, Ercel accomplished what Grandma Olsen was never able to do. She alone, and all by herself, accomplished the impossible task of converting Grandpa into a good Mormon again and convinced him once and for all, he had to eliminate his horse bite medicine (his Akvavit and Irish Whisky) he had hidden in the horse barn, his stout (if you can't float a silver dollar on it, it isn't stout enough) boiled coffee, and all his tobacco plugs and cans of snooze, from his diet. Like my dad's Grizzly Bear story, for some unknown reason, I suddenly felt sad and very sorry for my wonderful Grandpa.

Dad believe it or not, also finally and reluctantly gave up his vices, except for his Bull Durham cigarettes he claimed would be too much of a shock for his system. But, to his credit, he did agree he would begin working on a *stop smoking program* only seconds before their negotiations reached the *that's it divorce stage*. It took Dad almost two more years of constant suffering before he finally quit smoking cold turkey, and gave up his bull Durham hand rolled cigarettes. So, after all was said and done, Ercel, in the name of prohibition and the Mormon church, and as a single handed vice squad, not only cleaned us of all our vices, but cruelly closed down Dad and Grandpa's beer still *Root Cellar Speakeasy*, and converted it into producing her legally approved *Root Beer*. When several of our church going neighbors complimented Dad and Grandpa on their behavioral improvements, Dad bragged he and Grandpa had *re-seen the light* all on their own, and decided to become better Latter Day Saints. I remember telling him, "Never under estimate the power of a good women either, Dad." It was Ercel who deserved all the credit.

Ercel also saw to it, the floors in that old farm house got new linoleum and rugs, the leaky roof received new asphalt shingles, and the interior and exterior of that old house was given a much needed new coat of paint. The only difference between Ercel and Grandma Olsen, as for as spit and polish housekeeping was concerned, was the "Scandinavian Yellow" exterior house color Grandma loved was changed to an "English White" that Ercel preferred. Grandpa's bed mattress, that had become infested with bed bugs, was burned and Ercel remodeled his room with newly painted walls, new curtains, and additional furniture. She even went to the extreme of setting up a weekly Saturday night bath schedules for all three of us men, whether we needed it or not. To this day, I still think an angel named Grandma Olsen had a hand in all these revisions because, in my mind there was no doubt about it, she was in cahoots with Ercel to save us from a life of sin and a fate worse than death.

The Christmas of 1934 was by far my most exciting Xmas I ever had, bar none, because it was the year I got my wonderful new red-balloon-tired bike I wanted so badly. Every time we went into town, while Dad and Ercel and Marilyn were shopping somewhere, I would stand in front of Charlie Nielsen's hardware store staring at that bike in the window by the hour, day dreaming about owning it someday. It cost a small fortune then ($20), so I would figure for hours on end about how I could earn money enough to buy it someday. Every once

Junior, Freddie, Ercel and Marilyn - 1935

in awhile, Mr. Nielsen would step outside his hardware store to answer any questions I had, and then he would allow me to come in and touch the bike if I would shine it for him afterwards. He even gave me a picture of the bike to hang on my wall, so I could day dream more about it at home while lying on my bunk looking at it. I think one of the *maddest* fist fights Tex and I ever had was when he rubbed out the tire tracks Grant Lundgren's balloon tired bike made in the dirt when he rode by one time that I was saving to look at. Anyway, as long as I live, I will never forget that wonderful exciting Christmas morning when everyone had finished opening their present (everyone got only one present in those days) and Dad, just like it was an after thought, wheeled out the same beautiful red balloon tired bike that was in Charlie Nielsen's hardware store window, and said, "Well I'll be darned, look what I found in Grandpa's room with your name on it."

When Ercel married my dad against her own mother's strongly worded advice *not* to marry him, it was a total commitment on her part. It was her savings, her salary and her good name as a first grade school teacher on their bank loans that made it possible to make all the improvements on the old farmhouse. It was also her savings that bought back their water shares so more crops could be raised again, and it was her savings that paid for my wonderful balloon-tired bike. She even financed a new chicken coop for a new batch of chicks, and a new potato cellar to store their first crop. Interestingly, she never approved of Grandma Olsen's white Leghorn chickens so she bought a hundred Plymouth Rock chicks for the new henhouse and all those little chicks grew into large speckled black and white chickens that laid large brown eggs, and were a much bigger fryer than a Leghorn. Ercel even had a hand in changing Dad and Grandpa's farming emphasis from only dairying and sheep ranching, to also diversify into potatoes and sugar beets. Unfortunately, the market prices for farm products during the depression was so low they barely broke even on everything they tried. One thing was obvious, if it hadn't been for Ercel's small teaching salary (and her savings) during those poverty stricken years, we would have never made it through the Great Depression.

NEWS RELEASE

March 1935, Germany formally denounces the clauses of the" Treaty of Versailles" forcing its disarmament, reintroduces conscription, and announces its intention to create an Army. The Nuremberg Laws withdraw German citizenship from Jews and prohibit inter marriage with Aryans. In America, the Rural Electrification Administration is established; the Social Security Act, the Soil Conservation Act, and the Works Progress Administration are all signed into law.

On May 2, 1935, my second little sister, Winifred was born, and since her mother Ercel had wanted her brother Warren who was a doctor in Nephi, Utah, to deliver *"Freddie"*, Dad took Ercel and Marilyn to Fountain Green and stayed with them until the big day. Grandpa and I, and *Old Bob*, Dad's Border collie dog, were then left home to care for the sheep that were lambing in a nearby pasture at the time.

Edna, Marilyn,Grandma Allred, Freddie and Homer J – 1935

As long as I live I will never forget the very same freezing night *Freddie* was born, we were suddenly hit with a freak snow storm blizzard that left us with nearly two dozen shivering new born *dogey* (orphan) lambs inside our farmhouse, all huddled around the kitchen stove trying to stay alive. While Grandpa was constantly bringing in more and more dogey lambs from the pasture to the house, I kept racing out to the corral with empty root beer bottles to fill with warm milk directly from *Old Bluee's* four spigots, put rubber nipples on the bottles and race back to the house to feed all those hungry little dogey lambs, only to race back to the corral again to fill more bottles for

another batch of lambs Grandpa had just brought in. By morning, there was at least eight inches of new snow on the ground and we had lost well over a dozen of Dad's prime ewes, but fortunately we managed to save most of their lambs. Grandpa told me he found one mother ewe that died giving birth, but he couldn't find it's lamb, and to add even more misery, *Old Bob* had disappeared. The next morning,

Nibbly the Lamb — 1936

miracle of all miracles, we found my dad's wonderful Border Collie sheepdog *Old Bob*, nearly buried in snow, all wrapped around that newly born missing lamb like a blanket.

That *almost human* sheepdog had unbelievably kept that little lamb alive all during that miserably cold night, with its body around it for heat.

Dad came racing home the next day and he and Grandpa skinned the dead lambs of the mother ewes who survived, and tied their little pelts on the backs of our dogey lambs without mothers to trick the live mother ewe into adopting a different lamb. It was worth the try because it worked some of the time, but when it failed, I was given the responsibility of raising the lamb. One of those little dogey lambs my dad gave me to settle up some back wages, was not only intelligent, but was blessed with a wonderfully likable out-going personality. Like my dad's sheepdog, *Old Bob,* if she could talk, she would have been almost human. I named her *Nibbly* because she was always trying to communicate with me by nibbling my fingers and knuckles and rubbing against my leg. She seemed to be able to communicate with all animals, and she wouldn't take any guff off of anyone, and especially Old Bob. When she was old enough to join the larger herd, she looked like just another cotton ball in a sea of cotton balls herded along by Old Bob, but if she felt that dog was being a little too pushy, she would fly out of the herd and butt a surprised Old Bob, head over heals. Believe it or not, she would then look over at me in her "So there too" attitude, stick her nose in the air, and strut back into that sea of cotton balls, and disappear.

When Old Bob was not on the mountain or desert range with my dad and the sheep, he adopted Grandpa Olsen as his personal responsibility, and began acting as both his seeing-eye dog and his companion. I will never forget the time Grandpa and Old Bob limp-walked up to John and Carrie Hansen's place for a visit. John Hansen's eyesight was nearly as bad as Grandpa's and they were both leaning against a log-pole corral fence admiring John's green alfalfa fields, and Grandpa said, "Johann, Jeg tink one of your Holstein kus has bloated and

> ### NEWS RELEASE
>
> ---
>
> *October 1935, Italy invades Ethiopia. Britain and France lead the League of Nations to impose sanctions against Italy, but oil is not included as an embargoed product, and Italy is not prevented from moving troops through the Suez Canal.*

fallen down." John squinted and said, "Oh my God, Ole you're right, she's down and can't get up." They both climbed the pole fence and began limp running towards the bloated cow until John suddenly stopped and began to laugh so hard his sides hurt. He took off his hat and wiping his forehead said, "Ole, that's not a bloated cow, that's my wife, Carrie, painting the Monroe Mountains", and doubled over laughing again. Carrie might have been a little on the overweight side at the time at 250 plus pounds, but she was also a very talented landscape artist. And there she was, sitting in the middle of that alfalfa field on an oil cloth with her easel all by herself, wearing a black and white polka dot dress, painting those beautiful Utah Mountains. Grandpa always thought the world of Carrie and John Hansen, and all ten of their wonderful children, and he always enjoyed visiting with them. I found this poem in Grandpa's Old Norwegian Sea Chest he brought from Norway in 1874 (and had Dad will to me) that Carrie and John Hansen had written to honor his 86tthh birthday, and read at his birthday party on April 10, 1936.

> April 10, 1936   86th Birthday Anniversary
> To our dear neighbor and Brother Olsen,
> There is someone who is precious
> There is someone who is dear
> Not alone upon his birthday
> But each day of all the year;
> So we send our hearts devotion
> With our wish for many another
> Cheerful, bright and happy birthday
> For our neighbor and our brother.
> Dear brother Olsen
> With your upright living,
> Good will, honesty, whole heartedness
> And genuine good neighborly spirit
> You encourage and help us all.
> So
> Keep your heart a singing,
> Others hear thy song,
> And your cheerful mission
> Helps the world along.
> Your friends and neighbors,   John and Carrie Hansen

Monroe Grade School, 4th Grade - 1934

My fifth grade Teacher at Monroe Grade School gave me an assignment to first write, and then give an oral report to the class and parents visiting our school in November 1935, on the "Italian-Ethiopian War" and I found my speech in a box of my dads things he willed me after he passed away in 1987. This is my oral report.

"Ladies and Gentlemen, Mr. Davis, Fellow Students,."

"By the papers and my library study, Italy seems to have started the trouble. Italy says she has got so many people that she has to have more room to put her people on and says if England joined in this, it would be another World War. Mussolini said his answer was war. Italy is well equipped with modern guns and things while Ethiopia has some savage like men who have the old time fighting spirit with knifes and spears. Hili Silassi has got an Army but we do not know which is likely to win for Ethiopia has men who are used to there country and that is where they are fighting. The Italians do not know that Country at all so it looks bad for them there."

"The population of Italy is 42,100,000 people while the population of Ethiopia is 10,000,000 and the square miles are 350,000. The square miles in area of Italy are 120,000. The climates of Italy in general are temperate and extreme heat and cold are not great. The northern part where the sea is least felt has the largest temperature range in weather, annual and daily. The southern part of the peninsula and Sicily vary about 25 degrees between summer and winter. Indeed this southern portion with its hot dry winds is more like Africa than like Europe."

"The climate of Ethiopia is, the days are sunny ecepte in the summer rainy season from mid June until the last of September. The country is so high that even though it lays only a few degrees north of the equator, the climate is bracing. Though the soil is still tilled in the most primitive fashion, it is so rich that it gives generously of beans, barley, millet, wheat, sugar cane, cotton, tobacco and hops and often yields several crops a year."

"Italy is the best prepared for arms but Ethiopia is a little the best self supporting. Ethiopia trades to other countries and gets its food that way. Italy does the same thing. They raise corn and wheat, which are the chief grains, rice, barley, oats, beets for sugar, and vegetables. Mulberry trees raising silk worms are Italy's chief industry."

"The leag of nation is trying to stop the war because war means death and blood shed when they can just about talk them out of it. So the leag of nation have tried to do that. They are placing sansions on Italy now. The leag of nation is a group of men

from each country which form the leag. These men are supposed to keep peace in the world. This leag is trying to stop the war by talking them out of it. If they won't they will place sansions on Italy are whoever starts the war. This leag meets in a little city named the Netherlands in Holland. The building they meet in is a building named the heag. The leag does not want war because it means blood shed."

"The British (John Bull), is getting mad because the Italians are fighting around their Somaliland so they are sending their Somaliland army down to fight Italy. He said he would force Italy if he had to. Ethiopia is having trenches dug around adis ababa so that the Italians cannot surrender the city. They have been fighting for two weeks."

"The Ethiopians color is a dark brown and the Italians color is more like ours. There language is different there, government is different, education and religion is different. The Ethiopians talk a great deal like the Arabians. It is kind of a chattery talk. The Italian language is Latin. Latin declined and the speech of the common people became more vigorous and by the fifth century the lingua Romana or language of Rome as it is called now has entirely displaced the pure Latin.

Thank you."

We also had an old red rooster on our farm that had it's own personality, but unlike my pet lamb *Nibbly*, it's personality was like a bully's. That ornery old red rooster actually thought it owned the Gravelbed farm and wasn't afraid to let everyone know it, including all the other livestock. Unbelievably, my stepsister Marilyn, fell in love with that stubborn knot-headed rooster and for some unknown reason named him *"Bruce."* The interesting thing to me was, Bruce tolerated everyone in the family except Marilyn, who he treated like his slave and wouldn't even let her out of the farmhouse. Whenever Bruce caught Marilyn outside, he would either chase her back into the house or corner her on a hay wagon somewhere screaming for someone to come save her. I heard Dad say one time it was all because Marilyn had red hair and that red rooster wasn't about to tolerate more than one redhead on *his* farm.

Finally Dad had enough and said he was fed up with that rooster's obnoxious behavior and the way he treated Marilyn. Well, a week later when we were having our family dinner one Sunday, Dad turned to Marilyn and asked, "How do you like the chicken?" Marilyn said, "I think it's delicious Dad", and he said, "Well, it should be, it's that ornery old red rooster you called Bruce." Oooh boy, I'll tell you Marilyn was absolutely stunned by Dad's statement and left the table screaming, "I can't believe you would ever do such a terrible thing, you murdered the only pet I ever loved", and ran to her room sobbing, "I hate you monster, you murderer", and slammed the bedroom door. Dad just sat there shaking his head in disbelief and said, "For the life of me as long as I live, I will never understand women."

Like Grandma Olsen, Ercel also wanted a clean water well close to the farmhouse with a kitchen pump on her sink, so she insisted we dig down a 100 feet this time. Dad asked the same well digger, Doad Farmer, to dig the well and he arrived with his forked sticks, repeated the same water witching act, theatrics and all, and ended up in the exact same spot we dug before. Unfortunately, after Doad had dug down a hundred feet, the bottom of the well was still only damp sand. Dad was so disgusted, and not realizing the potential safety hazard he might create, he put a flimsy wooden cover over the well opening rather than waste time backfilling the hole.

As I recall, it was round my seventh birthday that Dad first promised me a Shetland pony for my birthday, and for the next three years as a joke he thought was hilarious, he would wake me up before sunrise every *April Fools* day (a week before my birthday) and shout, "Come down to the barn and see you're Shetland pony." I know your thinking I should have been smart enough to see through his same joke year after year, but I would always think "Oh boy, maybe this is the year he's not fooling", and leap out of bed, race to the barnyard to see my new pony, only to hear him yell "April Fool" again, and bust out laughing. Well, it not only irked me, but Grandpa, Ercel and Marilyn also got a little tired of Dad's joke on a little boy, so they called the family together for a secret meeting. As agreed, Ercel's assignment was to *prime Dad* by telling him he better do something about backfilling that dangerous open well or, as Ercel told Dad, "You mark my words, one of these days 'Old Patty' (one of our work horses) will end up on the bottom of that well", and Dad, bless his heart, answered exactly as expected, "Yah, yah, I know. I'll get to it one of these days."

I got up at 4:30 am on April 1, 1936 (April Fool's Day), because Dad always got up at 5:00 am to start his chores (and pull his joke on me) and raced into he and Ercel's bedroom screaming at the top of my lungs, "Dad, Dad, Old Patty fell in the well." Dad always slept in his long handled underwear, and I will never forget to this day, him waking up suddenly and frantically yelling, "What, What, What, Oh my God", and leaping out of bed, running wide open hell bent for election, silhouetted in the moonlight hurdling furniture, towards the back door (with me following) to the well outside. Fearing the worst, he was frantically peering down that dark well opening, trying to locate *"Old Patty"*, when I stuck my head out the house back door and shouted, *"April Fool."*

By then, all the rest of the family were up, and everyone gave me a big cheer before they cracked up laughing. Grandpa laughed so hard when he saw the stunned look on my dad's face, he couldn't eat his breakfast that morning, but Dad for some reason was real quiet. I know he was trying hard to be a good sport about everything, but finally he couldn't take it any longer and said, "I don't see one damn thing funny about any of it", and stomped out of the house to the corrals carrying his coat and hat. One thing for sure, it cured Dad of ever sucking eggs again, and he never pulled another April fool's day joke on me, but come to think of it, he also never gave me a Shetland pony.

I will always be grateful to my dad and my grandpa and grandma Olsen for teaching me the right character traits every child should live by. My dad's lessons in honesty and doing the right thing, really struck home with me when I was eleven years old and found two $20 bills rolled up together in the weeds. Dad and I had just come out of a matinee movie one Saturday afternoon when I found that small fortune, and I ask him, "What should I do?" He said as a way of testing me, "What do you think we should do?" and when I said, "We should find the rightful owner and return it." Dad grinned and said, "That's what I knew you would say."

NEWS RELEASE

March through May 1936, German troops move into the Rhineland, which has been demilitarized by the treaty of Versailles. France and Britain do not resist The Italian Army occupies Addis Ababa, ending The Ethiopian War and signaling the collapse of the League of Nations as a political force for world peace.

Clyde Gleaves was the town marshal then and after I explained to him what had happened he said, "We'll keep this quiet and if no one comes in to report their loss within the next thirty days, I'll return this money to you to keep." As it turned out, Mr. Simonsen came in to report the loss the very next day and when he told Clyde the exact amount, there was no doubt he had lost it. When the marshal told Mr. Simonsen that I was the one who turned it in, he was so impressed with my honesty and doing the right thing, he drove out to our Gravelbed farm and gave me five silver dollars as a reward. I'll tell you, I was ecstatic because it was the most money I ever had at one time, and proved once and for all, honesty does pay.

Dad also taught me to stand up for my rights and beliefs and not cave into bullying from anybody. He gave me a pair of boxing gloves one time for Xmas, and we used to practice boxing together in case I would need to defend myself, and I'm glad he did. There was a bully in our sixth grade class who had all the other boys in our home room intimidated into

NEWS RELEASE

In 1936, the United States Army consisted of 140,000 men.

doing whatever he ordered them to do, except me, and that was because I completely ignored him and tried to avoid any confrontation with him as long as possible. My turn finally came one day when he pointed his finger at me and ordered me to bring him a pan of warm water and some soap to wash his hands with before we went to the lunch room, or he would "kick the living crap out of me." To this day, I have never understood why *road rage* feelings will sometimes flare-up in people, and this time it happened to me. I literally came unglued over his obnoxious dictatorial personality and bullying everyone around, and told that knot head to get his own damn water. Oooh boy, I'll tell you, he came at me with both fists swinging like a buzz saw, and much to his surprise, I tore back into him like a chainsaw. Like two Roman gladiators, our fight to the death was on full bore when our home room teacher, Mr. Baker, came running in the room to save my life, but interestingly, when he saw I had already bloodied the bully's nose and was starting to get the upper hand, he left the room to let us have it out. Well, impossible as this may seem and everything was all over and done, I was the winner of that fight that day and believe it or not, the now dethroned bully ran home bawling like the cry baby he was all along.

The interesting thing to me about that little drama of life was how my intimidated school buddies reacted after I won the fight. Believe it or not they all concluded, if a skinny little kid like Homer Junior can lick a big bully like that, anybody can. From that day on, they all stood up to the bully and his rein of terror came to an screeching halt. Maybe I unintentionally helped them gain a little self confidence that day, who knows? Anyway, that boyhood experience occurred over seventy years ago, and when Joyce and I were in Monroe visiting relatives the last time and were taking our evening walk, that same ex-bully saw us sauntering towards him on the sidewalk. Unbelievably, he crossed the street to avoid visiting with us, and began pretending he was looking at something in a store window. He and I are both in our eighties now, so all I would have said to him anyway was, "Before we go at it again Glade, let's take a couple of weeks to get in shape first."

Speaking of lacking self confidence, I still remember the time the sixth grade boys softball team challenged the seventh grade junior high school boys team to a *do or die* game, and wouldn't you know it, just as my turn came to bat, up walks the three prettiest girls in my class I admired the most, namely Dorothy Ridd, Genial Lundgren and Dorothy Mortensen. When I saw them standing there watching me I suddenly had a terrible panic attack because I knew I would strike out and die a horrible death from embarrassment. I remember taking a deep breath, closing my eyes and swinging the bat as hard as I could on the first pitch. Whooee, you can believe this or not, but as miracles will happen when you need them the most and least expect them, *I hit a home run.* Everyone there watching were so stunned by that miraculously lucky hit, it was deathly quiet until I rounded second base, and all of a sudden, the cheers from my teammates and the three beautiful girls was deafening. I know you won't believe this either, but during that wonderful one minute of fame, I honestly felt I was Jack Armstrong, "The All American Boy", himself. It was an exhilarating experience and just shows to go you what can happen if you have absolutely *no* self confidence and your guardian angel feels sorry enough for you to think, "Wow, that little boy could sure use some more self confidence right about now."

It was also in the sixth grade I experienced my first case of puppy love and I developed a crush on a pretty little girl in my class named Dorothy Ridd. Unfortunately, she never paid the slightest bit of attention to me, so Aunt Maude told me I should give Dorothy a really nice gift for her birthday that year to let her know my true feelings. I remember coughing up a whole dime of my hard earned wages (one days pay for herding cows) for a beautiful string of beads that were on sale at JC Penney. Unfortunately, a really embarrassing experience occurred for both of us when she tried them on. Wouldn't you know, the rotten bead string broke and she lost the beads.

I asked Dorothy to go to a really good movie with me because there wasn't one woman in it. It was called the *"Sand Hogs"* starring Victor McLaughlin, and it was all about a crew of real *sweaty hard working tunnel stiffs*, digging that dangerous soft ground Holland Tunnel under the Hudson River in New York City. To add insult to more insult, she said she hated the movie and was sorry she ever accepted my beads and my invitation to that terrible show.

During our earlier grade school years, Dorothy always wore her hair in braids and since I was fortunate enough to be assigned the desk right behind her, I would go to all the trouble of dipping her hair braid ends into my ink well to get her attention. It seemed like nothing I ever did interested her in me, so finally in desperation, I wrote her a love note in our sixth grade home room class, held up my hand to go to the bathroom, and placed the note in the pocket of her coat hanging in the hallway and waited quietly for her tearful response. The note read, "I love you truly. Signed, Guess who?"

My Dad said one time, "For the life of me, I will never understand women", to which and I can't agree more. Instead of assuming I was the author of that love note and tearfully running into my outstretched arms to ride off with me on my red balloon tired bike into the sunset as I had fantasized, she engaged the services of two of my *former* good friends, Tallmadge Nielsen and MacRay Clowered, as her detectives to find out who wrote that note. To add to my already mounting embarrassment, her detectives even had the gall to announce to the whole school, their prime suspect in the case was me. Luckily, my two cousins, Ted Tuft and Tex Olsen, immediately volunteered to be my lawyers, "pro bono", and their lawyer advice was, "Take the fifth", which I did. As far as I know, the case was never solved, but the good news was, everyone had a lot of fun with it (except me) and Dorothy got rid of me once and for all, and I never bothered her again. I think Tex had so much fun defending my case; he began thinking seriously about becoming an attorney some day. Years later, he became a good one.

Dorothy Ridd, my first love 1941

In fact, several years later after he had his own law practice, I asked Tex if that little drama of life sparked his interest enough to become an attorney some day. He said "That case and one other high school incident were the two main experiences that really inspired him to study law." He said, he and Johnny Collings bought a Model "T" Ford for a song to impress the girls and, as luck would have it, actually got it running. It wasn't until they took their Model 'T" out for a test run down main street in Monroe, they discovered they had advanced the spark a little too far and the car backfired every so often as they putted along, scaring all the horses half out of their skins and the daylights out of everyone else. Hamner Smith was marshal of Monroe at that time, and as they banged along Main Street and passed in front of the town's combined jail and office building, Ham stepped outside and arrested them for disturbing the peace, and even ticketed them $5 for speeding. Tex said that he and Johnny were not only shocked by their arrest, but were completely discombobulated (a legal term) by the horrendous amount of the speeding ticket, so they demanded a jury trial and told Ham they would defend themselves to the death. All this confused and delayed the legal establishment even more, and when the county judge learned they were only sixteen years old, he excused himself saying it was a Juvenile Court matter.

Well, as it turned out, the only juvenile judge in central Utah lived over a hundred miles from Monroe, which delayed scheduling of their trial even further. By the time their case finally reached the court calendar, Tex and Johnny had spent so many hours researching the applicable laws and ordinances involved, they were well prepared to present their arguments. They each stood up and gave a brilliant one hour dissertation regarding their case to the court, and summarized it as follows; "There are no laws or ordinances in the City of Monroe regarding 'disturbing the peace and/or speeding', therefore any arrests and/or ticketing thereof is illegal, and the charges against our client-selves should be dropped." When the judge asked Ham Smith if this was correct, he was stunned and said, "I'm sure it's in the City Ordinance somewhere, your honor", and after a considerable amount of embarrassing page rustling and wasted court time, Ham was embarrassed to admit there was no wording to that effect in the city's ordinance, and the judge dismissed the case. Tex Olsen and John Collings were so pleased with the legal system working in their favor that, after serving in the Armed services during World War II and graduating from the University of Utah's Law School on the GI Bill afterwards, they both became practicing attorneys.

Homer C. Olsen — 1938

I still get a lump in my throat when I think about my late dad, and what a wonderful father he was to me, and how much I appreciated him instilling in me the same character traits he lived by. Dad was a very kind compassionate man with a wonderful sense of humor and he loved talking to people. He was a friend to everyone he met and I have never known anyone who didn't think the world of my dad. He always enjoyed talking and giving free sincere worthwhile advice to everyone that asked for it, and he really believed and practiced the "Golden Rule." (Do unto others as you would have them do unto you). My dad missed his calling early in his life as a top notch low pressure salesman he later became, selling insurance to people who respected his trustworthy advice. I know he would have been much happier and been much better off financially than he ever was trying to grub a bare subsistence living out of the Gravelbed farm. He was also a no nonsense person who was honest almost to a fault, and he strongly believed everyone should take full responsibility for their actions.

Dad's formula for success was very simple. Combine a good work ethic with a good education (which he missed), serve an apprenticeship for skill and quality development, and always live and work by the meaning of the words, integrity and responsibility in all your endeavors. It's the same formula for success I've tried to live by all my life. One thing my dad didn't believe in though, and that was *welfare of any kind* because it ruined incentive to work in people, and he especially didn't believe in allowances for children, including me. He always said, "You want money, work for it" and paid me 10 cents a day to herd the milk cows along the county road, 10 cents a row to plant, thin, weed and/or harvest potatoes and sugar beets and 25 cents a day to herd the sheep on Joe Town Hill. When I manned the hay mower, side rake and/or dump rake using with a team of horses, or tromped hay and run the derrick horse, I was paid 50 cents a day for what Dad called, *field farm work*. My salary's always included board and room, but I had to buy my own cloths. All my normal morning and night milking and feeding chores were considered *pro bono type jobs* I would be doing for nothing anyway. We both kept accurate time records, but Dad usually paid me in lambs, calves and/or pigs instead of money because he wanted me to have my own cattle and sheep herds, and be a successful rancher like his older brother, Orson someday.

When my dad and mother were divorced in 1926, the judge ruled Dad would have custody of me until I reached the age of 12 and was mature enough to decide which parent I wanted to live with until I was eighteen. Unfortunately, the court had no way of knowing how I would feel when I reached the age of 12 on April 7, 1936, or that I had forgiven my mother for kidnapping me four years earlier. Aunt Maude had apparently told my mother I was extremely underweight for my age and height, and my mother had kidnapped me thinking I was slowly starving to death. Interestingly, that suspicion was confirmed by the school nurse the same year I was kidnapped and was enrolled by Mrs. Jorgensen in the third grade of a Salt Lake City public school.

> **Lesson learned:** *All children around twelve plus or minus, are so trusting and naive they can easily be talked into agreeing to almost anything, both good and bad, thinking they are doing the right thing for the people they respect. I really loved both my dad and my mother, despite how they felt about each other, and all I ever wanted to do was please both of them so they would be proud of me.*

I wrote the following two letters to my mother in my farmhouse attic room to thank her for the birthday money and the picture she sent me of herself on my 12th Birthday, April 7, 1936 and the other on May 27th to tell her I would see her soon..

April 4, 1936

Dear Mother,

Mom — 1936

I am writing this letter to thank you for the nice Birthday present you sent me. That sure is a nice picture of you, and with the one dollar bill I have makes eleven dollars I've saved up. I sold my lamb for five dollars, and then I got five dollars reward for finding forty dollars. Now you sent me a dollar so I now have eleven dollars.

I am coming along fine in school. We have been studying the Civic Organizations of Monroe and I am through with the Lions Club and am starting on the Literose Club.

We have talked it over and I think I will be coming down to stay a few weeks after School lets out. I shall write another letter when I am coming.

This party I am having is the first party I have ever had alone. I've had it with Tex every year so I guess I'm going to have quite a celebration. I have invited some girls and boys and when they get here I'm going to brag on the picture of you.

Write and tell me what you are doing now and what Ted and Jess are doing. I guess Jess is hard at work on his airplanes isn't he and I guess Ted is busy carving people out of soap. It has been pretty windy up here for the last week or two. Yesterday it took the top off of Aunt Bertha's shed and blowed a barn over in town. I even blowed a couple of trees over here and a fence. One of the trees that blew over lit on the electric light wires and stretched them like the dickens. So you can see how bad it was. It is time for me to go to bed so I'll have to quit for tonight.

With love,

Junior

May 27, 1936

Dear Mother,

Our school let out on the 22nd of this month and I got promoted to the seventh grade. I don't know whether I can come right yet because I have to get a job to earn some money from somebody. You see I only have five dollars left because I bought clothes with the other. Then when I do that I'll stay down for a month and then come back. Dad isn't so hot about me coming down but he owes me a vacation so I guess I'm coming.

I may be down the same time Roger is but I have to get some money before I come. You don't have to send me any because I'll get a job from Dad or some neighbors. I guess it's about time to quit now.

Yours truly,

Junior.

Shortly after that second letter was mailed, I was offered a really good job by Pete Willardsen, to pick peas for him at the astronomically salary of $1.00 per day for only ten hours work. When I reported for work I found out Pete's pea patch was really several acres and there were at least a dozen other kids around my age also working there for the same pay. After the first weeks work, we all lined up for our six days pay and Pete said he only paid bi-monthly and would pay us at the end of the second week when he figured we would have the picking job completed. At the end of the second week, one of the fathers of another kid smelled a rat and showed up that last Saturday morning demanding his son's first eleven days pay. Believe it or

Marilyn, Freddie & I – 1938

not, Pete had the gall to tell him he never intended to pay any of us kids anything for all twelve days work and dared him to do something about it. Whooee, I'll never forget Pete's wife running out to the field where we were working, screaming to high heaven at the top of her voice, "Pete's a killing him, Pete's a killing him!" We all raced back to Pete's farm house to save our friend's dad and lo and behold, it was just the other way around. Pete Willardsen was so badly beaten and crippled up by our friend's dad he couldn't get out of bed for over a week. That dirty rotten rat deserved all the beating he got because, as it turned out, none of us kids were ever paid a dime for what we had earned. Needless to say, I'm thankful we still have our un-enforced slavery laws in place in this day and age, to prevent this sort of thing ever happening again.

Tex & me – 1936

According to the diary my two sisters gave me, on June 16, 1936, my best friend and double cousin, Tex Olsen, and I caught the Greyhound bus at Cove Fort, Utah and traveled all the way to Los Angeles, California by ourselves for a memorable vacation with Grandma and Grandpa Weimer, my mother, my half brother, Rodger, my Uncle's Ted and Jess, and my

Ted Weimer – 1936

Aunt Beth. We rode on Uncle Ted's motorcycle and took our first airplane ride in an open cockpit *"Waco"* biplane with him. We even went swimming in the Pacific Ocean and visited the *Funhouse* on Santa Monica Pier, and built model airplanes and fire cracker cannons with Uncle Jess. I remember my Aunt Beth giving me free piano lessons that summer and Grandma and Grandpa Weimer taking us to double feature movies with milk shake afterwards, twice a week. Towards the end of the summer, my mother and "Doc" Staley suddenly rented a home near the beach in Venice and Rodger and I were quietly moved from Grandpa and Grandma Weimer's house to the new rental. Tex was then sent back to Monroe alone on the bus without my knowledge, and suddenly I woke up with a start to their scheme with, "Oh my God, I've been kidnapped by my mother again."

My mother registered me in the seventh grade at Venice High School near where we lived as *"Junior Staley"* this time instead of *"Junior Brim"* and I was immediately given an IQ Test by the school that I flunked and I mean really flunked. I remember being scared half to death by that big school and I was so completely *discombobulated* and confused by what my mother was trying to pull and with what was happening to me, I couldn't think about answering any test questions. You guessed it, my test score immediately placed me in the *dumb kids* section of the seventh

NEWS RELEASE

July 17, 1936, Civil war breaks out in Spain. The Fascist forces, seeking to overthrow the elected government, are led by General Francisco Franco and supported by Italy and Germany. The government "Loyalists" are supported by the Soviet Union.

grade at the beginning of the school year. Well wouldn't you know it, a couple of weeks later, and apparently from habit, I turned in one of my homework papers to the teacher authored by *"Junior Olsen"*, not *"Junior Staley"* as my mother had ordered.

Venice High School was the largest school I had ever seen in terms of student population and not too many teachers and/or students ever got to know one another. When my teacher couldn't find a *"Junior Olsen"* in her attendance book, she reported me to the school principal saying she had an unregistered student (meaning less tax money for their school) in her class. The next day, the principal came to our *dumb kid's* class room to ask *"Junior Olsen"* to hold up his hand, which I did, and he took me to his office. Still not recognizing me, he re-signed me up again as a new student and gave me the same IQ Test I had flunked. Oooh boy, I know you won't believe what happened next. This time I was relaxed and more confident and really concentrated on answering all their test questions the best I knew how and unbelievably, I must have *cooled* the IQ Test. Why? Well because this time *"Junior Olsen"* was assigned to the *smart kids* section of the seventh grade.

You guessed it again. A rather serious problem developed soon afterwards because *"Junior Staley"* was still a registered student there also, and the only thing I could think to do to solve the problem was to go to the *"smart"* students room one day and sign in as *"Junior Olsen"* and be absent from the *"dumb"* students room as *"Junior Staley"*, then reverse the process the next day and so on. Believe it or not, this little charade went on for at least three weeks until finally my math teacher who taught in both the smart and dumb rooms, figured out *"Junior Olsen"* and *"Junior Staley"* were the same person. I remember, she took me by the hand to the principal's office

Jr Olsen – 1936

and he was stunned by her analysis and refused to believe what she told him because of the tremendous difference in the two Test scores. That fact alone he said, was proof enough I had to be two different people. According to him, it was absolutely impossible to have two major differences in scores on that infallible Stanford IQ test; no matter how many times the same person took it, simply because of the way it was designed.

Well, to shorten this unbelievable little drama of life, my mother finally (and reluctantly) confessed to avoid any further embarrassment, and admitted I was both people and a compromise was reached. The fictitious non-person student named, *"Junior Staley"*, was simply placed in the *"smart student"* classes in Math and Science, and in the *"dumb student"* classes in English and History. The other young student I accidentally had given his real name back to named *"Junior Olsen"*, by a simple stroke of a pen, simply ceased to exist and peace and quite prevailed once again, except for me.

NEWS RELEASE

October 25, 1936 through November 3, 1936, Italy and Germany sign The Rome-Berlin Axis Agreement. Germany and Japan sign the Anti-Comintern Pact later Italy and Japan will make a similar Agreement against communism. FDR is elected to a second term as U.S. President with Henry Wallace as his Vice President. (My dad's only comment was," Lord help us")

Living in Venice, California during that period was fascinating for a young farm boy from the high desert country of central Utah where everyone was either of English, Scandinavian, German, Scotch, or of Navaho Indian descent. I had never seen a black person, or an oriental person, or even many Mexican people before I went to California and it was interesting to me to see how clannish all the various ethnic groups were and how they always congregated into their own *"gangs"* every recess and after school the same way they do today. I remember there were no Scandinavian gangs for me to join at that time, so I signed on with the only gang that would have me, a *Japanese* gang. My diary lists my best friend at Venice High School was named, *Tomatso Utsukie,* whose family owned a nursery I thought was a fascinating business. I remember *Tomatso* and I would make cookie cutters for our mothers in the school's tin shop together and we would talk about everything in general, but mostly about the similarities between the sheep and dairy business and the nursery business. Later on one of the Italian kids there finally asked me to join his gang, but only if I passed their initiation test. When he told me all I had to do to pass their test was steal something from a store, I told him I wasn't interested in joining his gang because I was organizing my own *spread* and no one had to steal anything to join my *outfit.* To this day I still wonder occasionally, whatever happened to those kids?

Grandma and Grandpa Weimer 1934

Apparently something serious did happen between "Doc" Staley and my mother around mid-term time because my mother jerked Rodger and me out of the Venice school system on March 4, 1937 and moved us to an apartment in Culver City, to be near Grandpa and Grandma Weimer. We were then re-registered in the Palms School system in Culver City as Rodger and Junior Staley again and I barely graduated from the seventh grade in that school. Rodger and I always walked to and from school in Culver City and one day we saw an ambulance rapidly pulling away from our apartment building so we asked a man standing outside what happened. He said, "Some women in there tried to commit suicide." When we walked into our apartment, we saw Doc Staley (for the last time) hurriedly packing all his clothes to move out, and asked him where our mother was. Without even looking at us, he answered, "She went shopping and you two boys are supposed to meet her at Grandpa Weimer's house later." We walked on down to Grandpa's house, and when my mother finally arrived in a Taxi, I noticed she was wearing a long sleeved blouse, but I could still see her bandaged wrists. It was then I knew she was the women in the ambulance.

During the winter of 1936 and the spring of 1937 in Culver City, California, it rained constantly and Venice Blvd. literally turned into a fast flowing flood channel. I also remember squandering all my reward savings ($5) on midget race car parts to build my own race car someday, and, like the Salt Lake kidnapping experience, I survived another school year by the skin of my teeth by graduating from the seventh to the eighth grade *on condition.*

Chief Guide Philip Brim - 1939

Thinking back now, I thought it was interesting that just prior to moving to the Palms school from Venice High, the smart kid my mother had re-named *Junior Staley* was promoted to the "**X**" group (the smartest group in the seventh grade) in all four categories. My diary entry on February 1, 1937 stated, "I never knew I was smart before", but apparently my *hard drive memory* had erased again with our school change from Venice High to the Palms School system in Culver City, California. My mother filed for divorce from Doc Staley (her fourth husband) after the attempt to end her life and moved the three of us back to Nevada to live with Philip Brim (her ex-third husband) and remarried Philip Brim (making him her fifth husband) when her divorce from "Doc" Staley was finalized. Philip had recently been promoted by the Bureau of Reclamation to his new job as Chief Guide on Boulder Dam, but was still living in his shanty construction workers home he built himself in McKeeversville, Nevada.

Junior and Rodger Brim — 1937

Shortly after we arrived, Rodger and I stupidly decided we would hitchhike the seven miles without permission, or shirts or hats in a 110 degree weather from McKeeversville to Lake Mead, to go swimming. As you've already guessed, I passed out from heat prostration about halfway down the highway to Lake Mead, but fortunately was able to hail down a passing tourists car just as I fainted, and those wonderful people from Kansas immediately took us both to the Park Ranger's First Aid Station at Lake Mead and saved my life. I remember waking up an hour or so later with cold towels and ice cubes packed all over my body and looking up at a lot of worried people staring down at me, just as Philip asked me, "How do you feel?" The Park Service Rangers had notified Philip where to find us and he came down from work to take us home. I'll never forget the stern lecture he gave both Rodger and me about the dangers of desert heat and the importance of wearing proper clothing and drinking lots of water during summers in that hot desert climate. It was also the first time I heard about salt pills and the dangers of dehydration.

Grandma Weimer wrote the following letter to me on July 6, 1937. while I was in Boulder City, Nevada from her home in Culver City, California, shortly after that desert heat stroke experience,

July 6, 1937

Dear Junior,

Your letter came some time ago and I was so pleased to hear from you. My, it must be terribly hot up there. We have had it very warm here too but the last two days have been some cooler. Ted read your letter and said he was going to write to you and send you a picture of his Motorcycle. He thinks quite a lot of it and he has had quite a lot of fun on it.

Grandma Weimer

He has it running and in good shape now. Have you been able to run your little car? I hope you have because I know you would enjoy it so much.

Did you have a nice time on the fourth of July? Ted went swimming down to the beach and then went to a show at night. Grandpa and I just lay around all day then at night we went down to the beach to watch fireworks. They weren't much this year, lots of people down there though, too many to have fun. Beth went camping but is home now and is out teaching piano. Have you been able to practice any on the piano? I hope so, and then you won't forget. How is little Rodger getting along? Tell him to write to me too. It will be good practice for him and we are always so pleased to hear from you boys. I'll answer too and tell you anything you want to know about us down here. Kenny still comes over and so does Paul and Jim, the same old crowd but you like them don't you as we do. It seems funny to have school out but Ted and Beth are enjoying it. Well I must close and do up the dinner dishes before Grandpa gets home. It's almost time for him to come home. Grandpa goes to night School now down to the L.A. School. Pretty good don't you think? Well bye for now and write me real soon.

Grandma.

Philip & Ruth Brim - 1939

One of the best things that happened to me during the summer of 1937 was getting to know and respect Phil Brim for the high caliber person he really was. Of all the men my mother had married and divorced, he was the only one who really and truly loved her, faults and all, and always took her back and forgave her for all her shenanigans. He was a quiet Montanan who never bragged or talked a lot, but when you got to know him, had many talents and was truly a hard working tunnel stiff with skills as an ironworker and powder man, and believe it or not, was not a bad cowboy poet. He also had talent as a writer of Zane Grey type stories and even sent one of his stories to the editor of Collier's magazine and received the following answer, "You have talent Phil. If you will dust this story off a little for our magazine, we will buy it from you to print." I think he got all the *second opinion* recognition he wanted because for some unknown reason he never followed through on that letter. For all this, my mother still treated him like a dog, but he never complained.

When the "Six Companies" began building Boulder Dam in 1931, Phil Brim was one of the first men Frank Crow hired as a "highscaler." That job without a doubt, was the most dangerous on the project, but the good news was, it was the second highest paying job on the Dam at $9.00 a day, (highline operators got $11.00 a day) and Philip said he needed the money. That particular job required Philip and his crew to hang over the 600 foot high Black Canyon cliffs on a rope in 125 degree heat, and drill and blast the weathered rock away with jackhammers and blasting powder until a keyway was formed in the canyon wall to seat the abutments of the dam itself.

Philip told me a *close call* story one time about a highscaler who caught a young surveyor in mid air that had fallen off the rim of the canyon to his certain death, 600 feet below. He said the highscaler heard a shout from above where he was hanging on the end of a 100 foot rope drilling powder holes, and saw the man falling towards him, so he kicked himself out from the cliff wall and, as luck would have it, caught the young man in mid air. I don't know why I never asked him the highscaler's name at the time, or why he never bothered to tell me. I remember in 1960, twenty five years later, when

High Scalers - Boulder Dam – 1932

I was the Kiewit Company's project manager building the Titan I Missile Base near Camp Beale in Marysville, California, and was having lunch in Lincoln with John Duff, our surveyor. Interestingly,

Front View, Boulder Dam — 1941

Boulder Dam — 1941

John told me this same highscaler story that happened when he was employed by the Six Companies as an Instrument man on a surveying crew, and it was his rear chainman that fell over the edge of the cliff and was caught in midair by a highscaler. After he finished his story I asked John if he remembered the name of the highscaler that caught his chainman and he told me he would never forget his name because he was a *hero* in his opinion. He said the man's name was *"Philip Brim."*

It was my Stepfather, Philip Brim, who introduced me to the excitement of working in the Heavy Engineering Construction Industry by showing me every nook and cranny in the Boulder (now Hoover) Dam explaining why everything was designed and constructed the way it was when the

Dam was built. I remember, my little brother, Rodger and I followed Philip around that gigantic project like two pups, asking stupid questions while soaking in everything he said. I was fascinated by the design and all the fantastic construction engineering involved, and even more impressed by the high line and the huge eight cubic yard concrete buckets they used to deliver wet concrete, to build that magnificent structure. To this day, I still marvel at the magnitude of the Boulder Dam project and the professional excellence the project manager, Frank Crow, and his highly qualified staff used to plan, organize, coordinate, and synchronize the building of that magnificent dam over a year ahead of schedule.

Boulder Dam — 1937

Peter Kiewit once told me he thought the duties of a project manager on a heavy engineering project like Boulder Dam, were similar to those of a conductor of a symphony orchestra. He said they both must coordinate and synchronize the skilled efforts of so many different people with so many different talents and skills, towards the common goal of producing *beautiful music*. Frank Crow would have been a master symphony orchestra leader according to that definition, because he did a fantastic job of coordinating and synchronizing all those different construction workers necessary skills and talents that were required to construct that wonderful *"Symphony in Construction"*, the Boulder Dam Project.

Jr. and his Midget Racecar — 1937

I remember in 1930, Dad and I drove his 1927 Chevy coupe over to the flour mill in Ellsinore, Utah, with sacks of wheat to grind flour for Grandma Olsen, and we were stopped at a railroad crossing counting a long string of freight cars being pulled by a steam engine named the *Sevier Valley Creeper*. While we were sitting there counting cars rumbling by, I asked Dad what they called the man who drove the steam engine, and he answered, "That's a Civil Engineer." To this day I still remember looking up at my dad and very seriously saying, *"Dad, that's what I want to be someday."* The Boulder Dam Project is what civil and construction engineering is really all about, and standing there by Philip Brim in 1937 looking at that magnificently built project, I knew it really was what I wanted to do, that is, if I couldn't be an aeronautical engineer.

After Rodger and I moved to Boulder City with my mother and she and Philip went back together again, Philip helped me put my midget race car together with the lawn mower engine, four wheels and axels, and the steering mechanism I spent my last $5 on before we left . We also did a considerable amount of traveling during the summer of 1937 in Philip's new Plymouth, and even drove all the way to Philip's parent's ranch in Sheridan, Montana, to explain why he remarried my mother. We even toured Yellowstone Park on the way back to Culver City to explain the same thing to my mother's parents, and found my cousin Tex there visiting Grandpa and

Grandma Weimer. Like me, he *could hardly vaite* to help test my midget race car, and experience a ride he would never forget.

The following letter was written by Grandma Weimer in Culver City, California, to my mother and Philip in Boulder City, Nevada, August 20, 1937

August 20, 1937

Dear Ruth and Phillip,

Well Ruth honey, I haven't any news to tell you. Maude hasn't sent Tex's bus fare yet but we expect it so they can leave Tuesday morning. The boys are quite anxious to come up there now. Junior can't think of anything else, only his little car and Tex is very anxious to see it too.

Elizabeth Weimer — 1936

Ruth honey, you will have to get a piano for Junior just as soon as you possibly can because that kid is so talented. Beth and I were very much surprised to see him play so well and read so well. Beth said he was playing music two years ahead of himself and could play it well too. Junior said he would study his music in Boulder and then he would play it in his mind and he didn't forget. Ruth you ought to subscribe to that "Etude" magazine that would give him lots of information until you could get him a piano. He certainly has talent and now is the time to bring it out. He gets so much pleasure out of his music. Well Ruth, I must close now. I haven't got any work done and Beth is teaching so I must get busy.

Loads of love from all of us.

Mother

I wrote the following letter on August 23, 1937, to my mother (now legally Mrs. Philip Brim) in Boulder City, Nevada. while Tex and I were still in Culver City visiting Grandpa and Grandma Weimer.

August 23 1937

Dear Mother,

Tex got here a week ago, two days after Rodger left. We haven't gone to the beach only once so far. I got your letter and the music today but I wish you had sent the other book too but it's alright anyway.

Tex wants to come up to Boulder City to see the midget in about another week because he will have some money by then. We're both pretty near broke and Tex's money comes next week. I'm sure glad you got that flywheel pulley because it (the midget) will have more power with it. What has Philip done on it so far? I sure wish the midget was here, so does Tex, but he wants to go down there too.

When you send the money write and tell me how many pairs of socks and shorts and things. Ted hasn't got his new Motorcycle yet but will have it by next month. He has pretty near a hundred Dollars saved up now.

Tex says Grandpa Olsen has to pay rent to live in his own house to Dad and Ercel. Tex said Grandpa was chopping wood and a stick flew in his eye. He says they were all pleasantly surprised when they heard about my midget, except Ercel.. I can't think of any more so I'll have to quit now

You're Brat Yunior

Tex, and Rodger and me after a fight

Philip Brim's *Robison Crusoe* shanty home in McKeeversville was basically a corrugated tin covered two room shack consisting of a small bedroom and a combination kitchen-dining-front room plus an outdoor "two holer" privy. I'll tell you, things got pretty crowded around there and more than a little nerve wracking when company came. As you can see, Rodger and I had just stopped one of our many fist fights long enough for this picture to be taken (to stop the fight). But I will say one thing, Philip had the most wonderful outdoor shower ever built. Believe it or not, it was nothing more than a four foot square box, seven foot high, made up of 4 by 4 corner posts decked over on top to hold a 55 gallon sun heated water barrel. For privacy, corrugated tin roofing was nailed on three sides and a door, but the *secret* was a six inch diameter sprinkler head that sprayed a luxurious relaxing deluge of solar heated hot water.

Me and Tex 1937

Tex and I had a terrible argument over who would fine tune my famous midget race car on its maiden seven mile run down to Lake Mead. To settle the argument, Philip suggested we just flip a coin, and the loser would drive second rather than first and you guessed it, Tex won. So still sulking, but trying to be a good sport about it, I setup my clipboard to record test data, while Philip drove the Plymouth behind Tex and my midget racer down the hill. I remember Philip questioning my wooden 1 x 2 brake as *under designed*, but I argued something that simple would obviously work. As it turned out, Philip's

Tex and the Midget Racer - 1937

analysis was correct because Tex wore off the *drag end* of my well engineered wooden brake almost immediately by fine-tuning the lever. From then on, he was completely without brakes and I'll tell you, things really started to get exciting as he began accelerating down that steep Lake Mead hill.

As Tex began gathering more and more speed, a second design error suddenly surfaced in the car's steering mechanism and I noted on my clipboard, *direct steering is way too sensitive for high speeds*. All the while I was recording *design reminder changes* to myself, old *White Knuckles Tex* kept accelerating towards warp speed and I noticed that only a slight movement of the steering wheel would immediately careen the car off the road into one of the adjacent borrow pits. In fact, when Tex only *nudged* the steering wheel to only make a minor correction, the car would *zing* out of that borrow pit, careen across the paved road at high speed into the opposite borrow pit on the other side of the road. It became painfully obvious to both Philip and me it would be impossible to steer a straight line down a paved road at the high speed old *Wide Eyed White Knuckled* Tex had reached using my current steering system.

As we continued following the now *Goggle Eyed* driver named Tex helplessly watching in hypnotic fascination as he *zinged* from one side of the paved road to the other, disappearing in a rooster tail cloud of dust in one borrow pit, only to *zip* out of that dust cloud seconds later to zing across the road and disappear again in another rooster tail cloud of dust on the opposite side. Finally,

Tex, Jr., and Spot — 1937

after watching numerous ping pong crossovers shaking our heads side to side in disbelief, miracle of all miracle's, old now *toilet relieved* Tex finally shifted his brain into gear long enough to *key off* the engine and use it's compression to slow the car down somewhat, thus averting a disaster. The unfortunate news was, Tex *couldn't vaite* to slow the car and attempted to accelerate its slowdown by dragging his feet, sparks flying and all, to wear off the soles of both his shoes. To add even more interesting design reminders for my clipboard, when the car finally slowed enough to steer on the paved road, it passed over a railroad crossing and *Old Terrified* Tex unbelievably caught both his smoking sole less feet in the railroad tracks and wrenched them back under the two rear wheels to sprain both ankles and painfully engage his knee caps as brakes. The now famous race car finally slid to a screeching, wrenchingly painful, hide burning halt and as the curtain slowly fell on this exciting race cars test drive and the unanswered questions came to an end, *Old Cripple* Tex bashfully hung his head to giggle, "Damn, I wish I hadn't won that flip." Rumor still has it to this day; the two parallel grease marks on Lake Mead highway slightly downstream of the Hoover Dam's railroad crossing on Lake Mead Highway placed by the knee caps of a famous Utah race car driver, are still there as tourist attractions for all to see.

For some unknown reason, standing there next to Tex and my hot little midget race car, looking into his silver dollar eye balls, studying his dust laden sage brush hairdo with the toilet relieved aroma of his overalls with the missing knees, I got that same *de-ja-vu all over again feeling,* and was suddenly time tunneled back to our *black powder in the wood pile incident,* all over again and try as I might, I couldn't help it and busted out laughing so hard my sides hurt. Tex was not only stunned, but shocked I had the unmitigated gall to laugh when he knew he was dying, and swore he would get even with me if it was the last thing he ever did, come hell or high water.

Fortunately, aside from hurt feelings and two badly sprained ankles and smarting skinned off skid marked knee caps, he really wasn't hurt too badly. In fact, after a stinging lye soap scrub down in Philip's hot deluge shower and a well deserved good nights sleep, he settled right down. Unfortunately though, when we caught the bus to Monroe with Tex still on crutches, unbeknown to me he was still sulking and carrying a grudge against me for laughing when he finished the race car test. I guess his stubborn, never forgive and never forget Norwegian–German genes began working overtime because, Oooh boy, did he ever get even, with change to spare.

The following letter to my mother in Boulder City was mailed from Aunt Maud's house in Monroe, to tell her about my accident. I fractured my hip when I fell off one of Uncle Orson's spirited wild horses, named "Old Mugs" that Tex coaxed me into riding to get even.

August 23 1937

Dear Mother,

Tex and I got here OK yesterday at about 8:00 o'clock and the telegram came at 9:00 o'clock. When I got here I got on old Mugs (a really spry wild Horse) and started up to Ted Tuft's house and got to racing Tex (bareback with a nose rope loop for a bridle) and went to stop and stopped so quick I fell off and hurt my hip. Aunt Maud got worried and took me to the Doctor and he said it was or had been dislocated and he was afraid the pelvis was broke so we had to X-ray it but it wasn't. So he just taped it and my back and my stomach too and said it would be alright.

I went over to Dad's, and he asked me to stay there, and I said I believed it would be better if I stayed here, and there was nothing more said about it. Today I got Grandpa a quart of wine when I went to Richfield and he was sure glad. I told him you and Philip would be coming down to see him next month and he was sure tickled.

I saw Ridd's today and they haven't changed much except Beverly and she's grown taller. So has Stanley grown tall but Nolan hasn't changed much. Sterling has changed most of any. Freddie sure has grown. I could never imagine her that big. Ercel has got gray hair now and don't seem to talk much. I haven't even stayed over there one night. I won't stay there a night either.

I wish the midget was here. I haven't got any toys left. I got my bike though and my goggles. My sled is still left over there. I weighed 86 pounds on the Doctors scale today so I'm only two pounds underweight. I can't think of any more so I guess I'll have to quit. Tell them all hello.

Lots of love to all, Junior.

PS Ruth, I believe everything will be alright so you won't have to worry about it. I'm glad to have the Boys together so I think it will be alright. I'll write a long letter later.

Love, Maude

After we arrived in Monroe, Tex and I were pretending we were an Indian hunting party chasing buffalo on two of Uncle Orson's wild ponies bareback (with only a single *half hitch* Indian rope as a bridle), and I accidentally bounced off. Somehow the bridle slid off my horse's nose, and I was trying to reach down to my pony's nose while hanging on to its mane (while still racing wide open), to re-loop the bridle. Wouldn't you know it, I made a perfect tailbone landing on the hard pan county road and fractured my hip. The good news was, the Doctor who taped up my fractured hip told me, for a thirteen year old I was only two pounds underweight for my height (5"1") and weight (86 lbs), which was encouraging.

While I was recuperating, Dad came over to Aunt Maude's to see me several times and we had long discussions about everything that had happened since I left. In the end, Dad talked me into moving back with him and Grandpa, so once again to please the other parent I loved, I wrote my mother telling her Rodger could have my midget racer (which he sold immediately) saying it would be in the best interest of everyone concerned for me to stay with Dad and Grandpa, and go to the eighth grade in Monroe that year. I also felt really good about getting my real name, Homer J. Olsen, back again.

Tex & Brothers — 1941

Dad promised me I could have my own room in the attic if I would move back with them, so we built a stairway on the outside wall of the farm house to the attic together and planked over the open joists with fence siding for a floor. Ercel and the REA had already run electric power to the Gravelbed farm house while I was gone, so I wired my own new room for lights, built myself a sawhorse desk, setup some wooden fruit boxes for book cases and shelves, and re-setup my WW I army cot from my old kitchen bedroom, and "*Viola*" I was in business. I had already spent all my savings, but Dad said I had a few livestock left that were still mine plus my bike and my sled, and he even gave me my old job back at the same 50

cents per day. All in all, I felt really good about starting my life over with my real name.

After attending those two large California schools, coupled with that last transferring experience, I developed a dislike for all public schools in general, except for my shop classes. I remember during the winter semester in 1937, I made some quilting frames for Ercel,

Joe and Bud Hansen - 1937

a pair of skis for myself, and a really nice sewing table for my mother, which she immediately hurt my feelings by insultingly giving it away. I also became interested in Boy Scouting during the winter and spring semesters and spent nearly all my free time working on merit badges. Ercel made me a pair of semaphore flags so I could stand on my dad's hay stack and Evan Hansen would stand on his dad's haystack a mile away, and we would practice signaling

Monroe 8th Grade — 1938

semaphore messages back and forth after chores until it was too dark to see each other. The next day we would meet on the school bus to figure what we were really trying to signal each other.

In February of 1938, our Boy Scout troop hiked several miles up Monroe Mountain in knee deep snow to try out the skis we had made in shop class. Our Assistant Scoutmaster, Angus Jay Newby, (called A.J. or Jay) was the only adult that accompanied our small troop and unfortunately, he was the only one injured. He had fallen on a sharp snow covered rock while cross country skiing, and painfully severed the chord just below his right knee.

To this day I'll never forget that tough old Scotchman stubbornly refusing to go into shock despite the pain, and how he calmly called us kids together to tell us he was going to give us a practical lesson in *First Aid and Rescue*. He then showed us how to apply a tourniquet on his leg just above his knee and how to make a stretcher out of our skis and our coats, and finally, how a group of thirteen to fourteen year old boys could *easily* move a wounded patient on a ski-stretcher off a mountain to get help. Thanks to his remarkable leadership abilities and his calm coaching and encouragement, we all managed to keep our

> **NEWS RELEASE**
>
> *December 12, 1937, Japanese forces attack the U.S. Gunboat "Panay" straining U.S.-Japanese relations*

heads *screwed on right* and struggled all the way down the mountain with him on our ski stretcher, to a doctor. We were absolutely exhausted, but were extremely proud of what we had accomplished and the unforgettable lesson we had just learned.

> **Lesson learned:** *Anything can be accomplished when qualified experienced leadership is combined with inspired motivated teamwork.*

I remember one weekend while we were in the eighth grade, my cousin, Ted Tuft, and I decided to go jackrabbit hunting with our 22 caliber single-shot bolt-action rifles our dads had given us for our birthdays. We knew there were jillions of jack-rabbits running around

Ted Tuft — 1938

in the hills west of Monroe, but to our complete surprise, we ran across a coyote caught in a trap by only one of its toes that was only minutes away from chewing itself loose. The bounty on coyotes in those days was an unheard of $5 a pelt (which was a fortune to us), so Ted and I decided the right Boy Scout thing to do was, shoot the coyote so the trapper could collect his bounty. We then went on about our business of hunting for jack rabbits, both thinking about what had just happened. All of a sudden the *rotten hand of greed* suddenly appeared unto us and erased all our good Boy Scout training and in unison, we both came up with the same conclusion. "*That's our coyote; because it would have gotten away anyway.*"

Well, to make this little drama of life shorter, with Satan's encouragement and help we skinned and buried the coyote's carcass and took it's pelt into town to Mr. Forbush, the fur buyer, to collect our huge $5 bounty, but unfortunately Mr. Forbush smelled a rat and became suspicious. To stall for time he said, "Boys, I'm sorry to tell you this, but you skinned the coyote the wrong way and ruined the pelt, so now all I can pay you is $1 instead of the $5 you had coming." When we asked him, "Why?" he said, "Well, you're supposed to peel the pelt off a fur animal like a pullover sweater, not like a blanket the way you skin sheep or cattle", which is what we had done. Well, as you can imagine we were disappointed, but we were satisfied with his explanation and walked out happy with our 50 cents apiece. After all we reasoned, 50 cents was a whole day's pay working for our dads.

Oooh boy, I'll tell you the following Monday morning at school the *you know what*, really hit the fan. I remember Miss Sorensen, our home room teacher, came running over to our desks looking very worried and said, "The principal wants to see you two boys in his office right away." When we got to the principal's office, both scared stiff, there stood Clyde Gleaves, the town marshal, Mr. Forbush, the fur buyer, and the trapper with our school principal. Apparently the trapper's dog had sniffed out the coyote's carcass we had buried and the suspicious trapper had gone to see the fur buyer and they both had gone to the marshal with their suspicions. When they asked us what happened, we immediately confessed and told them everything exactly what happened. The marshal explained that technically we had stolen the trapper's coyote pelt worth $5 by taking the carcass out of his trap, then skinning it and selling the pelt, so we were both guilty as sin as far as he was concerned, we were nothing more than a couple of lousy crooks. We told them we would return the $1 we were paid by Mr. Forbush, and would work off any other damages we had caused the trapper, if they would promise not to tell our dads what we had done. We said, "Whatever the cost, we don't want our dad's to know we are nothing more than a couple of lousy crooks."

Well, after stroking their chins for a moment, the marshal told us to wait outside while they discussed our sentencing and fifteen minutes later, called us back in to hear their verdict. The marshal said no one would press charges against us and no one would tell our dads, if we would return the $1 to the trapper, which we did, and we would each pay an additional $1 to the trapper for damages. The trapper said he knew we didn't have any money so he would agree to let us work it off at the rate of 10 cents an hour for ten hours each of hard labor around his house and yard, to pay off the $1 in damages. The fur buyer had already given the trapper the other $4 he had coming, so after we all agreed and shook hands, the marshal said he now considered the matter closed.

Ted and I rode our bikes for the next two weeks to school instead of the school bus, so we could put in our one hour of hard labor every night for ten nights working off our damages, and would then hurriedly ride our bikes home to do our own chores like nothing had happened. Interestingly, neither one of our dads ever said a word to either one of us about the matter, so we assumed they were never told we were a couple of lousy crooks. Two months later, just after I had finished milking my favorite milk cow, "Old Bluee", I turned to pour my full bucket of milk into the ten gallon creamery can and, Oooh boy, there stood my dad and Clyde Gleaves, the town marshal. I'll tell you, I literally froze from fright thinking the marshal was after me, but Dad just grinned and said, "Clyde's not here to talk about coyote pelts, he's here to buy a cow", and all of a sudden it dawned on me, *Dad knew all along*. He must have figured I learned my lesson because nothing more was ever said to me about it afterwards, by him or anyone else. One thing for sure, Dad was right about me learning a lesson from that experience. From then on, except for business loans I've paid back with interest, I have never taken a dime from anyone I didn't earn by working hard for it.

Well, after that skidmark along the highway of my life, my stepmother Ercel decided it was high time I *seen the light* like my dad and my grandpa and become a good Latter Day Saint again. I hadn't been to a Sunday school since Grandma Olsen passed away

Freddie & Doll – 1939

(Uncle Orson and Aunt Maude weren't Mormons) and after that coyote incidence, Ercel figured I really needed some religious rejuvenation. The Mormon Church sponsored the Boy Scouts then, which I enjoyed, so I agreed to go to Sunday school occasionally to maybe become a better Scout. Well, to add more misery, when the bishop heard about my life of sin and degradation and discovered I was now thirteen years old, he unilaterally scheduled my baptism and made me a deacon in the LDS church. I remember having an infantigo infection below my right knee at the time, so he scheduled me last so as not to *dirty the waters*, and from my point of view, he nearly drowned me.

To this day I still think that bishop deliberately held me under that dirty last person water a lot longer than was really necessary.

Oooh boy, to pile even more fuel on Ercel's concerns, my disgusting inquiring little mind and my constant stupid questioning about anything and everything got me in trouble again, only this time with my Sunday school teachers while they were telling us all about the *immaculate conception* and the *golden plates*. The bishop angrily reported my embarrassing questioning of the Holy Bible and the Book of Mormon to my parents and to this day I will never forget my dad's anger and loudly demanding, "Who in hell's name do you think you are questioning the Holy Bible and the Book of Mormon the way you do?" I said, "Dad, all I asked them was, 'How did they know for sure those things really happened the way they are written?" I was hurt

Ercel, Winifred & Marilyn - 1939

that Dad felt I should suddenly accept everything I was told at face value without any proof or logic, when he always taught me otherwise. I guess when the Lord combined my Norwegian stubbornness on the Olsen side with my bone headed German on the Weimer side; it created my embarrassing inquisitive personality that rubbed some people the wrong way. I immediately resigned and/or was kicked out (your choice) of the Latter Day Saints Church shortly after that confrontation with my dad and Ercel, and only went to the Boy Scout meetings from then on. I remember telling my dad, the Ten Commandments were all the religion I really needed from then on anyway. From my point of view, if you believed in the Ten Commandments, about all the churches had left to sell to the congregations was guilt, and I already had enough of that to last me a lifetime.

Maybe it was my imagination, but after that church confrontation, I got the feeling my stepmother Ercel, and even my dad to a certain extent, began thinking of me more as a hired hand around there than one of the family. I also had a funny feeling Ercel had decided, as the Mormon's say, I was *not one of them* because she began acting very coldly towards me.

I knew she hated my mother for the way she treated my dad and for kidnapping me, and I knew she didn't like Aunt Maude because she was my mother's sister who she thought, was in cahoots with my mother to kidnap me. It was after my 14th birthday I was assigned more of Dad's regular farm work duties with no increase in pay that I began to feel they were trying to work my tail off as punishment. While everyone else in the family got to go on trips and picnics to Fountain Green or to Fish Lake as a family, Grandpa and I always had to stay home to do all the chores, look after the live stock and do all the farm work. But, like Dad said, "Somebody has to stay home and take care of things." I knew he was right, but why was it always Grandpa and me?

Aunt Bertha noticed it too because she secretly invited Grandpa and me up for a huge feast at her house, that even included some hand cranked home made ice cream, while everyone else were picnicking somewhere. I asked Ercel one time why she didn't like my double cousin and best friend, Tex

Granpa

Olsen anymore, and she said, "Because he's a Weimer." I thought to myself, "Oh my God, so am I. No wonder she doesn't like me." When I caught the flue herding sheep on Joe town hill that year and another time when I came down with the mumps, Ercel sent me over to the Weimer's (Aunt Maude's house) to be taken care of by them until I was well enough to come back to work. It wasn't hard for me to conclude, I was not only overworked, but was unwanted, unloved and was just another unwelcome mouth to feed around there, as far as she was concerned.

Homer C. Olsen - 1940

To add even more misery, I really messed things up while herding a few head of sheep along a ditch bank loaded with fresh green clover while everyone else was picnicking somewhere and Grandpa and I were home alone. Dad told me before they left, "If any of the ewes start to bloat get them out of there in a hurry." And added, "If one of the ewe's bloats and drops, measure one hand spread from its hip bone towards its head, then rotate the same hand, one hand spread down towards its feet, and stab an air hole in its stomach at that point with your pocket knife. If you don't do it right away to release the trapped stomach gas, the ewe will die." I remember I was in the field alone with thirty head of sheep, giving them a real treat along that clover lined ditch bank while Grandpa and old Bob were working some where else, and one of the ewes suddenly bloated and dropped to the ground. I ran over to stick her with my pocket knife just as another ewe dropped, and then another. I must have panicked when that last one fell because I immediately thought the whole herd would drop if I didn't get them out of there fast, and I took care of that first. When I ran back a couple of minutes later to stick the three fallen ewes, it was too late to save any of them. I was devastated because I was

Grandpa Weimer Family – 1934

personally responsible for losing all three of Dad's prime ewes. Grandpa thought I did the right thing under the circumstances, but my dad was furious.

Grandpa Weimer – 1937

It was around the end of July in 1938 that I decided ranching and farming was definitely not my cup of tea and not what I wanted to do for a living the rest of my life. I figured if I didn't make the move to leave Gravelbed soon, I would be trapped in the same *no win poverty cycle* my dad was trapped. As much as I loved my dad and respected his strong character traits, I could never figure out why he didn't have the self confidence or intestinal fortitude, to pick up and leave that God forsaken losing farm operation, and start over again somewhere else. Grandpa Weimer moved his whole family out of Marysvale, Utah in the early thirties to California just like the dust bowl Okies, and startedover as a janitor in the MGM Studios. When he retired years later, he had worked up to the rank of *"Chief Grip"* building movie sets for MGM pictures, and ended up much better off than my dad ever did as a livestock dirt farmer in central Utah. It wasn't until my dad finally began selling insurance and got rid of that poor farm, he ever made a decent living and began saving towards his own retirement.

My mother called me from Boulder City around the middle of August in 1938 to tell me Philip had qualified for government housing because of his position as chief guide, and they were moving to a nice big two bedroom home on Denver Street. She also

Dad & Ercel — Picnic — 1939

said the Boulder City School District had added a ninth grade to their school year so I wouldn't have to ride a bus all the way to Las Vegas, if I would like to come down and attend school there

Weimer Family Reunion - 1938

in September. Philip even said there was space behind the Denver Street home for a small shop building that we could put up for Rodger and me to build things. Their offer sounded just too good to pass up, so I told my dad I was going to drag up and get a lay of the land around Boulder City, Nevada. He said, "You won't be coming back, will you?" I said, "Dad, I don't know for sure what I'm going to do, but I know one thing; there are a lot better ways to make a living than being a farmer." He just looked at me and said, "What was good enough for your Grandpa is good enough for me."

Uncle Orson and Aunt Maud drove down from Monroe to Boulder City around the middle of September in 1938 and bless their hearts they brought my red balloon tired bike with them I really needed for my paper route job.

NEWS RELEASE

September 15, 1938, British Prime Minister Neville Chamberlain meets with Adolph Hitler at Berchtesgaden where Hitler demands annexation of German areas based on "self-determination." Czechoslovakia is divided without its consent in the Munich agreement Chamberlain, convinced of a diplomatic victory ,calls the agreement "peace in our time" Most of Western Europe is wildly enthusiastic over this peaceful settlement In response to uprisings in Sudetenland, in September 1938 martial law is declared in Czechoslovakia..

Uncle Orson was a veteran of World War I so they were on their way to the American Legion Convention in Los Angeles that year, and to visit Grandpa and Grandma Weimer. Since Philip Brim was also a World War I veteran, we decided to go down to the Convention with them also, and it turned into a wonderful "Weimer Family Reunion." It was the first and last time I ever saw the whole Weimer side of my family together in one place at the same time.

I wrote the following letter to my Dad and Ercel from Boulder City concerning my decision to stay with my mother and Philip and attend High School there. This was probably the most difficult letter I have ever written because I still loved my Utah Family, despite all the imagined feelings they had towards me.

September 6 1938

Dear Dad and Ercel,

As you probably already know I have decided to stay here and try their School out and if you could send a few of my things down with Aunt Maude if she comes or c.o.d. if she doesn't. When you send my Money (from the Pete Willardson "hoeing peas" job.) you can send it in the mail and not with Aunt Maude. I know after you read this letter you're going to be awful mad and won't ever write to me again, but I don't want you to feel that way because I like to hear news about how everybody is and what's what. I have a paper route delivering the Examiner every Sunday for $2.00 a month and I think I can get a job at the Airport next summer.

Gertie — My Cow — 1938

This Fall could you sell my sheep and "Peanut"(my calf) and I'll sell "Gerty"(my cow) to you for $15.00 and you can give my pig to Freddie because I never really earned the pig because I didn't work all summer. If Aunt Maude doesn't come, Marilyn can have the sled and Freddie the peddle car. Try and sell my skis for about $1.25 if you can. It has taken me two hours to write this much and I think Philip wants to add a line.

This has been a very hard letter for Junior to write as he thinks a lot of both his Dad and his Mother. He is a good kid and takes things seriously. You probably want to have him with you just as we do but I don't believe you will be mad at him. He and Rodger go swimming 4 or 5 times a week

My Pig — 1938

and are like two fish in the water. We will take good care of him and I believe I can get him something to do over at the Airport. He is afraid you would be mad at him and not send his things but I told him that you were not that kind. It is sure hard on children when the Parents are divorced. They are always afraid that if they please one parent they will make the other one mad. Be sure and write to him as he wants to know all about his Monroe family.

Yours, Philip

P.S. Tell Grandpa "Hello" and try and get a picture for me of Freddie and Grandpa and all of you because I want to put them in my album. I'll try and make the Medicine Chest for you someday Ercel if I can. Who's the new Scout Master?

Yours, Junior.

I think the most interesting things about Boulder City High School from 1938 to 1942 was everyone in my class were *Seniors* for four years. Prior to 1938, all of the classes above the eighth grade had to commute by bus for 23 miles to and from Las Vegas, every day to attend high school. In 1938 the school board added the 9th grade to the Boulder City School System and in 1939; the 10th grade and so on until we reached the 12th grade to

9th Grade — 1939

graduate with a full fledged four year high school by 1942. The ninth grade class shown in the adjacent picture stayed seniors for the four years and twenty five of us (15 girls and 10 boys) were the first High School class to graduate in 1942.

It has always amazed me what teenagers will come up with sometimes for something crazy and stupid to do. I remember around the first of October in 1939, a group of us were standing around on campus one morning before school started and someone came up with the bright idea of having a "ditch day" and not going to school that day. That ridicules idea caught on like wild fire and for some ridicules unknown reason, most of our sophomore class and some of the freshmen, all took off with their

April Fool's Day - 1941

lunch buckets, walking towards the Colorado River cliffs several miles east and downstream of the Dam. The cliffs were at least a hundred feet high at our planned location so, I'll kid you not, climbing down those nearly vertical cliff walls to the river, was no easy task. I remember the boys split up to find the easiest descent for the girls, and eventually, everyone made it and we had a wonderful time picnicking on the Colorado River, playing games, investigating Indian hieroglyphics, and swimming in a warm cave pool under the cliffs. Frank Shelton and I were the only paper delivery boys our boss, "Biz" Bisbee, had to deliver the "*Boulder City Review Journal*" evening newspapers, so we knew

Pasadena JC

we had to get back and left our group in the early afternoon. The others were all having too much fun to worry about anything anyway. Frank decided to take a more dangerous looking (to me anyway) shortcut back to town to save time, but I decided to retrace my original steps back to Boulder City and we split up shouting, *winner takes all.*

It was nearly dark by the time I jogged back to town to pick up my bike and papers, and I didn't finish delivering all my papers to my 165 customers until after ten o'clock that night. When I finally got home, lo and behold, there were a dozen police, park rangers, and worried parent's cars parked around our house waiting to talk to me about where the rest of our group were stranded and/or kidnapped. They said they had sent searching parties out looking for us around the Lake Mead area, and were really surprised to learn we were only a few miles downstream of the Boulder Dam on the river. I marked their maps where Frank and I had left our classmates and they all drove away so Philip could give me the chewing out I deserved, and they could talk to Frank Shelton. The next day, the Park Service flew a small "Piper Cub" up and down the Colorado River and located the rest of our group huddled and shivering around a camp fire on the bank of the river exactly where we marked their maps.

Fortunately, no one was hurt and the group had used some good judgment by staying put and keeping their campfire burning all night, rather than risk climbing up those high cliffs and crossing the desert in the dark. Unfortunately, a few of the search parties looking

> **NEWS RELEASE**
> _____
>
> *March 1939, Adolph Hitler tears up the "Munich Agreement" he made with Neville Chamberlain and Germany annexes the remainder of Czechoslovakia. Hitler puts pressure on Poland to adjust the Polish corridor, which separates Germany from parts of Eastern Prussia, Britain and France pledge aid to protect Polish independence.*

> **NEWS RELEASE**
> _____
>
> *The Spanish Civil War ends on March 28, 1939 with victory by Franco. Spain will remain neutral in the coming European conflict. Italy invades Albania on April 7, 1939 and Italy and Germany conclude a military Alliance on May 22, 1939. Germany and Russia sign a nonaggression pact and Germany demands a free hand against Poland on August 25, 1939.*

for us earlier had gotten lost themselves, so even more search parties were organized to look for them. Needless to say, the whole town of Boulder City was in an uproar over our adolescent stupidity and extremely poor judgment. I'll tell you, we were not only grounded, but were severely punished psychologically by our teachers and everyone in town for that little caper. Frank Shelton's answer to my 2004 Xmas card *ditch day* question below, recalls his memories of that exciting embarrassing event.

3 January '05

Dear Homer

You asked if I still remember our "Ditch Day" on the Colorado River??, Yes, I sure do. At our last class reunion in '04, I described this episode with some of the reunion members. Helen French was at the reunion but was not on the Ditch Day journey. I recall us going out east under the power lines and down one of the canyons to the river. There was a hot (warm) water pool near the river. I'm not sure when we ate our lunch, but it was probably at the river.

As the afternoon passed I became concerned with getting back to Boulder City to deliver the evening newspaper. I decided it would take much too long to retrace our path, so headed upstream along the river on the Nevada side. Going was pretty easy until I reached an area that was a shear cliff from the river waters up the canyon wall. I decided to try and cross the area rather than going up the wall. I took my shoes off and left them behind because I would need every finger and toe hold I could get. I didn't want to fall into the river because an adult had fallen into the river and drowned due to the massive amount of cable and debris in the river below the Dam. Well, with difficulty and holding my breath, I crossed the shear cliff area and reached the lower terminal road barefooted. I was picked up by a person in his truck and rode with him to town and delivered my papers.

That evening, I went to a theater show and every so often, a parent would have me called out of the audience to answer his/her concerns about there ditch day dependent and where they were. I would like to hear your version of this affair.

Sincerely, Frank H. Shelton

Speaking of psychological lessons learned, I'm reminded of another experience around that same time when Fred Holland, Johnny Abercrombie, Frank Shelton and I drove over to see a Las Vegas carnival. I remember a beautiful scantily clad girl working there only five years or so older than we were, said to us, "For ten cents apiece, I will teach you boys a lesson you will never forget." We thought, *Wow, for 10 cents apiece this should really be interesting.*

We each handed her our hard earned dimes and followed her into a tent where she sat the four of us down in front row seats, and told us to wait for the show to begin. Pretty soon, here she came on stage in her flimsy little costume carrying a wooden stick and a knife, and just sat down on a chair and began whittling on the stick. We all sat there quietly watching in open mouthed fascination as she whittled away on the stick for a few minutes, then she looked seductively at the four of us and said, "Boys, you can mark my words, you will remember the lesson I'm about to teach you as long as you live. The lesson is, *Always, always, whittle away from yourself, never whittle towards yourself.* And that was it. She stood up, took a cute little bow and said, *Thank you*, and skipped off the stage laughing while we sat there with stunned

NEWS RELEASE

September 1, 1939, Germany invades Poland on land and in the air with an Army of 1,500,000. Britain and France mobilize but are willing to negotiate if German forces will withdraw. Italy remains neutral. Germany ignores the offer and Britain and France declare War on Germany on Sept. 3rd. Soviet troops who have invaded Poland from the east, meet German forces near Brest Litovsk and on September 29th, Germany and the USSR divide up Poland.

NEWS RELEASE

October 1939, Albert Einstein writes a letter to Roosevelt explaining the potential of an Atomic Bomb, the uranium atoms split, and Roosevelt denies Jewish refugees aboard the S.S. St. Louis entry into the United States.

looks and our mouths wide open. I'll say one thing, she was right about the lesson learned. None of us have ever forgotten what she taught us that day, I know I haven't.

I'm still very proud of the fact I was in the first High School graduating class at Boulder City High School, Boulder City, Nevada, on May 28, 1942. There were only 10 boys and 15 girls in my graduating class, and only 150 students in all four grades of the high school that year. In fact, there were less than 100,000 people in the whole state of Nevada in 1942. Reno was the largest City in the state with a population of 25,000, and you can believe this or not, Las Vegas was only second largest with a population of less than 20,000. I

Boulder City High School Teachers - 1939

remember you could buy that lousy bone dry alkaline desert land in 1942 for only two bits (25 cents) an acre, which still seems like a lot to me. I remember when I was discharged from the army in February of 1946, my mother thought I should invest my entire $200 mustering out pay in desert land along the "Las Vegas Strip" that was selling for a whopping $25 an acre and I was shocked that the land had jumped from 25 cents to 25 dollars an acre in less than four years, and said, "Mom, you've got to be kidding." Oooh boy, talk about lack of vision, rumor has it that same land is selling now for 25 dollars a square foot, but when you think about it hard enough, I was only 22 years old in 1946 so obviously, I was too young to know the three most important rules to making money in the real estate business are: "location, location, and location."

NEWS RELEASE

April 9, 1940 Germany invadesNorway and Denmark. King Haakon VII and his cabinet escape to London. Finland surrenders to the USSR on March 12th after a three month War losing 25,000 dead and 16000 square miles of land.

Besides having wonderful teachers and being part of a four year senior class, the best thing about Boulder High School during those years was the small class size. It not only gave us more individual attention, but nearly every one in the class had an opportunity to serve in some capacity as a class officer. When I moved there, I was the new kid on the block and spent most of the first year in the ninth grade bashfully getting acquainted. I didn't wear glasses then because only four eyed sissies wore glasses, even though the school nurse said I needed glasses badly when I registered for the ninth grade. I remember, I was so nearsighted at the time I recognized the other kids by the way they walked rather than by their features. I'll tell you, when I finally gave in and started wearing glasses, it was

Student Body President - 1941

Junior Prom - 1941

a fantastic awakening to suddenly discover trees were more than just blobs of greenery and actually had individual leaves. And miracle of all miracles, my classes began to make sense and I could even tell what my teachers were scribbling on the blackboards. I still remember my dad saying one time when we were herding sheep on the summer mountain range and I couldn't see a porcupine in a tree, "What's the matter with you, are you blind?" I don't think it never occurred to him when I said, "What tree?" I might need glasses. And besides, no one on the Olsen side of the family ever wore glasses, needed or not. The school nurse was right; I needed glasses for nearsightedness long before I ever started wearing them.

Needless to say, my school work suddenly became easier with glasses and my grades not only improved, but I began to enjoy high school. Besides doing better grade wise in my classes, I also signed on with the basketball and track teams and even served on the student council and the *pebbles* (school paper) staff. I also become interested in student politics and was elected vice president of the sophomore class during the second semester, president of the junior class during the first semester and, believe it or not, *I had the honor of being the first elected student body president of Boulder City High School* during the second semester of my junior year.

NEWS RELEASE

May 10, 1940, Germany invades the Netherlands, Belgium, and Luxembourg. The War in Western Europe has begun and Winston Churchill replaces Neville Chamberlain as Prime Minister of England. The US Army Signal Corps cracks the Japanese diplomatic code.

It was during my term as student body president, I began thinking seriously about what and where I wanted to go with my life. My wonderful science teacher, Harry Fuller, was my chief advisor and mentor at the time and I respected his counsel and advice even more than my own dad or Philip's opinions when it came to a career and/or college selection. My dad just wanted me to take over the Gravelbed farm after his demise and wouldn't discuss me doing anything else for a living. My stepfather, Philip Brim, thought I should take a hard serious look at the construction industry as my life's work, and took me through Boulder Dam many times to see for myself what real construction engineers and skilled craftsman could accomplish by working together to make a good living, but all I could think about was flying airplanes and maybe being an aeronautical engineer. Harry Fuller felt I had the qualifications to become an engineer of some kind, but said I needed to get my grades up to at least a B + average during my senior year, if I was serious about being accepted by any engineering school. My problem was, there wasn't enough hours in the day to get everything done I was involved in.

Homer J. Olsen - 1941

My pre-glasses days – 1939

I must have looked like a walking skeleton during my sophomore and junior years because, much to my mother's surprise, I grew like a weed. She thought, because of my slight build, I would stop growing when I reached 5"8" in height like her older brother Byron, but here I was already 6"0" tall and weighed only 127 pounds when I was a junior in high school. When I left Utah and moved to Nevada to live, I was only 5"3" tall and weighed a whopping 87 pounds with not one ounce of it muscle. I still laugh about Coach Miles asking me to play *wide end*

receiver on the high school's football team my junior year, because he thought I had such *good hands*. I asked, "What happens after I catch the ball and get tackled, Coach?" He shrugged and said, "You won't get tackled if you run fast enough." Mrs. Macdonald used to hire me to wax her floors, wash her windows, weed her garden and mow her lawn, because I was such a *good worker* (her words). She would shake her head in disbelief when she saw how skinny I was and worried so much about it she even threatened to go to the authorities to report my parents were deliberately starving me, and to see if she could adopt me, bless her heart.

Philip & Me — 1940

She was convinced my parents weren't feeding me and my mother had a terrible time convincing her I was eating like a horse. I guess my metabolism was a roaring jet engine in those days because no matter how much food I would shovel down, I would never put on any weight and would only grew a little taller. Wow, how thing change when we grow older. Nowadays, I can swallow one Rolaids tablet and I'll gain ten pounds.

My Bedroom Model Airplane Display - 1940

When I moved to Boulder City, I spent a lot of time building and flying my model airplanes in the city park and met another model builder and a great guy named, Donald Johnson. Everybody called him *Waddle* because he was extremely overweight compared to me, so from then on everyone began calling us the "Laurel and Hardy" team. Waddle and I became very

NEWS RELEASE

May 17, 1940. German Tank Divisions sweep into France who immediately surrenders the largest remaining standing Army in Europe, a month later. French forces are disarmed and Germany occupies over 60% of France. In August 1940 German planes begin a bombing offensive to destroy British Air strength and the Battle of Britain begins.

good friends and flew our model airplanes together for the next two years until his dad accepted a better job with the Kaiser Ship Yards, and his family moved to Albany, California. I remember we both entered our model planes in a meet at the Boulder City Airport one time, and my

original design rubber powered model airplane won a gas model kit as first prize. From then on, Waddle and I built gas powered model airplanes together and flew them from a dry lake bed adjacent to the Searchlight highway near railroad pass. I even built an eight foot wingspan glider (shown on the ceiling photo of my porch bedroom) and talked Gordon Spearman into using his larger gas model to tow-launch it from the dry lake for it's maiden flight by using a friction spool release idea we dreamed up. Believe it or not, both Gordon's plane and my glider were caught up in a thermal that day and we never saw my glider again. Gordon told me at our 55th High School class reunion in 1997, a prospector found his gas model in a desert mountain range near Overton, Nevada, (ninety miles from our launch site) in 1951, ten years after the launch, and had returned it to him. I still remember following my glider in Philip's '37 Plymouth for over thirty miles from the launch site that day and finally losing sight of it circling high over Lake Mead

towards the Grand Canyon. As far as I know, no one has ever seen or heard *hide nor hair* of it since.

As a token of my affections, I named one of my model airplanes after a girl I had a crush on named, Delores *Hope* Brown, but unfortunately her family (sensing a problem), packed up all their belongings and moved to San Bernardino, California, to obviously get her away from me. Luckily, another girl I liked named, Lois Putney, accepted my invitation to the Junior Prom that year, but wouldn't you know it, she also moved back to California shortly afterwards. Oooh boy, things like this make a person wonder if they should shower more often.

Hope Brown — 1940

My stepfather, Philip Brim, would drop by our model airplane work room occasionally to watch us build model airplanes and dream up designs of what the airplanes of the future would look like. He would always laugh and say, "You guys are living in the past; the airplanes of year 2000 will look like this." Then he would

Lois Putney – 1941

fold a sheet of typing paper into a delta wing type airplane, pointed nose and all, and sail it across the room. We thought he must be some kind of a nut case or something because anybody with half a brain thought the "P39" and/or the "P40" fighter plane were the *plane of the future* look and would laugh him out of the room. Wow, what vision that man had because he was right. Our planes today resemble his design and to think, he never even finished high school.

Phillip Brim – 1937

Philip also used to tell us kids how much he enjoyed his Chief Guide job at Boulder Dam for the Bureau of Reclamation, because it gave him a chance to kid around with the traveling public. He said a sweet old lady asked him one time where all the CCC boys were working now that they had finished building the Dam, and he told

told her, "They are currently employed raking leaves in the Petrified Forest." She walked away saying how happy she was they still had such good paying jobs. Another lady wanted to know what the Bureau of Reclamation was going to do with all the water after they took the electricity out of it. Philip told her one of their young engineers had come up with the brilliant idea of selling it to the City of Los Angeles for drinking water, to help pay for the dam. She said she was so happy to hear our government was finally using their heads again, by not letting all that good water go to waste.

Philip & Ruth Brim - 1938

Looking back now at my daily schedule during my junior year in high school; I wonder how I ever found the time to even sleep. I was not only taking all the pre-college courses they offered in high school, but was active in student government and was on the basketball and track teams and working two part time jobs after school to earn money for college. I had fourteen lawns to mow every week (for 50 cents apiece), and had hired two other kids to help me, plus another high paying 25 cent an hour delivery boy job in a flower shop. On weekends, I also had two other 25 cents an hour good paying jobs. One was alternately manning the Nevada and Arizona side tourist stands every Saturday at Boulder Dam, selling post cards and film, and the other on Sundays, was caddying at the Boulder City Golf and Country Club, where (during a break), I made my first and last *hole in one* on a par three hole. When you think about it hard enough, I was lucky at

golf that day, but was really lucky to be able to still maintain a C+ average in school with my heavy workload. How I found the time to still mess around with girls and model airplanes, along with everything else, was a wonder. Mr. Fuller was right and it was time I began rethinking my priorities and get my act together.

One of the things all children of divorced parents have in common is their fear of not being able to please both of their separated parents they loved equally. I never felt right about my mother changing my last name to whatever name of whomever she was married to at the time, because I knew it hurt my dad's feelings, and mine too. My last name was *Olsen* when I was born and it is still *Olsen* on my birth certificate. My Norwegian immigrant grandparents always told me I should be proud of my Scandinavian heritage and I loved my last name. I remember in 1932 when my mother kidnapped me the first time after Grandma Olsen died and dumped me and my little brother Rodger off at Mrs. Jorgensen's rooming house, we were both registered in school as *Brim* because she was still married to Philip Brim. When she and Philip parted ways and she married a knot headed magician con-artist named, "Doc" Staley, she registered me at Venice High School as *Junior Staley* and when I moved back to Boulder City in 1938 to live with Philip and my mother again until I graduated from High School, my mother insisted my last name be changed from *Olsen* to *Brim* again to *avoid awkward questions from neighbors*. After all she said, her married name was now *Brim,* and my little brother Rodger's name was *Brim,* when actually Rodger's real name was *Sorensen* since he was the son of my mother's second husband, but interestingly, she had never allowed Philip to adopt Rodger. So anyway, to keep peace in the family from September 1938 to September 1941, I very reluctantly agreed to be known as *"Homer Junior Brim"* at Boulder City High School.

NEWS RELEASE

Salt Lake Deseret News Story:, April 5, 1941: *Ole Kjolvick Olsen will be the oldest man in Monroe, Utah when he celebrates his ninety-first birthday on April 10, 1941 with family and friends. Mr. Olsen was born April 10, 1850 in Kjolvick, Rogaland County, Norway. He went to sea when he was twelve years old, sailing with the North Sea Herring fleet, which salted their catch on board and marketed them at Stavanger, Norway. His father died when he was eighteen years old and he became the head of the family, bringing his mother and two sisters to America as LDS converts when he was twenty three years old. They initially settled in Ephraim, Utah.*

Grandpa Olsen - 1938

Mr. Olsen married Hannah Kristina Swensen in the LDS Endowment house in Salt Lake City on October 24, 1879. After making their home in Ephraim for a short time , they moved to Monroe where Mr. Olsen built a home, farmed and freighted Sevier County home produce to Pioche and Ely, Nevada where it took ten days traveling with good teams of horses to make the round trip. Mr. Olsen well remembers the hardships of the pioneers and the serious Indian troubles, but he never was harmed.

He also worked as a carpenter and stone mason helping to build the Endowment House and the Manti Temple. He was a counselor to the Bishops of the Brooklyn LDS ward and has served as high priest in the Monroe North Ward for many years.

Mr. Olsen is in good health, he has been out of doors every day this winter and spring cutting the wood needed for heating fuel. His son, Homer has lived with him since the death of Mr. Olsen's wife on November 26, 1931. In his spare time, he reads the bible and the daily newspaper without the aid of glasses. He shook his head sadly when he reflected on the plight of his native country since the Germans invaded it, and was very distressed over it.

> *With Mr. Olsen on his birthday will be his four sons and one daughter, Joseph Olsen of Woods Cross, Nephi Olsen of Richfield, and Orson and Homer C. Olsen and Bertha Tuft, all of Monroe; 43 grand children and 21 great grand children. A sister, Mrs. Lena Guldbransen (age 85) lives in Ellsinore Utah.*

It was during the summer of 1941, I decided it was high time I let the world know that *Junior Brim* was not my real name, and on my own against my mother's strict orders, I registered for my senior year at Boulder City high school as **Homer J. Olsen.** I remember during the first high school assembly we had in late September of 1941, my good friend, Frank Shelton stood up and nominated Homer J. Olsen to be student body president during our senior year and everyone wanted to know who that was. I got up and explained to the whole school why my name was changed and that I had been doing some serious thinking about what I wanted to do with my life and what I had to do to accomplish the goals I set for myself. I told them I wanted everyone to remember me by my real name because Homer J. Olsen was the name on my birth certificate and would be my name when I went into the armed services and on to college after the war was over. I also told them I had to improve my grades to get into any college and I only had one year left to do it and I needed more time to study. I thanked everyone for giving me the opportunity to serve the previous semester as their student body president and that I felt both humble and complimented to be nominated again, but someone else should have the honor of serving as student body president next year. They all applauded me when I sat down, and Frank Shelton was nominated and unanimously elected student body president for our final year at Boulder City High.

I also made several other changes during that last year of high school to improve my grades. I told Coach Miles I wouldn't play basketball on the team any longer and most likely would not be on the track team next spring. When I turned in my equipment he

NEWS RELEASE

April 6, 1941 German troops invade Yugoslavia and Greece who both surrender within the next two weeks. On May 20TH German paratroopers invade Crete and the German Army invades the USSR on June 22, 1941. Soviet units on the frontier retreat.

High School

HJO Enlistment 1942

said he was sorry, but thought I was making a terrible mistake. I also quit my flower shop job and turned all my lawn mowing jobs over to my two man crew to handle after my little brother Rodger said it looked like too much work for him and he didn't want to mess with it. His disgusting attitude was, "Mom always gives me all the money I need anyway, so why should I work for it?" When I talked to my boss, Kelly Lyon, about leaving the Boulder Dam weekend job, he said if I would stay on, he would give me a different after school job developing film for him in his "Photo" lab. He said the photo job would be both educational and interesting, and would even allow me the time to do my homework between the various operations. I accepted his offer and it turned out to be everything he said it would be. In fact I really appreciated the opportunity he gave me to work with an older retired photographer and his wife (whose names have escaped me) that both knew the photography business like the back of their hands and I learned a lot about photography from them. I even had an

> ### NEWS RELEASE
>
> *November 5, 1941, the Japanese Imperial general headquarters issues plans for an offensive against the U.S. fleet at Pearl Harbor, British Malaya, the Philippines, and the Netherlands East Indies. On November 15, 1941 Special Japanese Ambassador Sabura Kurusu arrives in the United States to reopen trade negotiations. On November 26, 1941 U.S. Secretary of State Cordell Hull says Japan would have to withdraw from Indochina and China, and recognize the Chinese national government. Japan rejects his conditions and the Japanese Pearl Harbor strike force sets sail. Japanese embassies in the United States begin to burn secret documents on December 3, 1941.*

opportunity to work with a famous photographer named Cliff Segarbloom, who was working for the Arizona Highways Magazine at the time. And besides, 25 cents an hour (the minimum wage then) was a lot of money for a high school kid to make during those depression years.

High School Years

The upshot of all my efforts to improve my grade point average was encouraging. My grades improved dramatically and I ended up with better than a "B+" average during my senior year, a feat that was anything but easy when you're graded on a curve against two of the smartest kids that ever graduated from Boulder City High School. One of them was named Frank Shelton and the other was named Helen French and I'll always be grateful to both of them for all the help they gave me in improving my grades. As I recall, neither one of them ever got a grade less than straight "A's" in any of their classes during all four years of high school. Frank Shelton had already decided that Cal Tech was the school for him and he talked me into applying with him to take the entrance examination for the freshman class in September of 1942. According to our teachers, Frank and I were the only applicants at Boulder City High that met their qualifications and were approved by the Cal Tech admissions committee to take the entrance exam. We both took the test in March and, as it turned out, Frank passed and I flunked. I was terribly disappointed at the time and decided to go to Pasadena Junior College during the fall semester to get better acquainted with the Cal Tech area, and maybe take the exam again at a later date. Somehow, I found out I had done well on everything except the English essay portion.

The following letter from the Office of the Registrar at California Institute of Technology informing me that I had failed the entrance examination on March 14 (English & Chemistry) and 21 (Math & Physics). Thinking back now, I wish I had been able to take the easy science tests first because it was obvious they never spent much time checking the March 21st test results after I blew the English essay portion on March 14th. Who knows, maybe the results, and my whole life, would have been different.

Report Card
BOULDER CITY HIGH SCHOOL
194.1. - 194.2.

Name Olsen, Homer Jr. Class Twelfth

FIRST SEMESTER						SECOND SEMESTER				
Atti-tudes	SUBJECTS	1st. Tm.	2nd. Tm.	3rd. Tm.	Avg.	Atti-tudes	SUBJECTS	4th. Tm.	5th. Tm.	6th. Tm.	Avg.
	Civics	B	B	C	B		Am. History	B	B	B	B
	Physics	A-	A-	A-	A-		Physics	A-	B	B+	B+
	Solid Geometry	A-	A-	A-	A-		Trigonometry	A-	A-	B	B+
	Physical Education	A	A	A	A		Physical Ed.	A	B	A	A
	Hygiene	B+	A	B+	A-		Hygiene	A	A	A	A
	Times tardy	0	1	1			Times tardy	0	0		
	Days absent	½	3½	½			Days absent	2	8	1½	

Signature of Parent or Guardian

1st Term *Mrs. Philip Brim* 4th Term *Mrs. Philip Brim*
2nd Term *Mrs. Philip Brim* 5th Term *Mrs. Philip Brim*
3rd Term *Mrs. Philip Brim* 6th Term

Note: See reverse side of card for standards of marking.

HS Twelfth Year Grades – HJO

March 22, 1942

Dear Mr. Olsen,

Your entrance examination papers and your high school record have been carefully examined by the Admissions Committee of this Institute, and we regret very much to have to inform you that you are not among those selected for admission to the freshman class in September of this year. Nearly five hundred students took the entrance examination this year, and since the class is strictly limited to one hundred and sixty students, it was necessary to deny admission to a large number of highly qualified candidates.

We hope that you will not construe your rejection as any indication that you are not able to do college work. The fact that you were permitted to take the entrance examinations indicates that the committee felt your high school record was distinctly above average, and therefore, that you should be able to carry college work successfully.

Very truly yours,
L. W Jones, Acting Registrar

Coach Miles sweet talked me into rejoining the track team after my impressive 2 minute 8 second half mile trial run, so I agreed thinking I might just be lucky enough to win my athletic letter my last year. I had never earned an athletic letter, and I figured my best chance was at the Tri-State (California, Nevada and Arizona) track meet in Las Vegas, Nevada, that year. As I kneeled in my stating chocks, I shocked Luke Hinman, a fantastic under-motivated over confident natural born Las Vegas High School athlete who was kneeling next to me, by confidently saying, "Luke, I'm going to whip your ass today." Talk about surprised, he looked over at me almost in shock and said, "In a pig's eye you will."

High Jumping HJO – 1941

Well, to make this story shorter I didn't win, but with my good start I jumped out ahead of Luke and all the other runners, and was in front of the whole pack all during the first lap, but unfortunately run low on wind and faded

Lake Tahoe – 1944

into third place during the last lap. Apparently Luke and a Navaho Indian kid (with his mouth half full of rocks) from Arizona got their second wind about the same time I lost mine, and they took over the first and second place. The Navaho Indian (whose name has escaped me) and I, were still able to stick real close behind Luke all during the second lap, and to this day, I still think we motivated old Luke enough to not only win the race, but break the State of Nevada's High School half mile record that day with a run of two (2.0) minutes flat, a record I've been told, stood for the next twenty years. Anyway as it happened, we were no slouches either with our runs of two minutes and two seconds (the Navaho's time) and my best yet of two minutes and three seconds.

I also tried high jumping and broad jumping that year, but never placed better than third place in either of them with my high jumps of 5' 7" and broad jumps of 19' 6." All in all, the only sport I was ever good enough to win a blue ribbon was in swimming, but unfortunately, swimming was not an official High School sport in those days, so I never got my athletic letter. My brother Rodger, was able to get his athletic letters easily because he was a natural born athlete and good in all sports, like Luke Hinman, where as I had to work my tail off to do as well as I did.

NEWS RELEASE

April 18, 1942, Lt Colonel James H. Doolittle launches a strike on Tokyo from the U.S.S. Hornet, 800 miles off Japan. Their Plan was to Bomb Tokyo, and fly 1000 miles into China. Two pilots fall into Japanese hands and are beheaded and thousands of Chinese are slaughtered by the Japanese for helping the other Americans (Joyce's Uncle "Bud" Van Dorn was a crew member on the U.S.S Hornet at the time.)

I was also appointed photo editor for our school's annual during my senior year because of my photo-lab job experience and served on the student council, but I spent most of my time trying to improve my grades and worrying about how the war was going. I celebrated my 18th birthday on April 7, 1942 and from all the rumors floating around, I would soon be eligible for the draft. On May 28, 1942, I graduated from Boulder City High School and along with my two best friends, Frank Shelton and Helen French, was chosen by our teachers to give one of the three High School graduation speeches that year.

NEWS RELEASE

May 4–8, 1942, the battle of the Coral Sea. This is the first navel battle in history in which no surface ship sights the enemy. American aircraft find and sink the Japanese carrier Shoh and damage the Shokaku: the U.S.S. carrier Lexington is sunk and the carrier Yorktown is damaged and the Japanese suffer their first setback in the War. One of my Boulder City High School friends, Norman Ready, enlisted on December 8, 1941 and went down with the Lexington during that battle, but fortunately was rescued.

Homer J. Olsen's High School Graduation Speech entitled "The Opportunities of the class of 1942 in the field of Economics", May 28, 1942, Boulder City High School, Boulder City, Nevada.

<u>*Parents, Teachers, Students and Friends of the Graduates.*</u>

Have you ever stopped to ask yourself why this present War is being fought? Have you ever tried to analyze the reasons for any War? Most of us, I think have not. Some say this is a War between the have and have not nations. Others say this is a War between the political viewpoints of different economic systems, while others say it is a War of Economics. Any economist will tell you all wars are fought because of an economic reason. Doesn't this prove something? Doesn't this prove that something is haywire somewhere in our economic system?

It is entirely possible great readjustments will take place in our present economic system after this War is over. Tariffs, which have proven in the past time and time again, to breed distrust between Nations will most likely be lowered if not done away with entirely. No nation should be allowed to gain a cornerstone on the world's monetary system and a system must be worked out whereby the people of the World share in the resources of the World.

Now we come to the question, "What are the opportunities of the class of '42 in economics?" In order to be more specific, let

Homer J. Olsen - 1942

High school graduation 1942

Boulder City High School - Class of 1942

us choose and discuss one branch of Economics. Let us choose and discuss the field of Industry.

With the present War raging now as never before, man and women power is urgently needed in Industry. Never before have opportunities for employment and advancement been equaled. It will be during this present conflict that Scientists working under the pressure of War will develop better Steels, advance in the world of Plastics and Synthetic Rubber, and develop better engines, airplanes and any number of other things. These things will all be placed in the hands of the youth of today for further development.

As we are all aware, there is a definite shortage of consumer goods. It will be after we have won the War that people will again want the things they have been deprived of such as Radios, Automobiles, Refrigerators, Cameras, and numerous other articles. Even things like Colored Television do not seem at all unlikely for the future. Opportunities in the further development of these fields will be tremendous.

We are now entering into what may be called "the light metal era that may be illustrated by the intensified efforts to obtain Magnesium as shown here locally. The great possibilities of the Airplane have demanded a lighter metal for higher efficiency. The Automobile of tomorrow will also use lighter metals. It has been prophesied by Detroit Engineers the Automobile of tomorrow will appear externally like the common Lady Bug. The framework will be of *magnesium and aluminum with a plastic cover and the windows will be made of Plexiglas used now for gun blisters on Bombers. It will be powered by a small engine housed in the rear of the car fueled by a high octane or aviation gasoline. Radical changes may also occur in the Airplane. Examples of this can currently be seen in John Northrop's "Flying Wing" and the Davis "Manta Fighter" designs. Opportunities in these exciting fields are numerous.*

The roads now being built in China and India for Troop transportation will later serve to bring these people into closer contact with the outside world. With the better development of the Radio, the people of the world will come to better understand one another thus stimulating friendship and goodwill between Nations. With the better development of the Automobile and the family Airplane, tourist trade to all countries in general will boom.

Many of you are probably thinking, "Isn't it too bad this class should graduate into a world of conflict, and into a disrupted world torn by War." No ladies and gentlemen, our class doesn't think so. It's not that we uphold war but that we see on the horizon a very bright future. To me and to my classmates, the opportunities for us in the field of economic is very "rosy."

Thank you.

Tex came down from Monroe on the bus around the first of June of 1942 shortly after I graduated from high school so we could work together somewhere and save as much money as possible for our college expenses after the war was over. We both got jobs right away, thanks to my good friend and former teacher Harry Fuller, as electrician helpers building the Basic Magnesium Plant in Henderson, Nevada. Tex and I were assigned to different crews right away and I was in a crew with an electrician friend of Harry's nicknamed "Bud", who turned out to be my foreman and was the one who helped Tex and I get our Union clearances. Talk about probability, and

NEWS RELEASE

June 3-6, 1942, Battle of Midway, in one of the most decisive battles in world history, American aircraft finds and destroys four Japanese aircraft carriers. The Japanese sink the U.S.S. Yorktown. American Forces land on Guadalcanal on August 7, 1942 signaling the first major assault in the Pacific war.

I know you won't believe this, but the other apprentice in my crew named Mervin Brannon, had exactly the same eye prescription I had for both my eyes. How did I know? We got our glasses mixed up one day and neither one of us knew the difference until two days later when we found out our frames were different. Anyway, the three of us, Tex, Mervin and I, were all around the same age so we wanted to earn as much money as possible that summer before we went into the service and this was an ideal job for us.

Bud sent me over to the tool shed to get a *left handed monkey wrench* (as an initiation stunt) when I first started working at the magnesium plant and I was so eager to make a good impression, I high jumped the barricades and ran all the way to the tool shed and back again to report they only had *right handed monkey wrenches.* Unfortunately, on the *shortcut return* with that good news, I hurdled a concrete wall with rebar sticking up and somehow ripped the seat out of my britches on one of the reinforcing bars. You guessed it, from that day on I was known as *Sunny Butt* to everyone in the crew, but from my point of view, it was still better than being called *Yunior* and *hey you*, and I had passed their *apprentice electrician initiation* with flying colors.

Summer of 1942

The Henderson Basic Magnesium plant was a crash, cost plus, defense contract, so we worked six ten hour days at an unheard of $0.90 cents an hour plus time and one half for overtime, and were able to save $200 a month each on our jobs. I'll tell you, Tex and I put a lot of miles on our hot 1929 Model "A" Ford commute car, traveling to and from the Basic Magnesium Plant in Henderson during that hot enjoyable summer.

I remember I had a terrible time figuring out the *why* various unions claimed certain things as *only their work* on that cost plus, fast track, defense contract. The laborer's and operating engineers union were supposed to dig a trench for us electricians, but they did such a lousy job fine grading the ditch I picked up a shovel to level out the high spots and the laborer's union steward threatened to fine me for *using their tool.* Then I would grab a claw hammer to remove the humps and the carpenter's union steward jumped me for using *their tool*, and so it went. What was even more depressing for a conscientious electrician helper like me was to see so many experienced journeyman electricians constantly goofing off by hiding out day after day in manholes around the job, playing cards and/or just sleeping. None of them seemed to care one way or the other, who won the war or even if the job ever got built, and it made me sick. I

NEWS RELEASE

August 7, 1942: American forces land on Guadalcanal and Tulagi in the Solomon Islands. This is the first major assault in the Pacific War and the start of a six month campaign that will include seven naval engagements and over ten land battles. August 8-9, 1942. The Battle of Savo Island Japanese forces attack the American Navy supporting the Marine invasion off Guadalcanal and America suffers its worst defeat in a "fair fight" naval battle. The U.S .Navy withdraws after loosing four heavy cruisers, one destroyer, and 1270 men leaving 17,000 Marines on Guadalcanal without food, heavy equipment, and ammunition. The battle area becomes known as "Iron Bottom Sound."

asked them, "Why do you guys do this?" and their answers were always the same, they had run out of couplings, or conduit, or something else and therefore couldn't do their work. I assumed it was job supervisions responsibility to keep all the crews supplied with the materials needed, but finally I couldn't stand it any longer and borrowed my foreman's pickup truck and drove to the rail head myself and picked up several boxes of the correct couplings that were sitting there waiting for someone to deliver, and secretly stored them around the job. The next time one of our deadbeat crew members smilingly complained they had run out of couplings, I just delivered them their correct couplings and watched their shocked expressions. Needless to say, they really had broad smiles on their faces when I announced I was going to leave to do something worthwhile for my country, by enlisting in the Army Air Corps.

The world's best workman are the American blue collar workers and they deserve a fair shake, but some of these union people just can't seem to get it through their heads they *still have to earn that fair shake by an honest day's work*. The only way company's in the competitive businesses like construction contracting can justify paying the high wages we enjoy today in America, is by having highly trained, efficient hard working people with a good work ethic on their payrolls. If labor productivity slows, the companies will not stay competitive by paying these high union wages and their days as a non-productive business will be numbered. Unions in effect, can price their members out of their jobs if productivity is not maintained at a high enough level for the company to stay competitive. But on the other hand and like it or not, labor productivity is a two way street between the unions and management working together as a team because productivity is not all the fault of the unions. Management must take much of the blame and in my opinion; management's share of that blame is 90%.

Ted Tuft, Jr, and Tex – 1942

Fortunately I was able to start my fifty year career in the construction business from the very bottom rung of the craftsman-management ladder of a construction company and I received the best basic *hands on* training possible, with learning experience on each rung of the ladder, to learn how construction company's operate and projects are built.. I apprenticed with four different craft unions, up to and including the journeyman carpenter level, and thanks to the wonderful GI Bill opportunity our country offered returning World War II veterans, I was fortunate enough to acquire a degree in civil engineering from two of the best college's in the United States, Pomona College and Stanford University. I was also very fortunate to be hired by the worlds best heavy engineering construction company, The Peter Kiewit Sons Company, to begin climbing the management ladder from the bottom rung one at a time, to eventually reach the top rung in 1963 and found my own construction company.

Like it or not, even good hard working people will *goof off* on you if given the opportunity by supervision, and I am convinced to this day, at least 90% of the blame for poor labor productivity in the construction industry is not the fault o unions, but the fault of incompetent company management. Peter Kiewit himself once told me the lack of productivity on a job was 100% management's fault, not 90%, including the things beyond their control. He felt a qualified competent management team that always pays close attention to business, will anticipate any and all problems affecting their work place, regardless of the cause, and will adjust their operations to compensate for them, if and when they occur. I also will never forget one of my old bosses named Ward White, telling me that once a project is properly organized and running, the job superintendent's responsibilities boil down to being just a "gopher" (go for this– go for that). He said, "If that carpenter over there reaches back for a nail, it's your job to make damn sure that nail, or whatever else he needs to do his job, is there for him. If that carpenter doesn't know how to do his job but wants to learn, it's your job to teach him. If he doesn't want to learn his job, or refuses, then it's your job to replace him immediately with some one who will do the job."

Lesson Learned: *Since all construction companies in a competitive market use the same dollars and basically the same equipment to perform their work, the only difference between those who are successful and those who fail is due entirely to the competence of their management. Simply stated, company's run by competent management will succeed; company's run by incompetent management will fail.*

THE WORLD WAR II YEARS

NEWS RELEASE

December 7, 1941; Japan attacks the American fleet at Pearl Harbor, Hawaii. Almost 2,400 U.S. Soldiers and Sailors are killed; and another 1100 wounded. 19 U.S. ships, including 8 battleships, 3 cruisers, and 3 destroyers are sunk or badly damaged; 188 U.S. aircraft are destroyed Japanese losses total 29 aircraft and 6 submarines.

December 7, 1941. I have yet to meet someone who was at least ten years old in 1941 that doesn't remember exactly where they were and what they were doing on that fateful day. President Roosevelt called the Japanese sneak attack on Pearl Harbor on December 7, 1941, *a day of infamy* and even though it occurred over sixty five years ago, I still remember that cowardly attack and the wake up call and shock waves it sent through every home in America as if it were yesterday. Unlike today, nearly all the protesting America First isolationists and the conscientious objectors immediately became interventionists and America united in its resolve to destroy the axis powers and win the war. Japanese Admiral Yamamoto was reported to have prophesied after their Pearl Harbor attack, *I fear we have awakened the sleeping giant.*

Frank Shelton, Fred Holland and I decided to get up at 4:00 am on that fateful Sunday morning to drive the Brim family's new 1941 Buick Sedan from Boulder City to a place called Indian Springs seventy mile north of Las Vegas, Nevada, to see an air show. We had heard the Army Air Corps would be there from the Las Vegas Army Air field to do some stunt flying and show off their newest aircraft, so to aviation buffs like ourselves; we knew it was going to be a fantastic show. I remember we arrived in Indian Springs around 8:30 am and the air show started at 9:00, right on schedule, but just before 11:00 o'clock when the Air Corps planes were scheduled to perform, another Army plane suddenly appeared to pull up next to the other three Army airplanes. They all seemed to get very excited and hurriedly started their engines to fly back to their base in Las Vegas just as the shows announcer said the Army's part in the air show was unavoidably canceled, but they would continue with the other events as scheduled. To this day, I don't think he or anyone else there were aware of the Japanese attack until after the air show was over. It was while we were pulling out of the parking area when a driver next to our car suddenly signaled me to roll down my window and yelled, "Turn on your radio."

With our ears glued to the radio all the way back, we made it home around sundown to see everyone in Boulder City running around excitedly like chickens with their heads off. As chief guide on Boulder Dam, my stepfather, Philip Brim, had already been sworn in as a deputy sheriff and was wearing a badge with a six shooter on his hip. He told us the Army had already notified the Bureau of Reclamation they were going to mount anti-aircraft guns on Boulder Dam and that all the electric power for the street and neon lights in town had been ordered turned off and we were on *blackout alert* in case of an air raid. Someone had reasoned the Japanese battle fleet that hit Pearl Harbor would most likely be heading towards California, and bombing the Boulder Dam would not be out of the question.

NEWS RELEASE

December 8, 1941, Japan attacks Wake Island and the Philippines, and invade Northern Malaya and Kowloon. The United States declares War on Japan.

Needless to say, we were all very worried and nervous sleepers that night.

The following letter from my old buddy, Donald "Waddle" Johnson (age 17) was mailed from 1059 Shannon Street, Albany, California, to me at 1354 Denver Street, Boulder City, Nevada, four days after Pearl Harbor. "Waddle" and I used to build and fly Model Airplanes together from 1938 to 1940 until his dad was offered a better job at the Kaiser Ship Yards and moved the family to California.

December 11, 1941

Dear J.R.

I am sorry I haven't answered your letter sooner but I have been very busy with school etc. I got me a "Madwell Mite" and a "Clailand Viking" (Model Airplanes). I modified the Viking and put slots in the wings and I have the fuselage done on my "Super Crate"

How is everyone down there and how do you like the War? I hear over the radio you had a Blackout down there last night. We had one up here Monday night and have all our instructions in the event of an Air Raid. We are having Air Raid drills in school now. All the neon lights are out in the city and it looks kind of funny.

I see by the papers that they are putting (Gordon) Spearman up for Allstate and the fellows played a pretty good game against Vegas. We finished up our season here with a

Dinner at the Lions Club and I won a ticket to the Big Game at Stanford (worth $4.40) so Mom and I went to Palo Alto on the train and had quite a time.

I don't think I will get down for Xmas vacation. We were going to come down but Pop doesn't think he can get time off now. They have Armed Guards over at the Ship Yard and are going to get about six Anti-Aircraft Guns. Well, that's just about all so I will close now.

You're Pal,

Donald Johnson

During the following week, all of the Boulder City High School grade 12 boys nearing draft age gathered in groups to decide what we should do. Should we all enlist immediately or wait until we are drafted? We all wanted to get in the service as soon as possible to help win the war against the Axis powers, but what should we do to be of the most help to our country? Only three boys in our high school decided to enlist immediately, Norman Ready and Bill Ewing joined the Navy and Charles Bingham

NEWS RELEASE

December 11, 1941 Germany and Italy declare War on the United States. The United States ends its neutrality in Europe and declares War on Germany and Italy. On December 22, 1941; the British and American Combined Chiefs of Staff agree to give the War against Germany priority over the War against the Japanese in the Pacific .Germany begins a U-boat offensive along the East Coast of the United States in January, 1942.

1941 Geology field trip with Mr Fuller

enlisted in the Army Air Corps. After a great deal of discussion and advice from parents, teachers and friends, the rest of us decided to stay in school and get our high school diplomas the following May, and then wait for the draft. Our former and most popular teacher named, Harry Fuller, the one we considered our mentor, was currently working as a geologist for the Bureau of Mines, and he often took Frank Shelton, Fred Holland and I on geology field trips with him. He argued that most of us at seventeen weren't even close to the draft age of 21 yet, and we still needed a lot more education and maturity to be of any help to anyone. He felt that even though we were patriotic and wanted to enlist immediately, which he thought was commendable, we still needed a lot more experience, training and growing up to do, before being effective as service menand women. Even if we were not called up right away after we had graduated, he felt we should continue pursuing our goals in life and try to acquire all the college credit we could before we were drafted. Any college credit we acquired, combined with all the ROTC training we could get in before being inducted, would result in much more productive service assignments, and would benefit both our country and ourselves a lot more in the long run. His arguments were the most logical course of action, and the majority of us decided to follow his advice.

Mrs. Udell's Boarding House – 1942

After graduation from High School and working the summer of 1942 in Henderson, Nevada as an electrician apprentice, I moved into Mrs. Udell's boarding house in Pasadena, California with Tommy Godbey as my room mate and registered for all the pre-engineering classes and ROTC training I could

at Pasadena Junior College, to prepare for my upcoming life in the Army. I remember around the first of October after a "You're Future and the War" assembly for draft age male students, I received a mailer from my counselor entitled "Thumbnail Sketches of Enlisted Reserve Plans of Our Armed Forces." The brochure described the various plans for the Army, Navy, Coast Guard, and the Air Force, and stated that the Enlisted Reserve Corps plans were devised to recruit potential officer material and to keep such

Enlisted reserve

candidates in various colleges for further training and future usefulness. It emphasized that an Enlisted Reserve status ***was not a scheme for dodging the draft*** and when you were in the Enlisted Reserve, you were in the Army. It was a plan to give you more training so you could

Mrs. Udell's Boarding House – 1942

be of more use to your country and sounded exactly like what I was looking for.

The Air Corps Enlisted Reserve *Plan B* interested me the most because it was setup for citizens of the United States, upper division students, married or single, over 18 and under 27 years old, who were physically qualified for ground duty and/or air crews. *Plan B* meant I could enlist as a private in the Air Corps Enlisted Reserve for later appointment as an

aviation cadet, and could continue in college until called up for duty. Candidates for air crew commissions were required to take intelligence and aptitude examination, while candidates for ground duty training were required only to submit transcripts of their college records. It also required a minimum of two years of college credit, plus certain prescribed courses that were essential for ground duty training. Candidates for air crews were given classification tests following their call up to active duty to determine the type of training they are best qualified, such as bombardier, navigator, or pilot training. At that time, I felt I met all the qualifications required except the two full years of college. They also told us, no new names would be added to the list after December 7, 1942 so my decision was of the essence. Rumor also had it, the draft age would be lowered to 18 by mid October of 1942, and I was concerned draftees from Utah and/or Nevada were always processed at Fort Douglas, Utah. There was a rumor going around (later proven false) that everyone inducted at Fort Douglas would automatically be sent to the Infantry, which I didn't relish because of my flat feet. I remember I was trying to decide whether to enlist for cadet training immediately and hopefully become a navigator in the Air Corps or enlist in the Army Air Corps Reserves and maybe get another year of college credit under my belt before being called up. After they read my letter, I got the feeling my dad and my stepmother Ercel, interpreted my thoughts as unpatriotic and were hurt by my letter, but then they hurt my feelings too by wrongly interpreting what I wrote when all I wanted was their expert advice on what to do.

Ted Tuft & me - late 1942

I wrote my dad from Pasadena Junior College while living at Mrs. Udell's Boarding House, to ask his opinion on what I should do about enlisting versus the draft, and received the following answer.

October 8, 1942

Dear Junior,

We received your letter of Oct. 3ʳᵈ and we are always glad to hear from you. I should have written sooner but I have been so busy harvesting the crops, I haven't found the time to write. We were quite shocked to hear how you feel about the Armed Forces. It seems no one can plan on anything anymore. I don't know what to say, you know best what to do. I know that if I knew I had to go into the service in the near future, I would join up now.

If you can join up now in the Army Air Corps and still be able to stay in school until you complete your courses this year that really wouldn't be so bad, but you know best what to do. I think you have the right idea. We can hardly think of it but it has to be

I would sure like to go deer hunting this fall but you can't get bullets anymore. I mean any at all, so I guess we won't go. I was on the mountain after the sheep last week and it's sure been cold up there. The lambs look good though.

Tex and that little girl from Joseph are getting quite thick. Orson said that when Tex drives the car through Joseph, the car wants to turn in at the girl's house when he passes. You ask what Evan Hansen thinks about the Draft; he said he is going to join right away. Lynn Hansen is also going to join and is trying to get in the Air force too. Well, I don't know of any other news except we are all well. Grandpa is holding up very good. So I will close for now hoping to hear from you al soon.

As Ever, Dad

The following letter is from my step dad, Philip Brim in answer to my request to my mother to fill out and sign all the forms I mailed them so I could join the Army Air Corps as a Navigator.

October 10, 1942

Dear Junior,

We received your letter yesterday and I am going to try and get this in the mail so you will get it by Saturday. Your Mother is so wrapped up in her Bookkeeping and typing lessons that she is as happy as a Lark. That makes me feel good also. She is so efficient and quick to catch on that I know she will be way out in front of the rest of the class in typing. Dan at the Green Hut Café is teaching her Bookkeeping and when he does anything he does it right.

This afternoon I'm going to Las Vegas for the "Coordinating Council" Meeting to see the County Commissioners about getting a little money for the Boulder Library. It seems that the County supports the Las Vegas Library so we think Boulder should have a little financial support also. I was supposed to go to a Luncheon at the Biltmore today given by the T.B. Foundation but Mrs. Dodge, the Chairman, went to work for the Basic Magnesium people today so the luncheon was called off. It did some good though as I cleaned up and put on my suit. This "Coordinating Council" job has turned out to be quite a chore this fall. We are making arrangements for the Halloween blowout, have a hut for the Soldiers to catch rides from, had about sixteen drives to raise money and tomorrow there is a meeting with the State heads of the OPA which I should go to.

The Boulder Football Team did not do so well against Ely. The first half Ely could not make any gains until they tried a "sleeper play" that worked and caught the Boulder team napping. In the second half Ely made their points by the pass route. The Boulder kids are weak on the passing game, both in offense and defense. They can hold their own against any team when it comes to a running attack but need to learn how to open up. Mr. Nellis is helping Simpson with the coaching now. I know that will help. I suppose your Mother told you that Jack Cobb is staying here this week. He and Rodger were "counting up" last night and they have both earned their letters, they say. Next year they will both be in the backfield.

I'm sure waiting to hear that you have signed up as a Navigator. Last night's paper said that the Draft Bill for eighteen year olds would be passed next week.

Yours, Philip.

I wrote the following letter to my former math teacher, friend and mentor, Harry Fuller, to ask for a letter of recommendation to join the Army Air Corps. It was written while I was staying at Mrs. Udell's "Room and Boarding House" at 160 North Bonnie Street, Pasadena, California while attending Pasadena Junior College.

October 15, 1942

Dear Mr. Fuller,

Perhaps you're a bit surprised to hear from me, but I'm writing this letter to ask a favor of you. I'm writing to ask you for a letter of recommendation to the Air Corps Reserve. I'm enlisting in the Air Corps as a Navigator and I'll try to explain what brought me to this decision.

Several weeks ago representatives of the respective Armed Forces of our Country came to the College and in

Young Ole

an Assembly discussed our future and the War. It seemed generally agreed by all including the Dean that at least half of us would be drafted and in the Army by January. They then started explaining the plans by which men could finish College at least this year. The Navy explained their V-1, V-5, and V-7 plans, the Army their enlisted reserve plans, etc.

After the Assembly, I made an appointment with the Naval Aviation representative. Because of my eyes (near sightedness) he told me I might as well give up all idea of flying for the Navy. I then made an appointment with the Army Air Corps rep. and was told I could probably be a Navigator. Still later, I talked with a Cadet Navigator who wore glasses and he told me eyes really don't play such an important part any more as long as ones eyes are brought up to normal with glasses it's OK.

By joining the Air Corp Reserve I can remain in School as long as there is no urgent need for me. I might even be able to finish College at (I'm not sure of this) the Army's expense. Providing, of course, my grades are kept up at all times. But, on the other hand, I might be drawn out at the end of the School Year or sooner.

The advantage of joining now are, It's along my line, I'll be in the Army by January anyway, I'll get practical knowledge along my line, and maybe get an Education at the Army's expense. I'll need my folk's consent (which I have), a letter of recommendation from the Dean of Men, Dean of Records, and two prominent Citizens other than Relatives. I'm in the R.O.T.C. now so I'll have to have my Colonel's signature, plus my Councilor and the Dean of Records signatures on my application.

Just address the letter "To whom it may concern" and put your position under you name. That is if you'll write the letter.

The subjects I'm taking are French, Engineering Drafting, Analytical Geometry, Calculus (which isn't as bad as I expected. I'm pulling down a C average in Calculus which is good for me), Chemistry and English Composition. Schools OK here but gosh it's big. There's about 7000 Students on this Campus. The only Teacher I've gotten to know and talk to is my Chemistry Teacher. I kind of like College in a way. When you have a free period you can go home or anything you want. I start School at 9:00 AM every morning and am free from 10:00 to 11:00 AM every day except Friday when I have a Chemistry Lecture. I'm free from 2:00 to 3:00 PM which is my lunch period.

I see Frank Shelton almost every Saturday and Sunday. He's taken me all around Cal Tech. It's certainly a wonderful School. Some of the guys that go there are freaks because all they do and think about is working problems. Judaist priest, if that's all there is to life, I quit. Frank's room mate is a swell kid. He's from Poland and speaks with a sort of English Cockney accent and it's difficult to understand him.

As you probably know, Tommy Godbey is rooming with me. He seems to be doing all right in School but he doesn't seem to ever have much homework. He's been out with a cold for the last four days. Mary Jane Carter and Marjorie Bissitt room about three blocks from here. Helen French was over a few weeks ago from USC. She lives about fifteen miles from me. A kid I went to School with in Utah (grade School) lives a block from me. He's working at Lockheed.

I've met a lot of fine people since I came down here. In the rooming house where we live there are two other kids who are taking Aeronautical engineering and we have had some interesting discussions. One is from Alma, Michigan, the other from Burbank, California. Both are swell fellows. There are others here also. One from Phoenix, Arizona, two from Seattle, Washington and three or four others from different parts of California. They are all swell guys.

I have a job working Saturdays and Sundays now. I waited for a month and found I didn't have enough to do those days so I ask for a job and got it. I'm a soda jerk at the restaurant (Van De Kamp's) I've been eating at. It's about a block from the house and pays 50 cents an hour which helps a lot. I never realized how much it costs to live before and it's amazing how the little things add up. I can't think of anything else to say except please answer my request as soon as possible. Thanks a million.

As Ever, Jr.

PS Tell Bud hello for me. My address is Homer J. Olsen, 160 North Bonnie, Pasadena, California

The following letter from Harry Fuller on October 18, 1942 is in answer to my request for a letter of recommendation from him to the Army to become a Navigator in the Air Corps.

October 18, 1942

Dear Jr.

I am enclosing the letter of recommendation. I was glad to write one for you and hope it helps you. It was hard for me to write one and tell all the good things I think about you and have it sound like it wasn't all bologna. I honestly do think you have a lot of fine qualities and I think you will succeed in whatever you go into.

I received a letter from Frank Shelton not long ago and your two letters gave me my worst pangs of regret for quitting teaching. It is such things as your letters that are the real rewards of teaching and when I thought that there would be no more of my students to hear from in the years to come it really made me have a sinking feeling.

Sincerely, Harry.

I submitted all the letters and materials requested with my application for appointment as an aviation cadet, to become a navigator in the Army Air Corps, on October 30, 1942.

Shortly thereafter, I took a battery of written tests including a thorough physical examination (my flat feet didn't seem to worry the Air Corps) and apparently passed everything except the eye examination. A week later, the Army notified me that I was too nearsighted to be considered for flight duty training as a navigator or anything else other than 'ground service' in the Army Air Corps. I was devastated. To make matters worse, when I got home for Thanksgiving vacation that year, my draft papers were waiting for me. I registered for the draft in Boulder City, Nevada, and the next day I decided to enlist in the Army Air Corps Enlisted Reserves *Plan B* program immediately when I returned for final exams at Pasadena Junior College.

I enlisted in the Army Air Corps Enlisted Reserves as a private, Army Air Forces, *Plan B* program, on November 30, 1942, shortly after I returned to Pasadena. I had made an appointment earlier with my ROTC commanding officer at the college to ask his advice when I flunked my eye examination for navigator and he suggested I look into the

NEWS RELEASE

November 8, 1942; Operation Torch, the Allied invasion of North Africa begins with Eisenhower as commander. British troops under General Montgomery attack German lines at El-Alamein on October 23, 1942. German forces occupy the remainder of France on November 11, 1942.

NEWS RELEASE

November 12-15, 1942; a Japanese reinforcement effort of eleven destroyers and 13,000 troops in transport ships approach Guadalcanal while their carriers to the north of the Solomon's provide air cover. At the same time, 6000 American troops are on their way to reinforce the Marines on Guadalcanal In a wild confused Naval battle, the American cruiser "Atlanta" is lost, the "Portland is wrecked and the "Juneau" is sunk by a submarine. Despite the losses, the Japanese replacement effort is turned back as they lose two destroyers and a badly damaged battleship, leaving the Japanese garrison on Guadalcanal virtually isolated.

Air Corps Class "C" Pre-Meteorology training program currently being set up at Pomona College. He said it was a *crash training program* that didn't require two full years of college like the "B" Plan, and I should be able to easily pass the minimum "20/100" eye chart requirement for ground service officers. Under that program, I would graduate in a year and a half as a 2nd Lt. Ground Officer Meteorologist. I mailed my application to join that interesting program the next day after enlisting in the Army Air Corps Enlisted Reserves.

HJO Enlistment 1942

NEWS RELEASE

November 19, 1942 ;(my brother Rodger's sixteenth birthday) Soviet forces move to encircle German troops fighting for Stalingrad. By February 2, 1943 the remaining German troops in Stalingrad surrender. The effort cost an estimated 200,000 German lives. On November 30, 1942 the Japanese sink the U.S. Cruiser "Northampton" and cripple the Cruisers "New Orleans" and "Minneapolis" in a major naval battle off Guadalcanal. This is a major tactical victory for the Japanese but no Japanese reinforcements are landed.

On December 28, 1942, I received the following letter from Pomona College in Claremont, California.

December 28, 1942

Dear Mr. Olsen

Your application for the pre-meteorology training program has been received, checked for completeness, and forwarded to the Joint National Recruiting Committee which makes the selection of candidates. The address of this committee is WEATHER, University of Chicago, Chicago, Illinois. The Committee will notify you directly of their decision. The notification will reach you considerably sooner than it does us, so nothing would be gained by addressing inquiries to us as to the status of the application in the interim.

We are asked to tell you that the Committee realizes that many candidates are under considerable time pressure from their Draft Boards and that every effort will be made to speed up action on the applications. Even so, our information at present is that it is likely to take as much as four weeks for notification from the Committee to reach you. Requests for special action on particular applications probably cannot be granted. Should you care to make such requests, however, they should be addressed to the Chicago address.

Should candidates be inducted into the Armed Forces after their application is on file but before they are notified of the results, they should send the following information as soon as possible to WEATHER, University of Chicago, Chicago, Illinois: Date of Induction, Army Serial Number, Army address. An attempt will be made to have the candidates selected held for the Meteorological training.

We appreciate your interest in the program and hope that whatever decision that is made will be the best one for you.

Sincerely, Edward Sanders, Assistant Dean

When finals week was over, I submitting my fully executed "Reserves" eligibilities cards to the Dean of Records and the Military Liaison Agent at Pasadena JC, to prove I was better than a "C" average student, and moved back to Boulder City with the folks. I knew

I would be called up before I would be able to finish another semester so I decided to get a job and work until my call up orders were issued. I had done everything I could for the time being and there was nothing left to do now but wait. The good news, I was a private in the Army Air Forces and no matter what Chicago (or the draft board) decided, I would be around airplanes somewhere helping win the war. Better yet, I would be getting some excellent *hands on* experience in the field of aeronautical engineering. After all I reasoned, that was the field I wanted to be involved in as my life's work when the war was over.

Army reserve

NEWS RELEASE

January 2, 1943; (my dad's 45th birthday) Buna falls to the Americans ending the Japanese threat to Australia and clears the way for Macarthur to drive up the coast of New Guinea while Admiral Halsey moves through the Solomon Islands creating a two pronged offensive against the Japanese base at Rabaul, New Brit.

The following letter from my mother at 1354 Denver Street in Boulder City was written while I was moving out of Mrs. Udell's Rooming house to return home and work at the Magnesium Plant again until my "call up."

January 2, 1943

Dear Junior,

I got your letter yesterday and was so happy to hear from you. Everyone is asleep so I thought I would answer while I'm waiting for them to get up. Rodger didn't have to work today and Philip is working graveyard shift for a full month so I'm keeping quite by writing a letter and found I was out of paper, so I'm using Philips stationary.

I am enclosing your Bank statement that came yesterday. I couldn't figure out the enclosed revised schedule of service charges for awhile but if you notice the columns, Philip said with the amount you have on deposit, you would have to write 27 checks before they would charge you anything. You never write half that many so I don't imagine they will charge anything.

The Café was supposed to be open today but I went down last night and they said it will be about Tuesday or Wednesday before they will be open. They are repainting the whole place besides putting in new linoleum in the kitchen and coffee shop. It is really going to look nice when it's finished.

Mom

You still may hear from the application you sent in (Class "C" Meteorology Program) but if you don't, I think you will make it on the screening test. Whether you know it or not, you are outstanding in my mind. While I'm thinking about it, I sent to Sears and got a large mothproofed bag to keep your clothes in. You said something about your coats fitting your Dad. Junior, I paid too much money for those things to have you give them away. I want you to send everything you can't use yourself home to me. Your coats and suit, I'm going to put in this mothproof bag and keep for awhile because this War may be over before you know it and if it isn't and you grow out of your clothes, then is the time to decide who will wear them. So please Junior, don't give them to anyone including your Dad. I want them all sent to me. Not only that,, it will seem like having part of you just to have your clothes to take care of. You see Junior, we mothers are a funny sort of people sometimes and it will mean a lot to me. So be sure and send them all home to me won't you..

I am glad you had a good time while you were in Utah. Have you seen Ted and Grandpa Weimer since you got back? Rodger ask me again to remind you about your model airplane motor. (Rodger wanted me to give him my motor so he could sell it) There's no more news that I can think of so bye for now. Here's a Dollar Bill, have lunch on me today.

Loads of love, Mother

The following letter is from my cousin Ted Tuft, who was living at home and attending the University of Utah at the time, while awaiting the draft.

> *January 1, 1943*
>
> *Dear Cuz,*
>
> *Well, the vacation is nearly over and my marks still haven't arrived. Evidently they are giving me the third degree by letting me worry over them for awhile. How did you find PJC? How did you come out with the Meteorology deal? I hit a snag in this CPT outfit. It seems they are about full for awhile. It looks as if I'll just wait to be drafted then make my efforts like a drowning man snatching at a straw.*
>
> *The radio is jumping up and down with the vigor of the announcer at the Rose Bowl stadium. I guess you are at the game having a time for yourself. This kid is hibernating this year due to financial strain of late. Last night Tam and I walked down town to watch the drunks and damn near got in a fight. Luckily he couldn't catch us.*
>
> *I guess you have learned of the death of Dorothy Mortensen's mother. She died up here in a Hospital last Thursday at 10:00 AM. I don't know what was the matter. We were surprised to hear about it.*
>
> *Well, I will be re-registering I guess. Damn, that little habit gets expensive. Sixty four bucks a semester is no laughing matter. Rite whin you git time.*
>
> *You're Cuz. Ted Tuft*

The following letter from my cousin, Pvt. Wayne B. Olsen, was written while he was assigned as a clerk in the Induction Headquarters at Fort Douglas, Utah. He had enlisted in the Army on November 24, 1942.

> *January 11, 1943*
>
> *Dear Junior,*
>
> *I received your welcome letter a couple of weeks ago and I've been going to answer ever since then and now I've finally gotten around to it. Boy, I'm tired tonight. I was on 'fatigue' duty and I scrubbed and mopped with the best of them. Everyone gets some of that. I bet a days work on a farm would kill me off.*

Well, I'm getting along pretty good nowadays. I bought a Bassoon and it sort of set me back a dab but then I can always get my money back as they don't depreciate like a car. I can toot away in the basement to my hearts content. I can get in the Army Band any time I want but I think I'll stay where I am for as long as possible. Do you blame me? I go home every weekend. My sister, Helen had a new baby boy and they don't know what to name him yet. I have two nephews now. I got a three day pass for New Years and I went to Richfield and stayed with a friend of mine named Kieth Jensen. We had a whale of a time. I took three girls and Keith took two others from Ellsinore and we had a '30 Chevy coupe we had to crank. You can imagine the time we had. There are six dames for every 4F down there. I missed the Train back and was supposed to report for duty at 8 AM on 01/04/43 and I pulled in at 4PM.that day. I really got told off by the Top Kick but all is well now.

We've had Gas Mask Drills and soon we will go through actual 'Gas' drills at the Fort. We are not inducting for the next ten days so we're catching up on drills etc.

When you go into the service, take only enough clothes to last three days. You will have to send it all home so don't bring your golf clubs, ski's etc. I never took anything but what I had on when I came in. They give you a toilet kit, razor and all. Bring your own soap though. I have all my 'civvies' at home in a trunk now so I can wear them again when I get back. I really don't mind being in the Army at all. People treat you like you were winning the war yourself. I can go to Officers Training School in two more months if I want but as long as I'm here close to home like I am, I think I'll stay where I am.

I surely hope you can get in that School (AAF Class 'C' Pre-Meteorology School at Pomona College) like you mentioned in your letter. Every time I think of you I think back to when we both lived at 'Brookland' and how we both used to play games together. Remember when the limb broke on the Cherry tree and Grandma Olsen chased us half way to Monroe and gave us a licking with a Sunflower stock. And when we sailed boats in the irrigation ditch, and tromped hay, and built a railroad in the garage, etc. etc. those were the days. I guess I was pretty cross eyed then too.

Well old pal, I guess I better close. Hell yes, take it easy until you're called – I don't blame you. Believe it or not, it's like summer here too but a little chilly now and then. Take it easy and let me know how you make out.

Yere ole pal and cuzzin,

Wayne

Fortunately while waiting to be inducted, I was able to get my old apprentice electrician job back at the basic magnesium plant in Henderson Nevada, only this time I was assigned to an elite "motor test" crew. Interestingly, I was the only *helper* picked by my old boss for that highly motivated skilled crew of one electrical engineer, one electrician foreman and four of their top journeyman electricians working at the plant. Our crew's job assignment was to check out all the control panels in the plant for wiring accuracy and re-wire them as necessary, then test run all the units to make sure the plant

NEWS RELEASE

March 2-4, 1943; Battle of the Bismarck Sea. Fighter Bombers from the Fifth Air Force spot a 17 ship Japanese convoy attempting to reinforce the Lae Salamaua area of New Guinea. They sink 8 transports and 4 destroyers. An estimated 3000 to 5000 Japanese soldiers drown. American forces lose 2 bombers and 3 fighters.

equipment run properly. It was a fascinating job and I learned a lot, but unfortunately, it only lasted one month for me. My orders to report to the induction center at Fort McArthur, San Pedro, California on February 12, 1943, arrived only days earlier, but the good news was I had been accepted for pre-cadet training in the Army Air Corps Class "C" Pre-Meteorology Training Program at Pomona College, Claremont, California. I would now be on active duty in the Army Air Corps as a soldier of the United States of America where I could do something worthwhile to help win the war.

The following letter, dated April 14, 1943, to my Utah family in Monroe, Utah, was written shortly after our Army Air Corps Detachment of 230 "Student" Air Corps Meteorologists were organized and settled in at Pomona College, for the "Class "C" Pre-Meteorology" Training Program.

April 14, 1943

Dear Folks,

I received your package and thanks a million. I really had a swell birthday but frankly I don't feel a bit older. Gee, just think, I'm now 19 years old and if everything goes right and I'm lucky, I'll be a 2nd lieutenant when I'm twenty. Aunt Maude sent me an Angel Food Cake and Rodger sent a box of Candy, so my roommates and I had a big party. We consumed what you sent (it was very good by the way) and all the rest in nothing flat. I got a photo album from Tex, suntan ties and handkerchiefs from Mother and Philip and a writing kit from Dorothy. I was really well remembered if you ask me.

Rodger was in a car accident and the two other fellows he was with were hurt badly. He got out without a scratch. One kid was sitting on Rodgers lap at the time so he acted as a cushion. He went through the window and cut his forehead and blood was all over Rodger and he vomited from the sight of so much blood. Mighty lucky kid if you ask me.

I haven't been getting the number of letters from you as I used to, but I guess it's because I have slacked off too, but I have a good reason. It's getting practically impossible for me to keep up on my correspondence, but just because it's my turn to write, you don't write. Please get rid of that idea. Gosh, just hearing about what you talked about at the supper table, any little thing you consider unimportant, is interesting to me,

Pvt Olsen – 1943

I believe you know my usual routine so I'll tell you what I did over the weekend. I took Helen French to dinner and to a play in L.A. We saw the play "The Junior Miss" and it was certainly funny. Sunday, I spent studying and in the afternoon, I went to a picture show called "Air Force."

Oh yes, I nearly forgot. We were paid on my birthday for the first time since I enlisted and everyone celebrated whether they knew me or not. I was paid $180.43 and with deductions for food, schooling, insurance, etc. it came to $93.41 clear. Gosh, that's the most spending money I've ever had so (you know me); I sent $50 to Mother to put

1943 Pre-Cadet Meteorology unit, Pomona College

away for me. We go on base pay as buck privates of $50 a month from now on. Up until now we were paid $2.75 a day subsistence and it only cost us $2.00 a day. It made a nice comfortable excess. Living off post the way we do, things like haircuts, cleaning and laundry, shows etc runs way higher. It costs nearly $50.00 a month to live and I have to pay $11 and something for insurance alone. My Army insurance comes to $6 and my separate insurance I've been carrying is $5 a month. If I can save $10 a month from now on I'll be lucky and doing very well.

It's raining this afternoon or we would be drilling right now. They didn't have any shows for us to see so we are excused. Some of the fellows are finishing up their shots. We've been doing a lot of "ceremonial" drills lately – I feel a full dress parade in the wind soon. Maybe our friend the General is coming back for a second look, who knows. At any rate we'll put on some kind of a show soon.

Gee, just one more month left to go and I'll see you. I wish I could make it for Freddie's birthday but it's impossible. Did Grandpa get his Birthday card from me?

In Geography class we've been studying a lot about "Weather" lately and I find myself looking out the window and identifying clouds and trying to see what causes all this rain. I

all my Pomona College roommates 1943

think their cyclonic but they could be orographic – no, their drizzly so they must be cyclonic. See what I mean, I'm going nuts. Geography is interesting but lord they move fast. This "Cadet Program" is the hardest I've ever had to work. I hope I don't flunk out.

If I finish this course I'll have to take my "Officer" physical exam and frankly I'm a little worried. My eye sight is no better (A 20/100 reading for nearsightedness is the maximum to stay in this program) but maybe, going this far and all, they might let me finish. Well, I think I better join the chow line. Write soon

Love, Jr.

We were all standing at attention one day and Sgt. Copeland, our drill sergeant, asked if anyone in our group had any *Guide* experience. Like any *smart eleck* without brains enough to keep his mouth shut, I popped off with "Yes Sir, I was a guide at Boulder Dam once", although all I actually did was sell postcards and film and answer dumb tourist questions.

I remember hearing several muffled snickers from soldiers behind me as Sgt. Copeland marched stiffly over and bounced his chest off mine. We both stood there stiffly at attention with our bellies and noses touching while he glared at me for what seemed like an hour and I sweat blood thinking, "Ooh boy, I've really done it this time." Well, unbelievably and all of a sudden, he stepped back with a twinkle in his eye and said, "O.K. Private Olsen, you're the right guide of Squadron "C", about faced and marched stiffly away. Wow, believe it or not that meant everyone in our Squadron had to stay in step with me from then on and had to mimic my unique sheepherder's *moseying sagebrush sashshay* rather than the regular Army's snap step. I'll tell you, "C" Squadron's new marching style, combined with Dean Smith's *peppershaker hop* topped off with his occasional *Montana road apple side step*, resulted in a unique marching style never seen before, as we marched to our classes together singing, "The night that Patty Murphy died, I never shall forget."

> **NEWS RELEASE**
>
> *May 1943; In Washington D.C., FDR and Churchill agree in principle on Operation Overland, the cross channel invasion of Europe, and set a tentative launch date of May 1, 1944. On June 30, 1943 American forces invade Rendova Island and on July 2, invade New Georgia Island in the Solomon's. Resistance continues until August 25, 1943*

It was while our squadron was learning to march *my way* I got so well acquainted with two of my best army buddies. One of them was named Frank Wiggs, who marched directly

Dean Smith – 1943

behind me and was constantly out of step and blowing his nose and stepping on my heels. For some reason he was apparently unable to synchronize the split second timing our Squadron's new unique marching style required, and especially when I would try out my impromptu Montezuma quick step as a surprise morale builder. My other good buddy, Dean Smith, must have thought he was a reincarnated pepper shaker from the way he marched. He was always a half step out of "sync" with everybody else, but to his credit he tried hard to *sashshay* along in stride with the rest of us, that is except for the times he would launch into a *St. Vitas dance* maneuver for no other reason than to swat at circling bees and hornets. I guess when you think about it hard enough, my constant spinning around to sock Frank for his nose blowing-heel stepping coughing-snorts, coupled with Dean's sporadic pepper shaker sidesteps; did add personality to our squadron's unique marching style. Our frustrated drill sergeant, Sgt. Copeland, spent an ungodly amount of time with the three of us trying to teach us how to march like soldiers, but he always ended up shaking his head in disgust and asking Frank Wiggs for a cigarette. Frank never smoked because of his asthmatic condition, but he showed a lot of class by carrying a loaded pack of cigarettes in his shirt pocket for moochers and I can't remember how many times Sergeant Copeland fell for Frank's exploding cigarettes stunt, or how many times we were ordered to march double time for the next mile as punishment. I do know this however. Sgt. Copeland was convinced Frank was deliberately carrying those loaded cigarettes just to trick him, but when you think about it hard enough, maybe it explains why Frank Wiggs was the only soldier I've ever known during WW II that stayed a buck private the entire time he was in the service. Our theatrics were probably childish to some people, including me now, but they were good laugh moral builders at the time.

AAF Pre-Mets - Pomona College – 1943

I'll never forget the time our PT Instructor, Sergeant Potter; called me out of the ranks to lead the whole detachment of pre-cadet soldiers doing calisthenics in any exercise of my choice. Believe it or not, as I looked over that sea of 230 men all dressed in white "T" shirts, I was suddenly *time-tunneled* back to the sea of cotton balls that made up my dad's sheep herd on the side of the mountain grazing, Wow, I thought to myself, I wonder what it would look like to see 230 men doing *synchronized finger exercises*. Without considering the consequences and just for the hell of it, I demonstrated my straddle legged, arms forward, elbows bent upward with my index fingers extended, along with the cadence required finger exercise positions.

From my point of view, I'll tell you when that entire 230 man detachment began doing my finger exercises in locked cadence it was such a spectacular demonstration it only lacked fireworks for improvement. Sgt. Potter had apparently taken his break somewhere else while we were exercising because his hysterical *who flung dung* act never hit the fan until several minutes later. So in retrospect when you look back on the whole thing from a more optimistic point of view, and discount my lack of common sense and monumental stupidity as a physical fitness instructor, it was not only a memorable, but an inspirational experience beyond compare. Just being able to stand up there and watch that sea of *cotton balls* exercising their fingers in synchronized harmony, was breath taking. When Sgt Potter returned, I'll tell you, he not only flipped his lid, but never forgot how impressive it was either. He deleted all my weekend passes for the next two months and never asked me again to lead another fitness exercise or anything else for that matter, after that life saving rescue demonstration I participated in with *Old Bird Legs Nevins* in the Pomona College swimming pool.

Which reminds me of my other *foul-up* when Sgt. Potter had our "flight" (platoon) line up at the College swimming pool for a life saving lesson and asked if any of us had passed the Red Cross life saving exam in our civilian lives. I remember only two hands were raised of the forty soldiers standing there, mine and Pfc. Richard N. Nevins, who also bragged he had been on the Yale swimming team. Sergeant Potter seemed unimpressed, but said, "OK, Private Nevins, you pretend to be a hysterical drowning man in the pool and Private Olsen, you dive in and rescue him to show everyone here how it should be done." Well, I didn't know *"Birdie"* Nevins (called *Birdie* because of his bird legs) very well then and never realized what a conscientious perfectionist and stickler for detail he really was or even how stubbornly dedicated he could be in playing his part in our little rescue drama. I nonchalantly dove in the pool like Johnny Weissmuller would in a Tarzan movie, and casually swam over towards him thinking he would stop his ridiculous yelling and thrashing around after I rolled him over on his back, and I would just tow him back to the pool's edge amid all the applause.

Birdleg Nevins 1945

Whooee, not *Old Birdie*. I'll kid you not, that knot head could easily have won the Academy Award for his fantastic performance as a *Hysterical Drowning Man* that day. Just as I was about to roll him over to tow him back, he got a combination head lock-dead man's choke hold on me, and to this day I'm still convinced he deliberately tried to drown me by holding me on the bottom of that pool. If I hadn't been thirsty enough to drink half the pool dry that day and hadn't gotten mad enough to stomp his gonads flat on the bottom of the pool, I would have been a goner. Everyone watching our thrashing survival frenzy act that would have made an *ocean feeding frenzy* look like Lake Placid, were holding their sides laughing when I finally swam back without *Old Birdie*. I remember looking up at Sergeant Potter and saying, "Sarge, let me be the drowning man this time and have *Birdie* save me", to which he laughingly agreed.

Well, to make this little drama of life shorter, I immediately got a combination death grip-head lock-choke holt on *Old Birdie* when he tried to roll me over and you guessed it, he ended up drinking the other half of the pool dry before I felt sorry enough for him to turn him loose. Since it was now obvious that neither one of us could save the other, our grand finale only amounted to both of us doing an *embarrassed little curtsy* as we stood there shivering in the empty swimming pool, in appreciation of all the thunderous applause and laughter from our shipmates. Sergeant Potter was so impressed with our ridiculously competitive rescue demonstration, he made Birdie and I *partners for*

NEWS RELEASE

May 11, 1943, American forces invade Attu Island in the Bering Sea, Alaska. The Japanese garrison fights to the end then launches a suicide charge ending in a hand to hand struggle in the U.S. line. Only 29 Japanese soldiers survive.

the remainder of the Metro Program, and like it or not, from then on we were stuck with each other.

The interesting thing about having *Old Birdie* as a partner was, neither one of us could get the upper hand on the other long enough to whip the other, no matter how hard we tried. For punishment, Sgt. Potter had stuck me with Birdie as my boxing, jujitsu, and wrestling partner and no matter what it was, we always ended up in a *breakeven tie* in every bout.

30 mile hike in the army, flat feet become a problem

I remember telling my stubborn knot headed partner one time, if we could just learn to cooperate and quit trying to prove we were better than each other all the time, we both might amount to something in this man's army. But *Oooh Noo,* not *Old Birdie,* he said he was better than me at anything and everything, and all he had to do to prove it was, "Nail me when I wasn't looking." Well, as everyone who knows me can verify, I'm an easy going person and all my life I've tried very hard to be the friendly easy going compassionate human being from good old fashioned stubborn Norwegian-German stock that I am, so obviously my answer back to him was always the same, "In a pig's eye you will."

I also remember the time we were both on the firing range trying to get qualified in the various firearms, and this time it was for the M-1 Carbine. As usual, *Birdie* and I were stuck with each other so he was assigned to my target pit first to record my bull's eye target hits, and since I was such a good Utahan hunter, I figured there would never be any misses for Birdie to record. Well, apparently *Birdie* never got the message because he kept waving *misses* for me when I knew I had made some good shots and I became suspicious. Lo and behold, he was even waving my inside-liner bull's eye shots as complete misses and was only giving me points for center perfect *bull's eyes*. Well when I found out I wouldn't be able to qualify with only one cartridge clip left for my gun, I figured about where his helmet was located in the target trench and nonchalantly emptied my gun all along the top edge of his trench, showering rocks and gravel all over him. Whooee, talk about getting mad over nothing, Old Birdie flew out of that trench with fists swinging and swearing at the top of his lungs, but fortunately I was able to pacify him by thanking him for ruining my chances of qualifying, and not to worry about it because it was my turn to man his target. Well, as I've said before, everyone knows I'm an easy going, never forget-never forgive, type person that is maybe a little on the stubborn side, but I would do almost anything to get along with anyone who would reciprocates in kind. Unfortunately, try as I might, it was difficult for me to be my normal compassionate forgiving self when I was up against knot heads like *Old Birdie*, even though I still liked the guy. Despite all that, my easy going nature just wouldn't let me give him the benefit of the doubt on his bull's eye liner-shots either, so I judged him exactly the same way he judged me. After all, in professional football, you touch the inside edge of the outside line, and you're out too. Anyway, when all was said and done, I still think it was a crying shame neither one of us qualified that day, especially

Army 1943, Pomona College meteorology program

since we were both pretty fair shots. The sickening part about this was, it was all because of *Birdies* knot headed stubbornness. You said mine too? *No way*!!!

Philip Brim called to tell me a sweet little old lady named Eleanor Roosevelt had personally ordered the Bureau of Reclamation in Boulder City to fire every registered Republican on their payrolls and remove them all immediately from government housing, and that he had just been fired. All the "damn dumb democrats", (one word to my dad) remaining were then locked into their civil service jobs as loyal Democrat voters (or else) from then on with the Bureau of Reclamation. Philip Brim was one of the first and best construction men hired by Frank Crow in 1931, the project manager on Boulder Dam, and he continued working for Frank on many different assignments until the Dam was nearly finished and was appointed the Bureau's first Chief Guide. Philip said he had already been

> ## NEWS RELEASE
> ―――――――――――――――
> *July 10, 1943; Allied forces land in Sicily under General George Patton's command and on July 22, occupy Palermo. Benito Mussolini resigns as leader of the Italian government. On August 17, 1943, U.S. troops enter Messina, Sicily as the last German troops withdraw to the Italian mainland.*

hired by the 3 Kids Mining Company as their powder man over of all the blasting, and that he and my mother had moved out of their government home on Denver Street to a rental home in Las Vegas. Several years later, Boulder Dam was renamed the *Hoover Dam* in honor of President Herbert Hoover, the engineer president who envisioned all the Reclamation Projects in the first place. It's unfortunate that President Hoover, that exceptional Stanford engineering graduate who did such a wonderful job on relief work in Europe after World War I ended, wasn't a better politician when he became president. Franklin D. Roosevelt falsely ended up with all the accolades and the credit.

I wrote this letter to my Mother and Philip just after they had made an offer on a home in Las Vegas and were still in the process of leaving their government home in Boulder City.

September 8, 1943

Dear Folks,

I received your letter and was glad to hear from you. Gosh, I hope you can get that house in Las Vegas. It sounds swell, especially with a basement and all.

We received our grades of the last final from Chicago the other day and here are my results. The national average for Calculus was 54, Pomona's average was 66 and mine was 60. The national average for Physics was 56, Pomona's was 64 and mine was 64. The national average in Vector Mechanics was 72, Pomona's was 78 and mine was 78. As you can see I'm only average here now and all my grades are "C's." Now comes the bad news, I flunked the easiest test of all, the History tests. It wasn't as bad as I first thought because the Army only grades three ways; F to D+ is inferior, C- to B+ is ordinary, and B+ to A is superior. Well, I had a D+ in History and now I have 6 weeks to pull it up to a C (which shouldn't be too hard) or I'll be recommended for "wash out." Don't worry about it; I'm sure I can bring it up enough to pass.

I'm telling you they really had me scared for awhile. They are also giving us a special class in English Comp. and History so I think I'll learn something. One thing nice about the Army, their tolerant if you show signs of wanting to get it and they think you can make it. Otherwise they don't mess around with you.

On Labor Day, our outfit acted as Honor Guards to General Currie in the Coliseum. It was really swell and I thought the General seemed pleased with our Marching and Calisthenics demonstration (which I heard from prejudiced sources was better than the graduating cadets). At least our C.O. was beaming. During the Calisthenics demonstration two of our fellows made mistakes and, although the General and the other big wigs laughed, the Sergeant hadn't planned it that way so they are getting a lot of roadwork this weekend as punishment. I feel a little sorry for them because they were trying so hard and being a bit nervous and all, they didn't hear one of the commands.

I saw Grandpa Weimer there and he seemed to think our outfit looked pretty good. There were 350 cadets who got their "bars" that day. Gosh, I wish I were one of them. Aunt Maude sent me a fruit cake the other day and it certainly disappeared fast. Fruit Cakes are one of her specialties. I better write her soon and thank her.

The Engineers and Language ASTP Students are on furlough now so we more are less have the run of the College to ourselves. As you know, there are 500 women and 65 men on Campus and at Dances it is Paradise. All around the sides are gals instead of fellows and darn cute ones too. This is really Paradise, no kidding.

Well my car has to sit now until the 21st because I have no more "A" gas stamps. Sergeant Rowan gave me six gallons to take two fellows and myself to the Coliseum but that's gone now. We didn't have enough trucks to carry everybody. It's just as well; I've got some work to do on it anyway.

I got a nice long letter from Tex the other day telling me his routine at Miami. He's just taking plain basic training right now but I don't think he'll be there only about a week longer. He will be shipped to some College for five months schooling in elementary Physics and Math. Well, I've run down so –

Love, Jr.

Hollis Hartley – 1943

One of my eight "suite" mates at Pomona named Bruce Tanner was quite a ladies man according to some of the stories I heard about him. He used to sneak off base and then would come crashing back half looped in the wee hours after we had all turned in from studying and rudely wake everyone up. He also had an annoying disgusting habit of constantly combing and re-combing his hair in every mirror, every window reflection, every fish pond, bird bath, and even every mud puddle we passed, and it about drove all of us nuts. Finally, two of my brilliant roommates, namely Hollis Hartley and Dean Smith, felt things had gone on long enough and engineered a fantastic *Mouse Trap* that consisted of only three parts; an Army bunk, a truck tire inner tube, and an entry room door. The bunk bed, belonging to

133

Old Hairdo himself, was hung out of their second story bedroom window with the rubber truck inner tube that was stretched across the room and attached to the entrance door knob. The tricky part was to *very carefully*, remove the hinge pins from the door after the trap was set so only the slightest touch of the door knob from the outside, would spring the trap.

Dean E.Smith – 1943

Well, you guessed it, when Old Hairdo stagger crashed in loudly around three in the morning and *sprung* his trap, Whooee, I'll kid you not, all hell suddenly broke loose. He not only instantly sobered up, but his trap's spectacular crashing sounds literally woke up the whole camp. As the bunk began accelerating towards the ground from the second floor window, towing the tightly stretched truck inner tube attached to the entry door knob, the door itself accelerated even more rapidly to reach a "Mach 2" speed (well almost), and *literally exploded* when it hit the outside wall window. There was no doubt in any of our minds, it was the most spectacular, the most magnificently engineered installation and academy award winning finale any of us will ever witness again. After recovering from the shock and his cold sobering nights sleep on the floor, *Old Hairdo* angrily packed his duffle bag the next morning and moved to another barracks, mumbling something like, "Nobody appreciates me around this damn place anymore." The rest of us quietly took up a collection to furnish and install a new door and window, and peace and quite reigned once again.

NEWS RELEASE

September 3, 1943; Allied forces land in southern Italy and find almost no resistance. Italy surrenders on September 8, 1943. Allied forces then land near Salerno and are met by heavy German artillery and small arms fire.

At least four of our remaining seven man suite had a real talent in music. I remember Dean Smith, Hollis Hartley, Ralph Bryan and Bob Heil formed a barber shop quartet that sounded so good and professional, we decided we should have their wonderful harmonizing voices recorded. I was elected manager of their group so I arranged with a recording studio in Hollywood to cut only one record (it was all we could afford) of them singing, with the idea of duplicating more records later, and set a date. Well when the big three day pass recording weekend finally arrived, the five of us traveled over to Hollywood together, and made our *historical* recording. To celebrate afterwards, we went to an Art Linkletter show and a USO dance later, and in general, had a wonderful time. In fact, I even got to dance with a famous movie star at the time named, Marsha Hunt. The next morning we all drove back to the studio to pick up our recording before driving back to our Army Base, and Ooh boy, wouldn't you know it, I accidentally sat on the gold record while getting into the car and mashed it to smithereens. I was devastated, but despite my sincere apologies, (and Herculean efforts to keep from laughing), I was immediately fired as the group's manager and ever since have suffered from agonizing ostracized silent treatment as my punishment. I developed a terrible inferiority complex over it, especially after no longer being invited to any of their rehearsals and/or concerts. I heard via the grapevine they had expanded their quartet into an eight member *octet* by adding Bill Graham, John Nunan, Chuck Hattersley and Bob Johnson, and were even having concerts for the Pomona girl's at their dormitories. One thing for sure, I've never lived down that little drama of life because not one of the original group has ever forgiven me for busting their gold record.

Roommates at Pomona College AAF Unit 1943

Believe it or not, I was even blasted over it again at our sixty year 2003 Metro Reunion in Claremont, California. It was good lesson on *How **not** to be remembered.*

NEWS RELEASE

November 1943 – January 1944, Allied troops in Italy attempt to advance against stubborn German resistance between Naples and Rome. The Allies assault one of the defensive positions, the Gustav line, for five months. The 36th Texas National Guard Division is repulsed with heavy losses while attacking the Gustav line from across the Rapido River on January 20, 1944.

My folks failed to tell me when they moved to Las Vegas that my little brother Rodger had gotten into several fist fights with the Las Vegas High School's football team because he was a star player on the team they hated the most, namely Boulder City High School. When the Las Vegas coach even refused to let him play football with the Las Vegas team, Rodger quit school altogether and with my mother's silent backing, bought a motorcycle and joined the *Hells Angels* motorcycle gang. You guessed it; he got into trouble with the law right away and Philip told me later the judge gave Rodger two choices. He could join the Armed Services right away or go to jail, his choice, and he enlisted in the Navy at the age of 17 with my mother's and Philip's consent and blessing.

Rodger was called the *Sophomore Whiz* because he got to play first string varsity football for the Boulder City High School team. In fact, he and Jack Cobb were the only

Rodger, the Sophmore whiz – 1942

135

two sophomores that ever made the varsity team as for as I know and as it turned out, he wouldn't have graduated from high school until he was 19 anyway because of the repeat year he earned from being shuffled from one school to another by my mother. Rodger's schooling was a learning disaster, but fortunately he was a natural born athlete and it was the only thing that saved him. He had lost all interest in going to school except to play football.

I mailed the following letter to my Mother and Philip in September of 1943 shortly after they re-settled in Las Vegas and I was still stationed at Pomona College in the Pre-Meteorology Program.

September 27, 1943

Dear Folks,

I received Philip's letter today and the others last week. I'm glad you're starting to write me again. I was surprised to hear Rodger is going to join the Navy so soon, but I suppose your right. He probably would have been drafted anyway (He would be 18 after his junior year). I would have liked to have seen him finish High School first though.

We took our Government Geography exam last Saturday morning and as usual it wasn't as hard as I imagined it would be. I probably didn't do too well on it, but I think I passed. In other words, I'll be here until Xmas for sure now. Rumors have been flying around thick and fast, as to our future here. Many seem to think, including some of the non-coms, we will be reclassified and sent some place else within the next two months. I don't think so – I've gotten so I don't believe anything the Army says anymore until it's officially posted on our bulletin board.

My 1938 Hotrod – 1943

I think I have about pulled my History and English up to a C- level now so I think I can breath a little easier for awhile. We take (that is we, who are on probation) a final in English Composition within the next two weeks to see what's what.

I went to a dance last Saturday night. The faculty here put on the floor show and was it good. I've never laughed so hard before I don't think. Dr. Jaeger, our Math Professor, used to be in vaudeville so it was natural for him. He's an old man but gosh what a sense of humor – everybody likes him. My date was sure swell. She's about the only one I've met here that I felt like dating more than once.

I worked on my hot car all afternoon Sunday, cleaning etc. I broke the spring in the left door lock so I took that all apart hoping it had just slipped off. It was broken so it looks like there's another three dollars shot for a new lock The guy down at the Garage said he'd put a spring in it and re-rivet it for a dollar and a half so that's not so bad. I'm having the brakes relined at the same time.

Gosh, I hope I get a furlough in November because I won't get to see Rodger off if not. It looks like he won't get much use out of my car now, doesn't it? I got a letter from Tex the other day and he's still in Florida. He's shipping out to some College within the next week. He seems to be having fun in the Army, at least his letters sound that way.

I can't get over all the free time they've been giving us lately. In fact, I'm getting suspicious. I've had three hours free today and tomorrow I'll have two – it's amazing. The C.O. thought our outfit was getting pretty sloppy so today I was promoted to Flight Lieutenant, for a day, and was told to drill our flight for an hour or so. Later, he came out and told me to get on the other side of the field and yell the commands. Boy was I hoarse because it's the first time I've given commands since ROTC. Well, I gotta go to study hall. Write soon.

Love, Jr..

NEWS RELEASE

November 28, 1943. At their first big three meeting in Tehran, FDR, Churchill and Stalin confirm their decision to invade Europe on May 1, 1944.

The following letter, from my old Boulder High School buddy and former room mate at Pasadena J C named Tommy Godbey, was mailed from the Navy base at Port Hueneme, California on December 21, 1943.

December 21, 1943

Dear Little Honest Homer,

Naturally, as any fool can plainly see, I can plainly see, you didn't know you were writing to a Rdm3/c when you called me a Sc/2. Shame and stuff. A Rdm3/c makes $78 a month (same as a Buck Sergeant in the Army) so figure it out for yourself.   Seriously though, I really am proud of you. Any man who can stay in the Army ten months with as good a record, as I'm sure you have, is everything I've always said and told everybody *he is. You deserve more than any old Corporal Stripes and I think were robbed out of a good thing when they did whatever it was to take the commission from you. But, you did get what you said you were hoping for, the 'free Education' and all.*

I know how it is with the hometown and confidentially, ah agrees. I had 16 days and I never got out of there once, not even to Lost Wages. I didn't even have many dates, it was Hell.

We're pretty lucky so far, the 'Waves' haven't invaded our territory yet. When they do I'm leaving, yes sir, I don't like them – much. That was a good one about the 'prune pickers jumping mud puddles and singing 'Oh what a beautiful morning' The boys up here got a big kick out of it. We need natural humor like yours up here a lot.

Tommy Godby – 1942

Say Homer Junior, did you have any run in's with the 'Black Widows' when you were home. I met a girl from 'Twinville' or 'Barneyville' who said she had fights with them (the Barneys) lots of times. She said, 'Boy was I glad I had my brass knucks'. I laughed so hard I thought she would lay into me with her 'brass knucks'. I met her at the 'Pass'. As they say 'I got a kick in the ass at Railroad Pass'. She belongs to the 'Ranger Girls' now and in spite of the name she was not on the side of the Law. She knows little Teckie and said that all the Olsen's were stuck up that she knew, but that she didn't remember you very well.

I would sure like to see you again and I'll be in Pasadena both Xmas and New Years and maybe once or twice in between. If you could be there on New Years it sure would be swell. I'll be there Friday till Monday probably. I'm sure looking forward to it and if Mary Jane stands me up I'll kick her aferendum and just go across the street to Mrs. Whosits and get a good girl. Say I'm really sorry to hear about you hurting your leg. You will really be missed by the team, especially the Basketball team. Well, I'll be seeing you.

Your Pal and Admirer,   Tommy

I surprised everybody in Monroe by driving to Utah in my '38 Ford Coupe for Xmas in 1943 without telling anyone I was coming. I had sprained my ankle playing touch football of all things, and was on crutches the whole time. It was really embarrassing because everyone in Monroe thought I had been wounded in the war until I confessed, but I had a wonderful time anyway. Except for the harrowing trip up and back through winter blizzards in a car driven by a cripple, the Xmas of 1943 will go down as one of the best ever. A friend of mine from Monroe I went to grade school with named MacRae Clowered was in Air Corp flying cadet training at Santa Anita (near Pasadena) at the time, so we rode home together in my car sharing our "A" gas rationing stamps and driving duties. On the way back we slid off the road in a snowstorm near the summit of Clear Creek Canyon a short way from the Cove Fort, Hwy 91 intersection and were forced to turn around and retake highway 89 all the way down through Panguitch and Zion Canyon to reconnect with Highway 91 at St. George. It was a longer route, but by driving all night at breakneck speed, we made it back to our two bases by 5:00 am, three hours before being declared AWOL.

My 1938 Ford – 1943

The following three letters, all dated January 3, 1944, were written by my dad, , my stepmother, Ercel, and my little 8 year old sister Freddie, shortly after I returned to my *tough duty* AAF base at Pomona College.

January 3, 1944

Dear Jr.

    We have about 5 inches of snow now and it's still coming down. I think we have enough snow now to make a snowman. We were worried about you going that Sunday. I was afraid you would run into some snow but I didn't think it would be that much. over the pass.

    I sure hope you haven't gotten this cold that's going around now. Elwin Clowered said Macray has it. We have all had it but are better now. Grandpa's cold is not quite alright yet. He still has those spells he had when you were home quite often now.

    I guess Ercel told you Tex has started flying now so I won't tell you. I don't think she told you he has a $25 a month raise in his pay since he started to fly. I think I better close for tonight. I'll write more next time

                       Love, Dad.

January 3, 1944

Dear Jr.

We were glad to learn that you arrived in time even though you had some difficulties in making it. Believe me we are having snow now. There was about three inches this morn-

ing and now tonight it is coming down again. It really looks like winter is here.

We have all had the flue since you left but we are alright now. The Xmas tree is still in the house and we hate to take it out. We surely had a wonderful Xmas and it was very complete thanks to you for making it that way. I don't think I shall ever forget that surprise

First furlough 1943

of you standing at the front door in all my life. It will go down in the family history as one of the outstanding events.

Aunt Maude was here today and said Tex has taken his first flight in an Airplane. He is surely thrilled. We had Dinner down there on New Years Day and we enjoyed it very much. I suppose you've noticed by the Reaper, yours and McRae Clowered's names are listed under Central News. By the way, is McRae a Cadet? You see, I didn't put the article in the paper and I was just wondering.

I'm glad your foot is getting better. It is hard to be disabled like that. Marilyn went with Melvin Teiljen to the dance in Ellsinore New Year's night. I don't know whether she had a good time or not. She didn't act too excited.

Tina and Elliott Larsen received the Purple Heart award for their son Dean. He was the one that was killed at Pearl Harbor. It was surely hard on them.

I'll close now with tons of love,   Ercel.

January 3, 1944

Dear Jr.

How are you? I wish you were not going over so soon. Mother has gone to get some flowers for a Ladies funeral. We all wish you a happy new year. We are learning writing in school. Marilyn is sick with the flu. Mothers had it, Dad is getting it. Grandpa seems to be getting the namoneya. Daddy says that but I don't know .Well, I had better close for now.

With love, Freddi

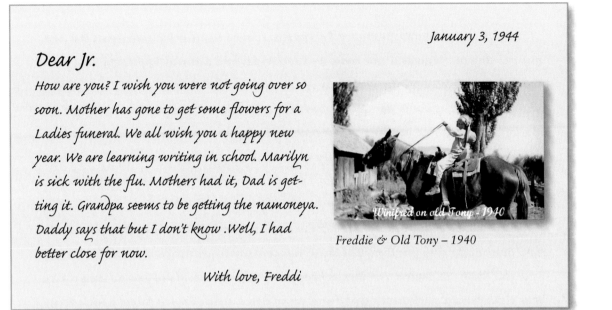

Winifred on old Tony - 1940

Freddie & Old Tony – 1940

The following letter is from my Boulder City High School buddy, Pvt.1/c Frank H. Shelton, ASTU 3922, University of Utah, Salt Lake City, Utah.

January 3, 1944

Dear JR,

How are you? I wish you were not going over so soon. Mother has gone to get some flowers for a Ladies funeral. We all wish you a happy new year. We are learning writing in school. Marilyn is sick with the flu. Mothers had it, Dad is getting it. Grandpa seems to be getting the namoneya. Daddy says that but I don't know .Well, I had better close for now.

With love, Freddi

January 7, 1944

Dear JR,

I was glad to get your letter and hear from you and will be more prompt in answering from now on. We are busy as Hell here and are carrying a big load this term but my gawd it is interesting. We are taking Internal Combustion Engines (6 units), Strength of Materials (5 units), Metallurgy (4 units), Kinematics of Machines (4 units), plus a bunch of Labs (Heat Lab & Strength of Materials Lab.) and Military PE. That's enough.

I think the schedule is pretty well arranged. It gives us all Friday afternoon free and only one class on Saturday so this term we have Friday and Saturday nights off. This place has surprisingly little to offer in the way of entertainment but I really had a good time New Years. A girl at the 'U' here (and a corker of a good looker and just smart enough to be a lot of fun) invited me to her house that night. She has two sisters and they also had fellows. It was her Dad's birthday so they were having one helluva blowout. There were three other families there and we all had plenty to drink. I've even been over to her place a couple of times since..

That damn Tommy Godbey, and after only three weeks of School he gets a promotion. Doesn't that cork you though? I think you and I will go through this whole War as Privates. Tough 'TS' I guess. I'm glad to hear you got some time off at Xmas to spend with your Utah family. I got three days off and went Home. Helen French threw a little shindig on Christmas Day and there was Johnny (AWOL) Abercrombie, Fred (Souse) Holland, Eileen (Glammer Girl) Sweeney and Marge Bisset, all there.

I'm sorry to hear about your Meteorology deal closing but if it isn't going to produce, get the hell out of it and into something else. This program I'm in gives a pretty good course but you don't know from one day to the next if it's going to close or what the hell you'll get out of it. At any rate, I'm enjoying these advanced courses. Give your finals hell, might as well, you don't have anything better to do right now.

If you see old Lady French around, slap her on the back and say Hello for me. Wishing you the best of Luck.

You're Pal, Frank

When I left my motor test crew apprentice electrician job at the Magnesium Plant to report for active duty on February 12, 1943; I tried to talk another apprentice buddy and good friend, Mervyn Brannon, into enlisting with me in the Air Forces, or the Navy, right away instead of waiting to be drafted into the Infantry at Fort Douglas. He told me his draft papers had arrived around the same time as mine did during Thanksgiving of 1942, but he was given a hardship deferral because of his dad's fatal heart attack, and decided to work as long as possible to save money for his mother. He was allowed to continue working until October of 1943 before he was finally drafted and was inducted into the Army at Fort Douglas, Utah and sent to Fort Benning, Georgia for his Basic Infantry Training.

Mervyn mailed the following letter to me from Fort Benning, Georgia on January 16, 1944, while he was going through his basic infantry training

January 16, 1944

Dear Sunny-butt

I got your card and believe it or not, I was glad to hear from you. Hoo-boy, have I been busy lately. In fact we just finished a tactical two week bivouac. If you've ever spent a few nights in fox holes and pup tents you will probably know why I tend to do some bitching in my letters.

We had one grand week last week. Gosh, it only rained four out of the five days. One day we even saw the Sun. Wet and cold it was and how. We all lived in the cutest pup tents. Four shelter halves spread over a hole in the ground. My bed was nearest our so called entrance so we used my blankets for a door most of the time. I spent a couple of nights in a fox hole. A fox hole is just a hole in the ground and when it rains it's a miniature swimming hole. There is nothing like a swim in the morning especially when you have some nice cold "C" rations for breakfast. It was TS but most of us lived thru it. You should be here Yunior, and then we could laugh at each other when we begin to cuss out the Army.

Just think, I only have a week more of Basic Training. Boy o Boy will I be glad when it's over. By the way, do the glamour Boys in the Air Corps have any Basic? We have 13 weeks of it, four of which are on bivouac. I might get to a School afterwards, but only God knows what's going to happen when you're in the Army

We're attached to the Infantry School here at Benning. That means we have Infantry Basic Training. The next time you're in a nice warm bed and about 10:00PM, think how nice it would be to be dragged out and marched until 6:30 AM. Then imagine it is cold enough to freeze the water in your canteen. That's an example of one of the things we have had thrown at us. Our favorite pass time is digging fox holes. The Lt. says "Boys, in two hours a tank will arrive here and drive over your fox holes so dig them deep." We dig like confused bastards and we dig them deep. Then in two hours they say "Hey men, you can fill them in."

By this time you probably think all that Brannon guy can do is bitch. Believe it or not, I like the Army. All this training isn't hurting me but it sure is giving me a going over. I hope they send me to School but I think I might end up in combat. That's the favorite sport of the 2ⁿᵈ Lts around here, to tell us we had better get on the ball or we'll wind up in combat.

I sure hope I get sent out West. There are only 250,000 Soldiers at Benning so a uniform is unfamiliar. What I mean is the towns around here really throw it into the soldiers. It's nothing less than hi-jacking.

So you have a sprained ankle from playing touch football. We play tackle without equipment during "group games." So far we've only lost a few fellows. If there is anything you want to know about Georgia, forget it. Be glad you're in California. Try to write.

You're Pal, Mervyn.

I was terribly shocked and very sorry to hear in July my good friend, Pfc Mervyn Brannon, was killed during the invasion of Europe on Normandy Beach on "D" Day, June 6, 1944.

The following letter dated January 15, 1944 is from my cousin, Private Ted Tuft, 39916113, Ordnance CO. 13, 1ST Battalion, APO 7317, % PM, New Orleans, La. My address at the time was Private Homer J. Olsen, 19177784, AAFTD section 8, Pomona College, Claremont, Calif. Ted was shipped to the Panama Canal area and was stationed there the remainder of the War.

January 15, 1944

Dear Cuz

Your letter of the 7ʰ did a whale of a lot of chasing around but finally caught up with me. But, now damn it, I can't lecture as long and freely as I've done in the past due to censorship. As yet, I'm not overseas but will be soon. So, Doyle was snatched from under the apron of Dear Aunt Minie – what a sad case. You were lucky to finish that course. Why did they close it? I haven't any idea how far "Yale" is from here but no doubt it is a hell of a long way off.

Bethel and I are doing fairly well considering the handicap. I can't complain though, and it wouldn't do any

Ted Tuft in Panama 1944

good anyway. I personally feel that the duration and six months will hold untold safety and terrific boredom for me. I'll probably go to Egypt and repair the plumbing fixtures in the pyramids or to take the stinks out of the sphinx – Oh nuts. Write when you get time. If, and when you get home again, tell Grandpa Hello for me.

Well, be good and so long, Cuzzin Ted.

The following letter to me, dated January 19, 1944, is from my mother in Las Vegas regarding their trip down for my "Metro" graduation and what to do about my car. It was pretty obvious she wanted me to get rid of it but I wanted her to store my wonderful "hot" little car for me until after the war was over. In retrospect, I wish I had left it with my dad and my Utah family to store in the wagon shed on their farm.

January 19, 1944

Dear Junior,

I got your letter this morning and I am ashamed of myself for not writing to you last week. I have been putting in every spare minute I've had painting this darn picket fence. Jimmy (Jim Lee boards and rooms at their place) puts a few slats on every night after work and he has gotten so far ahead of me and my painting that I really have to hustle to keep up. I have only the length of three more two by fours to go and I will have the front, back and one side all painted. We are trying to get the fence and the gates built before we leave for LA so we won't have to worry about dogs digging up everything while we are gone. Time is really going by fast, especially since I started working. I have my fur coat all paid for except $23 and I can pay that off this week out of my tips. I'm just putting my wages away so I can have some money to come down there.

I hope your Dad and Ercel can get down there too. It would be nice but I think you should reserve a room over there for them. There will be Philip, Jimmy and myself staying at Grandpa Weimers and that is about all they have room for. Anymore people, I think would be imposing on them. We are planning on leaving here Monday night and that will give us a good visit with them. We will call you and let you know when we get there so that we can have time to visit with you or maybe you can come over to Dad's and we can get together before Saturday.

Rodger so far hasn't arrived yet (Rodger just finished Boot Camp and is on his first furlough) but I look for him maybe tonight late. I haven't heard from him since I sent his letters on to you. It takes about two days to get here. I don't know why I didn't think of it to have you leave one of your pictures for Rodger. I imagine he will want one and I don't want to give him mine.

I will be glad when you find out definitely just where you stand on this other course. I imagine it will be quite a relief to you. That's probably accounts for your tired feelings lately. It's a nerve strain not knowing just what you are going to be doing or where you stand and then too, you are probably studying too darn hard. That would also account for it. Maybe, when you get back here you should see Dr. Balcomb and have you eyes tested again and have your glasses changed.

What did the boy and his Mother decide on your car? Are they going to take it? If I were you, I would put that money right in savings or part of it anyway and the other in War Bonds. It will mean that much more towards your education when you get out of the Army. I got another War Bond of yours last week so now that gives you exactly $1000 in bonds, not bad. Then if you add what you get for the car to it you will be sitting on top of the world. At least you will have a good start.

It's getting late and I have to get up at five as usual, so I'll quit for now and honestly try not to go so long between letters again.

Loads of love, Mother.

Army Hike – 1943

All my Army letters mailed to my mother from the time Rodger enlisted in the Navy were mailed on to him to read, as his were to me, except my letters were destroyed by him after reading and my recollection of the events may be off somewhat. I remember around the end of November of 1943, the rumor going around that our crash meteorology program would be cancelled and we would all be reassigned, became a fact and we were given three choices on where we would like to be assigned next in the Army. In view of my nearsightedness, my #1 choice was the Communications Cadet Program, #2 was the Army Specialized Training Program, and #3 was, Weather Observer Training. All of us were then given much tougher physical examinations, including the reading of *revised eye charts* from behind closed doors, which meant I would no longer be able to memorize the eye chart down to the 20/100 level, while waiting in line with my glasses on. We were then told to wait for our new orders until around the first week in February when the results of our final written exams are known.

NEWS RELEASE

January 1944; Allied Forces land on Kwajalein and on February 17, land on Eniwetok in the Marshall Islands Franklin D. Roosevelt is re-elected for the fourth time with Harry S. Truman as Vice President. (Thank God Henry Wallace was replaced) Supreme Court rules American citizens cannot be refused the right to vote because of color. Congress passes the G.I. Bill of Rights. On January 22, 1944; and in an effort to outflank the Gustav Line, the Allies land 50,000 troops at Anzio Beach in Italy. The beachhead will be besieged for four months.

The following letters, dated January 22, 1944, are from my dad and Winifred, telling me they will be unable to attend my "Metro" graduation ceremonies on February 12th.

January 22 1944

Dear Jr.

We received your most welcome letter and were very glad to hear from you. We should have written before now but we have been so busy we haven't had time to do anything but look after Grandpa.

Grandpa is in a very bad way and we have had our hands full with him. I'll tell you, he has been down since the first of January and he seems to not be getting any better. Well you know, he has lost control of everything that way and he don't know what he is doing at all. He has gotten so bad that we can hardly handle him. We got the Doctor and he said his kidneys are gone and what the kidneys throw off goes into his blood stream on into his mind. He won't stay in bed and he doesn't know where he's going. The Doctor gave him some pills to quiet him down and now he doesn't do anything but sleep. The Doctor said if they could put in a pair of new kidneys, he would be fine, but they can't do that so it's just a matter of time. It's hard to say how long that will be. He is so hard to handle, we have to have help to take care of him.

We did so want to come down so bad this time to be with you on your graduation. It hurts to think we can't go as we did plan on it so much. We wrote to Aunt Bertha to see if she could stay with Grandpa but she couldn't because they have sickness too. She said Ted has his APO Address now.

> *I feel bad about it but things like that happen. I don't look for Grandpa to make it much longer. His mind is gone and he doesn't know anybody anymore. It's just pitiful. We have to even feed him now and we have been taking turns looking after him, Orson during the day, and me and Oluf during the night. Well, I have to close for now.*
>
> Dad

The following letter is from my eight and a half year old sister, who now prefers being called Winifred.

> January 22 1944
>
> ## Dear Junior,
>
> *Grandpa is sick. He seems to be a little better this morning. We are learning to print in school. Mother said I should print because I couldn't write good enough. Mother and Daddy sure do feel bad because they can't go to Calif. Maybe they can come if he gets better but there is not much hope. Be sure and come home as you have planned. We will write again.*
>
> With love,
>
> Winifred.

The following letter, dated January 25, 1944, is from my double cousin A/S Tex R. Olsen who is currently in flight training as a pre-cadet at Butler University, Indianapolis, Indiana. He ultimately graduated as a B29 pilot just as the War ended and like me, never saw overseas duty.

> January 25 1944
>
> ## Dear Junior,
>
> *Well Cuz, I've got enough flying time in now so that I could solo if the Army would let me. I just finished the ten hour course they give here and I sure hated to quit. We flew Aeronica Trainers, a 65 horse power plane. I sure had a lot of fun. They gave us mostly landings and takeoffs but a few spins, stalls, and then figure eights, rectangular courses and things like that to get acquainted with wind drift of the Airplanes track over the ground.*

Smilin' Tex 1942

The spins were what I liked. You get the plane climbing steep and then when you feel it stalling you pull the stick clear back into your stomach and kick the rudder the way you want to spin and hold it. Then when you look down the ground is going round and round. Your jaw feels like it weighs about 100 lbs. It seemed to me that all the pressure was centered in my jaw. When you want to come out of the spin you just push the stick forward a little and kick the opposite rudder. This puts you in a dive, so then just level her up.

The hardest thing for me to do was the landings. If the ground was built about ten feet lower I'd make perfect landings but until about the 9th hour I'd hit the ground and bounce and have to give her the gun again before I could land. It had the advantage of two practices in one landing but the Instructor sure did cuss.

I won't be here much longer. I ship out in two weeks for either Texas or California. I hate to leave here but I'm pretty anxious to see how I'll make out at 'Classification'. It's a lot tougher now than it has been because they've got as many Aircrew members as they can use so they've raised the standards quite a bit. I'm sure hoping I can make the grade. It would be terrible to wash out now. To make things worse right now, I've got the worst cold I've had in a long while, just when I need to feel my best. Here's Hoping.

What are you doing now? Did you get into something different? We've finished all our finals here and I didn't do too badly in Math and Physics but I was pretty poor in my other classes. My final marks are: Math 89, Physics 95, Geography 85, English 82, History 84, I'm pretty proud of that 95 because it was the highest in the class.

Boy, I sure would like to get a furlough. It's been about six months now since I left home and I'm sure homesick to see the folks. I think I'll call them this weekend but it's going to have to be collect. This Army pay just doesn't hold up for long. I'll write more later on.

Tex,   39917552,-(32- for short)

The following Article appeared in the Pomona College newspaper "Student Life" on Tuesday, February 8, 1944

"Metros to Graduate, Hold Formal Review on Saturday Morning, February 12, 1944, ending their twelve months spent at Pomona College with appropriate flourish, 173 Student Air Corps Meteorologists will participate Saturday morning in formal review and graduation ceremonies which will begin at 10:00 am on Marston Quadrangle. Farewell activities, to be well under way by a meteorologist dance at 9:00 Friday night, will be preceded by a reception given by President and Mrs. E. Wilson Lyon in the Student Union. Saturday morning at 10:00, Air Corps meteorologists, combined with members of the Army Specialized Training Corps, (ASTP) will be mustered on Marston Quadrangle for a formal review by Colonel R. C. Baird, Lt.Col. Franklin Rose and 1st Lt. DuBois. Graduation exercises, held in Bridges Hall of Music, will begin at 11:00 am when all departing Air Corps students will be presented certificates and a few will be awarded Bachelor of Arts degrees earned with credits completed in the Pomona course and added to others already held. Lt. Col. Rose will be principal speaker. 1st Lt. DuBois will act as master of ceremonies."

Washed out Cadet - Feb. 1944

When the orders were read for the following "communication cadets" to report to the commanding officer at Seymour Johnson Field, Greensborough, North Carolina, and Cadet Homer J. Olsen's name was read as one of them, I was without a doubt the happiest guy in the world. After all the orders and names had been *called out* and were told to report to their various assignment locations, Lt. DuBois added, "Now for the bad news. The following men have just washed out of their program assignments and will remain here for other assignments at a later date." Along with five others, I was shocked to hear my name read once again by 1st Lt DuBois and I suddenly felt devastated and I never felt so discouraged in my life as I was at that moment. My emotions had ricocheted from one extreme to the other in less than one hour, all because of my eye sight that my subconscious suspected might happen all along. My eyes were now worse than the 20/100 maximum established for ground officer's in the Army Air Corps and I was now no longer qualified to ever be an officer in the United States Army Air Forces.

When I graduated from the Class "C" Meteorology Program, I was 19 years old, 6'1" tall and weighed 175 pounds, and my Physical Achievement Scale Rating at 225, was right on the line between "Excellent" and "Very Good." All in all, except for my eyes, I was in the best physical condition I had ever been in my life. When I enlisted in the Army Air Corps Reserves on November 30, 1942 and called up for active duty February 12, 1943, I weighed 152 pounds, was 6"0" tall, and barely made "Good" on the Physical Achievement Scale. It just shows to go you what twelve months of intensive "cadet" physicall fitness training, good food, and burning the midnight oil studying, will do for the human body. When I told my folks I had washed out, my mother's only comment was, "Well, whatever happens, happens for the best." I was really hurt by that ridicules, fatalistic, non sympathetic remark at the time, but looking back on that experience now, and at the other disappointments I have had during my lifetime coupled with the adjustments I've had to make to compensate for those skidmarked disappointments along my highway of life, it was a brilliant remark.

Lesson learned: *As we travel down our various Highways of Life, many things can happen, both good and bad, which can detour the direction and dim the goals we have chosen for ourselves. The trick is to retake the right road after the delays have been resolved, and continue traveling towards our chosen destination in life with optimism and the motivation to achieve those goals we have set for ourselves.*

The following letter from Philip and my mother dated February 2, 1944, concerns what to do about my car that I wanted them to store for me until the war was over.

February 2, 1944

Dear Junior,

We received your letter and I have just time for a short answer before taking your Mother back to work. (She was working a split shift at the restaurant) If you are bringing your car home it will be nice for your Mother now that she is working. About the license, I don't believe I would get a California license as it would have a Nevada license here anyhow. I don't think service men have to pay a tax and if they do it could be transferred to my name as I don't have to pay taxes on cars being an ex-serviceman. At any rate, if you can get by without a "44 license until you get the car home, we can get one here.

Rodger left this morning on the 05:20 train. I don't believe it is possible for anyone to have a better time than he did while here. He was on the go all the time. He drove the Buick over to Kingman Friday night to see the Basketball game and on the way back the lights went haywire and six of them slept in the car. According to the paper, the Boulder Basketball Team has not lost a game this year. Boggess, Abercrombie, Bassett and some of the other boys are the team now. I saw Norman Ready the other day. He is here on leave and asked to be remembered to you. He was on the "Lexington" when it went down but survived. Will have to close now, and will be seeing you.

Philip

P.S. (from my Mother) Philip is just trying to save you paying Taxes on your car by it being in his nam, and it would do just that. At the same time he can sign it back to you at any time. Will write more later.

Love, Mother.

The following letter from my mother concerns more about my car that I wanted them to store for me.

February 3, 1944

Dear Junior,

I got your letter yesterday and am glad to hear that your tests are all over with. Gee, how the time flies. Here it is Thursday already and I am way behind as usual with everything I wanted to get caught up with before coming down there. You said to be sure and stop by on the 8th, but we plan to leave here late the night of the 7th so that will put us down there about six in the morning. I will call you from Grandpa's and then we can see when you will be free and can run over.

Rodger left to go back day before yesterday. I hated to see him go back but he did have a good time while here. It was a little different this time because he really likes the Navy now and before, when he left, I worried about it. I hope he is sent to San Diego for he will be closer and we can get down to visit with him once in awhile.

Rodger 1944

I sent your insurance off this morning because it was due on the 9ᵗʰ of this month, so that's taken care of again. Philip wrote his letter to you in such a hurry I got to thinking that maybe you might think he wanted you to keep your car there, but he thought that if you were bringing it home it would only mean buying a license twice. They sure check on plates here and won't let you drive on a California plate over a week. So if you get a chance to sell it and want to go ahead, you are exempt from taxes in Nevada, being in the service. I don't know whether you're considered a California resident or not.

We finally have our yard fence up and the first coat of paint on it. Jimmy (Jim Lee, their renter) started the second coat last night and it's really ornamental and adds a lot to the appearance of the place. I've got to quit now and get my beds made and get ready for work. Bye for now and we will see you in another week. It's been a year now since I was down there.

Loads of Love   Mother.,

1938 Ford Coupe

I agreed with them regarding my hot little '38 Ford Coupe with duel pipes and rear skirts, and signed it over in Philips name only to learn a short time later they sold it after Rodger left for the navy. When I questioned my mother as to "why?" she said they never thought I would survive the war anyway and besides, they needed room in the garage for their '41 Buick. She told me they got back the $600 I paid for it and the money was in our joint account if I ever came back and would need it. Oooh boy, after that compassionate little speech, I just sat there shaking my head in disbelief. My mother would never have sold my wonderful little car if Rodger was still home and had a use for it. I don't know what it is, but sometimes my mother really goes a long way out of her way to make people mad at her. But, on the other hand and you think about it hard enough, it was all my fault anyway.

I should have just left my car with my dad in Utah in the first place. He would have gladly blocked it up and covered it with a tarp in the wagon shed for me until the war was over, and all this heartbreak never would have happened.

NEWS RELEASE

February 15, 1944. Allies bomb the fifteenth-century Benedictine monastery at Monte Cassino. The building had been empty, but the Germans convert the debris into a new stronghold.

While our washed out *dirty half dozen* crew waited for new assignments, we pulled KP and other cleanup duties around Pomona College for almost a month after everyone else had shipped out, and wouldn't you know it, my dedicated partner Birdie Nevins turned out to be one the washouts. Believe it or not, he washed out of flight training for being too tall at 6' 3" and my other good buddy, Frank Wiggs washed out of flight training (as expected) because of his *asthma* condition. Anyway, since no one in the Army had told us anything about what and/or where our next assignment might be while we were doing our KP duties, leave it to old worry wart Homer to find out. I got permission to see our commanding officer, and honest to God and cross my heart, you won't believe this. The Army had lost all our personnel records after we washed out and as far as they were concerned, we had ceased to exist. Wow, we could have walked right out the back door into civilian life, (if

Metro Room mates – 1943

we could have ever started the Model "A") and no one would have ever been the wiser.

Fortunately, our commanding officer took a personal interest in our plight, and to correct their unbelievable mistake, immediately reinstated the six of us back into the Air Force and

transferred all six of us to the commanding officer at Minter Field, Bakersfield, California, to train as weather observers. I don't think he was aware that half of our group, including myself, had picked the ASTP as our second choice, although I'm sure he knew the ASTP Program had also been cancelled. Everyone in my Meteorology group who had shipped out earlier to their *first choice* ASTP Programs (roughly 90 of the 173 Metro graduates) including my good buddy, Ralph Bryan, shown in the picture had been reassigned to the 89th Division as infantry replacements. Rumor also had

Bryan & Homer – 1945

it that all Air Corps cadets washed out of flight training, and/or any other cadet training program in the Army Air Corps, were being reassigned to the 89th Infantry Division. Needless to say, our 'dirty half dozen' crew felt very fortunate we were still in the Air Force.

To quote the Army's own post war report on what happened to our Metro group, "Approximately 50% of the 173 enlisted men who graduated were transferred to the ASTP Reclassification Centers at Chaffey Junior College and Compton Junior College in Southern California. Reports indicate these men all qualified and passed tests for Advanced Electrical Engineering, Advanced Physics and Languages. However, the ASTP Program was also cancelled and these men were then transferred to Camp White, Oregon, for Infantry Training. Of the 50% remaining, approximately 20% were transferred to AAFCC at Santa Ana, California for classification and training as aviation cadets and another 20% were transferred to a pre-technical school at Seymour-Johnson Field, North Carolina for training as communications cadets The last 10% were sent in small groups to Williams Field, Arizona; Paine Field, Washington; and Minter Field, Bakersfield, California for training as weather observers."

As far as I know, no one in our Pomona College Meteorology Group lost their lives during World War II. Two members in our group were killed in action when they were re-called for the Korean War, one as a fighter pilot and the other as a weather officer in an unarmed B-29 weather plane, and both were shot down by Chinese-piloted Russian Mig fighters over North Korea. Overall, including those who saw military action, we all led charmed lives and were obviously protected by our guardian angels. Many in our group saw infantry battlefield action in Europe during World War II, and many flew missions over Japan and Europe. One Air Corps pilot recorded 15 missions over Japan in a B-29, another was a ball turret gunner in Europe who received the Distinguished Flying Cross with several Oak Leaf Clusters for 35 B-17 missions over Germany. Another member of our group received an Infantry battlefield commission, and at least two others were awarded purple hearts for battlefield wounds as infantry replacements in Europe. All in all, I think every member of the old 66th Weather Detachment, had exceptional wartime careers and they were all heroes in my opinion, except for Corporal Homer J. Olsen. I still have guilt feelings over receiving more from this wonderful country of ours than I have ever given back.

During our 'crash' 12 month Metro training period, 230 aviation students started in the program, but only 173 graduated, or nearly 25% washed out during our one year training period. I came very close to being one of the failure statistics because of my nearsightedness and poor schooling in English, and let's face it, I wasn't as smart as most of my buddies. They were undoubtedly the brightest group of men in terms of IQ scores, that I have ever been associated with. As I recall, a person had to have an IQ of at least 115 to become an officer in the armed services during WW II, and mine at 132 was very near the bottom of the Pomona College Metro list. I will always be very proud, and grateful for the opportunity to have even been part of that Metro Group, and to have been associated with all those wonderful people during our *one year* as aviation students. They were an outstanding bunch of guys and every one of them did exceptionally well in civilian life after the war was over. Nearly all of them re-registered at some college on the G.I. Bill after their discharge from service and became physicians, dentists, business executives, engineers, geologists, scientists, teachers, researchers, writers, musicians and surprisingly, even lawyers. According to Milt Houston, several were employed as civilians by the Department of Defense during the *Cold War*, and only three stayed in the service and made the military their career. Two of them became Weather Officers and retired as Lt. Colonels, and one was a Communications Officer who retired as a Full "bird" Colonel.

I wrote the following letter at 4:00 am on graveyard shift, April 6, 1944, to my mother and Philip in Las Vegas, while I was training as a weather observer at the Base Weather Station, Minter Field, California.

April 6, 1944

Dear Folks,

I got your letter yesterday and thought I would answer it now that I have a little time. I'm working graveyard shift and won't have much to do until 0500 o'clock now that I've finished plotting my weather map. We have a pretty good setup as far as shifts go. We work two nights at swing then two nights at graveyard and after we finish two days on day shift we get two days off. You sure loose track of the date though, and I never know what day of the week it is.

Night before last Rudy Vallee was here with his Coast Guard Band and they really put on a good show. They had a tumbling act with them that was the best I've ever seen. Anyway we all got a big kick out of the whole thing. I get a two day pass over next

Minter Field, BT 13 and me

weekend and I don't know what I'll do yet. If I don't get a date, I think I'll drop in and see Grandpa Weimer. I haven't heard where Ted (Weimer) is either but I imagine he is in Arizona or Texas. I don't think you knew that Ted Tuft (my cousin) is in Panama now and my other cousin, Boyd Allred, is in India. They both thought they were going to England.

BT-13 Minter Field – 1944

As time goes on I'm afraid I'm going to be stuck at this field for awhile because their shipping all the old timers out and their depending more and more on us even though we are not qualified observers yet. Sgts Greer and Spencer left for overseas last Friday which makes nine gone from our ranks in one week. They've practically had a complete turnover in personnel at this field since I got here. Gosh, every body is going overseas. The Army guys that go over now won't get back until the war is over. By the time the weather men are finally brought back I don't think anyone will care what my good conduct medal stands for and my chances for being a hero will just go "woof."

I guess I told you Ralph Bryan and all my other Buddies that transferred into the ASTP Program are in the Infantry now. They were all sent to Camp White, Oregon for training. Gosh, that was my second choice. I guess I have been pretty fortunate when it comes right down to it. I'll will be glad when April 15th has passed. I got 82% on the last test and all I needed to pass (for corporal stripes) was 70%. It was only a practice exam made up of previous exams, but I'm still worried.

Betty Glaser – 1943

I guess the last money I sent home answers your last question Mom, and thanks a lot for that card and five dollars. Boy, this is really a swell Birthday (my 20th Birthday was April 7, 1944). This pen is really swell for plotting maps when it's turned upside down. Betty (Glaser) sent me a shaving outfit with a note of irony in it about my starting to shave soon with it. She also sent a handkerchief to blow my nose in case I didn't like the smell of the aftershave lotion. Hah, very humorous. Please send my other two roles of film when you can. Film is pretty hard to get now and it's just getting old there at home. Well, so long and write soon.

Love, Jr.

Three weeks after I mailed the above letter, wouldn't you know it, my dedicated partner Richard *Old Birdie* Nevins and I were transferred from the "BT 13" Basic Flight Training Center at Minter Field, Bakersfield, California to the Air Transport Command

C 46 Transport – 1944

Pilot Training Center at the Reno Army Air Base near Reno, Nevada, on April 28, 1944. The Reno Air Base was the training field for pilots to fly the "C 46" Transport Planes over and through the Himalayan Mountains between India and China, by having them fly over the Sierra Nevada Mountains, back and forth, from Reno to Sacramento. Birdie and I were assigned to the base as weather observers with the responsibility of making balloon runs, gathering weather data, decoding secret weather telex data from various pacific and coastal stations, and plotting all that information on weather maps for our officer forecasters to prepare flight data for pilots. As it turned out, Birdie and I made a good team because of our knot-headed, competitive stubborn pride, combined with all our other dual character deficiencies. Neither of us would admit to the other, or anyone else, we were overloaded with too much work, and as it turned out believe it or not, we were the only *two man team* capable of handling all the duties of a *six man weather station team* specified by the Air Force. Much to our surprise, we impressed our commanding officer so much he recommended both of us for promotions.

I was unaware of it at the time my step dad, Philip Brim had been in a terrible accident on his job at the 3 Kids mine where he was *powder man* for the company, and his right foot had been blown off. Apparently there was a misfire in the mine and it was his responsibility to find the cause and fix it. He cleared the mine of all the other men and had gone back

NEWS RELEASE

May 11, 1944; Allied Armies in Italy begins an offensive that will smash the Gustav Line, allowing a breakout from Anzio and the capture of Rome on June 5, 1944.

in alone to investigate where the problem was when the "misfire" suddenly exploded. He was very fortunate to have even survived the blast and was in the hospital for over eight months afterwards hovering between life and death.

For some unknown reason, my mother felt it best not to burden Rodger or me with this shocking news so we were both unaware of his accident until several months later. My folks in Utah knew about it and innocently commented in a letter to me months later about it and Rodger learned of it in a letter from his Grandma Brim, Philip's mother in Montana, who wrote him while he was overseas, seven months after Philip's accident.

The following letters dated May 21, 1944, are from my stepmother, Ercel and my two sisters, Freddie and Marilyn in Monroe, Utah, and mailed to Private H. J. Olsen 19177784, at the Base Weather Station, Reno Army Air Base. We decided the last time I was home (Xmas of 1943) they would start calling me "Homer J." rather than "Junior" any more.

May 21, 1944

Dear Homer J.

Your letter came today and it was really very interesting. I suppose by the time it reached us your headaches were better, at least I hope so. (For some unknown reason I was having migraine headaches) Your really getting the shots aren't you? I can't imagine you getting any kind of a disease after all those shots you've had to go through. Just tell us what we are to do to ask for you to have a furlough and we'll do it.

I want to thank you very much for the Mother's day card. I did appreciate it so much and it was so beautiful. I had such a lovely day; I really don't think I rate it. Grandpa isn't very well again. He is getting so childish it's terrible. I surely feel sorry for him but he eats well. I think I'll drop Philip a get well card. I can imagine it must be tiresome lying there so long and maybe that would help pass the time if I did.

Marilyn, me & Genevive – 1944

Your Dad is shearing his sheep today and he isn't home yet and it's eleven o'clock at night. I think I'll ride out and see what's wrong. It worries me when he is so late.

I'm going to be Librarian at our school now and I'm so thrilled about it. I think it will be easier than the teaching setup I have now. We are right in the middle of the yearend reports and they surely are a job. We have just four more days of school and I'll surely be glad when it's over.

Lynn Hansen was just home on a furlough. He surely looks fine. Melvin Hansen doesn't go in until next fall but Joe goes in right away. His dad, John is glad because Joe has really been quite a headache to him (Joe was always getting drunk and in fist fights).

We had a terrible storm yesterday. It haled for about ten minutes and then just poured so long we were afraid of another flood. I wish I had my entire garden in and it would have gotten a good watering. Please write often and we will do the same. The reason I haven't written sooner is because I've been waiting for your Dad to write a letter too.

Loads of love, Ercel

May 21, 1944

Dear Homer J.

I just haven't had time to thank you for the identification bracelet and the perfume you gave me. (Freddie's ninth birthday was on May 2,)

Mother is making Marilyn a formal. She is just putting the lace on now. Grandpa isn't feeling so good the last few days. I just got home from a Birthday party today. It was a neighbor of mine that had it. I haven't an eraser so doesn't mind will you. We got a letter from Aunt Clara today. Janice has graduated (from High School). We wished we could see her. I better close for tonight. With all my love. P.S. Thanks for everything

Freddie – 1941

Winifred Olsen.

June 1, 1944

Dear H. J.

had a very good time if you consider sitting and talking. This summer isn't going to bad after all as far as money is concerned. I've got a job playing the piano twice a week for a dancing class for $1.50 and I'm cutting (seed) potatoes for Dad too. My girl friends have a new brain storm. There is an old vacant Café in town and they think the bunch of us can run it this summer. I'm not in favor of it and I don't think it will work.

There isn't any news except that Janice enters School (College) in eight days and Edna plans on going to the University of Utah next year. She hasn't made up her mind yet though. Mother, Winifred and Edith are out to the farm cutting potatoes today. Daddy lived out there while we were gone. Grandpa feels better or as good as can be expected for a ninety four year old. Well, that's about all so I'll close.

Love, Marilyn

NEWS RELEASE

June 6, 1944; D-Day. At dawn Approximately 150,000 Allied soldiers land on five beaches in Normandy in Operation Overlord, the largest amphibious invasion in history. By the end of the day, a foothold has been secured.

I received the following letters from my dad and Freddie while I was stationed at Reno Army Air Base shortly after the "D" Day invasion of Europe on June 6, 1944.

June 14, 1944

Dear Jr.

It has been some time since I have written to you but here goes. I have been so busy that I have hardly had time to write. That is what we all say, but we will just have to take time.

I have had Grandpa out to the Farm with me for two weeks now while I was planting potatoes and watering. There was just too much chasing back and forth to check on him. He has been quite a care lately. I have planted about 11 acres of potatoes this year so I'll have plenty to do this year.

Yes, we are quite worked up over the invasion. I hope now it won't be long until the War is over and our Boys can come Home.

Grandpa last picture – 1944

I'm going to take the sheep up on the Mountain tomorrow so they can be on the range. There isn't much money to be made in sheep are anything else the way things are setup now. Before long, the sheep and cattle men won't be able to make a go of it at all the way things are. They are all going behind now.

I hope you can come home on furlough before long again. Dale Guldbransen was Home not so long ago and he sure looked good. He is a Corporal now too. Will close for now hoping to hear from you soon.

As Ever, Dad

June 14, 1944

Dear Homer J.

How are you coming with your training? How are your Buddies getting along? Mother is making me a play suit. It surely is cute and Mother has made me a lavender dress too. She is going to make me and Marilyn a lot of clothes because school is out now. I got promoted to the fourth grade and Miss Brown is to be my teacher.

I sure like to play it a lot (her piano). It's a lot of fun. I'm coming along fine and think you ought to hear me. I hope you don't have to go over seas for awhile. Daddy wants this pencil and its bed time so I had better close for tonight.

I hope you don't have as bad a time as I did last night. I dreamed you went blind. I better stop.

Love, Winifred

Furlough – 1944

I was on a seven day furlough visiting my Utah family during the summer of 1944, when I saw Grandpa Olsen for the last time. I remember, the whole family drove me over to Cove Fort to catch the bus back to the Reno Air Base, and after I said goodbye to Dad and my stepmother and my two sisters, I turned towards Grandpa to say goodbye. Grandpa took my hand in both of his and with tears in his eyes he sadly said, "God bless you son, this is the last time you will see me." I was stunned. In all the years I had known Grandpa, I had always thought of him as indestructible, and it never occurred to me that someday my wonderful grandpa might be gone. We hugged each other, and choking back tears, I climbed aboard the bus to leave and as we slowly pulled away, I waved goodbye out the window to the family I loved so much, and tearfully looked again at my wonderful Norwegian Grandpa that had meant so much to me, and had played such an important part in my life. He was standing quietly next to my dad, and as he waved to me with his work wrinkled hand, I had a terribly sad premonition it would be his last farewell to me.

It was on April 7, 1945 while I was stationed at Fort Monmouth, New Jersey on detached service with the Army Signal Corps, Dad informed me that Grandpa had passed away quietly in his sleep on April 2, eight days before he would have been 95 years old. April 7, 1945 was my 21st birthday.

NEWS RELEASE

*June 15 – 20, 1944; Twenty thousand Allied Troops land on Saipan on June 15. In a battle known as the **Great Marianas Turkey Shoot**, by June 19, 243 Japanese aircraft have been shot down, while the Americans lost only 29 planes. The Japanese also lost 2 aircraft carriers, including their largest. On June 20, another Japanese carrier, along with 2 heavy cruisers, goes down. This battle cuts the operational strength of the Japanese carrier force in half and reduces its aircraft strength by two thirds.*

Shortly after I returned to the Reno Army Air Field from my Utah furlough, my sergeant pulled up in his jeep and said I had just volunteered for fire fighting duty because there were dangerous *spot fires* flaring up all over the Sierra Nevada mountains that needed to be *snuffed* out before they got out of hand. I remember he rounded up over six truck loads of volunteer soldier fire fighters, and we were all loaded into Army 6 x 6 Trucks with shovels, coveralls and helmet liners, and driven to the various spot fire locations on the mountain. I'll tell you, I came back with a tremendous respect for the Army's 6 x 6 trucks because that truck took us places on the mountain only a goat could travel.

Pvt H J Olsen – 1944

The interesting thing to me about that fire was when we put one out, another would flare up across a canyon somewhere, and when that one was extinguished we would have another flare up, and so on. It was obvious they were being set deliberately by some one, but who? It wasn't until daybreak the third day before our exhausted team of soldier firemen finally got all the fires out and we were sent back to the base and were told what happened. A Japanese submarine had surfaced off the coast of California and launched helium filled balloons carrying thermite incendiary bombs that drifted over the Sierra Nevada mountain range starting all those spot fires. Their *mountain inferno* idea almost worked, but fortunately we were able to put them all out before they got out of hand. To prevent any public panic, no mention of this incident was ever made in any of the newspapers until after the Axis powers had surrendered and World War II ended.

Fire Fighting Duty – 1944

> ## NEWS RELEASE
>
> *July 24, 1944 Allied Forces land on Tinian in the Marianas; it will be declared as secured on August 1, 1944. Guam and Tinian will now provide platforms for launching the new American B-29 Super fortress bomber against the Japanese home islands. Guam is secured on August 11 1944.*

The following letter dated August 20, 1944, was addressed to Pvt. Homer J. Olsen, Base Weather Station, Reno Army Air Base, Reno, Nevada, from my cousin, Pvt. Wayne B. Olsen, 128th Gen. Hospital, APO #62, c/o Postmaster, New York City, NY. (Wayne was now stationed somewhere in England).

> *August 20 1944*
>
> *Dear Cuz,*
>
> *I finally made it somewhere east of Salt Lake City for once and here I sit. Things are pretty good here and we're earning our money. About the only kick I have is that I'm sleeping next door to the Morgue, but that's nothing. The English people are swell so far.*
>
> *I only wish I had a bicycle here. I've finally figured out the schillings and pence's. It's easy after your gypped a couple of times. The scenery is beautiful and the weathers cool. The gals are swell.*
>
> *I suppose it won't be long until you're taking off for greener pastures. I hope you have as nice a place as I have it. I don't think the War will last a month or two the way things are going, except for the Japs. Write and let me know how you're doing and the family news.*
>
> *As Ever, Wayne*

It was around October 1, 1944 that our Station Weather Officer, Capt. Kenneth E. Street, called Pfc. Richard N. Nevins and me into his office and told us he couldn't decide which one of us should get the one set of Corporal stripes he had been authorized to promote one or the other of us. He said in his opinion we both deserved the stripes, but unfortunately he only had one set to hand out. Then, believe it or not, he held up several all day sucker sticks of different lengths, shuffled and leveled them at the top in his hand, and said, "Now I want each of you draw one straw, and the longest straw gets the stripes." We both drew straws and, Oooh boy, you won't believe this, my straw was the longest. I'll tell you, *Birdie* was absolutely stunned by my winning draw for those stripes, and was shocked even more that a lousy buck Private like me, and especially one named, Homer J. Olsen of all people, would

NEWS RELEASE

September 15, 1944, Admiral Nimitz, aiming at the Palau Islands, lands Allied Forces on the southwest coast of Peleliu, garrisoned by 10,000 Japanese troops. After seven weeks allied Marines and infantry dig the Japanese out of their caves, costing the Japanese 13,600 killed and 400 prisoners; American casualty's include1750 killed.

luck out and be the winner. Unbelievably, being the good sport he was and all, he sulked over his loss all the rest of the time we served in the Army together and even beyond into our civilian life. He argued logically that he deserved those stripes much more than I did because, (and they were all good reasons) he was three years older than me, he had already graduated from Yale and had a college degree in liberal arts (of all things), and I didn't, he was a private first class and a corporal rating would be the next logical step for him. Here I was, he said, only a lousy dumb ass buck private, and I should never be allowed to jump two steps in rank all at once, and I've forgotten all his other good reasons. Captain Street finally got tired of his whining and said, "Just chalk it up to *outhouse luck*, and let it go at that."

Promoted to Corporal, Oct. 1944, Reno Airbase

To this day, I haven't figured out why *Old Birdie*, having a Yale degree and being three years older than me and all, didn't go into the six month "B" Metro training Program in the first place (which was never canceled), rather than the eighteen month "C" Program. He was even more qualified for the "B" Program as it was and could have been commissioned a 2nd Lieutenant a year ago and been doing something worthwhile for the war effort by now. Wow, I would have given my right arm to have had his qualifications when I enlisted.

I received the following letter stamped "Approved" from my commanding officer, Captain Street, concerning my request for a three day pass to visit my stepfather Philip Brim in the Hospital in Los Angeles who was still recovering from his terrible misfire accident at the 3 Kid's mine.

```
Subject: Request for Three (3) Day Pass.
October 11, 1944

To: Commanding Officer, Headquarters Squadron, Reno Army Air
Base, Reno, Nevada.


1. Request that Cpl. Homer J. Olsen, ASN 19177784 be granted
a three (3) day pass effective Saturday, 14 October 1944, at
0830 PWT.
2. Cpl. Olsen has performed his duties in the Weather Station
in an excellent manner since being assigned on 28 April 1944.
3. The above mentioned soldier has not had a three day pass
since he has been on this base, and wishes to visit his step-
father recuperating at the Hospital of the Good Samaritan in
Los Angeles, California.

Kenneth E. Street
Captain, Air Corps.
Base Weather Station
```

The following letter is from my 16 year old sister Marilyn to Cpl. Homer J. Olsen, 19177784, Base Weather Station, Reno Army Air Base, Reno, Nevada.

October 22, 1944

Dear Homer J.

For the past week I have been picking up (harvesting) potatoes, which gives you the reason for not hearing from me. Picking spuds is really hard work and I'd hate to think that would be my life's work. I earned enough for my new winter coat and I also obtained horrid sunburn. About now it has started to peal and you would really laugh if you saw me.

I have been hearing from Evan Hansen rather regularly. This last week I received two letters. He is stationed in San Diego now and before he was at Burbank, California. He is going to a new school that has something to do with B-32's. (?) He seems to think he will get a furlough around Xmas time and if he does, I have a date for the Jr. Prom with him. That is a load off my mind as I would certainly hate to go stag.

School starts again next week and I will surely be glad. I'm already tired of the lazy life I lead. I'm gaining back all the pounds I ever lost when I was going to school.

Tina Larsen has a house full of deer hunters and they surely make a lot of noise. I hope they go back to the mountains tonight so I can get some sleep. The "Deer Hunter's Ball" was last Thursday night. I went with rather a funny guy but he at least wasn't drunk like everybody else. Honestly, I have never seen so many drunken men and women in one place in my life. It is funny we haven't had an accident yet, but there will be one, or more, before the season is over. I can't see how some of those guys would dare to go hunting. They are drunk most of the time.

Well, I still have a letter to write to Joy tonight so I'll close.

Marilyn – 1943

Write soon "Corporal." We all love your letters and you don't write often enough.

Love, Marilyn.

NEWS RELEASE

The Battle of Leyte Gulf rages against the Japanese between October 20 to 26, 1944 in the Philippine Islands. My half-brother Rodger Dean Sorensen was a F1/c on the LST 612 that took part in the Battle of Leyte Gulf and it was his first Invasion. The newspaper account on October 22, 1944 simply read, 'Units of the Sixth Army land on Leyte Island; MacArthur wades ashore at Leyte Gulf to announce "I have returned."

When the naval battle of Leyte Gulf ended on October 26, 1944, the Japanese had lost 4 aircraft carriers, 3 battle ships, 10 cruisers, 11 destroyers, 1 submarine and 10,000 men were killed. American losses were 1 aircraft carrier, 1 escort carrier, 2 destroyers, 1 destroyer escort, and 200 aircraft. In the "land campaign" that lasted until World War II ended, the Japanese lost their entire Philippine Army of 350,000 men holding the Islands. American losses totaled 62,000 casualties with 14,000 dead.

The following two letters to me were dated November 3, and 6, 1944, and are from my half brother Rodger D. Sorensen when he was made a Fireman 1st Class on LST #612, shortly after the battle of Leyte Gulf in the Philippines.

November 3, 1944

Dear Junior,

Well, I got two letters from you and was sure surprised to get them. One was a card and the $5 sure came, or will come in, handy when I get to where there is good libation.(I always sent my mother's cash gifts to me on to Rodger because I never earned them and she wouldn't call it a loan) It's few and far between paydays but when they do come ooh-boy. I guess I should tell you I made F1/c the first of this month that will put my rate the same as yours now because if I were in the Army it would make me a Corporal.

I can't tell you where I've been or what I'm doing. I can only hope that when you come overseas you don't get stuck on some of these Islands. I must stop and that's bad. Nuff said. I just got some letters that were written in September so you can see I've been pretty much on the go. So far I've got one Star I can put in my Bar.

You said you saw Beverly in your letter. How is she? Fine I guess. I haven't heard from her in quite some time now but I guess her letters are having a hard time trying to find me or something. The last letter I got from her, she sent me a small picture of herself and said in her next letter she would send a bigger one. I've never gotten it or any mail after that. I've just about forgotten what she looks like now. The last time I seen her was Jan. "44." Long time huh?

After your leave, Philip wrote and said you were giving some girl in Boulder the runaround by the name of Barbara. So I just about give up guessing the last name when what happens, I get a letter from you and find out who it was. It sure had me thinking.

As far as rates go, I'm trying and am just behind you each time. As far as bucking for "Mister", I think I'm right there with you. I think, or have hopes, of making Motor Machinist Mate 3/c in four months. That is if I stay on the Ball. I've handed in my test for it but in the Navy you have to wait four months between rates. (Pretty good deal huh?)

Don't mind the writing because I could say it is the pen, but you know me. I just came out of something big and I guess if you have been following the news you will know what I mean. Well, I'm running out of things to say so will close for now. Feel good, three pages is good for me

As Ever, Rodger.

November 6, 1944

Dear Junior,

Well here I am again with just a short note. The Censor finally broke down and said we can say where we've been. What I meant in my last letter about getting a "star on my bar" now I can explain. I was in the invasion of the Philippines. That is quite a hot spot, let me kid you not. Boy, I sure saw some planes hit the water pretty. Our Ship has two shot

down to its credit. One we got, hit the water about 100 yards off our ship and did it breakup. The Japs sent over quite a few planes but our gun fire was too much for them I guess because it got to where, if they sent three over only one went back so that wasn't so bad.

I can't remember or not but I don't think I said I made my new rate F1ST/C

Barbara Reid – 1945

but if I did there it is again. Not much has happened since my last letter so there isn't much to say. You drew a picture or had one taken of you with Cpl Stripes well, what do I do but go on Liberty (I only wish) and got a picture taken of me – so here it is... (a blank space follows) Well, I'll close for now because of nothing else to say.

As Ever Rodger

Secret Radar Machine we worked on at Harvard

Around November 1, 1944, the Army Air Corps announced they needed volunteers to setup and man radar weather stations in northern China and elsewhere with secret high altitude gathering equipment to learn more about *the high winds aloft* (called jet streams today) never encountered before by our aircraft. The High Command needed trained personnel to find out why our B-29 Bombers were encountering such strong head winds on their high altitude bombing runs between Tinian and Japan that were causing aircraft losses from fuel shortages. They further stated, "Those volunteers who pass a rigorous written examination will be given crash seven months training before going overseas that would involve three months of *electronic theory* at Harvard University's Graduate School of Electrical Engineering in Cambridge, Mass, two months of ground forces *practical application* training at Fort Monmouth, New Jersey with the Army Signal Corps, and a final two months of Air Force *rigorous training* at Chanute Field, Illinois." Upon graduation, volunteers will be issued new MOS numbers,

Harvard, record snowstorm, Dec. 1944

staff sergeant stripes, and overseas shipping orders. I immediately volunteered for this training because it sounded like something right down my alley that I could do for my country.

As it turned out, of the twelve soldier applicants who took their rigorous written examination at Reno Air Base, only three of us passed and were accepted for training, namely Pfc. Richard "Birdie" Nevins, Pvt. Nicholas W. Richards and myself. Since I was the only non-commissioned officer that passed the test, I was placed in charge of my three man squad boarding the train in Reno that steadily increased to an even dozen trainees as we passed the various air bases across the country. Five days and six nights later our troop train we swore was used during the Civil War, arrived in Boston and we reported to the officer in charge at Harvard University, December 1, 1944 as ordered. We were then assigned to the 66th AAFBU, housed in "Dunster House" at Harvard University, Cambridge 38, Mass, just before one of the worst snow storms in Boston's history, struck with a vengeance.

Harvard - me and Nick Richards, Feb. 1945

My partner, *Birdie* Nevins, bless his pea picking heart, was still sulking over the stripes issue so Pvt. William Alfred Johnson, another good Pomona Metro friend and I, decided we should be roommates (Rm. E-33) to rejuvenate the old "Olsen and Johnson" copycat skit called '*Hell's a Poppin'*', hoping we could put some life back into our group. Birdie and I were both fed up with each other and, as luck would have it, I never saw much of him afterwards because the love of his life happened to be going to a nearby woman's college called *Vassar*. In fact, none of us saw much of Birdie after his tearful reunion with his *Cloe'*, except in our classes.

My other good buddy, Pvt. Frank Wiggs, was unfortunately one of the applicants who failed the written exam to go to Harvard, and unbelievably was sent to China by the Army anyway to teach the Chinese weathermen how to use our *secret equipment* he had never seen while we were sent to Harvard (and Fort Monmouth, and Chanute Field) to learn about this new secret equipment. I didn't see or hear from Frank again until after the war was over and we both had registered at Pomona College on the GI Bill. He told me a Japanese submarine had sunk the ship to china with all their secret weather and radar equipment, so he was re-assigned to a military police unit in Tsingtao, China for the remainder of the war.

As a little side story, Frank asked me while we were at Pomona College after the war, if I remembered the young draftee at Fort MacArthur that couldn't say *crap if he had a mouth full of it*, we called "Little Lord Fauntleroy?" When I frowned, he said, "He was the one that was driven to the induction center in a chauffeur-driven Cadillac with his mother." I said, "Oh yes, he was the guy with the Dutch Boy haircut and derby hat wearing knickers and a white shirt with a huge bowtie?" Frank nodded, "That's the guy." and went on to say his MP unit made a surprise raid on a local house of ill repute in Tsingtao, China one time, to sweep up all the drunken love sick service men while they were still discombobulated (a legal term) trying to pull up their britches. After their loaded *hoosegow truck* was on its way and the dust had cleared somewhat, Frank said he saw one of the sickest, sorriest dirt bag piles of human debris passed out cold in a corner he had ever seen, so he gently rolled him over with his foot to see if he was a goner or not.

Mary Marshall & Frank Shelton - Jan. 1945

Lo and behold and believe this or not, there lay Little Lord Fauntleroy himself (aka Michael T. Mahoney) wheezing his last gasp of a miss-spent life. Michael slowly opened one of his bloodshot eyes and when he recognized Frank, he whispered hoarsely, "It's a small world, isn't it Frank?" Frank said he cracked up laughing so hard he hurt, but finally answered, "Yes it is Michael and you want to know something? You have come a long way."

After we were settled in at Harvard University, I looked up one of my best friends from Boulder City High School named Frank Shelton, who was currently attending an Army Ground Forces training school at Amherst College for additional courses in engineering while waiting for his officer training Tank School classes to begin at Fort Knox, Kentucky. I remember we spent several enjoyable weekend passes together dating the girls at Mount Holyoke College near Springfield and rehashing our fun days delivering *Boulder City Review Journal* newspapers together, plus reminiscing over the good old days when we were growing up at good old Boulder City High in Nevada. Frank graduating as a 2nd Lt. Tank commander from Fort Knox just as

Bill Johnson – 1944

the war ended in Europe, but continued training for the upcoming November 1, 1945 scheduled invasion of Japan, until President Truman had the two Atomic bombs dropped on Japan that ended World War II. Like me, Frank never got to see any overseas duty and after his discharge, he returned to Cal Tech. on the G I Bill to get his Doctor's Degree in Physics. During his civilian career he was instrumental in the development and testing of our countries nuclear and smart weapons systems. To me, Frank Shelton was the smartest kid that ever graduated from Boulder City High School and the most brilliant person I have ever known. I will always be grateful to Frank Shelton, not only for his support during my high school years to help me improve my grades to college entrance level, but for his friendship as well. He is my kind of a guy.

Jr & Frank Shelton - Spring 1945

Since I was a hotshot electrician apprentice with the McNeil Construction Company in 1942 constructing the Basic Magnesium Plant in Henderson, Nevada, prior to my enlistment, I brazenly assumed the Harvard electronics course would be a snap. Oooh boy was I wrong or was I ever wrong. I'll kid you not; it was just the opposite, and turned out to be an extremely tough *nose to the grind stone* three months *crash* course I barely made it through by the skin of my teeth.

NEWS RELEASE

On December 16, 1944, Germany launches the "Battle of the Bulge" with an attack in the Ardennes Forest during one of the most miserably cold winters in Europe. Germans massacre 390 American prisoners of war in Malmedy, thereby enraging the American to take very few Germans as prisoners. The Battle of the Bulge becomes the last major German offensive during World War II.

In fact, when that electronic theory course was over, I had serious doubts about my ever making it through the communications cadet program I had washed out of for poor eyesight.

But the good news was when completed, I had accumulated another 13 units of college engineering credits by successfully completing their graduate electrical engineering course in Electronic Theory.

I thought it was interesting that one of my Metro room mates from Pomona College named Phil George was at Harvard attending some of the same classes I was. He was the same guy I bought my hot little '38 Ford coupe from for $600 at Pomona, and he had just graduated from the communications cadet program in North Carolina I *might*

Dec. 1944, Harvard

also have, if my eyes were in better shape. The only difference between us was, he was now a 2nd Lt. and I was a Corporal. When I saw him in the classroom and he recognized me, I moseyed across the classroom to say hello and shake hands, and surprisingly he just glared at me, stiffened to attention, and said, "Don't you recognize an officer when you see one, soldier?" At first I thought he was kidding, but when I saw he was really serious, I snapped to attention, glared back at him and said without saluting, "Not without my glasses, SIR", about faced, and marched back to my chair on the opposite side of the classroom. We never spoke or looked at each other again. I remember sitting there afterwards feeling a little hurt, but mostly thinking about how interesting it was how some people's personalities will change so drastically when they are given a promotion or a power title of some kind, and just chalked it up as another lesson learned, while traveling down the highway of life.

Lesson Learned: *A true leader will never rub a subordinate's nose in their imagined importance.*

The following letter from my little brother Rodger to his parents was mailed from his ship located in the Philippines Islands somewhere.

December 2, 1944

Dear Folks,

I received your letter today so while I still have a little time, here goes. I might not get this finished but I will do my best. I got a letter from Mrs. Cobb too and I see where they have moved to California. She said that Jack has been boxing in the ring at boot camp, and hasn't lost a fight yet. He's really doing well for himself.

Oh yes, Phil you said in your last letter you saw a picture of the invasion of the Philippines. We (LST 612) were there only I guess we missed the picture taking. I saw a copy of that picture too and that was LST 242 not 219. Where you saw 242 then 608, well between 608 and the next LST is where 612 was. So now, if you keep that picture, you can point to that blank spot and say, "Yep, that's where 612 was but she pulled out too soon and missed her picture." Nope, I guess I won't get to finish this letter; I have to go back to work.

Here it is now the evening of the 2nd and I'll try to finish There isn't anything I can tell you here anyway so I'll tell you about my "Post War" plans and it's a good one. I was reading a book about boats and I ran across one that I would really like to have. It's not too big, only 26 feet long, and has a small cabin. It's something I've always wanted and when the War is over I feel pretty sure I can get it. As far as taking care of it, that will be easy if it has a Diesel or Gas engine. What do you think about that?

December 19, 1944

Well, here I am again just to let you know I'm still O.K. I got your letter today, the one you wrote on Thanksgiving Day. As you say Phil, if you can eat as much as you say you can you must be feeling pretty good. I got a letter from Grandma Brim and she said you had been in the hospital for eight months. That's a long time but then time is really flying for me. It doesn't seem like eight months since I was home last. I think it's a good idea to save all those invasion pictures, Philip. I'd like to see them when I get back. There isn't much that I can say but when the censor tells us we can write home of anything I'll let you know.

Philip, I sure hope you can make it home for Xmas. It will make it a lot easier on Mother. I think she will like it a lot better. I hope Junior can make it home too As for me; I'll be there in spirit. P.S. I got the paper clippings on Boulder happenings. Thanks a lot for them. Well I can't think of anything more to say so will close for now.,

All my love, Rodger

The Christmas of 1944 was the first time I ever experienced homesickness while I was in the Army. We were all issued three day passes over the holidays that year so my roommate Bill Johnson, invited me to visit his relatives in Bangor, Maine, with him to check out Bowdon College and maybe register there after the war was over. We were both invited by one of his relative's to their Christmas party that evening, but all I could think about was my own two families and how my little brother Rodger was handling Xmas in the raging South Pacific war, and if any of my buddies in the 89th Infantry division survived the "Battle of the Bulge." I began feeling so depressed, I excused myself and went to bed early that evening so I could bawl myself to sleep. The

NEWS RELEASE

On December 26, 1944 the Allies break the siege of Bastogne and the Ardennes offensive is ended. The Germans lost 100,000 men and 800 tanks in this final major Battle of the European War called the "The Battle of the Bulge."

next day I invited Bill to bus over to Freiberg, Maine (on the New Hampshire border) with me to visit my cousin Reba Olsen Farnsworth. She is one of Uncle Oluf's daughters and was married to Filo T. Farnsworth's (the man who invented television) nephew so I was fortunately able to spend part of my Christmas leave with some of my own relatives. Like Bill'e relatives, Reba was a very gracious hostess and she and her husband (who managed a lumber mill there) went out of their way to make us feel at home away from home. Interestingly, Reba told me Filo T. Farnsworth was also living there in Freiberg at the time and was doing *top secret laboratory research work* for the government.

The following letter is from Lt. Edward L. Weimer to his mother and dad from an air base somewhere in China where he and the four engine B-24 bomber he flew halfway around the world, were stationed. Lt. Edward L. Weimer was my favorite "Uncle Ted", and was my hero during my younger years.

January 30, 1945

Dear Mom and Dad,

First of all, I want to thank you for the letters and sending Milton's address to me. I have been out on what you might call an enforced hike for two weeks and on getting back to the Base I was in a rather poor mood so your letters really did wonders for me.

Lt Ted Weimer - China - Jan 1945

There were fifteen letters waiting for me. Incidentally that is the only word I'd had from home in the last two months.

I see by your first letter that John has bought Jess's place. I think that will be pretty nice all around. That is a nice neighborhood and in a few years should build up into quite a community. Tell them all hello for me. Incidentally what is Jess doing for himself these days? Give him my regards and tell him to drop me a line.

This is quite a place over here. I lay around for two weeks then we get a bunch of missions assigned us and they work us to death. We ran into a lot of bad luck on the last one. Almost didn't get back from it. Everything went according to schedule. We bombed the target and headed for home. About three hours out #3 engine went out on us, after monkeying with it awhile it picked up again and we flew on for another hour when suddenly #3 and #4 went out. On increasing the power settings I could only get half power from #1 engine. I called back and had the crew put on their chutes and throw everything overboard they could get their hands on. Incidentally, I was flying co-pilot on this trip. They do that when you first come over until you get used to flying in this country, then take your own ship up.

Anyway by this time we were right amongst the mountain peaks. I gave the order to bail out then and took the plane while the pilot got on his chute then I got out of my seat and put mine on. I noticed the radio man was still at the radio hollering "Mayday", told him to get out again, and then turned to help the pilot. He was half out of his seat by this time and motioned me to get out of the way so I turned and dove out the bomb bays. If I had been in command I would have given the order to bail out much earlier. We were way too low for jump-ing. My chute opened when I was about 300 feet above the ground which didn't give me much time to pick a landing place and I landed in a pile of rocks which shook me up some. It was dark then so I rolled up in the chute and went to sleep.

Capt. Ted Weimer – 1944

The next morning I found the radio man, he was O.K., and we hiked on over the hill and found the pilot. He had gotten out alright but his chute didn't open soon enough. We had some natives help us bury him there. About noon the rest of the crew came hiking over the mountain so we started back. It took us around five days to hike over the mountains about a hundred miles to a village where we could get a GI truck. We stopped at quite a few small villages. The Chinese people really treated us like Kings, gave us guides and food. After getting a truck we drove for about five days, then caught a plane and ended up here at the base on the 12th day. It was quite a trip. Hope I don't have to do it again. That sort of brings things here up to date.

Lt. Edward L. Weimer - #0778632

375 Bomb Squadron,

#308 Bomber Group.

I met a cute little Irish girl at a USO dance for service men and women in Boston while I was stationed at Harvard, and she invited me to her home for an Irish home cooked dinner the following weekend with her family. I hadn't had a real home cooked meal for some time so I gladly accepted her invitation and besides, I wanted to get to know her better. The problem was, I didn't realize she lived in a really tough part of Boston at the time called "Skully's Square", and when I got off the subway at that Square, it was nearly dark and despite the snow patches it still looked like a slum area even to me. As I walked down that semi-dark street looking for her house number, I suddenly ran into six or seven *dead end* looking teen age Irish boys blocking the sidewalk and one of them with a big mouth said, "Let's beat up on this Soldier." At first my throat felt a little dry, but as I stood there listening to that loud mouth bully and his gang of yapping hyenas spout off their hatred for anyone wearing an American uniform, I felt that same road rage feeling building inside me I felt during my bully fight in Monroe,

Bangor, Maine - Xmas 1944

NEWS RELEASE

February 4 – 11, 1945; the big three meet at Yalta and make a number of decisions, including that a conference in April will prepare a charter for the United Nations; that the USSR will enter the War against Japan; that Germany will be required to pay reparations to Allied Nations; that Germany will be divided into zones of occupation by the USSR, France, Britain and the United States; that the USSR will obtain the Kuril Islands, a part of Japan, in violation of the Atlantic Charter.

Utah. I remember thinking to myself, "If this is the way I'm going to die, that pile of crap with the biggest mouth is going with me." I walked slowly over towards that pile of human garbage with the big mouth and stood close, glaring at only him and no one else, and waited for his move. I don't think he realized until then I was bigger than he was, or maybe it was my *rage to kill* look rather than *fear* on my face he expected, but all of a sudden his mouthing simmered down to a hoarse whisper, and slowly he, along with the others, stepped aside. I remember walking through them without saying a word or looking back, down the street thinking about what Old Man Crawford told us kids when a mean bull charged him in Uncle Orson's pasture. He said, *"Never let a mean animal know you're afraid of them because if you do, they will kill you."*

NEWS RELEASE

February 19 – 23, 1945, the Invasion of Iwo Jima. With the Air Force and the Navy providing aerial bombardment, the U.S. Fourth and Fifth Marine Divisions assault Iwo Jima, in the Volcano Islands of Japan, where the Japanese have garrisoned 21,000 troops and built extensive defense works. A beachhead is made the first day costing 2,400 casualties, including 600 dead. It takes four days to reach the summit of Mt Suribachi, from which a photograph of a squad of U.S servicemen hoisting the flag will become the basis for the Iwo Jima Memorial in Washington, D.C. The operation continued until the end of March and the last remaining 200 Japanese soldiers surrender and the rest die in Battle. The Marines suffer 6,800 killed, 18,000 wounded; they will receive 27 medals of Honor.

The following letter from my half brother Rodger (R.D. Sorensen, F1/C – LST 612) to my mother and Philip in Las Vegas, was written shortly after the invasion of Iwo Jima. The code wording "and another I can't spell" told the folks, who were reading the papers, his ship had participated in the Iwo Jima invasion. (Rodger told me later his ship was not involved in the actual invasion because they only made ammunition haul runs to Iwo Jima at the time).

> *March 8, 1945*
>
> ## Dear Folks
>
> *Well here I am again with not much news. How is everything around Vegas and Boulder in the way of news? Not much I can say here but I can tell you the Invasions I've been in now. They are Leyte, Mindinio, and Luzon and all of them were "D" day stuff. I've been in two on Luzon, one on Batton (spelling?) and another I can't spell at all. They are the ones that have been in the paper for at least 30 days so I can tell you about them now.*
>
> *Love to all, Rodger.*

After we graduated from the Harvard portion of our training, we were sent to Fort Monmouth, New Jersey for the second phase of our training and placed on detached service with the Signal Corps of the regular U.S. Army. I'll tell you, it soon became painfully obvious we were not welcome because the *Old Army* soldiers felt the Air Force *glamour boys* were nothing more than a bunch of goof offs barely equivalent to the *lousy draft dodgers*. Well as you've guessed, it didn't take long for a civilian soldier like me as the ranking non-com and the spokesman for my

NEWS RELEASE

March 10, 1945, Approximately 300 U.S. B-29 Bombers drop 1,667 tons of thermite incendiary Bombs on Tokyo, burning a major portion of the city and killing hundreds of thousand of Japanese in the raging fires.

squad, to get crosswise with the regular Army's Top Sergeant. To punish me for talking back when I should have been listening, he said, "I should bust you back to a buck ass private again soldier, but luckily I can give you twice the punishment by leaving you with your two lousy stripes." He then put me on KP (kitchen police) duty for a month working for the Italian prisoners in the company's kitchen during the hours I wasn't in training, and the second month, on CQ duty (charge of quarters) on night duty. I soon found out Corporal Stripes were the highest rank you could be and still do KP, and the lowest rank you could be, and still be assigned CQ duty. My friendly top sergeant, bless his heart, had graciously eliminated all hope I had for a three day pass while I was stationed at Fort Monmouth and his compassion was especially noteworthy when all the never ending rain storms we had were taken into account. He had thoughtfully prevented me from wasting any of my hard earned Corporals pay at any of the local watering holes down town that were probably flooded anyway.

I was on KP duty at Fort Monmouth working for the *Italian prisoner master chefs* on April 7, 1945, when I received the terribly sad news my wonderful Grandpa Olsen, had passed away on April 2nd. He apparently had slipped on the ice the previous winter while doing his farm chores and had broken his hip. From then on he was bedridden and without his daily exercise, had gotten progressively worse until the end. If he had only lived eight more days, he would have been 95 years old. I was in the mess hall peeling potatoes when I got that sad letter from Dad and I must have broken into

Winifred & her piano – 1944

tears while reading it. As the mess sergeant walked by, he said, "Those are potato's you're peeling corporal, not onions." I answered, "I know Sarge, I just got the sad news from home

my grandpa had just passed away. He was the finest man I have ever known." April 7, 1945, was my 21st birthday.

Two weeks after I received the sad news about Grandpa, our whole country was shocked to learn President Franklin D. Roosevelt died in Warm Springs, Georgia. Vice President Harry S. Truman was immediately sworn in as President of the United States, and a month later on May 7, 1945, Germany surrendered to the Allied Forces in Europe. I was on CQ duty the night of May 8, 1945, when a returning soldier from Europe I was processing bunk space for, told me the War in

Europe had ended. Our country could now direct its full attention and all its might and power towards destroying the last remaining Axis power, the Japanese Empire, and put an end to World War II. After I completed my KP assigned punishment of working for the Italian prisoners, I thanked my now good friend, the top sergeant, for giving me the opportunity to work with such motivated, hard working, and extremely happy to be in America, group of guys. The Italian prisoners took care of all the kitchen duties in the various company mess halls at Fort Monmouth and in my opinion, were truly master chefs. They were the best cooks and prepared the best meals I ever had while I was in the Army, and I can honestly say, it was a pleasure working for them. Several of the prisoners told me when I left for Chanute Field, their goal was to move to America after the war was over and become American citizens and open their own restaurants in the United States. I hope they did and I hope they became American citizens. This country certainly needs more qualified, hard working, motivated people like them.

Freddie's bike 1944

I thought the field training we received at Spring Lake, New Jersey (near Fort Monmouth) was very enjoyable and educational because it was similar to my last motor test crew electrician apprentice job. It was strictly a *hand's on* type training that involved operating and maintaining the same top secret radar equipment we would be operating in the field, so to me the Signal Corps training was more meaningful than learning theory. We were also given an interesting overview of the Signal Corps own equipment the Army ground forces were using in battle, so all in all, if you combine our training with all the excellently prepared meals by the Italian prisoners, I really enjoyed our training at Fort Monmouth. Believe it or not, I even took a

Cpl HJO & Squad - Chanute Field, 1945

liking to the top sergeant and we even shook hands when he wished me luck at Chanute Field, when I left. Interestingly, after all the speeches we heard about "a slip of the lip will sink a ship", when I picked up a copy of *Popular Mechanics* magazine before boarding the train for Chanute Field, believe it or not, there on the front cover was a picture of our high altitude *Secret Radar-Weather gathering machine*. I wondered to myself, "Oooh boy, I wonder whose lip slipped this time?"

It was around the middle of May in 1945 when the remainder of our Fort Monmouth squad arrived at Chanute Field, Illinois, for our final two months of crash coarse training. It was also my first encounter with the "Super Flying Fortress" known as the B-29 bomber and I can truthfully say, it was love at first sight. I knew they wouldn't let me be a pilot or a navigator because of my eyes, but they hadn't turned me down as a flight engineer on a B-29 as yet, so I applied for the job, but unfortunately my worsening eyesight let me down again. The flight surgeon said, "When are you going to get it through your thick skull Corporal, your nearsightedness is approaching 20/200 and you will never be approved for flight duty on any aircraft." I was so disgusted, I seriously considered joining the combat engineers, but after my *beer bull session* with a real combat engineer at the NCO club who had been wounded in battle, I changed my mind. He pulled up his pant leg to show me his new wooden leg and for some unknown reason I decided to finish my current training and accept whatever fate had in store for me.

Vicky Prodan, Univ. of Illinois 1945

The University of Illinois had a big spring dance around the end of May and a bunch of us "Chanute GI's" were invited to attend. As luck would have it, I met a cute little girl from Chicago named, Vickie Prodan at the dance who was a sophomore working towards her degree in clinical psychology. Vickie and I seemed to hit it off very well I thought, and we had several fun weekend dates afterwards during the two months I was stationed at Chanute Field. In fact I developed such a crush on her I even checked out going to the U of I engineering school on the G.I. Bill after the war to be near her and work towards my degree in aeronautical engineering. Unfortunately, the University of Illinois informed me they were only accepting entrance applications from Illinois veterans, so I decided the best thing for me to do when I was discharged from the service, was to re-register at Pomona College. I felt at the time, I could get all my degree work behind me sooner by going to Pomona because they would recognize all 64 of my service units as college credit.

Vicki & me – 1945

Unfortunately, Vicki and I then began to slowly drift apart through all this and sorrowfully wrote each other our separate "Dear John letters" around the same time. Like two ships passing in the night, our letters sadly crossed paths on the night mail trains going in opposite directions, and passing quietly in the night.

The following "Easter Greetings" card from my Uncle John (Lt. Comdr. J. B. Weimer, USN) was mailed to my mother in Las Vegas while he was preparing for the upcoming invasion of Okinawa. Uncle John was captain of the supply ship "Missoula" (APA-211) at the time, and had also participated in the Normandy invasion of Europe on June 6, 1944. I had an agonizing feeling Uncle John felt he wouldn't survive the war and would be killed during this upcoming battle for Okinawa from April 1, to July 1, 1945. In his position as captain of the USS Missoula, currently assigned to Task Force 58 (code named "Iceberg"), he knew the Battle of Okinawa would be much worse casualty-wise, than the Normandy invasion, and he mailed only this card, quoting Luke 24:5-7 from his Bible, to his sister, Mrs. Philip Brim at 223 N. Bruce Street, in Las Vegas, Nevada, on March 15, 1945.

> *Why seek ye the living among the dead?*
> *He is not here, but is risen:*
> *Remember how he spoke unto you when*
> *he was yet in Galilee, saying, the son of*
> *man must be delivered into the hands of*
> *sinful men, and be crucified, and the third*
> *day rise again. Luke 24:5-7*
>
> *From John,*
> *Lt. Comdr. J. B. Weimer, USN*
> *USS Missoula (APA–211)*
> *Fleet Post Office*
> *San Francisco, Calif.*

OKINAWA – THE FINAL ASSAULT ON THE EMPIRE
April 1, 1945 to July 1, 1945.

(Including excerpts from British author, Simon Foster's book of the same title)

Even more than Guadalcanal, Leyte and Iwo Jima, this sixty mile long island in the Ryukus Islands Chain typified the nature of the savagely fought Pacific War. The invasion of Okinawa by American Forces in April 1945 was the climax of the campaign against the Japanese that had begun more than three years earlier. It was the largest and most complex amphibious operation undertaken by the Americans in World War II and the most fiercely contested action in all the island-hopping campaigns that had taken the Americans to the shores of Japan. Okinawa lies only 325 miles from the Japanese mainland and hence would make a superb staging area from which the B-29 bomber fleets could pound Japanese cities, and from where the inevitable and costly invasion of Japan itself could take place. Its capture was vital and so too, for the Japanese was its defense, as part of the Absolute Defense Zone. The Japanese 32nd Army was created specifically to turn the island of Okinawa into a fortress. The American Task Force 58 launched the invasion of Okinawa (code named "Iceberg") on April 1, 1945 and there followed 81 days of continuous fighting. The 32nd Japanese Army general allowed the Americans to get a beachhead only because, unbeknown to him, Admiral Nimitz and Halsey had discovered and destroyed all the Japanese "Kamikaze" PT boats that were hidden in adjacent island coves, armed and ready to attack the American invasion fleet during their most vulnerable amphibious unloading operations. Once the mistake was known, he began following a policy of absolute resistance over every yard of the island and attrition became the nature of the conflict. By the end of the campaign for the island in June, Allied casualties were over 50,000 men, with 22 ships sunk, more than 250 damaged, and over 500 aircraft lost. Few if any of the defending Japanese surrendered, including civilians and the 77,000 man 32nd Japanese Army ceased to exist. Tom Brokaw's book lists the Japanese losses at 99,000, including the Kamikazes, plus 160,000 civilians, many of whom committed suicide. Simon Foster, the author of the book entitled, *"The Final Assault on the Empire"*, quotes one of the navy personnel involved, "The Japanese put up one hell of a fight, throwing everything they had left into this battle including all their Kamikaze planes. Nature also played a part in the battle. A hurricane played havoc with our forces."

The invasion of the Island of Okinawa was in every respect a miniature of the ferocity and savagery of the upcoming invasion of Japan herself. The loss ratio on the invasion and capture of Okinawa was over five Japanese (including civilians) killed for every American serviceman lost in battle. If America had been forced to invade the Empire of Japan, at least one million American servicemen would die conquering Japan and at least five million Japanese military and civilians would die defending their homeland. President Truman made the humane and *right decision* by ordering atomic bombs be dropped on Japan to stop this upcoming slaughter of so many lives. Approximately 80,000 Japanese died in Hiroshima and 60,000 Japanese died in Nagasaki when the two atomic bombs were dropped. Their sacrifice to convince their emperor to surrender and end World War II saved the lives of at least 5,000,000 more of their countrymen and the lives of at least 1,000,000 American servicemen.

Over 54,000,000 people died on both sides world wide during World War II, all because the Axis powers made the *wrong decision*, in the name of war. To this day I am convinced World War II would never have happened if Winston Churchill had been the

British Prime Minister instead of Neville Chamberlain during the 1930's when Hitler was flexing his muscles. If only the League of Nations had shown some "*intestinal fortitude*" during the 1930's and had taken a stand against Hitler and Mussolini, World War II would also never have happened, and all those lives would have been saved. Lord help us here in America if these gutless left wing socialists that are gaining control of the Democrat Party, ever gain control of the United States of America. It would be "*deja vu*" all over again, only this time it will be our grandchildren, and their children, and their children's children that will be called upon to defend and correct America's own national socialist party's mistakes, like their grandfathers were called upon to correct the *wrong decision* the German national socialist party made by starting World War II.

The following two letter, dated May 16, and June 18, 1945, were in the same envelope from my younger brother, Rodger D. Sorensen, F1/c on LST 612, to his Folks during a breather after their initial invasion of Okinawa in April.

March 16, 1945

Dear Folks

Well, here I am again with little or no news. I received several of your letters and was glad to get them. Thank you also for the newspaper clippings. Today is a big day on the 612. Today we are having a big party and, no kidding, it is really swell. For instance for Dinner we had our pick of food of Chicken, Turkey, or Ham with all the trimmings including ice cream, cake etc for desert.

You are probably wondering how come all this, well, the Ship has been in Commission for one year today. As yet I don't know but I hear we're to get a Pamphlet on everything the Ship has done for that year. If we get one and I can send it home, it will be nice thing for you to read and keep

It's now June 18th, Maybe I'll have time to finish this letter. I received your note and the letters from Junior, Ted and Jess. Thanks for them. Tell Junior that whatever he does, <u>stay in the States as long as he can.</u> He might think it is tough there now, but no matter how tough it is, it's Heaven compared to here. Well, I got to go and due to the War there is a paper shortage. I'll close for now

.   *As Always, Rodger*

I wrote the following stupid letter to Philip and my mother from Chanute Field, Illinois not knowing Rodger was envolved in the Okanahwa invasion and before we were advised our program to set up "radar-weather stations" in northern China had been canceled. I also wasn't aware of the impending divorce between my mother and Philip, which probably explained their lack of mail to me.

May 24, 1945

Dear Folks

It has come to the attention of the oldest son of your family that you, although not consciously, have sadly neglected said son in matters pertaining to mail. For eighteen days, the afore mentioned party has not received any type of mail (catalogs, cards, etc.) from any relatives, friends, or otherwise. Needless to say, the said party is rapidly approaching hysteria and at the moment is slobbering violently. If this condition is not relieved the party we both have in mind may develop a complex so severe his career in the Army may be affected. Thank you for your immediate reply and cooperation in this matter.

Sincerely Yours,

Homer J. Olsen, 19177784

Corporal AC

Box 1258, Brks. 463, Sqdn. M

Chanute Field, Illinois

As Always, Rodger

After we completed our final training at Chanute Field on July 21, 1945, my commanding officer called me into his office to tell me the weather stations they had planned to set up in Northern China to study the *high winds aloft* problem were no longer necessary with the capture of Okinawa and the program had been cancelled. He then asked me where I would like to spend the remainder of the war and since I thought he was kidding, I said, "Las Vegas Army Air Field, my folks live near there, Sir." He said, "You got it" and we saluted and I marched away thinking, "Ooh boy, I'll bet this is another April fool joke."

185

When I picked up my orders, unbelievably I really was being transferred from Chanute Field to the Las Vegas Army Air Field, (called Nellis Air Force Base now) in Las Vegas Nevada. It was also the last time I saw any of the *secret radar equipment* I had been sent to Harvard University, Fort Monmouth and Chanute Field for seven months to study and learn about. All of a sudden it occurred to me that two of my three years in the Army Air Forces had been wasted on one cancelled training program after another that was canceled, and now I wouldn't be able to do anything worthwhile to help win the war. I was devastated.

But, on the good news side, I was very fortunate to have been able to accumulate 64 units in college credits towards my engineering degree from all the various Army technical training schools I attended, which would make me a junior in college if and when I re-registered as a civilian. I will always be grateful for that education and training I received in the service, and especially for the GI Bill help I received later towards my degree in engineering. To this day I still have guilt feelings over not doing my part to have earned my keep and to help win the war like my little brother Rodger and my cousins, uncles, and many friends, who were heroes for the sacrifices they made to win the war. Rodger always told my mother I was the lucky one in our family, and he was certainly right. My whole life has been blessed in so many ways, and much of it I didn't deserve because I didn't earned it by doing something meaningful to help win the war.

Cpl HJO – 1945

As I suspected, my mother and Philip had another parting of the ways before I was transferred to Las Vegas Army Air Field, without telling me or Rodger anything about it. When I arrived in Las Vegas I was introduced to another one of my mother's new boyfriends named Charlie Hestler, who had already moved into her house to become her *sixth husband*. He was currently a roulette dealer at one of the casinos and she had already initiated divorce proceedings against her *ex-fifth husband*, Philip Brim. I visited Philip later at his apartment and really felt sorry for him and the way he had been treated by my mother. He said they hadn't gotten along since he came home from the hospital, and his hobbling around on a wooden leg didn't help things any. Despite all that, Philip said he still loved my mother, and was supporting himself by driving a Gray Line Tours bus to and from Death Valley, giving desert and geology lectures to the tourists. Knowing my mother, I'm sure she met this exciting roulette dealer while Philip was still lying in the hospital for eight months recovering from his terrible accident in the 3 Kids Mine.

On August 6, 1945, the "Enola Gay", a B-29 bomber flying from Tinian, dropped an atomic bomb on Hiroshima, Japan. Three days later, on August 9th, another atomic bomb was dropped on Nagasaki, Japan and on August 14, 1945, Japan accepted the terms of an unconditional surrender. On September 2, 1945, General Douglas MacArthur officially accepted the Japanese surrender on board the battleship USS Missouri in Tokyo Bay and World War II finally and officially came to an end.

The following letter from my little brother Rodger to his folks, was written while his ship was still anchored at Okinawa shortly after the Pacific War had ended. I thought it was interesting the Navy Censors still wouldn't allow any letters mailed from his ship, to mention where they were, what they were doing or what they had accomplished.

August 17, 1945

Dear Folks

I received your letters this morning so I guess now is a good time to catch up on letter writing. I'm sure glad to hear Jr. is close to home. Now that the War is over, maybe he can stay there at home. You say you would like to see me just walk in like Jr. did. Well, someday you will and I hope it is soon. The way the Navy has its point system it would take me three and a half years to get out. I only have 21 points now and you only get six points a year. It looks bad from that stand point but I don't think that will last to long. I have hopes of getting out within the next two years.

I got Jrs. Letter today also. He gave me the Boulder news and I'm afraid I wouldn't be of much help to him in trying to tell him who to go out with in Boulder. Talking about the Buick, the girls sure went for that car when I was there. I'm glad you picked out some nice clothes for me. No I didn't write to this girl yet I just got the letter with her address today. I'm writing you Mom, then Jr. then her.

Do you think you have enough tools to build a Boat with me? If you have and want to go in with me we can either buy or build us a Boat. What do you think? Well Mother, I'd like to be around so you would have someone to make tapioca pudding and pie for. I'll close for now and will answer sooner than I did this time.

You're loving son, Rodger.

I spent my final six months in the Army Air Forces stationed at Las Vegas Army Air Field making radar targeted weather balloon runs from a trailer mounted radar station located in the foothills near the Base. The balloon runs were basically made with a box kite type target covered with aluminum foil to reflect radar signals, plus a box of weather instruments called *Rawinsond* to gather wind speed and weather data. All this equipment was then tied to a helium filled balloon (that some people called UFO's) we followed by radar until the balloon, before bursting would sometimes reach an altitude of 100,000 feet. We would then plot all the wind speed readings at the various altitudes and all the weather data we received for the officer forecasters to brief the flight crews. All the balloon runs were made from 6 to 8 o'clock in the mornings and 6 to 8 o'clock in the evenings when the desert winds were light, seven days a week. I was basically free the rest of the time, so to keep from

going nuts after I had read all the good books in the library, I bought an old Harley Davidson 84 motorcycle for $300, and got a high paying 50 cents an hour civilian job at a Standard Oil station in North Las Vegas, greasing and fueling cars and trucks.

Oooh boy, I remember one day my captain at the base came in for gas, and while I was fueling his car and cleaning his windshield, he kept looking at me funny. Finally he said, "Where have I seen you before?" and I said, "Hell, captain, I work for you out at the base." I'll kid you not, when he finally figured out who I was he about flipped, and demanded to know what in *Keeerists* name I was doing working at that gas station. Well, leave it to dumb old honest Homer, and my unique ability of putting both feet in my mouth at the same time, I said, "I was looking for something to do to keep

My 84 Harley – 1945

busy." He angrily said, "After you finish your morning balloon run, I want to see you in my office, and we'll by damn, figure out something for you to do to keep busy", and sped off in such a screeching hurry he burned half the rubber off his rear tires. Well, to shorten this skidmark story a little, I pulled KP for a couple of weeks in the mess hall and spent

another two weeks working as a hunt and peck typist in our weather station until the captain finally forgot about me. My old boss at the Standard Station sweet talked me into coming back to work again because of the manpower shortage, only this time I was a little smarter about things. I hid in the lube shop whenever someone from the air base drove in for gas.

Anyway, as they say all good things will eventually come to an end, but this time,

Las Vegas AAF – 1945

Oooh boy, they came to a screaming screeching halt. Unbeknown to me, a new spit and polish Colonel had recently taken over the command of the Las Vegas Army Air Field and had put an armed guard with a K9 police dog out in the sticks guarding our trailer mounted radar station, the same evening I chose to putt out there on my motorcycle from my Standard Station job to make my 6 pm balloon run. To make matters even worse, I was unfortunately wearing a "T" shirt and a pair of Levi's as my uniform because of the overtime work at the station, and I'll tell you, when I saw that armed guard and his snarling snapping police dog, I nearly messed my britches when I spilled my motorcycle in the sage brush. The guard hollered

Halt Halt Halt, three times and cocked his gun to shoot, which didn't scare me half as much as his snarling dog did while trying to get loose to chew me alive. Whooee, by the time the 2nd Lt. Weather officer I worked for finally arrived in his jeep to identify me, the guard already had me blind folded and tied to a fence post to save the firing squad some time.

I'll tell you, from that day on until I was discharged, I was not only ordered to resign my high paying civilian job and wear full dress uniform full time, but had to pull a three shift work schedule (three days duty on each of the shifts, and three days off after nine straight days working), decoding and plotting weather maps, besides making my regular scheduled radar balloon runs every morning and evening. My captain said he only allowed me to keep my corporal stripes because of my important job, and wouldn't allow me to join any of the down town celebration after the war in the Pacific was over. As it all turned out, I was on all night CQ duty at Fort Monmouth during the VE Day celebrations and on swing shift duty at Las Vegas Army Air Field during the VJ Day celebrations, also as punishment.

The following letter from my high school buddy, O/C Frank Shelton, 1st Co. Class 89, Armored OCS, Fort Knox, Kentucky, was written to me while I was stationed at Las Vegas Army Air Field awaiting discharge. It was now just a matter of time until we would all be civilians again.

October 27, 1945

Hello Ole,

I have been going to write you for some time now, but you know how those things are, first this then that. Things here are proceeding along as well as can be expected, this being O.C.S. But all in all, I have been enjoying most of it and the time is simply flying by, all of which helps. I believe I wrote you once since I got here but, not remembering when, I'll just start and may repeat some things.

When we started in Class 89, before the cessation of hostilities, there were 64 of us to begin with. There were about 20 in the Tank Destroyer OCS and the rest in Armored. We attend nearly all classes together except for a few specialized ones. With eight more weeks to go there are now only 40 of us left which means a third have been eliminated. At the end of the sixth week nearly everyone who might wash out appears before the Board of Review and brother they can wash you out for anything. We lost a couple for academic reasons but most of them wash out for what they call "suitability."

Our barracks are three story brick buildings, the nicest on the Fort, which helps a little. The mess halls and offices are on the first floors, the study halls and supply rooms are in the basements. There is also a PX and barber shop in the building. We live on the second and third floors. Louisville is 30 miles from here and that is the major attraction on weekends. Transportation is by bus and quite cheap. We get off on Fridays at 5 pm until 11pm Sunday. So far I've taken one weekend trip down to the mammoth caves and had a swell time. I've also gone to the races at Churchill Downs a couple of times. There are plenty of different places to go.

The courses here move fast and are plenty concentrated. So far we've had Wheel Vehicles, Instructor Training, Tank Mechanics and Operation, Company Administration, Communications, Military Law, Small Arms, and Tank Platoon Tactics. We are now deep in the mysteries of big bore weapons, 57's, 75's, 90's, and 105 mm cannons. We have been firing more ammunition than any of us are worth. They are quite free with it now that the War is over.

There is of course all the chicken that goes with it. Our barracks are inspected every day, and they gig you with anything. It only takes 6 gigs to put you in on the weekends. I have been in only once, however this week, I drew CQ duty. That's why I'm here now writing this letter. Remember when the War in Europe was over you had CQ duty that night. We can get around to doing all those little things we put off anyway.

How are things around Las Vegas? Do you expect to be there sometime yet? What are your chances of getting out of the Army? I don't think I can get out any sooner as an enlisted man or an officer. It figures around late spring or early summer next year either way for me under the point system. I'm going ahead and completing this unless something definite comes up in the way of letting two year olds out sooner. They discharge you right out of OCS through the Fort Knox Separation Center if you become eligible. I really have nothing to loose by staying around here. We have signed no waivers like the classes that started after the War ended have had to do.

I will give you Donald Johnson's address if you do not have it. Sgt. Donald L. Johnson 39042202, Co. K, 60th Inf. A.P.O. 9, postmaster New York, N.Y. Drop him a line if you get some time. I suppose you know Johnny Abercrombie is over or on his way to Japan. He really hated to leave Vi but if you know John, he's glad to travel around. When I graduate from here, if I do, I expect to go overseas and am looking forward to it. I don't particularly care where but the European deal sounds better. Did Katy go back to School? I imagine she did. Well, I've about run down so will close. Drop a line when you get in the mood.

You're Pal, Frank

The following letter from my cousin, S/Sgt Wayne Olsen, was written after he returned from England and was assigned to a headquarters detachment at Camp Crowder, Missouri.

October 29, 1945

Dear Cuz,

I wrote to your folks to get your current address. I received word from them today and I was sorry to hear you were scheduled for overseas movement. If you do go you shouldn't stay very long as I know you've got around 31 points. Anyway you should be discharged by next spring just on your length of service. I don't believe you'd be one to sign up in the Regular Army as I believe most of us Olsen's are civilians at heart.

Boy, I'm so fed up with the Army that sometimes I don't give a damn for anything. From the looks of things, I should be discharged in six more weeks. I was transferred from my last outfit as they are scheduled to go overseas again and my point score kept me from that fate. My old Colonel slipped me another stripe and orders came out transferring me to this outfit. At present I'm working in the infirmary helping to discharge the lucky ones. It is like a vacation after what I was doing in my last outfit. We work four days and take off two days. I take trips to nearby cities from Tulsa to Kansas City. I'm right in the Ozarks and yes there are Hill Billies here.

I guess I never did tell you when and how I got back to the States. We left southern England on a train on June 23rd and 17 hours later arrived in Glasgow, Scotland and boarded the Queen Elizabeth, set sail June 24th and arrived in New York City on June 29th. I was given a 30 Day leave plus travel time and arrived in Provo July 7th and Boy did I lead an easy life for a month. I ended up getting engaged with a girl who lives about 5 blocks from my folks. She wants to get married next January but I don't know. I want to get located first. It looks like I'll be a civilian before Xmas. I may get one of those Army Staff Cars and paint it when I'm discharged. I'll need one.

I returned to the 128 GH here at Camp Crowder on August 10th. The rest of them shipped out a week ago for some POE. Well old pal, it has been quite some time since we used to herd cows for Grandpa. Those were the days. Do you think you will enter College next fall and finish things up? If I had any sense I'd go to College for three more years and I may still do it – who knows? I've only had one year at Weber College in Ogden. Write soon and let me know how your doing – also your romantical status. I promise to answer right back. Here's wishing you luck.

As ever, yer cuzin S/Sgt Wayne B. Olsen 39902273

The following letter from my brother Rodger to my mother in Las Vegas, Nevada was dated November 28, 1945 while their ship was anchored in China.

November 28, 1945

Dear Mom,

Well, here I am again, I'm in China as you can see. This Xmas card is a little better than the one we had last year. I'm going to send a couple of bills, a $100 bill in Chinese money and a $100 bill in Russian money. Any money I send home from now on put it away because I want to keep it all.

I had some pictures taken of myself while here so I'm sending you three of them. I hope

Rodger & 2 buddies in China – 1945

to hear from you soon. I haven't heard from you in three months. Oh, the small money enclosed is invasion stuff we used at Okinawa.

As always, Rodger.

The following letter dated December 3, 1945 is from Lt. Dean E. Smith, 0-877327, Detachment B, 120TH AACS Sq. APO 980, c/o PM, Seattle, WA. Dean was one of my good guy room mates at Pomona College when the Meteorology Program was cancelled and we were both chosen to be communication cadets for training at Seymour- Johnson Field in Greensboro, North Carolina. Unfortunately, I washed out for being "Too nearsighted to be a ground officer in the Air Corps" and Dean went on through the Communication Cadet Program, including additional schooling at Yale University, to graduate as a 2nd Lt. in the Army Air Corps. This letter was addressed to, Cpl. H.J. Olsen, Las Vegas Army Airfield, from Dean's current assignment at Adak, Aleutian Island Chain, Alaska during a winter blizzard and he was feeling depressed over which one of us came out the best in the long run. As it turned out, Dean was the only one in our Metro Detachment that reached the high rank of "Full Bird Colonel" after deciding to stay in the Air Corps Reserves for another twenty five years after the war.

December 3, 1945

Ole, you son of a (looks like a bisquit?),

I just finished re-reading your letter and am now gazing at the dent in the wall where I beat my head every night thinking of how you're (looks like trucking?) off and how I wish I were home doing the same thing. Tonight's another one of those nights. The rain is coming down in sheets and the wind is rocking this hut around like a Doll House. Someday I'm going to come back up here with an Atomic – driven Blower and start blowing all this wind right back where it came from. It would really be a pleasure after the months of discomfort this wind has caused me.

Dean Smith – 1943

Like the weather, life on Adak seems to go on and on. I get up in the morning at 7:45 usually and engage in a daily race against the 08:00 breakfast deadline at the Officers Club. Then back to make my bed and off to the Station. I've been handling Supply, Maintenance, and personnel for the past four months. I guess I told you I lost my Crypto MOS two days after V-J Day. The Office problems are essentially the same, but the variation provides a little interest. There are usually two or three requisitions or memorandum receipts on my desk every morning. Don't know just how but I've been roped into signing every property accountability record that comes through this outfit. As a result I've signed for about four million dollars worth of Communications and Housing Equipment. Damn near everything on the Air Base except the Runways.

Then about 10:00 AM Joe Doakes comes in and wants his mos changed or John Doe dashes in breathlessly and says he has to have an emergency furlough immediately since his collie is having pups. Maintenance inspections, transportation problems, supply records, and visits to our eight outpost's fillup most of the rest of the day. The off-duty hours are a little brighter although not much. The Air Base Officers Club has a Mess Hall plus a room with six each chairs, w/arms, upholstered, model 437-J and one each Divan, hard, leather covered. Another room has one each table, ping pong, with legs, model 14-L-2, and one each table, pool, sloping top, with extra small pockets.

The four Officers at the Detachment play quite a bit of ping-pong, mostly doubles, but we spend very little time in the Cub. Most of it is spent reading, seeing an occasional

Movie at the local Cinema (The Bill this week is "Birth of a Nation", an "Our Gang" comedy, and Rudolph Valentino in something or other) sacking up, or wasting time writing to guys who take months to answer.

Things are looking up for enlisted men, three years and six months service will get you out of the Army on January 1, 1946. But for us eager bastards that wanted to go to Cadets, the score is 70 points or four years service effective 1/1/46. If they keep on lowering points and time for Officers like they have, I'll be eligible on May1, 1946. You should be getting the glad news much sooner. Let me know just how you stand.

I heard from Swalwell the other day. He's been a civilian since October 11th, the lucky dog. That last issue of "Follow Through" was the best one yet. The boys are spread around to every corner of the Globe. Lucky me – the only one of the bunch who drew the Aleutians. Oops sorry, John Carrawan is up here too, I forgot.

I haven't heard from Veta for four or five weeks. Guess she's given it up as a bad job and I can hardly blame her. A platonic friendship doesn't provide much material for keeping the mails hot, or the two people concerned either for that matter. Hey, that sounded like a lot of fun, the trip to Utah by Motorcycle. Those babies must freeze your gonads off on a wintry day though.

We just got a new Officer in from Atka, an Island 100 miles east of here. Atka is one of the two or three islands in the chain where there's an Aleut village. We were shooting the breeze last night trying to find out from him just what the Indians did for a living. He said that in the summer they fished and –you know what – but that in the winter it was too cold to fish. Rough life, one of them actually came home to Atka on furlough from the States last month. Well my boy, my heart bleeds for you being stuck there in Vegas and all. But then, maybe you can get a furlough one of these days and can get away from it all too

Lotsoflove, Dean.

I had my last furlough in the Army around Thanksgiving in 1945 with my Monroe, Utah family. It was also my final long trip on my 84 Harley motorcycle and it certainly made me appreciate having an enclosed car during cold weather. Everyone got to ride my hot Harley motorcycle and we had a lot of fun with it, but I still missed my '38 Ford coupe my mother sold without my knowledge and approval. I remember

Dad and HJO & Fishlake – 1945

Aunt Maude and Uncle Orson invited me over for supper one evening and while I was *putting* along on my motor over to their place that evening, some dumb old farmer approaching me in his car was not only driving on the wrong side of the road, but wouldn't dim his bright lights. I figured; OK if that's the way you want to play mister, let's play *chicken,* and I turned my one light on high beam and headed straight towards him on a collision course. Well, to make this little drama of life shorter, just before we were about to collide head on, I swung off the road to the right into an adjacent borrow pit while that dumb old farmer swung to his right into his right hand borrow pit adjacent to the road. I'm sure we both got the thrill of a lifetime out of that little episode, and after I parked my motor in back of their home for supper that evening, I could hardly wait to tell Uncle Orson's family about my experience. Uncle Orson wasn't home yet when I got there so fortunately, I decided not to tell my exciting motorcycle story until he arrived. Ooooh boy, I'll tell you, when Uncle Orson walked in through that front door, he was really mad, and I mean furious. He said if he could find that knot headed kid on a motorcycle that run him off the road, he would not only tear him apart limb by limb,

Freddie & Marilyn – 1944

but joint by joint. I decided right then and there to keep my big mouth shut and mentally chalked another lesson learned while traveling down the highway of life,--and devouring Aunt Maude's wonderful home cooked meal.

Lesson Learned: *Silence is golden some of the time and even more so, most of the time.*

The following letter is from my dad in Monroe, Utah while I was stationed at Las Vegas Army Air Field.

> *December 19, 1945*
>
> Dear Homer Jr.
>
> Well, here I go again. I'm writing this while the rest of them are wrapping Xmas presents, I thought I would drop you a line or two. We are sending you're presents on the same mail as this letter. We received your gifts ok we won't look at them. I have a hard time keeping the rest of them away from them until Xmas.

> It sure has been awful cold here. It has been as low as 12 below zero here. Last night was 4 below. I have been sorting potoes for some time now. Its sure cold in the potato pit. We have all been down with the flue but we are better now. I wish you could come home for Xmas but I guess you can't this year.
>
> Maude said Tex has moved again and they don't know where to send his presents until they hear from him. Look for your presents soon because they are on their way. Will close for tonight.
>
> As Ever, Dad.

The following letter with return Address "China", is from my little Brother, Rodger D. Sorensen, who is now a Mo.M.M.3/c (motor machinists mate, third class – same as a buck sergeant in the Army) on the USS LST 612, % F.P.O. Frisco, California to our mother concerning his frustration and shock over just recently learning of her third divorce from his stepdad, Philip Brim.

> *January 19, 1946*
>
> ### Dear Mom,
>
> Well here I am again. I received some mail at last. This is the first mail the ship has gotten since September of last year. I hope you liked the pictures. I'm glad they came out as good as they did. China is the first place we have been where you can get pictures taken.
>
> You say you are wondering why you didn't hear from me. Well, you see I didn't get any mail for awhile then I get one from Philip telling me about the divorce. That hit me pretty hard, and then I got mad because of not letting me know sooner. I figured then that I would stop writing to everyone then I'd have no reason to get mail. I kept to my word about not writing to anyone up until today. I received a few letters the last two days and did the senders make me feel like a heel. So I'm writing.
>
> I have one thing I want to know and that is, what is the deal on the Buick? I thought it was in Philips name but you say you got it. Before I say anything I would like to know the whole story on everything. I think Philip needs the car the most because of his leg. It's going to be hard for him to get a job now with all the men getting out of the service, but then I don't know the whole story yet. As you can see, every time I think about it I get mad so I'll drop it here for now.

You ask me about the different Countries I've seen. That is a subject or something I'd rather not write about now. Maybe someday when I'm home and if you get me in the right mood, I'll tell you a lot about them. I will say though that Junior is darn lucky to have never come over here. The only good part about it is you can say I've been there and I've seen half the world.

You asked if I would be in China very long. Not too long I don't think. We are taking Japs back to Japan now and when that's done; I don't know what we will do. China is about the best place we have been to yet or since Pearl Harbor anyway. I have a few souvenirs for everyone though, Jerry, Junior and you and Philip and me.

You might be able to help me some, I don't know. You see I'm supposed to get out of the Navy in June as far as I know now. I'm going up to talk to an Officer tomorrow about getting out sooner to support you now that you and Philip are divorced. If they ask about Junior, I'll tell them he is going to College as soon as he gets out and can't very well do both. So if you can help maybe I can swing it. I said I'd get out in June – that's a maybe. You see I thought I was in for the duration and six months but I found out the other day I'm in until I'm 21 which is another two years.

Me being in the USNR Reserves, there is a chance I can get out on points, but I'm going to see if I can get out on supporting you. I'll write you and tell you exactly what to do after I find out about it for sure. You might have to write and say you need my help – but don't write until I find out.

The way it is now you have to have 24 months over seas duty before you can get a leave and I only have 20 months now so I still have another 4 months to do over here any way you look at it. Well it's getting late so I better close now and hit the sack. Hoping to hear from you soon.

You're loving Son, Rodger.

When I had acquired enough points for discharge and was handed my orders to report to the Separation Center at Fort MacArthur in San Pedro, California, on February 6, 1946 for discharge, as a going away present I installed my last novelty store "*Auto Scare Bomb*" in my captain's Jeep at Las Vegas Army Air Field. To this day, I still wonder if he was really that sorry I was leaving, or was only pretending, and why I thought this childish scare bomb stunt was so hilarious at the time,.

The following letter dated February 7, 1946 from me, "Pre-Mr." H.J. Olsen, is to my mother in Las Vegas. It was mailed from Grandpa Weimer's home at 3415 Mentone Ave, Palms, California, while I was waiting to be processed for discharge from the Army at Fort

Macarthur, San Pedro, California. My Honorable Discharge papers indicated I enlisted in the Army Air Corps Reserves on November 30, 1942. I was inducted for active duty on February 12, 1943 and discharged from the Army Air Forces three years and one day later on February 13, 1946.

February 7, 1946

Dear Mom,

Just a note to let you know the latest news. As it stands now I won't be home until next Monday or Tuesday. There seems to be such a backlog at the Fort that I can't even start "processing" until Sunday. We reported on the 6th and they just took our records and gave us all passes until Sunday morning.

I haven't been over to see Grandpa Weimer yet although I plan to before this pass is up. We have been staying here at Wilshire and Western at the YMCA for the last two nights. It's only 50 cents a night and since all the fellows are here we have a lot to thrash over. I couldn't help but smile at the way things have turned out.

I haven't been over to see Grandpa Weimer yet although I plan to before this pass is up. We have been staying here at Wilshire and Western at the YMCA for the last two nights. It's only 50 cents a night and since all the fellows are here we have a lot to thrash over. I couldn't help but smile at the way things have turned out.

I was inducted in Roster 138 on February 12, 1943 and now I'm being discharged in Roster 139 on February 13, 1946. Also, I've been assigned to the same Company and would have even stayed in the same Barracks had I not taken a pass. Maybe I oughta write a book someday. After I start to "process" it will take at least 30 hours before I can walk out as a civilian so it will most likely be three years and one day since I reported at Fort Macarthur and will be discharged from the same Fort Macarthur.

There sure were a lot of guys there I knew. Practically everywhere I went someone would yell 'Hello' and we'd reimburse one another on various facts. About all the guys I came in with are getting out, some I haven't seen in some time. This last week is really going to be one to remember I can't think of anything else at the moment except, it sure feels swell to know I can live a normal life again soon.

love, Jr.

Unlike our induction, we were all given thorough discharge physical examinations, and it was the first time the Army officially noticed I had flat feet. The Army doctor who examined me said, "There is no record of your having flat feet when you enlisted so this must have occurred while you were in the service. I'll give you a 10% disability." I said, "Doc, that would be dishonest, I was born with flat feet." I remember he looked shocked to me, but I think he was just surprised by my answer. He chuckled, and as he turned to shake my hand, he said, "OK corporal, we'll forget about your flat feet, and I'd like to shake your hand and wish you success in your civilian life."

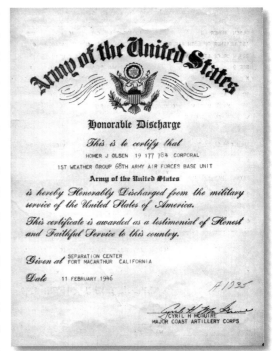

army discharge 1946

After we had completed all our discharge paperwork, we were asked to stop by the paymaster's desk to pick up our $200 mustering out pay and our *ruptured ducks* (discharge pins). An Army major standing near the desk said, "The United States Army will give any of you who will re-enlist now a one stripe promotion as a bonus for staying in and those of you who wish to join the Enlisted Reserves, will not lose your current rank if you are called up again for active service." I thanked the major, but respectfully turned down his kind offers. When he asked why, I said it had only taken me three years to make corporal and I thought I could do that well again by just starting over from scratch, if it

becomes necessary. I thought it was interesting how many buck (three stripe) sergeants, corporals, and even first class (one stripe) privates, took him up on his Enlisted Reserves offer. Less than five years later when the Korean War flared up, thousands of experienced non-com WW II veterans up to the rank of tech (five stripe) sergeants that had signed on as Enlisted Reserves, were re-called for active duty.

When the war was over, I learned for the first time that not one of my relatives lost their lives or were wounded during World War II. Some of them, like my little brother Rodger and my mother's three brothers, Uncles John, Ted, and Jess Weimer, were involved in savagely fought combat action against the Japanese in the Pacific. In fact Uncle John Weimer even saw combat action in both war areas, the Normandy "D" Day invasion of Europe and in several Pacific war invasions against the Japanese as captain of a supply ship. Many of my cousins were sent to the

European and Pacific theaters, but for the most part they were assigned to non combatant units as support personnel and were never in actual combat. My cousin Tex Olsen graduated from flight training as a B-29 Bomber pilot destined for Okinawa for the planned November 1, 1945, invasion of Japan, just as the war ended. My good friend, Frank Shelton, graduated as a 2nd Lt Tank commander and was destined for the land invasion of Japan just as the war ended, but like me, they were discharged from the service without seeing any overseas duty. I know my Utah and Nevada families were embarrassed (as I was) that I never spent any time overseas doing something important and worthwhile for the war effort, and were particularly embarrassed I never did anything but attend training schools for two of the three years I was in the service. It especially bothered my dad and my stepmother when they saw so many of their neighbors with gold stars hanging in their windows for sons lost in battle. I feel terribly sorry for everyone who lost loved ones during the war and I will always be grateful to all veterans for the sacrifices they made for our country and the world, to save freedom from extinction. If it had not been for our men and women in uniform in the armed forces during World War II, we would not have any of the freedoms we enjoy today and everyone in America should thank their lucky stars we still have people like them protecting our democratic way of life. Lord help us, if we forget the sacrifices they made to save our sacred constitution and our freedoms. Over fifty four million people died during World War II, of which six million were Jews and millions more were Christians killed in the Holocaust, all because of mistakes made by the spineless League of Nations and our gutless politicians during the 1930's who failed to take a firm stand against fascism. This wonderful country of ours, the United States of America, despite the negative activism bordering on treason by the few, is still the envy of the world for what we have accomplished as a nation under a democratic constitution framed to provide freedom for all its citizens. Let us never forget:

FREEDOM'S SOURCE

It is the soldier, not the reporter, who has given us freedom of the press.
It is the soldier, not the poet, who has given us freedom of speech.
It is the soldier, not the campus organizer, who has given us the freedom to demonstrate.
It is the soldier, not the lawyer, who has given us the right to a fair trial.
It is the soldier, who salutes the flag who serves under the flag, and whose coffin
is draped by the flag who allows the protestor the right to burn the flag.
Were it not for the brave there would be no land of the free (Author Unknown)

WORLD WAR II STATISTICS

Total American Service men and women in Uniform = 16,100,000

Total American Service members killed in Action = 291,557

Total Service members killed in non-theater accidents = 113,840

Total Veterans still living as of November 11, 2003 = 4,400,000

Estimated WW II Veteran deaths during 2003 = 338,536

Estimated WW II Veteran deaths per day = 1,056

NEWS RELEASE

November 11, 2003: *Conscious of the rapid rate at which World War II (that ended **September 2, 1945**) veterans are dying, project leaders at the National World War II Memorial site said they will finish construction in March and hope to open it to the public in early April. The dedication Ceremony is scheduled for **May 29, 2004**. (Amazingly, only 59 years later)*

THE COLLEGE YEARS

Pomona College Metro Returnees -1946

When the spring semester at Pomona College began in February 1946, there were 17 former *Metro* students (including me) waiting in line to register at the schools Admission's Office. We had all just been discharged from the United States Army Air Forces and were anxious to complete our educations and get on with our lives. Fortunately for all of us, Pomona College knew us from the pre-cadet Meteorology program we attended there in 1943 and accepted all 17 of us without any reservations, including our Army technical training elsewhere as college credit. This immediately gave us a whopping 64 college units with a Junior class level start to graduate sooner and could attend the University of our choice much sooner to obtain our degree in our chosen field. Nearly all the colleges we had requested entrance information other than Pomona, had reservations about accepting our service technical training as college credit.

When Bowdon College in Maine finally recognized my spring semester roommate Bill Johnson's service credits, he switched to *plan B* and transferred to Bowdon in June of 1946. I elected to stay with *plan A* and continued on at Pomona College through summer school and the following year with another good friend, Claude E. McLean as my new roommate,

Metro Reunion - 1946

to graduate with a BA degree in mathematics and geology on June 16, 1947. Surprisingly, I was then accepted by Stanford University's Graduate School of Civil Engineering the following September, and five quarters later graduated with an MS degree in Civil Engineering with a Structural Engineering option on April 6, 1949.

Unbeknown to me a family crisis occurred in late 1948 involving my younger brother Rodger that forced me to leave Stanford early in 1949 to look for work to help him meet his mounting legal fees. Luckily, I was hired immediately as an engineer trainee on the Friant Kern Canal project near Porterville, California by the Peter Kiewit Sons company. I remember my faculty advisor and teacher at Stanford, Dr. Donovan Young, told me I lacked one-three unit course in Structural Engineering of meeting all the Master of Science requirements for Structural Engineering, but mailed my degree to me with that option listed anyway. Several years later, I ran into Professor Young at the Engineers Club in San Francisco and thanked him for his *benefit of the doubt* on my MS degree *way back then*, and he said, "I just wanted you to know that school teachers are also human and that some of us even have a heart." Wow, what a guy, but Oooh boy, there I go again, getting ahead of myself.

I mailed the following letter to my mother at 223 N. Bruce Street, Las Vegas, Nevada, shortly after registering at Pomona and settling in Smiley Hall, Rm. 202, at Pomona College, Claremont, California.

March 4, 1946

Dear Mom,

I got your letter with the $75 money order today, thanks a lot. When you sell the Motorcycle (my model 84 Harley-Davidson) take out that amount plus the 21.90 and what else I owe you. I can cash the checks ok from here so just put the rest in my savings. You better take out a commission for selling it too. As for the laundry, that would really be swell if you wouldn't mind. It takes two weeks to get laundry back here and boy, what a lousy job. I'll get a laundry mail bag and send you a present soon.

While I'm thinking about it, what was wrong with the Motor anyway? I figured the sprockets were badly worn and that, along with the stretched chain, accounted for the slippage. The back brake does need relining but maybe you can sell it without doing that. I didn't think the back wheel was bent although I knew about the small dent in the rim. That happened when I was showing Frank Shelton how to ride a Motorcycle and he crashed into a curb. His little brother was the one that wanted to buy it, not Gordon Spearman

The reason I need a little collateral in the Bank now is because of how slow the Veterans Administration works. Most of the fellows have had to wait over six months before they receive their first subsistence check. It usually takes three months for them to determine whether you were in the service and eligible for the GI Bill or not.

Not much of anything has happened around here to speak of. I still haven't received some of the books I ordered, but I'm not behind anyway. I've seen a few Basketball games (Pomona invariably gets beat) and a Concert. My dates have been fairly cheap. My present experience has a car plus a knack for losing bets; consequently she pays for most of our dates, bless her heart. I sold that other sport coat to Bill Johnson for ten dollars the other day for poverty stricken reasons but it was too small anyway. This school is as bad as the Army in some ways. Too many ex-officers on the faculty I guess. Anyway we have to wear ties and coats to all the evening meals and be very polite etc. But, it's good for me, I guess.

Love, Jr.

Pomona Reunion - 1946

Shortly after I mailed the above letter, I got a real good job as a *bus boy* at *Frary Hall* dining room at Pomona College for the evening *formal* dinner meals. It was a perfect job for me at the time because it helped me save on my cleaning bills by not having to wear my good pants and sport coat and it included one free meal plus a welcome $10 a month salary. I still had to wear my levis with a white shirt and tie, but the school furnished our little white coats and aprons as uniforms for us that were big enough to catch spills. My mother sold my *84 Harley* motorcycle for $300, which is what I paid for it, but I soon found I couldn't get along without some means of transportation. So, like the boat owner when he buys and sells his first boat, I began experiencing the same *happiness/grief* and turned right around and bought a used Indian "Chief" motorcycle for $300. The good news was, it was in better shape than the Harley and I was able to sell it later to Jim Burden for $600 to pay down on a 1941 Ford V8 Sedan for $1100.

The following letter was written while I was rooming at Smiley Hall (aka Schenley Hall) at Pomona College.

March 4, 1946

Dear Mom,

I just thought I would send you a note along with this "deed" (pink slip for the Harley) and also a little of what I owe you. I know I still owe you about $50 on the Motor but I'm not sure of the exact amount so in the next letter tell me and we will get that all straightened out. I'm also returning some of this stuff I won't need down here. It's the first time I've tried on these sweaters and they are so small I can't get into them. I re-

Marti West & me, 1946

ceived the letter telling about sending my laundry bag down the day after I bought this new one so now you know how all that came about.

I had a very nice weekend. This girl I told you about (Margaret West) that has a car invited me to her place for the weekend and with nothing else to do, I went. Her folks were very nice. One of the other girls I knew gave me a white shirt that had belonged to her brother that was killed in the war and Mrs. West washed and ironed it for me. It was a bit yellow be-cause it had been sitting so long but it looks fine now. I broke the bank when we were playing Roulette and won six thousand dollars playing golf Sunday afternoon. To bad we weren't playing for real money. I had a really good time but I wish she would simmer down a little. Gadfrey, the other night I took a girl I knew from Elko, Nevada to a Basketball game and Wow, what stony glares. So goes life I guess. I like her but I just don't want to get too involved right yet.

Well, it's time to go to my Descriptive Geometry class so I better close. Be sure and let me know how much I still owe you on the Harley. I want to keep my Accounts straight with everybody and please don't deposit any of your money in my Bank Account. Tell everybody hello.

Love, Jr.

When Rodger called to tell me he had just been discharged from the Navy my first reaction was, "Damn, I wish he had re-enlisted" because the Navy was starting to make a man out of him away from his mother, and I knew he would stay out of trouble by staying in the service. And not only that, he could get his high school diploma in the Navy while he was deciding what to do with his life. Instead, I kept my mouth shut and volunteered to give him a ride back to Las Vegas on my *new-used* Indian Chief and came close to wiping both of us out in a freak accident.

We were putting along together towards Las Vegas around 70 miles an hour on highway 91 outside of Barstow, California, when all of a sudden the front tire on my motorcycle blew out causing it *to knife edge* from centrifugal force between the front forks. Strangely, and all of sudden, everything began to take place in slow motion and all I could think about was keeping that blown tire from binding in the front forks and spilling us end over end into a hospital somewhere. Fortunately, this little drama of life occurred in a sandy area with little traffic at the time, so I figured the best thing to do was, turn the engine key off, keep the engine in gear, stay off the brakes, and slowly edge the motorcycle off the highway onto the sand dunes to let it spill us safely. When we *finally* slowed down to around 20 mile an hour without the front tire binding, I yelled to Rodger seated behind me to bail out, and crashed the motor into a desert shad scale bush, in a huge cloud of dust. Wow, in what seemed like an hour, all this occurred in less than three minutes, but best of all, except for an ugly cut over my right knee, we both escaped without injury. Rodger hitch hiked back to a small desert gas station we had passed and telephoned our now ex-stepdad, Philip Brim, who drove down to Barstow in a borrowed pickup to haul the two of us and my motorcycle, back to Las Vegas.

My eleven year old sister, Winifred, wrote this letter around the same time I rode my motorcycle up to Utah to help Dad and Ercel with their sugar beets and potatoes. Her letter dated May 22, 1946 and Ercel's letter dated June 30, 1946, were mailed together, after I returned to Pomona for summer school.

> *May 22, 1946*
>
> Dear H.J.
>
> I guess I should have written before this sooner, but I guess I didn't have time. I have been sick quite a lot of the time. School is out now and am I glad. We are almost done with the spring house cleaning. Me and Mother went out to the farm and cut potatoes (for seed planting) today and I earned one dollar. We only cut till noon.
>
> There isn't much news to tell so my letter won't be very long. Daddy and Marilyn went to Provo and we left them on the sidewalk after they got their eyes tested and they

Winifred Olsen

couldn't see a thing so we had to come and lead them to the car. They have got their glasses now.

Marilyn is graduating (from High School) and she surely has lots of presents and cards. I am hurrying very fast over this so it's not very good writing.

Love, Winifred

Sunday June 30, 1946

Dear Homer J.

I imagine by now you are back at School and in full swing and I imagine it seems kind of good. But to us it's kinda lonesome around here. They finished the beets the day you left about 2:30 in the afternoon. Now they have been cultivated and watered but they do need some more weeding done.

The potato harvesters – 1944

The potatoes are coming up very nicely and your Dad has that patch of hay north of the house all ready to haul and its really looking good. I have the house all painted but windows to the north and two to the west. Now the question is, what shall we paint the foundation? You suggested the roof green. Look around and see if you can find any suggestions then write them to us.

Oh yes, I at last located some Levi's for you. They aren't just quite the right size you ask for but Daddy said they would be alright he thought, so I'm mailing them today. We had a very nice time at Cedar. In fact we have chosen the place to take our trip next summer when you are home. It's up at Cedar Breaks and it's certainly a beautiful place.

Tex went to Salt Lake this week to see if he could find some place to stay. Monnie is going up to the U. (University of Utah) next winter too. Anna Q. (Nielsen) said they've (Tex and Monnie) decided to be married the first week in August. Marilyn said Anna Q. told her. Well, I'll close now; I hope you made it back without any trouble. Write to us.

As Ever, Ercel (for all of us)

My new room mate, Claude E. McLean and I, along with Frank Wiggs, Jim Burden and Jim Block, decided to enroll in summer school in 1946 to catch up on some required courses and insure our graduation the following year. Fortunately, all of us found good paying part time jobs as construction laborers right away building housing for married veterans. When Jim Block proposed marriage to Mary Betty Zarn (and she accepted), we helped him build a honeymoon cottage on his lot near the campus, but the best job of all was building private airplane hangers at the Cable Claremont Airport as construction laborers. All three of us wanted to learn to fly so Dewey Cable (bless his heart) agreed to only charge us $5 an hour to rent his airplanes plus another $2 an hour for an

Flight Training - 1946

instructor. We agreed to take half our $1 an hour concrete laborers pay in flying time and the other half in cash, and as it turned out, the three of us soloed in eight hours each flying Dewey's new 65 horsepower Aeronica Champions he had purchased for his flying school. Best of all, we picked up some badly needed school funding, and enough college required

Solo Certificate!

course units to guarantee our graduation from Pomona College in June of 1947.

The following letter from Ercel concerning the marriages of so many of my LDS friends and relatives in Utah insinuates, "Forget your career and education goals. *Tojour Lamoure,* marry now and start your families."

August 13, 1946

Dear Homer J.

I suppose you've about decided you don't have any folks. We've been so neglectful in writing to you because everyone is so busy. Well, the house is painted, also the garage doors and the picket fence, and it really looks different around here. But I still haven't done anything about the foundation because we can't decide what colors we want.

Well, it won't be long until we are all back in school again. Marilyn is thrilled about the B.A.C. and we have her clothes nearly ready along with the other things she has to take with her. And to think that Winifred will be in the sixth grade this year just isn't believable.

Last Wednesday they had Anna Q's Nielsen's wedding down here on the lawn in front of their home. It really was a swell affair. Tex and Gene Mendonhall were ushers. Monnie and Virginia Richenback and Winfred Dykes were bride's maids. Athalee Bell was the maid of honor. It really was a nice wedding. Athalee Bell is to be married to Gene Mendonhall before long. Monnie has a boyfriend in the Service that she has gone with for about ten years and he is to be home right away. He really wants to get married but they seem to think Tex has the inside track (quote from Monnie). Do you remember Mary Olive Sawyer? She surely is a beautiful girl. Remember, she was engaged to a fellow that was killed just before the War ended. Anyway, I talked to her the other day in Richfield and Jay Hansen proposed and gave her a Diamond last Saturday night and is she thrilled. Macray Clowered and Maris Larsen were married last Saturday morning and moved right away to Cedar City where he has a new job with O.P.A. Hartley Newby has bought a home here in Monroe so now all he needs is one more year of College and a girl. He can easily get a job as his degree is teaching.

Bert Caseman was home. Boy does he look swell and is taking his last year at A.C. (Utah State). Aunt Maude said Stan would like to take a trip to California then he could take Jerry with him back to Jess, his Dad. Jess just doesn't have time to come and get him and they want him to start in Kindergarten this year. Of course you can't tell how things will work out.

You did very well during your last term and we are really proud of you. I can imagine you are looking forward to the School year opening up so all the girls will be back. I'm especially glad too that you're staying with that School until you finish as I'm sure you will get just as good a job as going to the other one. I hope I've told you all the news. This is kind of a funny letter so please excuse me. Well, I'll close for now. Write soon.

With Love, ErcelW

The following letter from Ercel was written while I was dating a girl named Sue Brady at Scripps College.

November 10, 1946

Dear Homer J.

I think if I had written to you every time I have thought of you since we received your last letter, you would had more letters than you would have had time to read. So now here goes for a volume and I hope I won't tire you because it's Sunday afternoon and I'm telling you it's just plenty lonesome around here.

Your father has his beets and potatoes up, and he has been helping Bert Christiansen get his up and it's so stormy and cold they are working today while the sun is shining. They are really afraid they will freeze in the ground So many people still have theirs in the ground and they can't get any help to harvest them.

I want to thank you for the lovely birthday card, you just don't know how much it meant to me but I'm really afraid I don't rate it. And the gift was so nice, you made a very good choice and always seem to know what I would really like and need. Thank you so much.

I was really pleased to hear about Sue (Brady) and I'm sure she is a very fine girl if you have chosen her. I suppose by now she has met your Mother and your plans are to spend Thanksgiving with her folks. Would it be asking too much for you to bring her home with you for Christmas? We'll have such a good time together and we will all be able to meet her. I suppose her folks would rather have her home but if it can be arranged we would certainly be pleased to have you bring her home with you. Your plans, when you left last June, were to come home for Christmas this year, remember? Believe me, I don't forget and I start looking forward to it from the minute you leave. I'm sure hoping you will both be able to come home.

Marilyn is enjoying her school so much, but she tries to do too much, and has been working in the library on the side and accompanying too, so she has been ill. However I called her last night and she is alright but she is of a high nervous temperament and tries to live too much in one day. She has gotten pretty good marks so far, but I'm afraid she will have a nervous breakdown if she doesn't slow down. She has been to the Doctor because she had an infected sore on her face that was so painful the Dr. gave her penicillin and told her blood was low and she would have to quite down or she wouldn't be able to finish her schooling. But then, I guess it's quite a temptation to have so many boys around and perhaps she goes out a little too often. But of course they have to be in at a certain hour.

She hasn't come home once with Nolan yet because it just doesn't work out that way. She says he really doesn't have very much fun down there but I imagine she told you all about everything in her letters to you. She told me she had a wonderful letter from you telling her all about Sue. It must have pleased her very much from the way she acted.

We went to Norris Gould and Geraldine Levi's reception the other night and it was quite an affair. I believe he is glad to be married. Bert Caseman is getting married during Thanksgiving time. Aunt Maude seems to think Tex and Monnie are really serious. I guess you knew Athalee Bell got married to a Mendonhall fellow from Richfield. I believe Marilyn and Calvin (Tiejen) have quit. I'm not sure because she hasn't said, but I believe he was kind of jealous about her going out with other boys at school.

Winifred is really working hard on the piano trying to memorize two pieces to play for you and Marilyn and Sue when you come home for Xmas. We are all making plans so don't disappoint us. If you could plan with Marilyn on which Bus ride we could meet you both at Cove Fort at the same time. I tell you I am just living for it. I've been so lonesome since Marilyn left I've hardly been able to take it. Of course I realize it's all as it should be but Oh it's terrible and this house seems as big as a barn. Marilyn said you sent her a kerchief and how she liked it. She said she had a wonderful birthday.

I want to thank you again for the wonderful gift and card. It does mean so much to me and someday you will know. Should I write an invitation to Sue to come for Xmas? Or will you ask her? If you will promise to write more often, I will. Let us know as soon as you can about Xmas. Your Dad gave me this pen for my wonderful birthday.

Tons of Love. Ercel

Unfortunately, Sue Brady and I parted ways shortly after we made our Thanksgiving weekend trip to Las Vegas on my Indian Chief motorcycle for her to meet my Nevada family. Ooh boy, I think she was shocked to learn we were not the well balanced mentally, *well off financially* family she had expected. As I recall, we were putting along on the highway back from Las Vegas to her dormitory at Scripps College, when we mutually agreed to call it quits, but I still think she is a wonderful girl. Unfortunately, I wasn't her kind of a guy and she wasn't my kind of gal, so when you think about it hard enough, "Whatever happens, happens for the best", as my mother used to say.

Apparently I wrote a long feeling sorry for myself letter to Vicki Prodan, my Chanute Field girl friend who was about to graduate from the University of Illinois in clinical psychology, and the following letter was her reply. Surprisingly, she still liked me despite the way we ended our relationship, and she was still rooming at the same boarding house on 605 South Fifth Street, in Champaign, Illinois.

NEWS RELEASE DURING 1946

Truman Seizes mines and railroads as millions of workers strike for better pay; the Atomic Energy Commission is established and A-Bomb testing begins at the Bikini Atoll; the "cold" war begins and War criminals are tried at Nuremberg, Germany. Birthrates in America begin to soar.

December 4, 1946

Dear Ole,

To say I was surprised to get your letter last week is putting it mildly. To tell the truth, I'd put you down as past history months ago. But nevertheless, it was a pleasant surprise.

Your letter sure sounded dismal, not really like you at all and you don't sound very happy Ole, and I'm really sorry. I can't say I envy your courses but wait until I tell you mine later on. You should have known without taking all those psych tests that you are best suited for outdoor work. After all, you always said you liked to be out in the open air, like "This traveling by bus sure cramps my style."

That flying club sure sounds like a good deal. It's an ideal way to learn to fly. Johnny (her cousin) is taking a flying course at the University now and he goes up quite often. Have you soloed yet? I guess what you said about your buddies in the Army is true with almost everyone. You go through so much together and then think you could never lose sight or touch with each other. But civilian life is so different that it's almost like a separate existence. Johnny thinks he knows your friend Ray Daniels but he's not sure and I've not run into either of the fellows you mentioned. I guess they're not psych majors.

I can sympathize with you about your indecision on what to do after graduation next year. I'm exactly in the same fix myself and I'm a little worried. It's practically impossible to get a decent job in psychology without at least a Masters Degree and I don't want to go on to graduate school just yet. I've about had my fill of school and anyway there is no more money. When I was home Thanksgiving I went up to the State mental hospital at Elgin about twenty miles north of Aurora, to see about an internship there.

The psychologist there came down to talk to us a few weeks ago and it seemed worth looking into. The work would be interesting but the pay is small. Still it would be a wonderful experience and I'm trying to work up some enthusiasm. To tell you the truth, I just don't want that job but I like to eat.

I don't know what's the matter with me, but for the first time since Mom died, I'm homesick. I didn't want to come back to school Monday and I can hardly wait for Christmas vacation. I guess it's because I'm lonely and at home I feel as if I belong or something. The whole time I've been in college I haven't really made a single close girl friend. I've made lots of friends, but none real close. I guess that comes from living in a private home instead of the Dorm all that time. I've four term papers to write in the next two and a half weeks so I can type them over Xmas vacation. What a rotten bunch of courses I've got this term – Industrial Psychology, Personnel Tests and Measurements, Culture Patterns and the Individual, Charities and National Culture Societies. The only interesting one is Clinical Psychology and I love it. We've made a couple of field trips to Institutions.

Vicki Prodan - 1945

I'm sorry you and your girl busted up; according to Soo, that was the "principle of least interest" operating. However, I disagree with you about keeping them guessing. That's alright for some people, but as for me, I like to know how I stand with people. It gives me a sense of security. And anyway, if she treated you that way, she wasn't worthy of you.

You know Ole, I've never told anyone this and maybe I shouldn't even tell you, but it took me a lot longer to get over you than I think anyone knew. It wasn't until the beginning of summer school that I started dating again. Since then I've gone with half a dozen fellows or so but mostly nothing serious. I don't know, but after a few dates, I get rather bored with them and seem to know all there is to them. There is only one fellow I could get serious with and he's a graduate student in Clinical Psychology. I'd just as soon not go with anyone else so I think I'll just take it easy this next semester and see what happens. Being cautious is one thing you taught me. Come to think of it, you taught me a lot of things about being careful and watching myself. Just the same Ole, it was wonderful loving you and I will never regret it. I don't know about you but I meant all the things I wrote you at the time, and no matter how many more times I may fall in love, the first time will always hold a special magic.

Going to the Rose Bowl is a standing joke around here. Sure, I'd love to go but there's a slight matter of a train ticket, etc. Are you going to be able to get a ticket? We're really thrilled and very proud of our team this year. They played beautifully this fall season. Well, I'm at the end of my paper so I'd better end too.

Love Vicki.

I mailed the following letter to my Utah family shortly after my 23rd birthday on April 7, 1947, prior to my graduation from Pomona College on June 16, 1947.

April 20, 1947

Dear Folks,

First off, I want to thank you for the Birthday present of ten dollars because it sure came in handy. All this flying and the proms etc. that have been coming off lately have been sort of pressing. Which brings up another thought, and that is I'm really getting old according to the calendar and my receding hairline and shaving schedule. I guess I am getting along in years but darned if I feel very old. I'm still just a kid, mentally anyway. The only time I notice it is when I see what beautiful young women Marilyn and Freddie are turning into.

Well, quite a lot has happened since my last letter home. I flew my "solo cross country" flight as I said, up to Las Vegas in one of the planes (a 1938 Porterfield) here at the Airfield. Mr. Cable wanted me to try and sell it for $1300 but other than a couple of nibbles I didn't have much success. He even offered me a $25 commission and I'm still sweating out one last fellow who's still thinking about it. If it goes through, that $25 will almost pay for my Private License and the little flying time I have left to go.

The trip up there was really nice. I landed at Barstow to refuel both coming and going and was really surprised to see how cheap it was. I made it up to Vegas in 2 hours and 50 minutes at a cost of $3.68 which is much cheaper than a car. I beat that record on the way back with a time of 2 hours and 40 minutes. Flying is the way to travel in my estimation. The scenery was beautiful and I got a chance to fly over places along and off the Highway that I always wanted to see.

My stay at Vegas was pretty interesting from several points of view. First, I spent a lot of time trying to roundup a job for this summer and I think I got just what I had hoped for. I thought the ideal job would be as an Engineering Aide either as a rod and chain man on a surveying crew or in an Engineering office, anything that would give me some experience in Civil Engineering. I talked to some fellows I knew on a surveying gang and they introduced me to their foreman who sent me to their main office. You could have knocked me for a loop when I saw who was in charge of the hiring. He was a fellow named "Dutch" Barton who used to fly Model Airplanes with me at the dry lake all the time. He was very sympathetic and interested in what I wanted to do and gave me a great deal of encouragement in getting the job I wanted. At present, I almost think it's in the bag. Mr. Fuller knows all the big shots over there and he's pulling for me so now all I have to do is wait until Schools out and keep my fingers crossed. Another thing, that job would give me an opportunity to meet all the fellows I would be working with when I finally get out of School. I've halfway decided I'd like to make my Home in Boulder City. In fact, I'm all hopped up right now on buying a Home there.

Cross Country Flight to Las Vegas - 1946

Things in Vegas are about the same I guess. Rodger is getting married the middle of May and will live in my mother's house in Vegas. Charlie Hestler and Mom are moving to Reno right after I graduate, at least for the summer to work at Lake Tahoe. That leaves me looking for a place to board and room, hopefully in Boulder City since I hope to get a job there. I still owe $400 on my car but I hope to get that paid off this summer.

School is as monotonous as ever and my grades are terrible (only a "B" minus average) but I will graduate and that's the main thing. I've succeeded in destroying my chances for another early marriage by breaking off with another girl (Sue Brady) but that's life I guess. Somehow, I have got to win that bet with Marilyn. Maybe someday I'll find a girl I can get along with for a whole semester and if I do, by damn, I'll marry her. Maybe there is something wrong with me or I'm too hard to please- I don't know.

I got a letter from Tex about the University of Utah but I still haven't written to the Professor he suggested. Stanford said they will let me know if I'm accepted in May, and the University of Nevada has already accepted me. The University of Illinois says their still considering my application. At any rate, I'm pretty sure now of going to some Engineering School by this next fall.

Well, that seems to be about all I can think of for the present except we have had some of the most beautiful Weather, especially for Beach Parties. I'm even starting to get a little tan. Thanks again and write me soon.   Love to Everybody, Homer Jr.

1947 reunion of the Pomona College Class "C" Meteorology AAF Detachment

Shortly after the above letter was written, I had another death defying experience while building up flying time towards my private pilot's license. It all started when Dewy had my flight instructor, an experienced pilot and excellent flight instructor named Ruth Johnson, who also was a Women's Air Ferry pilot (WAF) during WW II, take me up for my final checkout. I remember during our flight, she complimented me on my flying and after I had completed everything but the spins, she said, "OK, one more to go and you're on your way with my stamp of approval." We climbed to three thousand feet and I stalled our little Aeronica Champion into the perfect spin towards the ground until she said, "Very good, now pull her out and let's go home."

To this day, I have never figured out why I nudged the stick forward slightly after I straightened out the spin, instead of slowly pulling the stick back to ease us gently out of the dive. When I stupidly nudged the stick forward slightly while diving straight down towards the orange groves, the plane suddenly made a slight *outside loop* maneuver that caused Ruth in the back seat to not only pop out of her improperly buckled seatbelt, but suddenly smack into the cabins roof bruising her forehead and fall forward (and down) onto my shoulders. When that happened, she squashed me into the instrument panel, and Oooh boy, you'll never guess what happened next. Like a domino chain reaction, as I fell forward I rammed the planes throttle to full speed forward, and into a screaming, straight down, full blown power dive. I remember frantically scrambling to help Ruth get back into her seat, as the plane kept accelerating, and all of a sudden, it was all *deja-vu all over again* and everything began to take place in slow motion, like the motorcycle incident. I remember looking at the redlined airspeed indicator and thinking, "Ooh my God, the wing will *rip off* if I don't cut the throttle and ease us out of this dive." In my *slow motion dream movements*, I remember struggling to reach the throttle to cut the power with one hand, while still trying to lift Ruth enough to ease the stick back gently with the other hand, and fortunately, we slowly began to level off. When the curtain finally fell *hours later* on my slow motion movement award winning act, complete with the Clara Bow fluttering eyelids and all, the plane had leveled off and another exciting little drama of life had come to a breathtaking end. While I was checking all our planes instruments, and Ruth was buckling her seat belt properly this time, the altimeter indicated we were still a safe three hundred feet above the orange groves. Wow, talk about outhouse luck, we had used only 90% of our altitude, pulling out of that death defying dive.

After we had climbed to a higher and safer altitude and exhaling our last few sighs of relief, I looked back at a disheveled looking Ruth Johnson, with the nasty bruise on her forehead, and in a smart alec, sarcastic tone of voice, said, "So tell me Ruth, how did you like those apples?" She glared angrily at me for a moment, but then, and you can believe this or not, she busted out laughing so hard her eyes welled with tears. I handed her my clean handkerchief, and she finally stopped laughing long enough to shrug nonchalantly to say, "Fantastic!!! So tell me, Homer J., what are you going to do for an encore?" I said seriously, "Ruth, if I don't do my spins over again and do them right this time, I'll never fly again." She nodded and said, "OK, let's do it", and I did them perfectly this time.

If this exciting little drama of life had ended here, I'm sure I would be remembered as a much stronger person than I really am. Unfortunately, while we were flying back towards the Cable Claremont Airport, I began thinking about the *close shave* we had just experienced, and Ooh boy, suddenly I began feeling airsick, and I mean really airsick. In fact it got so bad, I finally had to tell Ruth to take over the controls, and I weakly hung my *chalk white pale face* out the side window and embarrassingly began *"slipstream spraying"* the whole left exterior side of that little Aeronica Champion. I'll tell you, and you can believe this or not, that award winning sickness act of mine, complete with crossed eyes, runny nose and all, was the straw that broke the camels back as far as Ruth Johnson was concerned. After she *bounce landed* back onto the Claremont Airport runway, she angrily ordered me to clean and polish both the inside and outside of that entire airplane. In fact, thinking back about it now, the last time I saw Ruth Johnson was when she stormed off towards Dewey's pilot's lounge after her lousy landing, shouting something back to me that sounded like, "Boy am I glad I don't have to mess around with you anymore."

The following letter from my stepmother Ercel to me just prior to my graduation from Pomona College. It was the most beautiful, heartfelt letter I have ever received from her., and she told me for the first time, her true feelings how she really felt about me as her stepson.

After I read her letter, I felt ashamed of myself for the cruel stepmother comments I made in the past about my imagined feelings and thoughts she had about me.

June 8, 1947

Dear Homer J.

I've not been able to get up courage to write to you before; I've been so disappointed in the fact that, through all the effort and all the planning and all I've done, I can't go to you're Graduation. I feel defeated as well as disappointed. It's always been my idea that if you try hard enough you could do most anything and I've failed so far. Listen, I'm not giving up until the 11ᵗʰ hour.

I'm so proud of you. No one knows just how I feel and I can't tell anyone as they just don't understand and being in my position, I've had to keep still when otherwise I would have liked to have told you. Of course your Mother comes first, as of course she must but I can say this, you will never have anyone who appreciates your real true value more than I do. I couldn't think any more of you if you were my very own son. I can say, neither you're Dad nor your Mother realizes just what this Graduation means to me. As I never had a Son, only you, and to see you accept that Diploma would show me you're hard earned reward. I'll be with you in spirit every minute. To think you have been accepted by Stanford gives me a thrill because I see you gaining that absolutely by yourself. You gained it without any help from anyone. I think that's why I appreciate you too, and through it all you've lived clean and now days that alone is invaluable. So, if I don't get there don't blame me too much; I

Ercel May Olsen - 1973

just must have you know how proud I am of you and how I appreciate your thoughtfulness towards me at all times. I must say again, I feel as if I have failed you by not helping in more ways than I have.

Now when you have read this letter, please burn it because if members of your family should get it they would be angry and they would think perhaps that I haven't a right to feel as I do towards you. Perhaps I haven't but I still feel that I have and it will just cause trouble if you don't burn it. Just keep the things I've said in mind is all I ask.

We received your announcement this morning in the mail and it was grand. I hope you received the box we sent. There was quite a little ceremony that morning as we got it ready to mail. We felt as if you were with us. I wish you could come home for a day or two before you go to work. Can't you? I must close.

P.S. Just got your letter this morning. Listen, you didn't hurt my feelings I'm not that way. Last night Dad and I talked the whole thing over but it does look very discouraging about coming down there. It really does. But I'm not giving up yet. You've surely done a lot of planning and I can imagine what a wonderful time we would have.

Tons and tons of Love, from your proud Mom (#2)

During the fall semester of 1946, a few of us "Metro's" accepted the Sigma Tau fraternity at Pomona College's invitation to join because we had heard they were a great bunch of guys with a lot of camaraderie. All that turned out to be true, but I was really turned off by the medieval initiation rites new recruits were forced to endure to become members. To be a good sport, I tolerated them when I went through their initiation, but when two of my good buddies, Frank Wiggs and Don Reedy, both mature WWII veterans joined and were forced to go through the same ritual, it turned my stomach.

The Sigma Tau Fraternity had a rule, if one member thought another member was getting out of line during the initiating phase, he could yell *"low blow"* and get to swat that person's aferendum with his paddle, and that person could then swat back to show you he got the message and learned something. Well, we had one guy in the fraternity everyone called *Earthquake Magoon* who I thought bordered on insanity because of his obvious enjoyment administering sadistic torture on new recruits. Every time he would bust his paddles for some unknown reason on one of my buddies, I would yell *low blow* and bust my paddle on his aferendum to teach him a lesson and, in accordance with our rules, he

Sigma Tau Fraternity - 1946

would return the favor to indicate he got the message by busting another paddle on me. Well, the trouble with *Old Earthquake* was, he never quiet got the message because he would almost immediately return to his maniac ways and I would be forced to yell *low blow* all over again, and so it went, over and over. You can believe this or not, you're choice, but *Old Earthquake* and I ended up that day in much worse shape than any of the new recruits during their initiation. In fact, when you think about it hard enough, both our *aferendums* ultimately resembled a three dimensional rainbow montage blending of a black and blue mosaic landscape intertwined in bright orange overtones, all beautifully and artistically overlain with a frosting of imbedded splinters. When I think back now about those two *Artistic Masterpieces* we created on each other s hind ends that day, I wonder why we didn't frame and hang them next to each other in an art gallery somewhere for everyone to admire. Well, when all the initiation *hullabaloo* of my two buddies was over I was turned off by fraternities in general and wished I had never joined them in the first place. In my opinion, these secret hazing clubs on college campuses is not only stupid and ridiculous, but should never be allowed on college campus.

Speaking of the childish stunts and hilarious *saga's* of past escapades members of the Sigma Tau fraternity were involved in and told (and re-told), some of them were nearly of archive caliber. One interesting story they told occurred during a Xmas vacation when one of their members asked his fraternity brothers to *completely* service his Model A Ford for him as a Xmas gift while he was home during the holidays. Well apparently his bored *stuck on campus* buddies looking for something educational to do, decided to not only service, but completely dismantled his Model "A", and using block and tackle attached to the roof of Smiley Hall, lifted all his car's parts up to his third story window and put the Model A back together again in his room. You guessed it, when their fraternity brother returned from his Xmas break and discovered his *completely* serviced and ready to drive gift was delivered inside his room, instead of showing gratitude as expected, he went into an embarrassing unglued orbiting shock. They told me it took him from January until the following June working by himself, (having hurt his buddies feelings and all) to re-dismantle the car in his room, re-lower the parts from the third story window to street level again, and put his Model "A" back together.. For some unknown reason, that little story struck me as an excellent *'hands on'* attention freezing teaching method to solving tough engineering problems.

That particular story apparently motivated another Sigma Tau group looking for an educational experience, to *carrot stick* lead a burro from a farmer's pasture nearby, up and into another fraternity buddies third floor room in Smiley Hall, and shut him in while their friend was out on a hot date. As it so happened, I was studying in my room downstairs on the first floor when the poor guy staggered *home* from his hot date, I'll kid you not, all hell suddenly broke loose upstairs when he switched on the lights and saw that little donkey contentedly munching on his homework papers. Unbeknown to him, the burro had also been munching on green clover in a pasture all that day, and when old *what's his name*, began shouting and tugging on the burros halter rope to pull him out of his room, the burro panicked and developed a terrible case of what those of us raised on a stock-ranch call, *The Skowers*. When we heard the ruckus upstairs, we all assembled as an audience outside his doorway to see the show, and you can believe this or not, the hypnotic fascination we experienced while watching that memorable little drama of life unfold before our very eyes, was indescribable. That panic stricken little burro suddenly began bucking, kicking and hee-hawing frantically while '*old hootenanny*' cussed, shouted and yelled, hanging onto the halter rope for dear life frightening the little burro even more. I'll kid you not, that little donkey all by itself, literally kicked every stick of furniture in that room into fireplace kindling and Oooh boy, you won't believe what happened next. After that little furniture demolition derby finally ended, to make matters even worse the burro suddenly shifted gears into a green clover *skowering mode* and began spinning, high tail and all, on the tightly held short radius halter rope to begin *spray painting* beautiful sine waves on all four walls. I'll tell you, that whole rooms color (and aroma) began resembling the renowned world famous masterpiece entitled, "*Entwined Montana Road Apple, on four Walls*" by the famous Chinese artist, "*Who Flung Dung.*"

Oooh boy, anyway when *old what's his name* finally developed the where with all to drag that ornery little burro out of his room and onto the third story stairway landing outside his doorway, that *Damn Dumb Democrat* symbol like the triple D congressman today, stubbornly refused to descend the stairs in a cooperative manner. Instead, in one fell swoop, that little burro leaped all the way in one fell swoop from the top landing down to the next stair landing below, with *old hootenanny* hanging on to the halter rope for dear life. You guessed it, that maneuver only magnified the problem and they both tumbled together, head over heels on every jump thereafter, to each stairway landing below, to a final bone crushing landing on the street level floor below. Amid deafening applause, and a final thank you gesture for their appreciative audience, old crippled *saucer eyes* and the triple D burro, painfully staggered to their feet for their closing bow, mumbling something to the effect, "We'll get even with all you basket weavers if it's the last thing we do", and the curtain fell on another award winning performance. The dean of men, trying desperately to keep a straight face, ruled the Sigma Tau fraternity was guilty of an illegal act of terrorism and to cover the cleanup and repair costs, fined every fraternity member (except the two main characters) equal amounts as punishment. With this decision, any and all legal claims that may or may not be filed in the future were nullified, and peace and quiet reined once again at Smiley Hall.

A bunch of us were discussing the unfairness of the Sigma Nu Fraternity running an unchallenged candidate for Student Body President (Jack Bradford) for the 1947 school year, so we decided to run someone from our fraternity as well to give the election a little excitement. You guessed it, not one in our fraternity members wanted any part of politics because of what the press might do with our sleazy backgrounds. Now what do we do? Well, I think it was Don Reedy who said Earthquake Magoon would be late signing up for his classes that year, so *Viola!!* unbeknown to him, we unanimously chose Earthquake as our perfect *peoples choice* political candidate. Why? because he was the most unqualified person at Pomona College for the job, and he would prove once and for all if elected, over fifty percent of all American voters are so damn dumb they will elect a *yeller dog* as president of the United States if the dog has a money hungry Public Relations staff, and funds enough to throw away on all the *Brouhaha the PR people dream up*. Fortunately, some of our veteran members were pilots during the war so, to get out the vote, we rented a small airplane from Dewey Cable and began bombing the girls dormitory area of the campus with leaflets spouting *Vote for Earthquake Magoon, the peoples most unqualified choice for Student Body President*. Believe it or not, the girls fell for our *Brouhaha* campaign *like hogs for slop* and when Old Earthquake himself arrived and discovered what we had done, to his shocked surprise and embarrassment, the sophomore girls began following him around campus like he was Frank Sinatra, or somebody important. Well you guessed it, Earthquakes tear jerking "I don't want the job", speeches generated thunderous applause, and were always the same, "I did not choose to run, I will not run if asked, and if I am elected, I will not serve." Whooee, fortunately Jack Bradford, the most qualified candidate for the job, won the election by the skin of his teeth, and with sighs of relief from all of us that Jack had won despite our stupid political shenanigans, peace and quite once again reined at Pomona College.

Lesson Learned: *It is terrifying to think how easily our Freedoms and our Democratic form of Government can be manipulated and even overthrown by unscrupulous ultra-wealthy scoundrels who can so easily buy control of our media and informational services. They can then brainwash the unconscious uneducated unconcerned uninterested voting public enough, to gain control of the illegally elected (?) robot following talking faces in the legislature, to control our senate and congress,(and judicial), and even the administrations of our various federal and state branches of our governments, with just their unearned fortunes and their professional unscrupulous Pubic Relation Staffs.*

Pomona College was the first place I ran into any of the liberal far left type students, which was interesting because they all seemed to come from such well to do families. One thing for sure, they were all educated way beyond their intelligence because they all belonged to the same radical campus group called "Students for Wallace." I remember when Franklin Roosevelt picked Henry Wallace as his vice president running mate during his third term in 1940, my dad began praying nothing would happen to President Roosevelt because "Lord help us" if Henry Wallace ever got to move up a notch and become the first real Socialist Party President of the United States. Fortunately, Roosevelt *seen the light* and got rid of Henry Wallace and chose Harry Truman in 1944 as his vice president running mate during his fourth and last short term as president. One of the female radical members of the "Students for Wallace" kept bugging me to join their group and finally after listening to her verbal garbage much too long, I told her of my dad's depressing experience during the 1930's with her New Dealer hero, who was then the Secretary of Agriculture at the time, and how that experience converted my dad into a dyed in the wool Republican from then on. I told her how proud everyone in my family was to be an American citizen and how fortunate I was to have been born in this wonderful land of freedom where everyone had an opportunity to better their lot in life, if they were motivated enough to get a meaningful education and work hard to succeed.

When she told me she was ashamed of all the money her grandparents had willed to her, I suggested she give it all to some legitimate charity and make her living like the rest of us, by working hard for it. Fortunately, she never spoke to me again. My dad's only comment about people like her who seem to suffer from "*social hypochondria*" (the more wealth they accumulate, the un-happier they are) was, "Some people will holler even if they are hung with a new rope."

The following letter to my mother and Rodger in Las Vegas was mailed one month prior to my graduation from Pomona College to invite them to the ceremony.

May 12, 1947

Dear Mom & Rodger,

I got your two letters today and thank's a million for the ten dollars; it sure came at a good time. I'm sorry I haven't written sooner but then that sprained wrist (from busting paddles) gave me a good excuse for awhile. Just seems like there isn't much worth saying anyway. Right now I'm sweating out graduating because I'm doing so poorly in Econ and I'll be lucky to get a "D" in that course, but I can still graduate with that. I had to go see the Dean the other day about not getting on the ball, so we had a nice long chat about gambling in Nevada and the high price of food. He's quite a joker.

Speaking of graduating, it's not far off (4 more weeks). I don't think there will be any trouble at all getting rooms down here because their asking all but Seniors to leave so their guests can use the rooms. Otherwise

Pomona College Graduation - 1947

224

there would be quite a housing shortage since we have 230 in my graduating class. I think the folks from Utah are coming down. The commencement exercises take place June 16th so let me know when you can come so I can reserve the rooms. I hope Rodger and Vi will come too and then we can all go back together.

Things are about the same as ever around here. Right now we are in the middle of big plans for our "Senior Party." (I was social chairman for the Senior Class) We've taken over a place called "Fullers Ranch" down by Corona for all day and the evening for swimming, dancing and Barbecue. I hope it all turns out O.K. because we've put a lot of work in to it.

We've had almost perfect weather lately with only spells of rain. It's really the prettiest time of the year now with everything so green. I still have another four hours of flying time to go before I get my Private License but I hope to have all that out of the way by the time you get here. Would you like to go for an Airplane ride?

Marti West, Pomona College 1946

Last weekend we had our big carnival and, if I do say so, our fraternity had a pretty fair stand. We cleared $40 which wasn't bad for a bunch of hair lips. We put on a corny freak show, but it was good for laughs. Only one other "stand" cleared more than we did and that was where the Student Body President, (Jack Bradford) and others stuck their heads through a target hole and people threw rotten eggs at them. They made $80 but, boy what a terrible mess and smell. They must have got quite a bargain on the eggs.

As for my love life, it's about the same I guess. I told Marti (Margaret West) I wouldn't mind being married to her if it were just for weekends because I sure get tired of her continual "yackety yak" on what I should do and how I should act and why didn't I ever grow up – ye gods. Reedy and I are going over to Tujunga this weekend to date a couple of Shirley's girl friends just for the ducks of it. We composed a ridicules letter about our being neurotics and we had heard about their psychiatric clinic and were applying for treatment – a lot of nonsense. Anyway, they answered which surprised us and they sounded as if they had a sense of humor, so here we go again - anything for a gag. Well, it looks like its sack time soo

Love to all, Yunior

April 7, 1947 - HJO's 23rd Birthday

When I graduated from Pomona College on June 16, 1947, I still hadn't received any admission commitments from any of the graduate schools of engineering nor had I heard anything concerning my *sure thing* summer surveying job. My brother Rodger and his new bride Violet and their daughter Joy (I called button nose) invited me to stay with them at my mother's house in Las Vegas they were living rent free if I would pay them board and room, which I accepted. Well, you guessed it. After I moved to Las Vegas, the Bureau of Reclamation advised me they had decided to only hire full time (democrat) employees, so there went my summer surveying job along with the University of Utah and Illinois approvals when they both notified me they were only accepting admission applications from *their state* veterans. That left me with no job and the University of Nevada as the only engineering school that would accept me. I decided not to mail my application to Cal-Berkeley after hitchhiking there on a B-25 bomber from Las Vegas Army Air Field to Hamilton Field prior to my discharge, because I just didn't like *the feel* of that school. I hadn't received any word from Stanford, but had doubts about being accepted there anyway, so there it was. It looked like the University of Nevada would be my engineering school to work towards a degree in Engineering..

You can believe this or not, but while I was looking for summer work I was shocked to discover how useless a Bachelor of Arts degree from a liberal arts college really is in the real world of work, unless it's in teaching or librarian work, and they even require further certificate study. Interestingly, there was always an embarrassingly long pause whenever I mentioned to the interviewer I had a BA degree from a liberal arts college and finally, they would all say the same thing, *"That's nice, but what can you do?"* It suddenly dawned on me, liberal arts colleges were created to teach *life style* and *baby sit rich kids,* rather than to teach *meaningful* educations for better jobs. Suddenly I became more convinced than ever I had to

Roger, Violet and little Joy

get an engineering degree if I wanted to earn a decent living some day for my future family.

After several job interviews, I was offered two jobs that sounded interesting from a gross pay point of view, and neither one of them required a college or high school education. One of the jobs was near Searchlight, Nevada working on the Parker Dam in 120 degree heat as a construction laborer, and the other was driving a Yellow Cab in Las Vegas. My younger brother, Rodger was already driving cab for the Riddle Yellow Cab Company, so I chose that job after hearing him brag about his high tips. Besides, it sounded a lot more exciting and interesting than pouring concrete in 120 degree weather, and it might even net more in the long run towards paying my school expenses when tips are included. I had to join the Teamsters Union and get a chauffeur driver's license to become a cab driver with the Riddle Yellow Cab Company, but I guess it was worth it.

When I joined the Union, I decided to attend the Teamsters meeting in Las Vegas as a new member one evening and, Ooh boy, was I shocked to learn how undemocratic and dictatorial that local really was. The Teamsters business agent turned out to be a loud mouthed bully I immediately took a dislike to and I remember wondering at the time how could a knot head like that ever get elected as the business agent in the first place. He told all the members that evening, he had decided to raise the monthly union membership dues to finance another raise for himself, and one of the members stood up and asked, "What are you being paid now?" Whooee, talk about a road rage temper, that business agent literally came unglued that anyone would have the unmitigated gall to question what he was being paid, and/or any other decision he made regarding union business. After his shouting tirade simmered down somewhat, he and two of his goons he called "sergeants at arms", walked into the audience to where the questioning member was sitting, picked the poor guy up by the nape of his neck and cold cocked him for asking what I thought was a legitimate question. They then dragged this poor guy over to the stairwell and tossed him down the stairs while the rest of us just sat there watching and listening to him roll down the stairs in silence. I'll kid you not, you could have heard a pin drop in that room when it was over and all I can remember thinking at the time was, "My God, Adolph Hitler really is still alive." It was the last Teamsters Union meeting I ever attended.

When I went to work for the Riddle Yellow Cab Company, I was assigned to what they called the "old ladies grocery store runs with 10 cent tips if you're lucky" day shift routes, but later on they gave me good tip runs out to the *Strip* and back. My best big tipper ($1) and steady customer, was a housewife who had a secret boyfriend working at one of the hotel casinos on the *Strip*. I would pick her up after her husband left for work in the morning, and take her to a hotel to meet her boyfriend and then drop by again around three in the afternoon to take her home in time to get dinner ready for her husband before he got home from work.

Another time, one of Tommy Dorsey's band members rented my cab for an all day tour of the area and at the end of the day his cab fare amounted to a whopping $20. When he told me real smart ass like, he didn't have any money and started to climb out of the cab at his hotel without paying, I slammed the cab door on him and asked the hotel bell hop to call the cops. Well, as it all turned out, he really was flat broke from gambling as were his friends in the band he tried to borrow from, so I reluctantly settled for five Italian silk ties he said were worth more then $4 apiece, and dropped the charges. A shyster divorce lawyer also gave me a $5 tip another time to shadow his client's wife's escapades, but I refused jobs like that after my first exciting encounter with one of her thug boyfriends, for fear of getting shot. After all, the tips I got from my drunken clients to and from the local houses of ill repute were only slightly less than the shyster lawyer's offer anyway, and I'll tell you, they were a whole lot safer.

You can believe this or not, your choice, but the best paying job in Las Vegas *tip wise*, was working as a *bell hop* in a major hotel. I remember thinking at the time; if you were fortunate enough to ever make $10,000 a year, you would be rich and the bell hops were making twice that amount, tax free. The blind man with his *seeing eye dog helper* selling pencils near my cab stand (who really wasn't blind by the way), told me he also cleared twenty thousand dollars a year, tax free. So my advice to anyone who wants to learn what really goes on in a big city, drive a cab, but if its tip's you want, be a bell hop.

To tell the truth I enjoyed working as a cab driver in Las Vegas during hat summer because, as a student of life, I got to meet and know many of those interesting people well, but for the life of me, never could figure out why their only goal in life was to find a *"live one"* (a high roller) to skin out of his money. My gold mining Grandpa Weimer used to tell us kids, "If only I could have scraped together enough money for another *stake*, I could have struck it rich." But, when you think about it hard enough, all gold miners are optimists, as are fisherman, and gamblers, and certainly all of us construction contractors. After all, *optimism* is what our economy is based on and what keeps the world spinning. Grandpa Weimer should have paid more attention to that old gamblers proverb, "If you're in need of a *stake*, always borrow from a *pessimist* because they don't expect to be paid back."

Two of my Boulder City High School buddies, Frank Shelton and Fred Holland, were also working near our home town during the summer of 1947, and since we were about the only WW II veterans left our age who were still single, we spent a lot of beer time together. I remember Ted Garret's mother was working at the Boulder City Hospital at the time and told us there were three newly hired single nurses around our age working there who were complaining there was nothing to do in Boulder City for laughs, so we told her, "Tell them, if they wouldn't mind babysitting three snot nosed, spoiled rotten little boys, their exhausted parents would sure appreciate a night off."

Well, you guessed it, she did tell them and the three nurses reluctantly agreed to baby sit the three brats to give their overworked parents their needed break. I'll tell you, when Mrs.

Garret drove the three of us over to where the nurses lived all squelched down in the back seat of her car so only the tops of our heads were showing like three small boys, and one of the nurses walked out in her bathrobe to take charge of the brats. Whooee, you guessed it again. When she opened the back door to let the three of us crawl out the back seat everyone had a good laugh, including the other two nurses who came running out to see what was so funny. We told them between guffaws, "If you three gals will get a little more dolled up, we'll take the three of you out for a steak dinner and dancing at the Railroad Pass Casino", and they thought it would be fun. Well, as things turned out, we were all soon well acquainted and we had a ball that evening. We found out all three nurses were single ex-Army officers that were just slightly older than we were and had just recently been discharged from the Army Nurse Corps and the six of us continued having our fun dates all during that wonderful romantic summer. Believe it or not, less than a year later, Frank Shelton and Fred Holland ended up marrying their two nurses, but I was so focused on getting through engineering school and getting settled into a real job before I made a commitment, I sadly and unfortunately lost track of my little nurse. That enjoyable romantic summer along the highway of life

Ruth Stitz, a 1st Liutenant in the Army nursing 1947

is behind me now, but I will always remember my little Norwegian nurse from North Dakota named Ruth Fostnes as one of the best gals I have ever known, and I'm still a little sorry I wasn't more mature at the time to appreciate her more. She was a wonderful girl.

The problem I had with most of the girls I dated in the Army and later on during my college years was, they all suffered from a terrifying disease called *"immediate nesting syndrome"* and wanted to get married *instantly, not later.* I had a real crush on the girl I met while stationed at Chanute Field that was going to the University of Illinois and later, I liked the two girls I went with at Pomona and Scripps College, and I really liked my little Norwegian nurse from North Dakota, but none of them wanted to wait for me to *mature*, as they put it. Besides, I had that funny feeling I was being rushed into something I wasn't ready for yet and all they really wanted in a man was a *"Prince Philip prop"* to round out their wardrobe with and use as an escort lover once in awhile. My stubborn Norwegian pride wasn't about to let any woman ever support me because I believe the man in a marriage should be the prime wage earner and should be allowed the time necessary to prepare for that responsibility before making a lasting commitment. But on the other hand she did have warts, as my dad used to say, and the fact of the matter was I just wasn't ready to settle down in 1947. I learned from my mother's numerous mistakes and experiences, marriage can be either heaven or hell, depending on the parties involved that may or may not be dream mates for the remainder of their lives.

Thinking back now, the only two girls I dated during my life that I really felt, honestly and truly loved me for my own obnoxious self, faults and all, were Vicki Prodan, the girl from Chicago I thought so much of while I was stationed at Chanute Field and mistakenly let get away from me, and my wonderful second wife, Alice Joyce Deyoe from Lewistown, Montana, the girl I met and married after my first wife and I were divorced. I still thank my lucky stars every day for having the good fortune to meet and marry that wonderful Montana girl who, besides being the love of my life, is also my best friend. She, and my three children with their wonderful little families, are my most valuable *possessions,* and are the reason I was put on this earth.

My mother, bless her heart, tried many times to help me with my college expenses by trying to give me part of her meager waitress salary and tips like she gave Rodger all his life, but I wouldn't accept her hard earned money except as legitimate business type loans, which I always paid back with interest. She was the only one on either side of my two families who offered to help me financially with schooling, but I always felt, with the GI Bill that paid my tuition, books and gave me a whopping $50 a month coupled with what I made on part time jobs, I could easily make it through college without any help from anybody, *if I stayed single.* It was depressing to me to see some of my veteran friends having to abandon their once in a lifetime GI Bill opportunity and give up their potentially promising careers, all because of a hurry up marriage, and having children before they could afford them. They became trapped in the same frustrating hand to mouth poverty existence all the rest of their lives like my parents, and I would have if it hadn't been for that wonderful GI Bill all war veterans were offered by our grateful government. As someone said long ago, "If it is not worth waiting for, it was not meant to be."

It was around the first of August in 1947 I received the fantastic news I had prayed for. The Graduate School of Civil Engineering at Stanford University believe it or not finally accepted my application for admission to the upcoming fall quarter as a graduate student in the school of civil engineering. I was ecstatic that I had actually been accepted by such a prestigious engineering school and I couldn't wait to call Frank Wiggs, who suggested I apply there in the first place, to thank him for his encouraging advice. After all, he argued, "You have everything to gain and nothing to lose." Who would have thought a sheepherder's dumb kid from the high desert country in central Utah would ever be invited to attend such an elite University as Stanford. It could only happen in this wonderful country of ours, the United States of America.

I remember while I was driving up from Las Vegas, Nevada to Palo Alto, California, I had an overheating problem suddenly develop in my '41 Ford, so I stopped by the Ford garage for an engine and radiator checkup (it needed a new radiator hose) before checking in at Stanford. I was then assigned to a four man room in Bldg, 212 of the old Navy barracks buildings Stanford had acquired for single veteran housing and renamed, "The Village."

Interestingly my three new roommates turned out to be two ex-officers, one Navy and one Army, plus one 4F civilian. The naval officer, Grove Holcomb, and I seemed to hit it off right away so we decided to have a beer together at the "Oasis" (the enlisted man's club) that first afternoon to get better acquainted. He was from a pioneer family that originally settled the Reno, Nevada area and a street in Reno is still named after his family. Since I was from Boulder City, Nevada we soon discovered we both knew many of the same people.

I remember we were laughing about how small the world really was and the guy sitting next to us at the bar chimed in with, "Where have I run into you two guys before?" He looked familiar to me too, so the three of us spent another picture of beer going over our lives together trying to figure out where we might have run into each other. Finally I asked him where he was currently working and when he said the Ford garage in Palo Alto, I busted out laughing and said, "I'll be damned, you're the guy that fixed my Ford this morning." Grover grinned and said, "Well anyway, as I was trying to say, it really is a small world."

Building 212, Stanford University - 1948

When I registered at Stanford I told my advisor I only wanted a BS degree in civil engineering, but he reminded me I already had a BA Degree in mathematics and geology from Pomona College and since I was now registered in the graduate school of engineering, I had to go for the Master of Science degree. Whooee, that shocking piece of news now unfortunately forced me to take both the undergraduate engineering courses I had missed along the way with the follow up graduate courses that were required, all at the same time during the same quarter that normally are taken at least a year apart. Now what should I do?. I only had a limited amount of funds left to finish my schooling with, so you guessed it, I decided to take 18 to 20 units a quarter to try and graduate before I went broke. If I had been halfway smart, I would have known I was overloading my class work schedule for a potential burnout, but fortunately I came from good stock and was gifted in being just dumb enough to not know I couldn't make it, and succeeded. Don't ask me how, all I know is, Stanford required a 2.75 grade point average (B-) minimum to graduate with a masters degree and when I graduated with my MS Degree five quarters later, I barely made it by the skin of my teeth with a 2.76 grade point average.

Stanford was by far the toughest school I've ever attended, including Harvard and Pomona, and I worked harder at Stanford for a decent grade than I have ever worked before. During those pre-meteorology Army Air Corps days, I thought Pomona College was tough, but these ex-servicemen graduate school engineers at Stanford who were studying for their master's and doctor's degrees, may not have been smarter "I.Q." wise than the Pomona group, but they were much more motivated to finish their schooling to get on with their lives and careers. Stanford also graded on the curve so to meet that hurdle, I couldn't afford to waste time and I gave up all thought of part time work.

Since I was the only enlisted man in our four man *suite*, I proposed we vote *democratically* for our room officers and we adopt a catchy room name like *the odd foursome*. Unfortunately, the spit and polish Army officer, Bob Johnston, couldn't accept the fact he was now a civilian and was no longer a 1ˢᵗ Lt. in the Army, so he insisted the ranking World War II officer should be the room's president without an election. Amazingly he had assumed Grove Holcomb was only an ensign in the Navy until I told him he was a two stripe Lt. equivalent to a captain in the Army, which set him back a notch or two. Anyway, to keep peace in the family, I campaigned on my own *Free Air and Water* platform as a *far left wing liberal with center plus or minus moderation and, far right wing conservatizm* candidate, and believe it or not, I won the presidency by an overwhelming one vote margin. The two officers and I voted for ourselves obviously, but the civilian, bless his heart, cast his vote for

Stanford Roomates - 194

me as the best candidate. Well, as I expected, our first cabinet meeting turned into a fiasco because only one person in our group, the naval officer, owned the rooms radio and a disagreement immediately arose over what type music we should listen to while we were doing homework. The Army officer and the civilian both preferred classical music and the Navy officer enjoyed country-western with Glenn Miller thrown in occasionally. I didn't care much either way although I must admit I enjoyed the radio *turned off* the most. As the compromise president elect, I called a special meeting to resolve the matter and proposed the owner of the radio should have his one vote re-weighed and increased from 1.0000 to 1.0001 and surprisingly, a 3 to 1 majority agreed. When this

new house rule was tested later on to settle the disagreement once and for all, you guessed it, I naturally voted with the radio owner because we were both from Nevada. Oooh boy, the two losers became so enraged over losing by only a lousy .0001 of a vote, they slammed their books shut and stormed off to the library to study by themselves. My good friend Grover, the Navy officer and I, then smilingly turned off the radio to finish our homework quietly without further any interruptions.

In the end, the 4f civilian, Lowell Napper couldn't stand the three of us any longer and moved out in a *huff* after the first quarter. My old Army and fraternity buddy at Pomona, Frank Wiggs, was a semester behind me because he had flunked the entrance test and missed the Harvard radar training, and had just recently graduated from Pomona, and when Stanford accepted his application, we invited him to be our new roommate which evened things out with two enlisted men and two officers as roommates. Interestingly, Grover Holcomb the naval officer, had deteriorated to a dirt bag by then like Frank and I were all along, but not *Old Bob*, he remained spit and polish military nearly the whole time we were roommates. Unbelievably, he had drawn chalk lines on the floor of our room to divide the rooms total floor area equally between the four of us and he had even waxed and mirror polished his quarter section, while our sections lay happily under a half inch of dust and lint. To make matters even worse, his bed was always neatly made up *Army style* with the top blanket stretched so tight you could bounce a quarter to the ceiling, while our bunks (called sacks) lay happily airing out unmade.

During those good old days, everyone wore dirty white *cords* (corduroy pants) to school because they were the "in" fashion at that time and Levi's were still thought of as work clothes. Old spit and polish Bob Johnston not only washed his cords to a brilliant white, but ironed them afterwards with razor sharp creases in both legs that was absolutely disgusting to us dirt bags. Grover and I finally couldn't stand it any longer so we borrowed Frank Wigg's car keys one day and took a pair of Bob's clean white razor creased cords from his bureau drawer to the parking lot and for orneriness, backed a dirty greasy tire track across the seat of his britches before returning them to his bureau drawer. I'll tell you, when old Bob discovered that tire track across the seat of his white cords, I'll kid you not; he absolutely came unglued and launched into an embarrassing screaming air socking tirade while charging up and down the hallway of our barracks, swearing he would find the dirty rotten culprits who were responsible for this heinous act by forensic science if necessary and would severely punish the guilty parties to the full extent of the law.

1stst Lt. Bob Johnston – 1948

Well, you can believe this little drama of life story or not, your choice, but our whole barracks population watched in hypnotic fascination as old spit and polish Bob, wearing his Sherlock Holmes hat and spying through his huge magnifying glass, painstakingly examined every tire on every car parked in the Village lot, looking for the culprit with the guilty matching tread. Unbelievably, he finally found Frank Wiggs' left back car tire was the *smoking gun*, but poor Frank, who knew nothing of what we had done, was able to prove beyond a reasonable doubt he couldn't have been involved in that terrible crime because he was in the school lab all that day, which confused *Old Forensic Bob* even further.

I guess for no other reason than looking guilty, Grover and I suddenly become Bob's prime suspects, soalong with all forty four other engineers living in our barracks who also failed his lie detector test, we also took the *fifth* during his inquisitions. To this day, I'm not sure if *Old Forensic Bob* ever felt he solved the case, but for some unknown reason someone in Building 212 unknown to me obviously carried a grudge against me for the next two quarters. Whoever it was kept installing auto scare bombs in my '41 Ford on a sporadic continual basis when I least expected them, but being the good sport and forgiving person I am and all, I suspected that heinous act was only to mistakenly teach me an unnecessary lesson for some imagined caper they wrongfully assumed I might have been innocently not involved in. Who knows?

Grover R. Holcomb was without a doubt *the lover* of our group because he had a mysterious aroma about him that attracted women like swarms of blowflies to Montana road apples. I remember telling him one time he could be a billionaire someday if he would bottle and sell whatever it was, as an after shave lotion for *real men*. Back in those good old days, the girls we dated wouldn't even let you kiss them goodnight unless you were engaged to them, so Grover, bless his pea picking little heart, would always carry a hand full of engagement rings in his coat pocket like Grandpa Olsen's peppermints, to hand out to his girls.

I still remember the time two of the girls he was engaged to simultaneously, one from Ely, Nevada and the other from Phoenix, Arizona, both arrived the same weekend to visit him. Oooh boy, and I'm sure you guessed what happened next. Somehow he had misread his calendar when he invited them and I'll kid you not, he almost panicked when he realized they would both arrive the same weekend. I told Grove I would gladly double date with him as any good friend would, but that was before I knew of his two women engagement. When

Grover & Homer - 1948

I discovered what had happened, I was so awe struck with hero worship and admiration of his intestinal fortitude, I just stood there shaking my head in disbelief, and wished him luck.

Leave it to *Old Lover Grover* to come up with some complicated cockamamie plan that would require such split second timing it was destined for failure from the very beginning. Believe it or not, he actually planned to have two simultaneous romantic dinners with both of his fiancés at two different hotels across the street from each other without either girl knowing about the other. He figured as an excuse, all he had to do to switch hotels when necessary, was tell one fiancé he was experiencing terrible reoccurring attacks of *Montezuma's Revenge* and she would understand his problem and sympathetically excuse him, and vice versa. Fortunately for *old quick step Grover*, phase one of his plan went off without a hitch. When he met his fiancés at the airport, there was a two hour difference in flight arrival times, so he was able to place his girls in separate hotels across the street from each other without either of them being aware of the other. It was when phase two of his plan kicked in that precise split second timing became a primary concern for any success. Unbelievably, he made dinner reservations at the

(Grove & Homer rehashing Grover's infallible? Strategy - 1948) two separate hotels only

thirty minutes apart, thus forcing him to excuse himself almost immediately after each early dining seating and a cocktail with *fiancé #1*, then race across the street to the other hotel dining room for another seating and hand holding cocktail and few minutes with *fiancé #2*, then back to the first hotel again to frantically *shovel dine* with *fiancé #1* for another very few minutes, and so on back and forth and over again. He must have looked like a ping-pong ball to the bell hops in the two hotels watching his strange behavior, bouncing back and forth across the street.

Over the years it has been my experience that even a well thought out plan will have a flaw somewhere and a contingency plan must always be prepared to avoid a potential disaster. In this case, Grover had not taken into account the extra time that would be required to pull off his two separate romantic candlelight dinners, without one or the other of his fiancés becoming suspicious. As it so happened, one of his two girls did become suspicious of his ever increasing time lapses between visits and she called me while I was doing my homework, and in a half hurt half angry tone of voice, asked where Grover was. I know I could have gone all day without saying what I did, but I answered her honestly and said what any good friend would have said to help cover his hero's shenanigans. I simply asked, "Which one are you?" and click, she hung up. Whooee, anyway when Grover came prancing back to her Hotel dining room doing his quaint little quick step with the road apple side hop, she decided to play along with him to find out what was going on. You guessed it, after his few minutes of small talk, Grover began fidgeting around again and suddenly announced the spirit had appeared unto him and he had seen the light to leave, she secretly followed him.

Well to make this story a little shorter, about an hour later Old Cripple Grover staggered back to our one room suite from his two girls (no holds barred) beating, and unbelievably, blamed me for everything that happened. I'll tell you, *the crapolla must have really hit the fan* when fiancé #1 saw him with fiancé #2 As I watched Grover imitating Jack Dempsey shadow boxing at the open door and listening to his tirade about me *putting up my dukes*, I busted out laughing so hard my sides hurt. Apparently a food fight had erupted between the two girls over who really hated Grover the most and all I could think of was how fortunate he was to have escaped with only two black eyes, multiple scratches and only a dozen or so ugly bruises, but with no broken bones. It could have been much worse so I said, "Grover, the way you look right now you couldn't fight yourself out of a wet paper sack, so why don't you just chalk this whole thing up as another exciting memorable experience along the highway of life, and let it go at that because after all, as my mother used to say, *"Whatever happens, happens for the best."* And with that, he sadly sat down and said, "Damn, and I really liked the one from Arizona" and unclenched his fist to let two badly bent engagement rings fall to the floor.

As time went by, Grover's romantic escapades began to take their toll and it became increasingly difficult for me to wake him up for our 8:00 o'clock engineering classes. In fact, about half the time I would just give up and start to drive off without him when all of a sudden, here he would come wide open, racing out of the barracks in his underwear carrying an arm load of clothes to put on in the back seat of my car. I tried curing his late for everything habit by picking up girls hitch hiking to their classes at Stanford to try embarrassing him into changing, but nothing worked. We always sat next to each other in our early morning engineering classes so I'll say this for Old Grove, his high school Latin *sleep training* class really paid off at Stanford. Unbelievably he had developed the uncanny ability to fall asleep almost immediately with both eyes open using only the eraser end of his pencil propped under his chin as a pillow. I remember Professor Clarke Ogelsbey asked him a question one time in our highway engineering class and when there wasn't any response from Grover other than a zombie stare, Clarke repeated his question a second time, and then a third.. Well, to speed things up a little, I reached over and nonchalantly *flicked* the pointed end of (*F. Wiggs, H. Olsen & Schizophrenic B, Johnston*) his pencil out from under his chin with my cocked

Stanford Picnic - 1948

finger. Oooh boy, you can say all you want about ringing church bells, but Grover woke up with such a resounding nose flattening, ear ringing, ball dribbling head bounce when his face ricocheted off his desk, it put Big Ben to shame. Fortunately, with his relaxed neck muscles and all, it was a blessing his head stopped dribbling after only 12 *big ben bongs*, because he woke up to answer Clark's question without a whip lash. Oooh boy, I guess I do exaggerate a little, but as my dad used to say, and our current Media has learned, "Never ruin a good story by the facts."

Besides being re-elected the *Free Air & Water* Party's compromise president of our four man room, I was also elected social chairman for Building 212 during the 1948 spring quarter. Apparently no one in our barracks wanted any part of the job and I wasn't present during the nominations to withdraw my name, so I was nominated by my *get even* roommate, Grover and was unilaterally and unanimously elected *draft board style* to the job. It was without a doubt the most thankless job ever dreamed up because no matter how hard or what kind of a social gathering I put together for our barracks group, I was always severely criticized. If the job hadn't been such a golden opportunity to meet good looking women, I would have resigned long before I was even elected.

The way I saw it, my responsibility as Bldg. 212's social chairman was to meet with all the various women's dormitory house mothers and resident assistants to organize our *"Let's get acquainted"* type picnics and social gatherings. Well as it turned out, I did meet a lot of really good looking women, but our first social gathering with the sophomore girl's dormitory at Stanford, and the second one we had with Mills College in Oakland, were absolute disasters. For some unknown reason, the sophomore girls seemed to feel they were dating their own fathers and our more mature war veterans apparently felt they were baby sitting their own air headed teenage daughters. We really weren't that much older than the undergraduate girls, but it soon became painfully obvious our years in the service had matured us way beyond the dippy, adolescent, mentally immature younger college girls, who were still in the giggling talking through their noses in a foreign sounding language stage they called *valley talk*. From then on, I simply organized social gatherings with only senior and/or graduate women students, and the working nursing school girls who were in their mid twenties. The only girls I dated that first year at Stanford were girls my own age (24) or slightly older who were either nurses in training or resident assistants working towards their master's degrees and/or teaching credentials.

The fall, winter and spring quarters at Stanford the first year seemed to zip by and my good buddy *Grover,* graduated with his Masters Degree in Civil Engineering in June of 1948, and went back to work for the Isbell Construction Company in Reno, Nevada. Bob Johnston continued on with Frank Wiggs and I as roommates, and remarkably, he began to relax somewhat and the three of us ended up as really good friends. Frank and I applied for summer jobs with the California Highway Department, District VIII, in San Bernardino, California, and we were both hired as highway inspectors on our advisor professor Bert Wells' recommendations, providing we pass the Junior Civil Engineers examination, which we did.

Frank was assigned to a Peter Kiewit Son's Company contract building a new highway to Palm Springs, California as a grade inspector while I was assigned to a George Herz Company contract near Loma Linda as a compaction and curb and gutter inspector on a highway widening job. Frank's mother, bless her heart, offered us room and board on her thirty acre orange grove ranch in San Dimas, which we thankfully accepted, and even though the commute was longer, cost wise it was a Godsend for both of us. Frank and I were able to save considerably more from our pay checks for school expenses because his wonderful mother, Mrs. Wiggs, not only gave us free rent, but charged less for our meals. Our highway Junior Civil Engineer inspector jobs paid a whopping $310 a month at that time so we both saved nearly $500 apiece on our summer jobs and even gained some valuable civil engineering experience for future résumé's and job interviews. All in all, we began to feel everything was falling into place (barring an emergency), and we could now make it financially to our graduation in June of 1949.

The following letter from my little 13 year old sister, Freddie in Monroe, Utah, was mailed to me while I was staying at Mrs. Wiggs room and boarding house at 1018 W. Cypress, San Dimas, California, working for the California Highway Department. My other sister Marilyn was getting married in July and they were all excitedly preparing for the big event.

June 7, 1948

Dear Junior, (Oooh boy, I'll live that name down)

Thanks a lot for my Birthday present, but I don't see how you can do it when you are supporting yourself and going to School and everything. I really appreciate your thoughtfulness and I have now saved up a lot of money. When is your School out so you can come Home? We are all so lonesome to see you and I can hardly wait until you get here. We can make homemade Carmel ice-cream like we always do, and go up in the Canyon and have supper.

Dale is here now and we have had a lot of nice times together. He really is a swell guy, so sweet and considerate. I think the wedding will be in July and it's really going to be a swell affair. They haven't got the wedding dress yet but they have Dales suit and the ring. They are going to live in Edith's house while she is in Fish Lake.

I surely am glad School is out because I was getting very tired of School. I bet you are to; at least I would if I were in your shoes. Well, that's about all the news for now.

Love, Winifred.

On my way back to Stanford for the fall quarter, I stopped by to see how Grandpa and Grandma Weimer were getting along in Culver City and maybe learn some interesting family news. Wouldn't you know it, Grandpa came to the door with a twinkle in his eye to tell me how proud he was someone in our family had made headlines. He handed me a copy of the *Richfield Reaper* (a central Utah newspaper) with headlines about a famous Rocky Mountain *asstronaught*. Interestingly, the newspaper article was mostly about my cousin Tex and his new bride, Monnie spending the summer of 1948 on their families Marysvale cattle and dairy ranch in Piute County helping Nolan "Spun" Olsen, Tex's younger brother with ranch chores and milking 21 Holstein cows. Apparently Monnie was constantly objecting to the repulsive smell radiating from their outdoor privy she felt was built way too close (for shorter winter runs) to the ranch house and since she had invited dinner guests from

Salt Lake City who were arriving soon, she asked Tex for the fiftieth time to do something about it. Well, unbeknown to *Spun* and to keep peace in the family, Tex poured a half bucket of kerosene into the *two holer privy* to dampen the aroma somewhat and Oooh boy, you guessed it. *Spun* stepped inside the *two holer* for a relaxing hand rolled bull durum smoke and nonchalantly dropped a burning match into the pit below, just as their dinner guests drove up the driveway.

Calif Hwy job - Summer 1948

Over the years this exciting little *saga of life on a Utah ranch* article has been re-written and re-told many times, but like many historical accounts it has been revised and re-written by biased authors so many times the facts of the matter have been warped and exaggerated beyond belief. The most credible account is obviously from the dinner guests themselves. Their verified eye witness accounts of a deafening mushroom cloud explosion suddenly occurring as they drove into the driveway that evening are unquestionable. As they watched in hypnotic fascination *Spun*, the star in the show with his pants at half mast flattened against the outhouse door, was blasted into orbit. When the now famous *Privy Asstronaught* together with his splintered door skid re-landed to a hide burning stop in front of his wide eyed audience frantically re-buttoning his britches he discovered his most valuable possession, the *Norwegian toilet seats* were ablaze. Like any cowboy-rancher would do while holding his pants up, *Spun* scrambled frantically towards the flaming privy screaming, *Save the seats, somebody get some water to help save the seats."* Years later when I asked *Spun* what his recollections were of that little saga along the highway of life, his answer was simply, "It made the paper."

Nolan B. Spun Olsen– 1948

As I recall, Grandpa Olsen was the one who told me it was the *Swedes* who first invented the famous *Scandinavian Toilet Seat,* but the Swedish design never caught on with the general public until many years later when the Norwegians came up with the idea of cutting a hole in the middle. Oooh Boy, anyway I still think to this day my wonderful double cousin, Nolan B. *(Spun)* Olsen was not only the last cowboy, but with his unique sense of humor was Utah's answer to Will Rogers because when he told his story's they were always about himself.

He told me one of their 600 pound Hereford calves got loose from their fenced in pasture one time and was running crazily, tail up and all, along highway 89 playfully dodging fast moving traffic and he didn't have time to saddle up his horse. When he tried to head her off and back into the pasture on foot, he wasn't fast enough so he asked his dad (my Uncle Orson); to drive his pickup truck alongside that speeding calf while he lassoed it standing up in the truck bed. Apparently he figured all he had to do was drop a looped rope over the calf's head and neck from the truck bed and lead it back to the pasture behind the pickup. Oooh boy, I bet you've already guessed what happened next. Spun and his dad nonchalantly cruised their truck up alongside that ornery heifer running wide open on the highway, and *Spun* casually draped the looped rope over the heifer's neck and Whooee, I'll kid you not, things really got interesting in a hurry. That ornery 600 pound calf suddenly stopped dead in its tracks with only a 175 pound *Spun* Olsen standing in the truck doing thirty miles an hour, holding his end of the rope tightly looped around his wrists.

As Spun recalled while in his hospital bed later during friends visits, "You can say all you want about how fast a rock zings out of a flipper, but I'll say this for sure, when that damn calf jerked me out of the truck bed, it was more like a bullet leaving a high powered rifle." From all accounts, he had instantly become airborne when the calf stopped dead in it's tracks and he smacked the highway pavement with such a resounding splat; it not only bloodied his nose, blacked both his eyes, sprained both his wrists, but skinned the hide off and bruised his knees and elbows so badly he couldn't walk for a week. The good news was, no bones were broken and his arms were pleasingly stretched an even foot longer. Spun's only comment was, "Hey, now I can tie my boot laces without bending over."

During the Fall Quarter at Stanford in 1948, our four man room was rudely taken over by Stanford as overflow administrative offices and the three of us were re-assigned (Grove had graduated) to an eight man suite in the same barracks with five new roommates. One of them named Paul Beroza, was undoubtedly the smartest guy I've ever known other than Frank Shelton, and had worked for Dr. Oppenhiemer at White Sands, New Mexico during the Manhattan Project as a soldier scientist to develop the atomic bomb. He told me he was working towards getting two doctor's degrees, one in Electrical Engineering and the other in Physics, to complete his education. As it turned out Paul and I hit it off from the very start and became good friends, and I will always be grateful to him for his help and expertise in explaining difficult engineering problems to me. For some unknown reason his advice and counsel made my homework seem easier for me after our discussions, and needless to say, he became a renowned engineering professor later on during his life.

Janet Whitehead – 1949

One of my other roommates in our suite was the strangest guy I've ever met. He apparently came from a very wealthy family because his parents had given him a *Rolls Royce* of all things, to drive around campus and unbelievably, he was also a card carrying member of the Communist Party. As I suspected, he had never held a legitimate meaningful job or ever had to work a day in his life, and like the Pomona girl, was obviously educated way beyond his intelligence. I remember we were all sitting around shooting the breeze one day listening to him spout off about how wonderful everything would be after his form of government overthrew our democratic form of government. Finally I couldn't stand it any longer and walked over to his desk and picked up his Rolls Royce keys, ans as I started to walk out he said, "Where are you going with my car keys?" I said, "I have a date tonight and I'm taking the *peoples car* out for a spin to show her around town." He glared at me and said, "Like hell you are; that's my car." When I reminded him of his passionate speech about no one owning property any longer and we would all own everything together equally, he said, "Oh that

> ### NEWS RELEASES DURING 1948
>
> *U.S. begins the Berlin Airlift after the Soviets seal off the city; Harry Truman and Alben Barkley are elected President and Vice President; the Selective Service Act becomes law; U.S. becomes a net importer of oil; Congress authorizes the Marshall Plan to help rebuild Europe; Whittaker Chambers accuses Alger Hiss of being a Communist; and the telescope at Mount Palomar is dedicated.*

only applies to you peasants, because I'll be one of the leaders after the revolution and will have a chauffeur-driven Rolls Royce and live in a mansion." We all busted out laughing and as we were filing out, I said, "Ooh boy, has he got another think coming. Guys like him will be the first people shot by the Communist firing squads." Not long afterwards he moved out of Building 212, apparently because he finally figured out he was wasting his time converting World War II veterans. I wonder what ever happened to that knot headed idiot?

Frank at Stanford

I remember around *Big Game* time in November of 1948, Frank Wiggs and I both had tickets and dates for the Stanford-Cal big game at Berkeley and my girl suddenly cancelled out on me at the last minute. Frank Wiggs' girl friend, Ann Hazelton, then got me a blind date with another "resident assistant" in her same girls dorm named Janet Elizabeth Whitehead that I had met earlier when I was social chairman, but figured she wouldn't ever go out with a dirt bag like me. I think Frank knew me better than anyone else, so he naturally agreed with my analysis and told Ann she was making a terrible mistake fixing me up with a wonderful girl like Janet. Well, contrary to his analysis and as it turned out, we all had a wonderful time that day even though Stanford lost the game to Cal by a sickening 7 to 6 score. Since I promised Frank I would try really hard to behave, I pretended I was Gary Cooper and played his quiet *yep* and *nope* role all day, trying *not* to screw up. In fact, my Gary Cooper behavior act worked so well even

Frank was (Janet Elizabeth Whitehead impressed until we passed a loaded hay wagon in flames on the Stanford campus.

Apparently some nut case from Cal had deliberately set the wagon on fire as a sick victory joke and I thought "Oh my God, this whole campus could go up in flames if that fire gets out of control." I yelled to Frank to stop the car, jumped out grabbing a shovel leaning against the wagon tongue, and began beating out the flames before they escalated into something dangerous. Frank was so embarrassed, disgusted, and enraged by what he thought was my *psycho behavior;* he drove the girls on to their dormitory without me and didn't bother to come back until I had the fire completely out. On the way home, he angrily told me I had better call Janet the next morning to apologize or he would never double date with me again. So, as he suggested, the next morning I called Janet to apologize and believe it or not, contrary to Frank's assessment, she and all the other girls in her dormitory thought I was a hero for what I had done. Well, you guessed it, Janet and I started whirlwind dating soon afterwards and one thing led to another until two months after we first met, I wrote the following letter to my Nevada family on January 22, 1949, to tell them I was now engaged to the girl of my dreams.

I blew my test, 1948

I mailed the following letter to both "Mr. and Mrs. Philip Brim" who unknowingly to me were interestingly back together again, and living at 223 N. Bruce Street in Las Vegas, Nevada. I became aware of my mother's breakup with Charlie Hestler, but was completely unaware of Rodger's murder arrest when this letter was written.

January 22, 1949

Dear Folks,

This time I really have some news for you so hang onto your hats. Janet and I are now officially engaged! She has my "Ruptured Duck" discharge pin, legion button, ASCE pin, Sigma Tau Fraternity pin, soap dish, everything I have including my heart and if that's not official, I don't know what is. As to how we will eat, when it will be (this summer for sure), and where (probably Seattle), I don't know. Only thing I know for sure is that she is the one for me. She will have her teaching credentials by June so if the worst comes to the worst, we can both work at least until we get on our feet and I can retire and keep house. As to where we will live, I don't know yet. I've gotten a couple more job offers. It hasn't been until now that I've gotten that "down and can't get up" feeling and that I *will have to start getting busy on this "job" business. The practical things can take care of themselves later, right now she feels the same way about me and that's all that's important now.*

The way it looks now, we will be coming home the last of March during spring vacation to bring a lot of my stuff home and for you to meet her and then go up to Seattle when schools out to "choke" – tie the knot. Gosh, she's such a wonderful girl though. She can cook, sew, and what a joker–always good for laughs, tall and blonde, blue eyes, whatta women. No kidding, I'm the luckiest guy in the world. She's as broke as I am and she has had to work for everything she has so tell Rodger I'm sorry about not landing a rich women for us. She's a fast runner too, and strong.

The guys just came into the room to listen to the Basketball Game on the Radio and its distracting at this point. Stanford's ahead of USF, 18 to 13 right now. Needless to say, everybody was plenty surprised and they are all either shaking their heads or my hand. We have had a couple of parties to celebrate already, so it's all over now but the shouting.

School is about the same as ever I guess. It doesn't seem very important anymore. I don't think I will be making any killing on grades anymore either, just so I get through now is all that's important. I was elected Social Chairman for the "House" again for this coming Quarter. They figured I had an "in" knowing Janet (she's a house mother at one of the girl's dormitory's) and that I could get them dates. I can't finish this letter now, this game sounds too exciting. FINAL SCORE: Stanford 65, University of San Francisco 55. Good Game…I gotta date, PS: Did Rodger hear anything from the State and is he working yet? How's Violet and "Button Nose"? write soon.

Love to all, Homer Jr.

I remember asking my good friend and mentor, Paul Beroza, if he would like to drive home with me to spend the 1948 Christmas Holiday with my Utah family, and he gladly accepted. Everyone in Utah, including my two sisters, had already fallen in love with Paul the previous September when we drove home to celebrate my youngest half bother "Baby Steve's" birth, and to build a baby crib in my dad's shop for him. I also found out from my Utah family at that time Charlie Hestler and my mother had split up after he tried to kill her with his handgun, and he had been arrested. Fortunately, he was a lousy shot and missed, but I'll tell you, I was really glad to hear she finally got rid of that nut case. Philip Brim, who had always loved my mother from the time they first met, came back to guard her during that terrible crisis period and maybe to try re- marrying my mother for the third time. From what little I was told, my mother was a psychological basket case, and especially after she learned (unbeknown to me) her baby son, Rodger, had shot and killed her own younger brother, Jess Weimer, in a drunken brawl. She needed a steady man like Philip around to lean on during that trying period and they were married again when her divorce with Charlie Hestler was finalized. That marriage made Philip Brim husband number *seven*.

Shortly after my mother and Philip received my engagement announcement letter of January 22, 1949, I got a frantic telephone call from them informing me of Rodger's upcoming trial for second degree murder. When they finally told me the story of what had happened, I was stunned, shocked and surprised beyond belief over their terrible news and became sick to my stomach after I hung up the telephone. Apparently Rodger and Uncle Jess had gotten into a drunken argument that degenerated into a fist fight to the death, and when Rodger was apparently getting the worst of the fight, he said he raced into the house to get a gun to scare Jess into giving up, but Jess kept coming at him and he shot him in self defense. Unfortunately, Jess only lived a short time in the hospital.

It was a terrible tragedy and a terrible waste of a wonderful man's life. Jess was in the Marines and Rodger was in the Navy, and both were in combat in the Pacific war and were *Heroes* in my opinion, but unfortunately, they had both developed serious drinking problems during the war. I was furious with my folks for not telling me sooner about what had happened, but they thought I would do something stupid like quitting school, and I couldn't be of any help anyway. Philip told me to drive up to South San Francisco and talk to his sister, my Aunt Mary, and she would tell me the whole story.

The following letter from Rodger's dad, R. D. Sorensen, was mailed from his cattle ranch in Idaho to Philip Brim in Las Vegas in answer to his request for financial assistance defending his son, Rodger in his upcoming murder trial.

January 24, 1949

Dear Philip,

I want to thank you for letting me know. I take the Salt Lake Tribune but I must have overlooked it. Weather conditions are so bad here that the mail is delayed some time for a day. It was 25 below zero last night.

I have a lot I would like to say but some times it is better to keep still. I really don't think any of us are qualified to judge a bad mistake and the best we can do is little enough. We all have responsibilities to meet and I think the sooner a young person realizes it, the easier it will be to go through life. I believe Rodger will or should try to repay every penny spent on his behalf and feel thankful his folks are going the limit to help him in his time of need. Philip, I think you have been too generous, both you and his Mother in times past but I suppose we are all pretty much the same when it concerns our loved ones. Give my best wishes to Jess for a speedy recovery. After all, I think he is really the loser. There isn't anything in a person's life that will take the place of good Health.

I hope you received the wire OK; I am not in too good of shape financially. Mortgage Companies don't like to give permission to sell Live Stock and the Market isn't too good right now. Tell Rodger to keep his chin up. How is the wife and my Grand Daughter? Why don't you folks write once in awhile? Now take me, well I can't write. Let me know what is necessary, it takes a little time for me to get things rolling. So long and let me hear soon.

R.D. Sorensen.

I mailed this long letter to my mother and Philip after my meeting with Aunt Mary, to tell them my thoughts and plans, and what I planned to do to help Rodger financially.

March 7, 1949

Dear Folks,

I'm sorry about not writing sooner than this but ever since my talk with Aunt Mary, things have really been hopping. I felt the first thing I should do is drop School to help out and that is what I have done. I had a long talk with my advisors, the head of the Department, and so forth to explain to them a situation had arisen making it impossible for me to continue with further Schooling and requested that I be granted an MS Degree at the end of this Quarter in "General" Civil Engineering. They were all very cooperative and it went through so I will get my Degree in two weeks. That was when I called you last. I figured the next thing was to get a job and that is what kept me from writing. Matter of fact, I still haven't for sure, got one but I have three or four deals cooking and one of them is sure to come through. I've been up to Frisco several times and the week before last I drove down to LA, and last week I was in Bakersfield, so you see I haven't been goofing off all together. Trying to keep caught up on homework on top of all that has just about taken all my time, including my "Janet" time.

I think things are shaping up pretty good though. The job I'm after, and I will know for sure by the time you get this, is the one with the Peter Kiewit Construction Co. as a Field Engineer. It pays $325/mo to start with a $25/mo raise at the end of three months and another $25/mo raise 6 months after that – a total of $375 in nine months. The salary is nice and the work is exactly what I want to do and there is a terrific chance to go places. I'll be on a Canal digging and lining job near Porterville California, which will take about two years to complete. There's 37 Bridges, 6 siphons, 6 outlets and 27 miles of Canal to dig and line in that time – strictly Heavy Construction. So far I've spent better than 4 hours in interviews from the Vice President (Tom Paul) on down to the Superintendent (Keith Wasson) so now they all know me. All I have to do now is wait for my Dear John letter. The other jobs were with the Guy Atkinson Construction Co. ($300/mo to start), Los Angeles County as an Assistant Civil Engineer ($355/mo to start – but I didn't like their assignments), or my old job back with the State Highway Dept. at $310/mo. Janet and I will come down to see you before I start to work. I would like to start working somewhere around April 1st.

Well, now you know what I have been doing. I might as well start with the talk I had with Aunt Mary. I must say, I like the way she talks, straight from the shoulder, and I learned a lot of things I never knew before that tie together and have made me understand you Mom, and Philip too, a lot better. She told me the whole story on Rodger and all that happened and from what she said, I'm not particularly worried about the outcome. I believe Rodger will get off alright. It's after that I'm interested in now. Mary spared no punches at all and I got the whole story on everything she knew about our family. She brought all the old ghosts out of the closet and I am in complete agreement with her now on what she and Philip have been talking about for years, namely Mom, you having that operation now.

I believe Mary is right in what she said about a lot of good will come out of all this in our family. I believe our family really is in there pitching together for the first time and I think we should clear up all the loose ends now and then all work together to pay them off. That means Mom; you're getting that operation now.

My idea is to begin working as soon as I can. I've got all the Schooling I need and want and from now on I am in the best position to help. I know I will never be able to repay you both for your help in putting me through School, I never would have been able to have gone otherwise and I also realize now is the time I can help out the most. As for Janet and I, we are still planning on getting married in June. She plans to teach High School for awhile until all of us get on our feet a little so I think we are pretty well set for now. When Aunt Mary finished her story, I decided the best thing for me to do was lay my cards on the table with Janet and let her know the whole story and what she was getting into. Her reaction was, let's get married now as planned and both of us work and live off her salary and send mine home to the family. I really had to blink on that one to keep the tears from flowing. She is undoubtedly the most wonderful girl in the world and I have never been surer that I was doing the right thing than I am in marrying her. Before now, I have been petrified by the very thought of getting married and then you meet a girl like Janet.

When I first heard about what had happened and Rodger being mixed up in it, I felt like wringing some ones neck for not letting me know sooner but now, I believe it was best I didn't know. I would have come whipping home and would have spent a lot of time getting in the way. I couldn't have been of any help then. I was completely knocked off my feet but I wonder if any of us would have reacted any differently than Rodger under the circumstances. I believe all of us feel partly responsible for the factors leading up to it. I was glad to hear about R.D. entering the picture and I believe he will be the one that will be of the greatest help to Rodger in getting over this thing. I think that is one of the "goods" that have come out of this family "Earthquake", as Mary called it. Some of the others are the drawing of the whole family together. I think Violet and Mom certainly understand each other better now. I know I certainly understand our family better. The thing now is for Mom to get that hysterectomy operation over with and then we all pitch in and get out of debt. I understand Rodger will go up to Idaho with his Dad (R.D.) until he has paid him back. Maybe at the end of that time, I can help the kid out.

Well, I've just about run down and it's getting late. This is my last week of school now, finals come next week and I'll be all through Friday, March 18th. We will probably see you around March 21st. I'll let you know the job situation the minute it breaks. Write soon with all the latest, including the present financial situation.

Love to all, Homer J.

The following letter to my mother and Philip, is the last letter to them from Stanford before going to work for Peter Kiewit Sons Company in Porterfield, California on the Friant-Kern Canal as an engineer trainee.

March 15, 1949

Dear Folks,

I got your letter yesterday and was glad to hear from you. Things don't sound as bad as I was thinking however, the way I figure, you still have payments of $98 to make a month which will be pretty steep until the car loan is paid off. I'll send as much as I can until June when Janet and I get married. I think I can pay you back about $500 on what I owe you before then which will pretty well take care of that loan. Janet and I will still have enough to start out on and with her working too, we will be setting on top of the world.

The job I was hoping for finally came through and I will be attached to the Porterville organization. My address until further notice will be just General Delivery, Porterville, California. It's the Canal lining job I told you about and I report for work as a Field Engineer on March 28th. I think I told you the pay range on that job was $325/mo to start and in three months a $25/mo raise and six months after that, another $25/mo raise, so you see, I'm pretty well set now. I talked to the last man I had to see (that makes five people I've seen now and over four hours of interviews) yesterday, a Mr. Browne and he said that since I was on sort of a training setup I could expect to move around quite a bit for the first year or so. They have the Garrison Dam in North Dakota and big jobs in Denver, Seattle, and Alaska as well as the Hollywood Freeway in LA. I could be assigned to all of them before my "Course" is finished. What they want to do is give all us "trainees" the maximum amount of experience and an overall picture of "Heavy Construction."

So far, I've been the only one hired although about six or eight have tried to get on with them from Stanford. I think what did it for me was my Boss last summer, John Cowgill, and Kiewit's Chief Engineer knew each other well and Johnny gave me a recommendation. Its politics I know, but it's nice when it works in your favor. My Teachers at Stanford and Pomona have also given me some nice little boosts.

Our trip schedule beginning next Saturday will go something like this.

1. Saturday – Stop at Porterville to show Janet the Kiewit job, check housing, see the Supt. of Schools about a teaching job for Janet, drive down to Mrs. Wiggs for dinner.

2. *Sunday – Drive to Las Vegas to see the folks there.*

3. *Tuesday – Leave early for Monroe*

4. *Thursday – Drive to Logan, Utah, Janet talks to one of her Bridesmaids.*

5. *Friday – Start driving back to San Francisco, and arrive Saturday.*

6. *Sunday – Drive to Porterville, to start work Monday, March 28, 1949.*

I think my "Final" grades have all held up pretty well considering. So far I have a B- in Sewer Design, a B+ in Hydraulics and Dams, and a B in Soil Mechanics with only two more finals to go on Friday. I think it will be clear sailing from here on. The head of the Department saw the first two grades and reviewed my past record and said he would stick his neck out and say I'd make it OK, So he signed my application to take the Professional Engineers Examination to get my license. I'll take the fist half of that exam on May 30th.

Well, it's about chow time and I thought this afternoon I would drive up to see Aunt Mary. She offered to let me board and room there if that job in South San Francisco came through with Atkinson but it didn't because their not hiring until June. I thought I would go up and tell her and say goodbye. We'll see you sometime Sunday evening.

Love to all, Homer J.

It's always been interesting to me how mothers of their youngest sons react to the women their sons marry. Grandma Olsen took an immediate dislike to my mother for stealing my dad, her youngest son, away from her. Grandma Brim had the same dislike for my mother for marrying her youngest son, Philip, and my mother took an immediate dislike to Violet when she married her baby son, Rodger and stole him away from her. When I introduced Janet to my mother as my future bride, I felt some of the same coldness developing between them and I think the following *thank you* letter from Janet to my mother after their first *get acquainted* visit, reflects that coldness.

The following letter from my future bride, Janet E. Whitehead, is to my mother, Mrs. Philip Brim at 223 N. Bruce Street, Las Vegas, Nevada.

Sunday, March 27 1949

Dear Mrs. Brim, (instead of Dear Ruth)

Home at last! We began to wonder last night if we would ever make it home. That last long stretch from Salt Lake City to San Francisco was rough. Ole came over for break fast this morning and left around noon for Porterville. It was such a beautiful day, sun shining and everything looking so green, he really hated to go. Except he was getting kind of bored having nothing to do and was anxious to get started working. I am going to miss him this Quarter.

We spent two nights in Monroe and then took Marilyn and Dale up to Logan. Ole stayed with them and I stayed with my girl friend and then we came on back here. We came into Palo Alto around midnight. I really had a wonderful time. He explained all about the Country and the rock formations and the early pioneers, etc. everywhere we went so I had quite an educational experience too.

Thank all of you so much for making our stay with you so enjoyable. I am very glad I got to meet you folks. I hope some of you can come to our wedding, but if not, that I will see you again.

Sincerely, Janet Whitehead

The following letter is from Mrs. Wiggs, Frank's mother (she was also my room and board land lady during the summer of 1948 while Frank and I were working for the California Highway Department) to Janet in Palo Alto.

March 29, 1949

Dear Janet,

You could never guess what I found on my chair in the front room when I went there after you and Ole left last Sunday. What a wonderful surprise. I know you will never know what it was so I will let you in on it – a wonderful box of salted nuts and all the most delicious assortments. Oh boy, cashews, filberts, almonds etc. If by any chance you know how they got there, be sure to give them my thanks. They are delicious and I certainly enjoyed them.

I was so glad you and Jr. stopped over here. I'd heard so many nice things about "Janet" from all the gang that had been in here. You know I am crazy about Ole, he seems like another son to me of whom I am very fond. I think you are two lucky people and I wish you both all the success in the world.

Thank you again for the delicious gift. I'll be looking for you both down here some weekend soon after June 25th. You know the room is always there ready for you.

Lovingly Helen Wiggs.

The GI Bill was without a doubt, the most cost effective welfare program the federal government has ever envisioned, when return on investment is taken into account. For reasons I'll never understand, only three million of the sixteen million men and women in uniform during World War II, bothered to take advantage of this wonderful gift opportunity from our grateful country, to better their lot in life. If it had not been for the GI Bill, I would never have been able to afford and/or obtain a college education, and it was the GI Bill that made it possible for me to be the first in my family on either side, to ever graduate from a college. I will always have guilt feelings over not doing enough during the war for my country to have earned it, but I will always be grateful to this wonderful country of ours for the opportunity I was given. Otherwise, I would have traveled down the same bare subsistence poverty cycle highway of life my parents, and my grandparents were forced to travel, for the remainder of my life. The only way someone trapped in a poverty cycle will ever have to escape the hog mire their trapped in, is to acquire a

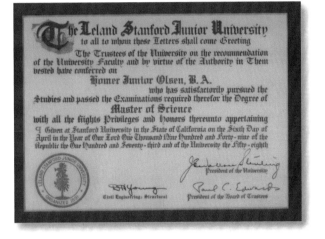

meaningful education that will lead to a meaningful job. A meaningful education will open up multiple employment opportunities in better paying job positions with opportunities for advancement, thereby improving their lot in life. A meaningful education, coupled with relevant apprenticeship training in an excellent company, will open up entrepreneurial opportunities to startup their own businesses, thus increasing their chances even more for a better standard of living.

"To furnish the means of acquiring knowledge is the greatest benefit that can be conferred upon mankind. It prolongs life itself and enlarges the sphere of existence." **John Quincy Adams**

Lesson Learned: *Give a man a fish and he will be at your door step everyday asking for another fish. **Teach** a man to fish and he will soon become independently wealthy."* (Author unknown)

The Leland Stanford Junior University mailed my Master of Science Degree in Civil Engineering with a Structural Engineering option to me on April 6, 1949 while I was working for the Peter Kiewit Sons Company as a $75 a week engineer trainee on the Friant-Kern Canal near Porterville, California. The next day, April 7, 1949, I celebrated my 25th birthday of reaching the goal I had worked so hard for, by working overtime on my new job. My Stanford Engineering Degree was the ultimate birthday gift.

THE KIEWIT YEARS

On March 28, 1949, I reported to Keith Wasson, the project manager on the Friant Kern Canal Project in Porterville, California, for my first day of work with the Peter Kiewit Sons Company. Keith was one of the four people who interviewed me earlier and had told Tom

Paul, Kiewit's vice president, he felt the company should take a gamble and hire me. When I arrived, he welcomed me aboard and introduced me to everyone in the office, including my first boss, Jimmy Garver, who was the excavation superintendent. Mr. Garver then gave me a tour of their newly awarded twenty-seven mile canal contract that was currently being organized to begin construction. He told me my first assignment as an engineer trainee would be working as a *grade checker* on the swing shift downstream of the cat and can and dragline operations, with a three-man structure excavation crew.

Monigan Dragline with it's 5 cubic yard bucket – 1949

After we had driven to my assigned location, Mr. Garver (who asked me to call him Jimmy Garver) introduced me to the two other crew members. One was the dragline operator named Jack Graves, and the other nicknamed, *Honeysuckle* Rose (because of his last name) who would be the oiler on our 38B Bucyrus Erie dragline the company had recently purchased. The swing shift *union foreman* I was to replace with my new title of *grade checker* was a guy they called *Wig* (because of his toupee), was being transferred to the upstream cat and can spread. Jimmy Garver made it a point to caution, me again *never go outside the right-of-way lines* shown on our drawings, and to report for swing shift duty at 3:00 pm the next afternoon. He then handed me a hand level to use on my job and said, "To finish your first day our project engineer, Major Lowe, has an engineering problem for you to take care of at his office."

When I reported to Walden "Major" Lowe (he was called Major because of his rank in the combat engineers during WW II), he handed me a set of plans for the concrete batch plant they were about to erect, and said, "I want you to design the concrete footings for this plant, and don't worry about the cost because we can't afford any differential

settlement problems during any of the concrete pouring or canal paving operations." I calculated and sketched what I thought was a *hell for stout* reinforced concrete footing design and after Major Lowe reviewed my calculations and my design drawing, he smiled and said, "It looks good to me Homer. We'll construct the footings exactly the way you've shown here on your drawing."

Cat and Can Spread on the Friant-Kern Canal- 1949

Thinking back now, I believe the most noteworthy thing I remember about the Kiewit Company after my first day was how impressed I was with their dedication and commitment to get the job built safely, on schedule and under budget. I also noticed during the following week, everyone on salary reported for work at 7:00 in the morning and didn't leave their job for home until after 7:00 at night. Saturdays were always set aside for superintendent's job planning, safety and schedule meetings, and as *a catch-up* day for cost reports and any construction engineering necessary. It was obvious to me, the Kiewit Company knew what they were doing and they were the kind of company I would enjoy working for.

When I reported with my two-man crew for work at 3:00 pm the next afternoon, I thought it was odd *Wig* had only completed half the work he told me the day before he

normally accomplished a shift, but I never thought more about it until he left saying, "Don't ever leave the canal right-of-way with equipment for any reason, if you value your employment", that I smelled a rat. The next structure excavation site was just on the other side of a *flooded pasture* the farmer there had over watered to

Concrete Batch Plant on the Friant – Kern Canal – 1949

continue grazing his cattle free a while longer before the canal was excavated, but instead I thought, "Oooh Boy, the company must want to test me and my crew."

We completed *Old Wig's* partially finished job two hours later and I asked Jack Graves what he thought about crossing the flooded pasture and after we walked around it he said, "We just might luck out, *if it's not too soaked.*" Well, as it turned out, it was *too soaked,* and our 38B dragline got stuck in mud half way across the pasture. Luckily, Jack was an experienced operator and was able to fill his dragline bucket with mud, swing the bucket around 180 degrees behind the rig, and little by little with a flat boom, *duck walk* our dragline out of the flooded muddy pasture and back on to the dry county road to think some more about it. When the crew asked me, "Now what do we do?" I said, "Well, it looks to me like we're caught between a rock and a hard place, so the way I see it, we're going to be fired for not doing our job by just sitting here, and if we leave our rightaway to get around that flooded pasture to try doing our job, we'll also be fired, so I think we should vote on it." Believe it or not, the vote was unanimous we get fired trying to do our jobs rather than just sitting around worrying about it and get fired anyway. After all, by trying to do our job who knows, we just might luck out and be able to move our rig to dry ground on the other side of that pasture pond without any problems.

38B Bucyrus Erie Drag Line with a one (1) cy bucket – 1949

It was almost sundown by the time I walked over to the farm house to discuss our mutual problem with the farmer that flooded our pasture. He was very cooperative and a little embarrassed about flooding our pasture, so he agreed to let us walk our dragline *off the rightaway*, down his barnyard driveway and cross his water filled irrigation ditch behind his barn somewhere. Unfortunately, he rejected my idea of digging a *detour* ditch around our dragline on the other side of his barn to simplify the crossover, but did agree we could dig ramps in and out of his ditch to maybe have a better chance of plowing across his full irrigation ditch to our dry work site. The ticklish part was crossing his full irrigation ditch in the dark and how *soaked up* his ditch banks might be.

Keith Wasson, Project Manager, 1949

As it turned out, his plan worked OK right up to the crossover phase, and of all things to happen, the *over soaked* ditch bank suddenly caved away as we turned to crossover and our dragline slid into the flooded ditch nearly tipping over. The farmer shouted it was *OK* to use his cedar fence posts stockpiled near his barn, so Honeysuckle and I raced back and forth putting his fence posts under the tracks while Jack struggled to keep the rig from tipping over. I remember we were all soaking wet shoveling like mad in that cold water filled ditch placing fence posts, when we suddenly heard a loud "Harrumph" from the opposite bank. Oooh boy, when we looked up and saw it was Keith Wasson, the project manager himself silhouetted in the moonlight, I'll kid you not, all three of us froze to attention to wait for his, "All three of you *dumb bastards* are fired." Instead, believe it or not, everything was deathly quiet until finally to our complete surprise Keith calmly said, "I see you boys have a problem here."

Well, before we could answer Jimmy Garver drove up just about then and Keith told me to go back with Jimmy to the shop to get the lowboy and bring back a D8 Cat from the job's north end to pull the 38B out of the ditch. Well wouldn't you know it, Jimmy Garver said he knew a really good *short cut* to the shop to save time and we soon found out his idea of a short cut was fjording an already swollen Tule River. You guessed it, that idea turned out to be another stupid mistake when his truck engine quit in the waist deep water smack dab in the middle of the river. By now, its eleven o'clock at night and my crew and I hadn't eaten since noon so I was not only hungry, soaking wet and freezing cold, but knew this would be my last day working for Kiewit. I remember thinking, "What in hell's name am I doing here like this sitting in the middle of this damn river with my feet up on the dashboard, when I'm going to get fired anyway?" To me that lousy river crossing idea of Jimmy's was the last straw, but he suddenly interrupted with, "Tell you what, I'll stay with the pickup while you wade on across the river and hitch hike the two miles back to the shop to bring a flatbed back with some cable to pull me out", which is what I did for the next two hours.

When we finally got to the shop, Jimmy elected to stay there tinkering with his pickup motor while Bob Powers, the graveyard shop mechanic and I drove the low boy up to the dirt spread to pick up the D8. The other mechanics were refueling and doing graveyard shift maintenance work at the time, so they helped us load up and Bob and I headed south with the tractor to *Homer's Screw up site*. Everyone had left for home earlier except my two man loyal crew waiting to help get the 38B back onto high ground. So to summarize this whole embarrassing mess I got everyone into, everything finally returned to normal again just as the morning sun rose over the hillside. Our 38B dragline was now sitting at its next excavation site on high dry ground ready to work again, the farmer's water filled ditch had been repaired and realigned with new ditch banks, and as Bob Powers pulled away waving *so long* with his Low Boy loaded with the D8, my crew and I shook hands all around with, "Hey, it was nice working with you guys, while it lasted." The three of us staggered home absolutely exhausted from our exciting sixteen hour shift and I took a hot shower, fixed myself some breakfast and after sleeping a few hours, drove my car down to the job's trailer office to pick up my first and last two day payoff check.

Unbelievably, as I walked up to the office trailer door, I heard several people inside howling with laughter while Keith Wasson was telling the whole embarrassing (now famous), *Homer's Screw-up* story. I heard him say, "You should have seen the trouble that kid got himself into last night, it was unbelievable." Reluctantly, I walked in and to my amazement, all the superintendents on the job came over to shake my hand and pat me on the back. Wow, Keith was right, it really was unbelievable. Ward White, the structures superintendent told me, "Son, when you finish what Garver's got for you to do; I want you to come to work for me." I said, "I don't know why you would want me to work for you when I'm now the #1 screw up around here." He said, "A successful construction company is made up of *can-*

do type people, and anyone who thinks *getting the job done* is more important than sitting around sucking his thumb just worrying about it, is my kind of a guy."

The remainder of my assignment with Jimmy Garver's dirt spread was without incident except for the time Peter Kiewit himself arrived for a job tour and dropped by our small *dirt spread* located ten miles down stream of the main earth moving operations, to inspect our work. I remember my dad telling me, "Whenever someone asks you a question you don't know the answer to, never be afraid to say, *you don't know, but you will find out.*" Well, when the PKS company car stopped next to our 38B dragline during our brown bag lunch at sundown, and Peter Kiewit himself got out with Tom Paul, the Los Angeles district manager and Vice President, Keith Wasson, our project manager, and two of our job superintendents, Jimmy Garver and Ward White, I'll tell you, we literally froze like three wide eyed frogs gasping for breath during a

Frank Wiggs, Ann Hazelton, and a 5 cy bucket

panic attack. All three of us were still suffering from *Sargentitis flashbacks* from our Army days anyway, so we automatically snapped to attention when they stepped out of their car. I still remember Pete and his group walking in Army style lock step to where we were stiffly standing at attention, and believe it or not, the very first question Pete asked me, I didn't know the answer. For some unknown reason my mind had gone completely blank, so I automatically said what my dad told me to say in a situation like this, and said, "I don't know sir, but I'll find out." The question Peter Kiewit asked me was, "What's your name, son?"

The following letter is from my old boss, John Cowgill, who was the State of California's resident engineer on the highway widening job in Loma Linda where I worked the previous summer. John's letter, offering me an opportunity to work for him in his new assignment as head of the Department of Advanced Planning in District VIII, San Bernardino, California, was very encouraging and interesting at the time. Needless to say, I seriously considered taking him up on his kind offer after my disastrous two day beginning with the Kiewit Company.

April 11, 1949

Dear Homer,

What happened to that trip down here "the last of March"? You sure passed us up. Since we didn't get to see you in person, I want to supplement my previous letter with a little added "info."

I have been given a new assignment heading a new Department within the District. The responsibility of our new Department is Advanced Planning. As you might surmise the purpose is to formulate an orderly and coordinated program of Highway improvement. Our principal concern will be with Freeways and urban routes. We will study, analyze and compare costs of alternate routings and designs to the end that a general alignment and design may be selected and agreements made with local planning commissions etc. well in advance of the detailed design stage.

If you care to broaden your experience in Highway Engineering by taking a tour of duty in this work, there is a job for you. It is my understanding that you are now on the eligible list for permanent appointment. Right? Please drop me a line to let me know if you are receptive.

Kindest Regards, John Cowgill

When I reported for duty at the Structure Concrete Division's warehouse office; Ward White congratulated me and my crew for lowering the structure excavation and fine grading costs to half what they were when we took over. He asked me how we did it and I told him Jack Graves, our *master* operating engineer, deserved ninety percent of the credit and Honeysuckle and I would split the rest. Jack Graves was truly an artist with a dragline bucket and he could carve out a beautiful safely sloped open cut excavation site within a tenth of a foot (one inch) tolerance with his dragline bucket. Old Honeysuckle Rose and I would then smooth out the buckets teeth marks with our *Mexican Dragline* hand shovels and the site would be ready for carpenters and ironworkers. We also increased our production from two to three excavation sites per shift by constantly checking and re-checking for errors and being more efficient during moves etc. to save time. I didn't mention to Ward I had discovered my $75 a week salary as an engineer trainee *grade checker* was exactly one half of what an operating engineer *union foreman*, like "Wig", made doing the same job so I'm sure my lower wages also contributed somewhat to our lower unit costs.

Ward White, Str. Supt. - 1949

Ward transferred Jack Graves and Honeysuckle Rose from the company's 38B dragline to a brand new 25 ton Lorain motor crane in the Structures Division and told me that his *on loan* engineer, Fergie Mitchell, would be returning to his regular estimating job in the Arcadia office the following morning and I would be his full time *Structures engineer* from then on, and gave me a cooks tour of their facilities. I thought it was interesting when he introduced me to his crew because everyone I met that day would smile and say exactly the same thing, "I've heard a lot about you", and then turn their heads to keep from laughing. It became painfully obvious, my reputation as a *world class screw-up* had spread like wildfire throughout the company after that flooded pasture fiasco, and then when my memory lapse episode with Peter Kiewit was added in it put me in the Guinness Hall of records. Maybe I should write a book someday called, "*How* **Not** *to make a Lasting Impression on your Boss.*" I'll bet if television were available in those days, I would have been asked to appear on some Today Show somewhere for everyone to ridicule my stupidity and I would have gained enough name recognition to maybe go into politics and become another Damn Dumb Democrat Senator or congressman, or maybe even sell my rights for a movie and be rich. Wow, maybe Buster Keaton or Charlie Chaplin might be interested in playing *me* in the movie. Oooh boy.

The following letter is from my 14 year old little sister Freddie, (Winifred) thanking me for her birthday gift and to bring me up to date on the latest family news. Apparently she still wasn't aware I had left Stanford and gone to work for Kiewit to help my brother Rodger out with his legal expenses.

May 6, 1949

Dear Homer J. and Janet,

I don't write often because Mother does most of the writing, but I do want to thank you for the nice present. One thing you always do to please a person is to send them money and let them buy what they want. You really shouldn't do things like that because you're going to School. I have such a wonderful Brother, and to be his Sister, and that I am the luckiest person in the world to have you.

The "Girls Day" we have at our School was wonderful. I was in a Dance with some others. It was a Ballet dance and we had dresses that were full and long to dance in. The theme was "A Girl can Dream." I had to play "Flight of the Bumblebee" afterwards on the piano during the Tea.

Steven crawls all over now really well. He pulls on all the lamp chords and scares us half to death. Mothers making him some blue corduroy pants like his yellow ones with little blue dogs on the knees and the pocket, and it won't be so hard on his knees when he crawls around. We had "Sevier Day" over in Richfield last Wednesday. That's when all of Sevier County gets together and has Soft Ball Tournaments. I wasn't on the team of the Eighth Grade, but we played Richfield and lost by one point. That's about all the news for now.

With Love, Winifred

Ward White told me when I started working for him that he liked to work people *mad* because their blood would pump faster when they were mad and they would do at least two days work for him instead of one days work. He said, "Mark my wards, thirty days from now I'll have you so mad at me, you will want to whip me." I said, "Ward, the last time I got mad I got whipped, so I don't get mad anymore" and he said, "You'll see" and walked away.

Canal Lining Machine for the Friant-Kern Canal - 1949

Well, I had always thought before now that my top sergeant at Fort Monmouth was tough, but Ward White made him look like a sissy. Ward worked my tail off 16 hours a day, six days a week for nearly a month and, *try as I might*, I couldn't do anything right to please him. Finally, one night around eleven o'clock while we were working late on a Delta Mendota Canal bid, I couldn't take it any longer and came completely nglued and slammed my fist down on my drawings with, "God Damn it Ward, I've had it clear up to my eyebrows with you and this damn job and I'm going to quit, but before I do I'm going to get a piece of you to take with me." He looked at me with a smirk on his face and said, "OK, if that's what you want, let's go out in the saw yard and see what you can do." At that time, I was 6"1" tall and weighed 185 pounds, so for a hair lip I thought I was still in pretty fair physical condition, but Ward White was a raw boned 6"3" giant made up of 225 pounds of solid muscle. When I led him outside into that dimly lit saw yard and just as I said, "This looks like a good spot to have at it", he grabbed me from behind before I could turn around, pinned my arms to my sides, and lifting me off the ground while laughing hysterically, shouting, "See, see, see, I told you I could make you mad enough to try to whip me", and wouldn't let me down until I promised to *talk it out* with him. Finally I told him I would stay on, but only if he would treat me like a human being from now on rather than some damn slave, and he agreed. From that day on until I was transferred to the Colorado job a year later, it was a night and day change and he not only began treating me with respect, but like I was his right hand man. Interestingly, I found out later he thought I was *too nice a guy* when I signed on, so he wanted to find out if I had any *Spunk*. For crap sakes, he should have known all Norwegians have *Spunk* when they finally get it through their thick skulls they are being treated like a dog.

Janet and I were married in the Green Lake Congregational Church in Seattle, Washington on June 25, 1949. I had requested a week off at the end of June when I started working for the Kiewit Company in March, with the idea they would charge it to my future vacation time, but was amazed to learn when we returned from our short honeymoon, I didn't receive a paycheck for that week because my three and a half months employment so far didn't qualify me for partial vacation time. As a result I had to borrow $60 for our first month's rent from Frank Wiggs since everything else I made had already been mailed home to my mother to pay off my loans and help Rodger, or squandered away on our honeymoon. Janet still owed $500 on her student loan at Stanford and I had borrowed $300 to buy her an engagement ring that she immediately lost or was stolen. Fortunately for both of us, Janet was hired by the Porterville School District to teach high school English for a whopping $3,200 for a nine month year short day job beginning in September, and that combined with my $325 per month ($3,900 for a twelve month year six day plus two hour overtime job), we figured we were in hog heaven and would be out of debt by our birthdays the following year. One thing for sure, Janet and I might have started our

The wedding party of Janet Whitehead & Homer Olsen's Wedding, 1949

married life with a negative net worth, but we both had college degrees now and good jobs, so our futures looked very bright and we had unlimited opportunity to improve our lot in life.

Up until that time, the Peter Kiewit Sons Company was primarily a dirt moving outfit and I don't think Pete was ever interested in having a structure concrete division within the company. Ward White apparently talked Pete into letting the company do all the

Two 34E Paving Mixers feeding the hopper of the Friant-Kern Canal Liner – 1949

structure concrete work on the Porterville job, including the reinforcing steel, instead of subcontracting it all out, because he knew from his own structures contracting experience, there was money to be made. From what I heard, Pete told Ward he would go along with him this time, but his future with the company would be based on how well the structure work came out when the job was completed, bottom line profit wise.

Ward accepted Pete's challenge and I'm glad he did because the structure concrete work on that job was not only finished ahead of schedule, but increased its job profit by a whopping

35% over what was originally estimated. I profited by learning everything I know about job planning and scheduling, cost keeping and estimating, concrete form and falsework design, labor productivity and safety, and managing a construction company like a business. Peter Kiewit was so pleased with the Structures Division's bottom line, he decided the company should stay in the structure concrete business after that job was completed. He was also impressed with all the improvements in the overall job's schedule management and the cost savings that resulted from less subcontracting interference problems on fast track work. The improved teamwork and better job coordination resulting from better job control lowered the labor costs on all job operations. All in all, it was a well run job by the project manager, Keith Wasson, but Ward White and his organization had a major part in making it the successful job it turned out to be. I was and still am, proud to have played a part in its success as one of the best Kiewit jobs.

NEWS RELEASES DURING 1949

General Motors, Standard Oil of California, Firestone Tire and other Companies are convicted of criminal conspiracy to replace electric transit lines with gasoline and diesel buses; NATO is established; Minimum wage is set at $0.75 per hour; and Tokyo Rose goes to trial.

Ward White may not have gone beyond the sixth grade in a public school, but he was a cum laude graduate of the great depressions school of hard knocks. To me he was one of the smartest men from a practical, common sense optimistic "get the job done, the sooner the better" point of view that I have ever known. He was too young for WW I and too old for WW II so he missed both wars, but he worked in Alaska building barracks for the Army as a contractor's job superintendent and bragged he never had any labor problems because he was also the Carpenter Unions business agent as well. He told me that in the early thirties, he made a living driving a bullet proof car from Canada south through Montana, Wyoming and Colorado to Oklahoma, delivering bootleg whisky. During the great depression, he also *rode the rods* on freight

A finished stretch of Concrete Paving on the Friant-Kern Canal

trains looking for work around the western states and ended up building snow fence in Wyoming with Roosevelt's WPA. He founded his own construction company partnership in Oregon after the war called, Lockyear and White, building bridges until this golden opportunity came along with Peter Kiewit. I was honored to be chosen as his first full time structures engineer to help him realize his dream of setting up the first Structure Concrete Division in the Kiewit Company.

Our canal Structures Division always held their foremen schedule and safety meetings on Tuesday evenings after work and one of my jobs was to prepare the foremen work schedules for the coming week. Our blackboard schedule had separate columns that I chalked each foreman's worksite location, and their anticipated pour quantities and dates each week. At the beginning of the meeting, I would read the unit costs each craft foreman had made the previous week and compared them with the estimated costs they were expected to meet. Ward White would then review each crews schedule with each of the foreman and resolve any questions regarding their unit costs and/or problems they might have in meeting the re-bar installation and pouring schedules. All that resulted in a reinforcing steel and concrete quantity and pouring date, time, and location, for the re-bar and concrete foremen to do their jobs. It took nearly split second timing to meet the

The Tule River Spillway in its infancy with my 1941 Ford Pickup

schedules we came up with because all the various crew sites were scattered along a *sliding* five mile working front and teamwork from everyone was absolutely necessary for success. Amazingly, once a foreman committed to meeting his crews weekly schedule, you could set your watch by it and believe it or not, every foreman met their individual work schedules because they knew exactly what was expected of them for the week ahead, when they left our Tuesday evening schedule meetings.

I remember thinking at the time; Ward would have been an excellent athletic coach because when I played high school basketball, I used to think Coach Miles really gave inspirational pep talks at half time when we were behind, but Ward had him beat. After all the questions regarding next week's schedule had been resolved, Ward would launch into one of his inspirational fire and brimstone speeches, and it was fascinating to watch the expressions on the faces of the foremen when he spoke. Every man in that room seemed mesmerized by his talk and when he finished; they leapt to their feet like an inspired football team raring to go out there and win. He might have been a character, but I'll tell you, he was an amazing character.

Time was always of the essence on the structure concrete portion of the Friant-Kern Canal job because staying out in front and never delaying either the dirt and/or concrete canal lining spreads in any way, was imperative to keep things running smoothly. Our structure work soon became scattered over a ten mile sliding front working area with our crews constructing various structures in various stages along the twenty seven mile project. Ward came up with a brilliant forming idea for the larger crawl through box culverts and

263

siphons running under the canal so they could be poured *monolithically*. How? by simply *hanging* the interior side and lid forms in one piece from double steel channels across the top. That idea alone saved us two weeks in move in and out, pouring, sandblasting, and curing time at each location. We even purchased 52 five ton flat bed farm wagons to move materials more efficiently and to save on trucking and material handling costs. I asked Ward one time how he ever came up with 52 as the exact number of 5 ton trailers we needed and he said, "Easy, there are 52 weeks in a year."

Anyway, by using all 52 of the farm trailers he purchased, we were able to park them loaded with the exact number of concrete form panels and reinforcing steel needed at the various structure sites, a day before the crews arrived to install them. When the forms were stripped and re-oiled after the concrete was poured and *spray cured*, they were re-loaded directly onto the trailers again for movement to the next site needed.

A Double Barreled Culvert Formed to Pour Monolithically

My job assignment was to make sure the exact amount of materials and small tools needed at each of the sites was delivered on the flatbed trailers *before* the construction crews arrived. I remember the truck driver assigned to me looked like the railroad civil engineer, *Casey Jones tooting* his *truck locomotive* along while towing a *train line* of loaded 5 ton flatbed trailers down the Canals *dirt railroad track*. As he *tooted* to different structure locations he would simply drop off the marked trailers loaded with the exact amount of materials etc. needed for that particular structure, then *toot* on down to the next location until his *train trailers* were all delivered.

Oooh boy, I still vividly remember the time I screwed up (accidentally of course) on the exact number of snap ties needed at one structure site, and when that crew's concrete pour was delayed

The 25 ton Lorain crane making a Bridge Deck Pour on Friant-Kern Canal

somewhat because of my mistake, Ward literally came unglued. He angrily stomped up to me in front of that crew and stood on my toes, nose to nose and belly to belly, so I couldn't back up and angrily thump his knuckles onto my chest while fogging up my glasses shouting at the top of his voice, *"Damn you Homer, I've learned you, I've learned you, I've learned you all I know, and you still don't know nothin'."*

It was during this same period my half brother Rodger's self defense trial in Las Vegas came to an end with a second degree murder verdict, but because of his distinguished service during the war against the Japanese in the south pacific he was only given a three year sentence in the Penitentiary at Carson City, Nevada. I have only shadowy recollections of his trial and what really happened between him and my uncle Jess Weimer that led up to his self defense trial because all the newspaper articles, correspondence, and other records of Rodger's trial during that time were destroyed by my mother. All I remember is the legal fees totaled over $15,000 and it wiped all of us out financially.

Philip began working on two exhausting jobs, one day and one swing shift, sixteen hours a day to earn additional money for Rodger's defense fund and my mother put in long hours on her waitress job to donate every dime she made in salary and tips for Rodger's fund. With Janet's teaching job to live on, I was able to pay off my college and engagement ring loan to my mother with interest, and was still able to help Rodger with his legal defense fund. The extra bedroom in their Las Vegas home was even rented to a room and boarder for even more extra money and Rodger's real dad, R. D. Sorensen, sold off part of his cattle in Idaho to contribute to Rodger's defense fund, with the stipulation that Rodger would personally pay him back with his own hard earned money (not his mothers, Philips or mine) after he was released from prison. Barring a catastrophe, it looked like we could pay all Rodger's legal expenses off in eighteen months, if we all continued working together as a team. To this day I think Rodger's Attorney did an excellent job defending him and I think Rodger was fortunate to get off with such a light sentence. As it turned out, he was paroled one year later on good behavior, but my Nevada family was never the same again.

C. F. Smith, husband # 8

A terrible catastrophe unfortunately did occur a few months later. Philip Brim was killed in a single car accident late one night while driving home from his second shift job. Apparently he had fallen asleep from lack of sleep and exhaustion and had driven off the highways into a concrete bridge abutment. Philip Brim was a kind, generous, compassionate hard working wonderful man who devoted his whole life to supporting my mother and raising Rodger as if he were his own son. Interestingly, Philip Brim's accident insurance policy coincidentally totaled the exact amount needed to finish paying off the remainder of Rodger's legal obligations when he died and to this day, and I'm sorry to even think this, but knowing the kind of a man he was I still wonder if his untimely death really was an accident. All I know is he was a good man and he didn't deserve to die like he did, or be treated the way he was by my mother during their unhappy marriage.

My mother married a fry cook named Charlie Smith shortly after Philip's funeral. I was told she met this man at one of the restaurants where she worked as a waitress, so that made

C.A. Smith, her husband number "eight." When Rodger was released from prison for good behavior in 1950, he immediately moved back to Winston-Salem, North Carolina where Violet, his wife was from, and as far as I know Rodger never made any effort to repay any of his Nevada family, or even thank them for what they had done, including his promise to R. D. Sorensen, his real father, to pay him back personally. My mother began acting very coldly

Mother, myself & Janet – 1950

towards me after that long letter I wrote to her and Philip after my Aunt Mary meeting, and especially after I sided with Philip and Aunt Mary and lit into her over the way she treated Philip. When I drove to Las Vegas in March of 1949 to introduce my future bride, Janet Whitehead to her, she refused to attend our wedding and from then on she literally cut both of us out of her life. That is, until she suddenly gave Janet and I a surprise visit in the late summer of 1950 in Fort Collins, Colorado, to *mend fences* (her words) on her way back to Las Vegas from North Carolina. That visit occurred just shortly after her con-artist *eighth* husband, C. A. Smith, absconded with all her worldly goods and disappeared while they were visiting Rodger and Violet in North Carolina. As far as I know, no one has never seen nor heard hide nor hair of him since.

The following letter was from Rodger to my mother (now Mrs. C.A. Smith, 223 N Bruce Street, Las Vegas, Nevada) and was written while he was living at 795 Chatham Road, Winston-Salem, North Carolina. He had moved there four months earlier to live near his in-laws after his release from prison.

May 6, 1950

Dear Mom,

Well here I am again. I guess you were thinking I got lost someplace. I have been on a spree spending money yesterday. We went to Sears and got our drapes and curtains, Joy some socks and panties and I got some shoes. (this pen writes bad because I dropped it in some paint). It's not the Parker 51 you gave me, it's a cheap one of Vi's.

Claypool got stuck for money here yesterday so I drew out $100 and paid off my bill there so now I own all my furniture. When my other checks come in I'll be able to pay off the car and still put $200 away then I will be out of debt and still be able to save $100 a month. I thought I'd just keep putting it in the Bank and forgetting about it for awhile. That way I won't owe anyone anything (here at least) and really get on my feet.

I sure was surprised to get that call and it was good to hear from you again. When you get things straightened out, come on out here only plan on staying awhile this time. We have more room now so you can stay here. I told you we were going to have a new Garage to work in didn't I, over the phone? Jim is going to have to move so he is just going to put up his own place. If he gets this peace of land we won't have far to move. Just behind King's stack house, the place you had coffee while you were waiting for me.

The weather has sure turned warm now. It's not too hot but it sure is sticky. When you get here we will take a ride out and see some pretty views. Things are sure pretty here now. I still haven't received the boxes yet but I don't really look for them until next week.

I was surprised to see that clipping about C. H. (Charley Hestler). I guess he will draw one to two on that one. If he does, he'll have to do one and a half in all. On that, you do it all. I'm sure glad I'm away from Vegas. I'm happier and I've gotten further ahead in the six months I've been here than I ever would have in Vegas. This makes me think, I haven't had a drink now in a year and a half. Not bad is it?

Well, I guess I've run down for now but will be waiting for your next long letter. Keep me posted on how C. H. comes out and all the news around there. P.S. Tell Charlie and Rita "hello" for us.

You're loving Son, Rodger.

Apparently Charlie Hestler, my mother's *sixth* husband, came back to Las Vegas to work again as a dealer and was caught stealing from the club he worked for, which is the worst crime possible in the state of Nevada. Since he had tried to shoot my mother earlier with a hand gun, the prosecutor subpoenaed her to testify against him. I never found out where the checks Rodger mentioned were coming from, but I assume they are from the "52-20 Club" ($20 a week in unemployment for 52 weeks from the Government while veterans look for work) while he was supposed to be looking for a job. Either that or my mother was still supporting him in some other unknown way.

It was after my mother was resettled in Las Vegas and working again as a waitress, she met her *"ninth"* husband, John Galloway. He was an older retired painting contractor and a widower who was suffering from tuberculosis and was a steady customer at the restaurant my mother worked. Apparently he took a liking to her and told my mother he would give her his home in Las Vegas, free and clear, if she would be his live in caretaker, and take care of him until he died and everything else he said he had would go to his grown children. Since my mother was still reeling from the Charlie Smith disaster and getting older herself, she gave serious thought to his offer and finally agreed if he would put everything in writing.

John Galloway did put his offer in writing, and they were married shortly afterwards. My mother sold her home on 223 N. Bruce Street in Las Vegas, to pay off her replacement car and clothes, (and to help Rodger) and moved into the caretaker's quarters of John Galloway's home as Mrs. John Galloway. She took really good care of that fine old gentleman as she had promised until he passed away a few years later. True to his word, she got the home free and clear, and as far as I know, John Galloway was the only one of all her nine husbands that ever left her anything after they were gone. None of the others had anything to leave her anyway and all of Philip's estate went towards paying Rodger's legal expenses.

In July of 1949, Tom Paul hired a guy named Jim Ward to be Ward White's assistant and understudy on the Friant-Kern Canal. Ward White told Tom he didn't need or want any damn assistant, but Tom ordered him to take Jim anyway to help him handle the Tule River siphon work that we all felt was a potential flooding problem. Ward White and Keith Wasson had already detoured the Tule River by a cofferdam half way across in order to begin work, so time was of the essence now to complete the structure work before the winter rains. Ward told me to make sure Jim Ward and Jug Jones, a general carpenter foreman that

Tule River Siphon

rode in with Jim, got all the materials they needed on a priority basis, which I did. The problem was, Jug kept ordering and reordering more and more materials than I had calculated he would ever need to build that structure and I smelled a rat. When I brought it to Ward White's attention, he figured I must have made a mistake somewhere and said, "Send him what he wants anyway. I don't care if he's over budget on materials or even on labor, because we can't afford not finishing that structure before the rains hit us."

To add a little more suspense to this story, my honest hardworking truck driver, bless his pea picking heart, told me on the *"qt"* that Jug threatened to fire him if he ever told anybody he never unloaded several truck loads of lumber at the Tule River siphon work site. He said, he was ordered to haul the lumber to a housing project near Porterville, and that a higher up in the Kiewit Company (he didn't know who) was in *cahoots* with Jug, to build six new houses with stolen materials and labor from Kiewit. When I quietly made a visual head count of the three separate carpenter crews working at the Tule River site, against the number listed on their crew time cards, it proved to me several carpenters and laborers were working somewhere other than where they were charged. After a great deal of soul searching, I decided to keep my mouth shut and see how big this mess really was. I suspected Jim Ward, but then maybe even Tom Paul himself, might even be the Kiewit *higher up* since Tom had hired Jim Ward and forced Ward White to take him as his un-needed assistant. I had the utmost respect for all the Kiewit people I knew, except Jim Ward and Jug Jones, who struck me more as *blowhards* rather than real *construction stiffs*. Beside that, they were all my bosses, so I would have lost the best job I ever had making premature unconfirmed accusations.

Well, as it turned out, I was able to get *the word* back to Jug Jones via my honest truck driver, that '*some people*' were *secretly* checking on him, and I noticed right away the missing carpenters and laborers began working again at the Tule River site. Better yet, I even stopped receiving requests for more lumber from Jug, and the siphon was completed ahead of the flood season, but the direct labor and material costs ended up well over what was originally estimated. Interestingly, all the foremen on the Friant-Kern Canal job that worked directly for Ward White and were not under Jim Ward's control, beat their estimated labor costs, while Jim Ward's crews all exceeded their estimated labor costs and lost money.

Homer's Folly # 1 makes it's debut on a Tule River Siphon Concrete Pour

During the preliminary coffer dam stage, Ward White and I were discussing various methods to construct the Tule River siphon and he asked me to design a concrete pouring machine that would distribute wet concrete anywhere we wanted. Since this was before the boom mounted concrete pumps were invented and we were too dumb to think it ourselves, we both felt something like conveyor belt delivery would be the answer because it would lower our pouring costs 50% by eliminating the *concrete buggy* crew. The above picture called *Homer's folly*, shows flimsy structure I came up with, and Ward had built in Sailor Hamby's shop. I still think it was a good idea, but the problem was, it would invariably break down in the middle of a pour and we would end up using the concrete buggy crew to finish anyway. Keith Wasson got so disgusted with my idea, he said, "Park that damn thing and just do the job the way we know will work."

During the late fall of 1949, it became obvious our Structures Division would finish all its work assignments well ahead of schedule, and despite the Tule River Syphon cost overrun, well below the original estimated costs. As my own assignments tapered off, I was re-assigned by Ward White to help with the estimating and bidding for more work with Major Lowe in his job office. Everything was looking up for Janet and me about then and we were both happy with our jobs. Best of all, we were also slowly working ourselves out of debt, but the only thing still bothering me about the Kiewit Company was their apparent memory loss concerning my scheduled salary increases and not living up to their commitments when I signed on.

When the Kiewit Company hired me as an engineer trainee, it was agreed I would be paid $325 a month ($75 a week) to start with the promise of a $25 a month raise after three months, which they ignored, then another $25 a month raise six months after that, which they also ignored. In other words, nine months after I started work, I would be making $50 a month more than my starting salary, or $375 a month ($86.60 a week), but would earn any additional raises on my own merits. When my first January pay check (nine months after I started) still didn't show any raise increases as they had promised, I figured I better find out if they were trying to tell me something, and made an appointment to discuss the matter with Major Lowe. From my point of view, if they really felt I was not *cutting the mustard* so to speak, I better stop wasting my time on this job and begin looking elsewhere for a job where my efforts would be appreciated. Well, to make this little story shorter, Major Lowe was terribly embarrassed when we discussed the matter and was very apologetic for not paying closer attention to the time and staying on top of their commitment to me. He asked Ward White to join us, who was also very apologetic, and they both gave me a $10 raise for a total of $20 a week, to rectify their oversight. Oooh boy, now I was the one who was embarrassed because I was now making $95 a week, or $8.40 more than I was entitled to per our agreement. Ward White even made me fell more embarrassed when he handed me a $200 bonus for doing such a good job as his structures engineer.

Lesson Learned: *Never tamper, adjust or ignore an employee's salary terms after an agreement has been reached. The employee will never trust you or the company again if they feel you deliberately tried to renege on the agreed commitment..*

In mid January of 1950, Ward White and I were sent back to Grand Island, Nebraska to attend Kiewit's Equipment Maintenance School and to learn more about the company's overall operations. Unfortunately, our Union Pacific train didn't reach Grand Island until after midnight because of extreme weather conditions and by the time we checked into our hotel; it was two o'clock in the morning. Somewhere between two and our six o'clock wake up call, a cat burglar tip toed into our locked room as well as several others by apparently using a hotel pass key, stole our wallets. I lost all my spending money ($65) and Ward lost all his poker playing money ($200) that first night, but fortunately the police found our wallets with our driver license and credit cards in a back alley garbage can, but never caught the thief. The good news was, Major Lowe called our hotel to tell us we were low bidder on both the ten mile Delano extension contract on the Friant-Kern Canal and the Poudre Supply Canal near Fort Collins, Colorado. I had estimated the structure work on both those jobs before we left, so if we hadn't lost all our money we would have really celebrated.

Well, you guessed it. When we returned Dan Bell, Kiewit's Denver District Manager, called Keith Wasson to ask for help building the structures on the Poudre Supply Canal that we had estimated. Ward always told us, whoever estimates a job should be required to build that job to *prove* his figures and since I was the one who estimated the structure work on the *Cache le Poudre* contract, he told me along with Jim Ward, Jug Jones, Ray McClarnin, Orville Saulfeld, Zel Mullican and George Hatfield, to start packing our bags to move to Fort Collins, Colorado. He said he and his remaining foremen would move down stream to Delano to build the structures on the Delano extension contract.

Wingwall entrance structure to the Long Gulch Siphon

One thing I learned right away about the construction business, you either report for work where they tell you to, or you quit. Janet tearfully and reluctantly gave up her teaching job she loved so much and we sadly packed our '49 Chevy pickup we traded our '41 Ford Sedan for, and moved. In late March of 1950, we arrived in La Porte, Colorado to setup our new office, yard and shop and just began constructing the six mile long Poudre Supply Canal along a hillside contour from the Horse Tooth Dam to the upstream end crossing the Poudre (Powder) River, to have all the craft unions suddenly go out on strike. The good news was, Ward White gave Janet and me another $5.00 a week raise as we left Porterville to help with our moving expenses giving us now a whopping $100 a week salary. I was so embarrassed over all these generous salary increases from Ward White we decided not to submit our expenses to the Kiewit Company for reimbursement. After all, Kiewit had been more than fair with us. Interestingly, it still hadn't occurred to me, my new $100 a week salary ($5,200) was still less than the ($7,100) per year we both made working our two jobs ($3,200 plus $3,900), so we had basically taken a cut in pay to move from Porterville to Fort Collins, Colorado. But on the other hand she did have warts, so if I had refused to move and got myself fired from this good job, we would have only had Janet's job to live on until I found another one and good jobs were not all that plentiful then.

During the five week strike, Jim Ward and I rescheduled all the structure work and concluded we had to double shift to meet our specified completion date and moved our concrete pouring operations to the second shift. To complicate things even further, all the non-com WW II veterans on our crew that had signed up to be enlisted reserves when discharged, were re-called for the Korean War. That left us short handed in both supervisory and our most qualified craftsmen.

I remember while bidding for more work in Porterville with Major Lowe (who was then a Lt. Col. in the Army Reserves), he said, "Homer, if you would be interested in joining the Army Reserves, I'll make you a 2nd Lt. in the Combat Engineers." And added, "All you'll need to do is come down to the Armory one evening a month to review and resolve engineering problems with the troops, plus spend two weeks on field maneuvers every year." I admit I was tempted because I never got the *gold bars* I wanted so badly during my Army career because of my poor eyesight. Major Lowe told me the ground forces would overlook vision problems because of their acute shortages of junior officer's with civil engineering degrees. Well, while Janet and I were discussing the pros and cons of his offer we were transferred to Fort Collins and had to turn him down. Looking back now, I guess I was lucky because Combat Engineers are the first troops called up in any war and like some of my crew, I would have been called up for the Korean War.

NEWS RELEASES DURING 1950

The Korean War begins when North Korea invades South Korea; Truman authorizes the development of the hydrogen bomb and begins calling up the Reserves; Truman orders the Army to seize the Railroads, and; the U. S. Population rises to 150,697,361 in 1950 including the 1,035,039 immigrants who entered the U. S. during the last decade.

After the five week strike was settled we went back to work on our tight scheduled short handed job and to help resolve our problems somewhat, I volunteered to work two shifts. After all I was used to working long hours for Ward White anyway and I thought I could easily handle my engineering duties during the day shift and still be able to take care of my concrete foremen's job on swing shift. As it turned out, pouring the structure concrete during the second shift was the most productive and efficient way to build the job anyway.

The day shift carpenter crews didn't have to work around my labor interfering crews, and the forms that were buttoned up at the end of the day shift and we poured the concrete that same night. The forms were then ready to strip (and reset) the next morning for a pour the following evening, and so on. That not only helped us save time, but also saved on labor and materials by fabricating less forms.

Well, you guessed it, my sixteen-hour-five-day-work week plus another eight hours on Saturdays to catch up on unfinished engineering was a lousy arrangement from

Constructing the Long Gulch 12 foot diameter Siphon

Janet's point of view. Why? Because we hardly ever got to see each other and I'm sure it was on that job Janet began having second thoughts about why she ever married me in the first place, but unfortunately in those good old days, the job always came first and wives came second, take it or leave it. To try keeping some peace in the family, Janet and I decided to pack our Sunday lunches for picnics on the job with our newly acquired little blond cocker spaniel we named *Powder* (after the river) and as an added bonus, I was also able to check out the job on how the concrete was doing. It was on one of those picnic luncheons while playing with our little pup near the Rist Creek Siphon, we discovered a hastily camouflaged stack of lumber in the underbrush adjacent to the job, I remember thinking, "Oooh boy, it's *deja vu all over again* and some dirty rat is trying to steal our lumber - *again.*"

After that shocking discovery, Janet and I parked our '49 pickup in the saw yard and drove the company's flatbed truck back to the *cache le lumbar* site to haul that hidden stack of lumber back to the saw yard where it belonged. To this day I still remember the shocked expressions on Jim Ward's and Jug Jones' faces the next morning when they saw that lumber in the yard again. It told me immediately what I had suspected all along on the Friant-Kern Canal, *They were the culprits..* I never said anything, but I asked our *saw man* to give me a confidential detailed delivery list of all the materials that was sent to each structure site from his yard from then on. Although more materials than I thought was necessary seemed to silently evaporate and although I continued looking for more secret hiding places for company lumber stashed around the job, I never discovered any more hidden material sites.

Lesson learned: *Maybe it was the way I was raised, but it made me sick to my stomach when I discovered I was working for a couple of lousy crooks. I made a promise to myself, even if I had to resign, I would never work with or fore either one of those two lousy crooks again I knew were stealing the company blind.*

On another subject, an interesting thing happened around midnight around the end of August in 1950 while we were pouring a twelve foot diameter siphon section on the Long Gulch siphon. You can believe this little drama of life or not, your choice, but my crew and

Building the Bifurcation Structure into the Powder River

I actually witnessed a real honest to God live *"UFO"* (unidentified flying object) pass directly over us. I remember seeing three red balls of fire approaching us in formation at a very low altitude and my first thought was, it was a three engine airplane in trouble that was about to crash. I yelled for everyone on my crew to look up, and as we all watched in hypnotic fascination whatever it was, it silently cruised directly over us and quietly disappeared behind a hill next to our work site. I ran to the top of the hill thinking it had crashed on the other side, but everything was dark and whatever it was, had disappeared. A newspaper account the next day reported several sightings that night, the first near Cheyenne, Wyoming, followed by more sightings near Fort Collins, then one in Denver, and another near the southern border of Colorado with the final sightings near White Sands, New Mexico. I had personally launched many weather balloons while I was in the Army Air Forces during WW II, so I always snickered whenever I heard people talking about these sightings, but now I know how they felt when everyone busted out laughing after they told their story. Why? Because everyone snickers now when I tell them my own UFO experience. I told my dad this story and he just looked at me suspiciously, and said, "Who knows? Maybe all these damn-dumb-democrats (all one word to him) have something up their sleeves they don't want to tell us about."

Anyway, my cost estimate to build the Poudre Supply canal structures held up fairly well despite the labor shutdown and other delays, including the additional $0.10 an hour raise they won by striking. Although none of these *beyond our control* contingency costs were anticipated at bid time and were not in our estimate, we were able to improve our labor productivity nearly enough to offset them by better planning and scheduling, using smaller well supervised crews and spreading out the work by double shifting. We also redesigned our concrete forms during the strike to allow more re-use with savings in materials and labor costs, but best of all, our structure organization began pulling together as a motivated

Touring the 12 foot diameter Rist Creek Siphon

let's get the job built team. To me that increase in morale was what offset nearly all the cost increases beyond our control. We not only made our mid October black frost completion schedule, but even finished with our structure concrete job profit close to what we had estimated at bid time, that is, up until the time I quit. What happened to the costs after that, I'll never know.

Ward White called Jim Ward in early October, to tell him we were low bidder on the final section of the Friant-Kern Canal into Bakersfield, that he called the "Shafter Job", and that job would make the total Kiewit built portion of the Friant-Kern Canal Project a whopping 110 miles. He also said they got more freeway bridge work in Los Angeles County and he needed him to come back to handle the structure work on one of those jobs.

Jim Ward turned to me and said, "Homer I'm going back to California, so you're directly in charge of this job from now on." I said, "That's fine with me Jim, but I want you to know right now, the minute you walk out that door, Jug Jones is fired." Jim stared at me for a moment with a surprised look on his face, then he said, "I've just re-evaluated your position in this company Homer, you are no longer in charge; Jug is." I said, "Jim, I quit", and walked out.

When I got home to tell Janet (who was now pregnant with our first child), that I had just quit my job, she was ecstatic we were moving back to California to have our baby. We packed up our pickup truck with our few belongings, turned in our rental key, picked up our final pay check at the Kiewit office and you can believe this or not, we beat Jim Ward back to Bakersfield, California. As we drove by the Shafter, California job office, we stopped in to visit the old Porterfield gang and talk to Keith Wasson. He said Dan Bell had just called him and they would both like to know why I quit, so I finally confessed to him all my suspicions on both jobs with my feelings about working for crooks. He listened quietly and when I finished, he said he and Dan Bell would look into it and as I got up to leave, Keith said he had a job for me if I would be interested in being the structures concrete foreman on the Shafter contract. He said the concrete labor costs had gotten completely out of hand on the Delano

Rist Creek Siphon being constructed on the Poudre Supply Canal

job after we left, and they were embarrassingly higher than what we made on the Porterville job. He concluded with, "Something is rotten in Denmark somewhere Homer and I would like you to find out why." He also said Tom Paul had transferred Ward White to the Los Angeles bridge job and assigned Jim Ward to this Shafter job as his new structures superintendent when he arrived. Oooh boy, I thought to myself, "This is going to be interesting."

When my *new* boss, Jim Ward finally arrived and coldly drove me to the batch plant to meet my recycled Delano concrete crew, I felt about as welcome as a road apple in a church punch bowl. I immediately found out I had a new reputation already as a *slave driving, headstrong, trouble making workaholic,* that was now being *spewed* around on the job by Jim Ward, rather than the easy going *lack of spunk screw up* guy I was formally famous for. I also lucked out by being assigned the notorious Teamster Unions *toughest steward bully* known only as *"Red"* (because of his red hair) as one of my transit mix truck drivers. Interestingly, *Old Red* had already been briefed by Jim Ward all about me and had immediately taken a real dislike to me. When the meeting was over, Red sidled up to me on the way out and said, "Homer, I guarantee you won't last long on this job." I was startled by his sincere heartfelt interesting remark and thanked him for his warm welcome, but when I left I thought to myself, "Oooh boy, that guy really does think he's *Jesus H. Keeerist* " himself.

I remember we were making a day time pour on one of the Shafter job structures when two of our transit mix trucks didn't show up with their fresh supply of concrete. When we were in danger of losing our pour entirely, I jumped into my pickup and started retracing the transit mix truck route and lo and behold, there in front of a small bar-restaurant sat two of our fully loaded transit mixers idly spinning. For some unknown reason I began to feel that same terrible *road rage* feeling building up in me while parking my pickup, and stormed into that bar seeing *"Red"* twice when I saw *Old Red* and the other driver sitting there slobbering down beers. I must have flipped my lid and really came unglued because I stomped over and spun Red around on his bar stool, shouting at the top of my voice, "What in Keerists name do you ass holes think you're job is around here? Our whole crew is out there waiting for you two knot heads to deliver that concrete, now God damn it, do it." The other driver jumped up and ran out to his truck, but my union steward bully friend only sauntered out while looking back saying, "Homer, mark my words, I'm going to get your ass fired." I said, "Red, I'll tell you what, let's you and me meet in Keith Wasson's office after work tonight and get this thing settled now, one way or the other, and see which one of us gets fired."

Well, when Red and I arrived at Keith Wasson's office for our after work meeting, the Teamster business agent and Keith, who seemed to have a good working relationship, were both there waiting for us. We both told our sides of the story and Keith told me Red was completely wrong in what he had done, but I had put him between a rock and a hard place with Red being the union steward and all. Then the Teamster BA told Red he better by God, not pull another beer hall stunt like that again or he would be fired by both Keith and himself, and that he better get it through his thick skull he was not the boss of the concrete crew, Homer was. Keith said he and the business agent had agreed the best option for the four of us was to put this whole thing behind us by shaking hands and let bygones be bygones. He also said, if Red and I didn't want to cooperate and build the job by working together as a team, he would be forced to fire both of us and they would appoint a new concrete foreman and a new union steward for the job. I looked over at Red and said, "I'll agree to working together as a team to get the job built, if Red will." Red said, "I'll go along with that and agree Homer is the boss of our crew." All four of us then shook hands and the meeting was adjourned. Believe it or not, I actually thought we really had settled things and had put the whole thing behind us, but I soon found out *Old Red* never was in agreement and never forgot his grudge with me.

When I took over the structure concrete pouring operations, it soon become painfully obvious the vibrators, and most of the other equipment was not only poorly maintained, but was worn out and obsolete. I heard via the grapevine a local man named McGinnis had invented a light weight, high cycle, electric vibrator that one man could operate, so I called him for a demonstration. As it turned out, his equipment was so far superior to our current cable shaft 2 cycle engine variety that required two men to operate and a mechanic to keep running, it was unbelievable. With Keith Wasson's approval, (thankfully, Jim Ward was ignoring me) I purchased the McGinnis generator equipment for the company and made all the necessary changes needed to use his high cycle vibrators. Lo and behold, fifty percent of our current concrete crew suddenly became obsolete and our costs immediately improved. In order to keep everything I had purchased in a convenient place for quick location movement and setup, I asked Sailor Hamby, our master mechanic, to build me a U-Haul type trailer to house the McGinnis 180 cycle generator, the high cycle vibrators and the flood lights we would need for night work. I also asked (actually begged) the Bureau of Reclamation to redesign their overly harsh concrete mix their *water-cement ratio expert*, Mr. Tuthill was so proud of, and after several heated and emotional discussions with Mr. Tuthill regarding his unreasonably dry mix ratios, he reluctantly agreed our current mix was too harsh, and added more sand, water, and cement to make it a smoother more workable mix. *Voila*, our rock pocket problems were suddenly resolved. Finally, I made personnel changes in the crew with new people who had a better work ethic, and like the Colorado job, began pouring all the concrete structures on swing shift. Believe it or not, our labor costs were soon even below the Porterville costs and Keith Wasson thought I must be some kind of a genius, but Jim Ward disliked me even more. Actually, those needed changes were only common sense, and it was my hard working motivated concrete crew that deserved the credit for our cost improvements.

It was during one of those late night swing shift pours that *Old Red* (in cahoots with an even more bitter Jim Ward) finally realized his dream, and got rid of me once and for all. I remember calling Ivan, the batch plant operator, on my pickup radio and telling him, I was not sure if that last four cubic yard load of transit mix concrete he had batched would be enough to finish the pour, and I would call him back later to confirm. As luck would have it, (or Jim Ward had planned) *Old Red* was the last transit mix driver on the run and when I saw his truck load would make it after all, I tried calling Ivan again on my radio to tell him to wash-up and call it a night. Unfortunately, Ivan never acknowledged my radio calls and since it was nearly midnight and we were over ten miles from the plant, I asked Red when he got back to the plant to wash up, to tell Ivan it was OK to shut down and let everyone go home. Red said he would, and I drove the two miles back to the Bakersfield apartment Janet and I were renting. I remember trying to call Ivan again on our home telephone because of a funny feeling I had, with still no answer, and even debated whether or not to drive back to the plant, but decided *Red* would do what he said he would do, and went to bed. Along about four o'clock in the morning, someone pounding on our front door woke me up and I was shocked to see it was Jim Ward. When I asked "What's going on?" he shouted, "The batch plant is lit up like a Xmas tree and Red and all the other drivers and the plant crew are sitting around playing poker waiting for your call to shut the plant down or batch out another load." I thought to myself, ooh boy, Red said he would get me fired and now I know he meant it, so I said, "Jim before you do anything rash, let me go back up to the plant right now to kick the living crap out of *Old Red* for not doing what he told me he would do." He said "No, it's too damn late for that now, you're fired" and handed me my two typed layoff checks the office girl had interestingly typed for him that afternoon, and left. Like a bolt out of the blue, *I seen the light* and to this day I still think Jim and Red should be awarded the

Academy Award for the excellent way I was setup for the kill, and for the beautiful job they did removing me from the Shafter job's payroll.

> **Lesson learned:** *For reasons I will never understand, some people are so jealous and resentful of other people trying to do the right thing for the company they work for, they will try to destroy them..*

One of the best lessons I learned during the great depression was to never worry about finding another job when you are laid off because employers are always looking for honest hard working people with a good work ethic during good times and bad. I remember my mother and my stepfather, Philip Brim, were never out of work during the depression years because they were good hard workers who were always more concerned about their employer's success than their own hourly pay and/or fringe benefit packages. They knew the company's success meant their own success and they also knew the jobs available then may not pay as much as they might think they were worth, but if you produced for your employer, your salary and your responsibilities always increased. Good hard working honest employees are always hard to find and small business employers especially, will always take good care of their key people. I knew I could find another job right away, but the rumors floating around that I was a *head strong, slave driving, trouble making workaholic,* were still bothering me. Ward White must have inherited my reputation (or mine his) because Tom Paul abruptly transferred Ward to another job, but in his case I think the motivation was envy and petty jealousy. None of Tom's project superintendents were anywhere near the money makers Ward White was.

My sudden *firing* on the Shafter job occurred in mid December of 1950 when Janet was seven months pregnant with our first child due around the end of February, and we both wanted to be settled in a nice place somewhere as soon as possible to have our little boy or girl. We were packing our things to move just as Keith Wasson called to say Tom Paul wanted me to work for him in the Arcadia office as an *engineer estimator trainee* at my current salary of $100 per week, if I were interested. Well, to get settled right away, I accepted Tom's offer and Janet and I found the perfect one bedroom rental cottage in an avocado orchard near Monrovia, California, as our nest egg nest. It was an ideal spot for our newborn baby and our cocker spaniel pup *Powder*, who loved ripe avocados, and we were near the top rated St. Luke's Hospital in Pasadena. I also thought at the time we had a qualified pediatrician, who told Janet her pregnancy was doing nicely, but the truth of the matter was, that unqualified horse doctor never noticed our little boy could be a difficult breach birth and was completely unprepared when little Jimmy was born.

What happened next was the most traumatic emotionally devastating experience either one of us ever had, and we were grief stricken for many months afterwards. Our perfect little eight and one half pound baby boy we named James Christian Olsen, unfortunately only lived two days after he was born because, they said, he was a *blue baby* and a valve in his heart didn't close properly. Apparently things like that were fatal in those days, but are considered a minor heart correction today. The facts are, Jimmy was an extremely difficult tug of war breach birth and Janet was in hard labor for over twelve hours and we were very lucky Janet even survived.. I worried myself sick over Janet's mental condition afterwards from grief and guilt she felt over losing little Jimmy. For some unknown reason, she felt it was her fault her precious baby died, which was ridiculous. It was that knot headed doctor's fault because he should have performed a cesarean immediately to deliver that little boy and I still feel Jimmy would be alive today if that birth had been handled properly.

After his demise, I felt little Jimmy deserved at least a decent burial so I asked a local protestant minister to say a few words in little Jimmy's behalf and carried his tiny little casket under my arm, sobbing all the way, to the Monrovia Cemetery. The three of us, the minister, his wife and I, were the only mourners at little Jimmy's graveside service and to this day I haven't fully recovered from his death and there hasn't been a month go by that I don't

Los Angeles Flood Channel Bridge work during 1951

think about that little boy and wonder where and what he might be doing now, if only he had lived. Fortunately, Janet's mother came down from Seattle for a few weeks to stay with her daughter, which was a Godsend for both of us. Without Grandma Whitehead's helping hand during that grieving period in our lives, I don't know what we would have done.

When I reported for my new *engineer-estimator trainee* job, in the Los Angeles district office in Arcadia, California, I buried myself in my work determined to learn everything I could about that side of the construction contracting business. I remember for some unknown reason, every concrete structures estimate I prepared for my immediate supervisor, Julian Gobel's review, he would always complain the unit labor costs I used were much too optimistic, and in his opinion were impossible to make, even though I showed him copies of our canal work cost reports to prove we had actually made them. He would have Paul Scroggs, Tom Paul's personally anointed top project manager, review them. When they came back after Paul's review, everyone of my carpenter unit labor costs were raised an even $0.10 per square foot and all my concrete pouring unit costs were always increased an even $1.00 per cubic yard, time after time. When I protested I had used the same labor unit costs we had made on the more difficult Friant-Kern and the Colorado structure work, and that my estimates were based on the same hourly ratio adjusted union rates, he just stared at me and

279

said he agreed with Paul Scroggs, my costs were impossible to make, whether we actually made them or not.

Well, leave it to an old stubborn knot headed Norwegian like Homer J. (me) to figure out a way to beat that theory, when we bid the Los Angeles River job, I took the liberty of adjusting all my legitimate estimated unit labor costs down an even ten cents and an even one dollar lower than I thought they should be, so when Paul Scroggs raised my unit costs after his review, the estimate would be where it should be. Oooh boy, apparently Paul Scroggs was busy with something and never had a chance to raise my figures his even unit price numbers, so when Julian finally called the job to ask why my estimate had not been returned, Paul's office girl just took it out of Paul's *unlooked-in file*, and mailed it back to Julian. Well you guessed it. In the interest of time, my low unit price structures bid was posted in the overall job bid submitted without Paul

The completed Bridge over the Los Angeles Flood Channel

and/or Julian's review (and increases), or even to my knowledge. Oooh boy, then to add on more insult to injury, Tom Paul wanted the job so badly he cut his markup on the bid at the last minute. I remember Pete Kiewit used to tell us, "The easiest money you'll ever make in this business is what you ***don't*** leave on the table", and as you've already guessed, we were the low bidder with an embarrassing amount still left on the table. Now what should I do?

Well, to make this story shorter, I drove down to the Los Angeles River job after it was awarded and confessed to Ward White, the project manager, what I had done and amazingly, he thought it was funny. He said, "Homer, even good men will only produce 30% of what they are capable of doing if they're not interested or inspired to produce more. As their supervisor, you therefore have a 70% window of opportunity to inspire your crews to increase their productivity so don't worry about it; competent leadership coupled with qualified craftsmen is the key to making good labor costs and I'll make you a bet right now we'll make the unit labor costs you've estimated." Lo and behold, Ward and his crackerjack crew did make my *too low* estimated unit costs by inspiring his crew. How? He told them my humorous (?) screw-up low estimate story, and that wonderful bunch of guys said they would bail me out of my bind by making my *low* unit costs, and by golly they did.

Lesson Learned: *Labor productivity can always be improved by combining skilled qualified craftsmen with competent supervisory leadership, and both are inspired to accomplish the task working as a team.*

During the spring of 1951, both the Cold War and the Korean War were escalating, and more and more defense work was being put out for bid on fast track work schedules. The Corps of Engineers advertised for the construction of a new 10,000 foot runway at the March Air force Base near Riverside, California that required exceptionally strict paving tolerances for the Air Force B36 and B47 bombers (the B36 was a flying wing and the B47 was the forerunner of the B52). The specifications required the new runway be constructed on a *crash* (the Russians are coming) short six month time schedule, including the new POL facilities and over fourteen miles of new utility lines so we knew it was a Kiewit job. Well, to meet the extremely short time period with all the strict tolerances and overtime required, we estimated the contract very conservatively and in fact, after we totaled our bid, I thought we had added so many contingencies we wouldn't have a snow balls chance in hell of being low bidder.

Much to my surprise, Tom Paul asked me to ride down to the bid opening with him and on the way to the Corps of Engineers office in Los Angeles to turn in the bid, he said he felt we should add another $160,000 for contingencies and additional markup before we turned the bid in, and asked, "What do you think?" I said, "Tom, I don't think we'll be low bidder anyway so you just as well add the $160,000." I'll tell you, he really got hot under the collar over what he thought was a *smart-aleck* answer, and said sulkily, "OK, then damn it I won't", and still mad, slammed the bid down on the Corps *turn-in* counter. Well, wouldn't you know it, much to my surprise and his too, we were the low bidder by $250,000 on a $6,000,000 job and Oooh boy, I'll tell you, Tom must have glared at me for a full minute. Finally he said angrily, "I hope you realize what you've done. You just cost the Company $160,000 by not telling me to put it in the bid." I said, "Tom, what I tried to say was, you might as well put it in the bid because I felt our bid was estimated too conservatively to be the low bidder." Then I crossed my fingers and added, "Tom, if you're really all that shook-up about it, I'll make you a deal. I'll make that $160,000 back for you on my structure items alone, if you'll let me run all the structure work that I estimated." He looked at me with the most shocked-puzzled-surprised expression on his face I've ever seen, and said, "OK smartass, you got a deal, but by damn if you don't make my $160,000 back for me by the time that job is built, your days with this company are over." Well, you can believe this little drama of life or not, but that is the true story of how I became the youngest *Superintendent,* at the ripe old age of 27, in the Peter Kiewit Sons Company, up until that time.

When I reported for work at the job office of Herb Studer, the project manager on the March Field job, it was *déjà vu* all over again. I got the same unwelcome bastard calf reaction I did from that *Old Army* Top Sergeant when I reported for detached service duty at Fort Monmouth, New Jersey, with the Army Signal Corps. I tapped my knuckles on the open door of Herb's field office, and he waved me in without saying a word, all the while leaning back in his chair eyeing me up and down. Finally he said, "So you're that hotshot kid Tom is sending me to do the structure work on this job." When I said "That's right" he said, "OK, let's find out what you can do. I've arranged with the Colonel here to shut down the runway for forty-eight (48) hours to give you plenty of time to open cut a electrical duct trench across and underneath the runway, place a duct bank of 48-four inch power and telephone duct lines, encase them in quick-set high strength reinforced concrete, backfill the trench and repave it with blacktop to reopen the runway for air traffic. I repeat, you have forty eight (48) hours to do the complete job, and your starting time is set for 8:00 o'clock tomorrow morning. Do you have any questions?" When I asked if he had any equipment I could borrow, or had made any arrangements for any of the materials needed, he said "No, you're the *wonder boy* Tom assured me would take care of all those details, that's you're problem." I thanked him for his cooperation and immediately went to my assigned office room and began telephoning.

Homer J. Olsen reporting for work

Fortunately for me, I had already lined up Dick Leland as my engineer, Zel Mullican as my general foreman and Earl "Spec" Coffee and Orville Saalfeld as two of my key foremen, all from the Friant canal days, so I informed them Herb had given us an exciting problem to see if we were qualified to do our jobs and we only had 48 hours to prove it. After I explained our challenging little test to them and we had broken the job down into its various work units, we each began running with our delegated piece of the puzzle to be ready. Lo and behold, the next morning at 7:00 am, my motivated team had our dayshift crew all lined up and raring to go with a backhoe and four ten

Typical power & telephone manholes

wheeler trucks, two compressors, concrete saws and paving breakers, all waiting with shoring materials stacked neatly nearby with a 10 KW generator and flood lights for night work, ready to go. The transit mix company, rebar and the electrical subcontractors informed me they were also *hot to trot*.

My Crackerjack Crew – March Air Force Base – 1951

At 8:00 am sharp, the runway was shut down and my motivated team enthusiastically began working a continuous around the clock three shift schedule until the runway crossings was paved over, completed, and reopened for air traffic, just two hours before our specified 48 hour completion schedule. The base Colonel was so impressed with my motivated crackerjack crew to help us out a little; he gave me permission to construct the manholes required on each end, during the day shift between takeoffs and landings, which we did. I'll tell you, when that exciting little job was completed, we passed Herb's *qualification* test with flying colors and he was more than impressed and agreed my crew was capable of doing the work we were assigned. We had proven to him that we knew what we were doing and much like my experience with the top sergeant at Fort Monmouth; New Jersey, Herb and I became good friends by the time that new runway contract was finished.

Concrete encasing miles of duct lines - March Field

The good news was, the total March Air Force Base contract was successfully completed ahead of the six month schedule and Herb Studer, the project manager who was in his late sixty's, decided it was time to cash in his chips and return to his home state of Wyoming to *hunt pheasants* the remainder of his life. Everyone on the job

Storm drain headwall at March Air Force Base – 1951

chipped in on a beautifully engraved double barreled shot gun to present to him just before his retirement speech, and that tough old construction stiff we all learned to love, got so choked up he couldn't give his talk.

Anyway, to get back to building my first job as a Kiewit structures superintendent, my *special ops* structures crew soon welded into a motivated crackerjack team and we went on to complete the fourteen miles of trenching and installed all of the underground duct lines, runway lighting, storm drains complete with manholes and headwalls, and building the new jet fuel, oil and lube facilities, ahead of schedule without interfering in any way, with any of the other operations. We also introduced several new construction innovations to save time and money, such as precasting all 400 runway lighting concrete bases and the smaller four foot diameter and under storm drain headwalls so the contract could be completed within the Corps fast track schedule. True to my finger crossed promise to Tom Paul, my structures organization beat our estimated costs by a whopping

Storm Drain Manholes at March Field

$250,000, and doubled our original estimated job profit on our structure work. It was not only equal to what was left on the table at bid time, but more than returned the $160,000 Tom was so shook-up about. Tom was so pleased when I passed both Herb's and his test he officially retired my *engineer-trainee* title and re-classified me as *structures superintendent*. Best of all, he finally increased my weekly salary to match that of a craft union foreman's

Airplane service station P.O.L. Facilities at March Air Force Base

$150 a week and even surprised me with a $500 bonus when the job was completed. As I requested, he even gave bonuses to all my weekly foremen of $200 each for doing such a good job. Tom Paul was an old pile butt from Michigan of Finnish descent who worked up through the ranks to the vice president level the hard way, and I'll tell you, he was anything but generous. Bonuses like this were a milestone in the Los Angeles District under Tom's command and I remember suggesting he give his employees a pat on the back once in awhile for doing a good job would also be a good morale builder, and he said, "Why should I? They're paid to do a good job."

In January of 1952 I was invited to the Kiewit Company's annual Top Managers meeting in Grand Island, Nebraska to learn even more about the company operations and to get better acquainted with the top brass. It was not only interesting and very educational, but what impressed me most was the caliber of people the Kiewit Company had working

NEWS RELEASES DURING 1951

Truman relieves MacArthur of his military duties, Americans begin building personal bomb shelters, the 22nd amendment is adopted which limits a president to two terms, 250,000 GI's are in Korea, the United States begins testing nuclear devises with live soldiers, flooding in Kansas and Missouri leaves 200,000 homeless, the first power producing nuclear reactor goes on line and the first transcontinental TV broadcast is an address by President Truman.

for them. The friendships I made in the company, beginning with that meeting, have lasted all these years and although many of them are no longer living, I still consider that old Kiewit gang as some of my best friends. It was at that meeting I learned Dan Bell, the

Denver District manager, had hired a private investigator to look into my *confession* to Keith Wasson concerning my resignation over Jug Jones's illegal activities, and they were all confirmed. Apparently Jug had plea bargained, and had turned back to the company, the ownership and sales revenue of all the houses he built in California and

284

Move-in day on the Antioch Freeway – 1952

Colorado illegally with Kiewit's labor and materials. The company then sold the remaining unsold houses and recovered all their losses and the charges against Jug were dropped. I was also told he was only fired as punishment and they were still looking into the involvement of the *higher up* in the Kiewit Company.

In February of 1952, Janet and I were transferred to northern California to help build a new six mile stretch of a four lane highway located between Pittsburg and Antioch, California, called the Antioch Freeway. I had estimated the structure concrete work on that job so I was assigned the position of structures superintendent under a job superintendent Tom Paul recently hired named George Primo. I had

Constructing Culverts under the Antioch Freeway

a feeling that many of the older supervisors in the Kiewit Company thought I was way too young to have the title of *superintendent*, but who knows, maybe it was just my *workaholic slave driving, trouble making*, reputation popping up again. For some unknown reason, I

My Crackerjack Crew on the Antioch Freeway contract in 1952

kept getting the same unwelcome *new kid from out of town* glaring look along with the same speech I got at March Field. George Primo told me in no uncertain terms, he was the boss on that job and that he was a world renowned earth moving expert with a BS degree in civil engineering from UC Berkeley, and the last thing he needed was a dumb snot nosed carpenter like me stumbling around messing up his job. Apparently he was unaware I already had one battle star

(March Field) on my campaign ribbon as a superintendent, but maybe I disliked the man right

away was because of his egomaniac bullying personality. On the other hand when you think about it hard enough, the real reason I disliked the man was because he graduated from Cal Berkeley.

Wing Wall construction for a 10 ft. diameter Storm Drain)

Anyway, I told George I was assigned to his job by Tom Paul to build the reinforced concrete structures within the costs estimated as rapidly as possible, and he could count on me and my organization to cooperate in every way, to make the Antioch Freeway contract a profitable one for the company's share holders.

Bridge Pier construction on the Antioch Freeway in 1952

One of the things that tickled me the most about moving to northern California was nearly all of my loyal foremen on the March Field job transferred north to the Antioch Freeway job with me except Dick Leland, who decided to be a city engineer and Bob Carlson took his place. I still remember the winter and spring of 1952 as one of the wettest years on record in northern California which really messed things up and caused a late startup on all our work. The good news was; Janet was pregnant with our second child due in May of 1952, and the rainy weather gave us the break we needed to locate a nice tract home to rent as our nesting place. Luckily, we found exactly what we were looking for on Garden Avenue in Concord that was fairly close to the highly rated Alta Bates Hospital in Berkeley and we were fortunate to find a pediatrician like Dr. Lamb, the finest in northern California, to look after Janet. I was determined she would never have to go through another traumatic experience like the last birth, and I made sure doctor Lamb was aware of everything that went

wrong during her first pregnancy. He assured me he would watch Janet like a hawk and take real good care of her and our new baby.

Sitting here like this, hen pecking these memoirs with one finger has a real time tunneling effect on me. Believe it or not, I feel sometimes like I'm writing my own *epic poems* like that other Homer who described Odysseus' adventures in detail during

Setting Bridge Girders on a Freeway Bridge – 1952

his ten year return from the Trojan Wars. Don't laugh, for some reason I was also named Homer and I'm recording my own epic wanderings, experiences, and hardships as they unfold before me like ocean waves crashing on my *skidmarked* highway of life.

Oooh boy, I must be cracking up. At the moment my memories are recalling all the different meaningful jobs I've held and the wonderful people I've worked for and with over the years that have made those jobs so enjoyable. Starting with my first good *50 cents a day* job in 1932 when I was 8 years old, to my last job as Chairmen of the Board of a company I founded and retired from in 1996 at age 72, all my supervisors had one thing in common.

They were all my kind of competent *"can do"* get the job done safely and profitably type people, except for two incompetent supervisors I worked for in the Kiewit Company. One was a *Shouter* (bully) and the other was a *Whiner* (cry baby) type and they were both poster boy examples of people who should never be allowed in positions of power over other people. Why? Because they are miserable to work for, they literally give ulcers to their employees, and they are disasters as money makers for a company. In fact I named my first ulcer, *George Primo,* after a *shouting bully* type by that same name Tom Paul hired as job superintendent

Pouring Deck on the Railroad Avenue Bridge- 1952

on the Antioch Freeway. I named my second ulcer, *Paul Scroggs,* after a *whining cry baby* of the same name also hired by Tom Paul as a project manager who couldn't make a simple

The finished Harbor Avenue Bridge on the Antioch Freeway – 1952

decision if his life depended on it, and blamed everyone else for his mistakes, but he's another story and I'm getting ahead of myself.

The Antioch Freeway Job turned out to be a nightmare to build and a profit disaster when it was finished; all because of stupid job management decisions by a knot headed incompetent job superintendent named, George Primo. I will never forget our first meeting of all the supervisors in March of 1952 when it was still raining cats and dogs, and George announced we would begin moving dirt with our scrapers the following Monday. I was so shocked I said, "You mean mud, don't you George?" Whooee, I'll tell you, he immediately came unglued and shouted, "Homer, I want you to get this through your thick skull right

Constructing a Freeway cross through tunnel – 1952

now. I'm running this God damn job and we will build it my way." to which I replied, "We've both been hired to make money for the Kiewit Company George, not to put on circus acts for our competitors. You're nuttier than a fruit cake to think you can load and unload mud in those scrapers, and even nuttier if think you can compact mud if you do unload it." From that day forward, our shouting matches over his screwball ideas began in earnest, and ended up being the first item on the agenda of every weekly supervisors meeting from then on. Unbelievably, he actually went through with his mud moving circus act in the rain, and as I prophesied, nearly every contractor in northern California was lined up along the fence in their rain coats holding their sides laughing. It was the most ridicules costly equipment damaging disaster I've ever seen, but fortunately one of Kiewit's competitors telephoned Tom Paul in Los Angeles to kid him about it, and George's stupid mud moving operation came to an end.

A pump house under construction on the Antioch Freeway

I could probably write another book about all the stupid management decisions and costly mistakes George made on that job that wasted even more of the company's money, but it would only make me angrier. It was none of my business to argue with him anyway, but when his screw ball ideas began affecting our structures schedule in building seven major bridges, two pumping plants, four large culverts, miles of storm drain piping and ninety eight drop inlets and headwalls, I couldn't contain myself. For some unknown reason my company loyalty and stubborn Norwegian pride just wouldn't let me stop voicing my opinions when common sense told me he was wrong. Anyway, I prevented him from fouling up our own structure operations somewhat, and we finished building most of our work that first year close to our schedule and our budget.

A finished cross through tunnel on the Freeway

The late spring inclement weather that forced our late startup, coupled with the complete lack of cooperation from George in meeting his targeted schedule dates, affected every operation on the job and in the end, my crew and I failed to do as well as we hoped and only matched my estimated costs. As the whole job turned out, we were the only department that broke even, while all the other operations all lost money, causing the overall job to suffer a substantial loss. It was a crying shame too, because the job could have been profitable if it had only been managed properly by someone who knew what they were doing. To make matters even more frustrating, George somehow convinced Tom Paul all the problems he had meeting his earthmoving schedules and costs were my fault because of my stubborn uncooperative attitude. Baloney, he went out of his way to do everything just opposite of what I suggested anyway. Without even hearing my side of the story, Tom shockingly replaced me with Zel Mullican (my assistant) to finish the remaining structure work on the Antioch Freeway and transferred me to a recently awarded East Shore Freeway job in Emeryville, California. It was during my move to that job my doctor informed me I had somehow acquired my first stomach ulcer, so I named it *George Primo,* in honor of the bully that caused it.

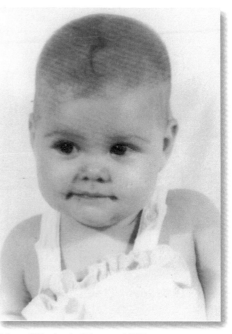

Mary Elizabeth Olsen – 1952

After I left, George Primo took complete dictatorial control of every operation on the Antioch job and it deteriorated even further into an unsalvageable losing job, *until finally* Tom Paul woke up. To save face, he unbelievably transferred his pet George Primo *Army Style* by recommending that incompetent nut case highly to Gordon H. Ball in Danville, as a construction genius and a fantastic money making project manager. Whooee, you guessed it, Gordon innocently hired George Primo on Tom Paul's bald faced lying recommendations. Then to save further embarrassment, Tom silently apologized to me by reluctantly raising (bless his pea picking heart) my weekly salary a whopping $25 a week to match the current union foremen's weekly rate of $175, and silently told me (?) I had *almost,* arrived as a structures superintendent. Even better, several of my loyal crackerjack crew from Antioch, namely Frank Wiggs, Orville Saalfeld, Ray Maclarnon, Bill Turnbough, and *Slop-it-in Sam* Elderidge, also moved to the Eastshore Freeway with me to help build the concrete structures between the Albany Race Track and the Judson-Pacific-Murphy's steel yard near the Oakland distribution structure.

The most wonderful thing that ever happened to Janet and me during the Antioch Freeway job was when our first beautiful little baby girl we named Mary Elizabeth Olsen, was born on May 8, 1952. I still remember that day as if it were yesterday because when Janet called me at work and said her water just broke and she was having labor pains, I nearly fainted from fright and I don't think I have ever driven a company pickup faster than that trip home that day. Janet had already called Dr. Lamb and had packed her little overnight bag and was climbing into our family's '49 Plymouth sedan we traded our '49 pickup for, just as I skidded into our drive way.

I'll tell you, we took off wide open for the Alta Bates Hospital in Berkeley, but by the time we reached the Caldecott Tunnel, her labor pains were much harder and more frequent and, I'll kid you not, I began praying, "Oh please God, give us a little more time to *not* give birth to our baby in this tunnel." Fortunately, my prayers were answered, and as we slid to a screeching halt at the hospital, two nurses raced out with a wheel chair and took Janet, who began giving birth at that very moment, directly to the delivery room.

Mary Beth and Dear Old Dad – 1952

As I parked the Plymouth, two accountant types from the hospital suddenly appeared, jerked me from my car by knap of my neck and demanded I immediately sign on the, *how are you going to pay for all this* line, and by the time I made it to the delivery room, I was the proud father of a beautiful brand spanking new eight pound healthy baby girl. I can truthfully say, I have never felt happier or more relieved in my life, than I was at that moment. Our beautiful new baby's birth was such an easy one this time for Janet I couldn't believe it, and needless to say, bottled beer and *'It's a girl'* cigars were passed around at our foremen schedule and safety meeting that evening, to celebrate the wonderful event.

Mary Beth and Great Grandpa Weimer

When I reported for duty at the Kiewit job office on the East Shore Freeway and met Bill Roach, the job superintendent, it was a night and day welcoming experience compared to my last two jobs. Bill was a big jovial Irish Catholic guy who had a wonderful wife and ten beautiful children he bragged about every Saturday morning during our scheduling meetings. Unbelievably he welcomed me like I was a long lost friend and said I would have his complete cooperation building all my structures as economically as possible. Wow, and you guessed it, I immediately took a liking to Bill and his staff and thought to myself, what a wonderful way to start a new job. I still remember to this day leaving his office convinced that this job was not only going to be a profitable job, but an enjoyable one for all of us to build.

Mary Beth and Grandpa Whitehead

Since the new East Shore Freeway would be built on a newly widened San Francisco Bay shoreline made up of over million cubic yards of dredged in sand fill from underneath the San Francisco Bay, all the bridge work would be delayed. I remember during our first Saturday morning superintendent's schedule meeting with Brad Lockwood, the project engineer; Otto Heppner, the office manager; Johnny Kaufman, the dirt superintendent and Bill Roche, we reviewed several options on how to integrate my structure work into the overall job's schedule economically. Since several of my Antioch crackerjack crew had already checked in, I made the suggestion I join the Carpenters Union and be the acting foreman of my all foremen crew to install all the initial storm drains and culvert extensions needed prior to placing the sand fill. I said we could also fabricate the forms and falsework we would need later for bridge work, but best of all, my crew would then remain intact and when the bridge sites at Powell Street and Ashby Avenue became available, my all foremen crew would split into separate crews and we would hit the work *full speed ahead*. Everyone agreed it was the best plan and gave me their, *fire at will Gridley*, approval.

Grandma & Grandpa Olsen

When I checked in at the union hall of Carpenters Local #37 in Oakland, California to sign on, much to my surprise I was welcomed like a long lost friend again, only this time it was because of my Norwegian last name. Interestingly, nearly all the members Carpenters Hall #37 at that time were of

Bill Roach, Job Superintendent – 1953

Scandinavian descent, and when I got a perfect score on both their apprentice and journeyman written and verbal tests, they were so impressed with my unlimited Scandinavian intelligence and my practical construction knowledge (that's a laugh), they immediately made me a journeyman carpenter and wished me luck as the new foreman in the Kiewit Company. As I left, I asked the business agent for three of his best heavy timber men for a rush job that I had in mind, and he sent me three of his best Norwegian shipbuilders named Ole Storstrom, his son Boyd, and Lars Larsen.

Bill Roach had just recently relocated the Pabco Paint Company's warehouse off the freeway's right-of-way to a newly driven pile area in the Bay next to the new Freeway, so the

NEWS RELEASES DURING 1952

*Dwight D. Eisenhower and Richard M. Nixon are elected President and Vice President, the "H–Bomb" is exploded at Eniwetok, Eisenhower visits Korea, subversives are prohibited from teaching in public schools, a Polio epidemic afflicts 50,000 Americans, Jonas Salk develops a polio vaccine, the "Big Bang" theory is described, pocket sized transistor radios and the first video tape are introduced, heavy snow storms in the Sierra Nevada mountains traps Southern Pacific trains **AND Mary Elizabeth Olsen is Born at the Alta Bates Hospital in Berkeley California, May 8, 1952.***

rush change order involved cutting an eighteen foot wide, fifteen foot high door opening on the Bay side of their warehouse to load cargo ships. For some unknown reason, the paint company insisted the doorway *header beam* be a 12" x 24" x 20' length Port Orchard cedar weighing over a half ton and when I showed what had to be done to my Norwegian crew

foreman, I said, "Ole, it looks to me like we'll have to cut a hole in the roof to drop a hook through to lift that timber beam while you post it, then we can patch the roof later." Ole thought for a moment and said, "Ohlmer, yust give the tre of us some block and tackle, and leave us be for two hours." Whooee I'll tell you, when I came back two hours later the job was completed without roof holes, and to this day I have never figured out (and they would never tell me), how the three of them were able to lift that 1000+ lb wooden beam up the fifteen feet and post it over the doorway, with only a block and tackle.

Relocating the Pabco Paint Company's Warehouse

In fact I was so impressed with their heavy timber craftsmanship I asked them to be part of my *special ops* crew, and they worked for me until all the bridge and structure work on the Eastshore Freeway contract was completed.

Lesson Learned: *Never underestimate the ingenuity of the American Blue Collar worker (the best craftsmen in the world) when it comes to doing his job. Just tell him what you want done and when you want it completed. He will do the job his way, the easiest way, and nine times out of ten, it will be the most economical way.*

Back in those good old days before Sewerage Treatment Plants were built, all the cities located along San Francisco Bay considered the Bay their own private *cesspool* and connected all their sewer lines directly to the same pipe lines and culverts constructed originally for storm water drains into the bay. It so happened, there was a large box culvert storm drain under Ashby Avenue that ran all the way from the Claremont Hotel and the Alta Bates Hospital in the foothills, down through Berkeley and past a slaughter house to the San Francisco Bay, and believe it or not, during the dry season that large culvert ran half full of wastewater.

Well, you guessed it. When it rained it not only ran full but was also under pressure and it was my job to extend all these box culvert and pipe storm drains into the bay another 150 feet or so for the new freeway's sand fill widening, so it goes without saying, Ashby Avenue became more than a minor problem. I originally thought a 60"diameter steel pipe punched through the side wall near the old bayside headwall would suffice as a detour pipe during the dry period, but much to my surprise, it ran full and under pressure from the first day we installed it. In effect, the whole Ashby Avenue drainage area had suddenly become a giant combination bladder prostate problem filling with wastewater faster than we could empty it with our constricting 60" detour pipe. Whooee, talk about a gamble, but fortunately for us we had clear skies and were able to complete the culvert extension on a fast track crash schedule just before the wastewater back-up would have really caused some home flooding problems. We were also lucky to convince Lloyd Marshall, our resident engineer, he needn't worry when the time came to remove our stoplog dam because, being an engineer and all, I had designed a secret weapon to remove it that

Culvert extension on piling prior to Sand Backfilling

was fool proof. Why? Because my infallible secret weapon was simply nothing more than a steel cable looped around the span centers of the wooden stoplog planks to *theoretically* snap the planks as they were winched out by a D8 tractor at the outlet end. The broken wooden planks would then (we thought) float out to sea in one gigantic flush and we would all celebrate with cold beers afterwards.

Culvert extension work on the Eastshore Freeway

Unfortunately during the winching operation, our steel cable suddenly snapped after breaking only two of the top planks and both state engineers watching our operation named, Loyd Marshall and Don Higgins, stomped off muttering, "Homer, you and your damned secret weapon ideas are driving us nuts."

Well, aside from all that, it left the four of us, namely Orville Saalfeld, (carpenter foreman), Bill Turnbough, (labor foreman), Art Loyd, (crane operator), and myself, (the crews screwup superintendent), sitting on the *riprap* beach rocks looking at each other, looking at each other mumbling, *Now what?*

Culvert Extension Pour on the Eastshore Freeway

Orville finally said, "Homer, if you can find a rowboat for Bill and me, we'll paddle up *Road Apple Creek* to check out what needs to be done." I told him there was no way I would let him do something like that because of the *bad air* they might encounter inside, but in the end, Art and I agreed with his plan if we could tie a rope to their boat to hurriedly haul them out when they signaled, and would paddle up there only during low tide to **re-tie** *the steel cable.*

Is this the way Orville and Bill looked Daddy?

As it turned out, Orville and Bill did paddle their row boat up road apple creek alright, all the way to *Stop Log Dam*, but on their own decided **not** to re-place the cable as agreed, and removed the top cinch anchors holding the side wall angle to let the planks hinge themselves out. Oooh boy, about the same time we heard their loud *"Thar She Blows"* inside and felt their tug on the rope to begin pulling, I'll kid you not, all hell suddenly broke loose. Believe it or not, a huge rumbling *tsunami* wall of surging, swirling wastewater suddenly thundered by us out the end of the culvert, showering planks, debris and garbage by us out to sea in the bay,

but no rowboat. Art and I frantically began pulling on the boat's tow rope, and I'll kid you not, when the rope suddenly snapped, we both had *frog eyed* panic attacks. Luckily, a Northwest #6 dragline was parked nearby with a two yard sand bucket attached so we immediately moved it to a sandbar semi-blocking the culverts flow during low tide, and began cutting a larger drain slot. Like a maple leaf twirling down a city street gutter during a *tunder and lightening* downpour, all of a sudden, out popped our rowboat with two of the palest, scaredest, death warmed over looking, toilet relieved guys we had ever seen lying flat as pancakes in the bottom of their row boat twirling out to sea. Apparently when our now famous *stop log dam* gave way, the sewage wastewaters surge had pinned their rowboat to the roof of the culvert and they were

All's well that ends well Daddy

stuck flat on their stomachs in their boat against the roof until the *tsunami* subsided. As luck would have it, they were fortunately not squashed or swamped against the roof because of the Dory's deep draft.

When things settled down and we all finished thanking our lucky stars how fortunate we were no one was hurt, I'm sure this *screwup story* will be remembered by

everyone as a hilarious keystone cop comedy, but I'll tell you, at the time it was anything but. We all gave a sigh of relief and I gave my crew the rest of the week off to regain their sense of humors while I chalked up another lesson learned while traveling down the highway of life.

Lesson Learned: *Life threatening situations can easily occur when poorly thought out "Joe Magee" ideas and cheap methods are used to try saving time and a few pennies. When it comes to safety, "pennywise and pound foolish" thinking cannot be tolerated. Believe me, **it's not worth it**.*

The Powell Street Bridge under construction in Emeryville - 1954

The new Powell Street Freeway Bridge was basically two long side by side four lane box girder concrete bridges for north and south bound traffic. At my request, the State's Bridge Engineers reluctantly agreed to let me split the two four lane bridges into four two lane bridges, providing we *re-welded* them back together again at no additional cost to the State, which we did.

Their cooperative agreement not only allowed us to roll our bridge shoring sideways four times using mine car wheel dollies rolling on 20 # rail, but also allowed us to reuse our forms more times for even more savings. We elected to pre-cast all the pipe headwalls and the lower half of the large drainage pipe headwalls to further simplify the drainage pipe placement and we slip formed all the *rolled* curb and gutters (unheard of in those days) to save even more time and money. As I recall, our only major job problem was, our equipment (other than the track laying type) was unable to maneuver on either the dredged beach sand

Sliding the Falsework sideways on the Powell Street Bridge

and/or the bay mud without getting stuck, so we purchased four surplus four wheel drive power wagons plus one extra for parts, and a half track at an Army Depot surplus auction for $1500 apiece. We then mounted "A" frame booms on all four of them to work off the truck's winches, like our March Field job, and *Voila!,* we had a small fleet of handy small cranes that worked beautifully in sand and mud without getting stuck Three of the power wagons were assigned to the pipe laying, headwall, and the concrete placement crews, and the halftrack was assigned to the mechanics for their equipment maintenance duties. The Judson-Pacific- Murphy Steel Company gave us all the *slag* we needed at no charge to make temporary roadways for our rubber tired equipment and we soon discovered slag makes good roads but a poor cofferdam material because of its porosity.

The Mine Car Dolly Falsework Mover

All in all, the Eastshore Freeway contract ended up very successfully, profit wise, as I envisioned, except for one incidence. A drunken pickup driver veered off the road underneath the northern Ashby Avenue cloverleaf bridge late one night and struck a corner falsework post, dropping a steel beam on a passing refrigerated truck. Believe it or not, on a probability of one in a million, that beam landed exactly crossways between the refrigerated trucks cab and trailer, causing the speeding truck to immediately assume the role of a berserk bull in a china closet with a pole strapped to its horns, as it thundered underneath and through the bridge, wiping out everything in its path. Honest to God, that truck took

Ashby Avenue Cloverleaf Bridge just before the Truck Demolition Derby

out all the remaining posts, dropping all the other steel beams, deck materials, reinforcing steel, and ended up crushing itself and the drunk driver's pickup like pancakes under all the debris. When I arrived at the scene around 4:00 o'clock in the morning, I was amazed by the amount of wreckage strewn along the highway, but very relieved that miraculously neither truck driver was hurt. With the help of the Highway Patrol, my crew and I began clearing the mess and by sunrise we had the freeway ready for commuter traffic. Everyone else involved, immediately headed for their lawyer's offices to file law suits against each other, the drunk driver, the steel beam that dropped first, and the two sea gulls that witnessed the accident. You guessed it, their trial lawyers convinced them the suit should be against the one with the deep pockets, the Kiewit Company.

I spent three days on the witness stand being grilled by the attorney's for the Nielsen Trucking Company, while they tried to prove the accident was my entire fault because I was building an *attractive hazard that* was literally begging for an accident to happen. When the jury finally finished hearing all the testimony, including the drunk driver's statement he never saw the bridge, let alone the flashing lights we installed, they ruled

I was the one at fault. Why? Because I couldn't prove exactly when we last wiped the dust off our flashing warning lights, and when the drunk driver proved he had no car insurance, no driver's license, no money or net worth, and concluded his *ambulance chaser's nightmare speech* with, "You can't get blood out of a turnip." So, when everything was all was said and done, justice prevailed once again and the *deep pockets* were fairly ruled as the guilty party and the Kiewit Company got stuck with buying a new refrigerated truck for the Nielsen Trucking Company, plus all the court costs and attorney's fees for both sides. The drunk driver was awarded his mashed truck back again, and Kiewit was awarded the bridge debris to reinstall.

Ashby Avenue Cloverleaf nearing completion on the Eastshore Freeway

The best thing that ever happened to me on the Eastshore Freeway job was, our second beautiful little daughter, Barbara Jean Olsen, was born October 15, 1953 at the Alta Bates hospital in Berkeley, California, with help from the

Mary Elizabeth & Barbara Jean Olsen – 1953

same Dr. Lamb that delivered her older sister. It was without a doubt, the second happiest day of my life and once again, cold beer and *It's a girl* cigars were passed around at our foremen's weekly schedule and safety meeting that evening to celebrate our beautiful little girl's birth. Barbara Jean was two weeks over due when she was born, so at nine and a half pounds, she was a much larger baby and a more difficult birth than Mary Beth, but Janet still made it through with flying colors, thanks to Dr. Lamb. I remember thinking what a different personality this cute little girl's first squawks conveyed compared to her older sisters. How did I know? Well because their first *squawks* when they were born sounded so different. I asked Bill Roach if he noticed it in any of his ten children when they were born, and he said, "Homer, no two human beings are alike from the day they are born to the day they die. Every one of my ten children's first squawks sounded

Mary & Barbara enjoying a shoe snack – 1954

differently at birth and they're growing up with completely different personalities and that's the reason I love each one of them so much." Wow, what a wonderful father.

Dear Old Dad & his beautiful daughters

We discovered shortly after we brought little Barbara home she was allergic to both her mother's and cow's milk, but fortunately, she tolerated soybean milk (and shoes) and soon became the same happy contented little baby her sister was. I remember when the hospital called me to bring Janet and little Barbara Jean home, I drove my "Peewee Keewee" pickup (named by Mary Beth) home to trade cars so they would have a more comfortable ride, and wouldn't you know it, I couldn't get that lousy '49 Plymouth started. Both Janet and our new little baby girl bounced and bawled all the way home in that rough riding "Peewee Keewee" truck. In fact, we decided right then and there to trade our old 1949 Plymouth in for a new car and bought our first brand spanking new family automobile, a 1954 Plymouth station wagon that turned out to be the perfect car for our little family.

The picture of Mary Beth and her dear old dad reading to her was taken shortly after I arrived home from an overtime concrete pour on the East Shore Freeway and was late for our story time. Little "Steamer Jean" (named by her mother because she always waited for a new dry diaper before she wet again) had already caved in and gone to bed, but Mary Beth waited up for me to hear her most favorite "Bre'r Rabbit" bedtime story. Unfortunately, I seldom made it home early enough to have dinner with them because of my job responsibilities, but I really tried to be home in time for our important story time before their bed time. I think sometimes I enjoyed our animated story telling time and the exaggerated character parts I played while reading, even more than my little girls. One thing for sure, I will always have fond memories of their happy early

Story Time with Daddy

NEWS RELEASES DURING 1953

The Korean armistice is signed; U.S. casualties include 25,604 dead. Earl Warren becomes Chief Justice of the Supreme Court. Nuclear fallout from an atomic test rains down on St. George, Utah. TV Dinners, instant ice tea and sugar smacks are introduced, Charlie Chaplin is banned from the U.S., Meteorologists give women's names to hurricanes Francis Crick and James Watson discover the double helix structure of DNA. AND Barbara Jean Olsen was born on October 15, 1953 at the Alta Bates Hospital in Berkeley, California.

childhood days, and reading the "Bre'r Rabbit" and "Hans Christian Anderson" stories to my little girls. They were such a wonderful and appreciative little audience and I'm sure it is the reason my girls were such good students during their school years and are such good readers (and writers) even now.

It wasn't too long after little steamer Jean was born we made an offer on our first home at 156 Lucinda Lane, Pleasant Hill, California. As I recall, it was a 1300 square foot mansion on a half acre lot, with a huge two car garage, three large bed rooms, a single bath, a kitchen and a front room with a dining nook, and it even had a brick fireplace and hardwood flooring. The owner accepted our offer of $12,500 and we took over his 3% veteran loan of $9,000 and borrowed a whopping $1,500 on a second mortgage loan from uncle Larry's mother, Mrs. Lindberg, at 6% interest (which was

"Bre'r Rabbit said to the Tar Baby"

horrendously high to me) and put up our life savings. Tom Paul thought I was nuts to buy

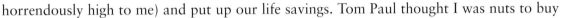

a home and said, "What are you going to do with it when you're transferred to another job?" I said, "I'll rent it out until I'm transferred back."

I used to get such a kick out of little Barbara "Steamer Jean" when she was first learning to talk. She would stand up in her crib after we had put them both to bed after their bedtime stories, and she would whine *Maammaa* over and over again a thousand times before going to

Mary Beth & Barbara enjoy Meem's third birthday

sleep. Janet would say, "I'm not going to answer her because if I do she will never lie down and go to sleep." After a hundred pathetic sounding *Maammaas* later, I couldn't stand it any longer and would answer in her mother's high voice with a quivering *"Wwhhaatt."* She would then angrily shout back, "No talkkadaa to you Daaadnn, talkkadaa to Mammaa",

and start all over repeating her "Maammaa's" over and over and over again. Whenever she thought I should be home instead of at work, Barbara (also known as *"Bowie"* because *"Meem"* couldn't say

Our Wonderfully Happy First Home on Lucinda Lane - 1954

Barbara) would stand out by the tree in the front yard for what seemed like hours to her mother, wailing, "Daaaaddnn, Daaaddnn" over and over again, to call me to come home from work.

All ready for bed and bedtime stories-1954

The horseshoe shaped road around our home named Lucinda Lane was filled with young families with dozens of young children. Every year the mothers would organize Halloween parades and parties for the children and they would all dress up in costumes and parade up and down that safe street, trick are treating, eating their goodies and playing games. Our oldest daughter, Mary Beth, was born with a remarkably lovable *take charge* personality and she used to stand in our front yard by the tree wailing over and over and over, "Chillddrenn, Chillddrenn, come to our house and play", hoping they would hear her. It finally got to the point that nearly every weekend when school was out and all their Dads were home, the neighborhood kids would all show up at our front door at 8:00 o'clock in the morning asking, "What are we going to do today Mary Beth?"

Bill Roach had an easy going approach to building construction jobs that seemed to radiate throughout our whole job, and it did wonders for my ulcer recovery. In fact, I still think the two years I spent working on the Eastshore freeway job with Bill and his crew, were the most enjoyable years I spent with the Kiewit Company. I worked with so many good hard working people on that job who later became lifelong friends, like Fred Cavin, who was with the

That's not Funny Dadden

Raymond Pile Driving Company at the time, and so many others I got to know so well. They all had a major impact on my life and on my career later on in the construction business. I

remember in 1954, I was given a job tour of the recently awarded Richmond-San Rafael Bridge during its early phases, and I met Bill Ziegler, the project manager, on the super structure portion. In April that same year, Bill called to invite me to lunch with him at the "Hotel Mac" in Richmond wher I met Rod Chrisom and Paul Bowen of the Judson Pacific Murphy Co, George Merriman

Let's Play We're in the Rose Bowl Parade

of Clementine Co, Paul Hilkowski from the Pacific Coast Aggregate Company, and Bill McGraf, who worked for the American Bridge Company. Interestingly, everyone in that group including me, were born in April, so you guessed it, from then on we had many "TGIF" *git together's* to celebrate our April birthdays. Believe it or not, that first 1954 luncheon at the Hotel Mac was the beginning of the now renowned club we named, "The April Club" (what else), that has become the major heavy engineering contractors social group it is today. It was also the beginning of the many lifelong friendships I've enjoyed with all those hard working, fun loving heavy construction stiffs who made up that wonderful little club.

Off to Church with G. W. & Mom

All the people shown in the adjacent group picture taken at the April Club's first Annual meeting at Mape's Hotel in Reno in 1964, are all sadly gone now except two members, Paul Hilkowski and myself seated next to each other at the far end of the table, but I will always remember those wonderful story telling good times we had together, and be grateful for my long friendships with all those wonderful guys. Many other qualified people have joined the April Club since then to replace those who have passed away, and to this day the April Club is still a

The April Club's first Annual Meeting at the Mape's Hotel in Reno, Nevada

vibrant group in the western states heavy construction industry. It is no mystery that eight Golden Beaver and associate construction industry awardees for accomplishments in the heavy engineering construction industry are members of the April Club. In 2006, fifty two years after I first became a member, I requested the Club reclassify me as a non-active lifetime founding member to create an opening for a former prized employee and Golden Beaver Awardee named John Shimmick, to join our elite group. I was honored and humbled to receive our industries most prestigious Golden Beaver's Management Award in 1995 for my career accomplishments, and was honored by the April Club with a Founder's Award when I retired, but I'm most honored to have known every member in that Club since its inception, as the hard working honest contractor friends who lived and breathed responsibility, integrity and quality built construction works during their lives. They were and are my kind of people.

It was in 1954 I also met Bill Ames, founder of the Miller and Ames Company, when he was Peter Kiewit Sons Company's insurance and bond underwriter. Bill and I became very good friends over the years and in 1963 when I left Kiewit to start up Homer J. Olsen, Inc., Bill became both my mentor and valued business advisor. My dad also thought the world revolved around Bill and unbeknown to me, asked Bill to keep a watchful eye out for me and our fledgling company when we first started in business. I will always be grateful to Bill Ames because we would never have made it as a construction company without his valuable advice and help during our early years.

NEWS RELEASES DURING 1954

The Supreme Court outlaws segregation in public schools, Mississippians vote to abolish public schools to halt integration, five congressmen are shot by Porto Rican nationalists, U.S.S. Nautilus is the first atomic submarine, U.S. and Canada announce construction of the DEW (Distant Early Warning) radar network, Eisenhower changes the Pledge of Allegiance to include the words "under God", children are inoculated with Salk's polio vaccine, Ray Kroc buys franchise rights from McDonalds, and the "Iwo Jima WW II Memorial Monument" is dedicated in Washington, D.C.

It was also on the Eastshore Freeway job, Bill Roach taught me the secret art of smoking cigars that he called *adult male pacifiers* to use as a prop to stall for more time to *review problems*, he invariably made the wrong decisions on anyway. As nice a guy as Bill was, he had a disgusting habit of blowing cigar smoke directly into the faces of the people he was talking to until finally, to defend myself in our coughing, eye watering meetings, I started smoking his same smelly five cent *King Edwards* to return the favor. I remember Brad Lockwood also smoked an even worse smelling cigar called *rum soaked crooks* that made me half sick just watching him smoke. I'll tell you, when Brad's cigar smoke was mixed in with our cigar contributions, it created such a thick cloud of dark toxic smoke that was not only stifling, but was dangerously damaging to our health. The best (thing to come out of all this was, our Saturday morning "cough, sneeze and wheeze" planning and scheduling meetings ended sooner and whatever decisions

Playing' Horsey' with Uncle Larry Lindberg

that had to be made, were made quicker, and we got to go home to play with our kids earlier.

To save face and compromise with my family, I switched to smoking a milder more expensive ten cent cigar called *White Owls*, and later on to a more milder variety called *Thompson's*, that were said to be less toxic. Unlike the marijuana smokers of today, I made it a point (like Bill Clinton), to **never** inhale my cigar smoke so my lungs wouldn't be damaged. Oooh Boy, was I ever wrong. After smoking my cigars for 45 years before quitting cold turkey, I sit here now, hunt and pecking these memoirs with emphysema and only one good lung, but as my dad used to say, "Only the good die young son, so the way I look at it, you'll live on forever."

Lesson Learned: *Don't Smoke! And if you do, don't light up.*

The upshot of all this was, the Eastshore Freeway contract turned out to be a very successful job when completed and I was invited to give a slide presentation at the January 1955 annual Kiewit Company managers meeting in Grand Island, Nebraska. Apparently my job presentation went over so well with all the company managers, both Homer Scott, Vice President and Wyoming District Manager, and Ivan Brunsbach, Vice

Powder, Mary Beth & Barbara play 'Vikings'

President and Washington State District Manager, offered me job's if I would move my family to their states to work for them. Tom Paul had just handed me a huge $1,000 bonus for doing

Ben Williams, Project Manager – 1955

such a good job on the East Shore Freeway, so I told both of them they should check with Tom first because I felt a loyalty to Tom, bonus and all, but said, "If either of you find out he wants to get rid of me anyway, I'll gladly consider your offers."

Well, when I got back to California, I found out Ben Williams, the project manager on the Garrison Dam in North Dakota, had already talked Tom Paul into *loaning me out* to him to help build their Stilling Basin in two years instead of the three years the Corps of Engineers specified. The main Garrison Dam contract would be completed and was going to be dedicated by President

Eisenhower in two more years, so Pete Kiewit, for tax reasons, wanted all the company work there, completed during the same year. When I told Janet we were moving to North Dakota, she literally blew her stack and said, "You can move up there if you want, but the girls and I are not moving, period." I said, "Well, it's too damn late for me to back out now because I've already told Tom I would help Ben Williams get the Stilling Basin job built in two years." For some unknown reason, Janet still couldn't get it through her head after five years of marriage, in the construction business you either report for work when and where you are asked to report, or you quit, period.

Well, you guessed it. When I arrived all by myself in Riverdale, North Dakota, in early April, 1955 (and missed my sister Winifred's wedding) to meet Ben Williams for my job introduction tour, I was not only awe struck, but completely intimidated by the immensity of that huge earthen Garrison Dam Project on the Missouri river, the largest earth filled Dam in the world at that time. Ben wanted me to be the general superintendent in charge of constructing the "Stilling Basin" portion of the project (#6 on the picture of the Garrison Dam Project below) which would require my crew and I to place, finish and cure over 200,000 cubic yards of structure concrete in two short five month North Dakota work seasons. I looked over at Ben and said, "Are you sure you picked the right guy for this job Ben? I don't think I have either the qualifications or the experience needed to handle a job like this." Ben grinned and said, "Homer, you have the qualifications, and you already have all the experience necessary to handle this job, so here is what I want you to do. I want

Winifred Olsen and David Dahl's Wedding – 1955

you to take a good hold of your nose with both hands, real tight if necessary, and take a deep breath. Now, while your holding your breath and your nose tight, blow as hard as you can until you feel yourself swelling up to the size you feel you need to be to handle this job." Honest to God, I *cracked up* laughing, and after I had regained my composure, Ben said, "Homer, every job, large or small, is built **one brick at a time.** The principles used to build any project, large or small, are the same and the only difference is in the size of the equipment."

Ben Williams had a fascinating easy going way about him that made everyone working for him feel comfortable. In my opinion, he was a born leader and I used to marvel at the homespun humorous way he had of convincing people to do a job his way. I don't remember him ever ordering people to do anything because he felt employees should use their own good judgment on how to do their job the best and most efficiently way on time. He would only tell them what needed to be done, when he wanted it done, and why their job was so important in the overall scheme of things. All in all, he was a likeable down to earth, homespun typical Montanan with a wonderful sense of humor, much like Will Rogers, and

Steve and Mary Beth – 1955

he used those gifts masterfully during negotiations with the companies clients, craft unions, subcontractors and suppliers. One thing for sure, I will always be grateful to Ben Williams for reaffirming what Ward White tried to teach me on the Friant-Kern Canal.

Lessons Learned: *The working stiff deserves a fair shake. Always be honest and fair in all your endeavors. The best and most economical way to build anything is to build it right the first time. Every job, big or small, is built one brick at a time, and to restore self confidence when necessary, hold your nose and blow hard until you swell up to the size you think you need to be to handle that job.*

After I regained my self confidence and released my *body building* air, I met with Ben's excellent staff and discovered they had already dreamed up several time saving ideas to speed up the job. We began negotiating credit type change orders with the Corps of Engineers to save both time and money, beginning with pouring the five foot thick concrete slab sections in 25 foot wide highway type lanes using standard paving equipment, rather than pouring the 50 foot square blocks as shown on their drawings. The Corps of Engineers also approved our pouring the 80 foot high retaining walls in 7.5 foot lifts rather than 5 foot, and the 24 foot slope walls in one 24 foot lift pour as I had done in California, rather than the three lifts they specified. These changes not only reduced the number of pours by making them larger, but best of all, saved valuable time towards our now feasible two year completion goal. We also purchased an *already built* batch plant from the upstream contractor to begin our work sooner and started our job by working two shifts, six day week. All the drilled piling, carpenter work, and reinforcing steel placement was then done on the

The Stilling Basin Job being constructed from the outsides towards the middle

day shift, while all the concrete place, finish and cure, was done on the night shift, like the Colorado job. Fortunately for me, three of my loyal Eastshore Freeway crew, namely Orville Saalfeld and Ray McClarrinon (carpenter foremen), and Bill Turnbough (labor foreman), moved to North Dakota with me, giving me three good dependable supervisors I could trust to build new crews when needed.

When we began pouring the highway strip pours with our paving equipment it took thirty continuous hours to complete each 3,200 cy pour, so Mel, our resident engineer, became worried we might get caught up in a *tunder & lightning* shower during the pour. I told him *never to worry* because we had invented a *top secret weapon* in our shop called *Homer's folly* to take care of that situation. Basically, our secret weapon was nothing more than a light steel trussed canvas covered tent, 50 foot long and 27 feet wide that would simply be placed over the pour by crane when needed to shelter the finishers and the wet

305

concrete. Well, as you've already guessed, I didn't take into account the *whirly gig winds* that accompany the North Dakota *tunder & lightning* showers, and when Mel demanded I unveil my secret weapon during a sudden rain squall, I yelled, "Open up the hanger doors boys, and roll her out."

Oooh Boy, I'll kid you not; I immediately learned I had missed my calling as an aeronautical engineer. A gust of wind caught that sucker just after we set her over the wet concrete pour, and Whooee!! I'll tell you, it took off like Chuck Yeager when he broke the sound barrier. Everyone in my crackerjack North Dakota crew stood goggle eyed, quietly watching in hypnotic fascination, as my secret *flying tent gracefully*

My Crackerjack Crew on the Garrison Dam Stilling Basin Job-1955

thermaled skyward towards the Missouri river, and disappearing behind an adjacent hill. I'll tell you, the curtain fell on one of the most spectacular *secret weapon* demonstrations ever seen, and our mesmerizing award winning show came to a memorable ending. As if on cue, my all Norwegian crew busted out laughing, applauding, and shouting, "Oh det var sin" (Oh that's too bad) as Mel, red faced and angrily disgusted, turned towards me muttering between clinched teeth, "Homer, you and your damned secret weapon ideas are driving me nuts", (Oooh boy, where have I heard that before?) and stomped off towards his office.

When you think hard enough about it, the Garrison Dam Stilling Basin is nothing more than a giant chute, 1200 feet long and 800 feet wide, equivalent to a 22 acre concrete slab that varied in thickness from 5 feet in the lower area to a 2 foot thickness near the top of the slope. The concrete slab itself is held down by 11,430 drilled anchor piling belled at the bottom to prevent uplift, and the walls on each side vary from 24 feet high on the slopes to a height of 84 feet along the bottom as the slab drops 170 feet in elevation, top to bottom. Multiple concrete baffles and a 12 foot high sill wall at the

Stilling Basin Structure when completed on the Garrison Dam in North Dakota

end of the structure was built to create a *hydraulic jump* to dissipate the tremendous energy the flood waters will generate while *chuting* down the Stilling Basin from the reservoirs Spillway above.

From my point of view the Stilling Basin was a fascinating job, not only for its immense size and huge equipment used, but also for its concrete mix requirements. It is the same mix design used to build the Boulder Dam in the 1930's consisting of 6 inch cobble stone aggregate in the larger footing and slab areas, to 2 inch rock size in the remainder. We premixed our concrete at the hill side batch plant we purchased from the Spillway contractor, using three 2 CY tilt mixers that dumped into a 40 CY gob hopper. The hopper mix was then dumped into the three 4 cy buckets on each of the low boy haul trucks to a 4500 Manitowoc crane with a 120 foot boom where the operator air hooked each bucket off the trucks to swing to the pouring crew. The wet concrete was then consolidated with one man lightweight Malan air vibrators invented (used for the first time on our job) by a mechanic named Red Malan.

My mother & family enjoying California without me

All and all, the job was a night and day change for a 31 year old general superintendent like me, especially when compared to my earlier bridge building days. Way back then (six months earlier), we used 1 cy concrete buckets (instead of 4 cy buckets) with 1 inch aggregate (instead of 6 inch boulders) in the mix, and placed the concrete with a 20 ton crane (instead of a 150 ton crane) using 2 inch diameter (instead of 6 inch diameter) vibrators to consolidate the mix. To this day, I still marvel at what Ben William's *nose holding self confidence builder* did for me, especially since I had so little self confidence only three months earlier.

After two months of batching it at the company's BOQ dormitory, I found a government rental and somehow talked Janet and our two beautiful little girls into moving to Riverdale, North Dakota to be with me instead of their best friends and Janet reluctantly rented our home in Pleasant Hill, and our little family was finally back together again in a partially furnished *unit* by mid June in 1955.

Unfortunately, a serious problem arose when the incompetent moving company we hired named, Allied Movers, lost our partial load of furniture on the way to North Dakota and was not found and delivered to us until the middle of August. Until that time, we were forced to live out of our suit cases and used empty blasting powder boxes as furniture. Luckily Ben's office girl, bless her heart, finally discovered where that lousy mover had either *stolen and/or lost* all our furniture and the paperwork in a Denver warehouse of all places. Well, when all those frustrations were combined with my six day, three shift work schedule, the stilling basin job was even more damaging to our marriage than the job in Fort Collins, Colorado. Except for Sundays, Janet and I barely got to see each other after she arrived, and after Labor Day, even our Sundays were lost when we began working three shifts, seven day

307

week, to save on our last good weather. In retrospect, Janet and the girls probably would have been much better off staying in California like she wanted all along.

Barbara Jean Olsen, age two-1955

The fast track schedule we dreamed up to build the Stilling Basin in two short seasons called for our first pour in mid June, and place 110,000 cy of concrete before the *black frost* shut us down in mid October. We would then fabricate all the wall forms we needed the following year in the mechanics luxuriously heated shop during the winter months. Ben always paid his weekly salaried people half salary during their *no-work* winter shut down months anyway, so I figured why not have an *all foremen crew* fabricate all the forms we needed while they were resting at full salary and we would be able to complete the Stilling Basin by mid October of 1956. As it turned out, the Stilling Basin was completed in two years as Pete wanted, but was not accepted by the C of E until December 1, 1956, six weeks behind our original schedule. Pete's tax accountants were ecstatic, but Pete as usual, only said he was pleased, but not satisfied. No matter how well you did on a job; Pete always said the same thing after reviewing your job cost reports, "I'm pleased, but not satisfied", and then add as desert, "Pay attention to business and business will pay."

Mary Elizabeth Olsen and Santa – 1955

Lesson learned: *That's true, practice does make perfect, and anyone can do better the second time around in any endeavor if attention is paid to the business at hand and something is learned from the first experience.*

As a little side story, after a typical North Dakota tornado had passed through our job and ripped the roof off our shop building, tipped over our light towers and knocked out all our power, I was down in the bottom of a flooded footing with our mechanics trying to get dewatering pumps going and someone on top shouted, "Hey Homer, how are you getting along?" I looked up and surprise of all surprises, there stood Pop Reynolds, one of my favorite Stanford professors. Unbelievably, he had dropped by our job at least a hundred miles out of his way to Iowa, just to say "hello." Wow, what a guy and what a wonderful surprise, especially since I never got better than a C+ in any of his classes. I said, "Pop, I can't believe you would go this far out of your way just to check up on a dumb guy like me." He said, "Homer, your veterans group may not have been as smart as some of my other classes, but that motivated group will always be my favorite class because of their maturity and motivation to learn and get on with their lives. You mark my words; I still think your class will end up much better career wise in the *real world*, than any of my other classes." Interestingly, some thirty years later in 1985, another favorite Stanford professor of mine named Clark Oglesby, said the same thing at a Golden Beavers Awards banquet in Los Angeles. Three of professor Oglesby's former students, namely Grove Holcomb, Gerald Clair and I, were reminiscing with Clark and laughing about the time Grover used the eraser end of his pencil as a pillow in his class, and Clark said, "Your class was probably the dumbest bunch I've ever taught, but I had more fun teaching you guys than any of my other classes, before or since and interestingly, you GI Bill veterans have turned out to be my most successful class, career wise. Maybe Stanford should re-analyze their *rich kid entrance requirements* and take a long hard look at letting more disadvantaged students with blue collar parents go to Stanford." We heartedly agreed with him, but added, "Unfortunately Clark, students like us in the disadvantaged category will never be able to go to a school like Stanford, even if we save every dime we make working full time during summers and part time during school years, without additional help from scholarships like the GI Bill."

Barbara Jean Olsen – 1956

Anyway, to get back to some of the major problems of building the Stilling Basin on the Garrison Dam, heavy spring rains delayed our first concrete pour until after the first of July. When that two week loss was coupled with other damaging delays caused by passing tornados and the *tunder and lightening* squalls rolling through along with more

Sledding in North Dakota weather, November 1, 1955

ground water than anticipated while drilling the belled piling, it all played havoc with our two year crash schedule. By the first of September we had only placed 40,000 cubic yards of concrete with only six more weeks of good weather left to pour out the other 70,000 cy needed to stay on schedule. Something had to be done.

I called an emergency meeting for all the shift supervisors the Saturday before Labor Day weekend and said, "We all know this job is in serious trouble, but before we talk about what we should do about it, I want everyone in this room to stop pointing fingers at each other and sit on your hands for the next two minutes without saying a word to think about of what we can do, **working as a team**, (I repeated it twice) to make up for lost time during these last few weeks of good weather" and at the end of the two minutes I said, "O.K., now let's talk about getting this job built." Well, you can believe this or not, but everyone in that room began coming up with good positive teamwork ideas while I chalked

them on the black board, and an hour later we all agreed on a *do-able* concrete schedule totaling at least 50,000 cubic yards of additional concrete placed by mid October, if we can **work together as a team.** To close our very positive meeting I said, "I want to thank all of you for all your hard work during the past two months and for all your good ideas here today. It has been a tough frustrating first two months and I know all of you are about give out so I think we need a short break. Let's take the remainder of this Labor Day weekend off to enjoy our families and beginning next Tuesday morning, we'll hit this job *wide open* at 7:00 am and begin working three shifts, seven days a week, until we've reached our 110,000 CY goal or we're froze out. I'm looking forward to seeing all of you here raring to go on your shift assignments next Tuesday morning. This meeting is now adjourned."

Reviewing a second Xmas list with Santa

The upshot of that meeting was even more encouraging because my motivated *espirit de corps* Riverdale crackerjack crew showed up the following Tuesday morning rested, motivated, and raring to go. Believe it or not, they did exactly what they said they would do and placed 50,000 cy of concrete during the last six weeks making a total of 90,000 cy in place the first season, just two 10,000 cy weeks behind our original schedule. Unfortunately, I stupidly gambled on the two more weeks needed, hoping the weather might hold, but in the end, accomplished nothing. The black frost hit us with a vengeance in mid October as forecast and only kept getting worse, stranding our 4500 Manitowoc crane on the lower slab area for the winter. The ground was frozen solid by the end of October and my sending four D8 tractors down to help pull the Manitowoc up the 20% grade and out of the hole, failed because of the slick frozen ground. Four D8 tractors and the 4500 Manitowoc crane, all

When dressed warmly, sledding in North Dakota is fun

pulling together, just sat there spinning in their tracks while attempting to pull the grade. On November 1, 1955, the high Fahrenheit temperature for the day in Riverdale, North Dakota was a *minus 5 degrees* and the low during the night was *minus 30 degrees* Fahrenheit.

Despite my job failures, Ben Williams, the best boss I ever worked for in the Kiewit Company, gave me a $25 a week raise to an unheard of $200 a week salary, and when I was called back to California by Tom Paul to run the Crockett Interchange job, Ben gave me a fantastic $3000 bonus for my help in building the Stilling Basin. I was embarrassed in accepting that huge bonus because I didn't reach my promised first season schedule, but I'll tell you, my little family really appreciated Ben's generosity and we used that huge bonus to payoff our home's second mortgage and to buy additional furniture to make our home more livable. Ben was also the first person in the Kiewit Company to tell me anything about *key employees* owning company stock (Kiewit was a *closed* corporation) and invited me to buy a few shares. Wow, what a guy, so we took him up on his kind offer with the rest of our bonus and it was the probably the best investment I have ever made. For some unknown reason, the Los Angeles District seemed to think company stock was a deep dark secret they couldn't talk about.

State and Contractor Personnel pose at the Ribbon Cutting

It was around the middle of November, after our carpenter shop was set up in the mechanics heated building, and I had placed Ray McClarrinon in charge of my all foremen crew to fabricate the wall forms for next seasons work, I told Ben I was give out and hadn't had a vacation now for over three years. Believe it or not he said, "Homer, I want you to take a full month's vacation in Florida or somewhere to relax with your family." Wow, can you imagine Tom Paul ever saying a thing like that?

Anyway, we caught the Great Northern train from Minot, North Dakota to Seattle, Washington and had just finished a fantastic Thanksgiving dinner with Janet's parents in Lynwood, Washington, when I got an urgent telephone call from Tom Paul. He said he needed me right away to run the Carquinez Bridge Interchange contract in California (called the Crockett job) and he wanted me to meet Bud Waigand (San Francisco area manager) and Merritt Mason (the Kiewit Company's asst. chief engineer) for the ribbon cutting ceremony in Vallejo, California. Then he said, "I also want you to fly with them down to Texas to a bridge site on the Pecos River near Del Rio where the piers for the new Highway Bridge are currently being "slipformed", and see if us doing the same thing on the Crockett job is feasible", and hung up saying he had already talked to Ben Williams about releasing me and had his approval. Oooh boy, there went my one month vacation.

The upshot of all this was, Janet and the girls stayed in Seattle during one of the worst snow storms to hit the Northwest, while I flew down to meet Bud and Merritt in San Francisco for the groundbreaking, and on to San Antonio, Texas. I remember we rented a car with a full tank of gas and I'll kid you not, we never saw another service station all the way from San Antonio to the Pecos River on the New Mexico border, and barely coasted on fumes into a gas station in Del Rio. Whooee, I thought stations were spaced a long way apart in Nevada but this was ridiculous. Anyway, the Winkler Construction Company was currently

slipforming the first of two 240 foot high (25 stories) concrete piers needed to set steel truss spans over the river, so we *lucked out* and arrived at exactly the right time. Tom already had permission from the California Highway (Bridge) Department to slipform all 47 of the 40 to 125 foot high column bents on the Crockett job if we so wished and we wanted to learn all we could about this interesting construction method that was being used so successfully building grain elevators in the Midwest.

After I finished reviewing the Crockett job's *as bid* cost estimate, I'll tell you, I soon found out why Tom was so anxious to use the slipform method to build the column bents. Julian Gobles, Tom's chief estimator with Paul Scrogg's experienced help, accidentally left out all the *jump form* carpenter labor to fabricate, place and strip the forms on all 47 column bents other than setting up for the first pour. Not only that,

a 25 Story Slipformed Pecos River Pier

they also left out all the carpenter labor and the materials needed for all the deck edges and expansion joints. My discovery of just these two major estimating errors convinced me we had to come up with someway of minimizing the obvious job loss as much as possible. If the slipforming method showed promise there was no question about it, slipforming was the way to go. It would shorten the job's construction time and would at least save some of the job's overhead costs.

When we arrived at the Pecos River bridge site, both Bud and I felt we had to see the slipform actually working at its current 180 foot height location on the 240 foot pier, and the only way to the work site was to ride a loaded one cy concrete bucket as an elevator. I remember telling Bud while we were standing on opposite sides of the bucket gripping the lift cable, "Don't look down Bud, don't look down, whatever you do Bud, don't look down." Well,

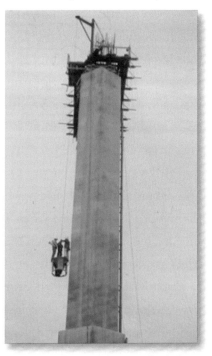

Don't look down Bud, Don't look down

about halfway up, Bud did look down and I'll tell you, he had a massive goggle eyed panic attack and literally *froze* while holding on to the cable. Fortunately for both of us in his paralyzed frozen fingers state, he hung on the rest of the way up to the slipform deck where we, believe it or not, had to literally *pry bar* his fingers off the cable. To make matters even more embarrassing, after we pried him loose he collapsed on the deck into a thumb sucking fetal position and stubbornly refused to ride the empty concrete bucket back down. For crap sakes, Bud knew as well as I did, it was the only way down to the ground, except jump.

All in all, a lot of good did come from Bud's award winning thumb sucking performance because it gave me both the time and an opportunity to study the slipform operation in detail and learn from the crew actually doing the work, all its idiosyncrasies. It also gave me the time to get well acquainted with two of Winkler's foremen in charge of the slipform operation, namely Howard "Chink" Harmon (called "Chink" because he was of half German and Cherokee Indian descent and came out looking like a Chinaman) and the other foreman named Ray Rogers, who both had experience *slipforming* grain elevators in the Midwest. When we shook hands to leave, they both said they would like to work for me on the Crockett job after their job here was finished, if I could use their help. I gave them my card saying, "I'm not here to

NEWS RELEASE DURING 1955

U. S. begins to send aid to Southeast Asia, Russia signs the Warsaw Pact, Polio cases drop sharply as a result of vaccinations, the U. S. Air Force Academy opens, Rosa Parks refuses to give up her bus seat in Montgomery Alabama, The AFL and CIO unions merge, Rock-n-roll music is declared immoral by moralists, Velcro, optical fibers, synthetic diamonds, and Crest toothpaste are introduced, Container ships begin to revolutionize the cargo-shipping industry, Disneyland opens in Anaheim, California, Kentucky fried Chicken is founded and Automobile stuffing becomes popular on college campuses

proselyte ant of Winkler's people, but if you two guys show up on my job four months from now, you're hired."

As it turned out, they both showed up in March of 1956 and I gave them the responsibility of teaching all the rest of us how to slipform 47 bridge piers safely and profitably on schedule. Believe it or not, hiring those two guys turned out to be a Godsend for all of us because when we started building all those piers, there wasn't any slipups (no pun intended) or mistake made, and we finished all our work on the contract,

Chink Harmon and Ray Rogers are standing upper right

including the deck work, *one year ahead of schedule.* In answer to your unstated question, "What ever happened to Bud Waigand?" Well, he starved out around sundown that same day on top of the pier and despite his whimpering prophecy of an impending disaster; he bravely rode the bucket to the ground huddled inside while I stood on the edge praying he wouldn't

Arne Glick & I posing with State Job Personnel

throw another St Vitas dance fit. After we landed, Merritt Mason and I took him to a local bar for a few stiff drinks to settle him down before dinner, and then laughing all the way back to our motel, tucked him into bed.

Kiewit's 80D Shovel equipped as its first Pile Driver

When we started work on the Crockett job, I called Russ Graff, the district manager for the Raymond Concrete Pile Company, to tell him we were about ready to start driving piling on the first stage work and he could move in the following week. For some unknown reason, Russ hadn't signed and/or mailed his subcontract back that Bud sent to him, and I soon found out why. He told me in no uncertain terms he wanted an additional $5,000 for each *move in and out* stage over and above his original quoted price at bid time, and I'll kid you not, I came unglued.

There were five stages specified on that job and that extra $25,000 he mistakenly left out of his bid was out and out extortion in my opinion and I told him so. He said, "OK, if that's the way you feel about it, drive the damn pile yourself", and trying hard to control my temper, I thanked him for that challenging opportunity, and said, "Russ, that's exactly what we're going to do." I called Norm Barnes (engineer transferred from the Gerwick-Kiewit San Rafael Bridge JV) and Larry Fischer (pile butt foreman) into my office and said, "I want you two guys to take that old 80D Northwest shovel in the yard and have Berkeley Steel build a set of pile leads for us, then buy a steam hammer and a boiler and put it all together as a pile driving rig for less than $25,000. We're going to drive our own piling on this job and you two guys will be in charge getting it done." As they started out the door, I also added, "And remember, if we don't make any money for the company by doing the pile work ourselves, Pete will fire all three of us. For our sake, I wish the three of us luck."

The Kiewit Company is now in the Pile Driving business

Lo and behold, that newly organized little pile driving operation not only made enough job profit to write off the $25,000 mobilization cost Russ wanted, but ended up with the best percentage return of any item on the Crockett job. You can believe this little frama of life or not, but this is a true story of how the Kiewit Company got started in the pile driving business.

The winter of 1955 and early spring of 1956 turned out to be one of the wettest years in northern California history and the central valley was nearly completely flooded, and delayed our work on the Crockett Interchange until the middle of April so I contacted the owner of a vacant combination service station-garage about a block away from our bridge

site and rented it as our office, yard and shop. Needless to say, it was an ideal covered wet weather area for our field office, fabrication shop, and the slipform training classes that we built a scale model of the slipform as a training tool to train our foremen and our future crew members during the rain. As it turned out, that rainy weather training period eliminated any confusion about how the *slipform worked* and once we started, everything went smoothly without a hitch to a safe completion of all 47 column bents on Christmas Eve, December 24, 1956, just a short six months later.

All systems are GO on our first Slipform Pier

Pier #1 Airborne with finishing scaffolds attached

When you think about it hard enough, the concept of *slip forming* is very simple. The form itself is only 4 feet high with two 4 by 6 inch walers placed one foot up from the bottom and six inches down from the top of the form. Double six inch steel channels are then placed across the top on four foot centers to tie the form together and make a working platform for the lifters, hydraulic jacks, and the rebar template frame. After the five ton hydraulic jacks that climb the smooth one inch rods have pulled the slipform high enough, a finishing scaffold is attached underneath to rubber float finish the continually poured partially set concrete as

it slowly emerges one inch every five minutes, or one foot every hour for 24 hours a day, until the pier is topped out. By working around the clock slipping an average height of 20 feet per day, it will take five days to slipform a 100 foot high pier.

Much like the first Wright brother's airplane in 1903, the slipform itself is controlled simply by twisting the frame with

Pier #1 successfully topped out,, all systems AOK

315

its hydraulic jacks, instead of levers. To plumb or level the form as it slowly rises, opposite hydraulic jacks are simply turned on or off as necessary. I remember telling Tom Paul one time that I was going to slipform him a 100 foot high pier as a birthday present that would

look like a giant airplane *propeller*. How? Simply by turning off opposite corner hydraulic jacks so the slipform could slowly twist itself halfway around (180 degrees) by the time it topped out at 100 feet. He just glared at me for a moment and said, "Homer, if you ever try pulling a dumb stupid stunt like that on me, your fired." Oooh boy, anyway I still think it's a crying shame Tom doesn't appreciate gifts like this of artistically sculptured masterpieces from his loyal employees. Wow, it might have even made interesting news at the Liberal Arts Colleges.

After the weather cleared and we had enough piling driven and footings poured to begin "slipforming" piers in July of 1956, I told Tom Paul and Bud Waigand we would complete the slipforming of all 47 piers by Christmas of that same year. They both busted out laughing, saying they hoped I was right, but (still guffawing) bet me a porterhouse steak dinner we couldn't make it because I was way too optimistic. Well, unbeknown to them and what they didn't know was, *Old Homer* and his crackerjack

Slipforming 2 Piers simultaneously

crew had already figured out how it could be done by simply pouring **more than one column bent at a time.** It just so happened the way all the interchange bridge ramps were designed, the column bents occasionally fell close enough together a working bridge could be built between them and we could slipform two, three, and in one case, four columns at a time with the same crew. After all we reasoned, the 4 foot high slipform only moves up one inch every five minutes and slipforming one column only requires placing an average of four cubic yards per foot per hour. So, we asked ourselves, why not pour eight cubic yards an hour to cut down on the boring-waiting time, and pour two columns at the same time with the same crew. Then we thought, hey the crew is still not all that busy, why not pour three or even four columns at the same time when possible. That would mean a tremendous savings in both time and money because each column pour,

Removing Slipforms from Piers

whether it was one, two, or four columns moving up together, only took five 24 hour days, and as someone famous once said, "An extra week saved here and there soon adds up." Well, talk about two guys being shocked and stunned at the same time, Bud Waigand and Tom Paul nearly fainted when they saw my crews pouring out the last four column bents, all tied together in one big slipformed pour on December 24, 1956 as promised, and discovered they had lost their bet.

Best of all, with all the piers now built we were now able to guarantee the completion of the Crockett job *one year ahead of schedule*. There was no longer any doubt in anyone's mind that if we had constructed all 47 piers by the standard jump form method and had to erect the deck structural iron in numerous short run stages and been forced to pour the roadway decks in

Slipforming four Piers simultainiosly with a single column pour crew

short sections, it would have taken a year longer to complete the bridge and we would have guaranteed ourselves a loss on the job. As it turned out, we only made 5% job profit when the job was completed instead of the major job loss Tom Paul had envisioned. When all was said and done, the 5% profit was did make was only because of the one year savings in job overhead costs and by driving the piling ourselves. It also helped job profit wise to sell all the salvaged form materials, scaffolding and small tools from the Crockett job to the recently awarded Central Viaduct job in San Francisco, for reuse because there were never funds enough in the original estimate to build 47 column bents by either method. One thing was for sure, by slipforming all the piers we held our losses to a minimum and saved valuable time.

Barbara & Mary Beth visit Dad's Job – 1956

As an added bonus when we rented the garage for the Crockett job, I inherited a small dog (a long haired dachshund mixture) with the garage. That little dog, for some unknown reason, became attached to me like no other pet I have ever had, including my pet lambs, and I named her "Rags" because she looked so much like a rag muffin. The whole time I was on the Crockett job, that little dog was constantly at my side both as my companion and my assistant. She always slept in the garage during the night guarding our equipment (and the food we left her) because in her mind that was her job, and after all, it really *was* her garage. I don't think I have ever become so emotionally attached to any animal, including my pet lambs and my calves when I was a young boy, as I was with that little dog.

On weekends, my girls used to ride out with me occasionally to check out the job and to play with Rags, and Janet would even pack an extra brown bag lunch for Rags to have at our picnic in the park. I always got such a kick out of little Rags when we toured the job together during the week because she would run out ahead of me to the work crews to

Daddy, we're going to need some more sand

warn them I was coming to check how things were going. Then she would hang around with the crew afterwards to congratulate them for doing a good job and to get another pat, while I walked towards another crews work area. Pretty soon, here she would come again to catch up with me, tail wagging and all, and run ahead to warn the next crew. She was such a wonderful little dog.

Ward White told me one time, "There are only two times in a man's life he's not worth a damn to you as his employer, and that's when he is building a house, or getting a divorce." I don't know about that, but I do know owning your own home does give you something else to think about besides company business. When we were building the Eastshore Freeway, my goal (besides getting the bridges built) was to get the landscaping and backyard areas paved and completed as soon as possible before we were transferred to another job. My little girls wanted their sand box finished first and Janet wanted her raised flower beds completed to set her plants, and so on. I tried building them both at the same time and would always bring a pickup load of beach sand home every weekend so my girls could play in their partially finished sand box for another week. Whooee, I'll tell you, it got so it became a weekly sand hauling chore just to keep their sand box partially filled and I still remember telling Johnny Kaufman, our job's dirt superintendent, he should hire my two little girls to move his dirt for him. When I told him they could move more sand in one week with their little sand buckets than his dirt outfit could

The unfinished backyard patio was an ideal birthday party area

in a month, he seriously considered hiring my *git the job done* production minded little girls to *show and tell* his crews how it should be done.

The Port Costa Brickworks was located on the Carquinez Straits near our Crockett job so after I had returned from the North Dakota job, I would stop by occasionally to

318

purchase a pickup load of their reject bricks from Bruce Johnston, their plant manager, for one cent apiece to finish paving our backyard patio. Three of my loyal crackerjack crew members volunteered (bless their hearts) namely, Orville Saalfeld, Marv Rogers and Bill Turnbough to help me pour the tetherball concrete court in the lower forty and to finally finish building the patio arbor over the brick paved patio for wisteria covered shade.

Cousins! Arne, Helen, Marybeth and Barbara

Our youngest daughter, Barbara Jean, has always been the *master chef* in our family, then and now, and believe it or not, to this day I still get a little choked up thinking about her little doll table all setup with her doll tea cups and saucers and those wonderful little mud pies she baked, just the way I like them, (burned on the outside and raw in the middle) in her own little doll oven. She always waited for me with her two dolls, to join them for her *home cooked dinner* when I

A tasty mud pie dinner party at Barbara Jeans house

got home from our Saturday's half day meetings. After we finished our wonderful mouth watering make believe mud pie meal, Mary Beth would top off our evening by inviting Barbara, dear old dad and the two dolls, to her cardboard box theater's opening night puppet show she produced and directed all by herself. I was, and still am, so proud of my two daughters and there is no doubt about it, I am the luckiest father in the whole wide world to have been blessed with my three wonderful children.

NEWS RELEASES DURING 1956

Dwight D. Eisenhower and Richard Nixon are re-elected president and vice president; the last Union Army Veteran from the Civil War, Albert Woolson, dies at age 109; The Polaris missile is developed; The Interstate Highway program is authorized; The first transatlantic telephone cable becomes operational; The Andrea Doria sinks off of Nantucket Island; The Methodist Church abolishes racism in its churches; Actress Grace Kelly marries Prince Rainier 111 of Monaco.

In 2006 I asked my 54 year old daughter, Mary Elizabeth, (born May 8, 1952) what she remembered most about our back yard on Lucinda Lane in 1957, and this is her hand written reply.

"Dad, I remember our back yard was a fantastic place to play. We had a brick ramp down to the lower forty where we would ride "Mr. Toads Wild Ride" down the ramp in our wagon, and down below we could play tetherball or dodge ball. Up the stairway there was a beautiful Almond tree and a sandbox on the patio. There were beautiful lavender wisteria flowers and grapes dripping down from the shade trellis and we had so many wonderful summer family barbecues and dinners and children parties on our backyard patio equipped with a large picnic table and a barbecue. I remember Xmas of 1956 as a shocking experience for me. On Xmas eve, I heard Santa rustling around in the front room by the tree so I quietly tiptoed out of my bedroom and saw you and mom putting presents around the tree. All of a sudden I was dumbstruck with the realization that it was my parents that were really Santa Claus. I was shocked by what I saw, but I didn't tell Barbara because she still believed in Santa and I didn't tell you or mom because I knew that you, Dad, loved playing Santa Claus. I just played along with everyone else for a couple more years until Barbara finally figured it all out for herself."

Mary Beth - Kindergarten

When we had our 1956 Christmas party at the Claremont Hotel in Berkeley to celebrate both the completion of all 47 bridge piers and the Christmas holidays, I discovered for the first time that Chink Harmon really had a drinking problem and to make matters worse, I also discovered when Chink got plastered he always ended up in fist fights at some bar somewhere. One of the wives at our Xmas party ran over to our table just as we were all sitting

Bethlehem Steel Company begins setting Structural Girders

down for dinner to tell me Chink and Curt Temple, my labor foreman, were about to go to fist city. I ran over to hopefully break up the fight just as fists began flying from both sides and, Oooh boy; I ended up on the bottom of a pile of six guys all trying to *Coldcock* each other. Arne Glick and Norm Barnes said they only jumped on top of the pile to save me if you can believe that, and by the time the cops finally pried all of us apart with our shirts half ripped off; we were nothing more than a bruised bleeding mass of limping human debris. Fortunately, by promising the hotel I would never hold another party their and would see that everyone got home safely; I was able to keep us out of jail.

What shocked me the most about that whole mess was when we were driving home, Janet asked, "Are you some kind of a big shot or something?" Surprised I answered, "What are you talking about?" she said, "All the other wives there treated me like you were someone important. Just what do you do anyway?" I was dumbfounded and thought, *Oh my God, don't tell me we've drifted so far apart we don't even know each other anymore,*

Bridge construction is not for sissies

and I couldn't believe this beautiful liberal Seattle girl I married that loved to cancel my republican votes, had absolutely no idea what my job was or what I was trying to do for her and our children. I looked over at this girl I thought I knew but apparently didn't, and shrugged, "I'm just a sheepherder's dumb workaholic son that's trying as hard as I can to make a decent living for my family"

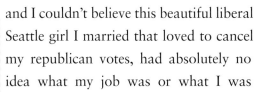

Setting steel girders at 125 feet

When the Bethlehem Steel Company began setting structural iron on the Crockett Interchange in April of 1957 and we began pouring the bridge deck behind them, I stayed on the job for the first few pours to insure our form ideas were working properly, and transferred to the newly awarded Central Viaduct job in San Francisco as project manager after turning the responsibility of finishing the Crockett job over to Norm Barnes. I also turned my little helper dog *"Rags"* over to Loren Krueger, our resident engineer, to look after for me since she was the landlords guard dog. One thing for sure, my leaving Rags that way was one of the saddest and worst decision I've ever made. Why? Well because I should have made a deal with the landlord to take her home for my girls. Loren Krueger

Homer's rolling platform to set & strip forms

told me later that little dog missed me so much while I was gone, she whined constantly and spent all her waking daylight hours looking for me around that job. Apparently, she had

climbed up on the high bridge girders somehow and tried walking a narrow flanged steel beam over towards the iron worker crew to find me and fell to her death 100 feet below. Loren told me my whole crew felt just as badly as I did over her death and they held a small graveside service and buried little Rags near one of the column bent footings near the side of the road. I visited her grave site one weekend all by myself and was so touched by the plaque they had attached to the column next to her small grave, I was sobbing when I left. The

Orville's overhang adjustable form for curved decks

plaque read, *"Here Lies little Rags, the Bridge Workers Mascot."* To this day I still get choked up when I think about that wonderful little dog.

For some unknown reason after the Crockett interchange was completed, Tom Paul forgot all about the estimating errors Julian Gobles and Paul Scroggs made on the job's original cost estimate, and blasted me for not making 10% job profit instead of only 5%. I said, "Tom, don't worry about it, I'll make the other 5% back for you on the Central Viaduct job." It was the first time I noticed Tom's attitude towards me had suddenly changed for the worse, apparently

because his middle management people had told him I was turning into another *head strong loose cannon* like Ward White. The rumor going around at the time was, *Old Homer* (age 32), is making too damn many decisions on his own without buttering up middle management first to get their approval, which was true. I knew if I had contacted Tom's golf playing non producing goof off's he called his middle management, about doing our own pile driving they would have immediately

Placing Reinforcing Steel for a roadway deck pour

given me thumbs down and had their attorneys sue Raymond Pile Company, and *really* delay our job. Worse yet, it would have cost the Kiewit Company their *golden opportunity* to drive their own piling and to finish the job a year ahead of schedule, profitably.

Tom even blasted me for purchasing two dependable 10 KW air cooled Onan generators instead of his middle managements choice of the inferior lower priced *Kato* water cooled generators requiring a full time mechanic to keep them running. Unbelievably, none of them seemed to appreciate the importance of us having a dependable, around the clock, power source for our three shift, five day, slipforming operations. I said, "Tom, if you can't trust me to make even common sense judgment calls on simple things like this when I'm building jobs for you profitably ahead of schedule, then you and I do have a problem." My God, he should have known me well enough to know I could never work under a stupid *penny wise pound foolish* government bureaucratic system he seemed determined to setup in the Los Angeles District. It was the first time I seriously considered leaving the Kiewit Company to start my own construction company, and looking back now, I wish I had quit then when the Eisenhower Highway Program was first busting loose. Who knows? Maybe Tom was trying to get rid of me anyway, like he did with Ward White.

Slim Martin & Homer Olsen-1956

Sometimes when I'm sitting here hen pecking these obviously un-exaggerated stories, I will recall even more *fascinating (?)* stories, and settling sticky job problems rapidly and fairly without involving middle management are some of them. I know it's infuriating to them I'm not a brown nose, but from my point of view, they would only multiply our problem and delay our work with their lawyer *chargeable hours* type thinking.

Pouring & finishing bridge roadway deck on the Crockett Interchange

I still fondly remember negotiating what I thought was an equitable enjoyable settlement agreement with an old "Portagee" gentleman on our Crockett job concerning his *wine still* he was defending to the death with his shotgun. As it happened his still was located in a small building that was sitting directly over one of our bridge footings the state had already bought and paid him for, but he was still stubbornly refusing to move because, he said, "It would ruin the quality of his wine to disturb his still." Well, we worked around him as long we could, but when it got to the point we needed to drive piling in that footing to begin the pier work to stay on schedule, I finally worked up nerve enough to get within shouting (and shotgun) range to suggest we meet and talk things out. Believe it or not, the old gentleman nodded in agreement and as the two of us sat down under his guard station umbrella eying each

Placing grout armor coating on the deck prior to finishing

other suspiciously, he opened up a bottle of his best home made *dago red* wine that I think is called *merlot* today.

I can honestly say I have never tasted a better wine anywhere than his home made wine, and by the time we opened our second bottle of his wonderful wine and had told each

other our life histories, I'll tell you, we were the best of friends. In fact, I began thinking his arguments made perfectly good sense because after all, they were exactly the same arguments Grandpa Olsen used during his coffee pot battle with Ercel, my dad's second wife. He said, "You mess around with a wine still (or a coffee pot) that has taken years to *brake in right*, you will never make good wine (or good coffee) again." In my semi-cross eyed condition, I slurred, "My new best friend, I agree with everything you've said here today one hundred and fifty percent and I think I have an idea how we might be able to solve our

A topped out deck pour awaiting final finishing & curing

mutual problem." He said, "So tell me my new good friend, what is this idea you have in mind?" I said, "OK here's what I think. I will *veerry carefully* pick this whole building up, foundation slab, wine still and all, in one big piece with my huge crane over there, without

disturbing anything you have inside. Then I will *veerrry carefully* set it on my huge lowboy truck, and moving *veerry slowly*, I will *gently* haul the whole caboodle up to your new home site and *veerry carefully reset it* exactly where you want it without disturbing anything inside in any way. How does that sound?" He thought for a minute while we both swirled and gargled a few more gulping swollers like real

The Crockett Interchange Bridge begins to take shape

wine snobs, then he said, "Sooo, my good friend, what will all that cost me?"

After pausing long enough for another good swig, I looked straight into his bleary four eyes through my blood shot crossed eye glasses and very seriously slurred, "Just one more bottle of your prize winning *dago red wine* to take home for our family dinner tonight." He busted out laughing and smiling broadly, extended his hand to shake mine saying, "Homer, my lifelong good best buddy and long lost friend, you just got yourself a deal." Well, believe it or not, your choice, but that is another true un-exaggerated story of how we

kept the Crockett job moving along it's fast track schedule without help from Tom's middle management. In answer to all your un-asked un-answered questions, "What did all that cost?" Well, it cost Kiewit around $1500, but Oooh boy, it cost me one whale of a splitting headache the next morning when I got up for work.

I remember another time we were given a change order to relocate an existing 21" clay sewer line that ran directly through another bridge footing near the Carquinez Straits,

with a 21" cast iron detouring pipe on piling that went around the footing. Well, I naturally assigned the work to the pile butts and the operating engineers because it was clearly their work, but believe it or not, the next morning there was some guy from the plumbers union parading around carrying a picket sign saying this job had been shut down for violating our labor agreement. I called Dimmler, the business agent for the plumbers union for a clarification and you guessed it, he said we were installing cast iron pipe that was plumbers work and because we had violated our labor agreement, he shut the job down. I said the pipe sits on piling below low tide elevation, so if he would check our labor agreement he would find the work was

We lucked out, most of the columns are in the right place

pile butt work, not plumbers. He got a little hot under the collar and repeated it was plumbers work simply because it was cast iron pipe period, and hung up.

So that's the new Carquinez Bridge

Anyway, when my crew started getting a little nervous working around the illegal plumbers picket parading around the job, without bothering Tom's middle management with the problem, I called for a union-management meeting with the business agents of the operating engineers, the pile drivers, and the plumbers unions to hash things out at the work site, and an hour later everyone showed up. You guessed it. When the plumber's business agent arrived with his bodyguard carrying a shoulder holstered handgun, it infuriated everyone else and when the discussion deteriorated into a cuss-fight shouting match, Dimmler's bodyguard unbuttoned his coat to lay his hand on his handgun, Oooh boy, that's when I figured something had to be done and pronto. I shouted, "Gentlemen, if we can agree there will be no precedent established here, I propose we do the following to settle this matter. The pile butts will drive the piling and install the pile caps, the operating engineers will swing the cast iron pipe onto the pile caps using a pile butt as a signalman, and the plumber carrying the picket sign will caulk the joints after the cast iron pipe has been placed."

Well, to summarize this little skid marked drama along the highway of life, the business agents discussed my proposal for a few minutes among themselves and we all

Norm Barnes & Homer Olsen are happy with the job

ended up shaking hands in agreement, and my crew went back to work. Thankfully, this little matter that could have become serious was averted, and my change order crew completed their work by the end of that same day. To this day I still wonder how much time and money would have been) wasted if Tom and his middle management group had become involved with their attorneys and screwed things up. Someone might have been killed.

Up until February of 1957 when Bethlehem Steel began erecting their steel girders we had a perfect safety record with no lost time accidents and it was my first experience with the American press on how they operate. A reporter for one of the bay area newspapers asked me for an interview one day and believe it or not, his first question was, "How many men have been killed so far on this project?" Somewhat surprised I answered "None, and we haven't even had any lost time accident" and when he acted surprised and disappointed, I added, "And not only that, the job is ahead of schedule, the State of California is pleased with our progress and our quality workmanship, and the Kiewit company is pleased we are making a

profit for their shareholders." Unbelievably, he stood up with disappointment written all over his face, closed his note pad, and said, "None of that will sell papers", and left.

Another time an advertising agency for the Ford Motor Company asked me for someone in my crew to pose as a typical American construction stiff standing next to his typical construction man's Marilyn Monroe type wife sitting in their typical construction family's new red Ford convertible. I said, "There are sixty typical American construction men working out there right now, take your pick."

The completed Crockett Interchange Contract shown in white-1958

Believe it or not, an hour later he came back disappointed and shaking his head, saying not one of the sixty men in my crew looked anything like typical American construction stiffs should look. Why? Well because they all looked to much like ordinary every day run of the mud hard working Americans. He said he would have to hire a male model from an acting agency in San Francisco that looked more like real construction stiffs should look, but he still wanted to take pictures on our job. Unbelievably, he came back with a big bellied hairy chested guy with a Brooklyn accent, cauliflower ears and a busted nose, wearing an open Hawaiian shirt and open toed sandals for shoes. Wow, talk about miss-casting. Anyway as a safety compromise after I insisted his model wear hard toed work shoes and at least borrow Orville Saalfeld's hard hat to wear backwards as he insisted.

Bud Waigand studies a Slipform

Well, you guessed it. After everything was all said and done, their advertisement only showed two *legitimate* construction items, namely Orville's backward hard hat that was too small for the model that made him look even more like an idiot, and our flasher light barricades alongside their new Ford convertible. It is unbelievable to me how far the people in the media have drifted away from the real world of honest reporting, but I guess in this day and age of disgustingly poor movies, lousy television and untalented loud noise making musicians, journalism schools are justified in teaching, "Never ruin a good story by the facts."

Lesson learned: *For field supervision to build construction contracts within budget efficiently, safely, and on schedule successfully, they must be given the authority along with the responsibility to make quick decisions. Wars have never been won, and Construction Contracts have never been built successfully with interferences from attorneys, politicians and/or government type bureaucracies.*

The $7,250,000 double deck Central Viaduct Freeway skirting the downtown business district in San Francisco is an elevated multi-lane double deck concrete structure, roughly 1.25 miles in length of box girder design. It required pouring 50,000 CY of concrete with over 2,000,000 square feet of formed concrete wall and deck area, and 13 acres of finished concrete roadway deck. It crosses over 25 streets that were required to be open for traffic at all times, and was

The double decked Central Viaduct Freeway we built in 1957

scheduled for completion by May of 1959, a short 18 months after the notice to proceed was issued.

HJO meeting with State Viaduct personnel

Well contrary to Bud Waigand's strongly worded advice to not waste our time trying to under bid Charley Harney in the city of San Francisco, my crackerjack crew and I quietly estimated the Central Viaduct job in our Crockett job office anyway. After all we thought, nothing ventured, nothing gained, and the job would fit our crew to a tee. We would also know all the job's problems by figuring the work ourselves and if we *lucked out* and were the low bid, we could hit the job running wide open and easily finish the work within the contracts tight eighteen month schedule. Bud frowningly gave our estimate his normal quick review with his encouraging "You'll never get the job anyway" signature and unbelievably, we were *low bidder*. Unbeknown to all of us, Charley Harney's one man outfit couldn't bid the job because he had suffered a minor heart attack at a USF basketball game just one week before the bid and the bonding company refused to issue him a bid bond. I asked Charlie several months later, what his bid would have been if he had turned it in and he said, with his fingers crossed behind his back, he would have beat us by 2%. The truth of the matter was, Charlie never totaled his bid after the bonding company refused his bond. Anyway as it all turned out when everything was said and done, the job was completed ahead of schedule and my motivated crew doubled our estimated job profit. How? By utilizing all the new ideas and easier

Tinkertoy falsewwork in place on the Central Viaduct

building methods we dreamed up during the estimating period and later properly planning, organizing and building the job. There was no question about it the Central Viaduct was by far the smoothest running job I've ever been involved in as job superintendent.

When I was transferred from North Dakota to the Crockett Interchange contract, I

would drive by some of our competitor's jobs occasionally to check out their bridge building ideas and much to my surprise the contractor on the Oakland Viaduct contract was using a light tubular painters scaffolding as his bridge falsework. I thought to myself, "Wow, he might be onto something, but it

Falsework being installed on the Viaduct-1957

looks way too light to be safe" and noted he used an ungodly number of braces and clamps to make it safe that only created more labor hours. I thought, "Why not design a heavier, stouter, and safer steel frame of a comfortable width that are still light enough for one man to handle?"

Wes Thomas's lightweight stem form design

When we were awarded the Central Viaduct contract, I asked Merritt Mason and Wes Thomas to come up with an engineered design of a stronger frame using a 1.90 inch diameter and heavier pipe tubing, and we took bids from four local fabricating shops. I then had several meetings with Tom Paul and Peter Kiewit, to hopefully gain their approval of our idea and our low fabrication bid, and finally reluctantly and filled with doubt, they agreed with my *tinkertoy falsework* idea saying, "OK, but if this idea doesn't work out like you say Homer, you're fired." We placed a $250,000 order with the Waco Scaffolding Company to *fabricate and test* our falsework design. When everything was all said and done, the savings ripple effect that idea had on all the other work involved was amazing. Homer's folly not only saved enough job labor to write off all the tinkertoy falsework's costs, but was responsible for at least 50% of the additional profit the job turned in when it was completed.

Column sweater form

As someone else said long ago, '*necessity is the mother of all inventions*; and my special ops crews came up with many other innovative labor saving ideas that also paid off handsomely, cost wise and time wise. They were all brilliant money saving innovations like the slip on and off *sweater* column forms, using lighter and more labor efficient deck stem forms, using elevated post holes for more efficient street crossing installations and removals, and they all paid off cost wise. Despite Tom's Arcadia's equipment department's protests, we lease purchased two newly marketed Austin Western hydraulic cranes with telescoping booms

Orville Sallfeld's elevated post hole design

to speedup the erection and the removal of our tinkertoy falsework from underneath low head room decks. Fortunately for us, every one of our criticized ideas that we came up with turned out to be time and money savers and made profit for the company's shareholders.

Fran Murphy, of the Murphy-Pacific Co. gave me quite a compliment one time when we were discussing over lunch the one time the many humorous problems we encountered while running our work. Being a good catholic and all, Fran actually felt I had not only been *blessed,* but had been given **the touch** by a higher power to be able to run my jobs so smoothly.

Engineering & Accounting department

Tom Paul even asked me one time, "Why is it you always start out with tough jobs, but always end up making them look easy?" I don't know about any of that, but I do know I was blessed with having the most loyal competent hard working foremen, skilled craftsman, and qualified engineers working for me than anyone in the Kiewit Company. Ray Gully called them my *relatives,* but I always proudly called them my highly qualified *crackerjack crew.* We worked on what I called a fifty-fifty basis and what's fair is fair. When it came time to share in all the accolades and screw-ups), equally that always occur on jobs they got all the accolades and I took responsibility for all the screw-ups. There is no doubt about it, I would never have made it as a job superintendent without their loyal support and I will always be grateful to that wonderful group of guys for covering my tracks for me and making it look like

I knew what I was doing. Some came and some went, and faces changed from time to time, but men like Orville Saalfeld, Marv Rogers, Ray McClarrinon, Bill Turnbough, Don Davis and "Chink" Harmon, worked with and for me on nearly every job I was involved from 1949 until my last job with Kiewit on the San

My wonderful Crackerjack Crew on the Central Viaduct Job in San Francisco

Mateo Bridge in 1963. I sit here now, at the ripe old age of 84, pecking away on all these memories with one finger, with the sad knowledge that most of my wonderful crew are no longer alive, but I will always treasure the friendships and good times we had working together

Homer Olsen, Job Superintendent-1958

building all those *easy* jobs. I guess I was always the youngest member of the group during those years, but the fondest memories I have other than our friendships was, we never built a losing job for the company all the time we worked together.

Apparently still sulking over losing his porterhouse steak bet and while we were 'punch listing' the final work on the Central Viaduct job, Tom Paul blasted me again for not making 10% job profit on the Crockett job. When I re-refreshed his memory of the estimating errors made prior to the job's bid and why we slip formed the piers in the first place to minimize the potential loss, he said I should have made 10% job profit anyway. His worst *below the belt* blow was when he completely ignored we not only finished the Central Viaduct job we estimated ourselves weeks ahead of schedule and had increased our estimated job profit from the $800,000 estimated to a whopping $1,800,000, a cool one million dollars more than we estimated, it really hurt. He*)* completely ignored giving any bonuses to any of my salaried foremen or even

NEWS RELEASE DURING 1957

"Sputniks", the first artificial satellite orbits the earth, President Eisenhower extends the "Truman Doctrine" to cover the Mideast, American scientists urge a ban on nuclear weapons tests, the first large nuclear power plant goes on line, and a civil rights bill passes congress

increased mine a little from the $3,000 Ben Williams gave me, I thought, "Why in Hell's name are we wasting our time working our tails off for a guy like Tom Paul when he doesn't appreciate anything we do for him or the company anyway. I must be nuts to still be working for this outfit."

The North end of the Central Viaduct contract nearing completion in San Francisco-1958

To keep my *money making* crew together and make sure they had weekly pay checks to take home, I took the liberty once again (while middle management was playing golf) to bid another job in our trailer office. Ooh boy, as it turned out we were low bidder on the first contract advertised to remove the trolley rails and remodel the San Francisco Bay Bridge for double deck automobile traffic. Interestingly, we even beat Charlie Harney again in a fair fight by his 2% and were low bidder on the Stillman Ramp portion of the Bay Bridge Project.

It was while starting that job to keep my crews busy working, I applied for and passed both the written examinations for the California Registered Civil Engineer's license and the Class "A" (Engineering) Contractor's license. Except for some financial backing I was now ready to startup my own construction company, someday soon.

Mary Beth in the fifth Grade

Even more interesting (to me anyway), Bill Ames of the Miller & Ames insurance company suddenly began showing up on my Viaduct job for his morning walks with me, before going on to his own office in downtown San Francisco. I remember jokingly asking him one morning, "Why are you buttering me up when you should be greasing wheels like Bud Waigand and Tom Paul?", and he laughingly admitted knowing I had picked up my two licenses and figuring I might be up to something. He said, "Homer, I know two contractors who are very familiar with your reputation as a *money maker* and they would like to hire you at a much higher salary than you're currently making with Kiewit, if you would be interested." I thanked Bill for that *confidence builder* but said if I ever left Kiewit, it would only be to start up my own construction company and one way or the other, I would make that decision before I reached my 40th birthday. Bill left saying, "OK, let me know what you decide and I'll help you find some good joint venture partners." Wow! What a guy.

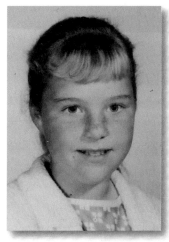

Barbara Jean in the third Grade

I'm still not sure if Tom Paul was aware of my conversation with Bill Ames, but when we started working on the new Stillman Ramp job in July of 1959, Bud Waigand was suddenly transferred to the Los Angeles District office in Arcadia, California, to be Tom's assistant and unbelievably, I was selected to take Bud's place as San Francisco Area Manager. Oooh Boy, now what do I do? While still in a state of shock over this sudden change in Jobs I'm sure Pete had hishand in, I turned over my company pickup and all the keys to the Stillman Ramp job to Orville Saalfeld to look after from now on, and moved to my new office on the ninth floor at 442 Post Street in San Francisco. For the first time in my current ten year career with Kiewit, instead of wearing a hard hat, khaki shirt & pants, and hard toed boots to work everyday,

The new San Francisco Area Manager & his wife

I was now required to wear a suit and a tie. Not only that, miracle of all miracles, Tom reluctantly (also Pete's doing) gave me my first salary increase in three years of $25 a week to a whopping $225 a week plus the keys to use a brand new Chevrolet company car. Wow, all of a sudden I was the *head honcho* over the most money wasting, non productive, un-needed non-essential, bureaucratic, goof off golf playing mis-managed middle management sub-districts in the company. It was also the highest position I ever reached on the Kiewit Company's totem pole. Apparently because of my reputation as a *loose cannon and a slave driver,* Tom and Bud had already transferred all the people requesting it to their Los Angeles office in Arcadia, California, to work for them so that left me with only four people on my staff, namely Dave Scott as chief

NEWS RELEASE DURING 1958

The first U. S. ICBM is successfully launched, "Nautilus" makes the first undersea crossing of the North Pole, NASA is established, U. S. launches its first satellite, the Boeing 707 goes into service, U. S. Troops are sent to Lebanon, and the Van Allen radiation belts are discovered.

estimator, Ev Clark and Wes Thomas as engineer estimators, and Jane Elliot as our secretary. The other half of the San Francisco office floor was manned by the Omaha Heavy Division under Vern Pew as west coast manager, Merritt Mason, assistant chief engineer, Martin Kelly, engineer-estimator, and Betty Meyer as their secretary.

The market for the heavy engineering construction was very slow at the time and nothing of interest was out for bid, but the cold war was escalating and we knew the (T-5) Titan I Missile Base contract near Beale Air Force Base would be advertised in the near future. I remember telling my new estimating staff we needed that missile contract badly, not only to insure employment continuity of our key field people, but to generate enough additional cash flow to pay our own non-productive salaries. I also told them we should begin now, even before the contract drawings are issued, doing all the preliminary work we possibly could to insure we're the low bidder on that project. I told them I thought it was ridicules to have overhead people like ourselves, wasting much of our valuable time commuting back and forth from Walnut Creek where we live to this high rent San Francisco office, and then do nothing all day but stare out of an office window pretending we are doing something important. This estimating office should be a close knit part of our company's *field operations team* that brings in our salaries

Barbara and Mary Beth as models

and be located next to our equipment yard and shop. It is much more productive to have estimator's office windows facing idle equipment we need to put to work, than staring through binoculars at un-shaded apartment windows. Every job has a *gimmick* and the trick is to find that gimmick to be low bidder. We should all begin now, dreaming up new ideas and better ways to acquire and build profitable work for our company

I also invited Tom Paul and Bob Wilson, (one of the good guys being groomed as Pete's replacement) to Concord, California to look at an ideal piece of property for our office, yard and shop near the Concord Airport and adjacent to a future freeway. I explained why I thought it was not only a good investment, but why we should move our sub district office there for our new office, yard and shop and surprisingly they not only agreed and bought the property, but had the building division construct our facilities for us while we concentrated on estimating the Titan I missile base. Bob Wilson told me later Pete Kiewit was so enthused with our moving the San Francisco office; he personally designed our new office, yard and shops, but gave us his blessings to proceed, full speed ahead.

I found this interesting *'all the family'* letter in my late mother's trunk that was written by Janet, dated January 11, 1960, and addressed to our Washington, Utah and Nevada families. Her comments concerning the hours I put in on my new job as Kiewit's new San Francisco Area Manager to acquire more work were certainly true, but thinking back now, I have no other person to blame but myself for turning my new *opportunity to goof off job* into an exhausting *earn your keep or quit,* type job. I could have easily done the same thing the previous manager did and play golf all the time and let some loose cannon (like Homer) do my work for me. After all, the beauacratic approach to promotions is, "Lay low, never stir up dust, and let things fall where they may." Unfortunately, I'm that rare kind of a person that would go stark staring raving mad in an un-needed un-productive un-necessary job.

January 11, 1960

Dear Family,

Well, things are about normal again after the holidays, thank god. Every year I blunder along getting a little worse every year through December. I still have Xmas cards to write believe it or not, to nice people that I want to write letters with their cards. Sometimes I wish I could escape somewhere from December 2, until after Xmas. I wrote my mother that I really need four holidays to celebrate Xmas. One for baking and festivities, one for presents, one for carols and music and the religious part, and the last for exchanging cards and letters and and catching up on all the news about old friends. How can one person do all those things right in three short weeks? Not me.

The girls seemed to have had a very satisfactory Xmas, which is the nice part to remember. Nobody thought Santa loved the other sister more than he did the first sister because each girl's presents were counted down to the last package to make sure they each had an equal number. Both girls were also reminded by their Dad that when one opened presents faster than the other, one would finish first and it wasn't Santa's fault the faster opener didn't have enough presents to open. Mary Beth had so much fun with her dear old Dad about Santa Claus this year. She's not a true believer anymore but she thinks

Dad still believes there is a Santa and plays along with him. She wrote him a note and left him a treat by the fireplace and Santa wrote a note back and thanked her for the

treat. But Santa answered in "real writing" that Mary Beth couldn't read because it was so poorly written – like Dad's real writing. Dad's such a big fraud

Everyone is well again, after having a couple of different flu's over Christmas. The way it turned out, it was a good thing we stayed home this year. We've really had some cold weather, more than we've had for the last four or five years. All the fuchsias, ferns, hibiscus, geraniums, and begonias are dead or look sick. The lower forty (of our half acre lot) is much colder than the patio – things look really bad down there. But, maybe the frost will get rid of some of the bugs.

Barbara - the campfire girl, 1961

Ole came home from Sacramento Saturday night at 12:45 with a suitcase full of dirty clothes. Sunday morning he left for Omaha at 6:30 with another suitcase full of clean clothes I had packed for him. It takes a lot of clothes to meet a schedule like that. The girls haven't even seen their father since January 3rd and they won't until January 16th. He's really burning the candle at both ends, but he says it will all be worth it if they can get more work. It is easier cooking when he's working late or gone and the girls and I get to go more places and do more things. We never know when to expect him even when things are normal and dinner is always late. But it is kind of lonely when he's gone all the time.

The girls and I went to see the movie, "South Pacific" Friday night. Mary Beth took off like wild fire after hearing all that beautiful music. She's learned all the songs and where they

Mary Beth - 1964

sang them and why – and she infects Barbara. We borrowed a record from our neighbor that had all the songs from the stage play and we really had a rousing South Pacific weekend. These are some of the wonderful experiences with children growing up. We've also "ice skated" several times lately. Barb is finally getting so she can get one foot in front of the other on skates. Mary Beth is fun to skate with because she can glide to the music - some of the time.

Over Xmas vacation we got the whole family, including dear old dad, to the Nutcracker Ballet in the city. Even Dad had to admit it was good although I think he would *rather watch football on TV. All he wants to do is lie on the davenport and he acts like he's been drugged or dragged out on something. I guess if I worked the hours he does everything would be an effort for me too. Yet I feel guilty going ahead without him so much of the time. We should cherish the things we can do as a family because we are together so little of the time anymore.*

Love to all, Janet.

I was in Grand Island, Nebraska attending the companies January 12, 1960 annual managers meeting when Dave Scott called and said our bid of $30,157,000 *was low* on the T-5 Titan I Missile Base near Beale Air Force Base, Marysville, California. The project consisted of three separate ten million dollar ICBM Launching complexes that were located near Lincoln, Chico, and the Live Oak Buttes, at the tips of an equilateral triangle with ninety mile legs, so we located our headquarters office near the center in Marysville. As shown at the left, each complex consisted of three missile silos, 120 feet deep by 45 feet in diameter, 16 underground supporting structures to house personnel, fuel equipment, and tracking antennas, all connected by a labyrinth of tunnels 60 feet below ground. Rather than do any tunneling, we elected to speedup the work by open cutting the entire site, which meant double shifting with our heavy earth moving equipment excavating and stockpiling for later backfill, over 600,000 cubic yards of earth at each site. When everything was all said and done

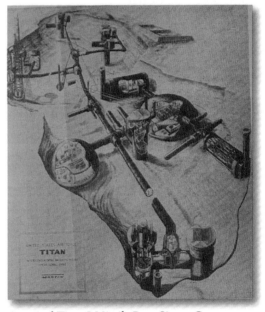

A typical Titan I Missile Base Site at Camp Beale – 1960

and all three complexes were backfilled and completed, only the entry portal, antenna silo lids and three launcher silo lids were visible, flush with the ground surface.

NEWS RELEASES DURING 1959

Nixon and Premier Khrushchev engage in a "kitchen debate" in Moscow, the first military advisors die in Vietnam, NASA selects the first seven U. S. astronauts, Alaska and Hawaii enter the union as 49th and 50th states, the micro chip is invented, Walter Williams, the last Confederate soldier dies at age 117, American Motors introduces the 'Rambler' to compete with small foreign cars

Shortly after I returned from the meeting in Grand Island, Peter Kiewit called to ask me as a favor to him, to handle the T-5 Titan I Missile Base job as Project Manager. When I asked if Tom was aware of this, Pete said Tom was and he wanted Jim Zack for the job, but he personally wanted me to handle the work because I was more experienced in *fast track* construction. I said, "Pete, for you I will gladly accept the job if you will let me pick whoever I want in the company for my crew" and he chuckled with, "You got it on one condition, you choose Ray Gully as your assistant." I said, "I've heard a lot of good things about Ray, so Pete, we've got a deal." I called home to share this exciting news with Janet and the girls, called Dave Scott into my office to tell him he was now the new San Francisco Area Manager, and began clearing my desk to transfer to a *real job back in the real world* again, humming "Happy days are here again."

Peter Kiewit, President of Peter Kiewit Son's Co.

While still packing for my families move to Marysville, California, Peter Kiewit flew in from Omaha in his surplus C-47 he had remodeled as his private airplane for a pre-job meeting in San Francisco with Bob Wilson, his first vice president, and Jim Sexton, the company's labor relations negotiator. Tom Paul flew up from Los Angeles with Bud Waigand and Paul Scroggs, in his company Cessna 310, and we all met for a dinner meeting in Pete's hotel suite to review how the missile contract would be handled. Pete told everyone there, I would be the Project Manager with Ray Gully as my assistant, and Paul Scroggs would be in charge of the Mechanical work using *Kiemech Mechanical* (a newly organized in house mechanical company) as a subcontractor. He then gave me the shock of my life when he said, "We are going to build this job Non Union and I want to know what each one of you *honestly* think about it?" Pete then questioned everyone around the table from the top down, with Bob Wilson first, then Tom Paul and on around the table on down the line until he finally got to me at the bottom of the totem pole. Honest to God, I got the shock of my life because every one of those top management people there answered his question exactly the same way as if from a script, saying, "You must have had a vision from Christ himself Pete. That's exactly what I think should be done." I was not only stunned by their answer, but shocked to learn for the first time what a disgusting bunch of *brown nosing yes men* this high powered bunch turned out to be, and especially Bob Wilson's spineless answer because I knew he knew better.

Anyway when Pete finally got around to me for my opinion, I took a deep breath and said, "Pete, if you pull a dumb stunt like that in the strong Union area where that job is located, I can guarantee you, we will be shut down the next day with a long crippling strike. If this is what you still want to do and plan to do, count me out and I'll go to work for somebody else." Oooh boy, except for a few *that's the end of old Homer,* snickers going around the table when I finished, I'll kid you not, Pete's face turned redder than a beet and you could have heard a pin drop in that room. Finally, after glaring at me for a full minute while I sat there sweating blood, Pete turned his chair around to squarely face me and stunned everyone there with, "Homer, I want to thank you for your honest answer. I'll give it more thought and we'll make our final decision at our 7:00 am breakfast meeting tomorrow morning in this same room. This meeting is adjourned."

Tom Paul and Paul Scroggs review the Titan I Missile Base Schedule

Well, you can believe this or not, but when we all met the next morning for breakfast, Pete shocked everyone in the room by announcing, "We are going to build this job Homer's way." Then he turned to me and said, "I've already setup a pre-job meeting for you with all the building trade unions at 10:00 o'clock this morning in the labor temple downtown. I want you and Jim Sexton to conduct that meeting and answer any questions the union people may have concerning this contract." After we all shook hands and Jim and I were driving to our union meeting, Jim turned to me and said, "Thank God

Homer, *we* got Pete to change his mind last night. My job would have been a nightmare if he had decided to go non-union on this job." I looked over at him and said, "Jim, I thank God too, but I also want to thank you for the strong support you gave me to help convince Pete to change his mind."

Our meeting with the unions went very well, especially after the rumors going around that Kiewit was going non-union were put to rest. Every business agent I had worked with in the past, gave a big sigh of relief and congratulated me on being chosen as the job's Project Manager. They also all assured me I would have their complete cooperation and they would personally see to it we were assigned their best craftsmen, and suddenly I felt even more anxious to get the job up and going. To have this golden opportunity to hand pick my own team of superintendents, engineers and foremen from within our company, and now having the full cooperation of all the craft union's, I knew we would chock up another profitable contract for our company and our employee shareholders.

My biggest shock on the job came when Ray Gully and I were hand picking our crackerjack team for the job in our Marysville headquarters office, and Tom Paul called. Apparently he was still sulking over my appointment as project manager by Peter Kiewit and decided to get even with me by appointing his anointed best friend Paul Scroggs as my boss with the title of *Job Sponsor,* as well as being the head honcho over Kiemech mechanical. To *handcuff* me from coming up with any more *Homer's folly* ideas, he also cut my spending authority down to a maximum of $25,000 on the job. In effect, he turned

100% of the general contractor's control and authority over the project to a whining subcontractor by removing all my *authority* as project manager, but still leaving me with all the *responsibility*. Wow, what a brilliant scheme. In one fell swoop, he not only guaranteed we would have a loosing job under Paul Scroggs supervision, but brilliantly tied my hands so it would all be my fault. Well you guessed it I came completely unglued over his vindictive reorganizing move and demanded he fly up to Marysville immediately for a final face to face meeting to thrash things out, once and for all.

Colonel Sherrard, Homer Olsen and Ole Lein discuss my scheduling proposal

Anyway, to make this story shorter, after the dust had finally settled and everything had been said and done, our shouting match was compromised somewhat by me agreeing that Paul Scroggs could keep his title as the job sponsor if it were only as a *toothless tiger* and he couldn't stick his nose into any of the civil work I was handling. I would then agree not to mess around with his mechanical operations except to check occasionally on his progress as our mechanical subcontractor. Fortunately for both Ray and me, there were no interferences anticipated between Kiemech's preliminary fabrication and the installation work with our civil work until 80% of our civil work was completed, so I quit worrying about it.

Marysville Crew - 1960

Ray Gully and I then proceeded to put our team together and I can truthfully say we were blessed with the cream of the crop in the company as our crackerjack crew, including many of my relatives as Ray called them. My own crew that answered directly to me (as chief delegater on the job) boiled down to only three people, namely Ray Gully as General Superintendent handling the field work; Brad Lockwood as Project Engineer, taking care of all the in house engineering and letter writing duties, and Don Davis, our Office Manager, looking after all the payroll and job accounting duties. Everyone else on the jobs indirect totem pole payroll, then worked for the three of them.

Digging missile silos with our 4500 Manitowoc

I remember we started with 26 engineering and accounting people in the Marysville office including the lift drawing draftsmen needed, to try and keep the three field trailer office personnel down to less than five people. When the design change order work (and claims) began building up to the 600 number during the last 20% of the job, the Marysville engineering and office staff had to be increased to 50 people to handle the deluge of additional design change paper work, along with working three shifts, seven days a week to stay on schedule. I'll tell you, if it wasn't for Brad Lockwood's fantastic administrative skills and abilities, and his management expertise he fine tuned during WW II in the south pacific as a three striper (Commander) Naval officer in the CB's, I don't think we would have ever been able to handle the flood of paper and additional field work their design changes generated. It was Brad Lockwood who taught me the importance of keeping accurate up to date documentation of all work performed on jobs, including daily job diaries from the jobsite supervisors, to stay abreast of the rapid changes on fast track contracts. We would never have been able to settle all our claims and our change orders equitably without Brad Lockwood constantly staying on top of all the cost impacts caused by all the design changes etc. without our job diaries, current cost reports, prompt replies to all the owner's correspondence, and constantly updating our critical path schedule. Wow, what a guy.

Homers Folly Orange Peel Forms being setup for a pour

When we started work on the missile base, to save time and to speed up the work, we subcontracted all the open cut dirt work to two earthmoving contractors to open cut the three missile sites as rapidly as possible and by the time the first "A" Site near Lincoln was excavated, we had the carpenter yard setup and were fabricating forms needed and had our hard rock shaft excavation crews working on a three shift basis, six days a week. We even had the *orange peel* dome forms setup ready to pour, before moving them for reuse to the other sites as the dirt work progressed.

I remember during breakfast one morning while peeling my daily orange, a *light bulb* suddenly clicked on over my head and, *Wow,* like a bolt out of the blue, it occurred to me the domed forms for the different sized powerhouse and control center could be split into two opposite 22.5 degree *orange peel forms,* and then simply rotate them for reuse four times on each of the two structures at the three different sites. That would give us twelve re-uses on each of the two dome forms and would save us a substantial amount on materials and labor costs.

Placing Rebar for a Powerhouse Pour

Oooh boy, here I go again without Tom's approval. I called Jim Wilton of Jacobs Associates (my brilliant engineering classmate at Stanford) to see if he could come up with a design along the orange peel idea for me. Well, bless his heart and his brilliant mind, he not only came up with the design, but also all the shop drawings I would need for Berkeley Steel to fabricate the forms, and as it turned out, the orange peel forms were not only designed and fabricated within Tom's $25,000 budget, but thanks to Jim Wilton and his fantastic engineering talents, he more than helped us with another *Homer's folly* cost saving idea for the company.

The Powerhouse being constructed on a Titan I Missile Site – 1960

It was on my 36th birthday (April 7, 1960); I received a telephone call from the Union Valley Dam to pickup Peter Kiewit who was flying in to visit our job, at a local crop duster's airfield. Well, when I picked Pete up, I don't think I've ever seen him before in such a foul mood, and when I jokingly thanked him for visiting us on my birthday, he about bit my head off with, "I just found out we are going to lose $6,000,000 on the Union Valley Dam and I'd like to know just how much we're going to lose on this damn job." I said, "Just the opposite Pete. You mark my words, we are going to make a killing on this job" and went on to say I was especially glad he picked today because everything was shaping up beautifully to make it another smooth running profitable job. He just glared at me and said, "We'll see."

Well, wouldn't you know it, the job was running smoothly an hour earlier when I left to pick him up, but when we returned to the "A" site for his job tour, all hell suddenly broke loose. One of the cat skinners who had never seen what Peter Kiewit looked like before, drove over to get a closer look and unbelievably drove over and cut the tunnel crews air hose with his tractor. Oooh boy, I'll tell you when that stupid stunt occurred, all the rock drills on

the job suddenly went silent and all the men working on the three silos stood up to watch Pete and yours truly, driving by very slowly, looking at each other, looking at each other. Oooh boy, to make things even worse, for some unknown reason this little drama reminded me of those hysterically funny keystone cop movies, and I busted out laughing so hard my sides began to hurt. Then to top that off while still guffawing, of all the stupid things I should have waited all day without saying, I said, "Pete, sometimes I think you really are a jinx. Things like this never happen when you're not here."

Slipforming Missile Silos on the Titan I Missile site

I'll tell you that was *the* wrong thing to say to Pete Kiewit because he literally came unglued and *flipped, his lid*. I'll tell you, he gave me one of the best *aferendum chewing outs* I've had since my Army days and from then on, nothing we were doing on that job was right, including *I wasn't cost conscious*

because I put the 2x4 wall studs in the mechanics shop on 16" centers instead of 24" centers like they do in Nebraska. After he finally left I asked Ray Gully if Pete was always that ornery and he said, "Are you kidding, Pete was in a good humor today. You should see him when he's really mad."

In order to save even more time and money, my *relatives* and I decided to *slipform* rather than *jump form*, the nine 45 foot inside

MAJOR NEWS RELEASE DURING 1960

The Soviets shoot down a U-2 spy plane, the U.S.S. Triton completes the first undersea circumnavigation, Eisenhower warns against the "military-industrial-complex" while Kennedy campaigns to close the "missile gap." Nixon and Kennedy debate on TV, John F. Kennedy and Lyndon Johnson are elected President and Vice President, Physicist Theodore Maiman invents the laser, birth control pills are approved, Quasars are discovered, the U. S. now has 2.17 million miles of surfaced roads, 2,515,479 immigrants entered the U. S. in the previous decade, and the U. S. population reaches 179,245,000,

diameter, 120 foot depth missile silos. After all, when you think hard enough about it, we were already trained experts from our Crockett job days and Chink Harmon, along with Wes Thomas, handled that operation beautifully and as luck would have it, by the end of 1960, just twelve months after our bid was submitted, 75% of the civil work on the three missile sites had been completed by my crackerjack missile base crews.

Unfortunately, while we were busting our tails trying to get the job built, little or nothing was being accomplished by our subcontractor, Kiemech Mechanical Company, all because of a whining, blame everybody else for his own mistakes, Paul Scroggs. Ray Gully said it like it really was, Kiemech was suffering from a terrible case of "Kiemechites", (a synonym for "cant-itis") and nothing was getting done in the mechanical department because of that terrible disease. Whenever I asked Paul Scroggs for progress updates, all I got were excuses and numerous reasons why something **could not** be done rather than ways it **could be** accomplished. He even used the excuse there were communist moles in his crew that were sabotaging his work as an excuse, which was the last straw as far as the Corps of Engineers were concerned. The Colonel in charge finally had it up to his eyebrows with Paul Scroggs and called me to say he was drafting a letter to Peter Kiewit, with a copy to me, demanding that Paul Scroggs and the Kiemech Mechanical Company be removed from the job for incompetence. I said, "Colonel, I'm supposed to be the figure head around here so I would appreciate it if you would give me a couple days to look into Kiemech's problems before you write that letter."

Open cut tunnel piping prior to backfilling

Completed piping installation inside a tunnel

Reluctantly, he agreed.

I packed my lunch bucket that same night and met with the pipe fitters union steward by myself for lunch on the graveyard shift in one of the "A" site tunnels where Kiemech was supposed to be installing piping. After reviewing some of the installation drawings with him, I asked if the communist charge Paul Scroggs had made was true and the poor guy went into shock that his boss would even think anyone in his mechanical crew were communists. He said, "Homer, like you, nearly all of us here are WW II Veterans and we are all proud we are American citizens. When we finish our lunch, I'd like to show you a few of the so called '*minor*' problems we've had to put up with on this site." Well, when we finished our tour of that tunnel they were supposed to be installing piping, I was the one that was shocked. The welding machines Paul Scroggs had ordered too late because of his price chiseling habits had finally arrived, but were delivered to the

Backfilling begins on the Titan I Camp Beale Missile Base-1960

343

crews without leads. When the welding leads were back-ordered and were finally delivered, they were given the wrong (and cheaper) welding rod to use. The piping Paul Scroggs gave them to install in the tunnels was either the wrong size or didn't meet the contracts quality specifications and were rejected. When that piping was replaced with the correct piping,

it was invariably delivered to the wrong location in the wrong tunnels, and when that was straightened out, they were never issued enough pipe supports to complete any one area when they did start to work, and so it went on and on. The truth of the matter was obvious. Kiemech's supervision above the union foreman level were incompetent and something had to be done immediately.

Four 1000 hp diesel engine generators in a Powerhouse

Apparently Ray Gully had telephoned Peter Kiewit directly to save me another agonizing fight with Tom Paul over his best friend, Paul Scroggs, because Pete called me early the next morning and wanted to know why the Colonel was

so unhappy with Paul Scroggs. I told Pete about my midnight tour and my frustrations with

Paul's *cant-ites* attitude and I even confessed how Tom had handcuffed me (unknown to him) in doing my job. When I said, "Pete, two people with different philosophies on building works can never run the same job at the same time so I wish you would just remove me from this job and let Tom and Paul Scroggs finish the remaining work." Pete said, "I'll take care of it", and hung up.

The next morning Peter Kiewit called me back and surprisingly said he had just fired Paul Scroggs and told me to take charge of

Al Kanzler C of E and Ray Gully, General Supt-1960

the Kiemech Company and do whatever was necessary to get the job done. I was stunned, but thanked him for giving me my authority back to do my job again and by the end of the day, I had cleaned Kiemech's house. I laid off every mechanical supervisor above the rank of union foreman and called our crews together to announce we were all now in charge, hook line and sinker, and have been given a golden opportunity to show the Corps of Engineers how mechanical work should be done. Ray and I immediately corrected all of Kiemech's penny wise and pound foolish materials and equipment procurement and their installation problems by putting our own competent *can-do* supervisors and engineers in charge of their work. We also put all the mechanical work on a three shift, seven day work week to make up for lost time, and low and behold, we began producing owner approved mechanical

Aerial view of one of the three missile launching sites being constructed in the vicinity of Marysville, California. The key photo below indicates some of the construction details:

1: Access road
2: Missile launcher No. 1
3: Missile launcher No. 2
4: Missile launcher No. 3
   (Each of the above consists of a missile silo, a propellant terminal and an equipment terminal.)
5: One of the connecting underground tunnels
6: Control center
7: Powerhouse
8: Air intake structure
9: Air exhaust structure
10: Entry portal
11: Antenna silo

The stockpiles of earth from the excavation will be used to backfill the area, covering all of the construction.

Aerial View

work safely and on schedule. Believe it or not, we suddenly began to look like a mechanical company that knew what they were doing.

The mechanical supervisors in Kiemech were replaced with our own competent hard working civil engineers to not only get the work done rapidly, but also to prove my long held theory that mechanical engineers are simply too detail minded by personality, education, training and motivation, to be production minded supervisors. On the other hand, civil and mining engineers are by nature motivated "can-do" type "A" personality people who think in terms of production and getting the job done in a safe, cost effective timely manner. It therefore goes without saying, civil and mining engineers with additional training in business law, construction engineering and management, and obtain apprentice training in the field with a good construction company,

"A" Site under construction near Lincoln, California

will always make the best supervisors, managers and owners of construction companies that are interested in making money.

Well, as you've already guessed, Tom blamed me for all of Kiemech's problems from the very beginning of the missile base job as I expected, and from then on until he died he never forgave me for getting his anointed best friend, Paul Scroggs, removed from the job. He said every problem they had was my fault because of my knot headed *always think I'm right* stubborn attitude. Oooh boy, the truth of the matter was, Paul Scroggs was a poster boy example of the worst type of supervisor possible for anyone to work for, and especially

"B" Site construction in the Buttes during 1960

on fast track jobs. Why? Because of his penny wise and pound foolish thinking, his constant whining and inability to make decisions and his blaming everyone else for his own stupid mistakes. He literally gave ulcers to everyone working for and around him, including me and I even named my second ulcer "Paul Scroggs" after that anal canal that caused it. Unfortunately for the company, Paul Scroggs (the whiner), and Tom Paul's other best friend he hired named George Primo (the bully), both turned out to be disasters as money makers for the Kiewit Company. I guess Tom is a lot like me in many respects. He's so full of stubborn Scandinavian pride he could never accept the truth about those two knot headed *best friends* he hired. I know it's hard to believe, but I've been told basically the same thing about myself, that my head was so far up my *afferendum* I couldn't see the light, which proves there are two sides to every coin and she does have warts, on the other hand.

Speaking of bullies, we had another obnoxious bully much like George Primo on the missile base at "B" site, only this guy was the pipe fitters union steward. For some unknown reason, he was always threatening (and tried occasionally) to beat up on my mechanical supervisors when they *politely suggested* he do the work he was hired to do. Our union agreement wouldn't allow me to fire him because he was their steward, so I was continually having shouting matches over the telephone with the pipe fitters business agent about replacing him with someone more cooperative and with a better work ethic. I remember Clyde Ingram walked into my office right after one of those frustrating shouting

"C" Site near Chico, California

matches with the business agent, and said, "I want you to meet this young engineer I've been telling you about." Clyde hired this young man right after he graduated from the University of Nevada as a mining engineer to be his tunnel engineer on the Union Valley Dam, and had asked me to give him some *diversified* training when the tunnels were completed. To this day I still remember looking up at this young man and thinking to myself, "My God, my prayers have just been answered."

The young engineer Clyde introduced me to named Stan Summers was 6' 7" tall and looked skinny at 270 pounds. I said, "Stan, how would you like to take a shot at running a pipe fitting crew on one of the missile sites?" When he said it sounded like a good job to him, I drove out to "B" site with him and introduced him to Bob Davick, the "B" site superintendent who would be his boss, and to his crew which included this bully who was the union steward. I'll tell you as long as I live; I will never forget the look on that steward's face when I introduced him to Stan Summers as his supervisor. He looked at me after shaking hands with Stan, and said, "Homer, I'm glad to see you finally hired a guy I can get along with." As we were walking away Stan looked over at me and asked, "What was that all about?" to which I smilingly shrugged, "It was nothing important." The interesting thing to me about that little drama of life was, the bully and Stan became very good friends and their crew ended up as one of our best mechanical crews on the job, safety cost and schedule wise.

After my crackerjack crews had adopted Kiemech and we were rapidly regaining lost time producing specified work, I turned my attention to our electrical subcontractor from

New Jersey named Superior Electric Company, who were dragging their feet. Apparently their way of doing business was to bid jobs at cost to get their foot in the door, then stop work and file a claim when there was a change in the contract, and not return to work until it was settled and been paid. Their business approach may have been fine on unimportant work where they came from, but was just opposite of my approach to *the Russians are coming* fast track defense contract work. Come hell or high water, I felt we had to get this important national defense contract built as rapidly as possible for the safety of our country, and we should argue later about the changes encountered. I told them they should continue documenting everything that was changed, but not worry so much about settling everything until the major work was completed and the costs, including impact costs, were determined. In the good old days, honest owners were always willing to settle contract changes equitably, *if* their bonded contractor delivered them a quality built job, safely and on schedule.

On the other hand she did have warts, so when you think about it hard enough, there is another side to the coin. Fast track contractors must either have a reservoir of *working capital* or know a compassionate banker who will issue them a *substantial line of credit* when working for a slow paying owner. As I recall, the Titan Missile Base was the largest contract Kiewit had ever taken alone without a joint venture partner to help with financing and nbelievably, we were into Pete's pocket a whopping $7,000,000 at one time before our progress payments finally began to catch up with our costs. I'll tell you, there are not many heavy engineering contractors in America with that kind of financial *staying* power.

After I wrote several breach of contract type warning letters to the Superior Electric Company that they ignored, I began holding up their *behind schedule* work payments to encourage them to get with it. Well, to make a long story shorter, they knew a higher up in the federal government back east to call for help, and in this case it was Les Kaufman's wife who did the calling. Les was president of Superior Electric at the time, and as it turned out, his wife had attended a girl's finishing school back east somewhere with Jackie Kennedy before she married Jack Kennedy. Well, you can believe this story or not, but she actually called the wife of the President of the United States for help. Her friend Jackie Kennedy then went to her husband Jack with the problem and President John F. Kennedy himself, personally called our Colonel at Beale Air Force Base on the telephone nearly scaring him half to death, and ordered him to personally hand deliver a whopping

My little family in Yuba City, Calif. in 1961

$1,000,000 check to me to hand to Superior Electric Company's job superintendent to help solve their cash flow problem. Wow, talk about fast *before claim settlement* action. I meekly handed Les Kaufman's superintendent the one million dollar check and said, "Now, will you please do the work you hired out to do?"

It was also around that same time I got my own pleasant surprise. Pete Kiewit discovered I was being paid less than Ray Gully and some of his other Omaha people that he had transferred to my job, so he unilaterally raised my weekly salary a whopping $75 a week, from $225 to $300 a week, to bring me up to par with his people. Tom was so enraged when he found out what Pete had done, he retaliated (unbeknown to me) by freezing my salary from that day forward, along with my already frozen Garrison Dam yearly $3,000 bonus amount. His only comment to me was, "Pete has really screwed up my districts indirect pay scale with stupid stunts like this." True to his word, it was the last increase in my salary and bonus (total yearly earnings) that my family would ever receive from the Kiewit Company until I resigned in 1963 and founded our own company.

Guppy fishing with Dave Scott's children

By the end of 1961, all the work on the Titan I (T5) Missile Base was completed and except for finalizing the outstanding change orders and claims, the contract was accepted eleven days ahead of the original schedule. Contrary to the Colonel's threat of removing Kiemech from the job for incompetence before my crews took over, the Corps of Engineers presented Kiemech with an award for their outstanding performance as the best mechanical contractor in the missile program, and despite the 600 design change that were added to the original contract that increased the original $30,000,000 bid to a whopping final amount of $57,000,000 with no time extensions, the Kiewit Company ended up as the only general contractor in the missile program to complete their contract ahead of their specified schedule.

An exhausted Homer Olsen with Dave Scott in 1961

As for me, I ended up completely exhausted when the job was finished and was even told by my doctor that I had not only developed another ulcer, but was a textbook example of *job burnout*. To reward myself for this outstanding accomplishment, I named my second ulcer, *Paul Scroggs,* after that whining incompetent with the same name that caused it and as it turned out, my ulcer was the only *thank you for a well done job* my crew and I ever received, other than a letter of commendation from Colonel Sherrard. But, as Tom Paul always used to say, "What are you hollering about; you're paid to do a good job."

I remember I was so down in the dumps when that job was completed, I wanted to quit the construction business entirely and just watch almond trees grow the rest of my life. To top things off even more, Janet flipped her lid and threw a tantrum when she discovered she was pregnant with our son Bob, which depressed me even more. To me her pregnancy was not only a blessing, but a God send and was the only good thing that has happened to us. For some unknown reason, I knew this little baby would be that wonderful little boy I had been praying for and I knew we needed to get re-settled somewhere soon, and hopefully it would be in our Pleasant Hill home to have the same Dr. Lamb who delivered our two beautiful daughters, also deliver this baby boy at the same Alta Bates hospital. I also hoped I might be offered my old goof off job back as the San Francisco Area Manager again to be able to spend more time at home learning to be a good father for our children again.

Unfortunately, my only job offer from Tom Paul was to *straighten out* the San Mateo Bridge job he said was slightly behind schedule and had some minor cost overrun problems. Somehow, and unbeknown to me, Tom and Pete had decided my most value to the company from then on would be as a *Troubleshooter* to clean up poorly run jobs and whatever talents I might have would just be wasted in middle management. Dave Scott had also developed a real liking for the goof off job I had given him and told Tom he wasn't about to give it up. So, in my depressed burnout condition, I accepted the San Mateo Bridge *Troubleshooter* job at my current salary to get my family moved and resettled in our Pleasant Hill home, *if and only if,* Tom would remove Charlie Pankow as it's *Job Sponsor* and I would have complete control and the authority, as well as the responsibility, to straighten the job out. Surprisingly, he agreed.

Charlie Pankow and I were good friends socially, but Charlie was one of those kind of guys who was so damn tight and penny wise

Bill Ziegler, Supt. Mike Uhl, RE, and Fran Murphy

pound foolish about things, he squeaked when he walked, and I knew sooner or later we would *cross swords*. Janet and I took a couple of weeks (our first *long* vacation in five years) to get our family moved, and were comfortably resettled again in our Pleasant Hill home by early March of 1962.

When I checked in at the San Mateo Bridge casting yard's trailer office, I'll tell you I was never so shocked in my life. Honest to God, over twenty percent (*20%*) of the time specified to build the bridge was already gone and only two percent *(2%)* of the bridge was built. To make matters even worse, the job was over *$1,000,000 in the red* and the rejected piling in their bone pile kept getting higher everyday. Wow, if this was Tom's idea of a *slightly behind schedule* and a *minor cost over run,* I'll eat your hat. Apparently everybody but me knew

Tom was so worried over the outcome of this Kiewit-Murphy-Pacific joint Venture, he would even put up with me running things to straighten the job out. For no other reason than the same brilliant management stupidity he used on the missile base, Tom had handcuffed Fran Murphy, the current project manager, the same way he tried to handcuff me with Paul Scoggs, only this time Charlie Pankow was Fran's *whining penny wise pound foolish job sponsor*. Shortly after I arrived to give Fran a helping hand, he announced he finally had it up to his eyebrows with Tom's stupidity and Charlie's tight fisted money interferences, and resigned to go to work for the Kaiser Steel company. Oooh boy, leave it to Tom in his unquestionable lack of any organizing talent, he decided to re-classify me as the *acting project manager* temporarily until he could find another genius like George Primo or Paul Scroggs to take over and guarantee the job would be a a major loss fiasco. Norm Raab, the chief engineer for the Bay Toll Bridge Authority, took Tom's reorganization break as an opportunity to replace his own *whining* Resident Engineer named Mike Uhl, with a younger *let's get the job built* engineer named Harry Reilich, as the job's new Resident

The Richmond Casting Yard - 1962

Engineer.

Slipforming 24" Pipe Piling for the San Mateo Bridge

I'll tell you, Harry Reilick was a Godsend for that Kiewit-Murphy-Pacific joint venture because unlike Mike Uhl, Harry was a qualified *can do* type civil engineer who believed the owner and the contractor should work together as a team in building the State's contracts. Like me, Harry wanted to see the job built safely, on schedule, and profitably for the contractor, and as things turned out, Harry and I not only became good friends, but were a great team to straighten out all the problems on that five mile, $14,000,000 trestle portion of the new San Mateo Bridge. Thanks to Harry's cooperative attitude and expertise, we turned the job around and finished the contract eight months ahead of schedule and unbelievably not only made back the million dollar loss when I first arrived, but increased the job's estimated job profit from the original as bid $1,250,000 to an unbelievable final job profit of $2,500,000.

Some of my Crackerjack Team and State Personnel

351

I remember thinking when Harry and I first started resolving problems on the job, it reminded me of my high school basketball coach's pep talks during a time-out, "Boys, we may be thirty points behind now, but by golly, we still have five minutes left to win the game." We spent our first week meeting with everyone working in the casting yard to hear their ideas

Loading Pre-cast Deck Units and Piling on a Barge

and review the shape the plant and equipment were in. Interestingly, the two major problems the crews doing the work were most disturbed about was Charlie's penny wise and pound foolish thinking way of doing things, such as his harsh *rock pocket* concrete mix design to save a cup of cement and his steam curing system that kept breaking down because of the cheap tubing he installed just to save a nickel. It became painfully obvious that major changes were needed throughout the plant to avoid a disaster.

On the good news side, the overall casting yard layout and their plant setup was almost an exact copy of the successful Lake Pontchartrain Bridge recently completed in Louisiana. I also thought Charlie's 24 inch concrete pipe pile's horizontal slipforming idea was brilliant because it was an efficient way to make piling and it got them the job in the first place. Fran Murphy told me when he left, "Basically, the root cause of all the problems in the casting yard are due to Charlie's pennywise and pound foolish way of thinking and all this job really needs to make it a success is to keep the bean counters noses off the job and you to give it the *Olsen Touch* you have been blessed with."

Well, the first *Olsen touch* change I made was in the casting yards supervisory personnel. Charlie obviously had too many Chiefs stumbling around looking for something to do and not enough Indians to do the work, so I cut the overhead costs by two thirds by transferring and/or laying off all of Charlie's supervisors above the union foreman level, and gave the casting yard superintendent's job to Chink Harmon and the office managers job to Don Davis and assigned the yards engineering duties to a newly hired young engineer named Dave Stacy. Fortunately, my old April club buddy, Bill Ziegler with the Murphy Pacific Company, signed on again as the field superintendent over all the pile driving and

Slipforming Piling on a 900 foot Casting Bed

bridge building operations. In fact Bill already had his combination iron worker-pile butt crew lined up raring to go as well as all the equipment he needed, so all he needed now was our pre-cast bridge units meeting the specifications, barged to him on schedule and, as he put it, "I'll take care of everything else."

We requested the union's permission to add to our labor agreement overlapping startup times on the two shifts to save daylight hours and increase job efficiency, and our request was cooperatively approved. With Harry's expertise, we also redesigned the concrete mix for the slipformed piling by replacing the *crushed Haydite* lightweight aggregate with a slightly more expensive kiln dried *rounded Basalite* aggregate and added another sack of cement, fifty pounds of dust fines, and additional water. *"Viola"* we had a smoother more buttery mix that immediately solved our rock pocket and concrete strength rejection problems. The sliding interior mandrel for the slipformed pipe piling was also lengthened an additional 20 feet to eliminate interior dropouts, and lo and behold, we began producing high strength piling in accordance with contract specifications that Bill Ziegler could drive without breaking. To add more insurance, Bill doubled the number of cushion blocks

Precasting Deck Units for the San Mateo Bridge

between the hammer and the piling and installed a hydraulic clamp in the leads to hold the

Driving Pipe Piling thru a Floating Template - 1962

pile steadier while driving. Lo and behold, we drove sixteen pile, 90 foot in length, that met the specification the first day.

I remember Jack Wagner, the pile butt business agent, stopped by our operation one day to complain about our unusually high pile driving production and said, "If Ben Gerwick had been low on this job, he would have shown some class and only driven eight piles a day." I said, "Jack, this job is a good example of what can happen when you have two guys like Bill and me doing something we don't know one damn thing about. Bill got all his pile driving experience as an ironworker and I got mine by herding sheep in Utah. So, as you can see, neither one of us are smart enough to know how many pile we're supposed to drive a shift." Jack just stared at us for a minute and then, shaking his head, turned and walked away muttering something we wouldn't care to hear.

Oooh boy, talk about real penny wise and pound foolish stupidity. In an attempt to save just a few pennies, Charlie installed a cheap thin walled tubing to transport hot curing steam from the boiler to the curing hoods over the concrete piling and deck units, but unfortunately in that marine environment, his cheap tubing had already rusted holes in the tubing to make it a full length *steam sprinkler* system rather than a *steam curing line*, even before the job started. That problem alone caused a major steam loss for proper curing, and guaranteed the rejection of the million dollar stack of un-cured rejected piling. By simply replacing the rusted tubing with heavier walled piping, and using a smoother buttery concrete mix, the slipformed pile rejection problem was solved.

The Gantry Crane Operators view of a Deck Pour

Apparently Charlie also thought a thin 2" layer of ballast under the cranes rails would be sufficient support for the 40 ton Gantry cranes, but once again, his penny wise thinking backfired. That lack of track support immediately created a twisting pumping action to develop when the loaded cranes moved over the rail lines and you guessed it, the twisting action in the Gantry's frame caused welds to begin to *pop,* resulting in even more downtime and delays and proving once again how costly penny wise thinking can be. That problem was solved by re-laying the gantry track ties and rails on a well tamped 12 inch minimum thickness layer of ballast, as Charlie should have done in the first place.

We increased the production of the 35 ton pre-cast deck units by 50% (from 8 to 12 per day) with several ingenious mechanical changes in the batch plant and gantry cranes themselves. The sprocket wheels on the mixing plant drives were changed in diameter to increase the belt speeds for material handling and concrete mixing, and the hydraulic pressures in the crane's motors was increased to give them more snap and speed. We even switched from petroleum based form oil to a whale oil (which was still available in those days) because whale oil, when used as a concrete form oil, didn't seem to break down under hot steam like the petroleum based oils, and the deck units popped loose easier without sticking. Finally, we increased the yard's crew size from 40 to 60 people, and put the job on two overlapping shifts to increase labor efficiency and save on daylight hours. Lo and

Stripping a Precast Deck Unit – 1962

behold, we began producing specification pre-cast bridge units and slipformed piling at a faster rate, and best of all we began to look like we knew what we were doing.

I received a copy of this letter from the Army Corps of Engineers at Beale Air Force Base, signed by Colonel Sherrard, and addressed to Peter Kiewit Son's Company in Arcadia, California. Colonel Sherrard, was in charge of our missile base contract and was the officer

I worked with throughout the job. Not that it matters, but I thought it was interesting Tom Paul never mentioned to me he ever received this letter.

16 July 1962

Gentlemen:

With the acceptance of all work performed by your firm on the Beale Titan I Missile Launch Base Facilities, I want to congratulate you on the project's successful completion. The accomplishment of a project of this type has been no small effort on the part of your organization and a great many excellent workman. The complexity of the project, the restricted work areas encountered, the criticalness of the construction schedule and the numerous changes demanded that you select a Project Manager possessing the ability to get things done while accomplishing the extensive coordination of activities. Your firm is to be complimented for your selection of Mr. Homer J. Olsen as your Project Manager.

Throughout the course of the project Mr. Olsen was continually abreast of the activities transpiring on all of the widely separated complexes. He spent numerous hours in the field acquiring firsthand knowledge of the operations and was able to schedule his activities so that he could be relied upon to be available for a multitude of meetings with Beale Area personnel. During those many sessions he participated with a firm open-mindedness and a positive attitude toward getting the job done although there were obstacles or changes impeding the effort. In numerous difficult situations wherein excessive obstinacy was being shown by others, Mr. Olsen remained tactfully firm and amiable with the result that disagreement areas were more quickly resolved and there was greater promotion of cooperation among the various organizations engaged in the overall effort. All of his actions and associations with members of governmental agencies and other contractors were characterized by a high degree of integrity which was promptly recognizable by all with whom he came in contact. His integrity permeated the project and had considerable influence on obtaining high quality workmanship.

The leadership shown by Mr. Olsen as your Project Manager has been most commendable. He has demonstrated that he is an asset to your organization and a credit to your firm.

Sincerely yours,
Joseph H. Sherrard
Lt. Colonel, CE
CEBMCO Liaison Officer

Robert Kevin Olsen one week old-1962

Two weeks after the Colonel's letter was written, I raced to the Alta Bates Hospital with Janet and my prayers were answered with the birth of our wonderful eight and a half pound baby boy we named Robert Kevin Olsen. I remember, while I was in the waiting room with a couple of other potential fathers, they kept trying out different girls names on each other while I confidently listened quietly for my boy. Suddenly Dr. Lamb came in with his nurse carrying Bob and announced, "You got your wish Homer, *IT'S A BOY!!!.*" Wow, I still remember yelling, *"YAHOO!"* at the top of my voice and picking up Dr. Lamb like my dad did with Grandpa Olsen to *Auteetot* him around the room, and started to polka dance with that wonderful doctor struggling to get away and shouting, "Hey, I just delivered him, you did all the work." I stopped dancing to take another good look at that wonderful little boy angel in the nurse's arms and said, "No Doc, Janet did all the work and she did a beautiful job on this little boy." It was without a doubt, the fourth happiest day in my life. The other days were when our first little boy and our two little girls were born.

It soon became painfully obvious during the

Story telling time with Bob-1962

construction of the San Mateo Bridge we desperately needed two more 500 ton BK barges to transport our pre-cast concrete units to the bridge site, to stay on Bill Ziegler's *crash* installation schedule. Fortunately, we were able to convince Tom Paul of our plight and, believe it or not, he was the only bidder at a Navy surplus auction on a 1000 ton barge worth at least $350,000 for the unbelievable price of $35,000 that met our needs much better than the two 500 ton barges. I had already told our tug boat captains to ignore Charlie Pankow's "Read my lips, there will be no overtime on this job" order, and work the *tides* instead of the *clock* so they could get over the sandbar on high tide without high centering on the sand bar, and be able to deliver more loads to Bill with our *too few* barges. Fortunately (and thank you Lord) our new 1000 ton barge solved our delivery problems and we were able to supply Bill Ziegler with even more than enough pre-cast units for him to meet his record breaking construction schedule. Believe it or not, Bill Ziegler and his crews began erecting

> ### MAJOR NEWS RELEASE DURING 1962
>
> *John Glenn is the first American to orbit the earth, the Cuban Missile Crises brings the U. S. and the Soviet Union to the brink of war, U. S. advisors in Vietnam are allowed to return fire, eye surgery is performed using a laser, Marilyn Monroe dies from a drug overdose, the first Kmart and Wal-Mart stores open, Wilt Chamberlain scores 100 points in a single basketball game, the first diet soda called Diet-Rite is marketed,* **And best of all, Robert Kevin Olsen was born July 28, 1962 at the Alta Bates Hospital in Berkeley.**

300 feet of completed two lane finished bridge per day and needless to say our casting yard, tug boats, and field crews, all began working together as a well oiled close knit motivated team.

As a little side story when our new 1000 ton barge was delivered to our casting yard dock for loading, Tom asked me "What are you going to name you're new barge?" We

Loading Piling on our new 1000 ton Barge – 1962

both happened to be standing next to Larry Fisher, our pile butt foremen, as he opened his can of *Copenhagen Snooze* for a quick lower lip re-charge, so while turning towards Tom with a grin on my face, I said, "Let's name it the *Copenhagen*." Tom looked at me like I was some kind of a nut case or something and said, "I've never been able to figure you out. Why don't you name it the Homer J. Olsen?" When I said, "What, you've got to be

kidding Tom, I wouldn't even give a name like that to my own son", he looked stunned and shaking his head, turned and walked away with, "I give up, go ahead and name the damn thing *Copenhagen*, see if I care." As far as I know the *Copenhagen* is still hauling freight up and down the west coast.

Shortly after we began moving along efficiently and finally getting some bridge work done, Charlie Pankow paid me a surprise visit. He said, "I see you hired 20 more men than I have in the estimate, how come?" I answered, "Charlie, we are now at the most efficient crew size to produce bridge units at a minimum cost and its imperative we stay ahead of what the field crews can place. We've more than doubled your estimated production by increasing the yard crew by only 50% and our unit labor costs are approaching half of what you originally estimated." When he answered, "Homer, I'm telling you one more time, get rid of those 20 extra people", I said "Charlie how's your wife and family?" Well, when he angrily answered, "Don't change the subject, I'm ordering you to get rid of those 20 extra men." I glared back at him for a moment to regain my composure and finally answered, "Did Tom ever talk to you after I took over this job?"

Mary Beth, Bob and Barbara waiting for Santa -1962

He shook his head with "No, why should he?" so I dialed Tom Paul and handed him the phone. Oooh boy, after their shouting match subsided somewhat, Charlie angrily *jammed* the telephone back at me and without a word, stormed out of the office trailer while Tom blasted me for embarrassing him that way. It was the last time Charlie Pankow ever visited our job and surprisingly, a short time later he not only resigned from Kiewit, but took the

Chink's Storage Yard Materials ready for Barge Loading

whole Building Division in the Los Angeles District with him to start up his own company. I ran into Charlie a year or so later and apologized while asking him if I was responsible for his leaving Kiewit so abruptly. He said no, he and the others had resigned over Tom's new unfair personnel salary policies.

For some unknown reason, that story reminded me of Harry Reilick's first day on the job. I remember when Harry arrived to take Mike Uhl's place as our new resident engineer he was wearing of all things, a brand

My Crackerjack Casting Yard Crew on the San Mateo Bridge – 1963

new blue suit, a white shirt and tie, and polished black shoes. Bill Ziegler, Ernie Bergstaler (Mr. Pile Butt) and I were standing there discussing how to pull and replace another *rock pocketed* broken pile Ernie had failed to drive again, and Harry stormed up in a demanding tone of voice, ordered Bill to have the crane operator swing him over on the hook to inspect the broken pile. The three of us looked at each other with, "Oooh boy, don't tell us they've sent us another lousy bureaucrat to help build the bridge?." Well, Bill casually looked over at Bill Richardson, our crane operator, and winked, then helped Harry get seated on the ball over the crane hook and signaled towards the broken pile. You guessed it, Bill Richardson swung Harry out over the San Francisco Bay and *just by accident* dunked him in the drink like a donut in a cup of coffee up to his shirt collar, and then apologizing, jerked him out of the drink and swung him on over to the pile to make his inspection. Whooee, I'll tell you when Harry finally swung back the bridge deck soaked to the skin, he had a completely different personality. Dripping wet and with a sheepish grin, Harry busted out laughing and said, "I know you bastards did that on purpose, but I asked for it", and sloshed off to his car to leave. The next morning he showed up wearing work clothes, hard toed boots and a hard hat

I think a beard would look good on you Dad

like the rest of us, saying, "OK starting now, let's begin working together as a team and get this damn job built." What we didn't know then about Harry Reilick was, he had spent more time in a Japanese prison camp during World War II than any of the rest of us spent

Building the final two lane side of the San Mateo Bridge- 1963

in the service. Like Don Davis, our office manager, he was captured in the Philippines and was in the death march, and spent the next five years as a slave mining coal for the Japs. Needless to say, after that discovery Harry Reilick and Don Davis were our War hero's, and the whole job became a dedicated team shouting, *pull the lever full speed ahead.*

From then on my job as troubleshooter and as an *acting* project *manager* was a breeze compared to some of the other jobs I've handled. My little brother Rodger was working for me at the time as an apprentice operating engineer and told my mother, "Junior has the easiest job in the world. All he does all day is drive around in a company car between

Chink's Richmond casting yard and Bill's bridge in Hayward, shooting the breeze with Harry Rielick." He was certainly right about that. I would tell Chink that Bill told me to tell him to get the lead out because he could build the bridge ten times faster than Chink could cast and deliver the units he needed, and Chink would answer with, "Oh yeah, you tell Bill he'll never catch up with me and he better get with it because I'll bury him with piling and pre-cast deck units."

Pre-casting 35 ton Deck Units for the San Mateo Bridge

I remember another time Harry Rielick and I were *shooting the breeze* with Bill Ziegler at the bridge site discussing construction problems, and Bill commented on how the *gawkers* driving by watching him drive pile, were backing up traffic. Harry said, "Bill, let me show you how easy it is to *really* foul up traffic, watch this", and he started pointing up towards the sky. Then he said, "Now you two guys join me pointing up like this and watch what happens." I'll kid you not, while all three of us were pointing at the clouds above, every passing car suddenly slowed down to nearly a stop, to look out of their car door windows and up where we were pointing.

When the line of cars began to stretch back nearly a mile or so and we heard police sirens in the distance, we put our hands in our pockets and walked behind the pile driver holding our sides laughing.

Oooh boy, anyway, to get back to the tug of war between Bill and Chink, the best day's production Bill Ziegler ever had building the bridge was 30 pile driven per day, 9 pile caps set and 18 deck units and 18 curb and handrail units placed, totaling a whopping 315 feet of completed two lane bridge built in one 10 hour day. With only four 900 foot long pile slipform beds and only 15 deck casting bed forms, Chink's crew could only cast a maximum of 20 – 90 foot pile and 12 deck units per day because it was all they could pour and cure in one day, but By using his storage yard area as a cushion along with a few work weekends, Chink fortunately was able to stay ahead of Bill's record bridge production without any delays.

I'll say one thing for sure about those two guys and their *crackerjack* crews. They put on one of the best bridge building shows I have ever seen and believe it or not, the five mile San Mateo-Hayward Bridge trestle, including the one million dollars change order Norm Raab issued for additional work, not only made back the $1,000,000 loss and the four months behind schedule time showing when Harry and I took over, but completed the job eight months ahead of it's specified schedule and doubled the estimated job profit by the time the contract was completed on August 1, 1963. When you think about it hard enough, it wasn't too bad for a bunch of hair lips like us.

Apparently, word got back to Peter Kiewit in Omaha, that I didn't have enough work to do anymore to keep me busy, so he asked me to fly up to South Dakota to see what the problem was on the Platte-Winter Bridge Kiewit was joint venturing with the Massman Construction Company. When I got there, I took a boat ride out to their floating rig on the

Homer & Old Mugs on a relaxing stroll

lake that was supposed to be driving a cluster of 5 to 1 batter, 48" diameter, 100 foot long pipe piling for bridge piers. Instead, believe it or not, the whole crew was just standing around sucking their thumbs and picking their nose. I recognized the foreman, Everett Pearson, right away because he had worked for me on the Garrison Dam Stilling Basin job in North Dakota, so I asked him, "What seems to be the problem here, Everett?" He said, "Homer, the Kiewit Company has really gone out of its way this time to screw up. They've picked up a job that can't be built." I said, "Well, we've got a contract to build this job whether it can be built or not Everett, so there is no if and buts about it and like it or not, *we've got to build it.*" He said, "Homer, we've tried everything we know how to do to get the 48" pipe pile down through that two foot layer of *hardpan* on the bottom of the lake and nothing has worked. We're even using the world's biggest pile driving hammer and we still can't get the pile down." Well, apparently Everett and his crew had decided it was impossible to break through *solid iron* and just quit trying, so I

Barbara and Mary Beth watch as Bob checks things out-1963

said, "Everett, the crews just standing around anyway, so for my benefit let's try once more, only this time I want you to send a diver down to feel the tip of the pile while your world's biggest hammer is pounding on it."

When the diver reported back all he could feel near the tip of the pile was a tingling sensation, it confirmed what I thought was happening all along. That 48" diameter pipe pile they were trying to drive weighed 1000 pounds per foot, so a 100 foot long pile would weigh a whopping 50 tons and the diver had just proved a pile that heavy would absorb all the energy their pile hammer could produce. I said, "Everett, the only way we're going to get any of these pile down through that hard pan layer is by *jetting them* down. Let's figure out where the pile tip lands on 5 to 1 batter after standing the pile vertically on that point, try blasting a hole straight down through the hard pan layer with our jets at full blast. When the pile breaks through the hard pan, tip the pile top back slowly into its template and continue jetting and tapping it on down to it's specified tip elevation with the hammer." Everett just shrugged and said, "OK Homer, if you say so, but I can tell you this right now, it won't

Bob helping his dad solve construction problems

work." Well wouldn't you know it, two hours later we had a pile down and by the end of the shift, we had another pile down and in place.

I said, "Everett, now that we know the job can be built let's get everything back on schedule by working three shifts when I locate two more good pile butt foremen to handle the other two shifts." I called Bill Ziegler at the San Mateo Bridge from their Platte-Winter trailer office, to ask if I could borrow Ernie Bergstaler and Jack Johnson, and after I explained to him the importance of having two more experienced foremen to help build the job, he said, "I'll ask

them, but I'm sure they will want their plane fare there and back paid plus their motel bills while in South Dakota.", I said, "Bill, tell them that won't be any problem." Well when Ernie and Jack arrived and saw what had to be done, I asked Ernie (Mr. Pile Butt himself) how many pile per shift he thought his crew could drive, he said, "I'd say at least four." Jack Johnson overheard Ernie and said, "If Ernie can get four, I can get five" and Everett Pearson, who was standing behind them listening, chimed in with, "Hell, I can get six." Lo and behold, the job suddenly began to move forward and believe it or not, the $600,000 loss showing on their last cost report suddenly began to melt away towards the plus side.

While I was waiting for Ernie and Jack to arrive, I spent some time reviewing some of their other operations on the Platte-Winter Bridge, and wouldn't you know it, the penny wise and pound foolish crowd were at it again. The concrete mix they were using was so harsh and dry the concrete couldn't be placed with their vibrators without rock pockets showing up, and everywhere I went, finishers were chipping and patching concrete. I was told it was the South

We sure straightened that job out fast, Dad

Dakota State inspectors fault until I asked the resident engineer, who said, "You've got to be kidding, your own damn people came up with that ridicules mix design to save a tablespoon of cement." Oooh boy, you guessed it and once again the problem was corrected by simply adding more cement, more sand and dust fines, plus some more water and *Viola*. Like mixing batter for a prize winning chocolate cake, the problem was solved again by using a more workable mix and the concrete and finishing foreman couldn't thank me enough for putting some common every day run of the mud sense, back into the job.

A little later I was in their shop talking to the master mechanic and a pile butt from the floating rig on the reservoir came in by boat to borrow the only cutting torch they had on the job. You guessed it; a cuss fight soon broke out between the mechanic in the shop and the pile butt because he also needed the torch for his work and wasn't about to give it up. I said, "My god, can't this job afford more than one lousy cutting torch?" The master mechanic groaned with, "Oooh boy, I'll let you talk to the front office about buying another one. They won't even give me the time of day." So before I left, I made sure both crews had their own cutting torches and I had the job superintendent's promise he would pay Ernie and Jack's travel and motel bills. When Ernie and Jack finally arrived and everything was taken care of and began running smoothly, I drove away with a good feeling about the job being a successful one, and caught my plane for home.

A Site Office Trailer - 1960

It was after I had finished going through my paperwork and mail buildup in the San Mateo Bridge trailer office, and saw my company bonus check for the year that really put the icing on the cake far me as far as staying with Kiewit or not. For some unknown reason, I felt Tom would show some class this year and increase my bonus in 1963 because I honestly felt I had personally done more than a little to bringing the San Mateo Bridge back on track, and even more to do in building the very profitable Titan I missile Base. Oooh boy, instead and much to my surprise and disappointment, my bonus was the same $3000 I received every year since Ben Williams first gave me that same amount in 1955 on the Garrison Dam. I was shocked because during the past twelve years that I had run jobs as either a superintendent or a project manager, my crews and I had turned in an average job profit of $1,500,000 per year, and I was considered one of Kiewit's top three money makers. Surely that would have entitled me to a bonus at least close to what the golf-playing middle management types were getting. Oooh boy, was I ever wrong.

Thinking back now about it, I must have really come unglued when I saw that bonus check because I telephoned Tom Paul, who refused to take my call, so I told Bud Waigand I was flying down to Los Angeles the next day to personally jamb that check up Tom's *aferendum*, or words to that effect. Well, you guessed it, when I stomped into Tom Paul's office, he had already hidden out somewhere and no one in his office seemed to know where, so I stormed into Bud Waigand's office and threw that crumpled up check at him shouting, "I've had it up to my eyebrows with this cheap lousy district, I quit."

I believe it was Ward White who told me one time there are only four ways to accumulate wealth during your lifetime. He said the three easiest ways were to marry it, inherit it, or steal it, and the fourth and only choice left for me, was to work hard making money for a good company and hoping to be fairly compensated. As far as I was concerned, that old Viking Code, *Those who pull on the oars will share in the plunder*, made good sense a thousand years ago, and made even better sense in this day and age. Under Tom Paul's new civil service policy where the money makers and money losers with same job descriptions are paid the same salary, it soon became painfully obvious I would never improve my families net worth as a *Troubleshooter* enough to purchase more Kiewit stock, or pay for any of my children's college educations, or even save a small nest egg to retire comfortably with some day.

Robert Kevin Olsen at one year

The two things I wanted most to accomplish during my lifetime was to first, escape the miserable locked in poverty cycle my parents and my grandparents were trapped in all their lives and second, to make enough money to give my family the things I never had while I was growing up. The answer was to obtain a meaningful education from a top notch school like Stanford, and apprentice with a good company like Kiewit, which I've done, and then 'Found' my own construction company to hopefully keep more of what I've made for myself. I was approaching my fortieth birthday and the decision to leave the Kiewit Company or not had to be made soon, while I was still young enough to put in the long hours necessary to succeed. If it so happened, Lord forbid, I was not successful, I would still have enough working years left to recover working for another company.

When I drove down to the San Mateo Bridge to see how Bill Ziegler was getting along, surprise of all surprises, there stood Ernie Bergstaler and Jack Johnson and honest to God, I couldn't believe my eyes, so I asked them, "What happened in South Dakota?" They said Kiewit reneged on their agreement to pay their motel 6 bills because some bean counter in the Omaha office rejected it, so they quit. Wow, talk about penny wise and pound foolish stupidity. Those two guys, along with Everett Pearson, were driving twelve 50 ton piles on a three shift day, which was more than they had driven all the previous month, and they were finally getting the bridge back on schedule into the profit column. Unbelievably, some knot headed head office bean counter picking his nose at a desk in Omaha had the unmitigated gall to pull a dumb stunt like this, and he let two of the most badly needed capable pile driving foremen quit over a lousy two bit motel bill. It was unbelievably ridiculous, but on the other hand she did have warts, so I guess when you think about it hard enough, it was really all my fault. I should have just given them a fancy title like *Pile Consultants* or *Lobbyist*, rather than a run of the mud, red necked blue collar title, like *Pile Butt Foreman*, and they would have been paid much more than they had asked in the first place.

A couple of months later Tom apparently figured I had simmered down enough to fly up from Los Angeles to talk things out, and the gist of our meeting (from his point of view) was, I was too good at my job as a *troubleshooter* to consider promoting me to a higher salaried position and he couldn't pay me more than I was currently making because of my new locked in *civil service* title. Without telling me in so many words, he said I had now reached my *glass ceiling* in the Kiewit Company and would never go higher on the Kiewit management totem pole, or even worse, I would never be paid more than I was currently making. I said, "Frankly Tom, I enjoy this challenging *troubleshooter* job, but if this new *civil service* and *craft union idea* is going to be your salary policy from now on, I quit. As I told you, I'll stay on this job until it's finished, but when it's accepted by the owner, I'm leaving." He glared at me for a minute andsaid, "Homer, you don't have guts enough to quit the Kiewit Company", and somewhat stunned I answered, "Thank you Tom, you just made it a lot easier for me to leave", and walked out. At least now I knew what Charlie Pankow meant when he said he quit over Tom's *new personnel policy* and rumor had it, Ward White also quit for the same reason..

D. O. D. and his two Rainbow Girl daughters

Shortly after our meeting, Tom left for his three month vacation in Europe while I saw to it the remaining punch list work to complete the San Mateo-Hayward five mile trestle portion of the bridge was completed and turned over to the California Toll Bridge Authority. Bob Wilson surprised me with a quick visit from Omaha while Tom was gone to try talking me into staying on and moving back to Omaha with the same title and salary. He said Pete figured Tom and I must have some kind of a personality conflict going between us, and thought moving me back to Omaha would solve the problem. I thanked him and Pete for their concern, but said his offer was too late for two reasons. My family would never consider leaving California again, and my decision to leave the company when this job was turned over to the State was chiseled in stone. Bob surprised me as he left by saying, "I prophesize a year from now you'll be crawling back on your belly begging for your job back", and both shocked and angry I said, "I might be crawling around on my belly looking for a job somewhere, but by damn, I'll guarantee you Bob, it won't be with this company." Interestingly, every year after that conversation whenever I've ran into Bob Wilson at the Beavers and elsewhere, he would apologize to me all over again for making that stupid remark

When the San Mateo Bridge contract was signed sealed and delivered, I transferred everyone working for me to other jobs within the company and signed my own payoff check. I remember sitting there at my desk, staring at my last paycheck from the Kiewit Company with my signature on it, and thinking about my fourteen and a half years working for that wonderful company building all those *easy* jobs. I thought about how much I was going to miss all those wonderful people I enjoyed working with and how fortunate I was to have had the opportunity to apprentice with such a fine company, but I also thought about how well prepared I was now to start up my own construction company. My little brother Rodger was certainly right when he constantly complained to my mother about me always having all the luck in the family, because it was true. Fran Murphy was also right when he said I had not only been blessed, but had been given the *touch* by a higher power, but aside from all that, there is no question I have not only been lucky, but very fortunate all my life.

Over the years several people have asked me the same question, "Where did you ever find the intestinal fortitude to quit such a wonderful company as Kiewit to start your own construction business?" My answer, without getting into a long dissertation and stay within what they suspected all along, was always the same, "I was so stupid at the time I didn't know what I was getting into." The truth of the matter is, I felt the opportunity of a lifetime had just been handed me on a golden platter and I never felt more confident about what the future would hold for me and my little family, and that I had made the right decision.

I cleared my desk, locked the trailer office door for the last time and, never looking back, drove my car onto a new lane on the highway of life, confident that I was steering us in the right direction. I dropped off my keys, my company credit cards, and my company car at Norm Barnes' house on the way home to turn in for me, and took my family out to a fancy Danville restaurant called *The Brass Door* that evening to celebrate this wonderful opportunity awaiting us. As far as I know, I am the only employee in the Peter Kiewit Son's Company that has ever fired himself.

THE HOMER J. OLSEN, INC. YEARS

After a well earned two weeks to readjust and get reorganized, I called Bill Ames for a meeting to discuss setting up our own company and he suggested I talk to Pat Gibbons of the Gibbons and Reid Company in Salt Lake City, Utah and Gordon Ball of the Gordon H. Ball Company in Danville, California. I had never met either one of these two gentlemen before and was surprised to learn they already knew everything about me and my construction reputation. Bill arranged for me to meet with each of them separately to describe what I had in mind and they both rejected my joint venture idea initially by saying the same thing. "We are not in the business of creating more competition for ourselves because we already have way too much", and wanted me to work only as their employee. Pat Gibbons said if I would be interested in the job as his California division manager in their San Mateo office, he would start my salary at five hundred dollars a week (nearly twice what Kiewit paid me) and give me ten percent of the pre-tax profit my district turned in as a yearly bonus.

Company sign – 1981

Wow, what a job offer. I thanked him profusely for that wonderful offer, but to show him how stupid I can be at times, I told him I had to get this "having my own spread" idea out of my system while I was still young enough to make a run for it.

When I met with Gordon Ball, he also only wanted me to work for him as his company's structures manager along roughly the same terms as Pat Gibbons, only for a lot less. After considerable discussion, and thanks to Gordon's vice president, Vince Smith, and his "Why don't we give Homer's idea a whirl?", (Vince knew me from his early years as a district engineer for the California Highway Department) Gordon finally said, "OK, Homer, to get a *money maker* like you on board, we will agree to joint venturing with you if you will agree to a 50-50 split on the job profits you bring in." We shook hands and I said, "You got a deal Gordon, and I promise you won't be sorry." Unlike today where lawyers make all the management decisions, in those good old days a handshake was a contract and Gordon and I hit it off from the very start as two honest partners who trusted each other. We went on to build 14 profitable joint venture contracts together during the next several years until Gordon sold his company to the Dillingham Corporation to retire and we went on our own. Sorrowfully, Gordon passed away not too long after he sold out and unfortunately, never had a chance to enjoy his retirement.

I will always be grateful to Gordon for his friendship and his invaluable support during those early years. If it had not been for his signature on our first few bid bonds, along with his financial backing and his equipment when needed, our company would never have grown as rapidly as we did. I remember we both put up $27,500 (that was all I could scrape together) and I got into Gordon's pocket over the next year and a half a whopping $175,000 before things began to turn around. By the time we finished our last BARTD contract together, I had paid him that amount back at least twenty five times over, as his share of our ventures, and as it all turned out, our decision to joint venture was a profitable one for both of us. I will never forget Gordon H. Ball, for his homespun down to earth "keep your head screwed on right" approach to bidding and building work, and for being such a good, honest, hard working friend and trustworthy business partner. He was my kind of a guy.

I thought it was interesting that my old Kiewit boss, Tom Paul, angrily telephoned Gordon Ball after he returned from his European vacation and learned I had actually quit Kiewit and made a joint venture agreement with Gordon Ball. He told Gordon he was making a terrible mistake messing around with Homer Olsen as a partner because he was disloyal and was only a lousy uneducated sheepherder when he hired me, and in general went out of his way to run my character into the ground. When Gordon laughingly told me about it, I said, "If it bothers you Gordon, we can still cancel out our deal and I'll go somewhere else." He answered, "Homer, don't worry about it. You may have worked for Tom Paul a long time, but you don't know him like I do. Tom highly recommended I hire a *construction genius* named George Primo one time that turned out to be an incompetent idiot and he cost my company a small fortune before I woke up and fired him." He said, "Tom running you down this way tell me just the opposite. You must have been one helluva good hand all the time you worked for him."

To limit our liability on our first job, Gordon and I put together an *item joint venture,* rather than a total risk *true joint venture,* and bid the construction of the new six-mile Stevens Creek freeway (Hwy 85) from the Bayshore freeway near Moffitt Field, through the city of Mountain View to the Skyline Blvd, as three partners, each doing his own specialty of work. The L. C. Smith Company agreed to sponsor the total job and do the dirt and blacktop (asphalt) paving, the Gordon H. Ball Co. agreed to do the white (concrete) paving, and the Ball-Simpson-Olsen group agreed to construct all the bridges, culverts and do all the storm drainage work. The name *Simpson* was added to our structures group because Gordon had a *tax-loss-carry-forward* he wanted to use up (which also encouraged him to Joint Venture with me) from a previous losing job he had with the late Milt Simpson.

With the help of our newly organized company's guardian angel, and the expertise of my constant shadow (my 18 month old son Robert Kevin Olsen), we submitted our *structures* work portion of the bid to be added to our two other partners' portions, and on October 3, 1963 we turned in our combined bid of slightly over $6,000,000.

> ## MAJOR NEWS RELEASE DURING 1963
>
> *President John F. Kennedy is assassinated in Dallas, Texas, Lyndon Johnson becomes President, the U. S. and the USSR set up a "hotline" to prevent accidental nuclear war, the nuclear submarine "USS Thresher" sinks with all men aboard, 200,000 march on Washington for civil rights, the Supreme Court rules accused criminals have the right to free counsel, the first lung and liver transplants are performed, the U. S. Clean Air Act becomes law, Instamatic cameras, touch-tone telephones and skateboards are introduced, and* **the HOMER J. OLSEN Construction Company is founded.**

Whooee, miracle of all miracles and believe it or not, our combined bid was low and our low structures work portion (totaling $2,543,000 of the total bid), got the job for all three of us. Our little company had just picked up its first contract and we were now in the construction business, hook line and sinker.

When some of my former crackerjack crew learned that Gordon and I were low on the Stevens Creek Freeway, they began dropping by one by one to congratulate us, and to nonchalantly mention things were no longer the same at Kiewit anymore without my dumb jokes, and wondered if they could work for me again. Wow, what a wonderful bunch of loyal guys. I told them I couldn't (and wouldn't), proselyte anyone from another company, but did nonchalantly say, "If Kiewit lays you off after you're finished with what you're doing, and you're

The completed Madison Avenue Bridge crossing Highway 80 – 1965

looking for another job, I'll be glad to 'snokker' with you." Chink Harmon was the first to sign on, and after we had Job #1 set up and running smoothly, I turned the job over to him to handle things as structures superintendent while my young shadow and I bid for more work. A short time later, we picked up the $660,000 Oregon Avenue-Bayshore Freeway Interchange in Palo Alto and the $675,000 Madison Avenue Bridge over Hwy 80 in Sacramento. Oooh boy, all of a sudden things were really starting to look up for our little company and now if we can just keep our heads screwed on right, we're on our way.

Around that same time, one of my favorite engineering professors at Stanford named Clark Ogelsby asked me as a favor to him, to drop by some evening after work and talk to his Construction Management class. Not knowing what to talk about specifically, I took slides of the various jobs I was involved in building after graduating, and made my presentation more along the line of a bull session than a speech. Ooh boy, I'll tell you, that group of kids turned out to be the sharpest bunch I have ever confronted and they had me pinned to the wall several times that evening with their intelligent questioning and hunger to learn. Honest to God we started our *bull session* at 7:00 pm that evening and finally at 12:00 midnight, Professors Ogelsby and Hank Parker both said, "Hey come on guys, let's adjourn. Homer's jobs start at 7:00 in the morning and all of you have eight o'clock classes."

As I gathered up my slides, a young man sauntered up to my desk introducing himself as Bill Young and said he would like to work for me when he graduated the following June. I said, "Bill, I don't know why you would want to work for a dumb guy like me. I've never said '*I don't know*' so many times in my life, as I did tonight." He said, "Yes, but you were honest about it." Well, needless to say after an answer like that, I hired Bill on the spot and except for the two years he served in Vietnam as an Army ordnance officer, he worked for me ten years before he felt the same cockle burr under his saddle I did with Kiewit, and quit to start his own construction company. To this day, I can honestly say, William P. Young was the sharpest and the most interested in learning all he could about construction engineering, cost keeping, estimating, bidding, and running work safely and profitably, plus managing a construction company like a business rather than a hobby, than anyone I have ever hired. It goes without saying, he also learned from the mistakes I made because he did a much better job of managing his own company, bidding, building and financially wise, than I ever did, and when he retired he ended up much better off than any of us.

I remember during November of 1963, while clearing the Stevens Creek Freeway of trees and buildings to begin work, I drove by a telephone company repairman working at the top of a pole relocating phone lines, and he yelled down to me, "Turn on your car radio." I was stunned to learn President John F. Kennedy had just been assassinated in Dallas, Texas, and when I got back to our trailer office, everyone on the job were in such a state of shock that I shut everything down to let them all go home while I sat at my desk choking back tears. It was unbelievable to me something like this could happen in this wonderful country of ours and like an incoming fog bank, I suddenly felt it was an omen of worse things to come. To me, our country never fully recovered from that catastrophe and continued deteriorating for the next two decades until the best President of the United States during my lifetime, Ronald Reagan, was elected president.

Our families 1963 Christmas letter to our friends and relatives was also our new company's startup announcement to describe where we were and what our family was doing at the time.

ANNOUNCING A NEW CONSTRUCTION COMPANY
YOUNG – AGGRESSIVE – QUALIFIED.
Christmas 1963

Our young son, Bob, symbolizes the big news in our family this year. After 14+years with the same company, we have realized our dream of having our own contracting business and "struck out on our own." We presently have a joint venture contract underway now called, Ball, Simpson & Olsen involving the construction of 16 freeway bridges for the State in Sunnyvale, California. We now have 15 employees, one 30 ton motorcrane, two trucks, three pickups, two generators, one shop trailer, one office trailer, misc. skill saws, small tools and supplies and are mortgaged to the hilt. By next Xmas, we will either be off and running or standing in the bread line. We'll let you know.

Mary Beth and Barbara are young ladies now at twelve and ten years old and their dear old flabby graying dad is continually amazed at how fast they are growing. They are both enjoying their Alamo middle school and { despite their fears of never ever meeting such good friends ever again that they had in Pleasant Hill, they have. Janet stays young, slim and

Bob's first haircut – 1964

agile chasing our seventeen month old boy named Bob around the house and yard, while dear old dad admits to his years and just smiles and watches. My advice to everyone is simply this. If you are going to raise a thundering herd of young boys, (and just one can seem like it at times) have them before your forty. Janet just reminded me, "There is a difference between boys and girls", but then, she has a Phi Beta Kappa pin, you know

We also moved from our home on Lucinda Lane in Pleasant Hill to a bigger home located at 18 Adele Court in Alamo this year. It got so dear old dad could never get into the one bathroom with all these women, so our new home has two and a half bathrooms, *no bedrooms or kitchen, just bathrooms – and a garage for the cats. Needless to say, dad got the half bath. We also have six walnut trees in our backyard. I keep thinking about that old story of the alligators, so if anyone wants walnuts, and walnut tree leaves in the fall, send money. Ooh boy, as my former employer used to say, "Homer, someday you'll go too far." I think I'm getting ridiculous.*

Anyway, the gist of all this is to let you know we are all well, happy and healthy even though we never seem to communicate except through Xmas cards once a year. We hope all is well with you folks and that next year will bring you the best of everything. Come see us when you can.

Ole

I always got such a kick out of my young son Bob, especially when he was around three years old because he wanted so much to help his dear old dad get a good start in our newly organized construction business. When we first started, I put a desk in the master bedroom of our Alamo home to use as my estimating work station, and used the bed to lay out plans and specifications. I also purchased a Monroe hand crank calculator and I still had my same old slide rule I used in high school, so all in all, things worked out fairly well. I also installed a small desk for my young son Bob to help me and we both went through reams of paper

Dear Old Dad and Bob check out job progress

figuring the lowest cost way to build things using different construction ideas we dreamed up together. After all, check estimates are very helpful and my *little shadow's* expertise helped eliminate any chance of error. As Peter Kiewit always said, "*The easiest money you will ever make in this competitive construction business is what you **don't** leave on the table during a bid.*" When I informed my two year old shadow of this interesting fact, he tried even harder to prepare more accurate estimates, and believe it or not, on the first three jobs we were low bidder totaling nearly $4,000,000, we left only 2% on the table. When you think about that interesting achievement hard enough, it really wasn't bad for a couple of hair lips working out of a bedroom office.

As a little *stretch break* during our long sessions estimating jobs, Bob and I would practice an old Olsen and Johnson, "Hell's a Poppin" skit that went something like this. Olsen (me, age 40) would say, *"Don't go through that revolving door"*, and Johnson (Bob, age two) would answer, *"But my foddo's in der."* Then Olsen would say, *"What's your father's name?"*, and Johnson would say, *"Berschh MxShhnert"*, Olsen's answer was, *"Bert McSnert, that's me!!"*, and an even more surprised little Bob (Johnson), would recognize this Bert McSnert (Olsen) really was his long lost father and with his arms outstretched, would shout, *"Foddo!!"* His long lost dear old dad, Bert McSnert (Olsen), would then go into a mouth dropping surprised act and respond, *"Son!!"*, and happily picks up his long lost son in his arms and polkas around the room loudly singing a ditty called, *"The Irish Washwomen.."*

I think we need a break, Dad

I remember Pete Kiewit telling everyone at our management meeting in Grand Island one time, "To be successful in this competitive construction contracting business, you must bid the work at the right price, build the work for the right cost, collect in full for all the work you do, and take good care of your assets." It was Ward White who preached, "Never fall in love with any job you're bidding because it can bankrupt you." Wow, truer words were never spoken. Unfortunately I developed a real crush on our fourth job (the Sacramento River Freeway Bridge widening) and had completely forgotten Pete's first and most important of his four success points, and left a whopping 13% ($180,000) on the table, all because I thought I

Placing 20 ton Girders for Sacramento River Bridge widening

had a brilliant idea on how to construct the job. That particular *Homer's folly* idea was so simple I knew our competition would also think of it, but didn't, and we ended up giving away all our advantage plus, as it turned out, even our markup. My idea was nothing more than an oversized straddle truck gantry crane running on 90# rails, powered by an Austin Western telescoping boom crane on top. Merritt Mason designed the whole thing for me primarily to install the 20 ton steel girders over the river rather than use a floating rig and/or building a dock pier in the river. We fabricated it in Gordon's shop and it worked fine, but unfortunately cost twice what we estimated to build. I remember after we were awarded the job, Gordon rightfully insisted we write off *Homer's folly* 100% as specialized equipment on the job, rather than using the standard depreciation rates I used in the bid. Anyway, as it all turned out that plus traffic delays and a few other cost over runs resulted in only a breakeven job. I also remember just before we submitted our bid,

Gordon said, "I think your bid is at least $100,000 too low, and I hope you put extra money in to cover traffic delays." Well, it didn't register with me at the time and unfortunately, being in love with the job and all, I didn't put his suggestions in the bid. So, and I know you've already guessed this, I found out the hard way it costs twice as much to work in traffic as it costs in a vacant lot. Gordon just shook his head in disbelief when he reviewed my final cost report (we only made and split, $5,000) and said, "Next time Homer, please do me the favor of keeping your head screwed on right when you bid for more work", and as a keepsake, willed me his 50% interest in Homer's folly. Unfortunately, I never found another job to re-use that *specialized equipment* on again.

Homer's Folly straddle truck crane pouring with four concrete buckets

NEWS RELEASES DURING 1964

Lyndon Johnson and Hubert Humphrey are elected President and Vice President, Johnson declares war on poverty and the food stamp program begins, Congress approves the Tonkin Gulf Resolution thereby escalating the Vietnam war, a 9.2 Earthquake and Tsunami in Alaska causes major damage, The Warren Commission report on the JFK assassination is released, Martin Luther King receives the Nobel Peace Prize, Southern senators filibuster for 75 days before the Civil Rights Act is passed, The Surgeon General links cigarette smoking with cancer, Head Start is established, the St. Louis Arch is completed. Beatle mania makes long hair fashionable for hippies.

Our Christmas letter to all our friends and relatives describes what and where we were at that time.

THE DAY AFTER CHRISTMAS – 1964

Its amazing how fast time slips away – here it is already one day after Xmas and we're still madly trying to finish writing our Xmas cards. For some reason shortly after Thanksgiving, Janet suddenly began ricocheting between the 'Xmas quivers' and some kind of a 'staring coma' and this morning she was doing both at the same time. I think it's time the kids and I pitched in and helped a little around here by at least doing some of the Christmas shopping. I see by the paper they're having some really good sales after New Year.

Barbara is 11 years old

Last year, I said we would report to you whether our little business was off and running or we would be standing in the bread line. I can now honestly and truthfully report to you; both our accountant and our banker think we are "off."

Seriously though, all things considered, I think our little Company has done pretty well for its first year in business. We have continued to acquire more contracts and equipment and more good people have joined our organization. We bid around thirty contracts last year and were successful on three of them for a total volume of $3,900,000. We have already completed half that amount and are now looking for additional work to stay busy. Beginning next year, (January 1, 1965) we will change from a "sole proprietor" status to that of a "closed corporation" which, among other things, will have the advantage of being able to offer a profit sharing plan to our key people in the organization. As Gordon Ball, our joint venture partner, tells me, "Now if you can just keep you're head screwed on right

Bob Olsen - 1966

---". Anyway, we are continuing to look towards the future with visions of sugar plums, and sometime around the holiday season of 1965, we will report to you again.

Our family's deductible medical expenses were nearly nil last year and our kids continue to grow like weeds. Mary Beth, at thirteen, is almost as tall as her mother, with Barbara Jean rapidly closing the gap at eleven years old. The doctor tells me Bob will top out at 6'3" which is pretty good for a two year old. (Janet just informed me that figure comes from some kind of a chart doctors use) Actually, Bobby is 39"tall; he is two and a half years old and weighs 39 pounds. Both girls are doing very well in school which proves they take after their mother, but Bob is still having a stumbling time distinguishing the English language from "gammel norsk" (the language of the Vikings) so he undoubtedly takes after me. All in all, I'm really proud of my little tribe.

We wish all of you a Happy Holiday Season and wish you would stop in for a visit when you're out our way. Who knows, we might still have some of that egg nog mix left that uncle Larry and I were nearly divorced over – uh, I mean by our spouses. Happy New Year!!

Ole

In May of 1965 we were low bidder on our fifth job, the $1,150,000 Hazel Avenue Bridge over the American River near Folsom Dam, and believe it or not, we only left $1,000 on the table this time. My three year old shadow really helped me prepare a good estimate this time and we were back in Gordon's good graces again. Best of all, that particular job gave us an opportunity to drive our own piling and purchase much needed equipment and bridge building materials for re-use on future contracts. We bought a Link Belt diesel pile driving hammer, fabricated the leads for it in our own shop, and mounted the whole shebang on our new 30 ton P & H motor crane. We also began standardizing our false work by purchasing 60 foot long, 24 inch wide flange steel beams and heavier timber posts and caps, to add to our bridge building inventory. Things were starting to look up again.

Our 30 ton Crane rigged as a Pile Driver

The Hazel Avenue Bridge over the American River near Folsom Dam was basically a four lane box girder bridge, complete with a covered horse trail that sloped from around thirty to fifty feet above the river. One abutment sat on the north side bluffs of the river with the south abutment on the other lower roadway fill side. To save trucking costs, we built a *heavy* haul bridge across the river with our steel beams for earth moving scrapers to haul fill directly from the bluffs to the roadway fill side, and after all the fill dirt was moved, the haul bridge was used to support our tinker toy falsework for the bridge work. To put frosting on the bridge cake when it was finished, 30,000 tons of granite *riprap* stone was placed on the lower side slopes for flood protection.

An interesting thing happened (I thought) while the resident engineer and I were having lunch to discuss placement of 30,000 tons of half ton rock needed on the fill slopes and by accident, we happened to overhear two Folsom Dam engineers at an adjacent table discussing an interesting riprap problem of their own. Apparently when they built the Folsom dam they quarried more half ton

Constructing Hazel Avenue Bridge over the American River

riprap than was actually needed and, as the reservoir filled, their excess stone was scattered around under shallow water in an area the Park Service was using as a public beach and small boat harbor. When the lake was lowered each year to catch the snow melt-off, the excess stone in the shallower water became a hazard for both the swimmers and the boating public, and they didn't know what to do about it. Well, you can believe this or not, but a *light* suddenly switched on directly over my head, and I *seen the light* my dad had prophesied I would see someday, but actually, the light I really *seen* was a contracting opportunity.

You guessed it, *Old Butt-in* Homer asked the two Folsom engineers if they would consider lowering the lake another six feet so the rock could be removed. When they answered, "It's a possibility, what do you have in mind?" I said, "If you will lower the lake, and the rock is approved by the Highway Dept. for our fill slopes, I'll move in a track loader and a D-8 with a rock rake, and clean up that area for you for nothing, *if you will give me all the rock I need, free of charge.*" Well, you guessed it. They both sat there with stunned looks on their faces for a minute, and finally they said, "It sounds interesting. Let's meet at the site at ten o'clock tomorrow morning and discuss this some more."

Homer and Marv Rogers – 1965

Well, to make this story shorter, everyone agreed with my terms except I was only allowed thirty working days (six weeks) to complete the job, which created another problem. I had hired the Fratianno Trucking Company to haul the stone riprap we would salvage because the company owner, Jimmy Fratianno, personally guaranteed he would deliver a minimum of 1,000 ton of rock per day to our jobsite for us to place, if I would give him the hauling job. Well wouldn't you know it, once we began loading his *'too few'* trucks that he furnished to haul the rock, he only delivered 400 tons a day and we were threatened with not only losing our rock gold mine, but losing money out of pocket on our whole rock slope item. I called Jimmy Fratianno to meet me at a restaurant nearby for lunch to discuss putting more trucks on the haul and he showed

Bob the Builder home from work

up with two un-invited muscle men in *T* shirts I assumed were his truck drivers. I tried to explain the predicament he had put both of us in by not delivering the 1000 tons of rock a day that he promised and said, "Jimmy, we are both small business men who are trying to make a living the hard way, by working for it, and we both have to look out for every nickel we make just to survive. The way we're going now, you're going to bankrupt both of us." He said, "So what are you going to do about it?" I said, "Well, if you won't perform as we agreed I have no other choice but to boot your ass off this job Jimmy, and I'll find someone else who will do the job." He just glared at me for a few minutes while I *saucered and blowed* my coffee and watched his two drivers put on a side show of flexing their muscles for some unknown reason.. Finally he said, "Homer, you don't know who I am, do you?" I said, "Jimmy, I don't give a good God damn if you're

Jesus H. Christ himself. What I'm trying to tell you is, I've got a job to do and I need people working for me that will get the job done. The way I look at it, if somebody can't or won't do the job they've been hired to do while they're on my payroll, they'll soon find themselves working for somebody else." Well, apparently my little speech struck home because he quit glaring, and grinning instead said, "Homer, I like you. I'll get you more trucks."

Well, the upshot of all this was, everyone came out smelling like a rose. The Bureau of Reclamation was pleased their problem at the Folsom Dam lake was resolved at no expense to them, the State of California was pleased they received sound granite rock for their slope protection ahead of schedule, and the Park Service was pleased they now had a safer swimming and boating area. Believe it or not, Jimmy Fratianno even ended up delivering more than a 1000 ton of rock per day and was pleased to discover he ame out better than he expected, and best of all, we ended up beating our estimated slope protection costs by a whopping $30,000. When I told this story to Gordon he said, "Homer, you don't really know who Jimmy Fratianno is do you?" When I asked, "Not really, is there something I should know?" Gordon answered, "He's a hit man for the Mafia that has allegedly killed thirteen men so far. In the crime world he's known as *Jimmy the weasel.*"

GI Joe Bob – 1965

I found this letter from Janet in Ercel's things she willed me that I think describes our family in 1965.

June 11, 1965

Dear Folks

It seems every week I think, next week will be easier and maybe I can get some letters answered, but can't because of some Camp Fire Girl's activity. I'll send you pictures of our spring activities that were in the papers. Believe it or not, we spend many meetings in rehearsals first for every picture, but I enjoy it. As long as the girls remain enthusiastic and want to earn their Torchbearer, I'll continue on with them for another year.

The girls have one more week of school Mary Beth's dance recital is tomorrow afternoon. She's in three dances, but her costumes are not as elaborate as they were for 'Cinderella'. I had to make an 'Obi' for her 'Japanese Dance' that four girls do together, then a sash and part of a hat for the 'Mexican Dance' I believe she does alone, and we furnished Bob's toy telephone for the 'Teen Dance'. We have a Camp Fire swim party on Friday the 18th, and we leave for a one week vacation at Stanford Camp near Lake Tahoe, on Saturday.

Ole has two new jobs in Sacramento so he's sending his whole outfit up there. This makes three jobs there now, counting Sterling's. Our Nash Rambler broke down again so Ole is finally trading it in on a new Ford for us, along with some more equipment for the company .Ole's lawyer and family are coming over Sunday for dinner and to resolve the profit sharing plan for his weekly people and his will. He just doesn't have time to do all the things he does, and I wish he could find a man to help him, at least to bid jobs.

Did I tell you my sister and I went to Seattle during spring vacation? Ole couldn't get away and I wanted to see daddy because he isn't about to leave home (her dad recently discovered he had bladder cancer).Uncle Larry was going to a four day meeting at Asilomar, so my sister said she and her kids would go to help with the driving with me and our kids. It was 'Mr. Toad's wild ride' all the way because the Rambler boiled and we had to have the radiator blown out. We brought mother back with us without any trouble but Bobby got car sick all over Mary Beth and we had to stop and wash clothes at Grants Pass, Oregon. We had nine in the car counting Bob, and you have to count him because he's lots of trouble when he's awake. Luckily he slept most of the way.

Daddy goes back in July to have another scope. He's still very busy and active and is practically the 'Mr. Kiwanis' of Lynwood and is forever rebuilding something in the basement. His name and picture have been in the paper over and over pioneering for a new church while mother does all the cooking, entertaining, cleaning up afterwards, typing his bulletins and countless errands, and daddy gets all the credit.

Rodger went to Arizona with Helen last weekend and his daughter, Joy came back with them. Apparently she had left her husband. I think they may get little Rodger too, but they want to do it through the courts so Violet can't keep coming back for him. Rodger's new wife, Helen is a smart girl. She has problems at times, but she is a whole lot smarter than Rodger and has kept him out of trouble and all his bills paid up for a long time now. He gets laid off during rainy weather so she has to plan on weeks without a paycheck coming in. Evidently, Violet is mentally ill and is the reason the court may award them little Rodger. She has been living with a string of young boys.

Ole was going to write his dad a note and send the results of his last two jobs, but I guess it will have to wait. He did copy off the bids and I'll include them. The one job made him sick that he left all that money on the table that he could have had. He seems to have sinus headaches and backaches a lot lately. I thought the new mattresses would help his back, but we've had them over three months now and he still complains. He never had ailments when we were first married, then the ulcer and tons of gelusel tablets started, and now this. Barb has been home with a sore throat for the last two days. I never know how sick she really is. She misses a lot of school and gets violently annoyed with me for suspecting she isn't sick. enough to stay home, but I still wonder as I wander.

Mary Beth's dance part was nice and I was sorry no one got to see it but me. Ole had to work and Barbara had to baby-sit. Larry and Barb and their kids would have come over, but Larry had an appointment. I took some pictures feeling like a doting mother running up to the stage to flash pictures of my 'little darling'. But she's getting remarkably accomplished and the only way I can 'show and tell' about her is to take pictures. The pictures I'm sending you are of her as the king in 'Cinderella'. The cape and crown, jacket and blouse took most of my spare time for a month, to get it all together.

Well, I'll close and get this library in the mail. Let us know when you can come see us.

Love, Janet.

It was on the Hazel Avenue job I was forced to do one the hardest things I've ever had to do. I fired "Chink" Harmon, one of my best friends and best supervisors I've ever worked with when he was sober, for drunkenness and not showing up for work. Maybe his drinking problem started because he was of Cherokee Indian descent and couldn't handle alcohol, or maybe it was because his binge drinking just kept getting worse over the years and he had lost control, but after we had two unnecessary equipment accidents because of his three and four day drunks, and not showing up for work as my Hazel Avenue job superintendent, I couldn't put up with it any longer.

In a lot of ways I think construction workers are like the hard riding cowhands of the old west. We work hard, but when an excuse to celebrate comes along, we play hard. Some people I know (including my first wife) think all us hardhats are just *lousy red necked drunks* because when we holed through a tunnel, or completed a critical job assignment or were low bidder on a job, we celebrated by getting plastered. The problem was, some of us (like Chink) couldn't handle it only so long and after a few years of binge drinking and celebrating, sadly become alcoholics.

Thinking back about it now, Chink was a text book example of what happened to me during the late sixties and through the seventies until my first wife Janet had it up to her eyebrows and booted me out of our house and filed for divorce. Like Chink, I had let *Old John Barleycorn* get *'too strong a holt'* on me by binge drinking with my buddies more and more often for fewer and fewer reasons until it finally got the upper hand. I remember halfheartedly trying to regain control by checking in at the St. Helena Hospital to dry out while trying to lose some weight, and Janet and I even went to a marriage counselor one time to try saving our marriage. Believe it or not, after our session with the marriage counselor was over, he recommended we both call it quits and just split the sheets. He said we had

grown so far apart over the years we no longer even knew each other and were just two strangers living together that neither one liked anymore. It became obvious to both of us our marriage wasn't worth salvaging and, as it has turned out, we are both better off now that we have split up and started new lives for ourselves. My mother even suggested I check into St. Helena Hospital one more time after our divorce to *try drying out* harder this time and I even sat through some of their AA lectures. The good news was, six months after our divorce was finalized I did quit drinking *cold turkey*, and miracle of all miracles, was

Celebrating John Little's 67th birthday with my April Club buddies

touched by a higher power at a *singles git acquainted* party at St. Francis Yacht Club. Believe it or not, I met and fell hook line and sinker for a beautiful Montana girl named Alice Joyce Deyoe, a divorced supervisor that was working for the Pacific Telephone Company at the

Inspecting our new 30 ton Motorcrane on a bridge job

time. She was (and still is), the wonderful girl I dreamed would be my perfect wife some day, and Joyce and I have now been happily married for 28 years. Ooh boy, here I go getting ahead of myself again.

Anyway, when we first began talking about incorporating our construction company, I told Gordon Ball and Bill Ames I felt the *'working stiff'* deserved a fair shake and I was going to setup our company along the lines of that old *Viking Code, (Those who pull on the oars will share in the plunder)*.

To accomplish this, I said I would sell stock to the proven salaried employees, give stock options to my key employees, and would setup a combination profit sharing and retirement plan plus a liberal health benefit plan for all my salaried employees. I said I would then run the company the most efficient way like the Vikings, as a *benevolent dictatorship*. Gordon Ball and Bill Ames apparently understood human nature much better than me because, unlike me, they never trusted everyone, and especially th*e* current generation of selfish, over mothered, spoiled rotten baby boomers. They tried talking me out of incorporating by warning me of all the potential problems I would eventually face with my (their words) *overly generous socialistic management ideas*. They warned, "Always keep control of your company and be sure you incorporate in a business friendly state like Nevada, not California." Well, as it turned out, it was advice I should have followed more closely.

Bill Ames introduced me to an overly liberal Stanford graduate attorney I reluctantly hired named, Kim Allison to handle all our legal work, and for some unknown reason I let him sweet talk me into incorporating in California instead of Nevada as Gordon advised and it turned out to be my first mistake. Nevada would have allowed me to have voting and non-voting common stock with me owning all the voting stock, whereas California would not. Also as a *foreign* Nevada business entity doing work in California, I could get *prompt federal court rulings* and settlements if and when differences occurred, whereas California with their overloaded criminal courts, would take up to five years to even get on the courts *civil case calendar* as a *local* contractor

NEWS RELEASES DURING 1965

*Johnson outlines his "Great Society" program and illegally (?) transfers the Social Security Trust fund to the General fund to finance it., Operation "Rolling Thunder" escalates the Vietnam war as B-52s selectively bomb North Vietnam, Anti-war protests breakout, and, draft cards are burned, State Police attack civil rights demonstrators in Selma, Congress passes the Voting Rights Act, Medicare is established, the first U. S. Space walk takes place, the "Big Bang" theory is verified, Mexico and the U. S. initiate the Maquiladora Program, miniskirts are introduced, the "Afro" hairdo becomes fashionable, the hippie cult "Flower Power" becomes popular, cigarettes require warnings (but not marijuana). **And the Homer J. Olsen Company becomes HOMER J. OLSEN, Inc. on January 1 1965.**

I found this 1965 Christmas letter I wrote in my dad's things he left me when he passed away in 1987. This letter summarizes what our family and our newly organized closed corporation were doing at that time.

CHRISTMAS LETTER– 1965

Our young, aggressive, qualified construction company now has another year under its belt. As Bob's expressions indicate, we are pleased but we are not satisfied. We are gratified by our growth, but concerned with where we are going. This past year was our first year as a corporation so we are still experiencing growing pains, but little by little, we are adding more muscle (Janet thinks stomach in my case).Like last year, we have continued to add more equipment and acquire more contracts, and best of all, more qualified people have joined our organization. We have now completed both contracts in the Sunnyvale and Palo Alto area and our last year's in place volume was 50% more than the year before. But the overall earnings picture, although on the plus side, is not where it should be. As a result, we are now asking ourselves all sorts of interesting questions. Are we trying to expand too rapidly? Is our muscle development keeping pace with our nervous system? Will good "Indians" make good "Chiefs"? What

Tippy & Bob - 1966

ball league are we best qualified to play in? Should we concentrate on being the best football team or just stick to tennis? Will Janet have hash or prime rib for dinner tonight? —and what will we have a year from now?

Mary Beth and Barbara have about reached a plateau physically, now that they have caught up in height with their mother. I think mentally as teenagers, they have regressed with all this hullabaloo, noisy records, fan clubs and the whole bit. It's amazing to me how teenagers go about expressing their newly found "pseudo-independence" stage in life. They are literally slaves to Madison Avenue and will buy anything that is supposed to be "in" at the moment. Bob started nursery school this year and has a new Beagle puppy named "Tippy." Janet spends most of her time being the trail boss over this herd ever since I started spending more and more of my time hiding out at work trying to get the jobs built and putting more work on the books. All in all, we're fine and looking forward to Christmas and next year.

We hope all is well with you folks and we wish you a happy holiday season and the best of everything next year. Skoal!!!

Ole

It has always amazed me how fast company gossip can travel, especially when a guy (and a trouble maker) like Zel Mullican spreads it around. For some unknown reason, Zel knew long before anyone else, exactly what was going on in the Kiewit Company when I was there, and after I left he seemed to know exactly what I was doing and what was going on between my partner, Gordon Ball and me. Honest to God, it wasn't an hour after I let

Chink Harmon go; I got a call from Zel Mullican in Los Angeles wanting to go to work for me as my general superintendent. When I told him I couldn't talk to him unless he was

unemployed and he said he had already quit Kiewit, I asked, "When?" he said, "Jist now." Well, I needed field supervision with Chink gone and all, plus we needed more work on the books to meet our increasing payroll, so I hired Zel to finish the Hazel Avenue bridge while I spent more time bidding for more work. A short time later, on June 15, 1966, we were low on the only two jobs we got all that that year, both the same day. We left $3,400 (0.6%) on the table on the $585,706 Stanislaus River Bridge in Riverbank, California and $20,000 (1.1%) on the $1,830,604 Jibboom Street Airport Freeway Bridges as a subcontractor for the Ball/Granite Joint Venture. Fortunately, some of the best guys I've hired like John Shimmick, Bob Witbeck and Al Gully came to work for HJO, Inc. about that time and helped build those two jobs.

Zel Mullican signs on with HJO, Inc

NEWS RELEASES DURING 1966

The Supreme Court issues the Miranda ruling, the Vietnam war continues, the black panther party is organized, the national organization for women is founded, Catholics are allowed to eat meat on Friday, the first endangered species list is produced, four H–Bombs accidentally fall from a B-52 Bomber over Spain, the Iron Cross becomes a fad with the beach set, the motor vehicle safety act is passed, acid rock dance halls introduce light shows with their acid rock music.

I don't know what made me think of this story, but it was kind of funny at the time, to me anyway. Gordon Ball asked me to JV the new Toll Plaza contract at the San Mateo Bridge with him and estmate all the concrete work, and he loaned me Buck Bailey to figure the remainder. Well, as good a friend as Buck was, he was also one of these guys who believed in horoscopes and fortune telling, and especially in lucky numbers like the number seven. Well, you can believe this or not, but after we finished figuring the costs for the various items of work and posted them on our spread sheets the total job cost was all in sevens, or divisible by seven, which I thought was interesting. Oooh no, not old Buck. He immediately got all excited and shouted, "Homer, somebody's trying to tell us something." I said, "Baloney Buck, let's take a break for a quick lunch before summarizing everything", and we drove up to a restaurant in Alamo .Well when we picked up our separate lunch tabs, Buck nearly fainted and said. "My God, my lunch tab is $7.77, now I know somebody's trying to tell us something" and to make things even more interesting, when I parked my old Nash rambler company car at Gordon's office, the speedometer suddenly rolled over to 77,777 miles. Wow, I thought, maybe Buck is on to something.

Well you guessed it. We both got so excited over our job estimate we bid all the unit price items and lump sum items in *sevens*. We bid the structure concrete for $70.00 a cy, the job's dirt work for $0.70 a cy, the structure excavation for $7.00 a cy, the clear and grub's lump sum item for $7,777, and so on until, believe it or not, the total bid was divisible by seven, which it should be if you think about it hard enough. Anyway, as is always the case, the Bay Toll Bridge Authority read every bid item on every contractors bid after their 2:00 pm bid opening ceremonies, so it wasn't until nearly 7:00 pm before they finally finished reading all the bidders items and ours, as it turned out, was last. Well, when Ben Ballala, the bid reader for the state finished reading our bid, he was laughing so hard his sides hurt and between guffaws he insisted on calling me personally with our results. When I answered the phone he was still laughing so hard he could barely talk, and

Our first annual Company Managers Meeting – 1966

said, "Homer, you came in exactly where you figured." I said, "Where was that Ben?" and switched on the speaker for Buck to hear our results. Ben said, *"You came in Seventh!!.*

The Bay Area Rapid Transit program we had been waiting for, finally advertised for bids in 1967 and HJO, Inc. immediately used up all its bonding capacity by making a *clean sweep* on four low bid Joint Venture contracts totaling $41,244,000, with three other partners called the Shea, Ball, Granite, Olsen group. After we were awarded the contracts, we combined the underground Powell Street Station and the Market Street Tunnels into one $24,419,331 contact for management efficiency, with HJO, Inc having a 10% interest in the two combined jobs. The J. F. Shea Company would do the tunnel work and be the job sponsor of the two jobs with Buck Atherton as project manager, and Homer J. Olsen, Inc. would build the underground station

Wow! We made a Clean Sweep of four Rapid Transit Jobs

with me personally handling the construction of the station as its job superintendent. When our joint venture partner's responsibilities were finalized, I scheduled our company's second annual management meeting in December of 1967 with all our shareholders to review our company's course of action on our work. The following is a copy of my closing speech at that meeting.

CLOSING THE GAP BETWEEN HINDSIGHT AND FORESIGHT

I want to thank all of you for your presentations here today. This is our second annual Supervisors meeting as a closed corporation and I'm sure we can all agree it was better than our meeting last year. With the soul searching we have done here today, I think we are even more convinced we are in a tough competitive business that requires constant attention

HJO Inc 1967

to business to survive. We have learned to remain competitive, we must constantly strive to do better tomorrow than we did yesterday, and use yesterdays experience, good and bad, to improve our performance tomorrow. In other words, we must close the gap between hindsight and foresight

I would like to spend some time along the theme of this meeting, and review our progress this past year as a newly founded construction company. With regard to hindsight, we should ask ourselves the following questions: Have we made progress in the past four years since we were low on our first job? Have we learned anything from our mistakes? Have we religiously followed the four basic rules for success in the construction contracting business that were spelled out for all of us by Peter Kiewit, as listed below

1. Bid work at the right price?
2. Build work safely, for the right cost?
3. Collect in full for all work done?
4, Take good care of **all** the company's assets?

At last year's meeting our guest speaker, Ward White, reminded us, "The most valuable asset any company has is its motivated, hard working, competent employees. Always take good care of your key people because they are **your most valuable**

asset." Amen, truer words were never spoken. It was just for that reason our company was set up as a closed corporation along the lines of that old Viking Code, "Those who pull on the oars, will share in the plunder" if our company is profitably successful from the efforts and the hard work of our shareholder employees, I assure you, they will be well taken care of by this company

With regard to item #1 of the basic rules, 'Bid work at the right price', we have bid roughly one hundred jobs in the last four years and have been low on only eleven. During this past year we have been low on only one of twelve highway jobs, but were low on four of the sixteen BARTD jobs we bid with far fewer bidders competing for the work. Best of all, we left only 2.2% on the table on the rapid transit work. The answer to the question "Should we continue bidding the BARTD work?" is yes, even though the profitable portion of this much tougher work is still questionable.

All four of the BARTD jobs were bid with capable joint venture partners who all ran check estimates prior to bid. To minimize the risk, we have subbed out all the specialty work that doesn't fit our organizations and equipment. Lord knows underground station and tunnel jobs are tough enough to build without also having to do the specialty work. So all in all, I think we have 'matured' considerably in our estimating and bidding department.

We said last year we would organize our jobs with the best people available and we would continue to attract better people to our organization. My dad used to tell me when I was growing up on the family farm, "Good seed plus the right climate for growth will always produce good crops." The same thing applies to companies. This morning we agreed it was motivated teamwork that carried a company forward, and our company will only grow as fast as our organization matures. Zel said in his talk, "We now have an organization to build on so we have made progress." Manning our contracts with the most qualified people and continually looking for more good people should be paramount on our minds as we mature and grow as a company.

One completed job last year met all four of the basic success points listed and that was the Riverbank job (# 6) where John Shimmick was job superintendent. We not only beat out 13 competitors, but that job was completed ahead of schedule while bridging a river during a wet season. Better

Stanislaus River Brg – 1967

yet, John and his crew made 25% more job profit for the company's shareholders than was originally estimated. I would like to read the letter I received from the Department of Public Works, County of San Joaquin, congratulating our company and John in particular, on the good job we did building their bridge over the Stanislaus river. (read letter) I think John and his crew deserve a standing ovation from all of us for the great job he and his crew did. I am very proud of this letter and all the men who worked on that bridge. It proves to me we are on the right track.

We said a year ago we were going to speed up our operations, shorten the construction time on our jobs to cut overhead costs, and increase our bonding capacity to bid for more work. Our best job this year was constructed in this manner while our worst experience ran overtime. We promised ourselves we would do a better job of documenting our position with regard to change orders and claims Those of us who have had to sit before claim boards this past year have been very embarrassed by the poor job we've done as a company in properly handling and documenting our paperwork It has cost us time and money we rightfully earned, but couldn't prove. It is extremely important we improve in this regard to save lost dollars we have earned.

We told ourselves last year we would improve both our safety and equipment maintenance programs, but unfortunately they are both in worse condition now than a year ago. Zel said equipment is like the human body, "As it gets older, it needs more care" That's all very true, but our equipment is less than three years old and most of it was purchased only two years ago. Yet through operator and driver misuse and abuse and flagrant maintenance violations, a lot of our equipment already looks shot. As for safety, Bob Sample hit the nail on the head when he said, "We are over due for a major accident because our frequency rate is way too high when compared with our unusually low severity rating." The law of probability is bound to catch up with us if we don't give more than just lip service to accident prevention. It is imperative we improve our safety performance and do all the preventive maintenance required on our equipment this coming year.

We said last year we were going to improve on our field labor costs by returning to the principle of small well supervised crews always working short handed, and we would plan and schedule our work more efficiently. We've made some progress here, but there is room for improvement. Like Zel said, "Brains and inspiration are good but more perspiration is needed. The cream always comes last and then only by pulling for all you're worth."

The value of time goes up every year with every craft union increase so we've got to appreciate the value of time more. There is no longer room for lost motion through poor planning, scheduling, material handling, or poor supervision. Peter Kiewit used to say, "Pay attention to business and business will pay", and it's becoming more and more meaningful with each labor increase. I'll never forget Ward White blasting a guy on the Friant Kern Canal who stopped working to light a cigarette. He said, "Smoke that damn cigarette on your own time, Every minute you waste smoking that cigarette costs me five cents." The craft union hourly rates since that time have more than tripled so now it's fifteen cents a minute..

This morning Bob Witbeck gave an excellent talk on material handling that brought out another important area we need improvement. Unlike manufacturing where production lines move work to the materials, the construction industry must move materials to the work and 35% of our labor costs are involved

Riverbank Bridge - 1967

in storing, sorting, moving, and hoisting the materials we need to build our projects. Anything we can do to automate material handling to save labor and time, should be done. If we need specialized equipment such as straddle trucks, forklifts,container boxes and/or packaging tools, we should and will get them. To remain competitive we must always stay alert to everything that will lower our costs and help us work more efficiently.

We've hashed over a lot of things we need improvement on here today and it has been good for all of us . Constructive criticism never hurt anybody. If we re-read all the 'good advice' talks from both this and last years meetings, and put them in practice, we cannot fail. But we do have a lot of good things going for us.

1. We have made money for the company over last four years.
2. We have increased our equity in new equipment.
3. We have increased or assets and lowered our liabilities.
4. We have proven to our clients we can build quality work safely, on schedule, and in strict conformance with the specifications

5. We have many good subcontractor (and contractor) friends in the heavy engineering construction industry who are helping us to succeed.

6. We have proven to our banker and our bonding company we can build quality work safely, profitably and on schedule.

7. And we have developed a reputation of honesty and dealing fairly with our employees, the general public and all we do business.

I am very proud of all these accomplishments. We could and should have done better in a few cases, but we have the right attitude and motivation to improve and expand our company in the future. If we practice what we have preached here today, two years from now when our current BARTD contracts are completed, I'm confident we will be well on our way. Our company reminds me of a pioneer sign I saw somewhere along the Oregon Trail one time, that read something like this, "The cowards never started, the weak died along the way, it was the strong who won the west." We must continue to develop muscle in order to grow as a company.

Thank you.

NEWS RELEASES DURING 1967

474,000 U. S. troops are now in Vietnam, 700,000 march in antiwar protest in New York City, the CIA illegally begins "Operation Chaos" to spy on antiwar activities and the "Stop the Draft" movement, Biologically active DNA is synthesized, the 'Atomic second' becomes the time standard, the microwave oven is introduced, granny glasses, Nehru jackets, and antiwar buttons make the scene, Psychedelic "Head Shops" appear, Dr. Martin Luther King, Jr. encourages draft evasion, Dr. Spock is arrested for antiwar activities and Muhammad Ali refuses induction into the armed forces.

Our young son, Bob, started first grade in 1968 after graduating from the Doris-Eaton Pre-School of higher learning and was rewarded with a new beagle puppy best friend named

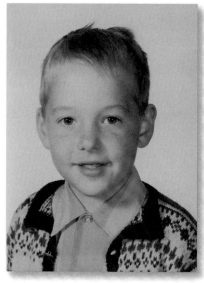

Tippy. Our second daughter, Barbara, also started high school that year at Monte Vista because she thought it was a good 'goof off' school compared to San Ramon and besides, she wanted to get away from her older slave driving sister. Mary Beth continued on at San Ramon alone as a straight "A" student, but the dumb jealous kids began calling her a 'geek' because of her good student reputation and ultimately destroyed her self confidence. So, in order to graduate a year sooner and to be nearer her younger sister for support, and get away from her strict dad and to college sooner, Mary Beth transfers to the easier Monte Vista High School. Much to my surprise and horror both girls and even their mother, began emulating the human garbage hippie crowd while I began worrying myself sick over what was happening to my little family and our marriage. For some unknown reason, *dumbing down* had become the *in* thing with those gullible sponge brained

Robert Kevin Olsen in 1968 at age 6

high school kids because of all the hog wash their anti capitalist, anti-war, marijuana smelling teachers were pumping into our children's precious rebelling little minds.

While all this was going on, our home began turning into a pig sty as my girls (and my wife) paraded around in sandals and/or barefoot wearing Indian headbands, wool sack dresses and farm overalls. In an effort to keep my daughters away from all those long haired, dope sniffing piles of human garbage boys they *cooed* were *hunks and artists*, I tried to keep them busy by backing them in a homemade clothing store they called, *"Toad Manor."* Finally, in a last effort to hang onto my sanity and my family until this ridiculous phase in their lives subsided, I hired a wonderful hard working black girl named *Lucy,* to muck out our pig sty of a house once a week, and went back to work with my fingers crossed humming a catchy tune called, *Pray for me, Argentina.*

Pauline and Bowie in clothes of the day

When Gordon Ball sold his company to the Dillingham Corporation, our company was booted out of his Danville office and we moved to a three room office in downtown Danville with very little working capital and bonding capacity left. The construction market was extremely tight at the time and I had re-hired too many of my old crew for the carryover work we had on the books, gambling on the upcoming Rapid Transit work as our savior. Every dime we had including our children's toys was invested in the outcome of the Rapid Transit contracts we had recently picked up with the Shea, Ball, Granite joint venture group. In fact, things were so tight at the time I was forced to freeze all my crew's salaries, and much to the disgust of my own family, cut my salary in half to $10,000 a year. I told everyone in our company, "Hold on to your paychecks as long as you can because we don't have enough money in the bank at the present to cover them."

To make matters even worse, one of my three partners on our two BARTD jobs in San Francisco suddenly out of the blue, called for another $300,000 in *startup funds* which required our company to come up with an additional $30,000 as our share of the working capital we didn't have. Our Joint Venture Agreement stated we had thirty days to comply with their request or we were out as a partner and they would not only split our 10% share of the profit on the jobs among themselves if it were a winner, but would nail our company for our full 10% share of the loss, if it were a loser. Well, talk about being caught between a rock and a hard place, we had already transferred all our loose change, small tools, steel beams, soldier piling and heavy timbers, to the joint venture for needed construction materials instead of cash for the first $30,000 contribution requested, so now what do we do?

My faithful burning belly pills and medicines

Well, we still owned $140,000 worth of mortgaged construction equipment that had been paid down to $60,000 so I figured maybe our compassionate banker would help us by refinancing the lot. Ooh boy, was I ever wrong. Like all bankers with hearts made of granite, he had to hold his sides in from laughing so hard as he showed me out the door. We had already sold HJO, Inc. common stock to all our key employees who wished to buy in, so as a last resort, I called an emergency meeting to let the shareholders, and everyone else on salary, hear the sad news straight from the horse's mouth. Honest to God, and this is a true story, after my emotional speech that left everyone in shock, like a gift from heaven, Bob Witbeck stood up and said he had confidence in our company's future and if all the other shareholders would approve he would appreciate an opportunity to buy $30,000 worth of HJO, Inc. common stock in the company. I have never been so emotionally touched by anything in my life as I was at that moment by Bob's generous life saving offer.

The upshot of all this was, a vice president friend of my old Kiewit boss, Tom Paul, in the Granite Construction Company named Bert Scott, apparently agreed with Tom that I was *the person* responsible for all the stampeding employees leaving Kiewit at the time, and agreed among themselves, now would be a good time to bury Homer Olsen once and for all. I'll tell you, when I walked into that meeting room with a certified check for our second $30,000 capital contribution, Bert Scott's face fell a foot and when my other two partners, Ed Shea and Gordon Ball, burst out laughing and handed me back my $30,000 check saying they had discovered it wasn't needed after all, Bert stomped out in an embarrassed huff. Ed and Gordon then told me they thought our company was an integral part of their group to build the underground station, and as a favor to them (because of my missile base experience), they wanted me to personally handle the construction of the Powell Street underground Station as job superintendent. Well, as you've guessed, I suddenly felt the weight of the world lift off my shoulders and accepted their offer with the reservation, *until I have the job running smoothly,* and I could then turn the superintendent's job over to someone else in my crew, to which they agreed. So, and you can believe this little skidmarked story along the highway of life or not your choice, but that is the true story of how our fledgling little company narrowly escaped early bankruptcy, by the skin of its teeth.

Gordon H. Ball

Gordon Ball was undoubtedly the best business partner and friend I have ever had during my construction career. To ease our other two partners worries about my back problems and general health, and to keep me on board as a partner–estimator-superintendent in their group even before we turned in our BARTD work bid, he put up a $100,000 life insurance policy on me to guarantee the partners I would survive the Market Street joint venture, if we were low bidder. He also gave us a Ball & Olsen subcontract to build the Elkhorn ($306,729) and the Jibboom Street bridges ($1,830,604) for his Ball/Granite joint venture on the Sacramento Airport freeway, plus whatever else we might make on a temporary earthmoving haul bridge over the San Joaquin River that I bid for $94,850. Then to top off the cake with a nice coating of frosting, Gordon also gave our company a 10% share in the job profits of the BARTD Balboa Park station ($8,630,000) for my *check estimate* and for loaning him Bob Witbeck to be his project engineer temporarily, and backed us with his bond signature on the ($1,119,003) Ball & Olsen BARTD/SPRR railroad bridge in Hayward.

Oooh boy, after all that wouldn't you know it, some how some way I threw my back out so while I was off work on a hot pad in bed with my slide rule, hand crank calculator, and a drafting board over my knees as my work table, I put together a structure concrete cost estimate for Gordon on the BARTD Oakland Wye tunnel contract ($15,706,167) that got his joint venture group the job. He was so pleased with my bedside cost estimate he gave our company a 2.5% interest in the job's profit that ended up giving us as our share a new ten ton fork lift and $146,000 in cash when the job was finished. All in all, and any way you looked at it, it was Gordon Ball who made it possible for me in my spare time (?), to bring in at least a million dollars extra in cash flow for our company during those critical 1967 through 1971 tight market years. Why?, because Gordon felt my 10% profit share in the Market Street BARTD joint venture work was too low for what our cash poor company was actually contributing to the venture, and he wanted to help me keep my talented crews gainfully employed while I was busy looking after Powell Street Station work as a combination troubleshooter / job superintendent.

As a little side story to describe what a *down to earth* no nonsense guy Gordon Ball really was, I'll never forget the time we had a claim settlement meeting with a cadre of stern faced State of California lawyers who arrived for an all out war with us in Gordon's office. I remember Gordon told Vince Smith, Dario Benidictus, his attorney, and me, to be sure we wore suits and ties like all them to not embarrass them, and after all the introductions and our failing disarming comments were made, we all sat down, and Gordon said, "OK, let's get down to business." Honest to God, and I know you won't believe this true story. Gordon took off his coat, loosened his tie, and as he sat down he leaned to

Bob training his dog 'Tippy' to do hand shakes

one side and let the loudest *Fart* I have ever heard, bar none. Whooee, I'll tell you that award winning act alone was funny enough by itself, but the stunned shocked expressions on all those stiff upper lipped lawyer's faces that were there for the kill, caused Vince Smith and me to bust out laughing so hard our sides hurt. Oooh boy, anyway, after Vince and I finally got control of ourselves and the brief case slamming, mutterings, and few snickers subsided, Gordon said, "Now that we've got this meeting back to earth, let's all take our off coats, loosen our ties, and get this matter settled." Unbelievably, we reached an agreement three hours later that would have taken three months to reach an agreement otherwise. Wow, what a guy.

CHRISTMAS LETTER – 1968

Holy cow! Another light year just greased by and it seems like I just finished singing "Auld Lang Syne", but then I've always been known to carry a note way too long (bank note that is – heh,heh, choke, yuk).

Anyway our two daughters started their own new exciting business this past year, strictly non profit like their Dad's, but it's with their friends and it's lots of fun (and hopefully keeps them out of trouble) and that is the most important thing anyway, they say (and Dad agrees). Their business is a teen age "home made" dress shop in downtown Walnut Creek, called "Toad Manor" that is chaperoned by their mother. Surprisingly, they are making enough to at least pay their store rent and, best of all; they are busier than little beavers learning the wonders of the capitalistic system.

Bowie & Meem

As for our own company, our banker said if we lasted five years in the construction business, he would begin speaking to us. This year marks the fifth year we have been in business, so I am now happy to report, we have reached the nodding acquaintance stage. If things keep going like they have, we should reach the handshaking stage sometime next year.

Mary Beth graduates from high school next June, Barbara Jean will be a junior and Bob will start second grade. It won't be long until our girls are off to college and Janet and I will be in our second childhood growing up with Bob, who is currently learning to read and write in the first grade. As co-author of this Xmas letter, he has earned the right to sign it with me and, as you can see, has added his own Xmas message.

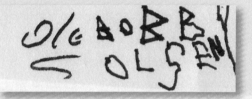

1968 Xmas card signatures

We are all fine and looking forward (Ooh boy, vi kan hardly vaite) to the upcoming "sensational seventies", and perhaps like you, thankful that there is only one more year left of the "sick sixties." We hope all is well with everyone and if you're by this way please drop in for a visit.

1968 Christmas card

While we were detouring the streetcar tracks on Market Street to open cut the Powell Street station, unbelievably we discovered sink holes under Market Street that were large enough to swallow ten wheeler trucks. Apparently the horseshoe shaped brick sewer underneath Market had *hour glassed* the backfill sand away leaving only a bedspring latticework of matted utility lines abandoned after the 1906 earthquake that had been encased in concrete to hold up the street. By the time the sink holes were refilled and the tracks were detoured I put in a 36 hour shift and was so exhausted I couldn't sleep from leg and back spasms and it was the first time I was told fatigue and stress were the root cause of my back problems, not arthritis. Anyway, in order to save commute time and get more rest between my regular twelve hour shifts, I rented a hotel room near the job and started having dinner and a few belts first to relax, with my binge drinking buddies at John's Grill. You guessed it, more home problems soon developed and Janet began wondering what I was trying to prove by working myself to death, and why she didn't marry her Whitman College boyfriend (that became a banker) in the first place, and me wondering if Tom Paul wasn't right when he said, "People in the construction business should never marry."

> ## MAJOR NEWS RELEASE DURING 1968
>
> *Robert F. Kennedy and Martin Luther King are assassinated, Richard Nixon and Spiro Agnew are elected President and Vice President, Chicago Police club demonstrators at the Democrat Convention, U. S. Troops massacre Vietcong civilians at Mai Lai, Vietcong launch the Tet Offensive, riots occur in 125 cities after King's assassination, Yale admits women, 6000 sheep die next to the Utah Dugway Proving Grounds from nerve gas, Pulsars are discovered, Enzymes which cut DNA strands at certain points is discovered, Congress recommends the U. S. adopt the Metric system, and the Mod and Deadbeat Hippie look become the latest "in" thing for the young people.*

After I was given the responsibility of supervising the construction of Powell Street station, I made a stupid error of promoting Zel Mullican from general superintendent to operations vice president to look after our other work while I was tied up in San Francisco and, Oooh boy, was that ever a mistake. Like my roommate in the Army Air Corps whose promotion to 2nd Lt. changed his personality for the worse, Zel's normal gossiping, trouble making personality also changed for the worse with his promotion to become an obnoxious dictatorial bully. To add even more insult to injury, his job costs began skyrocketing and several of my crew had either quit or were refusing to work for him any longer, so I took a Saturday off to look into his performance. When I checked back into the Danville office afterwards to catch up on some paper work, to my complete surprise there sat Zel Mullican at my desk, rifling through my personal files. I said, "None of what you're looking for is secret Zel, so all you had to do was ask me, and I would have handed you everything you wanted to stick your nose in to", and added, "Zel, for your information, I resent your rifling through my desk like some damn thief when I'm not here." He said, "I've been going through your monthly expense books and you're throwing company money away like some damn drunken sailor and it's got to stop." I said "Zel, I've just come from one of your jobs and for your information I salvaged enough she-bolts lying in the mud in one hour on that one job to cover what I spent on three of those monthly expense books you're crying about. Where I'm really throwing company money away is paying you a high salary for a job you're not doing."

Well to shorten this little drama of life, we ended up parting company and he immediately sued me for firing him and buying his company stock back for half what he thought it was worth. I then counter-sued him for not living up to our company's stock buy-sell

Janet, Ercel, Dad & Dick Shephard - 1972

agreement that everyone agreed to and had signed (including him) when they purchased stock, and for not accepting twice what he originally paid for his stock three years earlier. He knew damn well, our company's stock value was determined at the end of each fiscal year by an outside auditing firm, and his stock value was based on the company's book value net worth they determined. Well, as it all turned out, just as the judge was about to rule on the matter, Zel withdrew his suit against me and the company and accepted the company's audited stock price, so

I withdrew my suit against him. I have never heard nor seen hide nor hair of him since and the only comment I overheard about it from anyone was the time one member of my crew nudged the other and said, "Don't ever get on Homer's shit list."

The two Bay Area Rapid Transit contracts our joint venture group constructed underneath Market Street in San Francisco ended up not only a God sends, but gold mines for the Shea, Ball, Granite and Olsen joint venture. I was not only given the opportunity to plan and supervise the construction of the Powell Street underground BARTD station job as if it were a *troubleshooter* problem to enjoy solving, but my crew ended up increasing our station's estimated job profit by a whopping 50%, just by using new ideas and methods we all dreamed up together on the job. With John Shimmick's and Bill Young's talented construction expertise (Bill had just returned from Vietnam duty when the job started) and Merritt Mason's mechanical engineering expertise in designing *Homer's Folly* #7 idea, we lowered the station's excavation and loading of off-haul trucks down to a one man crew and our station excavation total costs to less than half that estimated. When the west end of the station was opened up enough for the tunnel work to begin, *Homer's Folly* was turned over to Shea's crackerjack tunneling crew as the *perfect head tower* to help lower their tunnel muck removal costs. All in all, when the two jobs were completed in 1970, the combined profits were more than double what we estimated at bid time. Best of all, I was handed a substantially larger, and very welcome check for HJO, Inc.'s efforts, along with our 10% share of the salvageable small tools, equipment and supplies on our well run, well built combined contracts. Our company was suddenly back in business again with working capital enough to bid and bond larger projects on our own.

I will always be grateful to the J. F. Shea Company, and especially to Ed Shea (whose father, Charlie Shea, was my step-dad, Philip Brim's boss on the Hoover Dam diversion tunnels), and to 'Buck' Atherton, for their cooperative attitude and welcome help. Fortunately our two organizations clicked from the very beginning and we made an excellent combined team to build those two contracts. It was also interesting for me to watch our two silent financial partners, Ball and Granite, quietly standing on the sidelines smiling enviously, as Shea and Olsen's *crackerjack* teams conducted their harmonizing *Irish Washer Women* symphony in synchronized construction and all in *Polka* time.

The following letter was written to my dad (and company director) on June 8, 1969 to bring him up to date on the company and family. Mary Beth skipped one year and will graduate from High School at age 17, and I was hoping Dad and Ercel could be here for her graduation.

Homer's 67th birthday party – 1991

June 8, 1969

Dear Dad,

I'm sorry we haven't written sooner but it seems like we are always so busy we lose track of time. We tried calling Ercel all day on Mothers Day and even into the evening, but couldn't get through. We're all fine and hope you are also.

I'm sending you a copy of our last financial statement for your file and information. I also made a run-down of our companies performance over the last two years based on the ratios bankers use to judge us by. Then I compared that to the average earnings of 39,000 contractors in the United States.(the first column) to show how we have been doing. The thing that really shocked me was when you finally get to where you show a profit, it's nearly all taxed away. As you will notice in my chart, the federal taxes plus the surcharge and the California taxes, all add up to 62% now and will most likely reach 67% (2/3) of everything we make by the end of next year. But, little by little, we're getting our heads above water and if we can keep from taking any losing jobs, we should be all right.

Mary Beth will graduate from high school next Friday night (June 13, 1969) and it still doesn't seem possible she is getting out so soon. She's already signed up for summer

Meem – 1967

school at the University of California at Santa Barbara, starting the 23ʳᵈ of June. We wish you and Ercel could be here for her graduation and we will gladly pay your way down and back. Virgil and Winifred Whitehead will be here also because their other grand-daughter, Helen Lindberg, is graduating from junior high the same day. I'll call you sometime Wednesday.

Since the Dillingham Corporation from Honolulu bought out Gordon Ball we have been pretty much on our own. We've bid with the J. F. Shea Company on two jobs and the Willamette Western Company (from Portland Oregon) a couple of times, but haven't come in better than second and we're bidding a $3,000,000 job in San Rafael with Willamette this coming Wednesday. We did get one job here in Danville the other day for $215,000 with the county on our own, and it's the first job (the El Pintado Bridge) we've gotten without any partners. So far this year we've bid 20 jobs and have been low on only two, and one of them wasn't awarded. The other was this county job. So, all in all, we've been second bidder six times and third three times. I guess it at least proves we're competitive, but unfortunately, if you're not low, it's better to be the high bidder and worry the low guy more. We hope you can make it down for the graduation. If not we'll see you in August for the board meeting.

As Ever, Ole

Bill Ziegler & Homer Olsen – 1986

Call it midlife crisis, or blame it on demons that infiltrated your body like some churches believe, or blame it all on where it really belongs. Namely on my apparent goal of self-destruction with ever increasing binge drinking drunks that caused all my stupid judgment errors. The late 1960's and the decade of the 1970's were without a doubt, the worst period in my life. I not only made numerous costly decisions and dumb drunken mistakes that not only guaranteed the end of my marriage to Janet in 1979 and all semblance of a *good father* to my three children, but resulted in substantial un-necessary losses for our company. Forsome unknown reason, I began binge drinking more and more often for fewer and fewer reasons with my buddies who like me, found good reasons to have these important *binge drinking* meetings that invariably ended up making fools of ourselves at some strip joint somewhere. Like it or not, by Christmas of 1979, I had become a full blown alcoholic badly in need of help and there was no doubt about it, whatever happened that was detrimental to my family and to our company during that period was 100% my fault.

Thinking back now about the stupid drunken stunts I pulled that are not funny anymore, I remember the time I put a "G" string a stripper gave me in Ray McClarrinon's suitcase during one of our out of town meetings that nearly caused a divorce when his wife unpacked his bag. Then there was the time my ultra liberal far left Seattle father-in-law, Virgil Whitehead, who was convinced all Scandinavians were behind the door when the brains were passed out, literally came unglued when I signed him up for membership in the Tempest Storm Fan Club, and she kept mailing him semi-nude autographed photographs of herself. While glaring at me suspiciously, he said, "If I ever find the knot

Barbara and Bob visiting the Whiteheads

headed Norwegian that pulled this *brilliant stunt*, I'll break his damn neck." I said, "Virgil, like you, I've never met a Norwegian that was smart enough to pull a clever stunt like that all by himself, but if I do Virgil, I'll shake his hand to thank him for you, but not hard enough to break his neck."

Bowie, Meem & Uncle Orson -1968

For one of the smartest guys I have ever known, Virgil had the dumbest and most useless college degree of anyone I've ever known. Believe it or not, he had a Masters Degree (MA) in Greek and Latin, but fortunately for his family's sake he became a science teacher at Ballard High School in the Swedish district of Seattle, instead of a waiter like most liberal arts graduates. He really hurt my feelings at our wedding by the way he treated my dad and my stepmother, like they were just poor white trash, and me like I was a lousy commoner marrying into royalty. But believe it or not, I still liked the guy, and especially his wonderful down to earth Missouri farm girl wife, Winifred Burch, who kept some sense of sanity in their family. To this day, I still remember Virgil glaring at me in disgust as he walked his daughter Janet down the isle towards the church pulpit during our marriage where my best man, Frank Wiggs, and I were waiting. I leaned over towards Frank and whispered, "Oooh boy, I've really made a terrible mistake Frank", and he whispered back, "No you haven't, Janet has, but unfortunately it's too damn late now for either one of you to squirm out of it." Anyway, I still thought both my Seattle in laws were wonderful people and I found as long as we never talked politics, religion, or I never said anything derogatory about the damn dumb democrats, and just helped Virgil with

Round 'em up and head 'em out – 1968

his chores and radio hobby, we got along fine. Uncle Larry Lindberg was a full blooded Swede from Ballard that married Janet's younger sister Barbara, and I really felt sorry for him and the way he was treated by Virgil and his wife Barbara. For some unknown reason Virgil disliked Swedes even more than us *brilliant* Norwegians and took out all his Scandinavian frustrations on poor old *Uncle Larry.*

I'll tell you, I nearly fainted from shock when I picked up a copy of a 1969 Life Magazine, and saw my youngest daughter Barbara Jean's picture on the front cover with two other hippy girls at Woodstock in New York. Apparently Bowie and her mother were in cahoots unbeknown to me and had approved and financed the

trip for her to that disgusting hippy event with her girl friend. I was also shocked when my oldest daughter, Mary Beth, unbelievably invited one of her radical college girlfriends home for the weekend to recruit my help in overthrowing our democratic form of government and replace it with communism. When Mary Beth began chasing around with all those creepy looking hippy radical *individualists,* who interestingly all look alike, and dressed like one herself was there watching when they burned down the Bank of America building in Goleta because their political science teacher told them to for a better grade, I came unglued. I jerked her out of the University of California at Santa Barbara, shut off all her financial help, and ordered her to get a meaningful job as a waitress somewhere until she finally grew up and become an adult.

Barbara graduated from Monte Vista High School in 1970 (a half year ahead of schedule), and the two of them moved to Hawaii, and once again dear old dad financed a clothing store business for them to hopefully keep them busy and out of trouble. They named their new store on Lahaina, Maui, *Hale Bikini* and custom designed, sewed and sold bikini bathing suits and beach wear for the next few years to hopefully learn something *meaningful* about the real world of business and to stop wasting their time (and their parent's hard earned money) at those touchy feely schools of liberal arts and misguided learning.

Until these liberal arts schools begin to stand for something more than *life style training* and *baby sitting day care centers for rich kids,* we parents are wasting our money and our children's valuable learning years by sending them to these schools of questionable educations. To me, it's a crying shame colleges like this seem to go out of their way to hire anti-American far left type professors that are ruining our young sponge brained children's minds (and our country's future) by pumping them full of rebellious hogwash. What our children really need is a *meaningful* job education to earn an honest living in a constructive field they will enjoy and make a constructive contribution to society while bettering their lives. To this day I sadly remember those sick '60's and 70's thinking, "Why am I busting my tail off for my family when they don't care anyway (except Bob) and why do I keep humming this tune called, *what's it all about, Alfy?* Will somebody please tell me.,what in hell's name is going on in this country???"

NEWS RELEASES DURING 1969

Neil Armstrong and Buzz Aldrin land on the moon, two black panther members are killed during a Chicago Police raid, millions protest the Vietnam War, B-52's bomb communist bases in Cambodia, the Charles Manson cult murders Sharon Tate and companions, the gay rights movement is launched, 400,000 attend the Woodstock music and arts fair, DUI Edward (teddy) Kennedy drives his car off the Chappaquiddick Bridge drowning Mary Jo Kopechne, tie-dying and bell bottom pant suits become fashionable for women, the first microprocessor is invented and a political cartoon strip called "Doonesbury" debuts.

My oldest daughter Mary Beth is now fifty six (56) years old, so I asked her for her thoughts on those "sick sixties" when she was a teenager. The following is her reply.

Dad, I think there must have been easier times to raise teenagers than during that period, and surely, the nineteen sixties presented more opportunities for family discord than any other decade in our history. In my early teenage years, the Beatles came to America; rock and roll music changed things forever and become a vibrant aspect of being a teenager. Fashions went wild with the most creative and silly clothes in history. The Baby Boomers were an enormous force in the evolution of the pop culture. The Pill was legalized and the sexual revolution swept the nation. Drugs were considered "cool" then (and now) and were everywhere, including school campuses. The Vietnam War started then and increased the division even more between the older generations and younger people. The counter cultural was immense and it affected everyone in our country, and even the world.

That said I shudder to think what it must be like raising teenagers today. They are all tattooed, pierced, their music is horrible, their clothes are atrocious, and hey, I sound exactly like my parents did when I was a teenager.

Jeg Elsker Det, Meem.

I remember driving home late one night about half looped from one of my important binge drinking meetings during the sick sixties and noticed the car behind kept following me closely all the way from San Francisco to Lafayette without passing. There was very little traffic during that early morning bar closed hour, so I thought to myself, "I'll bet that knot head behind me is going to try running me off the road to rob and/or roll me down that embankment up ahead" and Oooh boy was I ever right. All of a sudden, the beat up red van following me pulled alongside with two of the meanest looking long-haired piles of hippy garbage inside I've ever seen, sitting there glaring at me. I thought to myself, *My God, these guys are hit men,* and all of a sudden the same road rage feeling I experienced in Boston when the dead-end Irish kids jumped me, began swelling up inside me again. Fortunately, my

April Club meeting

timing was perfect because just as they sped up to swerve into my front tire to force me off the road over the embankment, I braked and turned my car towards the shoulder causing them to barely miss me and nearly go over themselves. I remember angrily shouting, "*OK, you two bastards have had your turn, now let's see what you can do*" and flipping my

lights on bright, I gunned my car wide open to shove them on over the embankment instead, just as they frantically *spun rubber* back onto the highway with me in hot pursuit.

Well, to shorten this exciting little drama somewhat, I rammed my accelerating car's front bumper into their slower van's left rear bumper, and shoved those two piles of crap up to nearly ninety miles an hour with them sweating blood knowing any way they turned, I would roll their van. I'll tell you, with my *road rage completely out of control* I didn't even consider slowing down for the next several miles, until finally my guardian angel, bless her heart, politely asked me to back off and get a grip on myself. As I began easing off on my speed, I watched in hypnotic fascination as they continued high tailing down the highway wide open at high speed turning north towards Concord, and steered my car south towards

Danville and home, recalling once again what old man Crawford had told us kids years ago when a mean Bull charged him. He said, *"Never let a mean animal know you're afraid of them because if you do, they will kill you."*

I may not have made Christians out of either one of those two piles of crap,, but I know one thing for sure. I cured them once and for all of ever sucking eggs. When I told Janet about my exciting little experience the next morning at breakfast, she just stared at me for a moment and said, "Well, at least I've learned about another *quirk* in your character I don't like", and left the room. Oooh boy, anyway I was still so pumped up, I re-told this same story to my friendly banker, Dick Hoffman, at our loan meeting that day and he laughingly said, "I would have done the same thing if they were really hit men, but unfortunately the way our legal system works in this day and age, they would have been judged as harmless young hippies *only trying* to kill you. If you had injured either one of them in any way in retaliation, you would have served time in jail for violating their civil rights."

Speaking of civil rights, it reminded me of the time a Black Mafia type guy named Charlie Walker tried to make some kind of a political statement by chaining himself to *Homer's Folly #7* on our Powell Street Station job. Fortunately, one of my binge drinking buddies at BARTD called me to warn the Channel (4) television station in San Francisco was *orchestrating a breaking story* for their six o'clock news program, by filming and interviewing an *activist* chained to our job. Oooh boy, who was it who said the media *only reports*, and *never creates* news? Anyway, when I looked out of my job office window and saw that Charlie was already chaining and padlocking himself to our head tower, I called the cops to arrest him for trespassing and had our mechanic cut him loose with a cutting torch, just as the cops arrived to pick him up. To this day, I will never forget the stunned puzzled expressions on the faces of the Channel (4) News people when they arrived to film their 'Scoop', only to see us working safely and efficiently on the new underground rapid transit station. As it turned out, Charlie got all the publicity he wanted later on, including his acting fee, by chaining himself to the Civic Center Station with another contractor, and even more name recognition after that when he was arrested for extortion in an FBI sting, and spent the next five years resting in a luxurious jail with free room and board.

It was in 1970 with the help of our company's auditor and financial advisor, Murry Regensburger and Ann Ewer, we made a complete review of our company's progress over the first seven years and were stunned to learn we were making a lot of money for everyone but ourselves. In fact, the only good thing about that first seven years was, we paid *zero* in taxes. Unbelievably, we were involved in many major joint ventures building 39 contracts that totaled over $68,000,000 worth of work with our various partners, and were doing over half of all that work ourselves, but our company's share of that volume completed was only $16,850,000 or (25%) because of our limited bonding capacity. Also interestingly, after we paid all our partners their shares we only collected a net total of $1,561,000 cash as our share of the 39 job profits, or an average of $195,000 per year for seven years towards paying our administrative and accounting expenses. That number, even more interesting, was the same job profit we made on our first job we built by ourselves, the SF Airport elevated roadway as a sole contractor. Luckily we used Gordon Ball's generous job equipment rental rates for our own equipment's back charges, and our salaried job supervision expenses were back-charged to joint ventures, so the total cash flow generated with our equipment and supervisors salaries with our share of the *job profits*, totaled our break even overhead expenses of $685,000 per year for that seven year period and was what saved us from bankruptcy. Like it or not, we were surviving on our equipment rental earnings, not our brains, talent, and construction expertise, which instead was being used to make our partners, bankers and insurance people rich. Obviously we weren't getting ahead this way, but on the other hand she did

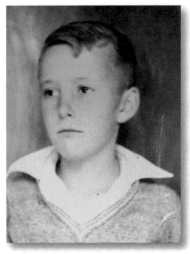

Homer J. Olsen at age seven – 1931

have warts (as my dad used to say), so when you think about it hard enough, we did help make our partners, bankers and insurance people wealthier while they were helping us learn the business the hard way business 101 warns, *how a cash poor company should **not** start* in business.

In 1970 the elevated concrete roadway bridge encircling the airport parking garage at the San Francisco International Airport advertised for bid, and after reviewing the plans and specifications, I felt it fit our company's organization to a tee, but unfortunately in spite of our success building BARTD jobs, Bill Ames was still refusing to write a bid bond for our company without a *cash rich* joint venture partner co-signing the bond. I told Bill a partner was not necessary and I wasn't about to continue paying his exorbitant premiums and high fees just for bond co-signatures any longer. When Bill asked me what my own goal in life was, I said, "Bill, all I've ever wanted for myself is to make just as much money off myself as you're making off me." When

Robert K. Olsen at age seven - 1969

I suggested I move the bonding portion of our account to a different insurance company I found that would write our *sole bonds* for us, but still leave him with the remainder, he stubbornly refused on an '*all or none*' basis. So, against my dad's advice, I sadly shook Bill's hand and moved our total insurance account to the Reidy and Casey Insurance Agency, with their promise they would write all the *sole bid bonds* we'd ever need.

Well, I discovered later Bill Ames was only bluffing and it backfired on him, but to his credit, he was becoming more and more concerned with my ever increasing binge drinking problem and my sanity in general when I considered opening an office in the Los Angeles area to bid work. Apparently he felt I had developed a crippling contractor's disease called, "*Big Shot Itis*", by trying to expand too rapidly. But then again, when you think about it hard enough, Bill's insurance company wouldn't have made as much off us and would assume *more risk* if we were allowed to build jobs alone. It all boiled down to a risk judgment call, "Can Homer cut it as a sole contractor, or not?"

The problem with all salesmen is they over *exaggerate* and will promise you the moon to get your business and their commissions. I soon discovered it was true of Reidy and Casey because I still had to re-sell our company by myself to our new insurance underwriters, all over again, to get the bid bond they promised. Bob Reidy introduced me to Hugh Shippey, the western head honcho for an eastern insurance underwriter, and I'll tell you, I have never had my resume and my small company's qualifications questioned so thoroughly in my life as I did by Mr. Shippey. He waded through my resume with a fine toothed comb and verifying calls from the time I was born to the present, and reviewed every job I was ever involved in bidding and/or building, including job tours of our company's current and completed contracts. We even had a few drunken dinner meetings together to get better acquainted, and finally Hugh Shippey and I become good friends. He said, "Ok Homer, I'm sold on you and your company now, but unfortunately our insurance guidelines are based on

Hugh Shippey & John Little negotiating with Walt the bartender)

liquidity and net worth and your company is just *borderline financially* to bid and build jobs of this magnitude without a partner, even with your families personal assets and kid's toys thrown in. This is the largest bid bond you have ever requested as a sole contractor so I'll

Bob & Dad – 1977

have to talk to my boss in New York to see if we can swing it." Well, his answer back from New York was "Maybe, but we're still inclined to play it safe and say NO", so Hugh said, "Why don't I meet you in Denver where you change planes and we can discuss this some more while we're flying to Los Angeles together for our company's meeting."

Well, as it so happened, their flight from Denver to Los Angeles flew directly over Grandpa Olsen's *Gravelbed* farm in the high desert (6000 ft elev.) country of central Utah where I grew up, so by the time they reached *Sevier County* and had re-reviewed my whole life, Hugh said, "I want you to look down at that desert country below us between those two mountain ranges. That's where this young man I've been telling you about was born and raised on a small sheep and dairy farm." A short time later while I was nervously sucking my thumb working on pins and needles in my office, Hugh called to invite me over for a lunch meeting in San Francisco to hear their final answer. When I arrived, Whooee and lo and behold, he smilingly handed me their *approved bid bond* on the San Francisco Airport's elevated roadway contract, and told me what his boss said as they flew over Grandpa Olsen's farm, "Anyone from that Godforsaken country down there that has worked as hard and done as well as Homer has so far, has earned our support. Hugh, let's gamble on this young man and write the bond his company deserves."

On May 21, 1970, ten bids were submitted on the San Francisco International Airport's elevated roadway contract and by the grace of God, Homer J. Olsen, Inc. was *low bidder* by 1.1%. Better yet, HJO Inc.'s low bid of $9,992,600, that increased with change order work to $10,904,219, was not only completed ahead of schedule and made $2,102,937 in total cash flow (the job profit alone was $1,579,194) for our company, but marked the beginning of Homer J. Olsen Inc. as an emerging highly qualified Heavy Engineering Contractor. Arne Glick, Don Hudson and Bill Young, made up my crackerjack supervision team that handled the construction of that San Francisco Airport job so efficiently and I will always be grateful to them, and to Hugh Shippey, for his conscientious analysis of our company's qualifications as an engineering contractor and his bull headed insistence his company would write our first large sole bid bond.

I always took great pride in the accomplishments of my crews during my fourteen years with Kiewit, but I take even more pride in my own small company's competent crackerjack crews that has constructed over 200 of our quality built projects totaling over a billion dollars at that time, safely and profitably, during the thirty year period I was president of Homer J. Olsen, Inc. They were my second family and I worried just as much about them and their family's well being as I did my own family. I have always believed *the working stiff deserves a fair shake,* and our company was founded on the principles and the philosophy spelled out in that old Viking code, *"Those who pull on the oars will share in the plunder."* We reached our goals over the years by religiously following the same principles I still call *Democratic Capitalism* working at its best as a closed corporation. When we became a corporation, I setup the most liberal salary and bonus schedules, stock and stock option plans, a generous medical benefit package and a retirement plan with the most liberal benefits for all our salaried shareholders far superior to any other construction company during our years in business. Except for the time I voted for Harry Truman, I've always voted Republican in every presidential election, but interestingly, Bill Ames and Gordon Ball still thought of me as a Socialist rather than the compassionate capitalist I really was who dealt fairly with everyone we did business with. They warned me, "All you're doing is encouraging your best people to quit as soon as they exercise their last ten year stock option, to startup their own companies to compete against yours – the goose who laid their golden eggs."

I guess the main difference between me and the Socialist Democrats is, I believe in sharing generously with those who *will work hard for a it* (pull on the oars), but unlike the Democrats, I will not share with those who are capable of working, but *won't.,* so basically the only difference between Democrats and Republicans nowadays is, the Republicans believe in jobs, the Democrats believe in welfare. I remember during the great depression, the tramps who came to our door for something to eat were called *Hobos* **if** they asked to do work for their food, but if they only begged for food, they were called *Bums* You guessed it, when the depression finally came to an end in 1942, all the *Hobo's* (Republicans) disappeared when they got jobs, but we still have *ever increasing* numbers of *Bums*, (Democrats) enjoying our country's costly unsuccessful overly generous welfare programs.

> ## MAJOR NEWS RELEASE DURING 1968
>
> *Robert F. Kennedy and Martin Luther King are assassinated, Richard Nixon and Spiro Agnew are elected President and Vice President, Chicago Police club demonstrators at the Democrat Convention, U. S. Troops massacre Vietcong civilians at Mai Lai, Vietcong launch the Tet Offensive, riots occur in 125 cities after King's assassination, Yale admits women, 6000 sheep die next to the Utah Dugway Proving Grounds from nerve gas, Pulsars are discovered, Enzymes which cut DNA strands at certain points is discovered, Congress recommends the U. S. adopt the Metric system, and the Mod and Deadbeat Hippie look become the latest "in" thing for the young people.*

I still remember the time when Carl Alt got mad at me and quit, he left saying, "If you can make it in this business Homer, any damn fool can", so I wished him luck and you guessed it, he went bankrupt on his first job. Carl forgot *profit* is not a dirty word and discovered it was important to add markup to the cost of doing his work (called profit) to stay in business. To be successful in the construction business it not only requires motivation, a good work ethic and experience in the construction trades, but also requires a *meaningful job education* and apprentice training with a good company (plus a rich grandfather for a backup bonding signature), and to top things off, religiously following Peter Kiewit's four points for success, namely:

#1 Bid work for the right price.
#2 Build work for the right cost.
#3 Collect for all work done
#4 Take good care of your assets.

After we completed the Airport job, I asked John Lamberson (who was still working for Bill Ames), "If a Montana road apple inherited several million dollars and asked you for a bond to bid a large complicated fast track heavy engineering construction job, would you write a bid bond for this unqualified manure pile to build such a tough job?" Surprisingly, his answer was an emphatic "**YES,** because the higher their net worth, no matter what they know, look or smell like, the lower the risk is for a bonding company." *Unbelievable!* For some unknown reason, most *owners* and 100% of the public Agency's still require construction bonds be submitted with their bids because the bonding company is guaranteeing them a *qualified contractor* will do their work. If their bonded contractor doesn't perform (something John apparently ignored), the bonding company is required to finish the project at no additional cost to the owner. The questionable conclusion is, the higher a company's net worth, the less qualified the contractor need be, whereas contractors who are *borderline financially*, must be highly qualified to be considered for a bond. As John Lamberson said,

It all boils down to the amount of risk the insurance companies are willing to take, and it's the cash money (liquid assets) the client has that talks, not his qualifications.

For some reason that story reminded me of the time I met the president of a large New York insurance company and put both my feet in my mouth at the same time. About a week before we settled on Reidy and Casey to be our new insurance carriers, John Luce of another company, invited me to a cocktail party to meet his company's president. Well, wouldn't you know it, after I shook hands with nearly everyone, I met a loud mouthed pompous anal canal I assumed was a used car peddler client of theirs and Oooh boy, believe this or not, he turned out to be the company president John Luce invited me to meet. He immediately launched into a verbal bowel movement tirade you wouldn't believe to impress me with not only his royalty and pedigree, but how hard he had

Bob – 1972

to work that almost brought tears to my eyes. He said he was *forced* to live in a huge Texas mansion his company gave him free and clear because his wife loved Texas, and he had to fly all the way from Texas to New York City in his private Lear Jet every morning to have his chauffeur driven stretch limousine take him to his luxurious top floor office suite in the highest New York building to go through his mail. To make things even worse, he said he also had to stay over night occassionally in his company furnished, maid and butler serviced pent house apartment because of his heavy letter dictating day and long staff meetings, before he could fly back to Texas again in his Lear Jet for a gourmet dinner his French chef had prepared for his lovely wife and himself. Wow, I was so choked up with emotion & flem I vomited.

He must have been pulling my leg, but unfortunately when I saw his Lear Jet parked at the San Francisco Executive Airport earlier that same day I took him seriously and said, "If I were a shareholder in your company, I would have you arrested and jailed for stealing from your shareholders, and I would demand the directors of your company immediately auction off your unnecessary New York apartment, your unneeded Lear Jet and stretch limousine and I would close down your high rent New York office. Then I would turkey walk your little ass all the way back to Texas into a small low rent ground level office near your home and cut your salary and fringes back to a level that was fair for both the company and the amount of constructive work you actually do."

Oooh Boy, red faced with anger and shocked that anyone would have guts enough to say the things I did to royalty, he turned towards John Luce and said, "Who is this ass hole?"

When John Luce answered, "He's the client we wanted that I was telling you about", he said, "Like hell he is, get rid of him", and stiffly turned and walked away.

CHRISTMAS LETTER– 1971

Hooo–boy, I flipped my back out again this morning and Janet said, "As long as you're going to lie there on a hot pad doing nothing anyway, you just as well make yourself useful by writing our Christmas letter." Soo, here goes. The only thing good about this lousy back of mine is, every time it flips out we are "low bidder" again and we could sure use some more work. The construction market this past year has been extremely competitive and for some reason, we seem to be able to build jobs faster than we can acquire them. In general, we are all fine and doing well, all things considered. Our family keeps getting a little smaller, and the house a little larger, because our two daughters both moved to Hawaii this past summer and opened a "Bikini and Beach Wear" store in Lahaina, on the island of Maui. Their dear old dad and mom are silently backing their store for them which is just what we need, another tax loss situation. We are proud of our girl's and their pioneering gumption at the age of 18 and 20, in what they are doing. Barbara will be home for Xmas this year but Mary Beth will stay in Hawaii to mind the store.

Our 9 year old son Bob is doing great in school this year. He is completely absorbed in baseball, and baseball cards, and has turned into a walking encyclopedia on big league players, U. S. Presidents, and world geography. He was in the peanut league last year and is really looking forward to little league next spring. Janet keeps herself busy as a volunteer at the school library, as publicity chairman of the library friends, assistant den mother of Bob's cub scouts, and taking various sewing and extension classes.

Last summer, we agreed to finance the construction of a deer hunting cabin on our three acre (10,500' elevation) lot on Monroe Mountain, Utah, for all our family to enjoy, if Dad and my youngest brother Steve would build it. Needless to say, it turned out great and we had a family reunion when it was finished in late August with all the Olsen tribe and family. Everyone showed up for the affair except our daughters who were tied up in Hawaii with their store. Wouldn't you know it, along came deer season in October with an early four foot snow storm that stranded many of the deer hunters (not us) and nearly buried our newly built cabin. Hopefully we will be able to use it again next year when it thaws out enough to find where it was built

We hope you have a Merry Christmas and a Happy New Year. If you're by this way, please drop in for a visit.

Ole

It was during the early 1970's, our company's three person board of directors decided that *going where the work is,* was no longer feasible and we should *diversify* our operations, but keep northern California as our home base. Many of the old timers in the company were retiring and the younger generation wives of our younger supervisors, were refusing to move their families to distant job assignments any longer. To resolve these problems we should continue working as *the* best contractor doing our structure concrete specialty, but by diversifying, would be flexible enough to build different types of engineering projects without moving from California and stay west of the Rocky Mountains. The Eisenhower Highway Program and the Rapid Transit Program we already knew was winding down, but the Clean Water Program was about to begin. To be competitive in this type work we needed to learn more about the intricacies of building the larger outfall sewers, pumping plants and clean water treatment facilities, including mechanical work. To learn quickly, joint venturing with experienced specialty contractors or hiring people that were qualified and experienced in these fields was the answer. It was during this *clean water* training period coupled with my dulling binge drinking sprees, I made my most costly judgment errors for the company.

> ## MAJOR NEWS RELEASE DURING 1971
>
> *The Supreme Court upholds busing School children to achieve racial balance,, voting age is lowered to 18, hundreds of Vietnam veterans throw away their medals to protest the War, Intel introduces a micro-processor, Texas Instruments introduces the pocket calculator, Amtrak takes over passenger rail traffic, Nixon freezes rents, wages and prices and devalues the dollar, Hot Pants and the "custom patch" for jeans become the "in" thing for young people*

Monroe Mtn Cabin – 1973

We first joint ventured with Bob Flora on six large diameter sewer pipeline jobs in the San Francisco area to gain profitable experience, but as it turned out, it was a complete waste of time and money. Bob Flora sponsored three of the six jobs we were low on while we sponsored three, and interestingly he lost money on all three of his contracts while we, inexperienced and all, made money enough on our three jobs to offset Flora's losses and all six of our ventures only broke even. What was interesting to me was, when the six jobs were completed; Bob Flora sued me for what he called, *book cooking shenanigans,* which was ridicules. Why?, because he felt he should have made $60,000 instead of only breaking even and amazingly, the presiding judge awarded him the $60,000 because it so happened, Bob owed his attorney, Quinton Kopp, exactly $60,000. Quinton then went on to become a judge himself not too long afterwards and as far as I know, everyone was happy with the settlement, except me.

Lessons learned: *Justice will always prevail because the winners are always attorneys. Don't ever underestimate the knowledge and inventiveness of your own crews because experienced American blue collar working stiffs (the best workman in the world) know more about construction than all the so called experts put together. Common sense and hard work combined with brains and construction experience, are the ingredients needed most to construct engineering works.*

The worst business decision I ever made was opening an office in southern California and hiring an old Kiewit mechanical engineering friend named Bill Mabry, to be our Los Angeles district's vice president, to build clean water treatment plants. I remember Bill's first job was a million dollar water treatment plant for the city of Poway near San Diego that ended up losing $45,000 out of pocket when it was completed, but since it was our first plant, I chalked it up as a learning experience. It wasn't until the Los Angeles office began getting nearly every job they bid, which meant they were bidding their work way too cheap, and began losing money on nearly every job they built, which meant they didn't have qualified cost conscious people running the work, I really became concerned. I telephoned Bill Mabry to meet me one Saturday at the Los Angeles Airport to tour his jobs and to work all that weekend to find ways to improve his costs. Well, Bill might have been an excellent mechanical engineer, but his *unworried* attitude about losing company money and his lack of knowledge of *why we were in business in the first place* shocked me. What really knocked me for a loop was when he said he couldn't meet me that Saturday was because he was going to go skiing. Oooh boy, trying hard to contain myself, I said, "OK Bill, ask Neal Boostrom to meet me instead, and I'll save postage by bringing your payoff checks with me." Unbelievably, by the time we cleaned up all his mistakes and completed all his losing jobs to close the Los Angeles office, my decision to hire Bill Mabry and open that losing office in the first place, cost our company a whopping $400,000. Bill Ames was right.

Lesson Learned: *Trying to expand too rapidly with the wrong personnel is not only expensive, but dangerous, bankruptcy wise.*

It was about that same time I had lunch with an old Stanford classmate named Oscar Holmes who also became a contractor after we graduated, and was currently in the throws of a bitter divorce. He told me a long sad story about his vindictive ex-wife and the excessive greed of the Wells Fargo Bank saying, "My ex-wife has tied up all my bonding to keep me from bidding for anymore work, my bank's loan officer thinks he can make a windfall for Wells Fargo by calling my million dollar note and auctioning off all the equipment I bought with it and have already paid down to $200,000. I also loaned Gerald and Kay Clair (his chief engineer) $50,000 to buy company's stock and my ex-wife now owns that note and is demanding immediate payment, which Gerald and Kay are refusing to pay." He said, "Homer, the bank's foreclosure will force me into bankruptcy if I don't pay off the loan within 30 days, and I've reached the point of no return. I guess what I need most now is some good advice on what to do, other than jumping off the Golden Gate Bridge." I said, "Oooh boy Oscar, you really are caught between a rock and a hard place, but the way I look at it, friends will always help each other in ticklish situations if possible. You and I have been friends a long time Oscar, so maybe this idea might work. *If* your ex-wife will back off enough to see that

Copenhagen 1973

her stock in your company will be worthless if she forces you into bankruptcy, and *if* she is willing to take your stock back from Gerald and Kay as full payment for their $50,000 note loan and will tear up that note, I will loan you $200,000 to payoff what you still owe on the bank loan. To pay me back later, you and I will then joint venture contracts together with you as the sponsoring partner, until you've paid my $200,000 back plus interest, from your earnings. How does that sound?" As I waited patiently, a completely stunned Oscar Holmes, that same tough marine officer who was so badly wounded in the battle for Iwo Jima during WW II, suddenly became so choked up with emotion he couldn't talk, and with tears in his eyes, reached across the table to warmly shake my hand in both of his, wheezed quietly, "God bless you Homer. I can't ever thank you enough."

Well, the upshot of this was, Oscar's ex-wife finally agreed with my terms and much to the shock and disappointment of the Wells Fargo Bank's loan officer, Oscar's note was paid off and in retaliation for the Bank's obnoxious uncooperative customer relations attitude and greed, both the O.C. Holmes Co. and Homer J. Olsen Inc., closed their accounts with Wells Fargo and moved to other banks. Our Holmes-Olsen Joint Venture was low bidder on the San Gabriel Canyon slide repair contract for $1,877,787 near Azusa, California a short time later and as agreed, Oscar paid HJO Inc back with interest when completed. I was so impressed with the work performance of some of Oscar's personnel, with his blessings; I told Gerald Clair, Ed Walker, Bill Coates and Frank Mock, they would be welcomed with open arms by the Homer Olsen Company if they ever decided to change companies. Believe it or not, a year later they all accepted my offer, and became valued welcome additions to our organization with their treatment plant expertise and experience. Oscar married an attractive wealthy widow he met after his divorce was finalized, and for health reasons, closed his company down to enjoy retirement.

To finalize Oscar's last claim on the San Gabriel Canyon joint venture, I met with the same engineers Oscar had negotiated a preliminary settlement, and after a couple of hours re-reviewing and re-compromising, we both agreed $100,000 was a fair settlement for both sides. When I arrived a week later to pickup our agreed check amount, much to my surprise there in the same conference room sat a half dozen state attorneys, instead of the engineers I had negotiated with, and unbelievably, the check they handed me was for $25,000 instead of the $100,000 agreed amount. I'll tell you, I literally came unglued and was not only shocked and angry, but really teed off and shouted, "What in hells name is this all about, I thought we already had an agreement for four times this amount and this check is ridicules. Are you people telling me your own engineers will

> ## MAJOR NEWS RELEASE DURING 1972
>
> *Richard M. Nixon and Spiro Agnew are re-elected president and VP, Nixon goes to China to establish political ties, the National Commission on Marijuana and Drug Abuse urges an end to criminal penalties for private use and possession of marijuana, B-52'S bomb Hanoi and Haiphong, the military draft ends, and the armed services become all volunteer, five burglars are arrested at Democrat Party Headquarters in the Watergate Hotel, Congress passes a Water Pollution Control Act, one third of the petroleum consumed is imported, Soviets buy one fourth of the U.S. wheat crop, Woodward and Bernstein of the Washington Post crack the Watergate affair.*

no longer have any authority to negotiate claim settlements and we'll be in court every month to even get our progress payments?" They coldly answered, "Times have changed Homer, the State of California's newly appointed Highway Engineer (an attorney instead of an engineer) feels revisions are necessary in the Highway Department", and went on to say, "Frankly, we feel your $100,000 settlement is fair for both sides and if you went to court you would most likely win, but it would cost you $75,000 in legal fees. The check we're offering you is the net amount you would receive after the trial, only we're offering it to you *now* instead of *later*."

I slammed my brief case shut and said, "Screw you guys and the mules you rode in on, I'll see you in court", and stormed towards the exit to leave, but thinking better of it at the doorway, turned and said, "You guys make me sick the way you relish stomping small businesses into the dirt, but as my final payment to never do any more business with you people, I'll accept your ridiculously unfair check of $25,000 if you will answer one last question. If I was a Peter Kiewit or a Morrison & Knudsen size company, would you have paid me the agreed $100,000 settlement?" They laughed and said, "Of course, the contractors you mentioned have top notch attorneys on their permanent staff and they have the resources and staying power to appeal a case like this all the way to the Supreme Court on principle alone if necessary, whereas you don't. It's time consuming and wasteful for the State of California to take on larger contractors like you mentioned, so in answer to your question, yes we would hand them their check for $100,000. Your company on the other hand, is too small to afford interferences to your cash flow because to do otherwise, you wouldn't survive. Take our advice Homer and face up to the reality of our times and accept our check for twenty five cents on the dollar." True to my word, HJO Inc. never bid another highway job with the State of California until many years later when they politely called to ask our organization to participate in their emergency bridge earthquake repair work.

> **Lesson Learned:** *Freedom and Fairness in Justice are always worth fighting to the death for, but unfortunately when the odds are insurmountable, it's better to surrender your sword – and slowly die like the coward you've become. Justice, fair or not, always prevails in the end because the winners are always attorneys.*

My oldest daughter, Mary Elizabeth, who was still in shock over her last deadbeat boyfriend breaking their engagement and stealing $5,000 from her Hawaiian store, closed down her Maui bikini shop and registered at the University of Hawaii to work towards her BA Degree, and wrote me this letter. It was the first time I learned she felt I loved her younger sister Barbara more than her while her younger sister Barbara always told me she thought I loved Mary Beth more. It was also the first times my beautiful talented intelligent oldest daughter Mary Beth I was so proud of running their store, told me how she really felt.

> *January 19, 1973*
>
> **Dear Dad,**
> A letter has been trying to form in my mind for the past few months so I guess I'll try and see if it comes out. I'm not even sure what's prompting me — probably a combination of many things, like a need for communications with you Dad, and questions I have and changes I'm experiencing that I would like to share
>
> Here I am, your oldest kid, not so young anymore, and soon I'll be 21 --- can you believe that? It really amazes me how many times I wished I hadn't been in such a hurry to leave home. I wish (like Bow) I knew both my parents better because most of what we shared the last few years I was home, was conflict, and I never felt the warmth and love and respect that Bow won for herself from you. I knew you respected me for what I was doing (shops etc), but never for what I was. I guess it can only to be expected when people don't know each other.

Ever since I was real young, I remember feeling this intense, almost fantastical need for freedom that manifested itself in so many ways. Things like, having to graduate from high school early, having to move out of our house early, even if it meant to a dormitory, and having to create my own life style that was functional for me. Why did I do this? I don't know. It was probably some deep psychological stuff that seemed natural at the time.

Actually, I think our differences are minor now and our conflicts have dissolved down to only a few. I respect and understand you and I know you're life style is right for you, but it is not for me. In my experience, I've found that I really have to want to do something before I can do it, and someone else wanting it for me is only frustrating. I don't know why I'm having such a hard time making my point and maybe what I've written sounds immature to you, and probably selfish, but I feel good where I'm at now. It's where I'm going that really interests me.

It's like this Dad. I rushed off to UCSB so I could be on my own and dove into university life only to come to the realization that college could really be hard. School had always been such a breeze before and it really was a struggle to try and balance my life. I had no perspective, no goals, and was just killing time taking required classes. I couldn't even keep it together taking dance as a major, something I loved. In short, I wasn't getting anywhere and just blowing a chance for at least some parental respect.

Well, you know the rest, I quit UCSB and split to Hawaii, and the Bikini shop idea came up between us, with another chance to test my worth. That learning experience was phenomenal, both materially and emotionally, and I learned a lot about myself. I know my weaknesses and what my needs are, and I know now there is so much I really don't know anything about.

I could apologize a million times to you for that whole R. C. bit, but we both know that I will be paying back dues on that mistake for a long time. (Note: The jerk she called RC was a dope sniffing deadbeat hippy boyfriend of Mary Beth's that absconded with over $5,000 of the stores operating capital, when she thought he loved her). I now live with the knowledge that no man I bring home from now on to meet you, no matter how superior or intelligent, you will be even more hesitant in showing your approval All I can say Dad is, my perspective was off for awhile there, but I'm much wiser now and I hope we are both mature enough to let it go as water under the bridge.

One thing I know now for sure, I don't want to be a seamstress, or even have another-shop, for the remainder of my life. It was a valid experience while it lasted that gave me insight into the business world and people in general, but I'm relieved it's over. It was just too much tension.

So here I am now. I enrolled in school (the University of Hawaii) at the last minute and I'm glad I did because two weeks of retirement was driving me up a tree. I really need outside stimulation and creativity, but I'm still plagued by the major question, what do I want to do for a living? I've been a partner in two businesses for nearly three years and I have accumulated nearly two years of college units in countless activities and interests, and now I've reached this void. I still don't know what I want to major in.

Mary Beth about 1982

After this semester, I will have fulfilled all the general education requirements necessary, so now I need a goal to work towards, and damn it, I'm drawing a blank. You don't know how much I envy you Dad, because you're a man who loves and lives for his work, and you're so challenged and enthusiastic, and so successful doing the work you love. I wish I could find work like yours that would challenge, and keep me growing and enthusiastic, that I could love to do, and would support me in the manner I've become accustomed.

All I know is what I don't want to do. I don't want to be a housewife with four kids, I don't want to be a seamstress, I don't want to be a celibate monk, I just want to keep growing and learning, and flexible, and to be happy. Any suggestions? Hint: Dad, I don't want to be an engineer, math bores me.(Mary Beth always got good grades, even in her math and science classes, in high school and was gifted with superior leadership qualities and a wonderful personality, so I suggested she think about combining civil engineering, business law and accounting, and take over running our company some day. Her answer, 'that's men's work').

I've been thinking a lot lately about being a teacher and have decided to go the extra year to get my masters and teaching credential. It certainly wouldn't hurt to have it as insurance. I love school and I keep forgetting that fact until I'm back again. I know I'm ready for college this time and I'm willing to give the time and energy it takes to get something out of it. I really want to finish and get my college degree, if for no other reason than to have a good educational background. Maybe the career interests will take *care of themselves and fall into place by then. I love dance and drama, music, literature, art and religion. I also love to write so maybe I'll discover a new and interesting career to pursue some day.*

I have one new development in my life. As you know, I never believed in God before, and now I do. I am surrounded by so much beauty and love here; it's easy to see the unity and the completeness of religion. I'm enclosing a wonderful article that I agree with on the subject that I would like you to read and give me your thoughts about. Sometimes I get so caught up in my own ideas I forget how others think about things.

I will always love you Dad, I know you don't often hear that because the "Olsen Policy" seems to be, never show affection and love. Well, that's another thing I've learned about myself. I can't live without love and affection, and I don't think you can either.

I love you Dad,
Meem.

It was during 1973, the One Hundred Year Anniversary of my *far far* (grandpa) Olsen's immigration to America that I took my family and my dad and stepmother, to the Norway farm grandpa called '*Vintravigen*', (winter cove) near Marvik, Rogaland County, Norway. It was without a doubt the best things I've ever done for anyone in my life because my 75 year old dad was so pleased he never stopped talking about that wonderful trip to everyone in Utah who would listen, as long as he lived. Dad got to see the same farm house and the same barn his own *far* (father), Ole K. Olsen, and *his far far* (grandfather), Ola Olsen built, and he met the descendants of the same family his father sold the *Vintravigen* farm to for $200 passage money for his *mor* (mother), Brita Kjolvick Olsen, and his two older sisters, Marta and Olena, while he worked as a crew member on their ship to America. Dad also got to meet his relative, Herr Johanne Kjolvick, who was Dad's same age and related to Dad's *mor mor* (grandmother) Brita Kjolvjck, who married my dad's grandfather, Ola Olsen, in 1844. Apparently Johann was an amateur genealogist as well as being a well to do fisherman-farmer, (his family's farm was 900 hectares) and had traced the Kjolvick family's genealogy back to 800 AD. I'll never forget the surprised and pleased look on my dad's face when Johann informed him he was related to four Viking Kings who, as I recall, three of them were named, Harold the Flat Foot, Harold the Blue Tooth, and Harold the Fine Hair who later became king of Norway and was killed during the invasion of England in 1066. If King Harold the fine hair had won that battle instead of losing his life, England would probably have been part of Norway today. But on the other hand he still might have lost to the Danish Viking, *William the Conqueror* later on. (if my memory of the Viking sagas is correct?)

We also traveled over to Sweden to see where some of my stepmother Ercel's relatives were from, and then on down to Denmark to tour the city of Ellsinore where many of my dad's friends immigrated from to settle in their sister city of Ellsinore, Utah. My youngest daughter, Barbara, who was registered at Evergreen College in Washington State for a fine

My wonderful Dad on the Norwegian trip

arts degree in languages, convinced her *dear old dad,* (me) the two schools were sharing college credits anyway and she should stay in Denmark to learn Danish at the University of Kobenhaven.

It was while we were in Kobenhaven, Denmark, I also had a relaxing *Akvavit* lunch with an old friend, Jens Thorsen who became president of the Monborg & Thorsen, Construction Company later, to reminisce over our fun days apprenticing as engineer trainees with Peter Kiewit Son's Company, and to discuss Barbara's decision. I wrote Jens a letter later while we were traveling through Germany to ask him to keep a watchful eye out for Barbara because of my worries over her attending the University of Kobenhaven all by herself. He answered he would, and after we completed our travels through Germany to see where my own mother's great grandfather (Peter Weimer) was born, we all ended up in Switzerland for the flight home after our wonderful three week European vacation.

As a little side story while in Switzerland, I visited the world headquarters of a large European company that was constantly mailing our little company expensive brochures and impressive business flyers, requesting an opportunity to Joint Venture work in the United States with us, and my suspicions were verified. Believe it or not, the world headquarters for this large impressive company turned out to be only a mail box and a one girl answering service, so I left my card for their CEO saying how impressed I was with their company's head office, and never heard from them again. Interestingly, people like this in the old days were called *con artists* and *loan sharks*, but nowadays they're called *venture capitalists*.

It was also during 1973 our little company survived a bitter court battle concerning the award of the BARTD Embarcadero Station under lower Market Street, and we were awarded the contract for $14,093,650 by the court. Initially HJO Inc. was the second bidder slightly above a broker type Building Contractor with a "B" (Building) license instead of the "A" (Heavy Engineering) contractor's license required, and their unqualified bid was rejected by the Bay Area Rapid Transit District. When we were awarded the contract as second bidder, the low bidder angrily filed suit against both BARTD and HJO, Inc. delaying the work long enough for our ornamental metals subcontractor to discover his bid was too low and filed bankruptcy to *cop out,* leaving HJO Inc holding the bag for his work, so now what do we do? None of the other ornamental iron shops in the area would touch the work with a ten foot pole unless we added an additional $200,000 to his bid price, which I thought was out and out extortion. You guessed it. I angrily slammed my briefcase shut (again!!) and said, "Screw you guys and the mules you rode in on, we'll do the work ourselves", and believe it or not, that is another true story of how a new division of our company called *The Viking Metals Company* was born, and Ernie Figley was hired to run this new company for us.

Looking back now, the best thing that ever happened to HJO, Inc. was when Gerald Clair, my old Stanford classmate and the best chief engineer estimator I have ever worked with, transferred over to our company from the Oscar C. Holmes Company and came to work for us during that tight 1970's economic period. It was also a God send for our company when such highly qualified and experienced engineering superintendents like John Shimmick, Bill Young, Ed Walker, Stan Summers, Dave Stacy, Bob Witbeck, Bill Coates and Don Hudson, all signed on with us. As an inspired motivated crackerjack team, they not only helped bid the work, but supervised the construction of $89,000,000 in total contracts during the first five

> ## MAJOR NEWS RELEASE DURING 1973
>
> *VP Spiro Agnew resigns amid charges of income tax evasion, Gerald Ford is sworn in as VP, U. S. ground troop involvement in Vietnam ends, The Supreme Court decision in Roe v Wade legalizes abortions, Senator Sam Erwin, Jr, heads the committee to investigate Watergate, Members of the American Indian Movement occupy Wounded Knee, South Dakota, Farm Labor represents five percent of the U. S. work force, CAT scan equip. is introduced, Homosexuality is no longer classified as a mental disorder, marijuana is used to treat glaucoma, the Skylab is launched, the first Arab oil embargo occurs, the U. S. dollar is devalued by ten percent, Chicago's Sears Tower becomes the worlds tallest building at 1,455 feet.*

years of the 1970's, and generated cash flow for the company of $15,000,000 after absorbing the Viking Metals and the Los Angeles districts combined losses of $800,000. Unfortunately, our union Viking Metals shop was unable to compete *price wise,* with all the low salaried non-union miscellaneous iron shops in the area, and like the Los Angeles district, they also lost a whopping $400,000 out of pocket before we were forced to close them down. The good news was, the successfully constructed Embarcadero Station supervised by John Shimmick and Bill Young, was not only a gold mine for our company, but is still considered the *jewel Station* of the underground BARTD Stations along Market Street in San Francisco. All because of HJO Inc.'s superior construction engineering expertise and craftsmanship, topped off with Viking Metals' quality designed, fabricated, and installed, ornamental iron and bronze *frosting* products.

I reluctantly hired Arne Glick because I still had an uncomfortable feeling about him from the Kiewit days because of his graduation from Cal-Berkeley, but with Bill Young's and Don Hudson's help and expertise, Arne did an excellent job running our first large *sole* contract, the San Francisco Airport, successfully. When he turned out later to be the perfect # 2 man for me to play the good guy-bad guy role (I naturally played the good guy) when we negotiated with unions and clients, I made him vice president of operations, Gerald Clair as vice president of engineering, and Henry Morehead as treasurer to handle the accounting and administrative office duties, while Kim Allison continued on as our company's attorney.

From then on, my crew consisted of only those four people with everyone else working for them. As we began accumulating more and more working capital, I purchased a bargain priced five acre piece of property in Union City alongside the Nimitz freeway for $100,000 with three older homes on it as our offices, and enough extra space for our shops and storage of construction equipment and materials, and closed the Danville office. I think it was the first time since I founded our company in 1963, I really felt things were beginning to fall into place.

With the *diversified* experience of all our people, we confidently began bidding and building different type construction contracts for the company. We negotiated a contract to build the new Great Western Bank building near 6th and Market in San Francisco, Bob Witbeck handled very successfully. I made Dave Stacy the head honcho over a newly organized smaller group to handle smaller jobs called the *Pucker String Division,* and they handled all the brick-paving and street reconstruction contracts. Ed Walker looked after most of our Clean Water Treatment Plants successfully and Stan Summers took over supervising the tunnel and airport work after completing the Fremont Bridge in Portland, Oregon on loan with a bonding company. John Shimmick and Bill Young shifted over from bridge work to concentrating on the tougher underground BARTD and larger pumping plant contracts while Don Hudson supervised the construction of the cement and gravel plant jobs and Bill Coates continued looking after railroad and various types of pipe trench work.

During the next twenty years, our company successfully diversified into building eighteen different types of work in the construction contracting business that varied from Tunnel work to Buildings, Airports to Clean Water Treatment Plants and Railroad track work to Highways Bridges and doing our own Pile Driving and Mechanical work. The experienced crackerjack people who made up our company's organization during that period were the most qualified, motivated and by far the best construction team I have ever worked with, bar none. I will always be grateful to them for all they contributed towards our company's rapid growth and reputation as a quality construction firm that lives and breaths the words skill, integrity, and responsibility. I told them I would help in anyway I could, but I only knew how to do one thing well, and that was *delegate,* and it was because of knowledge from their hands on experience, by personally estimating and supervising quality built construction projects safely, profitably and on schedule, that made our company so successful. Thanks to Ward White's teaching abilities, the most successful projects I ever handled as a job supervisor myself were the ones I estimated and supervised their construction.

It was during those lengthy gas lines of 1974, the San Francisco street car light rail replacement contracts were first advertised for bid, and once again I made the mistake of bidding work with questionable *experts*. I asked Marty Lummis, a local railroad contractor friend from my San Mateo Bridge building days, to joint venture with us on the rail work, but unfortunately he turned me down because of his heavy load of Southern Pacific Railroad work, but he warned me to never do railroad work myself because *it's too complicated for carpenters*. So, lacking self confidence, I asked the Railco Company in Oregon to be our *learning* partner on the Sunset Tunnel's Muni track replacement project that required all the work be done on graveyard shift when trains were idle. You guessed it; Railco accepted my 60/40% joint venture offer *if* we would be the sponsoring 60% partner and do all the work, which meant we would be teaching ourselves like the Bob Flora fiasco. Well, fortunately and

unbeknown to me at the time, Bill Coates already knew more about track work than Railco, so the only help they gave us was estimating a *bid way too low* leaving $150,000 (15%) on the table. Oooh boy, so anyway when everything was all said and done, my lack of confidence in my own crackerjack crews cost HJO Inc another $60,000 in un-necessary *tuition expenses*, but the good news was, unlike Flora, Railco didn't sue us.

Well, to rebuild my self confidence, I re-activated Ben Williams' secret formula of holding my nose and blowing hard until I swelled up to

MAJOR NEWS RELEASE DURING 1974

The House Judiciary Committee vote to impeach President Nixon, motorists experience gasoline shortages, a 55 mph highway speed limit law goes into effect, the ban on ownership of gold is lifted, President Nixon resigns and Gerald Ford becomes the 38th president, President Gerald Ford grants Richard Nixon a pardon, Congress passes an Election Reform Act and a Freedom of Information Act, the Symbionese Liberation Army kidnaps Patricia Hearst, money markets become available to small investors, and Hank Aaron breaks Babe Ruth's career homerun record. .

the size I thought I needed to be to do the job I was being paid, but wasn't, and we began bidding and building rail replacement jobs by ourselves without partners, and needless to say under Bill Coates' capable supervision, all the rail jobs were profitable. Interestingly, after word leaked out we weren't really as dumb as we looked, Marti Lummis called me to ask, "Homer, how come a company like yours that is manned by dumb carpenters, can all of a sudden out of the blue, start doing my complicated railroad work so efficiently?" I said, "Marti, I know you won't believe this, but we accidentally discovered the ties were already made of wood so we pretended the steel rails were also wood and strung them out along the ties like timbers. *Viola*, suddenly building railroads became as easy as building bridges."

From then on, I began delegating the work more to my crackerjack crews and kept my nose out of things my experienced competent superintendents already knew more about than me anyway. I let them do their own estimating and supervising with Gerald Clair's help, and began spending more of my time, visiting jobs to attend safety meetings, meeting with potential clients, and trying to prove to the bonding company's we needed more bid bonds to bid for more work to stay busy, and doing committee work for the AGC. Unfortunately, I also began binge drinking more while attending the late dinners with clients and contractor friends and really screwed up on the last BARTD upper Market street open cut contract we wanted and needed badly. Riedy and Casey started getting too greedy with their billings and *over charged* our company $60,000 (that must be my unlucky number) on that job's insurance premiums, and for some unknown reason I didn't re-check their figures and that one mistake cost us the ten million dollar BARTD job we wanted by $30,000. When I discovered Bill Ames had quoted the low bidder and all his other clients, $60,000 less than our insurance quote, I came unglued and fired Riedy and Casey as our insurance carriers.

Well, so now what do we do? The next day I bit my lip and called Bill Ames to *apologize and request a reinstate Homer* meeting and tossed my hard hat into his office for his response. Unbelievably, Bill shouted *Velkommen,* and he did the apologizing. He said everything that happened was his fault and he would bond us as a 'sole' contractor on any job we wished, *if* I could prove to him we had the cash flow, the equipment and the qualified people needed to handle the work. Since nearly all engineering contractors are *cash poor,* to help us meet the bonding company's *liquidity requirement* he agreed our yard inventory of re-usable steel piling, lagging materials and small tools with our banker's *line of credit letter,* were really *current assets.* After all, he said (repeating my previous argument), if all those things were cash we would *buy* the same things to build the jobs anyway. Wow, what a welcome change in attitude and there was no doubt about it, he really did miss our paying his insurance *billings.*

Armand Cassini & Big John Little enjoying lunch in Little Italy

It was while we were building the United Nations Plaza in San Francisco, I first met my good friend John Little, the owner of the George Reed ornamental granite and marble company. John was the best subcontractor I have ever worked with bar none because he was honest, hardworking, and qualified as a contractor who did his work on a schedule you could set your watch by. I remember the city asked John to find a long *solid* (no seams) block of black granite to make the new United Nations Plaza's monument, and he not only found the black granite they wanted somewhere around Hudson Bay in northeastern Canada, but carved, polished, delivered, and set it in place exactly on the schedule the city gave him. To this day, that same finished black granite monument is standing tall in the United Nations Plaza in San Francisco, California. Wow, what a guy.

John asked me to bid a *statue job* for him one time and when I asked, "Why don't you bid it by yourself?", he said, "Well for one thing Homer, you're honest and will be fair with me, but the main reason is, I don't have a general contractor's license. If you will act as the general contractor, I'll be your subcontractor and all you'll have to do is move in the stature and moon the inspector occasionally while I do all the work" Well, to shorten this story a little, John gave me his price and since I figured we wouldn't get the job anyway, I put $5,000 on top to cover the statue's moving expenses from Golden Gate Park (with a little left over for me) to the intersection of Market and Montgomery in downtown San Francisco, and turned in our bid. Lo and behold and believe it or not, we were the low bidder by $4,000 on the $44,000 job, so now what do we do? Well, luckily I had another good binge drinking friend named Adolph Battini, president of the Sheedy Drayage Company and the # 1 *moving and crane connoisseur* of San Francisco himself, who agreed to pick up and deliver the statue to its new location for us.

I know you will question my memory accuracy, but as I recall, Adolph had two of his guys drive one of his boom trucks over to Golden Gate Park at midnight when there was little traffic, and as they roared by the statue yelling and screaming like two pillaging plundering Vikings, they lassoed and jerked that sucker off it's stand and literally drug it all the way down Market Street behind their truck, sparks flying, skid marks and all, to it's new location, and had it ready to erect early the next morning. When I arrived, John and his crew were busy re-setting the *Phelan Statue* (a bronze likeness of the *squealer* that caused the California gold rush in 1849 in the first place), with it's arms outstretched and mouth wide open supposedly shouting, "Thar's gold in them thar hills." Anyway while the city's inspector and I were watching the crew work, for no other reason than to be helpful I said, "When I was in Salt Lake City the last time, I noticed Brigham Young's Statue was set with his back to the church and his arms out stretched to the bank. What's wrong with doing the same thing here?" The city inspector said, "Hey, the Mayor would love the statue facing his bank, let's do it." Well, knowing my big mouth and all, John glared at me while his crew repositioned the statue to face the bank, because he knew I might try adding even more frosting to the cake. You guessed it, to be even more helpful, I suggested the statue should also be lowered at least two feet so pedestrians could get the full impact, and the city inspector nodded in agreement once again.

Oooh boy, later on when a sulking John Little and I were having a beer to celebrate the successful

My Stepmother Ercel, Mary Beth and Dad at the graduation

completion of our tough little job, I'll tell you he really unloaded on me, and I mean cuss words and all. He shouted, "Damn you Homer, it was bad enough your twisting that *squealer* around to face the bank, but you could have gone all day long without telling them to lowering that sucker the last two feet. I had all my profit and overhead in that *granite base block item* you had the City delete from our contract and now I won't make one damn dime on this job." I smiled and said, "John, what I like most about you is the way you take troubling things like a man. Fortunately, I made a bundle on my share of that job, so *Skoal! John, the beers are on me.*" John just shook his head in disbelief (and disgust), and finally said, "Homer, I'll tell you what. In appreciation for what you've gone out of your way to do for me, and as a little going away present from me to you when you keel over, I'll make a headstone for you out of that damn block of granite I'm stuck with. What would you like your *epitaph* to say?" Whoowee, choking up with both emotion and flem, I tearfully answered, "John, I want to thank you from the bottom of my heart for this thoughtful gift. Just make a simple headstone with the *epitaph* reading, *"See there Joyce, I told you I was sick."*

To give you some idea of the stupid stunts binge drinkers can and will pull after a few belts, one of my binge drinking buddies named, C. Harper and I decided to joint venture a sewer pipeline contract in Sacramento and after walking the job two or three times during the day, we returned to my Danville office to adjust our estimate. Well, around 7:00 pm, we decided to adjourn for dinner at the Danville Hotel and I remember after sitting at the crowded hotel's bar waiting for our seating for about an hour slobbering drinks, Harper said, "This is ridiculous, let's go to my restaurant where we can get something to eat", and went to a telephone to make reservations. Well, when he came back and said, "Let's go, I've made reservations, but we've got to hurry", we took off *wide open* in Harper's car towards Jack London's Square for I thought our dinner. Believe it or not, we screeched to a skidding stop at the Oakland Airport just in time to catch our flight, and I can truthfully say I had

the best steak dinner I've ever had before or since, after checking into our four star hotel for the night. The next morning after breakfast, I called my first wife Janet to say, "Guess where I'm calling from?" and when she said, "It better by God, be a long way from here because the way I feel right now I could break your damn neck." I said, "I'm in Las Vegas" and *click,* she hung up. Oooh boy, and when Harper got the same reaction from his loving wife Connie we both said to hell with it, let's

My new USS Akvavit Motorsailor parked at dockside

stay a couple more days until they simmer down. Well you guessed it, we never turned in our bid, I barely broke even on the card tables and Harper lost $3,000 shooting crap, and after three days of fun and hilarity, we both staggered home to face up to the music and take the silent treatment, but Oooh boy, what a wonderful relaxing three day mini vacation from the harsh realities of life.

MAJOR NEWS RELEASE DURING 1975

Mayhem breaks out as U. S. leaves Saigon, the Vietnam war ends with over 50,000 American servicemen and total war deaths at 1,300,000 on both sides, President Ford escapes two assassination attempts, Jimmy Hoffa disappears, the Toxic Substance Control Act phases out PCBs, Lyme disease is identified in Lyme, CT., President Ford signs the Metric Conversion Act, Apollo 18 docks with Soyuz 19, Digital watches and VCRs are introduced, national unemployment reaches nine percent, Bill Gates and Paul Allen found Microsoft, and Vietnamese "boat people" begin to arrive in the United States

Mary Beth graduated from the University of Hawaii in 1976 with a useless BA degree in Fine Arts Puppetry and everyone in the family showed up in Hawaii for the occasion, including my dad and my stepmother. It was also the year I bought a used 34 foot Monk designed Motorsailor I named *AKVAVIT* (water life) built by the Skookum Boatworks in Port Townsend, Washington. For some unknown reason during a business trip to Bremerton, Washington to bid on a new Submarine dock at the Navy Base, I swung by Port Orchard to look at an interesting *for sale* Motorsailer in the marina. My God, to my surprise two young married kids were living on board with their six month old baby and I felt so sorry for them I gave them what they asked ($30,000) for their boat, to pay down on a two bedroom house

they really needed, and had the boat shipped to the San Leandro marina in California. My brother Rodger died suddenly of liver failure (and Alcoholism) in 1976 and it was also the

Mary Beth and Dear Old Dad at the graduation

year I experienced my first serious eye operation for a retina detachment and came very close to going blind in my left eye. In fact it was shortly after Rodger passed away and I had my eye operation I began thinking seriously about cashing in all my company stock and sailing my *new* 34 foot motorsailor sailboat single-handed to Hawaii, and beyond.

Mary Beth presented her Fine Arts Theater Masters Thesis (to get her MA Degree in children's theater) in a play production called, the *Last Unicorn*, at the University of Hawaii in 1977, and once again all our family was present. I said, "I'm so proud of you Mary Beth. You've always been such a good leader, planner and organizer, I think you should run our construction company some day" to which she grimaced, "No way Dad." Anyway I still wish she hadn't been so turned off math and science by her hippy peers and liberal touchy feely teachers, and had at least gone for a

Damn the torpedo's, full speed ahead

meaningful MBA Degree or something worthwhile. She has the personality the brains and all the qualifications necessary to be an engineer or to pursue an MBA Degree, or anything meaningful she might want to do to better her lot in life. As it all turned out, her MA from the University of Hawaii was a complete waste of time.

MAJOR NEWS RELEASES DURING 1977

President Carter pardons Vietnam War draft dodgers, Tokyo Rose is also pardoned, Carter makes "human rights" a part of the U. S. foreign policy, the neutron bomb is developed, fluorocarbons are banned as aerosol propellants, balloon angioplasty is developed for opening clogged arteries, insulin is produced from genetically engineered bacteria, the MRI scanner is developed, the Apple II personal computer is marketed, VHS recorders are introduced, "Star Wars" by George Lucas is introduced, the "Gossamer Condor" is the first human powered airplane.

Our second daughter Barbara kept busy traveling back and forth between Alaska working with her friend Pauline and to and from Europe leading museum tour groups for her college foreign languages credits at Evergreen College in Washington, (another playtime school) while our son Bob was making his dad proud as a model student at San Ramon High School in Danville, California.

There was a lull period in the clean water program that made 1976 and 1977 tough competitive years for our company, but fortunately Muni Railroad in San Francisco advertised street car track replacement contracts for bid that kept us going temporarily. As luck would have it we picked up six track jobs, two electrical duct trench and street reconstruction brick paving jobs, plus a new gravel plant for the Lone Star Gravel Company in Sacramento that fortunately kept us in business during that year.

The remainder of the family at Mary Beth's graduation

I was asked to give our bonding company, the Industrial Indemnity Insurance Company, a thumbnail sketch of our company and the following is a copy of the speech I gave at their 'Seminar on March 30, 1978.

Bill Eaglton asked me how we monitored our company so perhaps this slide will generate questions in that regard.

The construction business is a people business like no other and since all businesses have more or less the same financial and equipment capabilities, the only difference is how good one company's organization is compared to the other. My old boss, Peter Kiewit said one time, "There is no such thing as business failures, only people failures. Every time a business fails or succeeds, there are people failing or succeeding. Every bit of credit or blame for success or failure must be laid right at the feet of management, not to labor, not to chicken inspectors, not to the government, not to the economy, but to the management of that company."

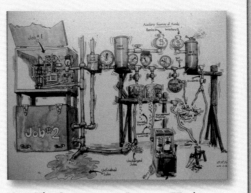

How The Construction Business Works

To be successful in the heavy engineering construction business, besides being profit minded, you must have experienced craftsmen, foreman, engineer-estimator-superintendents, and experienced cost control and accounting people. You must also have experienced legal advice and council and you must have the confidence of your banker and people like all of you in this room, your surety company. While it is true no one should withhold information from his doctor or his lawyer, it is also true no contractor should withhold information about his business from his surety and his banker. He should always keep them advised with quarterly financial statements cash flow projections and job cost reports, as well as audited annual profit and loss statements.

429

As a closed corporation, our employee owned company is basically setup along the same lines as that old Viking code (those who pull on the oars will share in the plunder) because all our key employee stockholders have 'a piece of the action' by owning stock. We believe in what I call 'democratic capitalism in action' because our company's goal is to build substantial estates for all the people who help our company grow. Unlike bureaucracies who think of their employees as only social security numbers, our employees, regardless of rank, know each other as friends. We not only strive to provide our employees with a safe and healthy place to work, but also strive for job continuity and security. We believe in fairness for all and in rewarding for superior performance, and we believe everyone from the bottom to the top of the totem pole, having a say in bettering our company's performance. Lord help us if the future management of this company ever lose sight of these beliefs.

Since I came up through the engineering and field operations ranks, my hiring and servicing policy leans more towards the project manager and job superintendent level, and in supplying them with whatever help they need to build their projects more efficiently and profitably. Larger and larger contracts are being let for bid nowadays that are much more complicated and have shorter time schedules. As a result the project managers have become combination engineer-estimator-superintendents and the motivating team leaders of these fast track contracts. Unfortunately, like qualified certified welders, people of project manager caliber are also in critically short supply, and finding and training good people to build these tougher contracts, is the answer.

It takes time to find good people, and especially good hard working qualified trained and experienced people who will work together as an inspired motivated team. Teamwork, and especially motivated teamwork, does not just happen, it only grows over time. To me, it grows from opportunity, from loyalty, from fair treatment, from friendships, and from a mutual respect for each other's abilities and expertise while working together towards a common goal. It was only after getting my engineering degree and fifteen years of apprenticing with another good company to learn this business I felt qualified to startup my own construction company. After these last fifteen years of running my own company, I look at our company's organization now as not only my second family, but as a motivated qualified team of hard working experienced people, all working towards a common goal.

I can't tell you how proud I am of the people who make up our company's organization. and if you will bear with me, I'd like to read the 1978 personnel summary of the thirty three (33) salaried people (twenty five of whom are shareholders), who make up our company.

1. Their average age is 41.6 years.

2. Twenty seven (27) have college credits of which twenty (20) have earned their college degrees and six (6) of the twenty have advanced degrees

3. Eight (8) of the twenty graduates are also registered professionally of which five (5) are registered Civil Engineers, one (1) a CPA, one (1) a practicing Attorney, and one (1) a licensed Land Surveyor.

4. Their construction experience totals over five hundred years and encompasses nearly every phase of the heavy engineering and the commercial building fields. It includes experience in everything from dams, tunnels, canals, highways, bridges, airports, railroads, treatment plants and buildings, to pile driving, iron work, slip forming, and mechanical work. As a group, they are exceptionally well qualified to build complicated fast track contracts of an unusual nature and their schooling in management techniques and training in construction engineering make them exceptionally well qualified to build rapid, multi-craft, high risk construction contracts, profitably.

Thank you for the privilege of being part of your seminar today, and thank you again for all your excellent questions during this presentation.

Thank you.

It was in 1978 I received the terribly sad news two of my business friends, Gordon Ball and Dick Shephard had suddenly passed away from heart attacks. Gordon sold his company to the Dillingham Corporation only a few years earlier and had just finished serving his management agreement to begin enjoying his retirement when he had his fatal heart attack. Dick had purchased his dream boat named, *Black Bart* only recently and had suffered his fatal attack while doing maintenance work on his sailboat. With my brother Rodger now also gone, and when another good friend, C. Harper suddenly passed away the following year in 1979 from pneumonia and Janet filing for a divorce, whatever optimism I had about the future suddenly disappeared. I began to feel my marriage, my business career, and my whole life in general was now all a waste and I should have stayed on Gravelbed farm milking cows and herding sheep all my life like my dad wanted me to. I had reached the lowest and most depressing period in my life.

Lesson Learned: *The problem with growing older other than deteriorating health, is, our travel lanes along the highway of life gradually begin to narrow, first to a slower lane and then to only a winding path as more and more of our friends, relatives, and business partners pass away, leaving a void in our lives that can never be replaced.*

I first met Dick Shephard in 1969 when Gordon Ball and I became interested in bidding the light rail rapid transit work for BARTD (Bay Area Rapid Transit District) and Dick was their corporate secretary who showed us around explaining their program to us. Interestingly, after our tour and lunch later, I learned Dick and I had a lot in common. He was not only a weatherman in the Army Air Forces like me during the war, but was sent to northern China in early 1945 to setup and man the same weather station I might have been assigned to study the high winds aloft problem (called jet streams today) with our secret radar equipment. If the battle for Okinawa had not ended two weeks before my final Chanute Field training was completed, and had not canceled my shipping orders, we might have run that Chinese weather station together. Like me, *Shep* was interested in sailing, and while we were on the San Francisco Bay one weekend on his sailboatnamed the *Black Bart*, I discovered he

Janet, my dad and my Stepmother Ercel, on the first train with Dick Shephard

was also a tried and true Scandinavian-American *Akvavit Skoaler* (binge drinker) just like me and my other good contractor friend, C. Harper. You guessed it, the three of us, along with several other good buddies, had many hilarious binge drinking wife worrying dinners together after work shooting the breeze at John's Grill during those fun years building the 75 mile long Bay Area Rapid Transit Districts light rail system.

Christmas Letter – 1978

Skoal!!! You can believe this or not, but I honestly felt I would have some exciting plundering and pillaging stories to tell everyone about sailing the AKVAVIT (water life) to the South Pole this past year, but unfortunately I was unable to untie the dock line knots to leave the slip. It not only takes more time to untie lines than I figured, but I also needed a lot more kroners to properly equipt my assault vessel to attack a fortification as formidable as the South Pole. And besides all that, I couldn't get a crew together because rumors were flying around town the skipper had flipped his lid. So anyway, maybe next year I'll have launched my one ship invasion fleet and will have some exciting sagas to tell.

Our daughter, Mary Beth, graduated from the University of Hawaii this past year with a Master's degree in Children's Theater (puppetry) and is currently pounding the pavement in New York with her friend Pam looking for work in their field and Pam got the plumb "Muppets" job they were both interviewed for. Our second daughter, Barbara, is also looking for work after being caught up in an economy "reduction in force" of state personnel in Alaska, so both girls will be home for Christmas. Our son Bob, is doing great in high school this year. He's also involved in Junior Achievement and got his drivers license this year. The Prop 13 cuts eliminated Janet's teaching job so she's taking several night school courses now, mostly in printing and lithography.

Our son Bob, was only one year old when we started our company, so I thought one way to describe our company's growth, was to equate it to his growth. At age(16) sixteen, Bob is a junior in high school now and is six feet tall and weighs 152 pounds. Interestingly, he is exactly the same height and weight I was when I enlisted in the Army Air Corps in 1942, only I was eighteen years old then. As with Bob, our company has grown a little taller every year in the industry, and we have even made the ENR top four hundred contractors list a couple of times. We are still trying to maintain our lean and mean and clean trim image, but with our youth as a company, we still have a lot more to learn.

This year will mark our company's fifteenth year in the construction business and despite a few traumatic experiences and losing contracts; I believe we have established a steady pattern of growth. This year will also be my thirtieth year in the construction business, so I guess (and I shudder to think about it) I'll have to begin planning my 'phase out' and eventual retirement.

Bob Olsen -1978

At our Thanksgiving dinner this year, my younger brother Steve asked, "Instead of giving our traditional thanksgiving prayer, why don't we go around the table and have each person state all the things he or she are most thankful for?" It was a stimulating way to have me, and I think some of the others, start thinking more positively, and it worked. After the first few humorous jokes of not having this turkey to kick around anymore had subsided, everyone suddenly become very humble, quite and emotional ---and thankful for all the many blessings we have and enjoy in this wonderful country of ours, the United States of America.. We all have so much to be thankful for. Have a Merry Christmas and a happy New Year.

Ole and family

NEWS RELEASES DURING 1978

Californians revolt against high property taxes and approve Proposition 13, Carter gives the Panama Canal to the Panamanians, Jim Jones orders cult followers to commit mass suicide in Guyana, the Airline Deregulation Act phases out regulations, 'Double Eagle II' becomes the first balloon to cross the Atlantic, Gambling casinos open in Atlantic City, Jogging outfits become fashionable and a cartoon called 'Garfield the cat' is introduced.

On April 2, 1979, I received the following letter from my oldest daughter, Mary Beth in New York. She was still trying to find work in either the theater or the Muppets, and apparently she and her younger sister Barbara, thought I was extremely depressed (which was true) and might even be suicidal.

April 2, 1979

Dear Dad,

How are you? I really wish you would write me or call. I feel like you could use someone to talk to and I want you to feel you can confide in me. You've done so much for me all these years and I want to support you now, emotionally anyway. Bow told me you were feeling very sad and depressed, and that you are in a crises situation and none of us know what will happen.

Psychologists say that when a person experiences change the concept of death comes up a lot for them. This is natural and is the old dying identity, so to speak. But it does not mean that you should take yourself too seriously. You are growing, and searching for an identity of sorts. Growth is always painful, even baby teeth being pulled is painful so new teeth can grow. You are not old Dad; you still have many happy beautiful productive years to live. You have three children who love you so very much, and who will never stop loving you no matter what you do. You are a great man Dad, not just good, and you have that spark that differentiates between the two. You also have my undying respect. Accept our love Dad, let it sink in. Embrace life and friendship while you have it. I love you and I always will.

Always your daughter, Meem.

My two daughters were right about my depression during that period because I always felt tired and down in the dumps, but not suicidal. The loss of relatives and so many good friends along with my failing marriage coupled with my feelings of management obsolescence and early retirement fears could have been part of the problem, but who knows, maybe it was just *mid life crises*. My dad called to request his retirement from our board for the good of the company and because he was now eighty one years old. He also felt the company's management structure should be changed to a five member employee-shareholder board, instead of our current three members of Janet, Dad and me, and closed with, "Son, I think you should delegate more and take some time off for health reasons."

When I told Bill Ames what Dad recommended, he said, "I agree, and I also think you should make Gerald Clair the new company president instead of your choice, Arne Glick, when you move up to Chairman of the Board. If you still want Arne as president, make damn sure the new board gives you an employment contract with the CEO title along with board chairman, because Arne will clean house of any and all competition, with you first on his list. Mark my words Homer, Arne Glick is not the man you think he is." Oooh boy, was Bill ever right and he obviously understood people better than me, especially the personality

Arne Glick, Mr. Aki, Homer Olsen and Henry Trainer

changes that can take place in some people when they are given a power title. Like my army friend, Phil George when he made 2nd Lt., and Zel Mullican when I made him a vice president, Arne's personality also changed dramatically for the worse when I mistakenly made him company's president and took my sabbatical. He not only turned into an obnoxious Hitler type dictator, but crippled our company even more by forcing some of our best money making superintendents like Bill Young, Dave Stacy and Bob Witbeck, to quit and start up their own successful construction companies.

In September of 1979, shortly after Arne was elected president and I was given my half time-half pay job title of Chairman and CEO with a ten year employment contract, Jim Wilton and I had a dinner meeting at Doro's restaurant in San Francisco to discuss a tunneling Joint Venture proposal from the Obayashi Company in Japan that Jim was familiar with. Unfortunately, we didn't adjourn our meeting (Jim left earlier while I stayed) until Doro's closing bell rang and the bar crowd and I went our separate ways. You guessed it, while unlocking my car parked on a dark side street I was high jacked and kidnapped by two young black guys, and barely escaped with my life.

As I unlocked my car to drive home, two young blacks in their late teens or early twenties suddenly appeared from nowhere, and the one pointing a handgun at my head shouted, "Give us your wallet and glasses." Fortunately, I had paid our dinner tab with my credit card so I still had the $200 in cash I had stopped at the bank earlier for expenses, and as it turned out that $200 saved my life. I handed them my wallet saying, "You can have the cash, but I need my wallet and glasses back because I can't see without them." Interestingly, after they split the $200, they seemed less nervous and surprisingly handed my wallet back, but kept my glasses saying, "Now give us your car keys and get down low in the front seat." After the guy driving got in and the other climbed in back to keep his gun trained on my head, we took off wide open towards Oakland, and surprisingly I wasn't afraid. Maybe being half looped helped, or maybe old man Crawford's advice, "Never let mean animals know you're afraid of them because if you do, they will kill you", was the reason. I said, "I was a cab driver a few years back, so I'll be glad to drive you two guys where you want to go, then we can go our separate ways", and the one driving shouted, "I'll do the driving dude, keep your head down." and that's when I began feeling nervous and thinking, "Ooh boy, what have I got myself into this time?." All the while the one driving was weaving and zigzagging around traffic at high speed to get on the Bay Bridge towards Oakland, I was hunkered down in the front seat wondering if I had enough insurance for my family to live on after I was gone, and where are the cops when they're needed. Finally, my two heroin addicts (as it turned out) pulled into a dark alley next to a warehouse off Powell Street in Emeryville, and got out to hand their dope peddler their two $100 bills for two badly needed heroin hits. For some unknown reason I still wasn't trembling with fear like I should, or would if I were an actor in a movie, so I waited quietly until their dealer drove away and my relieved kidnappers were enjoying their hits and began inching slowly towards the driver's side to escape. Oooh Boy, as bad luck will continue sometimes, just as I was about to start the car to escape without my glasses, I felt the cold barrel end of a gun pressed over my left ear through the drivers open window, and thought, "Oooh boy. Now I've really done it."

Well, after my captors were in the car again and I was hunkered down in the front seat, we began careening around street corners at high speed towards West Oakland while the two black guys discussed what to do about me. The one in the back seat waving his gun around argued, "I'm already a three time loser so it won't make any difference now how many more kills I have. Let's waste this dude." Fortunately for me, the driver apparently liked me a little because he said, "No, he's a good guy, let's --", and I butted in with, "If you two guys will give my glasses back and drop me off at the next corner, you can have the car." Whooee, all of a sudden we skidded to a screeching stop and the driver picked up my glasses, smashed them on the cars steering wheel, and threw the broken pieces at me screaming, "Get out." I'll tell you, when I jumped out I barely cleared the open car door as he took off wide open (to prevent the one in back from killing me), screeching two smoking tire tracks on the pavement, and disappeared into the night. Two weeks later, the Oakland police found my abandoned company car I had traded to them earlier for my life, wreaked and stripped in Oakland somewhere, and returned it to me for recycling.

Anyway, to summarize this exciting little drama of life, after the two new owners of my car dropped me off, I jogged along a dark unlit street up to McArthur Blvd., and with the pocket change they left me, I telephoned the Oakland Police from a motel pay phone to report my experience. By the time the police officer finished taking my testimony over coffee at an all night restaurant on Broadway somewhere and Janet arrived to pick me up, it was 4:00 o'clock in the morning and Ooh boy, was Janet mad or was she ever mad. As for as she was concerned, this little skidmark experience along the highway of my life was the last straw that broke the camel's back, and she booted me out of our house and filed for divorce. Unfortunately, I was unable to positively identify the kidnappers because of my poor eyesight without glasses, so the case was dropped and I moved in with my mother in Pleasant Hill and called for a special board meeting to request a leave of absence. On my mother's recommendation, I checked into the St. Helena Hospital's Alcoholics Ward afterwards to dry out and hopefully, start putting my life back together again.

If you've ever tried to negotiate a divorce settlement (or anything else) with lawyers who know less than nothing about running a meaningful business enterprise and/or business economics in general, you'll know it's a memorable experience. Unbelievably, both Janet's attorney and mine were like my stepmother (and some other people I know) who actually believed, if you have a million dollar construction contract, you will make a million dollars profit. After showing both attorneys our company's financial statements, and they both had taken their several hour course in business economics 101 from Murry Regensburger, our company's auditor (to increase their chargeable hours), my attorney finally said, "My god, I make more money than you do Homer, you're nuts to be in the construction business." Unfortunately, Janet's attorney never got the message that honest construction contractors only make an average net profit of 1% after taxes on their yearly volume, and the best of us only make 2%. Amazingly he was and is still convinced, I had several million dollars hidden out in Swiss Bank accounts somewhere because of the impressive volume of work we constructed, and therefore he reasoned, we should have made that amount in profit. Oooh boy, finally I told that bonehead he could have all the money he could find in any bank I hadn't already told him and everyone else, where we had funds. As far as I know, he's still looking for all that fictitious money somewhere, but fortunately it's on his own time.

When Janet and I were first married in 1949, we were both flat broke with a negative net worth and in debt up to our eyebrows, but we both had good jobs. Janet taught English at Porterville high school that first year while I worked as an engineer trainee for Peter Kiewit on the Friant-Kern Canal, and by living frugally, we scraped and saved enough together to pay off all our debts, and during the next 14 years, increased our net worth to $90,000 by the time we started our own company in 1963. Of that amount, $35,000 was invested in our home, car and personal property, and the remainder in Kiewit stock. When I quit Kiewit and sold our stock, Gordon Ball and I formed a 50/50 joint venture partnership, and when we were low bidder on our first job (Hwy 85) on October 3, 1963 we each put up $27,500 in cash (half of what Janet and I had left) to get the job started. Interestingly that $27,500 amount we put up, bought us 5,500 shares of Homer J Olsen, Inc., $5 par value stock that increased in value to $290.85 per share in the next 18 years, and increased our $27,500

MAJOR NEWS RELEASE DURING 1979

*The U. S. Embassy in Iran is seized and 52 hostages are taken, Carter engineers peace accord (?) between Israel and Egypt at Camp David, Diplomatic relations are established with Beijing, A near melt down occurs at Three Mile Island nuclear plant, U. S. Supreme Court upholds affirmative action, The Department of Education attains Cabinet level status, the first case of Aids is diagnosed, the inflation rate is 13.3%, Chrysler Corporation receives a 1.5 billion dollar federal loan, Oil embargo forces gasoline rationing, A black hole is discovered in the center of the galaxy, Skylab crashes to earth, and **after 30 unhappy years of marriage to a binge drinking red neck workaholic alcoholic, Janet files for divorce.***

investment to a whopping $1,600,000. When that amount was added to our share of the company's retirement plan along with our home and other assets, our total net worth reached $2,200,000 that we split equally when we were divorced. I told Janet's attorney (Janet never spoke to me again after she booted me out) if she would waive the alimony I would take full responsibility for our three children's college educational expenses and financial requirements, and she could have first pick of all our fixed and liquid assets as her half. Janet agreed, and after we paid our horrendously high and un-necessary legal fees, our divorce was finalized on January 22, 1981, sixteen months after Janet first filed her divorce papers.

For some unknown reason, I assumed Janet would want the family home we bought in Alamo, so I bought a two bedroom marina condominium in Alameda for myself for $165,000, and moved out of my mother's house with my sailboat and 1929 Model "A" Ford, to my new home. Oooh boy, after escrow closed, Janet decided she didn't want any part of our Alamo house, or the sailboat, or the Model "A", or the Utah mountain cabin, or the Pleasant Hill house (our first home) my mother was living in rent free, because all those things reminded her of me and when she thought about me, she got sick. Instead, she only wanted her car, cash for her 50% share in HJO Inc. stock, a new house free and clear she had found for $300,000 somewhere near Lafayette, and our free and clear Sycamore Valley acreage we purchased several years earlier for a potential multi-home development project someday. Unbelievably, she also wanted $3,000 for her cash value share of my 1942 $10,000 Army insurance policy. Anyway, for all that, she agreed to forfeit alimony and her half interest in the company's retirement plan, the Alamo house and our few remaining assets and liabilities. After agreeing to all her demands, I felt a little like Ole when he and Lena were divorced. Ole said, "Vi split every ting vi owned right down the middle. Lena got the tunnel and I got the shaft." But, as my mother used to say, "Everything that happens, happens for the best", and she was right. Our divorce was a blessing for both of us.

Well you guessed it. Without Janet's stock for support and me now having only a 30% interest instead of my former 60% ownership in our democratic company founded on that old Viking Code (those who pull on the oars will share in the plunder), I no longer enjoyed running the company like a benevolent dictator. After the newly elected five man board finished reviewing my request to sell some more of my shares to buy Janet her new $300,000 house and to pay off some liabilities, it was rejected. They had already set aside $800,000 to buy back Janet's stock, and when the company's new president, Arne Glick, unilaterally committed another $1,250,000 of the company's working capital towards building a fancy new office building to look more important and needed like a hole in our heads, it really tightened the noose on our company operations. My divorce, combined with my mistaken appointment of Arne as president, shocked everyone in the company and when Arne's new job assignment changed his personality into another Adolph Hitler, some of our key people gathered up their gear and quit, crippling our company further.

I can truthfully say, the loneliest, saddest, and most depressing Xmas eve I have ever spent in my life was on December 24, 1979 while sitting alone in my Alameda condominium staring into the fireplace and feeling my whole life had been a waste. As I sat there tearfully listening to Xmas carols and recalling (and *skoaling*) all the costly judgment mistakes I made during my lifetime, I got so plastered I passed out on the living room couch. Fortunately, my three children called on Xmas day to wish me a merry Xmas and bless their hearts, tearfully confirm they still loved me despite everything that had happened. I drove over to Pleasant Hill for a wonderful home cooked Xmas dinner with my mother and to re-hear her inspiring pep talks about quitting my drinking. Reluctantly (but fortunately), my good banker friend, Dick Hoffman, loaned me the $300,000 I needed to buy Janet her new house and finalize our divorce (at prime plus two with a three year payback), so all in all, things began looking up again. Better yet, my late friend's widow and a couple of divorcees I knew, began delivering casseroles (bless their hearts) to my Alameda condominium to keep me from starving to death and give my morale a boost.

Bob's High School Graduation

It was while living a stressful womanizing bachelor's life dating six different *Homer's Angels* six different nights a week an interesting thing happened. John Lamberson and I were having a quick drink after work one day and four young women in an adjacent booth sent us a round of drinks, so naturally we responded by sending them a round back, and continued talking business. Well, wouldn't you know it, when they sent us another round I said, "Hey John, I'm single now so let's move to their booth and get acquainted" and we introduced ourselves. Well, as it turned out, they all worked for the telephone company and I ended up inviting the one of Swedish decent named, Helen Dahlberg, to a Norwegian Club dinner party the following Thursday, and she accepted. Well, to make a long story shorter, besides being too young and immature for me, Helen wasn't my type and I certainly wasn't hers, but we stayed good friends and interestingly, she kept telling me about an older (age 52) divorced supervisor of hers in their telephone company office named Alice Joyce Deyoe, she thought was my kind of gal and I (age 56) should meet her.

In June of 1980 my son Bob graduated from San Ramon High School in Danville, California, while my mother and I were proudly watching him receive his diploma. As I recall it was shortly after his graduation ceremonies Bob announced he only wanted to major in business and accounting in college and wasn't interested in engineering and/or apprenticing with our construction company to run it some day as I had hoped. His mother wanted him to become a history teacher at some college somewhere so I said, "Bob, if you will shoot for an MBA Degree, I'll back you", which he did and ended up getting a duel major degree in Economics and History (to please his mother) fromSonoma State in Santa Rosa, California and an MBA Degree from the University of Southern California in Los Angeles (to please me). Bob is now happily married to Donna Barton Olsen and they have one child named Kyle James Olsen, and is busy running his own successful Accounting Firm servicing over 300 client accounts in Danville, California.

Well, as you've already guessed, it didn't take long for me to get sick and tired of womanizing and dating my selfish, whining, spoiled rotten *Angels* so I called Helen for a platonic dinner date to discuss setting up a *let's git acquainted* type party (with the idea of meeting her friend, Joyce) for unmarried couples. I told her several of my single male bachelor friends and I were sick and tired of being lonesome bachelors, and suggested we sponsor a singles working people's party for her hard working telephone company single girl friends, and my

Bob Olsen, his D.O.D.. and Grandma Ruth Galloway Weimer

hard working red neck bachelor buddies. Well, she thought it would be fun so I reserved a table for ten couples at the St. Francis Yacht Club around the middle of July in 1980 and to show some class, I choose lamb chops (actually mutton chops) as our gourmet entrée. Whooee, I'll tell you for a party that came within an inch of disaster, it ended up happily for the few survivors who stayed on for the mouth watering feast, but for me, the party ended up a *tunder and lightning* awakening. My dad always said I would see the light some day, and

A typical April Club meeting for a typical important reason

Oooh boy was he ever right. I finally got to meet that wonderful girl of my dreams named Alice Joyce Deyoe

As it so happened, our quarterly April Club luncheon was scheduled the same day at the engineers club as our singles dinner party at the Yacht Club, and when Helen called that morning to announce she had twenty (not ten) women signed up, I nearly fainted. In fact I was so discombobulated (a legal

term) by her announcement I completely forgot to tell her some of my bachelor friends had chickened out and there was no way I could deliver the ten single guys I promised. Ooh boy, now what do I do? Well, you guessed it, I stood up at the April Club meeting during *new business* and gave such an award winning passionate pleading speech it brought tears (of laughter) to the eyes of everyone in the room. None of them had ever seen anyone squirm, sweat, or heard them beg so emotionally as me and between guffaws, unanimously voted my speech the winner of the club's *hilariously funny* award. Finally, to help out a

friend in an embarrassing bind, one bachelor and three married members volunteered to pry their wedding rings off for the evening, and as promised, I confidently sashshayed into the Yacht Club that evening like John Wayne himself, with all my *giggling gang of nine* bachelors(?).

Oooh boy, when the nineteen early arriving women saw me and all my *giggling gang of nine* bashful sheepherders sashay into the Yacht Club doing their occasional road apple sidestep hops, they concluded immediately they had been *conned*. I'll tell you, all hell suddenly broke loose into a prize winning adult berserk behavior a two year old would envy, and after all the purse slapping, cuss shouting, hair pulling, and insulting gesturing subsided somewhat, most of the women and all of my scared married men scampered out,

The happy couple, Joyce and Homer-1982

leaving me holding the bag for all the damages and my *expensive mutton entrée*s, without a date. Worse yet, after enduring Helen's spirited cuss shouting and embarrassing gestures before she stomped out, I never saw, heard from, or had courage enough to ever call her again to apologize.

Oooh boy, anyway to shorten this exciting story a little, after the dust had settled somewhat and I was sitting discombobulated (I love that word) in the deathly silent Yacht Club lobby thinking to myself, "You really went out of your way this time to mess things up", the few survivors were nervously leaning against the bar sipping their drinks and whispering, "Now what?." Suddenly, like an angel from heaven the most beautiful well dressed fifty two year old young girl I have ever seen, sashayed into the lobby Montana style like Gary Cooper himself, and asked me where the Olsen–Dahlberg party

Homer J. courting his future wife,
Alice Joyce Deyoe

was being held. Oooh boy, I was so *awestruck* by her striking beauty I began stuttering like a fish bowl guppy and said, "Yyoou must be Jjjoyce?" When she laughingly nodded yes, I waved to our group at the bar to *light up the candles, the party's about to begin,* and escorted this beautiful lady from Lewistown, Montana, to a table seat next to me. Honest to God, and you can believe this story or not, your choice, but this is the true story of how I met that beautiful girl God sent to me from heaven to be my wonderful wife the remainder of my life.

After our spectacularly successful dinner with all the hilariously funny Utah sheepherder and Montana cowboy stories and Ole and Lena jokes as frosting, our *let's git acquainted* bachelor party came to a happy ending at Turk Murphy's on the Embarcadero, dancing up a storm until their 2:00 am closing hour. Unfortunately, with all the confusion during all the good night hugs, I nearly fainted when I got home to discover I had stupidly forgotten to ask Joyce for her telephone number. Oooh boy, I had also promised my son, Bob, we would take the jeep up to my Utah high mountain cabin (elevation 10,500 feet) the next day to fish for trout, do some hiking, build model airplanes together, and to just shoot the breeze whittling sticks and barbecuing steaks for each other. We took off bright and early the next morning with

Flying Model Airplanes is not for Sissies

me thinking I could find Joyce again someway somehow, and believe it or not, when Bob

See there Bob, I told you it would fly

and I returned three weeks later with our wide grins, stubble beards and pealing from sunburn to go through our mail, Oooh boy, there it was. A thank you note from Joyce for the wonderful time she had at our wonderful gourmet *mutton* party, with her telephone number and a post script saying, "Call me when you get back. I'd like to hear all about your fishing trip with Bob."

I'll tell you, despite our *fiasco first date* where I had to eat all her dinner and mine too because she got sick and heaved all over the outside of my car door while driving her home, Joyce and I had a fantastic whirlwind romantic courtship. During the next ten months while we were courting and getting better acquainted, the more I learned about her, the

more I loved her. Besides being the *looker* Uncle Orson rightfully said she was, she was also no ordinary run of the mud *shooter* and there was no doubt in my mind about her, she was my kind of a gal and I had fallen for her, hook line and sinker.

We were *gunk holing* one weekend on my motor sailor, the *USS Akvavit* on San Francisco Bay and I'll tell you she cooked me the best pot roast and wine dinner on that sailboat's little kerosene stove I've ever

Master Helmsman Joyce Deyoe on duty

eaten, bar none. When I complimented her on her cooking and she answered, "My mother always said the shortest distance to a man's heart is through his stomach", I proposed to

MAJOR NEWS RELEASES DURING 1980

ABSCAM uncovers bribery of public officials, Carter encourages pregnant women to avoid caffeine, The EPA superfund is created, Toxic Shock Syndrome is reported, Love Canal is declared a disaster area due to toxic waste, AT&T begins marketing 900 numbers, cordless telephone become available, the Hunt brothers fail in their attempt to corner the silver market, Honda announces plans to build an Auto plant in the U. S., the Moscow Summer Olympics are boycotted by the U. S., The Mariel Boatlift brings 125,000 Cuban refugees to the U.S., A keystone cop mission engineered by Carter fails to rescue hostages, the national debt surpasses one trillion dollars, Mount St. Helens erupts in Washington State, Ronald Reagan and George H. Bush are elected President and VP of the United States, and 4,493,314 immigrants entered the U. S. during the previous decade to bring the U.S. population to 226,542,203.and, **God introduces Alice Joyce Deyoe to Homer J. Olsen at a St. Francis Yacht Club July dinner party in San Francisco, California.**

Water life

her on the spot and we became officially engaged on my 57th birthday, April 7, 1981, on the poop deck of my famous motor sailor, *The USS Akvavit.*

I called my old Stanford buddy and room mate in Reno, Nevada, Grove Holcomb, to ask him to make all the arrangements for our marriage and to be my best man if he would promise to stay sober long enough to hand me the wedding ring when needed, and he agreed.

Gladys and Bob Oakland flew in from Great Falls, Montana to size me up and down and stand up for Joyce's dad who couldn't make it, and Stan Summers who lived at Lake Tahoe agreed to serve as our usher. Oooh boy, despite Grover's sincere promise to stay temporarily sober, I still had to hold him up during the ceremony, and after all the confusion of the wedding party's knee walking search for the ring he dropped just as the minister nodded, that we found of all places, in Grover's pant leg cuff, we were married on Joyce's 53rd birthday, May 23, 1981, at the Silver Queen Saloon in Virginia City, Nevada. You guessed it, in order to settle everyone's nerves after our exhilarating wedding ceremony, the entire wedding party adjourned to the Blood and Guts Saloon

Homer & Joyce are married, May 23, 1981

across the street for libations and a hilarious relaxing unforgettable reception to wish the happy bride and groom *Bon voyage,* as they rode off into the sunset on a razorback mule named *Old Jack. (true story?).* Wow, and it was a fantastically wonderful wedding!!

Shortly afterwards, and my recommendation and encouragement, Joyce decided to retire after 29 years service with the telephone company to be a housewife and we paid off my ex-wife's new home loan and my remaining divorce liabilities by selling both our townhouses, and moved back into the Alamo house with my promise to stop drinking and only smoke my cigars

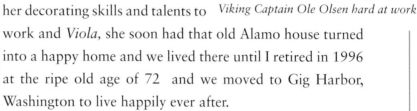

Viking Captain Ole Olsen hard at work

outside. Joyce immediately put her decorating skills and talents to work and *Viola,* she soon had that old Alamo house turned into a happy home and we lived there until I retired in 1996 at the ripe old age of 72 and we moved to Gig Harbor, Washington to live happily ever after.

The happy bride and groom in 1981

While we were still remodeling our Alamo home, Gerald Clair and Stan Summers suddenly appeared and said, "Homer, you've got to come back to work full time and run the company again. Without you, this company is going to hell in a hand basket under Arne Glick's iron fist, and we desperately need your leadership and God given *touch* again. Before you took your leave of absence to settle up your divorce, we picked up eight jobs (I got the Low Bidder Award that year) totaling $33,000,000 in new work, but now we're barely getting enough work to pay our water bill. Homer if you hadn't come back part time in September of 1980 to help us get that $50,000,000 west side job, we would only have picked up $10,000,000 in new work under Arne's command the last two years and the company would really be in trouble. We feel something's got to be done, and soon Homer, or we'll lose everything we've all worked so hard for." After Joyce and I discussed what we should do and she gave me her approval, I said, "OK, I'll be back to work full time, starting tomorrow morning."

Mike & Opal Holmes, Dad, Ercel, Joyce & Homer

MAJOR NEWS RELEASES DURING 1981

*Ronald Reagan and George Bush are sworn in as president and VP, Iran releases its U.S. hostages, The U.S. shoots down two Libyan jets, Reagan authorizes CIA domestic operations, Sandra Day O'Conner becomes the first women on the supreme court, Reagan signs the biggest tax cut bill in U.S. history, an assassination attempt on President Reagan's life fails, Reagan fires 12,000 striking PATCO employees ,two aerial walkways collapse killing 113 people at the Hyatt Regency Hotel in Kansas City, more women than men smoke cigarettes, the first test tube baby is born, IBM introduces the personal computer, VCR's become a household item, GM reports its first loss since 1921, space ship 'Columbia' makes her maiden voyage, **and best of all, Alice Joyce Deyoe and Homer J. Olsen are married in Virginia City, Nevada on May 23, 1981.***

Well, bright and early the next morning as promised, I reported for work thinking how lucky I was to still have the Chief Executive Officer's title (and authority), and began wading through a pile of paper the girls put on my desk. About an hour later, Arne's secretary

Back at work full time and catching up on paperwork

rushed in to tell me Arne wanted to see me in his office immediately, so I said, "You tell Arne my office is next to his, and my door is always open." I'll tell you when Arne stormed in, I can honestly say I have never seen so much hatred on anyone's face in my life as that man had on his for me. When he demanded, "What in Hell are you doing here?", I said, "Arne, it's interesting you would ask that question because I was going to ask you the same thing" and continued, "Close the door Arne and sit down, you and

I need to talk. "When I hired you in 1970 Arne, you told me you lost every dime you ever made working for Kiewit after you become the ruling partner in a Fresno paving company that went broke, and you literally begged me for a job. To help you out, I gave you a job with all our company benefits, and after you did so well on that Airport job, in appreciation I gave you a ten year stock option and paid you bonuses enough to exercise those options. Now you're stock and your share in our profit sharing (retirement) plan is worth well over a million dollars and for all that you hate my guts. Arne, I would like to know why?" When he wouldn't answer, I said, "I've been going through this pile of paper on my desk and I found this typed *agreement* you had our attorney prepare for my signature. The way I read it, you want me to sign over my CEO title and all my authority to you so you can have complete control running the company. For your information Arne, that will never happen."

Well to shorten this skidmarked story a little, when Arne correctly said, "No two people can run the same company at the same time doing the same job", and concluded with, "Homer, you should either quit or I should be fired to resolve this matter", I said, "OK Arne, you're fired." I'll tell you, Arne was so stunned by my unexpected answer he was quiet for a moment, but finally he said, "You can't fire me, the board is the only one who can fire the president of a company." I said, "OK, I'm still chairman of the board so to make it official, I'll call a meeting to fire you again", which we did. To this day, I still remember Arne storming out of that meeting vowing to sue me, and my answer back, "As far as I'm concerned Arne, when you walk out that door you just died." Unfortunately, none of us in the room that day knew, including Arne himself as a four pack a day smoker, he already had lung cancer and less than a year later, he died. My conscience still bothers me for making that cruel un-necessary remark when he left, but it also bothers me why I've always been so trusting of people and only see their good side.

The Happy Years – 1980 to 2010

The following is a copy of my 'State of the Company' speech at our shareholders meeting November 13, 1981.

THE STATE OF THE COMPANY – November 13, 1981

I know all of you are concerned about the recent changes in our company and I'm sure we can all agree the last two years will be remembered as years of worry and apprehension.

Two years ago we were essentially debt free and were in an exceptionally strong financial position for a company our size. Since that time we have built a fancy new office building for ourselves, bought several million dollars worth of new equipment, had one large job turn sour, and we are now in the process of buying back nearly 50% of our company from shareholders who have left the company for various reasons. So far, all this has been financed with our own company's working capital, and when it is coupled with the current tight economic situation and our apparent inability to obtain new work, it has been even more frustrating. And especially, since we have been second bidder on nearly $100,000,000 worth of work in our field this past year.

Fortunately for us, our bonding company and our banker are still supporting us and business cycles like this are temporary, so the only bad news is, our company's current situation demands we take immediate belt tightening measures to conserve our remaining assets until our company's financial situation improves. Therefore, effective immediately the following actions will be initiated.

1. All salaries will be frozen. If salary cuts become necessary, they will be only for officers and directors.

2. All bonuses will be eliminated until company earnings warrant their payment again.

3. To prevent further financial shock to our company, the current stock buy-sell agreement will be re-written and re-signed by all shareholders to allow the company a longer term buy-out schedule of payment (with interest) for any future departing shareholder.

In the olden days, journalism schools taught students to tell it like it is, with both the good news and the bad news, not just the bad news alone like the papers do today. The good news for us is, there is much we can be thankful for and can be optimistic about for our company. This past year will mark our 19th year in the heavy engineering construction business, and despite these last two 'spree spending' years, all nineteen of those years have shown successful steady growth. We were recently awarded job number 132, and the only bad news I can think of is, only 14 of those jobs (roughly 10%) lost money.

The good news is, many of the 118 other jobs we built beat their estimated costs enough to more than offset the losses on the 14 losing jobs. We still have $20,000,000 in carryover work on our books to complete, and since we first started in business, we've been the low bidder on $288,000,000 in contract volume (including our Joint Ventures) of which 75% or $216,000,000 is our share. Gerald's list of jobs to bid he discussed in his talk, is larger than last years list and even though we are in *a tighter market, I can assure you, we will get our share of that work to keep everyone in this company busy. As long as we religiously follow and continue adhering to Pete Kiewit's "Fundamentals for Success" in the construction business, by bidding work for the right price, constructing quality built work for the right cost, collecting in full for all the work done, and take good care of our assets, we **will** succeed. When this is coupled with our goal of building an aggressive, highly qualified, cost conscious, safety minded organization, our company is guaranteed a successful growth. To do otherwise, we will fail.*

I want to thank and compliment all of you on your bidding, building and safety performance this past year. I can't tell you how proud I am of everyone in this company and how happy I am to be back again, working full time as a member of this crackerjack team.

Thank you.

MAJOR NEWS RELEASES DURING 1982

President Reagan announces a war on drugs, U.S. Marines land in Lebanon on a peace keeping mission, Tylenol is recalled after seven die from capsules laced with cyanide, Barney Clark receives the first successful artificial heart, Herpes reaches epidemic proportions, The FDA approves human insulin produced by bacteria, The first successful gene transplant is performed in a mammal, The Boeing 767 makes it's debut, Reagan signs a bill removing "restraints" on S & Ls,. Aerobic videos become popular, Sun Myung Moon is sentenced to prison, and the Vietnam War Memorial is dedicated.

After everything was all said and done, only two stockholders of the twenty (20) shareholders left in the company refused to sign the new stock buy-sell agreement, mainly because of the extended buy-back clause, and cashed in their stock. When I expressed my disappointment over their lack of foresight and the potential of our company, especially when we should be pulling together, and that I took their actions as an insult to all of us, they only shrugged. It wasn't until I became aware those two were also in cahoots with Arne Glick to get rid of me and take-over of the company, I really came unglued. Surprisingly and even more shocking to me, those two shareholders turned out to be two of our company's trusted officers, namely Henry Morehead, the company's treasurer, and

Homer Olsen & Ed Walker discuss a rebar problem

Kim Allison, our company attorney. Lee Smith took over Henry's job as treasurer and I made the mistake of letting Kim Allison continue on as our hourly paid outhouse attorney while he was working for a San Francisco law firm.

The lack of vision those two individuals had in our company's future, along with their lack of confidence and trust in the quality and expertise of our company's organization was not only insulting but unbelievable. The most rapid growth our company ever had during its 43 year existence was during that 14 year period from 1982 to 1996 after Joyce and I were married and I had returned to work full time as the company's recovered

alcoholic president. Our company's stock value from the seventy one (71) completed contracts totaling $645,870,193 in volume during that period, steadily increased from the $290.85 per share value in 1979 (determined by the court for my divorce settlement), to

a new stock value of $2,241.50 per share that was split 50 to 1 to $43.83 per share by 1996. No matter how you look at it, I don't think we did too bad for a bunch of harelips.

After I returned to work full time and we had our spirited November shareholders meeting in 1981, our whole company become more focused as a confident qualified construction team and we rolled up our sleeves with new enthusiasm and determination to save the company we founded on the old Viking code I called,

Constructing the 2 mile underground reservoir under the great highway

"*Democratic Capitalism in Action.*" Unbelievably, we picked up five jobs in 1982 and eleven more in 1983 totaling $43,826,459, and only left 2 % on the table. Best of all, when the sixteen jobs were completed, we brought in a badly needed cash flow of $8,328,622 to put our company back in the black again. There was no doubt about it; our rejuvenated team was now back on track loudly shouting Otto Heppner's famous battle cry, *Pull the lever full speed ahead.*

I remember when we bid the $50,000,000 two mile long 50 foot square box culvert reservoir called the west side sewer transport system under the Great Highway using John Shimmick's brilliant belt excavation idea instead of haul trucks, I thought it was such a simple idea our competitors would also think of the same thing, but didn't, and we left a sickening $4,000,000 on the table. Oooh boy, then to discover we had a serious *hardpan* pile driving problem along with another $1,000,000 needed to buy a new 5 cy backhoe and the new crossover belt system, along with my divorce settlement problems, I'll tell you I began to sweat blood. Oooh boy, anyway thanks to my good friends and my highly qualified crews in the company and business associates like Jim Wilton, John Shimmick, Fred Cavin and his pile butt superintendent, Joe Hilton, we came up with some brilliant money saving ideas and solutions to all the problems we encountered.

Shoring for the 50x50 f.t Westside Transport under the Highway

The pile driving and impenetrable hardpan problem at elev. -35 was solved by *line auguring* through the beach sand and hardpan layer, then using a *vibrating hammer* to drive the sheet pile. John Schimmick's crossover belt excavation system and structure concrete form designs panned out even better than we had hoped and believe it our not, after the job was completed in mid 1983 and we had payed our Japanese partner, Obayashi, their 30% share of the job's profits for their signature on the bid bond and furnishing some start-up funding, we nearly doubled our estimated

MAJOR NEWS RELEASE DURING 1983

A truck bomb kills 241 Marines in Beirut, Lebanon, Reagan proposes a 'Strategic Defense Initiative" called Star Wars, U.S. Forces invade Granada, 63 die from a car bomb at the U.S. Embassy in Beirut, a highly addictive form of cocaine called "Crack" hits the streets, AT&T is broken up into a long distance company and "baby bells", Suspenders become fashionable for men, Martin Luther King, Jrs. birthday becomes a national holiday, and the Soviet Union shoots down a Korean Air Lines 747 killing all 269 aboard.

job profit and came out with a nice round $10,000,000 in total cash flow for our own company. It was one of the best job's we have ever built. .

During 1984 we were low on only nine small contracts totaling $9,014,338 because of the tight market at that time, but mostly because of a health problem I had that scared Bill Ames and affected our bonding. I remember I couldn't finish my *need more bid bond* meeting with Bill Ames one day because I felt terrible, and when I visited John Shimmick's West Side Pumping Plant job later to painfully walk the job with him, I was barely able to make it home to go to bed early. The next morning when I got up with the same intense

belly ache, I lied to Joyce I could *tough it out* at work, and bless her heart, she insisted I see our doctor immediately. Oooh boy, you guessed it, Dr. Zaharious took one look at me and said, "Can you make it to the hospital by yourself?" and when I nodded a yes he said, "I'll see you on the operating room table in one hour. You have a burst appendix and I've got to operate immediately."

About the only thing other than I spent eleven days in the hospital, I still remember about that operation is Dr. Zaharious coming into my hospital room afterwards to check on the black and blue area caused by my hemorrhaged appendix, and he said, "I wonder how this happened?" I said, "Don't you remember Doc, I came to while you were sewing me up after the operation and I accidentally rolled off the operating table while you were lighting your cigarette." He just stared at me coldly and said, "That can't be right, I don't smoke", and walked out without smiling to tell Joyce, "If that dingy husband of yours had waited just two more hours before coming in to see me, I couldn't have saved him."

It was also in 1984 Bill Ames invited me to go trout fishing with him at his *secret fishing hole* somewhere in northern California, and wouldn't you know it, his fishing hole turned out to be nothing more than a *stock pond* on Dick Fedrick's cattle ranch like we had in Utah to water our livestock. Dick apparently told Bill he stocked his pond with trout and you guessed it. After a long sun burning, unfunny joke telling day scratching insect bites and listening to dumb remarks like, *'Shouldn't we be using bate Bill?'* and *'Hey Bill, we're out of beer again,,* Bill finally groaned, "That did it. The reason the fish aren't biting Homer, is because you're a damn jinx. Let's go home." Well, after a short sulking hair raising high speed ride in his car Bill said, "I've never been skunked like this in my life before, and it's all because of you jinxing us. Jean expects me to bring some trout home – so -", and he

My wonderful wife Joyce and our three children – 1984

MAJOR NEWS RELEASES DURING 1984

Ronald Reagan and George Bush are re-elected President and Vice President of the United States by a landslide, The Reagan Administration cuts funding for the International birth control program, Geraldine Ferraro becomes the first woman to run and lose for Vice President , twenty two people are killed in a shooting at a McDonald's restaurant in San Ysidro, California, the AIDS virus is identified, Astronomers observe a distant solar system being formed, Apple introduces a "user friendly" Macintosh personal computer, The United States becomes a debtor nation, The Soviets boycott the Olympics in Los Angeles Trivial Pursuits and the Teenage Mutant NINJA Turtles become fads, screeched into the Susanville Fish Hatchery to come out a minute later with a beautiful string of nice sized trout for his lovely wife. Oooh boy, anyway while I watched Bill buckle his seat belt again he coldly *eyed* me with, "Homer, if you say one damn word to Jean or anyone else about this, I'll kill you" to which I answered, "You know me Bill, *mum's our code word*." To this day, I'll never forget the look on Bill's face when he handed his lovely wife Jean the fish to clean and she surprised him with, "Where did you catch them?." He said, "At the lake on Dick Fredrick's ranch, why do you ask?" Jean winked and said to Bill, "Honey, how do you explain the *Hatchery tags?*" I'll tell you, Bill's jaw dropped a foot and I busted out laughing so hard, I doubled up with, "See there Bill, Jean's broke our code already."

> ## MAJOR NEWS RELEASE DURING 1985
>
> *World Oil prices collapse and the banks heavily invested in oil production fail, TOW missiles are secretly delivered to Iran, leaded gasoline is banned, Federal tax credits for home solar installations are discontinued, the wreak of the Titanic is found, the scanning-tunneling microscope is developed, Coca-Cola brings back it's original formula as Classic Coke, Montgomery Ward discontinues its mail-order catalog, shoulder pads reappear in women's fashions, the cartoon strip, "Calvin and Hobbes" debuts and the SF 49ers defeat the Miami Dolphins to win the Super Bowl,*

Oooh boy, anyway to get back to company business, 1985 turned out to be another good year for us because we were low bidder on nine more contracts that totaled $47,204,466, including our largest treatment plant at the time, the $35,920,600 Modesto Wastewater Treatment plant. Stan Summers and Bill Coates handled that job very successfully and best of all brought in $4,795,263 in total cash flow for our shareholders on that one job alone. In fact the total net cash flow during that year that paid off all our bank loans and administrative expenses, was $7,549,919. There was no if ands and buts about it, Homer J. Olsen, Inc. was no ordinary run of the mud shooter when it came to building complicated heavy engineering construction contracts, successfully.

Unfortunately, 1985 was also a very sad year for Joyce and me because we lost my mother at the age of 79 from failing health and a sudden heart attack while she was stubbornly living alone in our Pleasant Hill home. I also lost another very good friend, mentor and business advisor, Bill Ames that I depended on for so many years the following year in 1986 from him having a sudden heart attack. The loss of my mother and Bill Ames, and then my own dad in 1987, was a devastating blow to me and it took me years to fully recover from their loss.

Everyone who knew Bill Ames contributed to a Scholarship Fund in his memory that three of us, namely

Bride & Groom, Barbara & Chuck Curtis

John Lamberson, Jeff Kasler and I setup for him at Stanford in his name, and $200,000 was raised to be used by qualified disadvantaged graduate students working towards their Masters Degrees in Construction Engineering at Stanford's Graduate School of Civil Engineering. Interestingly, that fund has now grown with investments and continuing contributions to well over $800,000 at the present time and like John and Jeff, I still have letters in my file from thankful scholarship graduates who had all been helped by the Bill Ames Construction Engineering Scholarship Fund.

Father of the bride and his two Daughters

On July 5, 1986, my youngest daughter Barbara and Charles Curtis were married and to this day I am thankful she found such a wonderful young man to be her husband and my son in law, as she found in Chuck. To me Chuck Curtis is not only an exceptionally well qualified engineer himself, but he has all the good qualities and character traits every father wants to see in his own son. Talk about an exciting wedding, I'll tell you I nearly had a panic attack when Joyce and I drove down to San Luis Obispo from Alamo to attend their wedding and got lost somehow while looking for the *right* church and nearly missed the ceremony. Fortunately, we had stayed overnight in San Luis Obispo fairly near the church (we thought) and were formally dressed, so luckily when we finally screeched to a sliding stop at the *right* church to walk my tearfully worried daughter down the isle a split second before the organist began

Jelsa Lutheran Church Ole K. Olsen was Christened in 1850

playing, '*Here comes the bride*', I was a nervous wreck. I can honestly say I have never been so relieved in my life as I was when that ceremony was over and we were waving goodbye to the happy couple leaving for their honeymoon.

After we finished loading the company up with more good contracts that we were low on

The boat dock in Marvik, Norwar near the Vintravigen farm

in 1986 totaling $46,312,378, and were out of bonding I did what I always do best and *delegated* all the work to my crackerjack crews and Joyce and I caught a Scandinavian Airliner from Seattle to Oslo, Norway for the trip I had promised her when we were married. After visiting *Vestre Akers* near Oslo where my *Mor Mor* (Grandma) Olsen (Hannah Kristina Swensen) was born in 1857, we caught the train to Bergen to *hydrofoil* down to Stavanger, Norway near where my *Far Far* (Grandpa) Olsen's island farm birthplace was near.

Visiting with Johanne Kjolvick

We caught the weekly mail boat at Stavanger for the fifty kilometers trip up the fjord to the small town of Marvik where Grandpa's *Vintraviki* (winter cove) farm was located nearby to visit relatives, hoping we could also stop at *Jelsa* along the way long enough to see the small Lutheran church where *Far Far* was christened in 1850. Grandpa told me when I was a young boy, his family always rowed across the sound in their family's row boat every Sunday to go to that small Lutheran church shown in the picture above. Unfortunately we couldn't stop at Jelsa

A plaque posted in New Paltz, NY

that day and were only able to take a picture of the church from our mail boat as we passed it on the way to Marvik on the other side of the fjord. Interestingly we were able to visit again with our oldest relative there named, Johonne Kjolvick who was 88 at the time, and he took us to see the same building Grandpa Olsen's mother (Berta Kjolvick, b.1817) was born and married my Grandpa Olsen's father in 1844. We only had two hours before the mail boat returned from its turnaround at *Sands,* so we hurriedly re-visited the home Grandpa helped his own father build on their *Vintravigen* (winter cove) farm, and barely caught the boat back to Stavanger. Interestingly when I tapped on the front door to say hello to the two hermits still living there (Herr Engstrom and his brother Ole), whose grandparents bought the property from my Grandpa, his welcoming answer was, "My god, you were just here the other day (Dad and I were there 13 years earlier). Why are you back so soon to pester us again?"

The Deyoe Family Coat of Arms

Well anyway, when Joyce and I made our trip to Norway to show her where my dad's side of the family were from, she proudly told me she was a French-American princess (with some Dutch sprinkled in) and that her dad's side of the family had immigrated to America as "Huguenots" and founded the city of New Paltz, New

York, and had also fought in the Revolutionary War. Wow, what a story the Deyoe family could tell. After we returned home from our trip I discovered there really was a Huguenot Historical Society in New Paltz, New York, and they cooperatively sent me a fascinating synopsis entitled "The Deyo (Deyoe) Family", published by the Deyo Family Association in New Paltz and the *excerpts* shown below are from the publication they mailed to me.

Fort de joux ,the tenth century Deyoe family Castle in the Jura mountains

"The history of the Deyoe family in America begins with a grandere named Christian because the impetus for reaching these shores was religious persecution in Europe. It is a Christian account, which begins in the New World with a man named **Christian Deyo**. The story of this remarkable and durable clan goes back to the tenth century when a chieftain held a fortress called Fort de joux in the Jura mountains, and continues until the 1600's when the descendents were forced to flee across Europe when their property was confiscated by the catholic King, Louis XIV to avoid martyrdom for their Calvanist (protestant) beliefs. The succeeding flight to America brought new adventures, a unique form of government, treaties with the Indians, and at last their refuge in a tiny settlement on the banks of the Wallkill in the shadow of the Shawangunks.

"Historic notes on the Origin of the family of Deyo in New York State , who are believed to be descended from the Sires de lou, Mountain Chieftains A.D. 1050, holding at Chateau de lou at the pass from France to Switzerland, knights of the Crusades, Kinsmen of Coligney, Huguenot Grandees. Their supposed descendent, Chretien du joux, became in 1677 a founder of New Paltz.

"Visitors to the street of the Huguenots in New Paltz cannot fail to notice a stone monument at the mini-square near the Hasbrouck and Deyo houses with a bronze tablet inscribed thus."

"To the memory of and in Honor of Louis DuBois, Christian Deyo, Abraham Hasbrouck, Andre LaFevre, Jean Hasbrouck Pierre Deyo, Louis Bevier, Antoine Crispell, Abraham DuBois, Hugo Frere Isaac DuBois, Simon Lefevre, the New Paltz Patentees, who driven by religious persecution from their native France, exiles for conscience sake, came to America after a sojourn in the Rhine Palatinate near Mannheim, here established their homes on the banks of the Wallkill, settled the country purchased from the Indians and granted by a patent issued by Governor

Edmund Andros on the 29th day of September 1677, and nobly bore their part in the creation of our free government."

The synopsis describes the Deyoe family as "A quite hard working people determined to ask no favors and able to take care of themselves. Characterized by their civic awareness and good neighborliness, the descendant's of Christian Deyo are noted for their good farmer abilities, silent until asked for an opinion, determination, and of good common sense. They were not afraid of work and labor is shouldered like a wreath of honor. Although William Penn gets the credit for his fair negotiations with the Indians, the Huguenot settlers of New Paltz were equally successful five years earlier. On May 26, 1677 five chiefs of the Esopus tribe, a branch of the Delaware's – Maysaysay, Magakahas, Nekahaway, Assineraken and Wawanis – made their marks on a contract for the sale of land to 11 Huguenots, including Christian and Pierre Deyoe. The purchase price was fair:"

One year old Joyce Deyoe

"40 kettles, 40 axes, 40 adzes, 400 fathoms of white and 300 fathoms of black network, 60 pairs of stockings, 100 bars of lead, one keg of powder, 100 knives, four kegs of wine, 40 oars, 40 pieces of duffle cloth, 60 blankets, 100 needles, one measure of tobacco, and two horses."

Alice Joyce Deyoe at the age of four

In accordance with a survey map of 1709, the *patent* was 39,683 acres of land and when combined with the conformation deed signed by 19 braves and 2 squaws and the royal grant issued by Governor Andros on September 29, 1677, it became the city of New Paltz, named after the patentees previous refuse called Die Pfatz. The settlers owned the land in common in a unique system of government based on sharing much like the Viking code – those who pull on the oars will share in the plunder. The patentees and their children tilled the land and divided all the produce equally, but the Duzine (old French for Dozen) had complete civil, military, and religious power. New Paltz was not incorporated as a township in New York State until 1785, but the *Duzine* continued to function until 1823, as the only form of government..

A majority of the Deyo family sided with the patriots in the American Revolution and put themselves on the line by signing the Articles of Association and fighting in the ensuing war. Among those signing the Articles on April 29, 1775 at the Inn of Ann DuBois in New

Paltz were: Abraham Deyo, Sr. and Jr., Benjamin Deyo, Christian Deyo II, Daniel Deyo, Christoffel Deyo, Henddricus Deyo Sr. and Jr., Johonnes Deyo Jr., John D. Deyo, Jonathan Deyo, Peter Deyo, Simeon Deyo Jr., Simon Deyo and Philip Deyo. Isaac Deyo signed the Articles at New Marlborough. The Articles of Association they all signed is as follows:

"Persuaded that the salvation of the rights and liberties of America depends, under God, on the firm union of it's inhabitants in a vigorous prosecution of the measures necessary for it's safety, and convinced of the necessity of preventing the anarchy and confusion which attend the dissolution of the powers of government, we the Freemen, Freeholders and inhabitants of the town of New Paltz, Ulster County, being greatly alarmed at the avowed design of the Ministry to raise a revenue in America, and shocked by the bloody scene now acting in the Massachusetts Bay, do in the most solemn manner resolve never to become slaves, and do associate under all the ties of religion, honor and love of our country, to adopt and endeveavor to carry into exception whatever measures may be recommended by the Continental Congress or resolved upon by our Provincial Convention for the purpose of preserving our Constitution, and apposing the execution of the several arbitry and oppressive acts of the British Parliament until a reconciliation between Great Britain and America on constitutional principles (which we most ardently desire) can be obtained and that we will in all things follow the advice of our General Committee respecting the purpose aforesaid, the preservation of peace and good order and safety of individuals and private property."

The major military events the Third Ulster County Militia, commanded by Levi Pauling, were involved in during the Revolutionary War were the invasion of Canada in 1775-76, fortification and defense of the Hudson Highlands at Fort Clinton and Montgomery, the burning of Kingston by the British in 1777, various frontier raids and the Sullivan campaign. I thought an interesting story of the Deyo family's history was when Josiah Deyo, the son of Christian Deyo III, was badly wounded during the Battle of White Plains against the British and was taken back to his home in Cherry Valley for his wife's care. When his young son, Chistian Deyo IV, who was 13 years old at the time, saw his father on a stretcher, he immediately shouldered his father's musket and marched all the way to Albany, New York to take his

Don Berry Deyoe,
Lewistown, Montana, - 1948

wounded father's place in the Militia. When he got to Albany, he found the Militia had just recently been transferred back to Ulster County he trudged all the way back to the Andrew

Brodhead homestead (then a fort) south of Ellenville at Lauren kill, to finally join up with his father's unit. .

Wow, what a family. Their fascinating history made me even more proud to be married to my wonderful wife, Alice Joyce *Deyoe*. They were a *work ethic* royal family with all the old fashioned American character traits that our forefathers had and used to build this wonderful country called the United States of America. The picture taken around 1948, is Joyce's father, Don Berry Deyoe, who was born in Iowa in 1903 and moved to Lewistown, Montana after marrying Joyce's mother, Opal Hannah Van Dorn. Joyce was born in the French Hospital in Lewistown on May 23, 1928.

Alice Joyce Deyoe at age eighteen

It was while watching some of our spoiled rotten over mothered embarrassingly uneducated liberal arts college kids protesting our country and our military on television, and comparing them to the *Deyoe* family and our country's WW II generations before them, I began wondering if any of our young people would ever have guts enough to fight and die for our country's freedom again. Sadly, I think not. Democracy is a fragile form of government at best, and when we reach the point where the majority of our citizens only vote for politicians who promise them the most handouts and will no longer *pull on the oars* to help pay their own way, then Democracy is doomed.. Socialism will then take over, but it will also soon fail because of an incurable human weakness called **Greed** and *Dishonesty,* and a ruthless dictatorship will take charge. When that happens, Lord Help us.

The Monroe Mountain Deer hunting Cabin we built in 1971

It was during October of 1986 Joyce and I drove our four wheel drive Jeep Wagoneer from Alamo, California to Monroe, Utah during the deer season to visit Dad and my stepmother, Ercel, and to checkout our Monroe Mountain cabin. As it turned out, we made such good time crossing the Sierras to Fallon, Nevada to stay our first night, we decided to continue on to Austin, Nevada. Well you guessed it, there were no rooms available there because of all the deer hunters so we continued on and halfway to Eureka, were caught up in an early snow storm and soon discovered there were *no vacancies* in Eureka either. Oooh boy, now what do we do? Well, while we were refueling our jeep in Eureka, a truck driver invited us to follow him in his snow tracks to Ely, Nevada, and as luck would have it after a blizzardly nerve wracking drive, we arrived in Ely around 2:00 o'clock in the morning, half frozen and half starved, and *Yahoo!!, one motel still had a vacancy.*

After a few minutes of anxiously pounding on the motel owner's office door and him finally sleepily answering, I said, "My name is Joseph and my pregnant wife, Mary, is about to give birth to a miracle child tonight. We would greatly appreciate your letting us stay the night in your manger for Mary to give birth to this miracle child" Whooee, I'll tell you, I have never seen a more surprised look on anyone's sleepy face in my life as on his at that moment, but suddenly his expression changed to *doubling up with laughter*, and between guffaws he said, "Joseph, I'll tell you what I'll do, if your emaculently impregnated wife Mary gives birth to her miracle child tonight in my manger, the tab for it is on me, here's your key", and as he sauntered towards his room, he laughingly shaking his head shouted, "Have a good night's sleep Joseph" and closed the bedroom door. Interestingly, Joyce didn't seem to appreciate my sense

Dad and Ercel during late 1986

of humor at that ungodly hour one bit. For some unknown reason between her *I'm freezing* and *We should have stayed home* complaints, Joyce moaned more when I sympathetically answered, *Push Mary, Push!.*

Oooh boy, anyway when we checked out of our *manger* the next morning, the Motel owner asked, "How much did Mary's miracle baby weigh?" I answered, "Well to tell the truth, it all turned out to be nothing more than a *vapor lock problem*, and nothing happened." He said, "Oh, Det var sin (Oh that's too bad), here's your bill." Well, you can believe this or not, but as we pulled away in our snow covered jeep with Joyce still muttering embarrassing comments about our memorable trip, the Motel owner was still shaking his head laughing, while waving farewell.

After our fantastic visit with Dad and Ercel and our relatives, and too much snow to check out our mountain cabin, Joyce and I sadly left Monroe to drive back home. We had a wonderful visit, but when we left this time, my dad forgot to say to me what he always said before, "God bless you son, this is the last time you will ever see me" and me trying to kid him out of it again with a big hug saying, "Only the good die young Dad. That means you

My wonderful Dad, Homer C. Olsen at age 65

and I will live on forever." Instead this time, like Grandpa Olsen did the last time I saw him, Dad quietly waved only a sad farewell, and suddenly I had that same terrible premonition it would be my dad's last farewell. To this day, I still remember choking up while we were driving over Joe Town hill and tearfully turning towards Joyce with, "I'm sorry to say this, but I think we just waved our last goodbye to my wonderful dad."

It was during the following April, Joyce and I received the very sad news my wonderful indestructible dad that I loved and depended on so much for his advice and council for so many years, had suddenly passed away at the age of 89 from a massive heart attack. I remember Dad calling me on my 63rd birthday, April 7, 1987, to ask me how it felt to be 63 and I said, "Don't you remember when you were 63 Dad?, I drove all the way from California to Salt Lake City to see you in the hospital after your gall bladder operation" and when he said, "Oooh boy do I, I've never had anything smart so bad in my life", I cracked up laughing with, "See there Dad, now you know how it feels to be 63 years old." It was only one short week after my birthday on April 13, 1987, we got the sad news from Ercel that my dad had just passed away the way he always said he wanted to go (from a fatal heart attack),

MAJOR NEWS RELEASE DURING 1986

*The space shuttle Challenger explodes killing all on board, The U.S. trades Iran arms for hostages, the federal income tax is restructured, the Iran–Costa affair is exposed, U.S. warplanes bomb Qadaffi's headquarters in Tripoli, random drug testing is introduced in sensitive jobs, the U.S. Supreme Court upholds affirmative Action hiring quotas to favor women and minorities, a hole in the Earth's Ozone layer is discovered over Antartica, a super conductive ceramic is discovered, thousands of small farmers go bankrupt, Wall Street is scandalized by insider trading, 5.4 million people form a chain from New York City to Long Beach, California during Hands Across America, **and Barbara Jean Olsen and Charles Curtis are married in San Luis Obispo, California July 5, 1986.**,*

while he was burning trash in his back yard. Like everyone else in the family and his many friends, we were all devastated by his loss and Joyce and I attended his funeral along with four hundred other good friends and relatives who thought so much of my dad. To this day I still miss my dad and I still thank my lucky stars I was raised by such a wonderful father and grandparents. I still feel any success I've had over the years was because of my dad and my grandparent's early character indoctrination, parenting and apprenticeship training, all combined with their old country work ethic, was what made it possible.

MAJOR NEWS RELEASES DURING 1987

Soviet premier Gorbachev and President Reagan sign an arms reduction treaty, America sends forces to the Persian Gulf to protect oil shipments, The Dow drops 508 points in one day, Gary Harts presidential ambitions end after sexual allegations, Jim Bakker resigns his PTL ministry after sexual liaisons with his church secretary, Hearings start on the Iran-Contra and the Webtech scandal, and the 'New Ager's celebrate "harmonic convergence" as planets align

When Dad reached 75 years of age in 1973, he was elected president of the South Sevier Senior Citizen's by campaigning for a badly needed building for their group's meetings. He told me he met with the American Legion to see if they would sell their dilapidated unused building the city felt was both an eye sore and fire trap to them for one dollar. Believe it or not, the Legion agreed providing they could use it occasionally for their own meetings. Well, to keep retired seniors with fixed incomes from being stuck with property taxes and mortgage payments and to encourage tax deductible contributions and volunteer labor donations towards remodeling their building, Dad convinced their directors they should *gift* the building to the City of Monroe. Well, to make this story shorter, the city bought the lot under the building from a local citizen and accepted the club's gift to make the refurbished building City of Monroe's own Senior Citizens Center. To this day I still feel my dad missed his calling as an *honest* politician who could accomplish

The Governor's wife, Dad, Ercel and me, with friends

anything worthwhile for the good of American citizens. His talent as a master negotiator resulted in unanimous agreements between everyone in the City, County, State and Federal Agencies involved. And it was a symphony in cooperative democratic teamwork performing for positive results, all in harmony, orchestrated and conducted by my dad, the master negotiator.

Dad told me they raised a total of $140,000 in cash (much of it his own), and when his amount was combined with the profits of the center's cake bake sales, park picnics, quilting bees, volunteer labor and local

The South Sevier Senior Citizen Center the Club Members Remodeled – 1979

business's tools and needed material donations, coupled with a local building contractor's free helpand expertise, they were able to re-model the American Legion's dilapidated building into the city of Monroe's new Senior Citizens Center shown in the adjacent picture, now known as the *South Sevier Senior Citizens Center* and to honor my dad, *The Homer C. Olsen Building.* Everyone involved in the buildings cooperative construction effort that I have talked to are very proud and very thankful for the monumental effort my dad made to get their new Center constructed. The Governor of Utah even named my dad, *Utah's Senior Citizen of the Year*, and honored him with the title of *Grand Marshall* in the lead car during 4th of July parade.

MAJOR NEWS RELEASES DURING 1988

George Bush and Dan Quayle are elected President and Vice President, the B-2 Stealth Bomber is unveiled, the USS Vincennes shoots down an Iranian airbus killing 290 people, 247 die when a Pan Am Boeing 747 is blown up by a terrorist bomb over Lockerbie Scotland, the junk bond dealer, George Milliken pleads guilty to felony charges, the US formally apologizes for the WWII internment of Japanese-Americans, studies determine an aspirin a day reduces the risk of heart attacks, and the white house aide, Donald Regan states Nancy Reagan uses astrology to plan her husband's activities.

Donna Barton & Robert K. Olsen-August 6, 1989

I'll never forget my 65th birthday party at Barbara and Chuck's Sacramento home because all three kids were there with their future spouses and they asked me, "Dad, you always told us kids you set goals to reach at certain time periods in your life that you called stepping stones. What is your goal now that you've reached the age of 65?" Without hesitation I said, "For Joyce and I to be completely out of debt and see all three of you kids happily married, but unfortunately Joyce and I have only reached the *out of debt* goal so far." Well, you can believe this or not your choice, but by the time that birthday party was over, Bob had happily announced he proposed to Donna Barton and she had accepted, and Don Kelly announced my *other* daughter Mary Elizabeth had

accepted his proposal. Wow, talk about a fantastic surprise and a wonderful birthday present. Chuck and Barbara were married three years earlier in 1986, so these last two announcements along with our being completely out of debt, made my 65th birthday party the *best one yet*. Robert Kevin Olsen and Donna Barton were formally married on August 6, 1989, in a beautiful Beverly Hills, California wedding and on November 22, 1989, Don Kelly and Marry Olsen were married in a beautiful Hawaiian wedding on the Island of Kauai in Hawaii. All Joyce and I had left to do now was, begin planning our retirement from H.J.O, Inc. to live happily ever after in the beautiful Pacific Northwest.

Mary Elizabeth Olsen & Don Kelly – November 22, 1989

We had already picked up two light rail jobs on August 20, 1987, and January 26, 1988, in Los Angeles called the LACTC- Flower Street Subway for $19,992,600 and the LACTC-Washington Street Track work for $26,153,500, together with the "J" Line Track work on November 1, 1988 in San Francisco for $17,262,363. On June 9, 1989, with the bonding signature help of a 70/30% joint venture partnership with Obayashi, we put all our eggs in one basket and were the low bidder on our company's largest contract, the underground $180,400,000 Oceanside Wastewater Treatment Plant underneath the San Francisco Zoo on Ocean Beach. As the 70% job sponsor and the builder of the project, I now felt we old timers could finally begin retiring from the company with much fewer ripples using the old *we worked ourselves in and we will work ourselves out*" philosophy. After all I reasoned, with all the cash flow that will be

MAJOR NEWS RELEASE DURING 1989

President Bush announces another war on drugs, the multi-billion dollar bailout of the failed S & Ls begins, American forces invade Panama to capture General Noriega, Hurricane Hugo devastates parts of the East Coast, San Francisco is struck by a severe earthquake, the Supreme Court rules that burning the US Flag is a protected right, the grounded tanker, Exxon Valdez spills oil into the Prince William Sound, Alaska, the National American Indian Museum Act requires the return of Indian remains to their tribes, Leona Helmsley is convicted of income tax evasion and tax fraud.

potentially come in, we would cause much less damage to the companies net-worth and/or bonding capacity with the company buying our stock back in yearly fixed amounts while we were still on the payroll helping build these last four jobs.

Ooh boy, was that reasoning wrong or was it ever wrong. As things turned out all my reasoning mistakes came to a head during 1990 and my well thought out plan for all us old timers to retire gracefully went to hell and back in a hand basket. For one thing, I was shockingly unaware how costly the owner's *new age ideas* would be for our company when they decided to add their design engineers as a third member on their management layered team. For some reason, these unqualified design consultant types had convinced the city of Los Angeles and San Francisco they would be much better *Construction Managers* than

Homer, Jack, and Stan go Halibut fishing in Canada

their *General Contractors* even though the Contractors had always been their most efficient *Construction Manager's* on Heavy Engineering Construction Projects in the past.

I had also planned on John Shimmick running the Oceanside Treatment Plant as Project Manager, but unfortunately he suddenly decided to quit just as the job was awarded to startup his own construction company, apparently because of my decision to let the younger generation of selfish inexperienced baby boomers run the company after we old timers retired instead of him, which was a major mistake. As the top money maker for the company and the

most qualified experienced construction stiff in the company and only ten years younger than me, John Shimmick was the most qualified to be company president after I retired and letting him go was the dumbest mistake I've made since I let Bill Young get away. To make things even worse, Bill Coates and some of the others loyal to John also quit to work for him and his new company instead of the *baby boomers* I appointed to run our company.

Oooh boy, then to pile on even more worries, I was suddenly forced to retire Stan Summers and Ed walker early for emergency health problems (Stan had a serious aneurysm and Ed had a heart attack), and everything I had worked for began slipping

MAJOR NEWS RELEASE DURING 1990

The US leads Operations Desert Shield after Iraq invades Kuwait, the "Keating Five" investigations begin, The Americans with Disabilities Act is signed, Home Schooling is popularized, the Supreme Court rules Native Americans may be prosecuted for using Peyote in religious ceremonies, killer bees enter the United States, Researchers grow human brain cells in the laboratory, Bungee jumping and Vietnamese potbellied pigs as pets becomes popular, after years of court battles, Gilbert Hyatt receives a patent for a microprocessor, and the US population grows to 248,709,873 as 7,338062 immigrants entered the U S during the previous decade.

away. How in God's name now are we going to be able to buy all their stock back and find the people needed to get these four last large jobs built without seriously crippling the company?

Well, to shorten this exciting potholed story along the highway, I quit sucking my thumb and dusted off Ben William's secret formula of replacing lost self confidence and held my nose tight and began blowing hard until I swelled up enough to resolve the problem of getting the job done, and amazingly it worked. I spent the weekend salmon fishing with some of my buddies to think of a plan of action and the following Monday morning met with my

Salmon Fishing in Canada to Troubleshoot a new Plan of Action

remaining crew members to review this new fascinating challenge, along with the *fishing weekend* idea's I thought would work.

Interestingly, like the Garrison Dam meeting, when we adjourned we all went back to work with a new enthusiasm and motivation to get the job done, come hell or high water. Jim McNinch took charge of the

Flower Street Subway job when John Shimmick left, Ron Llewellyn took over the Washington Street Track job from Dave Nosenzo, who took over Stan Summers' "J" Line job in San Francisco, and Gerald Clair handled the startup of the $180,000,000 Treatment Plant until Ron Llewellyn became available from the Los Angeles work. Since all jobs, large and small, are built **one brick at a time,** the $180,000,000 Oceanside Clean Water Treatment Plant was simplified even further by breaking it down into even smaller *brick units* for younger supervision assignments and more efficiency. Whenever my younger superintendents began feeling overwhelmed or intimidated by the magnitude of their job (like me on the Garrison Dam), I would say, "How come I'm the only one in this company that knows how good you guys really are?", and have them take the Ben Williams confidence builder test and say, "As a four year job, this Plant is only a $45,000,000 job four times, and those four 45 million dollar jobs can even be broken down into three smaller 15 million dollar jobs that are well within the price range all of you have handled before, so what are you worrying about?" Dick Brandt handled all the excavation work with Peter Althorn looking after the shoring work as the sand was removed and stockpiled nearby for backfill. The structure concrete work was then split into two equal sections that were handled very efficiently by Rob Pierce and Jim McNinch, and the mechanical work and final plant testing was professionally handled by Bill Johnson and

Look at me, I caught a 12 pound Coho

Chuck Schaller. The electrical and reinforcing steel work had already been subcontracted, so *Viola!* Despite all the designer errors and mistakes and lack of cooperation from either the city and/or their designers, that quality built prize winning Oceanside Wastewater Treatment Plant was still completed by mid 1994, one month ahead of schedule. Needless to say, I

will always be grateful to my *second family* for their loyal support and their professional performance during that critical company survival period constructing that potholed designed Wastewater Treatment Plant to rescue our medium sized well qualified heavy engineering construction company from extinction.

It was during the structure concrete phase while we were

The Oceanside Wastewater Treatment Plant approaching final Completion-1993

developing our *lift drawings* to show all the mechanical, electrical and embedded steel in a single concrete pour on one lift drawing, we discovered a multitude of embarrassingly incompetent design errors and interference problems that had been made by the design contractors CH2MHill & Bechtel, that were hired to design the plant for the City and County of San Francisco. To make matters even worse the City for some unknown reason, sided with their incompetent design engineers (who unknown to us were also assigned to the contract as project managers), by saying all the mistakes we found on their drawings were our problem to resolve at our expense. This strange ruling and interpretation forced us, because of the $25,000 per day liquidated damage clause, to redesign and correct the plants 4000 design drawings at our expense so the plant could be built on schedule. You guessed it, we filed suit and while the attorneys on both sides argued expensively back and forth, we were forced to assign our entire company's construction and engineering staff plus additional outside design engineering firms help occasionally, to redesign and to frantically build the plant within the time specified.

Homer and Joyce Olsen at Marcello's Restaurant, Danville, California - 1991

So now with our entire staff of engineers and construction people in our company assigned full time to the Oceanside Treatment plant and our bonding capacity maxed out, for all practical purposes we were out of business and the Treatment Plant was the only job we had during 1990 through 1991. My two full days of inquisition depositions by attorney's for the City and their *holier than thou* design firm, trying hard to intimidate and prove our firm was incompetent and inexperienced, was a failure. Interestingly, when they discovered our medium sized company had more engineering construction experience than all of them put together and I wasn't just a dumb sheepherder and had an MS Degree in Civil Engineering from Stanford plus a California professional engineering license, they changed their tune. Even more interesting when they also discovered I had recently been awarded the coveted Golden Beaver Award for lifetime career excellence in management by the Heavy Engineering Construction Industry and the referee judge told them they would lose if they pursued their suit, they settled our total *additional and unnecessary costs* claim to do their design work all over again for them, on the court house steps.

MAJOR NEWS RELEASES DURING 1991

Operation Desert Storm ends in 100 hours with Iraqi forces defeated, sexual harassment in the US Navy is exposed in Las Vegas at the Tailhook Convention, LAPD officers are video taped beating Rodney King, Bush unveils Goals – 2000, Texas Instruments produces the first optoelectrical integrated circuit chip, Clarence Thomas is appointed to the US Supreme Court amid charges of sexual harassment by a former coworker, Bush comes under attack for encouraging Kurdish and Shi'ite revolt in Iraq and then not supporting, and the bureau of Engraving makes paper currency more difficult to counterfeit,

After listening to our newly elected baby boomer board of directors constantly whining *I didn't trust them,* (when it was just the opposite), I finally and reluctantly agreed to accelerate my retirement at the 1990 meeting by stepping down at the end of 1993 when the Treatment Plant was completed except for the testing, as their exhausted 70 year old company president. I also agreed I would tear up my formally approved 1989 employment ten year contract per their request immediately, in exchange for a *toothless tiger* version (without the CEO title), called the "Founder's Agreement" and Oooh boy was that ever a mistake. My Founders agreements terms were basically the same otherwise so in 1993 I stepped aside and became the new half time, half salary, *powerless* chairman of the board until my yearly stock buyback payments were eventually paid off in full by 1999. My son, Bob, was working in the accounting department at the time and was approved by job title and time in service to buy stock if he wished, and he did. I honestly felt at the time I was doing the company a favor, current assets, net worth and bonding wise, by also transferring some of my stock over to my son Bob as an allowable gift. Unfortunately the new management team of scheming *want it all now* baby boomers greedily waiting in the wings, weren't about to watch us old timers bow out gracefully or for Bob to own any stock. They wanted all their unearned plunder immediately, not later, and thought like most baby boomers, to hell with the company's future (and their own jobs) or wasting their time waiting for the golden goose that laid the companies golden eggs in the past, to lay more eggs.

When we reached the halfway construction point in 1992 on the Oceanside Plant, we fortunately were able to release a few people to bid for other work and were low on four new jobs. Gerald and I were then able to continue again selling down our own stock in the agreed increments per year, and leave our remaining stock in the current asset column for financial and bonding purposes. To do otherwise, our stock would have been considered a major liability and would have negatively affected the company's financial ability to bid for more work until our claims were finally settled on the Treatment Plant. It was also during that period the new board hired an outside consultant to privately poll all the shareholders on their choice for a new president of the company and interestingly, the poll was a tie between Dave Nosenzo and my choice, Chuck Schaller. When Chuck's wife unbelievably refused to move their family from Sacramento to the Bay Area because their children would miss their friends, the board chose the less qualified, Dave Nosenzo to be the president and Chuck Schaller resigned, Oooh boy, there went another good man.

MAJOR NEWS RELEASE DURING 1992

Bill Clinton and Al Gore are elected President and Vice President, riots break out after acquittal of four white LAPD officers in the beating of Rodney King, four people die in Ruby Ridge, Idaho shoot out, Bush pardons officials for lying about the Iran-Contra affair, US Troops are sent to Somalia, Hurricane Andrew leaves 250,000 homeless in Florida, the newest atomic clock loses only one second in 1.6 million years, the US, Canada and Mexico sign the North American Free Trade Agreement and the US national debt now tops $3 trillion.

As a little side story in this lengthy saga of all the mistakes I've made to help insure the companies early demise, 1993 was also the fifty first reunion of my high school graduation class in 1942 from Boulder City High School in Nevada and the fiftieth anniversary of our Army Air Corps pre cadet Pre-meteorology units graduation from Pomona College in 1943. Believe it or not, who shows up for the High School reunion but my old girlfriend (who was now a widow) that I had a crush on in high school, but Delores (Hope) Brown. She's the lady sitting next to an uncomfortable me on my right with my lovely jealous wife, Joyce on my left. As I recall there were only 6 of my high graduating class of twenty five that showed up that year.

Hope Brown, Homer Olsen and Joyce Olsen-1993

My biggest surprise at the Army reunion was when *Birdie Nevins,* my old buddy and partner for my first two years in the army, began whining all over again about my promotion to Corporal by Captain Sweet, instead of him. Oooh boy, you'd think after all these years he was only kidding about not getting those stripes, but *Oooh Noo,* not old *never forget, never forgive,* Pfc school's Richard N Nevins. He went on to tell me when the War was over and he was discharged, he married his Pomona and Vassar College sweetheart, *Cloie,* and moved to Pasadena, California to live near his parents and went into politics to make a living. Interestingly, he was successfully elected to the State of California's Franchise Tax Board and from then on made that his lifetime occupation until his retirement. Well, after he served enough time on the board to be appointed Chairman he discovered I had incorporated our construction company in

Chloe & Birdie Nevins at our 50ᵗʰ Meteorology Reunion–1993

California, and I'll tell you from then on he had his crews audit our company's tax returns every year for the next twenty six years in a row, to hopefully find me in a mistake. In fact, his auditors were holed up in my office so long every year frantically looking for something to hang me with it became a joke around our office. Well you guessed it; not unlike having another child, I added another room to our headquarters office building just for Birdie's auditing crew to continue trying to catch me in a mistake, which believe it or not, they never found. In fact if anything, their audits helped our company because sometimes we *accidentally* over paid our taxes, and when they discovered we had over paid, they embarrassingly reimbursed us for our mistake.

Anyway, while Birdie and I were talking, I finally worked up enough nerve to ask him, "Birdie, tell me the truth, were those lousy corporal stripes of mine the reason you've stubbornly audited our company's tax returns every year for the past twenty six years?" Honest to God his unbelievable answer was, "You damn right it was. You were never qualified to wear those stripes in the first place, whereas I was and the captain should have given them to me instead of you." I walked away shaking my head in disbelief thinking, "As long as I live, I will never cease to be amazed how some people think about things."

MAJOR NEWS RELEASE DURING 1993

Eight Muslim extremists are arrested for involvement in the World Trade Center bombing in New York, after spending $30 billion, Star Wars (Strategic Defense Initiative) is cancelled, US troops are pulled out of Somalia, flooding along the Mississippi and Missouri rivers cause billions in damage, hundreds killed when Clinton orders ATF to raid the Branch Davidian compound in Waco, Texas, several foreign tourist are murdered in Miami, Florida, fifty percent of the American workforce is found unfit for employment, the orbiting Hubble telescope is repaired, and human embryos are successfully clone and line dancing becomes popular.

Anyway, to get back to the saga of our company's demise, Gerald Clair told me at age 69 he couldn't stand watching our company being destroyed by our current management baby boomer team's incompetence and greed any longer and asked if he could retire, and a copy of the speech I gave at his emotional retirement party is included below. Gerald and I were the last of the company's old timers other than Don Hudson, and Gerald was the last of my loyal hardworking dependable friends still on the payroll. His leaving left me with only my young accountant son Bob, and Dick Brandt for any company support and from then on my unsold stock combined with Dick Brandt's and Bob Olsen's stock only gave us muscle enough to elect three of the seven directors. Without Don Hudson's and Bill Johnson's support any longer after they sided with Dave Nosenzo and his promised welfare handouts, we were helpless in stopping the company's impending demise.

Homer J. Olsen's closing speech at Gerald E. Clair's retirement party on June 28, 1994.

```
    Most of the speakers before me covered Gerald's working
years with our company so well I think I'll just talk about
Gerald's early years, from the time he was just a little kid,
to when he signed on with our company.
    Gerald was born March 23, 1925 in Neligh, Nebraska and was
the youngest and only boy of three children. His two older
sisters were twins so you guessed it, he was nearly hen pecked
to death by women, namely his mother and two sisters, while his
dad worked at the Barbershop he owned and operated in Neligh.
```

Back in those days there were no pre-schools or kindergartens so he started school at the age five, skipped one class along the way, and graduate from Neligh High School in 1942, three months before he turned seventeen. Since he was too young to be drafted for WW II at the time, he registered at the University of Nebraska in September of 1942, and for the next year and a half, took all the pre-engineering courses he could.

In March of 1944, the same month he celebrated his 19th birthday, Gerald was inducted into the Army and was sent to Fort Benning, Georgia, for basic training and, since he was a big kid, additional training as a BAR 50 caliber rifleman replacement. From there he was sent to England and was assigned as an infantry replacement with the elite American 1st Division, known as Big Red One under General Anders' command. Gerald told me it was on 'D plus 60', when he landed on Omaha Beach (August 1944), to join his big red one Division that had already fought its way well into France. As he traveled along to join his unit through St. Lo, a city that was now completely destroyed, Gerald said he was struck for the first time by the abnormity of the war, and what he was getting into. It must have really been a sobering experience for a 19 year old kid to learn for the first time that more than 10,000 American soldiers had lost their lives in the battle for St. Lo, even more than were lost during the D-Day landing.

As we all know, it's like pulling teeth to get Gerald to toot his own horn about any of his accomplishments and/or experiences, and when I asked him to at least record for his children his war experiences, he would only shrug and say, "I was only doing my job." From what I've been able to piece together on my own, his European battlefield experiences during the first four months after his landing, must have really matured private first class Gerald Clair in a hurry. During the battle for Achen, Germany, Gerald was promoted (or had already been promoted) to Platoon Sergeant, was cited for bravery and awarded the Bronze Star. During the Battle of the Bulge in December of 1944, Gerald's unit was cited again for bravery, and Gerald was promoted to

Staff Sergeant and awarded his second Bronze Star. His second citation reads among other things, "For maintaining position during the Battle of the Bulge", which means his unit did not retreat. It was the Big Red One 1ST Division that turned the tide and stopped the advance of the elite SS Panzer Division, who lost over 800 tanks and 100,000 German soldiers in that last great battle of the war.

During World War II, there were roughly 16,000,000 American men and women in uniform, of which only 3,000,000 in the various branches actually saw real combat. The rest of us in the services then were either waiting for the upcoming invasion of Japan scheduled for November 1, 1945, or were serving as support troops around the world. Of the 3,000,000 servicemen who were in actual combat, only half were in the ground infantry forces that actually win the wars by advancing in battle and holding their ground positions. Gerald, as one of those unappreciated, under paid ground force infantrymen, is an American War Hero.

The war in Europe ended on May 8, 1945, and the dropping of the two atomic bombs ending the Japanese war in August of 1945, stopped the upcoming slaughter of at least a million American servicemen and over five million Japanese soldiers and civilians that would have died before the Pacific war came to an end, had we invaded Japan. With 90 discharge points to his credit, Gerald was discharged from the Army in March of 1946 (his 21st birthday present) and re-registered at the University of Nebraska in September of 1946. One year later in September of 1947, he transferred to Stanford where he got his BS Degree in Civil Engineering in 1949 and his MS Degree in Structural Engineering in June of 1950. It was at Stanford our two paths crossed for the first time, and all I can remember about Gerald Clair at the time was, I was the dumbest and Gerald and Jim Wilton were the two smartest students in our class.

In 1950 Gerald went to work for the California Highway Dept. for a few months until Peter Sorensen offered him a job as an estimator-trainee. Two years later Peter passed away unexpectedly

Homer's Garden – 1984

and Oscar Holmes, who was also working there with Gerald, made Peter Sorensen's widow an offer she couldn't refuse and bought the company to found the Oscar C. Holmes Construction Company. Gerald then worked for Oscar for the next twenty years from 1952 to 1972 as his chief estimator and vice president. In 1970, we bid with Oscar on a Joint Venture basis for a couple of years and in 1972 Gerald decided to come to work for us as our chief engineer. As you know, it was only a short time later he was promoted and began serving as our company's vice president of engineering and as a company director until his retirement.

As a little exercise in statistics, I ran a rather interesting analysis on how Gerald and I compared during the period we both held the same job of chief engineer for our company. From the day we were founded in 1963 until 1972 when Gerald signed on, I was chief engineer for HJO Inc. and I estimated and bid 232 contracts totaling $534,069,339, for an average per job size of $2,300,000. For some reason during those 456 weeks (9 years), I was only able to bid one job every two weeks and was low on only 53 jobs totaling $65,695,694

Joyce & Garden – 1985

in awarded contracts. In other words, for some unknown reason, I was only able to produce an average of $7,300,000 worth of work per year for our company during that nine year period.

On the other hand (she had warts), during Gerald's career with HJO Inc, from 1972 to 1994 (1144 weeks), he estimated and bid 1204 contracts at an average rate of 1.05 jobs per

> week that totaled $6,173,041,319 for an average per job size
> of $5,123,748. Wow, his bid performance rate was twice mine,
> while bidding twice the size jobs. Even better yet, Gerald was
> low on 125 of the 1204 jobs bid that totaled $723,344,570 in
> awarded contracts. So now you know, Gerald out-produced me as
> chief engineer by 500%, and averaged $33,000,000 worth of work
> for our company every year for 22 years.
>
> We would not be where we are today if it had not been for
> you Gerald. You are by far the best Chief Estimator, the best
> Engineering Vice President, and the best Company Director and
> friend I've ever had or worked with and we all thank you from
> the bottom of our hearts, for all you have done for us. We're
> going to miss you Gerald. We wish you happiness, good health,
> a long life and good luck during your retirement years.
>
> *Thank you Gerald, God bless you.*

It was only one month after Gerald's retirement dinner I was shredding yard *pruning* in my shredder-chipper for compost for our vegetable garden and I stupidly caught my glove in the shredder and lost four of my fingers on my right hand. For some unknown reason while thinking about everything else but what I was doing, I opened the plugged up exit chute which had a warning sign, *Turn off engine before opening*, to unplug it by simply swiping my gloved hand through quickly and Oooh boy, you guessed it. A chipper blade snagged my glove and instantly pulled my hand back into the machine. ZIP! Just like that, *four fingers on my right hand instantly disappeared.*

I remember shouting, "Oh my God, how stupid can I get", and running to the garden shed to find a towel to wrap my bleeding hand and something for a tourniquet, then to find Joyce to drive me to the hospital. Fortunately, Joyce hadn't left to go shopping as planned and, Oooh boy, she nearly fainted when she saw what happened, but bless her heart, she kept her head together long enough to drive me to the hospital emergency ward before bubbling over into tears. Interestingly, while I was quietly waiting for the hand doctor, a young girl who said she was a clinical psychologist suddenly appeared to ask if my parents were responsible for my accident or was it an equipment responsibility. I said, "No one is to blame for this accident except me and my own stupidity so please talk to my wife Joyce. She is the one who is taking this accident the hardest."

When the Doctor arrived he was amazed I still had any hand left and after complimenting me on my reflexes said, "Thank God you still have your thumb left on that hand because I think I can save enough of your other fingers to leave you with length enough to give you some use." I remember when they were getting ready to wheel me into the operating room on the gurney, Joyce and my son, Bob and his wife Donna, were standing there sobbing with their little chins quivering like harp strings, so to get them settled down and laughing again I called Joyce over and said, "Sweetheart, will you please do me a favor?" And as she leaned over between sobs, she said, "Oh yes, yes, anything, anything, what is it?" I said, "Please cancel my piano lesson today." I'll tell you, I knew right then Joyce and the kids would be alright because as they began wheeling me away and into the operating room, they were all howling with laughter.

Joyce and Homer Olsen waiting to Retire-1994

Since I was already on a halftime work schedule (six months a year) and couldn't write my own name anymore, Joyce and I signed up for a combination recovery-recuperating cruise through the Panama Canal for me to finally see the engineering feat I had always wanted to see, and flew to Florida to board our ship. It was while we were ocean bound towards the Panama Canal I received a ships call from Kiewit's vice president, Jerry Toll, in Omaha, Nebraska, to tell me, "Homer, you have been chosen by your peers to receive the coveted Golden Beavers Award for excellence in Management." Wow! It was not only unbelievably exciting news, but if true, was a Godsend for my moral at that time. I don't think I have ever been so pleasantly surprised or felt so pleased, humble, honored, proud, and thankful, all at the same time, than I was at that moment. To think I would even be considered for such a prestigious award known as the *Academy Award* of the Heavy Engineering Construction Industry, was not only unbelievable, but could never happen to anyone of my upbringing except in this great land of freedom and opportunity, The United States of America.

After our claim was settled in 1995 on the Oceanside Treatment Plant I met with our Board of Directors to tell them I thought it was time they let me retire. I said the last thing I

MAJOR NEWS RELEASES DURING 1994

The GOP wins control of both houses for the first time in 40 years, US troops intervene in Haiti, 14 smoke jumpers are killed on Colorado's Storm King Mountain, cigarette smuggling violence on the border forces Canada to lower its tobacco tax, CIA Agent Aldrich Ames is convicted of spying for the Soviet Union, United Airlines employees become majority shareholders, transistors containing no metal parts are developed, the new Interlink network allows spy agencies to access secret information from anywhere, 15% of the American families now live below the Clinton raised poverty level, and thousands of Cubans and Haitians escape to the United States.

**Homer J Olsen's 1995 Beavers Award Acceptance
Speech on January 19, 1995.**

Mr. President, Mr. Chairman, Honorable Speaker Dick Cheney, Fellow Awardees, Honored Guests, and fellow Beavers

I stand here before you tonight feeling very humble, very proud, and very grateful to the Beavers for this prestigious Award. This is my 46th year in the construction business and

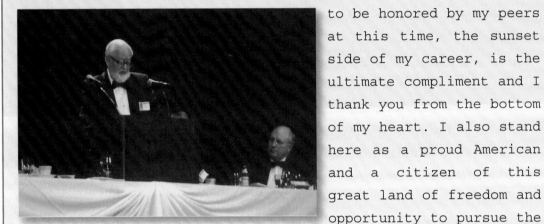

to be honored by my peers at this time, the sunset side of my career, is the ultimate compliment and I thank you from the bottom of my heart. I also stand here as a proud American and a citizen of this great land of freedom and opportunity to pursue the American Dream.

Beavers Award Speech – 1995

But the realization of that dream does not just happen. Besides good health, hard work and a positive attitude, it also takes proper guidance, education, apprenticeship and the

support of many mentors to achieve that goal. I have been very fortunate all my life to have had that support, so in my few remaining minutes of fame, I wish to acknowledge some of those wonderful people in my life to whom I owe so much, and share with them this coveted Award.

Dick Cheney & Homer Olsen – 1995

First I want to thank Ole Kjolvick Olsen and Hanna Kristina Olsen, my Norwegian immigrant grandparents, and Homer Christian Olsen, my dad, for raising me properly. It was during those early 1930's depression years I learned the true meaning of the words, responsibility, honesty and hard work. In the mid-1930's, it was Phil Brim, my step dad, who introduced me to this exciting business of Heavy Engineering Construction on the Hoover Dam and it was Harry Fuller, my Boulder City, Nevada, high school science teacher who encouraged me to pursue a degree in Civil Engineering. Thanks to the G.I.Bill, I was able to complete my engineering education after the war and was able to study under Master Teachers like Chet Jaeger at Pomona College and Clark Ogelsby at Stanford University.

In March of 1949, my lucky star shined brightly once again and I was hired by the worlds best managed construction company, The Peter Kiewit Son's Company. It was there I had the opportunity to work for leaders you would follow over a cliff like Thomas H. Paul, and apprentice under and with top project managers like Keith Wasson, Ward White, Bill Ziegler, and Ben Williams. I was taught how to estimate jobs by two of Kiewit's best engineers, Louis Trexlar and Vern Peugh, and I learned the business side of this business from the legendary master himself, Peter Kiewit. I will always be grateful to the Kiewit Company for those fourteen challenging years and I still cherish the many friendships I made while working for that wonderful company.

In August of 1963, I put into action a life long dream and founded the company I work for today, Homer J. Olsen, Inc. My head cheerleader and advisor at the time was my dad who also served on our Board of Directors for the next fifteen year. His advice and council was invaluable and I wish he were still alive and could be here tonight to share in this prestigious Award.

Another mentor and good friend whose council I welcomed was Bill Ames of the old Miller & Ames Company. It was through Bill Ames I met Gordon H. Ball, who later became a Joint Venture partner and good friend. Ball & Olsen ultimately went on to build sixteen successful projects together during those early years and I will always be grateful to Bill Ames, Gordon Ball and his second in command, Vince Smith,. for their invaluable help during that period.

Beavers Award – 1995

We have had many fine Joint Venture Partners over the years, too many to acknowledge here, but I wish to thank the J. F. Shea Company for their cooperative support on the Market Street BARTD work and the Obayashi Corporation for their help on the four contracts totaling some $280 million we joint ventured along Ocean Beach in San Francisco. I also wish to thank our outside consultants: Jim Wilton, Murry Regensburger, Kim Allison, Bill McInerney, and John Lamberson for their invaluable advice and council and my thanks go out to our many subcontractors and material suppliers who have worked with us so faithfully over the years.

Most of all, my eternal thanks goes to the dedicated, hardworking, talented people, both past and present, who make up the payroll of our company. They are my second family and deserve not only the lions share of this award, but the credit for our company's success over the past 32 years. Many are here tonight, too many to name individually, but I wish to recognize and thank one old friend, Gerald Clair, who traveled from his new home in North Carolina to be here tonight.

1995 Beaver Award

Gerald is our recently retired Vice President of Engineering, Director and Corporate Secretary, whose contribution to our company's success was invaluable, and I am happy he is here tonight to share in this award.

And last, I extend my heartfelt thanks to my wonderful family who are all here tonight, for their loving support over these many years. My everlasting gratitude goes to my beautiful and loving wife and best friend Joyce, to our two lovely daughters and their husbands, Mary and Don Kelly, and Barbara and Chuck Curtis, and our son Bob and his lovely wife Donna. I am so very proud of my little family and my company family. If it were not for them, and the others I have mentioned, I would not be standing here tonight. I now wish to ask my family, my company family and my friends who are seated at table numbers 8, 41, 49, and 84 to please stand and be recognized by the Beavers and share with me this coveted Golden Beaver Award.

1995 Beavers Award - my family

Thank you fellow Beavers. We all thank you from the bottom of our hearts.

MAJOR NEWS RELEASES DURING 1995

U. S. Troops are deployed as peacekeepers in the Balkans, Senator Bob Packwood (R) resigns from the senate amid sexual harassment charges, Robert McNamara calls the Vietnam War a grave mistake, O. J. Simpson is acquitted of the murder of his ex-wife and Nicole Simpson and Ronald Goldman, Melatonin is touted as the drug to a better, more energetic longer life, Louis Farrakhan of the nation of Islam, spearheads a million man march on Washington, D.C., a new state of matter is created: the Bose-Einstein condensate, A solar powered airplanes attains an altitude of 15,400 meters (50,000 ft), the federal government allows states to set their own speed limits on interstate highways, the closing of Smith Corona marks the end of the typewriter era, and **Homer J. Olsen receives the coveted Academy Award of the heavy engineering construction industry, The Golden Beavers Management Award for outstanding achievement in heavy engineering construction.**

would do was hurt this company I founded in 1963 with only optimism and a small savings, but it's now thirty two years later and we have not only created a debt free well qualified experienced company, but we have an excellent history of helping many hard working (*oar pulling*) employee shareholders become millionaires. In fact, my last count of the people this company has helped become millionaires not only includes most of our shareholder employees, but a few of our minority partners, subcontractors, banking, insurance and legal people who also helped us along the way. We should all be very proud, thankful and grateful for what this company has done for all of us that was founded along the lines of that Old Viking Code, *Those who pull on the oars will share in the plunder*.

I also told them, in order for me to smoothly hand over the reins of this company to our next generation of hard working (*oar pulling*) shareholders rather than selling out to another company or merging and/or going public to retire, I kept my own company ownership at a minimum by never purchasing any more stock than my original investment, nor have I given myself any stock options or excessive bonuses to be able to exercise those options, as I have done with all of you to increase your ownership and assume command of the company someday. I also believe no company president or anyone else in the company regardless of company size or type, should draw a salary higher than the president of the United States, and their salary and bonus schedules should always be based on the company's yearly performance. As many of you know, I have been on someone's payroll, either full time or part time, since my first job at the age of eight (1932 to 1995) for 63 years now and frankly I'm tired. During the last 32 years as the president of this company, I've never asked for any favors, but now I'm asking this board for one I think I deserve. My 1990 Founders Agreement stated the company would repurchase all my stock by 1999 so I could phase out and retire, but unfortunately, with John Shimmick and the others leaving, we postponed further payments to me until the Oceanside Plant was completed. The Treatment Plant work is now complete and we've settled all our claims and recovered those costs to give us an enviable *liquidity* and a debt free company again. We've also reached the point where all of you can stop taking *Old Homer* for granted any longer and let me retire to enjoy my few remaining years. My favor request is simply this, just accelerate my stock repurchase payments enough to catch up with the 1999 buy out agreement all of you signed. To my dismay and disappointment, my request was rejected.

Unknown to me, the current crop of baby boomer officers running the company had already initiated an irresponsible $10,000,000 *equipment-buying orgy* that would wipe out all our working capital and had even borrowed all our $6,000,000 line of credit from the Wells Fargo Bank. Unbelievably they were in a buying frenzy of replacing all the companys' current *free and clear* equipment, needed or not, with all new equipment. To make matters even worse in their thrilling spending spree of greed, they had also setup an overly generous unfair bonus and salary schedule for themselves that bordered on criminal. My God, and here I thought they had learned something about *the Olsen Way of doing business* over the years while working for the company. Oooh boy, in my hypnotic desire and uninformed haste to retire I wasn't thinking right and everything that happened was my fault. I should have at least insisted on them taking the WASL Test to see if they were qualified to graduate from kindergarten first.

Thinking back now, I was very fortunate to have been raised so frugally during the great depression of the 1930's on Grandpa Olsen's small high desert farm, and to have witnessed first hand how bankers seemed to enjoy foreclosing on small farms and businesses for missed interest payments. I made up my mind early in life to *never borrow* and be owned by bankers and/or loan sharks, like my grandparents and my dad. When I started this company, I did everything possible to keep from borrowing money and only rented or bought the minimum amount of equipment we actually needed when we had jobs for it. The equipment we did buy was purchased on a lease-purchase arrangement the first year and if we got a job for that piece of equipment the second year, we picked up the buy option and let the equipment help pay for itself, otherwise it was returned.

I remember telling the newly elected company president, the future of this company depends entirely on them re-establishing immediately our basic *Olsen Way* business principles and cost controls and religiously follow Peter Kiewit's four commandments for company success. I also said something had to be done immediately about lowering the company's bloated overhead costs and especially the unreasonably high salaries and bonuses the officers were currently paying themselves, and that I planned to bring all this up at the next Shareholders meeting. To me their salaries and bonuses were gross and should be tied to a company earnings formula similar to the one in my founder's agreement. This company will never survive if you continue this baby boomer philosophy of, *"It's our turn now"* and *"We want it all now."* To me the current management team seemed bound and determined to go out of their way to *"Stop the Olsen Way"of* doing business and had even put up a protest sign on the street corner. I had reached the point where I honestly felt they were determined to destroy our wonderful little company I gave them to run, while greedily feathering their nests.

Well, to summarize this embarrassingly sad demise story of the wonderful little company that made us all rich along the potholed highway of it's life, after all the shareholders had our breakfast together and before we adjourned for the shareholders quarterly meeting, the new president and the company's uninvited legal council suddenly stood up to announce there would be a short recess for the board to resolve a problem with Homer before the shareholders meeting could begin. Whooee, I'll tell you that was some board meeting. In order to prevent me from telling all the shareholders what was going on in the company, I was *fired* immediately by the board along with their trying to get my son Bob to resign, but wouldn't, and was fired anyway later on. Dick Brandt resigned as a board member and company employee shortly afterwards at the shareholders meeting.

The Company's Headstone – 2002

Apparently, I was fired for illegally (?) gifting and transferring some of my company stock to my son Bob to help him and (I thought) soften the financial impact on the company by my stock buyout. Oooh Boy, if only I had not torn up my 1989 employment contract to prove I trusted them and they replaced it with the toothless *Founders Agreement*, this *Coup d'e` tat* would never have succeeded. From all I can find out, my son Bob was fired because his last name was *Olsen*, and Dick Brandt quit in disgust over the rotten things they were doing to the company, to me and to all the other shareholders. That left Rob Pierce as the only legitimate contractor construction engineer type left in the company that understood the construction business since all the others in the company's hierarchy had turned into trial attorneys and bean counter types while feasting on the company remains. Sadly, the Homer J. Olsen Inc. company only survived five more short years before going into bankruptcy and closing down, still owing my son Bob and me our last two stock repurchase payments (totaling roughly $750,000 with interest), under that groups' incompetent command and poorly bid, poorly run, losing jobs in the construction contracting business, proving once again, **Greed**, *even in a business that was setup along the lines of that Old Viking (Socialistic) Code, will also fail.* Bill Ames and Gordon Ball were certainly right about keeping control of the company and that I was much too trusting and overly generous with our spoiled rotten, greedy baby boomer generation shareholders in the company.

Thinking back now over my 84 year life and sadly recalling all the mistakes I've made and

the lessons I should have learned along the skidmarked highway of running a construction company, if I had it all to do over again I really wouldn't have changed very many things. I probably should have spent more time learning more about business law and accounting rather than blindly following the advice of people I thought were experts in those fields. The company was initially setup wrong to begin with by my attorney, and should have been incorporated in a business friendly State like Nevada instead of California where I could have had voting and non-voting stock to keep complete control of the company. The profit sharing plan should also have been setup to buy departing and retiring shareholders stock back like the Keogh plan when they left or retired and perhaps even been setup to use a joint venture partner if and when needed. This would have minimized the silent partners and expensive signature

Joyce and Homer Olsen enjoying retirement- 2008

fees for bid bond approvals and saved considerable money for the company. But, that's all behind us now.

Were you hurt by way you were treated and what happened to the company? *Yes, I was terribly hurt.* Were the mistakes made your fault? *Of course, everything that happened on my watch that was detrimental to the company, to me or to anyone else around me, was my fault.* If someone asked you how you would want to be remembered, what would you say? *Well, Ward White used to tell me during my apprenticeship days, "Do the best job you can with the tools you've got to work with", but **I would prefer telling them the truth --. I always tried to do the right thing.***

THE RETIREMENT YEARS

A view of the Marina in beautiful Gig Harbor, WA., 1996

After Joyce and I recovered somewhat from the shock of being so rudely *fired* into early retirement in 1995, we rationalized enough to accept the company's action as a golden opportunity to begin enjoying our remaining years sooner and put our Alamo home up for sale. We had already looked into retiring in Nevada or Arizona, but when Joyce returned all excited about her visit with her high school friend Peggy Rafn in Gig Harbor, Washington and announced she had found our *dream home*, I flew up to check it out. Well you guessed it, there was no doubt about it being our dream home and the Puget Sound area really was God's Country. The owner-builder reluctantly lowered his ridicules asking price to accept what we sold our Alamo home for and we began packing for the big move. Bill and Paula Young, bless their hearts, sponsored a wonderful combination "Homer's Odyssey" retirement and moving away party for us and we were settled in our dream home by mid November

Our Pink Palace Home at 616 135th Street, Ct NW, Gig Harbor, WA

ber of 1996, just in time to weather the worst winter storm to hit the Northwest in the last thirty years. I think everyone can agree our Christmas letters to all our friends and relatives for the next few years describes what we were doing and going through while living in our new *dream home* in Gig Harbor on the Puget Sound that my sister Marilyn fittingly named, *The Pink Palace.*

GLEDELIG JUL - 1997

Whooee, I'll say one thing for sure. This past year has really been an exciting one for both of us and I can hardly wait to finish this letter to read about all the wonderful exciting things that happened to us.

Gig Harbor Storm - 1996

As you already know, Joyce and I officially retired last year and we moved in November to our new' dream retirement home' in Gig Harbor, Washington just before the worst winter storm in the last thirty years hit the Northwest with a vengeance. Joyce's mother, Opal, was here for Christmas at the time and I'll tell you, if you want to make your marriage more exciting, try living with two snowed in women during a five day power outage with only a fireplace for heat. It's a memorable way to do it. Whooee, talk about the Donner party. Anyway, when you think about it hard enough, it was kind of fun and was actually no more difficult than camping out in a sheep wagon on a Nevada desert during a winter blizzard.

All in all, when December of 1996 is thrown in, 1997 was also an interesting and exciting year. We hauled our sailboat, the USS Akvavit up to this wonderful boating country in April only to discover she leaked like a sieve apparently because of stouter water up here or something, but anyway she'll be ready

My Double Cousins

for gunk holing by next spring. All our travels this year have been confined to short trips because we've been so busy refurnishing and remodeling our new home, but we did spend a few days in Mendocino at the Heritage House in May for Joyce's birth day and then in September we flew down for Opal's 90th birthday party at Rossmoor. In October while Joyce was visiting our friends in Montana, I made a quick sneak away trip to Utah to visit my double cousins, Stan, Spun and Tex, that I hadn't seen in years.

Opal trying to keep warm

Our kids are all well and are very busy. Don and Mary are still living in Hawaii and have four successful black pearl shops going now. The last one they opened is in Miami Beach, Florida and the others are in Hawaii. Barbara and Chuck live in South Lake Tahoe, California, while Barbara is still busily involved with her Books Beyond Boundaries Company and Chuck is doing Consulting Engineering work and piloting his own Company Bonanza airplane to his assignments. Bob and Donna still live in Danville where Donna is a Master Teacher at the Alamo middle school. Bob passed all his tests for his CPA License and is currently working for an Accounting firm in Walnut Creek. Nope, we still don't have any grandchildren to brag about.

What have Joyce and I been doing? Well, we've been busy redecorating, refurnishing and correcting building errors made by the previous owner builder of this house for one thing. We've also joined the Welcome Club, an Investment Club, and the Navy League where we have made some wonderful new friends. We've also had the good fortune to have many of our wonderful friends and relatives visit us and I've even started a new company called Putterer's, Inc. and completely enclosed and finished the garage and shop area downstairs for future grandchildren toy building

Joyce's Front Room – 2006

projects. Our new company has also installed storage cabinets throughout those two areas downstairs, including a 7.5 KW Onan Generator fueled by natural gas, complete with an Automatic Transfer Switch to automatically start the engine if and when we have another power failure. I've even signed up for computer classes at the junior college and started building the radio controlled gas model airplane Meem and Don gave me for my 73rd birthday. Best of all, you should see the beautiful job Joyce has done on redecorating and refurnishing this place. It really has turned into a dream home.

Love to all. We wish you a very merry Christmas and a healthy happy prosperous New Year. We welcome a visit from you anytime.

Homer & Joyce Olsen

A Gray Whale fishing for Herring and Salmon in Canada

As a little side story, I remember one of the things I always thought was interesting about my fishing trips to Canada was watching how whales fish. I've heard many people comment on how dumb animals (including human) are because they're unable to think and/or communicate with each other, which is a lot of hogwash. I was very fortunate to have been raised on a *stock farm* where I was constantly around animals and I learned they are just as smart as we think we are (smarter in some cases) and like we are, they are constantly communicating with each other. How? By body language and many different sounds and grunts like humans before we invented a language. I thought it was not only fascinating, but brilliant the way three gray hump back whale rounded up a school of herring like cowhands working a herd of cattle. I remember Jim Wilton and I watched and listened in fascination with Jack, our guide, as three humpback whales worked a school of herring towards an underwater corral, and while two of the whale circled the herring into a vertical underwater *tornado funnel*, the third whale would swim underneath and up vertically

Hey, look at me, I Caught a 15 pound Coho

through the funnel with it's mouth wide open gobbling up herring until it broke the water's surface. Unbelievably, it would then trade places with one of the other *cowhands* below to

488 swim up from the bottom through the funnel, and so on until all three whales had a turn

gobbling up their share of herring. If that doesn't prove whales have intelligence and can think out a plan and communicate, I'll eat your hat.

I remember another time the three of us followed a pod of Orcas whale (also called killer whale) chasing a school of salmon into an underwater 'box canyon' corral and we decided to join them to fish uninvited. Oooh boy, you guessed it. Just as we dropped our unwelcome lines into their private fishing hole, as luck would have it Jim and one of the Orcas hooked the same salmon simultaneously and the tug of all wars was on. Whooee, I'll tell you the crapolla really hit the fan when Jim won the match by suddenly jerking the fish from the whale's mouth just as the enraged Orcas snipped off the salmon's dorsal fin. I don't think I've ever seen an angrier look on anyone's face than that whales face when it suddenly appeared on my side of the boat so close I could pet its nose. Whooee, it began *squealing* such a frightening stream of embarrassing cuss words in whale language we decided it was time to take off for home.

I'll tell you, this was one really mad Bull Whale

To emphasize further we were not welcome, a huge bull whale (the leader of the pod), suddenly appeared on the stern of our retreating boat *squealing loudly* and escorted us to the county line where he began thrashing the water with his tail several times to emphasize *'you two bastards are no longer welcome in our town'*.

GLEDELIG JUL – 1998

Formal Cruise Dinner

One of the problems with having early signs of Alzheimer's is trying to remember whose turn it is to write our Xmas letter each year and then to remember what we did. My lovely wife, what's her name, said it was my turn, so she must be right and here goes.

As I dimly recall the first four months of 1998, we were busy checking off punch list items as they were completed by our remodeling toy making company that we named, 'Putterers Inc.' who interestingly, were always low on our contracts. We were also fortunate in having many of our friends and relatives visit us again this year, but the bombshell surprise of all time was Joyce's 70th birthday present from our kids. It was a twelve day Mediterranean Cruise on the newly launched Royal Grand Princess. We flew by Scandinavian Airlines from Seattle to Frankfurt, Germany, boarded a Turkish Airline to Istanbul, Turkey (a story in itself) where

we boarded the largest Cruise Ship in the world at that time. We then made layover stops in Kusadasifor a tour of the ancient city of Ephesus, plus more tours of Athens, Venice, Naples, Livonia, Monte Carlo, and finally exhausted and happy, debarked at Barcelona, Spain. From there we flew to Copenhagen and home. Whooee, what a fantastic cruise.

Barnstorming Seniors – 1999

Unfortunately, Joyce's poor crippling arthritic back gave out on that trip and no amount of pills, therapy, or shots seemed to help relieve her pain. Her Neurologist finally recommended back surgery on the three damaged vertebrae that was successfully performed in early September and her back miraculously recovered and is pain free, but her nerve pinched partially numb left leg has not recovered, thus forcing her to use a walker. Since then, Putterers Inc. has installed an electric stair chair in the downstairs stairway, handrails in all the bathrooms, showers and the front and back porches to help us "honored citizens"(I love that description of us old fogies) get around a little better without falling.

Joyces' mother, Opal

Joyce's 91 year old mother, Opal, is as young as ever. She recently sold her Rossmoor townhouse and moved into an assisted care condominium at the Waterford in Walnut Creek. She was here in Gig Harbor for a visit in July when my April Club buddies were also here for a Special Meeting and you guessed it, she thinks I'm still a drunkard. Our kids are all fine. Don and Meem are still busy with their black Pearl shops in Hawaii. Chuck and Bowie live in South Lake Tahoe where Chuck is now working full time for the California Department. Of Water Resources about fifteen minutes by bicycle from their home. Bob and Donna still live in Danville where Donna teaches at the Alamo middle school and Bob is working for an Accounting Firm.

Love to All. We wish you a very Merry Christmas and a healthy happy prosperous New Year. Come see us when you can, we welcome a visit anytime

Homer & Joyce Olsen

When *Putterers, Inc.* completed its last rush remodeling Job (a Rock Retaining Wall to keep our home from sliding into the Sound) in early 1999 and I began enjoying building toys

for grandchildren, we began taking *Mini-Vacations*. Unfortunately our wonderful little pet named, *Sammy* suddenly passed away, but fortunately we were blessed to find a new little Norwegian Forest kitten (Maine Coon) at the Humane Society that also had a wonderful personality she named, *Tigger* to take *Sammy's* place.

In May, Joyce and I took our first 'Mini-Vacation' to Mendocino, California to celebrate our 18th wedding anniversary, Joyce's birthday and her miraculous back operation recovery, and to gorge ourselves with their wonderful food for three days at the Heritage House. We then drove on to Walnut Creek to celebrate three more gorging days with Joyce's Mother, our kids and long time no see friends, and in June (to cash in our

Santa's helper showing off his shop wares

duel Birthday gifts from our children), to stay at the 'Salt Springs Resort' in British Colombia for four more gorging gourmet food days. By now we both looked like two smiling Elephants, but believe it or not, in July when we got the most exciting surprise of all, it was without a doubt a 4th of July celebration all over again. Our Son Bob and his beautiful wife Donna called to bashfully announce during February of the year 2000,

!!!! WE WERE GOING TO BE GRANDPARENTS!!!! HIP, HIP, HOORAY !!!!

Joyce and Homer's hideout on Salt Springs Island

Whooee, while still choked up with emotion over this wonderful news and knowing good news travels fast, Joyce's mother, Opal, flew up from Rossmoor in August to get the word straight from the smiling elephant's mouths and she and Joyce flew on to Montana to spread the word even further. To top things off while both ladies were gone, Tigger and I tried to *batch it* alone and wouldn't you know it, we soon ran out of cat food and

mutton, the sink began spilling over with dirty dishes and suddenly there was no more clean underwear. When it got to the point I couldn't unplug any of our toilets and stop Tigger from biting, I called Joyce to ask her to come home to save Tigger and me from a fate worse than death.

Joyce & Homer showing off their new, Akvavit II

Ooh boy, anyway they say the two happiest times in a boat owners life is when he sells his old boat and buys another one. On November 7, 1999·, to prepare for our grandson's birth and future boat rides (we knew he would be a boy), we traded our 25 year old 34 foot motorsailor called, 'Akvavit' in on a brand new loaded to the gills, much easier to handle and keep up, 32 ft. Nordic Tug we named 'Akvavit II'. There was no doubt about it, 1999 was a wonderful year.

GLEDELIG JUL - 2000

Why is it the older we get the faster the months go by? I still can't believe this year is nearly over and I still have that funny feeling I just mailed last year's Xmas letters. Our year began with both a 'New Years' and a 'Fourth of July Celebration' all wrapped into one because our first beautiful little grandchild,

'KYLE JAMES SYDNEY OLSEN' WAS BORN. FEBRUARY 6, 2000

Proud parents with new baby Kyle

Wow! Joyce and I were so thrilled we did what any red blooded 'Older' American Grandparent would do and 'freaked out' about helping with diaper changes. We cowardly abandoned those two poor already exhausted parents and their tiny newborn baby and selfishly booked a three-week ocean cruise around New Zealand to celebrate little Kyle's arrival. Granted, it was a 'cop out' but we did enjoy the final two American Cup Races and touring the various Ports and countryside of New Zealand and the beautiful City of Sydney, Australia. On the way home we talked Opal, Joyce's 93 year old Mother and a former School Teacher, into flying back with us and giving us a crash course in 'caring for tiny babies'. Unfortunately Tigger our cat went on strike after several 'diaper pin sticks' and refused to play the part of 'Baby Kyle' any longer and Opal flew home – disgusted.

In mid April, Opal fell and shattered her 'good' hip but fortunately it was not serious enough to require a replacement like the 'other' side. She sailed right through her operation and recuperation period once again with flying colors and after only three weeks of 'Manor Care' and another two weeks of 'Home Nursing' visits, she was her old self again and back in her own Apartment. Joyce flew down to be with her Mother at the beginning when she fell and again to help her move back into her own Apartment. We worry about her down there by herself but Opal enjoys

Sidney Australia - 1999

all her good friends there and steadfastly refuses to move up here with us. Besides, she has two boyfriends.

They say Gig Harbor is a lot like Montana because it has only two seasons, namely Winter and Company, and we enjoy both. During June, July and August we were very fortunate in having a steady stream of our wonderful friends and relatives stop by to visit and tour this beautiful area. The weather was unusually 'good' this summer so we were even able to give nearly everyone a ride on our new boat,

the 'Akvavit II'- (Waterlife Too).

Unfortunately, it was during the month of September we got the shocking news that Mary Beth, our oldest daughter that lives in Hawaii, had Breast Cancer. Thank God it

was discovered early during her yearly mammogram examination and the operation only involved a right breast 'lumpectomy' and one lymph gland removal. She started chemotherapy in mid October and will follow that with radiation treatments next spring. Fortunately, Mary Beth is a very strong healthy girl who all her life has always had a positive attitude about everything.

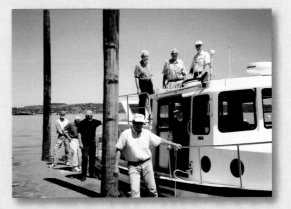

April Club Meeting - 2000

I know her positive attitude combined with all of us praying for her, will result in her complete recovery.

Love to all. We wish you all a very Merry Christmas and a healthy, happy, prosperous New Year. Come see us when you can.

Homer & Joyce & Tigger.

GLEDELIG JUL - 2001

Still stunned and in shock over the cowardly 9/11 attack that has re-stirred our vivid memories of the cowardly attach on Pearl Harbor and World War II that followed,

Mary and husband Don - she's cancer free!

we send mixed greetings and our prayers from our home to your home this year. It is our hope during this stressful holiday season, all is well with you and all your family

On family's good news this year, we had a wonderful family reunion in May to celebrate not only Joyce's birthday and our wedding anniversary, but, best of all, our daughter Mary Beth's VICTORY over Breast

Cancer, after nearly a year of chemotherapy and radiation treatments. Our prayers, along with Mary's positive attitude, were answered and we celebrated this wonderful occasion at a beautiful resort called the 'Aerie' in the mountains thirty miles north of Victoria, Canada. Whooee, it's the first time I think any of us have ever had a four-hour-nine-course-French dinner.

Baby Kyle at age one – 2001

Joyce's 94 year old mother continues to look younger every year and we are happy to report she has finally agreed to move to Gig Harbor to be nearer if she can have her own 'Partial Care Apartment. We are now on the Merrill Garden's Retirement Complex list in Gig Harbor

similar to her 'Waterford Apartment' she has now at Rossmoor. Joyce keeps busy with all her Clubs and Volunteer activities but still freaks out crossing the Narrows Bridge to shop at Nordstrom. Our kids are doing great. Bob and Donna are the perfect parents for little Kyle who is growing like a weed. Chuck and Bowie seem happy with their lives living at Lake Tahoe. Don and Meem, including all the rest of us, are so happy and so relieved with Meem's cancer recovery words cannot describe our feelings. Our family is so blessed.

Like last year during June and July, we were fortunate to have our wonderful friends and relatives stop in for a visit and a tour of our beautiful country. The summer weather was perfect again so we put more hours on our Nordic Tug gunk holing and motoring around Puget Sound.

Kyle's first birthday

In late August I returned from my fishing trip north of Prince Rupert, Canada with a bad case of 'Pleurisy' and Strep Pneumonia' which immediately put me in the hospital for eleven days. I'm home and feel fine now, but Whooee, I'll tell you, I've never had anything smart so bad in my life before, as that exciting little experience.

Well, keep a stiff upper lip and keep hoping for the best. We wish you a merry Xmas and a happy New Year and hope you can come see us soon.

Homer & Joyce & Tigger

Apparently when I came back from my fishing trip in 2001 with what I thought was just a bad cold, I was in much worse shape than I thought and once again Joyce saved my life by literally forcing me to go see our Doctor. You guessed it, Dr. Ostorgren immediately put me in the hospital and to this day I still remember having the most vivid dream about my dad visiting me while there it still haunts me to this day.

After Dr. Ostorgren finished checking me out, he said I had a serious case of *Pleurisy* combined with *Strep Pneumonia*, and immediately sent me to the hospital for a cap scan of my right lung. It was during the cap scan they discovered I had a serious infection between my inside lung lining and the interior side of my rib cage (how that could of happened I'll never know) that had produced nearly a liter of puss and was increasing rapidly. I remember three Doctors began arguing over what to do about the infection and one of them turned to me and said, "It looks like we'll have to split your rib gage down the middle of your chest in order to hinge you open enough to scrape and disinfect the infected area". I said, "That might work, but I can tell you this right now. I would never survive a stunt like that and I hope you can come up with a better plan than that". Well, one of the other doctor's must have taken petroleum engineering because he said, "How about just drilling a small hole between two of his ribs into his puss *oil pool* while being careful not to punch through the inside lung liner, and *pump out that pool* while giving him massive doses of antibiotics", which they approved. Well, you can believe this or not, but nearly a quart of *puss oil* was removed from my right lung area before I began to improve.

Halibut fishing is excellent in British Columbia

While they were *nip and tuck* pumping out my personal *oil well* for the first few days, I kept losing weight until I had lost nearly 20 pounds and my blood pressure dropped from 128/78 to 90/48. At that point my heart began tribulations intermittently and I suddenly had this vivid dream of my dad (who had passed away fourteen years earlier) walking into my hospital room to visit. I remember being happy to see him and we laughed and talked about all the fun things we did together when I was a kid until he finally stood up to leave and said, *"Are you ready to go with me now Son?"* I said, "Dad, I'd like to, but I still have so many things left to do I can't go with you now". He nodded and said, *"OK, let me know when your ready and I'll come back for you"*, and left.

When I woke up I'll tell you my dream was so *real* I was wringing wet from perspiration and I called my nurse in to tell her about it. She said, "Now I know you're going to get well. I've had several seriously ill patients tell me of similar dreams and when they answered, 'I can't go with you now because of important business, they always got better and went home from the hospital soon afterwards".

Interestingly, the important things I had to do before I could go with my dad was to stop procrastinating and write this book I promised my family, make sure my wife and family are well taken care of after I'm gone, and to finish setting up the three Olsen family grandchildren's

Angel Homer C. Olsen – 2001

scholarship trust's to help them acquire *meaningful job educations*. Interestingly, years later when Dr. Rowland, one of my three doctors laughingly told me they had a bet I would never leave the hospital alive, I said, "Damn Doc, I could be rich now if you had let me in on that bet."

GLEDELIG JUL - 2002

Homer, Joyce & Opal – 1992

Once again we send our greetings from our home to your home with the hope that during this Holiday Season all is well with you and your family. As always, our year has gone by very rapidly and it is hard to believe that our little grandson 'Kyle Olsen' will be three years old in just two more months.

Our New Year began by moving Opal, Joyce's young 95 year old Mother, to Gig Harbor on the 1ˢᵗ of February so she could be nearer to us. She is now comfortably living in an Apartment at a wonderfully well run and maintained 'Honored Citizen' Home near us called Merrill Gardens. She has 'Level three care' because of her age which means she gets her meals delivered to her room if desired, help bathing, laundry and cleaning service, medication and nursing care, and transportation to and from the Doctor if necessary, etc. In other words, she is now living like the Queen she is now that she sold her Condominium in Rossmoor.

Joyce and I were able to sneak secretly off in May for a few days to celebrate our Anniversary at the Kula Lodge in Hawaii, but I'm not supposed to tell anybody. Like last year, during June, July and August we were fortunate again in having many of our wonderful friends and relatives stop in for a visit and tour this beautiful area. The summer weather was perfect again this year so we put quite a few more hours on the

Anniversary in Kula

'Akvavit 11' motoring around Puget Sound with everyone. I finally got the Dingy painted and mounted on the swim platform so everyone can breathe easier about having a life boat we, named 'Tigger II'.

We had a wonderful family reunion in September at the Empress Hotel in Victoria, Canada to belatedly celebrate Joyce's birthday, but most of all, to celebrate our oldest Daughter, Mary Elizabeth's second year 'Victory' anniversary over Breast Cancer. Our

Mor Mor Joyce, Kyle Olsen & Far Far Homer – 2001

prayers were answered once again when she got her second yearly clean bill of health.

Joyce is healthy and doing fine. Our kids are also doing great. Bob and Donna are the 'perfect parents' for little Kyle who is growing like a weed. Chuck and Bowie also seem very happy living at Lake Tahoe. Don and Meem are doing great. Mary Beth finished her book and is now busy wit signing engagements from Hawaii to Chicago. I am so proud of all of them.

Love to all, and we hope you all have a Merry Christmas and Happy prosperous New Year.

Homer, Joyce & Tigger

Our oldest daughter Mary Beth wrote this beautiful testimonial for her sister's 50th birthday party on October 15, 2003, that I felt should be included in this book for posterity, entitled:

The Olsen Sisters, 10/15/2003.

My little sister Barbara turned fifty today—the one I carried around when she was one-year-old and I was two-and-a-half. I told everyone, "My baby. This is my baby". She of the naturally curly blond ponytail and big blue eyes; "Oh, she looks like a princess," strangers would exclaim. My brown eyes downcast, I nodded, brown hair bobbing, Always calm and observant, she would sit in the middle of the living room, serene and quiet as I ran around the room, a four-and-a-half-year-old doing cartwheels, turning somersaults, singing show tunes, kicking up my heels— anything to get attention and applause. At three-years-old, she already knew she was loved enough, and didn't have to work for it.

She had a pretty singing voice, though she didn't think so. I taught her songs so we could sing harmony. We put on shows in the garage, big productions

Christmas 1953

with make-up and costumes gleaned from my mother's cast-offs. In the backyard we would perform acrobatic feats of wonder using the garden hose and creating a circus for all the neighborhood kids. We were a team—we were sisters.

We discovered books together and became bookworms, each checking out fourteen books a week from the local library, and reading all twenty-eight before they were returned and exchanged for a new tower of fourteen each. We worked through Mary Poppins, Little Women, Jack London and all the Oz books, the Shoes books (Ballet Shoes, Skating Shoes, etc.) and A Wrinkle in Time. We loved fantasy and stories about girls who were heroes.

Neither one was popular in high school; we were both smart, and fell into the Geeks and Hippies segment of the teen-age caste system. Bored with normal activities, we opened our own fashion boutique at fifteen and thirteen, designed and sewed all our own clothes, and with the help of our friends we filled a whole store with our creations. We even made costumes for rock groups.

Sisters love shoes

Holding hands

College for me, Europe for her, then we came together again in the early 70's to open a Bikini Shop. We could do anything; we were sisters, and a team. Relationships and marriages followed, years of working in the theater for me, years of working in publishing for her. We were always connected, always close.

Then I was diagnosed with breast cancer three years ago, and she dropped everything to come and be with me and help. She cooked hundreds of meals and froze them, cleaned our house, top to bottom, and went with me to scary chemotherapy treatments. At forty-eight-years old, I finally learned what she had always known; that I was loved, I was enough; I didn't have to work for it.

We're growing up

I'm fine now, and she and I talk every week from 3,000 miles away. We're a deeply connected team, and our husbands joke about how lucky they are to have married the Olsen sisters. How could she be fifty? How could I be almost fifty-two? Well, that's the magic, she is really still my baby, and we're still singing songs together, putting on puppet shows in the garage, reading books and now traveling the world. Every time I think of her, whether we are together or apart, we are all these things. She has been there with me, through all of it. We know all the secrets . . . we were there. Together.

I threw a big party for her fiftieth birthday. Everyone was asked to bring a skit or poem or song. We learned the song "Sisters" from White Christmas and performed it at the party; at the end, the crowd applauded and

Bowee's wedding

someone yelled, "Do it again. We want to hear it again!" So we did. And I'm sure we'll do it again and again over the next fifty years. The Olsen Girls never quit because;

We're a team, forever and ever.
We're survivors.
We're sisters.

The Olsen Girls

As a breast cancer survivor, our beautiful daughter Mary Beth has also written and published two books of her ordeal with the help of her sister Barbara, entitled, *"Chicken Soup for the Breast Cancer Survivor's soul"* and *"Tools and Tips from the Trenches"*. She is currently busy with interviews and book signings and both she and her sister have become active in fund raising for Cancer Research. Needless to say, Joyce and I are very proud of our two daughters and their accomplishments. I know our prayers helped, but we also believe it was Mary Beth's positive attitude, her courage, her optimism about everything and her strength of character is what really saw her through that terrible ordeal.

GLEDELIG JUL - 2003

Once again we send our greetings from our home to your home with the hope that during this Holiday Season all is well with you and your family. Our year has gone by very rapidly and it is hard to believe that our little grandson 'Kyle Olsen' will be four years old in just two more months.

Joyce and I were able to sneak off for a few days in May to celebrate our Anniversary at the Empress Hotel in Vancouver, Canada but I'm not supposed to tell anybody. During June, July and August we were fortunate in having many of our wonderful friends and relatives stop in for a visit and a tour of this beautiful area. The summer weather was perfect this year so we put quite a few more hours on our Nordic Tug the 'Akvavit II' motoring around Puget Sound with everyone. We were also very happy to learn our wonderful April Club friends voted to make Gig Harbor their Annual Special July Meeting site for the next several years.

Opal's 95th birthday

This year is ending up as a very sad one for us. Joyce's 96 year old Mother quietly passed away on September 4th after a long and gradual health decline and only a month after we had moved her from her Merrill Gardens Apartment to a full care nursing facility. She was determined to reach her 96th birthday and then she just lost her will to live any longer and passed away six days after her birthday party. Her last request was to be buried next her Mother in Centerville, Iowa so Joyce and I flew back with her to Iowa where a beautiful graveside burial ceremony was conducted with her close family and friends. She was named 'Opal' after a jewel because she was a jewel of a person and she will be sorely missed by everyone who knew her.

Joyce is doing fine. She keeps busy with all her Church and Clubs and many friends. She still freaks out crossing the Narrows Bridge to shop at Nordstrom's, but otherwise she's

doing great. Our kids are also doing well. Chuck and Bowie are very happy living at Lake Tahoe. Don and Meem are doing well and have just opened another Jewelry Store on Balboa Island, California. Bob and Donna seem very happy and are the 'perfect parents' for little Kyle who is growing like a weed while waiting

Kyles Xmas- 2003

anxiously for Santa to come early with all his presents (and my Santa Helper's shop toys). We are so very proud of all our children, and especially our little grandchild Kyle we are obviously spoiling rotten.

I made the August fishing trip this year to Prince Rupert, Canada with all my buddies' despite my knee problem, and wouldn't you know it; everybody caught their four

day limit except me, which proves I really am a lousy jinx. Well you guessed it; I went ahead with my left knee replacement operation in October to eliminate 'the jinx' and am currently recuperating in anticipation of fishing next year. It's funny, and youcan believe this or not, but I do feel 'luckier'.

Love to all. We wish you a very Merry Christmas and a healthy, happy, prosperous New Year. Come see us when you can.

Xmas with Kyle – 2003

Homer & Joyce & Tigger

As another little side story, I remember around this same time my good friend, Murry Regensburger and I were fishing partners in British Columbia and for some unknown reason he wasn't even getting a nibble on his line while I kept reeling in fish like they were going out of style. Finally he said, "No wonder, you have the lucky pole", so .I traded fishing poles with him and wouldn't you know it, I began pulling fish in with his pole like mad, while he sat there like a dud without a nibble on my pole. He said, "Well, it's because you're sitting on the lucky side of the boat, that's why", so we traded sides and you guessed it again, he still didn't get a nibble while I kept reeling in fish. Oooh boy, by now he was almost in tears over his lack of luck, and in a quivering high pitched squeaky little voice like the whole world was out to get him personally said,

Hey look at that, my partner just got a bite

"I don't know why you guys invite me on these damn fishing trips anyway. All I'm good for is frying the bacon and eggs and washing dishes. The way I see it, I'm just a damn *Jinx* who has even *jinxed* himself, and was never cut out to be a fisherman". I said, "Nonsense Murry,

Enjoying a fishing trip feeding frenzy with my buddies

fishing is just like Safety in the work place, it's all about *attitude and thinking positively* about catching fish, or gold mining, or even gambling. To be successful in anything you do Murry, you have to think positive", to which his answer was, "That's a lot of crap".

I know you won't believe this, but honest to God, this is a true story. I held up my hand and said, "Murry, contained within this right hand of mine is all the power you'll ever need to change you're luck and all I have to do is lay this hand on your shoulder to transfer that power to you and you'll catch a fish". Well, and this is the unbelievable part, at the exact moment I laid my hand on Murry's shoulder, and *ZAP!!, a fish struck* his line so hard he nearly lost his pole overboard and Oooh boy, the fight to land his fish was on. You guessed it. A half hour later, the most stunned, excited, thrilled, seen the light and was converted, Murry Regensburger,

The Dolphin North's Mother Ship anchored in Works Passage

landed his *25 pound King Salmon* safely in the boat and unbelievably, his personality changed 180 degrees. Instead of his former polite, quiet, tip toeing, pigeon toed walk, the meek little Murry we all knew and loved, suddenly changed into a loud mouthed, uncouth, wind passing, braggart that almost made him impossible to tolerate. To make matters even worse (for me anyway) I lost my *power* with my shoulder laying hand demonstration and from then on never got a bite and became known to everyone as the group as a *jinx*. It has never ceased to amaze me how fast some people's personalities will suddenly change when they are *handed* a feeling of power. But then again, I suppose superstition plays a role because whenever I did catch a fish; it was always from my own lucky fishing hole near *Indian Rock*

My lucky Indian Head fishing hole

Around the first part of April in 2004, Joyce and I were invited to Newport Beach to see Mary and Don's new store and as it turned out it was a surprise 80th birthday party for dear old dad. Wow, my wife Joyce and all three of our children and their spouses went all out for my party and I was really touched, and I mean really, touched by their wonderful testimonials they gave at the party. There is no question about it. To be recognized by your business peers and loved and appreciated by your family is the ultimate compliment for any father, husband, and/or business entrepreneur. I can't tell you how much I appreciated all the love and effort that went into making the party such a memorable occasion and I'm so proud of my family. Following are copies of the talks

Homer and Joyce happily enjoying their retirement

my three children and my two sons in laws gave at my 80th birthday party on April 7, 2004. I was so touched by them I felt they should be recorded for posterity.

To Homer on his 80th birthday, by Chuck Curtis

It has been over twenty years since I first met you, Homer. Your warmth, generosity, interest and humor have always made me feel comfortable, loved and part of your family far beyond being your son-in-law. Your stories of growing up in Utah resonate with me and my own family's humble past and I love that you maintain the simple desires for happiness through friends and family. I also appreciate the skills and drive you have that made you successful in the engineering construction business, but mostly, I appreciate the love you show to Barbara and me and the rest of your family. Thank you Homer, for being such a wonderful father-in-law.

To my dear young dad on his 80th birthday, by Barbara Olsen Curtis

What is a father? The most basic answer to that question is, a father only contributes to the genetic structure of a child. If you're lucky enough to have a father who sticks around after the conception, that father also contributes to life in many other ways as well. I am one of the lucky ones because my father stuck around, a lot when we were little. He was so great when my sister and I were little, with lots of cuddling and reading stories and building things and telling stories and making faces and whistling, all designed to delight and enchant little girls. I loved my 'Dadden' so much and I knew he would do anything for me because he loved me.

Dad seemed to develop a mythic quality and all the stories about his childhood growing up with my grandpa and my great grandpa Olsen on the old Gravelbed farm took on a veneer of legend. They were not so much stories of youthful escapades starring the boy that grew up to be my father, but an epic chronicle of the old west with a hero named Ole K. Olsen, the great grandfather I unfortunately never knew. Later on as I grew older and into my teens, that mischievous adventuresome little boy in those stories seemed to look less and less like the angry distant man my father had become. I actually felt jealous of the fun that little boy in those stories had and I decided the life we were sharing with Dad then was boring because he didn't seem to have much fun with us. I understand now how busy Dad was then with his increasing job responsibilities and starting up his own business and building the many challenging construction projects for which he is justly famous. As a child and a young adult, I was obviously too self-absorbed to see, and be proud of, the passion my dad poured into his work.

After the divorce and the painful reconciliation later, I got to spend quality time with my dad. I guess sometimes it takes a tragedy to bring the best out in us and I am so grateful for those precious Thursday night dinners we had that brought Bob and me together with our dad. We talked and laughed together, just the three of us, and it was great. Later Dad fell in love with a vital fun-loving lady named Alice Joyce Deyoe, and she became part of our regular Thursday night dinners and I was happy my dad continued to spend the time with us, not as an obligation, but as people he loved.

Then I met Chuck, without whom I don't know how I could live. Chuck and Dad hit it off instantly and I felt even closer to Dad through his relationship with Chuck I felt I had given Dad a gift bringing Chuck into our family and I love basking in the warmth of their love and respect for each other. It wasn't until Dad started writing his memoirs I truly felt Dad had finally opened his heart completely to me. It was through the unfolding of his life the letters he copied into the pages and the pictures of relatives I never met but figured so prominently in his life, I discovered my dad. .I am so proud of him-so proud of the life he made for himself, often in the face of unbelievable struggle and hardship. I love him even more, knowing of the frightful challenges his family put him through- and how compassionately he dealt with heart breaking family tragedy.

I am one of the lucky ones because I have a Dad who stuck around and contributed so much to my life in so many ways. Thank you Dad for writing this wonderful gift for us. I will cherish your book with all my heart, knowing how much time and soul searching it took and how much love you've expressed by including us and completing this monumental project.

Dear Old Dad turns 80 on April 7, 2004, by Robert K. Olsen

Wow! Dad's 80 years old – that's a lot of years. A client asked me what my dad did to make it this long and how that was good news for me. All I could think to say was eat less and exercise more, which is what all the Doctors tell the Olsen's at every checkup. Dad has always had a positive attitude, not to mean he didn't worry, because he would go through four cigars on bid days when he thought we might be low, but he was always upbeat and in a good humor. I always think mental attitude is more important than medicine gives it credit for, look at Bob Hope, Henry Youngman, Milton Berle, and George Burns who never saw an excercycle and still lived much longer than the overeaters, smokers, and drinkers should statistically be expected to live.

My dad loves good wholesome food like barbecued steaks, lamb shanks, pot roasts, nearly all the cheeses, whole milk, homemade ice-cream, good strong coffee and fish like Salmon and Halibut properly cooked. He enjoys watching football and especially when

Stanford beats Cal and/or USC, and the 49ers beat the Raiders. He prefers Ford Motor Company cars and trucks and CAT construction equipment, and loves to go fishing for Salmon with his friends and solving construction engineering job problems. Put him in

Bob and Dad

a living room with a shot glass of Akvavit and a beer chaser and he's happy, but most of all, he enjoys his family and his friends the most. They can join him anytime to listen his stories.

My dad is simply a wonderful person. My sister's are always commenting on how conservative he is, but Dad is extremely generous and tolerant of people as long as they are trying. I think they even felt he was to the right of "Attila the Hun", but he is really only a Truman, Eisenhower, Goldwater, Gerald Ford, and a Bob Dole kind of guy, politically. These modest men (for politicians) really were about saying NO to all spending unless it was used for defense or putting Americans to work doing meaningful work. They opposed overspending, government giveaways, higher taxes, Foreign entanglements beyond stopping Fascism or Communism, and programs that have shifted the powers away from State and Local governments to Washington.

On the other hand, my dad has total disdain for the other guys, the ones who feel society owes a debt to constituents for past wrongs, who feel they should be entitled to greater rights and privileges due to inherited wealth, who feel America is not the land of freedom and opportunity, but a police state, and jurists who interpret bureaucratic proclamations law (or make it up themselves) .In summary, my dad is correct, and it's a shame I can't think of one politician in Washington like my dad's guys anymore.

It was great working for my Dear Old Dad because I was able to see first hand how generous he was with those who worked hard for him. It was part of the old Viking Code of "pulling on the oars will share in the plunder", but also to take good care of those who worked hard for him, the best way they knew how. Despite the really good years, and rewarding handsomely with bonuses and other incentives, my dad never paid himself more than the President of the United States made because he thought it was criminal to do so. He made twenty or more people millionaires who worked for him over the time he ran the company, with virtually every one of them making more than they ever would by working for another like company. He also spoke for the common man, saying in a humorous way what everyone was thinking, cutting the pompous down to size, and being eternally optimistic in the face of pessimism. He really was effected by the depression of the '30's and World War II, and he followed the basic thinking that business must give back by producing a quality made product at a fair price, and reward employees that make a company successful. It's those qualities plus his overall honesty that make me so proud of my dad.

My Beautiful Family

Finally, being a Dad like Dad is terrific. His happiest time he told me was when he was a little kid living with his own Grandpa and Dad on that old gravelbed farm in central Utah. You could tell from my Grandpa Homer C. Olsen's stories, they both loved little Yunior (my dad) and enjoyed being with and listening to him more than anything else. Grandpa Homer C. Olsen was also an incredibly generous people person but really didn't put that skill to use until he was 50 and began selling insurance, which to him was such an easy job because he enjoyed talking to people anyway. My dad learned a lot from those two wonderful men about being the supportive, honest, funny, kind and always being there as the same dad. I've always felt my dad would rather just spend the time with me listening to what I wanted to talk about – just like I am with my own son, Kyle. Happy 80th birthday Dad.

My dad is 80 years old today, by Mary Olsen Kelly

My dad is a great man and it has been my honor to have known him for fifty one of those eighty years. He possesses a rare combination of qualities; standup comic, politician, staunch hard working Republican, feminist, caring father, and a brilliant financial genius, but he is also visionary leader, successful business man, and an innovator in the field of engineering.

My dad and I have not always seen eye to eye. In my teenage and college years, we had little in common philosophically or intellectually, but even then I always respected him as a great leader and visionary. I was always proud of him and looked up to him and tried to emulated him because I admired his story telling expertise, his sense of humor and ability to make a room full of people howl with laughter over his perfectly timed jokes.

Dad & Meem – 2002

For the past few years as promised, Dad has been tirelessly chronicling his life into a book filled with the love and legacy of our family. All his treasured memories, all the photos and letters collected over a lifetime, are contained in this when finished. He has said many times he was doing this for us kids so we would have all the family stories and folk-lore in one organized volume. It's a monumental task, one that will take years to complete, but that doesn't stop him. Every day, Joyce says he goes downstairs to his basement office to work on his masterpiece. His commitment and focus on the task is legendary.

We have all tried to help Dad a little with ideas, editing, scanning photos and slides, and learning computer skills, but mostly it was support and appreciation and our love. He is the one who is doing all the work on the book, unbelievably by hunt and peck with one finger, filling page after page every day with his hysterically funny stories of growing up with cowboys and sheepherders in the ranch and farm high desert country of central Utah and Nevada, his years in the Army, his college years at Pomona and Stanford, and being a young engineer starting out in the world who ultimately starts up his own corporation and becomes part of building some of the largest projects in California

Meem and Don

I'm so proud of you Dad, and I'm filled with appreciation for the way you have shared your life with all of us. I know you so much better through this wonderful book. I love you Dad.

Happy 80th birthday Homer, by Don Kelly.

When I first met you Homer it was at was at your 65th birthday party in Sacramento at Chuck and Barbara's house. I had met the love of my life, his beautiful daughter Mary, not too long before. I was invited to the party but was a little apprehensive because Chuck said I would be facing the Olsen gauntlet. However the moment I met Homer, I found him to be instantly and incredibly likable. We wound up announcing our wedding engagement at the same time Bob and Donna announced their engagement. What a day! I was wholeheartedly welcomed and made to feel part of the family immediately.

Over the years I have been inspired by the way Homer ran his company and all the wisdom he shared with me about business. It's also always a pleasure to see his quick humor and wonderful laugh, and to be with him is a joy. I predict right now his book will be made into a major block-buster movie with Harrison Ford starring as Homer. And that's a true story.

Here's a salute to the worlds greatest Father-in-Law.

GLEDELIG JUL - 2005

Once again we send greetings from our home to your home with the hope that all is well with you and your family. Like every year, this year passed by us rapidly and believe

John Schimmick & Homer Olsen 2005

it or not, our little grandson 'Kyle Olsen' will be six years old in just two more months.

To prove we "Honored Citizens" lives can still be exciting, Joyce and I managed to sneak off to Los Angeles in January to celebrate the Golden Beaver Award in Management to John Schimmick, and then flew to Reno to party with the "April Club" and celebrate my 81st birthday early. Not unlike the year before, we "snuck off" by ourselves again in late May to quietly celebrate Joyce's birthday and our anniversary at the Empress and Aries Hotels in Victoria, Canada. We each took separate vacations in October. Joyce to Montana while I didn't go to Boulder City, Nevada, for my 63rd High School Reunion, as planned. Why? Joyce came back from Montana with the flue and after she shared it with me, I was too sick to travel. In December, we plan to fly to Danville for Xmas with our children, so all in all, things have not been too bad for a couple of hairlips.

Tex and Monnie Olsen are in the picture

During June, July, August and September, we were very fortunate again to have several of our good friends and relatives stop by to visit and tour this beautiful area. The summer weather was perfect this year so we were able to put more hours on our Nordic Tug, the 'Akvavit II', motoring around Puget Sound and showing everyone our new Tacoma Narrows Bridge during its construction. As always, we were very happy to see everyone and thankful they made a special effort to stop by for a visit. Once again, our special thanks go out to our April Club friends who were able to make the annual "Special" July meeting in Gig Harbor. Joyce and I feel we are blessed to have so many wonderful friends and relatives.

Joyce is doing fine. She still stays busy with her Clubs and her many friends and volunteer activities and still freaks out crossing the Narrows Bridge to shop at Nordstrom's, but otherwise she's doing great. Our kids are also doing very well. Bob and Donna seem very happy in Danville and are the 'perfect parents' for little Kyle who is growing like a weed. Bob's one man accounting business is more than keeping him busy and Donna is still

Tacoma Narrows Bridge - 2005

teaching at middle school. Chuck and Bowie are happy with their lives and are still enjoying their Lake Tahoe "snowed in" living. Don and Meem are happy traveling and are doing very well in their Jewelry Store business. Needless to say, we are very proud of all our children.

I missed the August fishing trip this year near Prince Rupert with my 'fishing buddies' and wouldn't you know it, they all caught their eight fish maximum take home limit the very first day. I knew right away they would miss me because it proved once and for all I really am a jinx. From then on they said their whole trip was an exhausting "catch

and release" five minute cycle, day after day. But the good news was, everyone cheered (or was it jeered) me when I announced it would be the last fishing trip I would miss if my son Bob would go with me and help slow the fishing down again. But now that I'm a potentially famous Author and professional grandson toy maker and all, it really is a sacrifice for me to fish again because I've got a book to finish writing and I'm way behind schedule building toys for grandchildren.

Kyle & Far Far - 2005

Love to all. We wish everyone a very Merry Christmas and a healthy, happy, New Year. Come see us when you can.

Homer, Joyce & Tigger

Roy, Bob & Stan show off Bob's first fish

Believe it or not I finally talked my son Bob into going fishing with me this year in Canada and despite his ' *this is a waste of time and money* argument, he had a ball. I'll tell you, when he caught that first 12 pound Coho Salmon and then a 30 pound halibut the next day, that was all it took to make him a true believer. At my ripe old age of 82, this really was my last year fishing with my buddies, all because I can no longer take the 5 am wakeup calls and late nights and binge drinking story telling bull seasons. Bill Young also threw in the towel that year after thirty years of sponsoring our group and putting up with my dumb jokes. Bill, it was fun while it lasted and I will always

be grateful to you for inviting me every year since 1980 to put up with my *bloviating*. As a potentially famous world renowned author and toy maker for grandchildren, it's been a real sacrifice for me to miss those fun fishing trips, but then maybe Bob will be interested in taking my place. Oh to be young again.

My last fishing trip breakfast with my fishing buddies

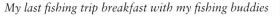

GLEDELIG JUL - 2007

Once again we send greetings from our home to your home with the hope that all is well with you and your family. Like all years, this past year whizzed by also and it's hard to believe our little grandson 'Kyle Olsen' will be eight years old in two more months.

Homer & David Olsen

To prove Honored Citizens can still enjoy some real excitement, Joyce and I drove in to downtown Gig Harbor in early April to celebrate my 83rd birthday, and then re-celebrated everyone's else's birthdays in April and early May with Mary and Don Kelly. Not unlike in the olden days of 06, we secretly snuck off again to quietly celebrate Joyce's birthday and our 26th wedding anniversary at the Grand Pacific Hotel in Victoria, Canada. Then in December, all our children and grandchild will be here for an early Xmas, so all in all, when you think about it hard enough, it has been so far, and will be, an exciting year.

During June through October, we were very fortunate again to have many of our good friends and relatives stop by for a visit and tour this beautiful area. The summer weather was perfect this year so we were able to put many more hours on the 'Akvavit II', motoring around south Puget Sound and showing everyone our new Tacoma Narrows Bridge that was completed and opened for traffic in July on schedule. As always, we were very happy to see everyone and thankful they made a special effort to visit us again this year, and our special thanks go to our April Club friends who were able to make another best to date annual Special July meeting here in Gig Harbor. This year marked the tenth Special April Club meeting here on the Puget Sound so Joyce and I feel we're very blessed to have so many wonderful friends and relatives who take the time to visit here with us.

Joyce is doing fine. She still stays busy with her Clubs and volunteer activities, and she still freaks out driving over our new bridge so I can drive her across to shop at Nordstrom's, but otherwise she's doing fine. Our kids are also still doing well. Bob and Donna seem very happy living and working in Danville and are the perfect parents for little Kyle who started second grade this year and is growing like a weed. Bob's one man accounting firm is more than keeping him busy and Donna is still teaching at middle school. Chuck and Bowie are happy with their lives and are still enjoying their Lake Tahoe

Tigger in the walker

snowed in living. Don and Meem are happy traveling more and are doing well in their Jewelry business. As a breast cancer survivor, Mary Beth and Don are busy selling Meem's book she wrote called, *Tools and Tips from the trenches,* with the help of her sister. Needless to say, we are very proud of our little family

In July, along with several members of Don Kelly's family, Joyce and her niece, Teresa White, went on an Alaska cruise ship tour to help and support Meem who was a guest speaker this year on the ship. Her subject was *Surviving Breast Cancer,* which was well received by the passengers, and everyone had an enjoyable time. Unfortunately, Joyce came down with a touch of stomach flue during the last two days of the trip and was placed under House Arrest, hand cuffs, ankle bracelet and all, by the Ships brown shirted Troopers (fearing the publicity of a communicable disease), which spoiled her trip somewhat. As a potentially famous single novel writer and a renowned Santa's toy maker helper (along with Tigger's experienced help), I have managed to keep busy this year. Hopefully my first (and last) book will be finished and in print by my goal of Joyce's 80th birthday celebration on May 23, 2008.

Donna and Joyce

We hope you have a Merry Christmas and a Healthy, Happy New Year, and will come see us for a visit next year when you can find the time

Homer, Joyce & Tigger Olsen

When I began writing this book in November of 2001 shortly after my dad's *dream visit* during my pneumonia hospitalization, I crossed my heart promised Joyce and my children I would finish it by Joyce's 80th birthday, May 23, 2008.

Like me, they all thought six and a half years to write such a boring uninteresting biography like mine was a ridiculously long time, but as it turned out none of them knew how computer incompetent, inexperienced and, let's face it, stupid I really was as a writer who flunked English in high school, to even consider doing such a monumental task as this book. As they say, ignorance is bliss and I'm hysterical so, as anyone who knows me well will tell you, "Once old Homer makes a commitment and a decision to accomplish something, his Norwegian–German genes will never let him stop until it's finished".

Homer and Joyce's American Dream Fulfilled

I'm now entering my seventh year hen pecking all these long sentience's, misspelled words ands misplaced commas with one finger, and for some unknown reason this past year my health has suddenly deteriorated at a much faster rate. I'm now allergic to many more things than just milk products and I've had more cavities and root canals. The glaucoma in both my eyes has increased to where my right eye pressure is over 22 and the *scatter test* indicates I've already lost half the vision in that eye. Doctor Taylor said "Something is going on in your body I don't understand, but we'll have to operate immediately to save the remaining vision in your right eye". Well, the operation by Dr. Pham was a success and the pressure in that eye has been lowered to 7 again, but the glaucoma in the left eye has suddenly increased and my hearing is continually getting worse. Take my word for it, old age is not for sissies.

Joyces' 80th Birthday Invitation

After my yearly physical checkup in April Doctor Ostergren reviewed all my lab work with me and said, "Everything seems to be normal except your PSA test shows a *sharp incline* this past year so I think the urologist should see you". Well to shorten this story somewhat, a worried Doctor Dean took 12 biopsies of my prostate and on May 16, 2008 informed me I had cancer and should begin my treatments immediately. I said, "Doc, my wife's 80th birthday party is scheduled for May 23rd so I would appreciate it if we could keep this quiet until her party is over before we begin. He said; OK let's begin your treatments on

June sixth and I said, "That sounds like a good date to me because we landed on Normandy Beach on *D Day* June 6, 1944 to save the world. It might be a *good omen*".

Well as it all turned out, Joyce's 80th birthday celebration at the Canterwood Country Club ended up as the *Mother* of all birthday parties and the nearly eighty people who attended are still talking about what a wonderful time they had celebrating not only Joyce's 80th birthday and several other May birthdays in the crowd, but also our 27th wedding anniversary. The invitation shown above was mailed to eighty of our relatives, old friends, and to our neighbors, and believe it or not, some of them came all the way from Montana, Illinois, Utah, Nevada, California, Hawaii and from all over Washington State to attend. Joyces' welcoming speech and the notice we left at the hotel for everyone checking in is combined as shown below

The Birthday Queen

Dear Friends and Relatives,

Thank you so much for coming to Gig Harbor for my 80th birthday and reunion of old friends and relatives party. We really appreciate your taking the time and going through all the hassle of traveling for this wonderful reunion of old friends and family who have not seen each other for many years. If you have already checked in at the Inn at Gig Harbor or elsewhere, no events have been scheduled for Thursday, May 22, .and you are all free to enjoy the local scenery and restaurants on your own. The hotel desk clerk will be happy to assist you and answer any questions you may have concerning the area.

On Friday, May 23, you are all cordially invited to attend a relaxing summer evening gourmet "dress code" (no jeans) 80th birthday celebration dinner party for yours truly at the Canterwood Country Club on Friday evening, beginning at 6:00 pm. A separate dining room

Homer and Aunt Katy

with outside entrance has been reserved for everyone in our group together with a surprise program and Rocket's type floor show directed and produced by our daughter, Mary Olsen Kelly.

On Saturday May 24, all the MEN from out of town who wish to volunteer for a death defying boat ride on the "USS AKVAVIT II" commanded by my husband, Homer Olsen, the world famous incontinent Norwegian Barge Captain, along with a well deserved relax-

USS Akvavit II – 2000

ing nerve settling Akvavit skoaling luncheon, please report in two separate boat groups of 10 or less each. The first boat group will report to slip number A 23 at the Gig Harbor Ma- rina at 10:00 am and the second boat group will report to Shenanigans Restaurant (3017 Ruston Way) on Tacoma's commencement Bay at 11:30 am, where the "USS AKVAVIT II" will hopefully arrive with the first boat

group simultaneously at 11:30 am. An Executive Board Room has been reserved for the

men's luncheon hosted by Captain Slim, for the nerve settling story telling luncheon that unfortunately must be adjourned by 2:00 pm for the harrowing boat ride back to Gig Harbor with the second boat group and our afternoon naps. Transportation to and from Shenanigans and the Gig Harbor Marina, will hopefully be arranged by the two groups.

Freddie an David Dahl and Mary

For all the WIVES and significant others from out of town, our two beautiful daugh- ters and world renowned hostesses, Mary Olsen Kelly and Barbara Olsen Curtis, are sponsoring a leisurely afternoon luncheon for the LADIES who wish to enjoy a relax-

Kyle at mic

ing summer day reminiscing with old friends at the excit- ing Green Turtle Restaurant overlooking the harbor in Gig Harbor. Please meet in the lobby of the Inn in Gig Harbor for transportation assignments at 11:00 am for this exciting event that may last until 2:30 pm.

We can never thank you enough or ever tell you how much we appreciate everyone coming to Gig Harbor for Joyce's 80th birthday celebration and wonderful reunion of family and friends. After our enjoyable brunch breakfast together on

Sunday, May 25, with all those who can attend at the Inn in Gig Harbor, we will sadly bid you a fond farewell; with the hope you will all come see us again soon. Vi Elsker Deg. (we love you)   and that's a true story

GLEDELIG JUL - 2008

Once again we send greetings from our home to your home with the hope that all is well with you and your family. Like all years when we get older, this past year whizzed by and it's hard to believe our not so little any-more grandson 'Kyle Olsen' will be nine years old in just two more months.

Birthday Cake

To prove that even Honored Citizens can survive some real excitement occasionally, Joyce and I drove my wonderful present, a new Diesel powered Jeep, downtown in April to quietly celebrate my 84th birthday and wouldn't you know it. In May our children, Mary and Don Kelly, Barbara and Chuck Curtis and Bob and Donna Olsen, hosted, produced and directed an award winning musical revue at the Mother of all surprise sit down dinner party's for Joyce's 80th birthday at the Canterwood Country Club. Unbelievably, and honest to God this is true, a total of 80 wonderful friends and relatives came all the way from Canada, Montana, Utah, Nevada, California, Illinois, Hawaii and locally, to make it a memorable family reunion as well. The next day Joyce hosted a luncheon for all the out of town ladies while I took all the men for a boat ride

Theresa and Steve's beautiful family

to an Akvavit luncheon at Shenanigans Restaurant on Commencement Bay in Tacoma. Whooee, I'll tell you, all the people around here are still raving about that fantastic party, including us.

During June through October, we were very fortunate once again to have many of our old friends and relatives stop by for a visit and a tour of this beautiful area. The summer weather was almost perfect this year so we were able to put many more hours on the 'Akvavit II', motoring around the southern end of Puget Sound showing everyone our newly completed Tacoma Narrows Bridge etc. As always, we were very happy to see everyone and thankful they made the special effort to visit us again this year. Our special thanks go to our April Club friends again who were able to make another best yet annual July special meeting in Gig Harbor.

Ladie's Birthday Lunch

We also thank Dean and Jean Smith, my old Army buddy and his wonderful wife, for making a special trip to see us and help put the finishing touches on my book entitled, Skidmarks along the Highway of Life. And thanks to you too Bowie for all your invaluable help getting it edited and printed. Joyce and I feel we are blessed to have so many wonderful good friends, relatives and children who always take the time to come see us.

Joyce is doing fine with her walker. She still stays busy with her Clubs and volunteer activities, but she still freaks out driving over our new bridge so I'll drive her to Nordstrom's to shop. Our kids are also doing well and needless to say, we are very proud of them and all their accomplishments. As a potentially famous writer and a future renowned Santa toy maker helper (with Tigger's expertise and help), I've managed to keep busy. My first (and last) book is finally finished thanks to everyone's encouraging advice and help, and I'm happy to say it's now in print and will hopefully be mailed by February as late Xmas presents to friends and relatives. Have a Merry Christmas and a Healthy, Happy New Year, and please come see us next year when you can

Vi Elsker Deg, Homer, Joyce & Tigger Olsen

Anyway, to get back (finally) to this last sunset years chapter of Homer's too long Odyssey of life, while shuffling through old files I ran across this photograph of the old farm house Grandpa Olsen and his father-in-law, Hans Swensen, built over 125 year ago on the old

Gravelbed Farm. Like Grandma Olsen's egg money bowl, while staring at this photograph of that wonderful old homestead where I lived for the first formative twelve years of my life, I was suddenly *time tunneled* back into all those happy years raising pet lambs and calves again, and helping Grandpa with chores on that old farm. To top things off, Joyce even found my Stepmother Ercel's misplaced long lost *secret hand cranked home made Carmel ice cream recipe* in the trunk that I scanned as it was written, for posterity.

Ercel's Secret Ice Cream Recipe – 1982

Whooee, sitting here like this thinking back about that wonderful homemade hand cranked ice cream again makes my mouth water. In fact all these wonderful recalled memories remind me again of how lucky I was to have been raised on Grandpa Olsen's Gravelbed stock and dairy farm by my wonderful hard working immigrant Norwegian Grandparents and my dad during those great depression years. I wish there was some way I could thank my dad personally, and my Grandpa and Grandma Olsen other than in my dreams, to say how much I appreciated the love and all the valuable advice, council and apprenticeship training they gave me. But most of all, to thank them from the bottom of my heart for sharing that period in their lives with me when I really needed them the most.

As we approach the sunset years of our lives, Joyce and I are very happy and content with what we have accomplished over the years. We have made mistakes, but the good news is, our children have all turned out exceptionally well and we have accomplished all the goals we had set for ourselves along the fast lane of our skidmarked highway of life. Our retirement travels around the world have proved to us beyond any doubt, there is no

Grandpa Slim, Luke, and Grandpa Don Kelly enjoying lunch

other nation on this earth that gives its citizens the freedoms and the opportunity to pursue and reach by working hard, their fondest dreams than our wonderful country, the United States of America. I will always be grateful to this great land of freedom and opportunity that offered all the WW II veterans the wonderful GI College Education Bill to obtain a meaningful college job education, to help them fulfill their American Dream. There is no doubt about it; I would never have accomplished any of the things I have without the help I received from the GI Bill.

Kyle J. Olsen at age Eight – 2008

Joyce and I have now reached the age (81 and 85) where we fortunately have been able to save more than we will need from here on for a comfortable retirement the remainder of our lives and can now give back to those who helped us along the way. We are convinced the only way our country's young people in this day and age will ever succeed financially and escape being trapped in poverty cycles is to acquire a meaningful professional (not liberal arts) job education. Opportunities of all kinds will then open up for them on their chosen career paths if a meaningful job education is acquired early in their lives before they become lost souls.

After we gained the approval of parents and grandparents, Joyce and I set up three meaningful job education Scholarships Trusts for the grandchildren in our family whose grandparents (and their great-grandparents) helped me when I was a child to reach that first rung on the ladder to success. The three meaningful job education Scholarship Trusts we founded are for 42 listed grandchildren in the

Mikelle Olsen with her toy – 2007

Olsen family whose forefathers (now deceased) helped me during critical periods in my own life to escape the poverty cycle my own parents and grandparents were mired in. Joyce is doing the same with her half of our estate for the Deyoe side of her family.

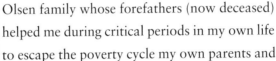

Arnie & Anne Lindberg Family

The three Trusts for the 42 grandchildren are very similar to the GI Bill our government setup after WWII for veterans like me who would never have been able to acquire a college education otherwise, with the primary goal of providing an incentive and motivation to set their career goals early in life. The Trusts will only provide enough funds to encourage and motivate the participants to begin, and hopefully finish, their college educations before they reach the age of 25 with individual yearly amounts of $6,000 each for four years plus a $5000 Graduation Bonus used to motivate them to finish and acquire their degrees. The combined overall contributions made to the three Trusts for the 42 participants of $29,000 each now totals $1,218,000. If any of the participants elect not to participate or continue their college educations, their remaining Scholarship amount will be forfeited and the unused portion of their initial $29,000 will be distributed equally among the (Pam & Jeff's Family in Casper, Wyoming – 2000) other

The David Olsen Family – 2006

participants equally who continue and will maintain a B- (2.75) minimum yearly grade point average until they graduate. Since the three Scholarships will only partially cover their college costs they will be required to earn the additional funds needed by working summers and part time jobs during the school year like their grandpa Tex and I did to make ends meet with the GI Bill, proving it can be done. If any unused and/or undistributed funds are left over in the Trusts after the youngest of the participant graduates or did not begin his college education before the age of 25, they will be contributed to a legitimate Charity and/or University, and the Trust will cease to exist.

The three separate Scholarship Trusts we set up for my sister Winifred and her husband David Dahl's 13 grandchildren, my double cousin (brother to me) Tex and Monnie Olsen's 13 grandchildren, and for our own

Pam & Jeff's Family in Casper, Wyoming – 2000

grandchild Kyle and my former in-laws 15 grandchildren we named The Viking Enterprises Scholarship Trust. The early results of these three plans have been fantastic. Only four participants have forfeited their scholarships so far of the 42 participants and two of the four who have already graduated from college are continuing on through medical school to become doctors. Joyce and I have never been so pleased and as proud as we are now in helping these wonderful young people get a jump start on their meaningful college job educations while they are still young. Their wonderful heartfelt letters thanking us for our help and encouragement brings tears to our eyes.

The Erik Horne Family – 2002

Joyce and I are also in the process of creating two more meaningful job education Scholarship Trusts: one in her late father, Don B. Deyoe's name at Montana State's School of Mechanical Engineering, and the other Trust has already been set up in both our names at the Stanford Graduate School of Civil Engineering for Master of Science Degree's in construction engineering and management for qualified, disadvantaged sons

Brandon Olsen & his toy tank – 2007

and daughters of our country's war veterans and blue collar parents in the construction industry. Both Trusts are setup similar to the GI Bill, and it is because of that Bill's help we are now able to give back for the many blessings we received along the way to make our lives worthwhile.

Jared and Conner Olsen – 2007

My wonderful wife Joyce and I believe we were all put on this earth to do something meaningful and worthwhile during our lives to help better the lot of mankind in some small way, and that I believe we have done. I chose Civil Engineering as my life's work because it is an exciting, fascinating profession that not only designs, but constructs the many infrastructures needed for the betterment of mankind. Where else can someone get that wonderful feeling of accomplishment for doing something worthwhile than in actually constructing needed infrastructure projects? To this day I still get a feeling of pride and accomplishment when I drive over bridges and highways and seeing the clean water treatment plants and the rapid transit facilities I helped build. There is no doubt in my mind my MS degree in Civil Engineering along with my active participation in the Heavy Engineering Construction Industry was the right professional choice for me. Joyce and I have been blessed in so many ways and we will always be grateful for having had such a rich life experience, such a wonderful family and so many good, longtime friends along the way while we traveled down this exciting Skidmarked Highway of Life.

Joyce and Homer retired and still happily married

"To furnish the means of acquiring knowledge is the greatest benefit that can be conferred upon mankind. It prolongs life itself and enlarges the sphere of existence."

John Quincy Adams

THE END

JUST A FEW OLE, LENA AND LARS JOKES

(as told by Homer J. Olsen at Safety and Shareholder Meetings)

1. Ole went to the Doctor for his annual physical examination and when completed the Doctor said 'I've got some bad news for you Ole, you've got terminal cancer and you only have six months left to live'. After Ole got over the shock of hearing this terrible news, he walked around town the next day shaking hands and saying goodbye to all his friends, telling them he had picked up a bad case of Aids and would be a goner within the next six months. Well it didn't take long for the Doctor to get wind of what Ole was doing and he immediately called Ole on the telephone to demand an explanation why he was telling everyone he had Aids when he had Cancer. Ole said, 'I didn't want anybody messing around with Lena after I was gone'. Oooh boy, anyway Lena happened to be dusting furniture nearby and overheard Ole's conversation with the Doctor and I'll tell you, she literally 'blew her stack'. Well, to make this story shorter, after the shouting match simmered down somewhat, Lena stormed out of the room with the parting shot, 'I can hardly wait to walk on your grave'. Ole, still hot under the collar, immediately telephoned his Mortician friend and said, 'Thorvald, do you still have that list of things I gave you to do after I keel over?' Thorvald answered, 'Yah shure, right here in front of me'. Ole said, 'I want you to add, I want to be buried at sea'.

   A short time later the Doctor called Ole into his office and said, 'Ole, I've been reviewing my accounts receivable and I notice you've run up a pretty high unpaid balance with me and I'd appreciate it if you would pay this bill before you keel over.' Ole said, 'Doc, I not only owe you, I owe everyone else in this town and there is absolutely no way I can pay off that bill in the six months I have left to live.' The stunned Doctor thought for a minute, tapped his pencil on his desk while stroking his chin, then got up to pace back and forth in front of the window with his hands clasped behind his back like Bank Loan Officer's are taught to do, and finally turned and said 'I'll tell you what I'm going to do'. To which Ole said, 'What's that Doc? '. The Doctor said, 'I'll give you another six months'.

2. Ole won a *raffle* ticket to a Senior Citizens Saturday night dance and met a very spry widow named Inge who turned out to be an excellent ballroom dancer and loved to Polka and Fox Trot just as much as Ole did. In fact they hit it off so well, Ole invited her up to his apartment for an after dance drink. When they got to the front room of his place, Ole said 'Inge, you sit here on the couch while I go into the kitchen and fix us a couple of drinks'. Well, when Ole came back with the drinks, Inge was nowhere to be seen. Ole began calling her name and looking for her in the two rooms along the hallway until he reached his own bedroom at the end of the hall - and nearly lost his false teeth in amazement. There she was on his bed, laying flat on her back, stark staring, stripped with not a stitch on, bare hind end and all. You guessed it, Ole did another 'double take' nearly spilling their drinks, Inge looked up seductively and said, 'Get aboard Ole'. Well, the next day at lunch Ole told this same little story to his buddy Lars and Lars curiously asked, 'So then what happened? , and Ole answered, 'Nothing happened Lars, by the time I got back from the lumber yard she was gone.'

3. Ole rode into town on an old wobbly bicycle one day and it was obvious to everyone that saw him zig-zagging down the street, he was anything but an experienced bicycle rider. Lars happened to be leaning against a tree in front of the barber shop whittling on a stick watching Ole fall from one side of the bike to the other several times and he said, 'Ole you're going to break your neck if you don't park that thing. Whatever happened to the car you used to drive and why are you riding that broken down old bike anyway? 'Ole stopped his bicycle in front of Lars so he could catch his breath and said, 'It's kind of a crazy story and a little hard to explain, Lars. A couple of hours ago

my car broke down a few miles outside of town and when I got out and raised the hood to check the engine, up rides this good-looking woman on a bicycle who just stopped and stood there by her bike watching me work on my car. Well, when I walked back and forth to the trunk of the car to get different tools to work with, she started acting crazy and saying terribly embarrassing things to me even though I ignored her and pretended I didn't hear a word she said. And then when I kept ignoring her, she jumped in front of me and took off all her clothes and shouted, 'Ole, you can have anything you want'. Sooo I took her bicycle.' Lars studied on this interesting fact for a minute and said, 'You did the right thing Ole, I don't think her clothes would have fit you.'

4. About a thousand years ago, two of Ole and Lars's distant relatives, who were also named Ole and Lars, were hired by a Viking construction contractor to help build a bridge from Greenland to Nova Scotia. One day Ole received a 'carrier-pigeon-fax' message from Lena saying, 'Congratulations Ole, You yust become the father of a newly born ten pound bouncing boy! ' Well, Ole was ecstatic and passed out cigars and' Akvavit' all around their construction camp in celebration of the event, but Lars didn't act like he was very happy for his good friend. When Ole confronted Lars about his negative attitude, Lars blurted, 'Ole we've been away from home on this lousy job for over three years now. Doesn't it strike you funny that Lena would have recently delivered a newly born baby boy? And, hasn't it occurred to you that maybe you're not that little boys' father? ' Ole studied on this interesting fact for a minute or two and then looked back at Lars with a really disgusted look on his face and said, 'Sooo, what's the big deal Lars? There's five years between me and my little brother.'

5. When Ole and Lars's distant relatives returned from their Viking trip to Greenland, their share of the plunder left them both very well-off' financially and they could have lived comfortably the rest of their lives. But unfortunately, as with anyone with too much money and behind the door when the brains were passed out, Ole and Lars felt they could 'expand their estates' by following the advice of a fast talking loan shark (called 'Venture Capitalist today), and put all their liquid assets into several exciting high-risk lucrative investments. Well, you guessed it. In less than six months, their 'Loan Shark Con-Artist' friend skinned them out of their entire hard earned fortune and, once again they were flat broke and looking for another way to make a living.

One day, while returning from a job interview, Ole noticed a 'Bounty Hunters Wanted' sign tacked on a spruce tree and turned to Lars and said, 'This could be a real 'Contracting Opportunity' for us Lars'. The notice, signed by the local Sheriff, stated in effect that, 'Whereas, it is obvious to all Norwegians that there is an over abundance of Swedes in the world, etc. etc.' and concluded with a statement that the County had voted unanimously to pay Three Hundred Kroner cash on the barrel head for every Swede pelt delivered to the Sheriffs Headquarters within the next 120 Calendar days. Well, to make a long story short, Ole and Lars signed on and did very well for the first two or three weeks. They were teammates on the 'School for Vikings' Relay Team during Basic Training and were still fair to middling runners so they were still able to catch most of the older crippled Swedes early in the game. Unfortunately, that supply soon began to dry up and their 'cash flow' tapered off to the point Lars began to lose interest and recommended they close down their shop. Well, as always, Ole was the 'Optimist' in all their ventures and sweet-talked Lars into hunting out the rest of that day and at least staying on until after breakfast the next morning. 'Then, he said, if we don't bag any more Swedes, I'll drag up with you and we'll call it quits'. As it turned out, that day was also a waste of time and they were 'skunked' once again, but were so exhausted from chasing the younger 'faster runner' Swedes, they could hardly crawl into their sleeping bags that night. Around midnight, Ole was awakened from a deep sleep by the snap of a tree twig and as he rolled over, he noticed off to his left a pair of giant feet supporting two 'redwood tree' sized legs that were connected to the biggest Swede he had ever seen in his life. That particular Swede was at least 10 foot tall and was holding a huge 'one-ton' stone, high over his head waiting for the signal to bash Ole into kingdom come. To make matters even worse, when he raised up on one elbow and looked to his right, he noticed there were a dozen more 'giant' Swedes lined up holding spears, axes, and huge boulders waiting for the signal to bash Lars into kingdom come. Well, as you can imagine, Ole was 'ecstatic with excitement' with what he had seen and was barely able to contain himself as he quietly slithered in his sleeping bag over to where Lars was sleeping. When he got there, he poked Lars in the ribs with his elbow and whispered hoarsely, 'Lars! Lars! Wake up, we're Rich!!

6. Ole belonged to the Local 'Pile Butt' Union in the San Francisco Bay Area for over forty years and had spent most of that time working on the Docks building Wharfs and Shipping Terminals. As he worked, he used to watch the beautiful Cruise Ships come and go from their Terminals and dreamed that someday he would be able to take a trip around the world on one of them. In fact he seriously planned on it when he retired because he knew he had more than enough money in his Union retirement fund to live like a king the rest of his life with enough left over to travel in luxury. Well, the big 'Retirement Day' finally came and Ole put on his best suit to go down to the Union Hall to pickup his 'million dollar' retirement check. Instead, he got the shock of his life. The funds in the Union Pension Plan that was touted as being safer than 'Fort Knox', were all gone, and even though Thorvald, the current Business Agent, patiently tried to explain the root cause of the trust funds demise was simply from normal human judgment errors coupled with a poorly conceived investment program, Ole still felt violated, angry and disappointed. In fact he was so angry he interrupted Thorvalds explanation and demanded to know if there was anything left at all in his retirement account and if so he wanted it all in cash immediately. Thorvald said, 'Ole if you will sign this release form, I'll give you one hundred dollars cash'. Ole signed, took his 100-dollar bill and stormed out of the Union Hall, sadly concluding he had no other alternative but to cancel his lifelong dream of a 'World Cruise.

A couple of weeks later, Ole was flipping through the local newspaper and noticed a Travel Ad that said, 'Three month round the world cruise, all expenses paid - 100 dollars cash'. On a whim, Ole called the telephone number listed and was assured the Ad was legitimate and if he wished to go on the next cruise, all he had to do was show up at Pier 46 at midnight with his $100 bill. As you can imagine, Ole was ecstatic and quickly accepted the offer and said he would be there ready to go at midnight. Well, when he showed up at Pier 46 with his $100 bill, the place was pitch black and as quite as a graveyard. Ole concluded he was obviously the butt of a cruel practical joke. But, just as he was about to leave, a voice in the darkness whispered 'Is that you Ole?' and he said 'Yah, det er me'. Then the voice in the darkness said 'Hand me your $100 bill Ole', which he did and immediately felt a sharp blow to the back of his head.

The next morning, when Ole come too, he discovered he was stripped to the waist and chained to an oar on a Viking Ship. He also noticed two giant 'Viking Warriors', both dressed in full regalia, at the stem of the ship. One of them was beating cadence on a drum and the other one was cracking a bullwhip over the bare backs of all the other oarsmen-passengers seated next and across from him. When the Viking with the whip noticed Ole was conscious, he came over and said, 'Ole, when I pop you on the back with this Bull whip, you're supposed to pull on that oar and you'll notice as we go along, I always pop you on the back in the same cadence as the drum beats'. Well, as you can imagine, Ole was a little clumsy at first and got a few extra whip marks across his back to show for it, but finally he got the hang of how things were supposed to work and by the time the ship reached the Farr lone Islands, he felt fairly confident as an oarsmen. In fact, the entire crew began to develop an 'esprit de corps' and, as they slowly came together as a team, the ship began to move with efficiency and professionalism.

Ole really had to give the 'Shipping Company' Owners their due because, true to their word, their ship traveled nonstop all the way around the world just as they promised, and returned he and his fellow passengers back in exactly three months to the same spot on Pier 46 from which they had departed. In spite of all this, Ole felt uncomfortable about 'something and decided to ask one of the other passenger-oarsman for his advice when he got the chance. As he and a fellow oarsman named Lars were standing on the dock watching that beautiful Viking Ship depart under the Golden Gate Bridge with its new load of 'passenger-oarsmen', Ole said, 'Lars, there is something about this trip that has been bothering me and I'd appreciate your advice on what I should have done about it'. Lars took note of Ole's worried expression and said, 'Sure ting Ole, I'll be glad to give you my very best advice, what is it that is bothering you?' Ole said, 'Which one of those guys are you supposed to tip Lars, the one with the Drum or the Whip?

7. When Ole and Lena were married, the minister reviewing their m license with them before the wedding said, 'I see by your Scandinavian name Ole, you got a little Norsk in you?' to which Ole answered 'Yah, Yah, Jeg common fra Norge.' Then the minister turned to Lena and said, 'And, I'll bet you've got a little Norsk in you too, Lena., am I right?' And Lena said, 'Yah, Yah, Det er right, Ole couldn't vaite.' After the wedding Ole and Lena drove over to Minneapolis for their honeymoon and along the way, Ole began feeling amorous and real sneaky like, placed his hand on Lena's knee. Lena looked over at Ole, winked and very seductively said, 'You can go further if you want to Ole'. Sooo Ole drove on to Duluth.

Well to make a long story shorter, Ole and Lena eventually ended up in Canada on the last day of their honeymoon and were stopped on their way back by a U..S. Customs Border Agent who asked to see their passports. The Customs Officer studied Ole's passport for a minute and said, 'It says here your blond, your blue eyed and your 6'- 2" tall and weigh 200 Ibs. Is that you Ole?' And Ole said, 'Yah, Yah, Det er Meg'. Then he turned to Lena after studying her passport and said, 'It says here your hair color is strawberry blond, you have green eyes, your 6'-8" tall and you weigh 275 Ibs. Is that you Lena?' And Lena said, 'Yah, Yah, Det er Meg'. The Customs Officer was amazed by her statistics and, looking up at Lena., said, 'My god Lena, You should play with the Green Bay Packers.' And Lena said, 'Oh no tank you. Ole's packer is the only one I play with.

8. Ole and Lena were given a 'Cruise Ship Tour' of the South Pacific Islands on their 25th Wedding Anniversary by their children but unfortunately, halfway through their tour, their ship hit the top of an under ocean mountain and sank. Even more unfortunate, everyone on the ship perished except Ole and Lena who somehow managed to wash up alive on a lush deserted Island somewhere in the South Pacific. Ole remained optimistic through all this because he 'knew' that someway-somehow they would eventually be rescued so he spent every day sitting at the top of a coconut tree scanning the horizon for passing ships. After about six months of this, Lena got tired talking to herself and climbed to the top of the tree where Ole was sitting, snuggled up next to him and said, 'Ole you got vat jeg vont and Jeg got vat you vont, vy don't ve get together?' Ole looked at her with this incredibly surprised look on his face and said, 'You got Snoose?'

9. Ole and Lars formed a Dairy business partnership and were doing fairly well for a couple of hair lips, all things considered. In fact, things were going so well, Ole signed up for an Adult Education class at the local Agricultural College so they could 'fine tune' their business even further and took some course entitled 'Lower your Taxes, upgrade your herd, and improve your milk production' all at the same time. Among other things, Ole learned he and Lars would be much better off 'owning' a registered purebred Holstein Bull rather than going 'outside rental' as they were currently doing. Well, to make a long story short, Ole and Lars drove over to North Dakota to the Live Stock Auction and submitted a 'low and only bid' of $1,500 and brought back a handsome 'Blue

Ribbon' Bull to service their hundred head of love sick cows. Unfortunately, they soon found out why they were the only bidder and why they got their Bull for such a reasonable price. When they turned their newly purchased Bull into the pasture with their love starved Dairy herd, he sleepily surveyed all the excited giggly cows, yawned, wandered over to a large shade tree, smelled the flowers, lay down and went to sleep. Lars was furious and threatened legal action but once again Ole's cool head prevailed and they decided to call in their local Vet for his opinion before doing anything drastic. After a lengthy and expensive examination, the Vet concluded there was nothing physically wrong with their Bull and that it was most likely a psychological problem. He felt that problem could easily be resolved by mixing a powerful new aphrodisiac called 'Livestock Viagra' with the Bulls oats during his next meal. Well, as you can imagine, the results were more than fantastic, especially after Ole took the liberty to double the recommended dosage. If a Hollywood Studio had made a movie of that event that day, their $1,500 Bull would have won an Academy Award for his performance. He not only serviced all 100. Love starved Cows not once but twice, and then went back for thirds on the good-looking ones. Lars, who looked as if he had just witnessed a miracle, stared at Ole in wide eyed amazement and said, 'My god Ole, that was the most incredible, fantastic performance I have ever witnessed. I wonder what's in that stuff we fed the Bull?' Ole said, 'I don't know Lars, but I can tell you this. It tastes a little like peppermint.

10. Ole and Lena were invited to a costume party and Lena had a terrible time deciding what costume to wear. Finally she decided to go as a 'raisin cookie' since it was the simplest, quickest, and the least costly costume because it consisted merely of going nude and wearing a raisin in her navel. Ole of course, always wore his 'Viking Warrior' uniform year after year and, since he wanted to leave for the party early to get a good bar stool, he was dressed and ready to go. When Lena kept trying on different raisins in front of the mirror, Ole finally lost his temper and demanded that Lena either leave for the party now or they would stay home. With that, Lena sprang to her feet, grabbed a raisin from the costume pile marked 'loose but comfortable', and ran down the stairs putting the raisin in her navel as she ran. Unfortunately, the 'loose' raisin fell out when Lena reached the bottom of the stairs and rolled into the coat closet. When Ole reached the closet, Lena was on her hands and knees patting under the coats and jackets for her raisin and tearfully explaining she could not go without her costume. Ole laughed and said, 'Lena, don't worry about it. Just back in on your hands and knees and tell everyone you're a Parker House roll'

11. As we are all aware, many of the wonderful 'Saga's' of this Great Country's 'Past History' are currently being revised to meet the new 'political correctness' standards almost to the point where the original facts have been distorted enough to completely change the real 'true story' . For example, the story of John Paul Jones standing tall on the bridge of his ship as it was sinking and as the water crept over his collar button, shouting to the victorious British Officer, 'I have just begun to fight', stops too soon. The equally famous 'statement' made by that great Norwegian-American Sailor, Lars Guldbransen, who was stationed in the crow's nest of John Paul Jones' sinking ship during that battle, has unfortunately been deleted from all our current History Books. When John Paul Jones made his famous statement, it was the great Lars Guldbransen who said loudly, 'Why is it there is always some dumb son of a bitch who never gets the word'.

Unfortunately, a similar deletion occurred in that Great Historical 'Saga' known as 'Custer's last stand' during the 'Battle of the Little Bighorn'. As all of you 'History Buffs' will undoubtedly recall, General Custer and his Battalion of 'Horse Soldiers' were stationed at an Army Cavalry Encampment in North Dakota called Fort Mandan, at the same time as the local Indians were being allegedly accused of not making their Mortgage payments. General Custer, as you remember, was given the assignment of teaching those Indians a lesson. Well, besides the good fortune of having a crack Cavalry Battalion under his command, General Custer had the luck of having assigned to his command a Great Norwegian-American Indian Guide named Ole Swensen - who like Lars Guldbransen, was equally unfortunate in having his famous historical comment deleted from the current editions of our wonderful Country's History Books. To their credit however, our current History books still accurately report General Custer was very impressed from the outset with the Mandan Indians determination and character he was ordered to chase, catch and bring to Justice. As you recall, he chased them out of North Dakota towards Montana to the West, then South into South Dakota, and then West again into Wyoming and finally North into Montana. It was there the exhausted Cavalry finally pulled up for a rest at the site of the future 'Historical' battlefield called, 'The Little Bighorn'.

After General Custer gave the order to dismount, he turned to his trusted guide and said, 'Ole, while the rest of us are setting up our tents, I want you to ride out and get a lay of the land and, if possible, find out where all those frigen Indians are hiding'. Well, to make a long story short, a couple of hours later a very troubled and worried looking Ole Swensen reported back to General Custer and said, 'I've got good news and bad news for you General, which do you want first?' The General replied, 'I've always felt every report should end on an optimistic note, so give me the bad news first'. Ole then said very seriously, 'General, there are at least a thousand hostile, well-armed Indians over that ridge and they are all itching for a fight. It is my considered and humble opinion that our chances of surviving this upcoming Historical Battle are less than a snowballs chance in hell'. General Custer said, 'My God Ole, after a report like that, what could be the good news?' Ole's expression immediately turned to one of happiness when he said, 'General, the good news is, we won't have to go back to North Dakota'.

12. Ole got a job as a fireman in a small North Dakota town and it wasn't long before his superiors recognized his leadership capabilities and he was promoted to Fire Chief. The only problem with the job, at least from Ole's point of view, was the scarcity of fires in that little town made the days seems terribly long, and especially when there was nothing left to do but play gin rummy. One day Ole read a story in the local newspaper about an oil fire in Texas that even the great Red Adair called 'The Mother of all Oil Fires' and had even stated, 'It was a fire that was impossible to put out'. The article went on to say the management of the oil company was continuing their offer of a fifty thousand dollar reward to anyone or any firm that could put the fire out. Well, as you can imagine, Ole was intrigued with the challenge of putting that fire out and when he asked his crew if they would like to make an easy fifty thousand dollars, they jumped at the chance. In fact, they were all so excited about this adventure, it only took an hour to get packed, their truck loaded and on their way, hats pulled down, spirits high, sirens blaring, lights flashing and speeding wide open towards Texas.

When Ole and his crew left that little North Dakota town, it created such a stir that one of the local news people telephoned another newspaper in South Dakota to watch for the 'Brave Norwegian Fireman from North Dakota who were unselfishly traveling south to put out an oil fire for the Texicans'. Well, you can imagine the stir that headline made throughout the Midwest and as their fire truck made pit stops in towns along their way through Nebraska and Kansas, they were met by local politicians and dignitaries, wined and dined by all the towns people, and escorted through all the various town squares by the local High School Bands. The national media finally picked up on the story as they approached the Oklahoma line and almost immediately, through worldwide TV coverage, the world's attention was focused on the 'Fearless Viking Norseman' from North Dakota. In fact, by the time they reached the Texas Panhandle, there were more Media Limousines and Helicopters loaded with 'Prime Time' news commentators and talk show performers than all the local people and livestock put together.

Ole and his crew, although impressed, continued on their way full speed ahead, sirens blaring, lights flashing, determined to put the poor Texicans fire out and collect all that easy money.

Finally, as they traveled deeper into the heart of Texas, Ole saw for the first time the billowing black smoke and the immensity of the challenge they had taken on. Lesser men would have paled at the sight but Ole, who had inadvertently forgotten to visit the men's room earlier, blindly yelled to Lars, their driver, 'Full speed ahead'. Lars 'floor boarded' their Fire Truck and, squinting through a greasy windshield, headed straight for the center of that huge black mushroom cloud of smoke.

As the 'Fearless Vikings' Fire Truck careened on towards the blazing inferno, the streets jammed with wildly cheering, hero-worshipping crowds of Texacans and Oil Field workers who quickly opened the security gate for them to speed towards the source of the fire. But a few moments later, when the cheering spectators began to realize the careening, speeding fire truck was heading directly for the epicenter of that roaring inferno with no letup in speed, a hushed silence fell over the crowd followed by a shocked collective gasp as the fire truck disappeared inside the raging inferno. The deathly silence that followed was nearly unbearable until someone noticed the smoke slowly subsiding and yelled 'Hallelujah' and everyone began to realize their terrible oil fire had finally been put out. A tremendous roar erupted from the crowd as the fire and smoke cleared even further and a soot covered fire truck with six goggle eyed, toilet relieved, terrified Norwegians slowly came into view. There they were, those brave 'Fearless Norseman' from North Dakota, all rigidly sitting in their Truck with the brims of their fire hats burned off, staring straight ahead like chalk faced zombies, while their fire truck slowly wind-vaned around and around. As miracles will happen when combined with unadulterated luck, Ole and his crew had high centered their fire truck on its exact center of gravity directly on top of the burning wellhead which had then cut off the flow of oil and 'snuffed' out the fire. The owner of the Oil Field was ecstatic and personally helped Ole in his stiff legged decent from the truck while his Oil Field crews 'cooled down' and closed the well head valve. As they walked along together, he kept shaking his head in disbelief and told Ole, 'I have just witnessed an act of bravery that has no equal anywhere in history', and said over and over how appreciative he was and kept thanking Ole and his crew on behalf of all the people of Texas for their tremendous act of bravery and unselfish sacrifice. When they arrived at the office and he had run out of words of praise, the Owner handed Ole his fifty thousand dollar bonus check and asked, 'What are you going to do with all this money Ole?' Ole wiped his eyes and shook the soot out of his hat, cleared his throat and said, 'I don't know what we're going to do with most of it but I can damn sure tell you the first thing we're going to do with some of it'. And when the Owner asked, 'What's that?' Ole said, 'We're going to get the brakes fixed on that damn fire truck'.

13. After a couple of weeks of R & R in the great state of Texas, which was sandwiched between numerous Banquets, Testimonial Dinners and Talk Show appearances, Ole and his crew decided they better head for home. Lars suggested they take a different route back to North Dakota so they decided to drive their Fire Truck north on the eastern side of the Mississippi River for a change in scenery. When they drove into the great State of Missouri and saw all the mules grazing in the fields, Lars turned to Ole and said, 'Ole, have you ever wondered why all the mules came to Missouri and the Swedes went to Minnesota?' Ole said, 'It's obvious Lars, Missouri got first choice'. Lars laughed and said, 'Do you know how to tell a level headed Swede, Ole?' to which Ole grinned and answered, 'that's another easy one Lars. Level headed Swedes are the ones with the snoose running out of both corners of their mouths at the same time.' And then Ole asked, 'I'll bet you never knew why the Swedes only charge four Kroner for a haircut, did you Lars?' And when Lars said, 'I'll bite Ole, Why?' Ole said, 'Because there's a law in Sweden that says Barbers can only charge one Kroner per side'. Lars cracked up, and then said, 'I see by the paper

that the Swedish Hospital in Ballard, Washington has made a major medical breakthrough, Ole'. And when Ole asked, 'Oh yeah, what's that Lars?' he said, 'they've finally figured out how to transplant Hemorrhoids successfully'. Ole cracked up and then Lars said, 'I also read in the same paper the Swedes in Minnesota are reporting an early arrival and successful conclusion to their' I 000 man march on Washington D.C.' to protest Norwegians telling 'Swede' jokes'. Ole said, 'No kidding. How far have they marched so far?' Lars, looking very serious said, 'They were sighted just outside of Seattle, this morning.' Ole caved in laughing at that one and finally said, 'Lars, I heard 'Sven the Svede' was fired from his elevator operator job after only one day because he couldn't learn the route.' Lars chuckled and said, 'Speaking of Swedes Ole, Do you know why Medical Centers pay such high prices for Swedish Brains?' Ole said, 'No Lars, why do they?' Lars' eyes twinkled as he said, 'They've never been used.' Ole said, 'Hey Lars, I read in the paper the same 'Elevator Operator' Swede from Minnesota became a race car driver and entered the Indianapolis 500 but lost because he had to make 75 pit stops - 3 for gas, oil and tire changes and 72 to ask directions.' Lars cracked up again but then Ole got a serious look on his face and said, 'Lars, I think we are being a little too hard on the Swedes. After all, they do deserve credit for inventing the toilet seat. Lars acknowledged that was true but he said, 'you must also remember, it never sold well because of a rather 'embarrassing technical problem' until several years later when the Norwegians came up with the idea of putting a hole in it.'

14. When they reached Iowa, Ole was so impressed with the beautiful green farm country; he sweet-talked the others into stopping for a few more days of R&R, 'Because', as he said, 'We've earned it'. Then the next day for excitement, while the rest of the crew were 'doing the town', Ole and Lars decided to go to a Cattle Auction at the local Stockyard and see the Texas Longhorns that were being auctioned off that day. Since Lars or Ole were from Hereford and Black Angus country, neither one of them had ever seen a Texas Longhorn before so when several of them were turned into a pen, Lars turned to Ole and said, 'By golly Ole, I don't think those cows have an ounce of meat on them'. 'In fact', he said, 'they look more like a gunny sack full of deer horns attached to a rack of horns, than beef cattle'. Ole said he couldn't agree more and when Lars said he was going to go into the corral with the cows to see if there was something besides bone under their hide, Ole thought it was a good idea. Well, unfortunately Lars wasn't aware that all those Longhorn cows were raised on Texas thistle weed and sagebrush and were not used to the lush green clover they were being fed in Iowa. As a consequence they had developed; what is known in Cattle and Farm country as; a bad case of 'scowers'. Well, as you can guess, when Lars began poking around with a 'stick-tester' in the herd of Longhorns they became very nervous and agitated as Lars continued to poke every cow. One of the most 'agitated' finally let out a 'beller', spun around and lifting her tail and let fly a 'perfect shot' that hit Lars right between the eyes. Ole of course, was a witness to this little drama of life and, as you can guess, doubled up with laughter when this happened and 'cracked up' again when Lars came sputtering out of the pen muttering, 'Boy, was I lucky that time'. Ole handed Lars a towel still laughing and said, 'In all honesty Lars, you don't look very lucky to me', and bent over holding his sides again. By this time Lars was getting a little peeved with Ole's lack of sympathy and, real disgusted like said, 'To hell I wasn't. If hadn't had my mouth open, it would have got all over me'. (According to my Dad, this is a true story)

15. Lena and her friend Helga went shopping one day at the mall and as they walked down the various isles, Helga noticed something unusual about Lena's earrings. Not wanting to appear too curious she waited until they stopped for lunch and said, 'Lena, can I ask you a personal question?' Lena said, 'ya sure Helga, what is it?' Helga asked, 'Lena, why are you walking around with a suppository stuck in your ear?' Lena reached up and took the suppository out of

her ear, looked at it and said, 'Oh my God'. Helga said 'Oh my God what Lena?' Lena said, 'Oh my God, now I remember where I put my hearing Aid. After Lena and Helga finished their lunch, Lena said, 'That Chocolate Cream Pie looks delicious, Helga, lets live it up and split a whole pie.' Helga thought it was a wonderful idea and when the waiter said, 'Do you want me to cut it into eight pieces or six?' Lena said, 'You better make it six; we're both on a diet,'

16. Speaking of hearing Aids, Ole and his friend Lars were having Lunch one day at the local Diner and Ole said,' You know Lars, I paid over $5000 Dollars for this Hearing Aid and it's the best investment I've ever made. You can believe it or not but, I can actually hear a feather drop a mile away.' Lars said, 'No kidding, what kind is it?' Ole said, 'it's twenty minutes to one.'

17. Shortly after they were settled in their vacation 'Mirror Lake' cabin, Ole and his two buddies, Lars and Thorvald decided to go fishing in their 'Boston Whaler'. A 'pea soup' fog covered the Lake the morning they left the dock but fortunately, using a compass, good judgment, and the red paint 'cross' they had the foresight to paint on the bottom of their boat the previous year, they were able to find their old fishing hole, anchor, bait their hooks and begin fishing. As they sat quietly the fog began to rise over the lake, and as they looked towards the shore they saw a longhaired 'hippy looking guy' in a dark red robe watching them. Then he waved and when they 'neighborly' returned his wave, he stepped off the shore onto the water and walked towards them. When he reached their boat, he introduced himself to the three goggle eyed Norwegians as 'Jesus Christ' himself, and asked if they had sustained any injures in their lifetimes they wanted healed. Well, Ole was the first to regain his composure and said, 'Yes Sir, I began my career as a Professional Football Player for the Minnesota Vikings but I was forced to retire early because of a broken shoulder. My friend Lars here was on the Olympic Ski Team but unfortunately blew his knee out on a practice jump and had to give up his lifelong dream of winning a gold medal. Then our good friend Thorvald, at the other end of our boat, won an insurance claim alleging that he was injured years ago while working on a Construction Job as an Operating Engineer. So, as you can see, we all welcome your kind 'offer'. Jesus then laid his hands on Ole's shoulder and 'low and behold' it was immediately healed. Then he lay his hands on Lars's knee and miraculously it was healed, but as he approached Thorvald to cure his ills, Thorvald put up his' dukes' to defend himself and yelled, 'Don't touch me, I'm on permanent disability.'

18. Lena went to the local medical clinic for her annual physical examination and as she was about to leave, her Doctor called her in his office and closed the door and said, 'Lena, I don't know how to tell you this but I've discovered that your pregnant'. Well, as you can imagine, Lena was shocked beyond belief because at her advanced age, she knew her child bearing years were over and that the Laboratory obviously had her records mixed up with some other patients. So she said, 'Doctor, that is impossible. I'm 90 years old and my husband Ole is 95 years old. You have got to have made a mistake somewhere.' The Doctor said he had checked the Lab tests several times, including the 'Rabbit' test, and he was sure he was right. He said, 'You can call it a miracle if you want to Lena, but I am convinced, you are pregnant'. Lena sat in stunned silence for a few minutes after the Doctor left and then a feeling of anger overtook her and she couldn't wait to find a telephone and tell Ole a thing or two. When Ole answered the telephone, Lena shouted, 'you old coot, do you know what you did to me?' When 'a somewhat taken aback' Ole, answered, 'No, what?' she said, 'You got me pregnant'. Ole said, 'Who's this calling?'

19. When Ole was a young man living in the 'Old Country' his love of Scouting took him to many 'Jamborees' throughout Scandinavia and it was on one of these trips he met and became good friends with a Dane named Lars and a Swede named Sven. In fact, they became such good friends

that they made it a habit in their later lives to go fishing together every year, usually at a different lake in a different Scandinavian Country. This particular year, they decided to fish at a lake in Finland, which unbeknown to them, was being invaded by the Russian Army. It was while they were seated around their campfire singing and telling stories after a wonderful 'fresh fish' supper that a patrol of Russian Soldiers stumbled on their camp and arrested them as spies. Well, try as they might to make their case, they were quickly convicted, sentenced and tied to fence posts in an adjacent cow pasture for execution. As they were being blindfolded and the firing squad was loading their rifles, the Russian Officer asked Lars, the Dane, if he wanted to say a few words before he was shot. Lars thought for a minute and said, 'No, but if it's all the same to you, I'd like to sing the Danish National Anthem'. The Russian granted his wish and then turned to Ole, the Norwegian, which is known worldwide as a nationality that won't take crap off anyone, and asked if he would like to say a few words before he was shot. Well, as you can imagine, Ole was still fuming with anger. He not only felt their Civil Rights had been violated, but they had been given anything 'but' a fair Trial, so he stuck out his chin and said loudly, 'I not only want to say a few words, I want to give a Speech'. When Sven the Swede heard that, he leaped to his feet and hollered to the Russian Officer, 'I want to be shot before that guy starts his speech.'

20. Ole and Lena returned home from church one Sunday morning after a spirited lecture by the Lutheran Minister, and after lunch, sat in the living room knitting, reading and thinking about the Minister's message that morning. Finally, Lena lay down her knitting and said, 'Ole do you really believe there is a hereafter?' Ole looked over the top of his Sunday paper, thought for a minute and said, 'Lena, I have no reason to disbelieve what the Minister has told us and the Bible says there is a hereafter so, yes, I think there is a hereafter.' Well,' Lena said,' I'm not so sure and I think we should make a pact right now that the first one of us to go should come back and tell the other whether it's true or not.' Ole rattled his paper, turned the page and said, 'O.K. Lena, you got a deal.'

Well, to make a long story short, Ole passed away first and three days after the funeral; Lena was sitting in the same living room knitting and a little light beeped on near the curtain. Lena asked, 'Is det you Ole?' And Ole answered, 'Yah, yah, dets me.' Then Lena said, 'Ole, tell me the truth. Are you having a good time?' to which Ole answered,' Oh Lena, You wouldn't believe what a good time I'm having.' Lena said, 'Oh Ole, please tell me what you did the first day there and then the second day and even the third day up until now?' Ole said, 'Well O.K, let's see, the first day I slept in until ten o'clock, had brunch breakfast, and then I moseyed up to the top of a beautiful grassy knoll and lay on my back in the warm grass and watched the beautiful birds lazily circle overhead until it was time for lunch. Then, after leisurely eating a wonderful lunch, I strolled into a beautiful garden and was introduced to a harem of the most beautiful females I've ever seen, so I spent all that afternoon and all that night making mad passionate love. The next day, I was really tired so I slept in again, but spent the remainder of that morning watching the clean, crystal clear water, cascade over the sparkling granite rocks and smelled the beautiful flowers until it was time for another delicious lunch and another afternoon and night of mad passionate love.' Lena interrupted at this point and said, 'Oh Ole, heaven must be such a wonderful place.' Ole said, 'who said anything about heaven. I'm a Jack Rabbit in Utah.'

21. Ole and Lars were two old WWII Veterans sitting in their rocking chairs on the front porch of their Retirement Home one afternoon watching the ladies stroll by and Ole turned to Lars and said, 'Lars do you remember that stuff they called 'Salt Peter' the Army used to put in our coffee to try and simmer us down before we were given a three day pass?' Lars said, 'Yes, now that you mention it Ole, I do remember them giving us that stuff.' And Ole said, 'you want to know something Lars. I think it's finally beginning to work.'

22. One of the many job assignments Ole had during his lifetime was as a traveling salesman with the Massy-Ferguson Farm Equipment Company selling Tractors to the local Farmers in North Dakota. As everyone knows who has traveled the back roads of this great country, and especially in the Midwestern States, the farm roads follow Section Lines with sharp right angle turns at their intersections. This of course makes them very dangerous to drive at high speeds which is exactly what Ole was doing on this particular sales call and rolled his car over several times, ending up in an irrigation canal upside down and under water. Fortunately, Ole survived drowning and only recovered because his head happened to be in a trapped bubble of air inside the car, but he was still in pretty bad shape. Both his right arm and leg were broken and he was trapped inside of his car upside down, breathing only from that rapidly diminishing air bubble. Lesser men would have panicked and given up but Ole, always the optimist, somehow managed to break the car window, squirm through the opening and make it to the surface and to the muddy canal bank before blacking out from pain and exhaustion.

     When Ole came too, he noticed an old farmhouse about a mile away and figured by using his good left elbow and good left leg as motive power, he could make it to that house in about four hours, or at least by sundown, and he could get some much needed help. Well, to make a long story short, Ole's optimism paid off and he was able to painfully drag himself, inch-by-inch towards that farmhouse in the time he estimated. As the sun began to sink in the west, the Farmer who lived there had just finished his supper and had stepped out of the kitchen on to the front porch to settle himself in his rocking chair with his pipe, when he noticed Ole slowly dragging himself towards the farmhouse. As the Farmer watched Ole and this little drama of life unfold before him, he became fascinated with Ole's determination. So after about an hour of rocking and puffing on his pipe and studying Ole as he slowly dragged his crippled body to within talking distance, the Farmer said, 'You look to me like a 'Traveling Salesman' that could use a little help.' Ole stopped his painful struggle for a moment and, gasping for breath said, 'You can say that again and I would be mighty obliged to you if you would put me up for the night so I could get a little rest.' The Farmer rocked back and forth some more while he studied this request and then answered, 'I would be glad to put you up for the night, but I have to make a confession to you.' When the exhausted Ole weakly asked, 'What's the confession?' The Farmer tapped out the burned tobacco from his pipe against his boot, and said, 'I don't have a daughter.' Ole, was momentarily surprised but true to his profession immediately regained his composure and said, 'How far is it to the next farmhouse?'

23. Ole called his friend Lars on the telephone and said, 'Lars, I see by the paper the deer hunting season is open in the Central Utah Rocky Mountains and they say the 'hunting' is excellent this year. What do you say we go out there for a few days and get our deer?' Lars said, 'Good idea Ole, I haven't had a good venison steak in ages.' Well, as is typical of the mainstream press nowadays, the facts of the matter were just the opposite of what had been reported in the paper and the deer hunting was the worst it had ever been. In fact, if it were not for an occasional 'brush' shot, Ole and Lars needn't have bothered bringing their hunting rifles because they never saw a deer during the whole trip. But, here again, Ole was the one who always remained optimistic and suggested to Lars they split up, swing around the next knoll from opposite sides and scare the deer out of the brush by simply 'rattling' the bushes. Well, to make a long story short, Ole came around the right side of the knoll and when he noticed the brush shaking off to his left, he fired his hunting rifle at what he thought was an escaping deer. Unfortunately, when Ole raced over to tag his trophy, he was horrified to discover he had accidentally shot his best friend Lars. As you can imagine, Ole was both stunned and shocked and nearly panicked before two other hunters arrived with their jeep and they hauled Lars to the Emergency Ward of the Richfield Hospital. While Lars was in the operating room, Ole paced the hallways wringing his hands and muttering how terribly sorry

he felt over this horrible thing that had happened to his best friend. Finally, the Doctor came out of surgery looking very grim, and slowly shaking his head said, 'I'm sorry Ole, we did everything we could but we were unable to save your best friend, Lars.' Ole was devastated and sobbed, 'Doc is there anything, anything at all, that I should have done differently before I brought him here, so you would have had a better chance in saving his life?' The Doctor looked at Ole sadly and said, 'Yes there is Ole. It would have helped if you hadn't gutted him out first.'

24. While waiting his turn for a haircut at the local Barbershop one Saturday morning, Ole read an Article in the Field and Stream Magazine about an exciting Grizzly Bear Hunt in Northern Idaho. When he got home and told Lena about the trip and how much fun it would be for them to go together, and that went over like a lead balloon with her. She said, 'I can guarantee you one ting for sure Ole. If you want to go on a trip like that, you can go alone.' Well, to make a long story short, Ole signed on for the whole tour package and caught a plane from Minot, North Dakota to Boise, Idaho to meet the rest of his Tour Group for their exciting trip into Northern Idaho.

The first leg of their tour was a scary Helicopter flight from Boise to an isolated wilderness area in northern Idaho, then by Horseback and Pack Mules into the backcountry until it become even too rough for the horses. From there, the final leg was on foot with backpack through the thick mosquito infested underbrush to where huge Grizzly Bear were reported to live. At the end of the 'Horseback' phase of the trip most of the 'Yuppy' types had lost interest in seeing Grizzly Bear in the wild and had gone home, leaving only Ole, the Indian Guide, and two other Norwegians to carry on. But even this little group dissolved a few days later when the two Norwegians 'drug up' after the Guide announced the trail ahead was so rough they would have to travel the remainder of the way on their hands and knees through 'yellow-jacket" country. Even Ole was tested to his limit a week later when the Guide announced they would have to travel the very last and final leg of the trail through snake infested wet mud and a rough Poison-Oak section, on their stomachs.

Well, it goes without saying, Ole stood firm and insisted they go on because he had paid to see a wild Grizzly Bear in its natural habitat and besides, by golly, he wanted his money's worth. The guide told Ole that was all fine and dandy but he was 'dragging up' because he had seen a lot of Grizzly Bears in his lifetime and it wasn't that big a deal anymore. The guide said, 'If you want to go on alone Ole, so be it. In fact'. He said, 'Right there in front of you are a set of fresh tracks of a 'monster' Grizzly Bear. If you really want to see what you come all this way for, just sneak up to that big fallen log up ahead and peek over and I'll guarantee, you'll get the thrill of a lifetime.' As the guide began to leave and Ole ignored giving him a 'small token of his appreciation', the guide said, 'Ole, do you know the difference between a Norwegian and a Canoe?' When Ole said 'What?' the guide said, 'A canoe will tip' and left.

After the guide was gone and Ole was alone with his thoughts, it suddenly occurred to him there was a terrible risk in what he was about to do. If it had not been for the freezing weather and how badly he 'smart' from poison oak infection, the yellow-jacket welts and the mosquito bites, he would have headed for home. But, when it's all said and done, the ultimate motivator that gave Ole the strength to carry on, was the thought of having to return home and face Lena and admit he'd failed. Or, even worse, to admit he had not gotten all that he had paid for.

Ole painfully crept to the fallen log and, trying with all his might to control his fear, peeked over the log. At that very moment, almost as if on cue, a monstrous 2000 pound Grizzly Bear, rose up on its hind legs to its full eighteen foot height, opened its huge gaping mouth showing all its sharp slobbering fangs, and gave a tremendous roar that echoed back and forth through the timber like a clap of thunder.

After Ole returned to his home in North Dakota, he telephoned his good friend Lars to meet him for lunch at a local restaurant so he could tell him about his 'Exciting Bear' trip into

Northern Idaho. When he got to the last part of the story about the 'Huge' Grizzly Bear standing up on its hind legs and 'roaring', to demonstrate he stood on his chair, raised his arms high over his head, and gave a loud head turning 'roar' himself, then suddenly and seemingly embarrassed when the crowd noise ceased, sat back down. Lars, of course, was very impressed with Ole's fantastic story, including his demonstration, and said, 'Boy, oh boy, oh boy, Ole, that must have been something. So then what did you do?' Ole looked at Lars with a strained expression on his face and said quietly, 'I crapped my britches.' Lars blinked and said, 'Well, I sure don't blame you one bit for that Ole. 1 would have done the same thing under the same circumstances.' Ole said, 'No, I mean just now, when I stood up and roared.'

25. Ole and his Swedish friend, Sven Svenson, had a date to play Golf one Saturday morning and as Ole left the house, Lena said, 'Be sure your home by six o'clock this evening Ole because I'm fixing your favorite pork roast, boiled potatoes, and green peas for supper.' Ole said, 'Don't ever worry about me being late for a supper like that Lena' and left with his golf clubs and singing his favorite song, 'A little bit of Lefse goes a long way.' Well, Ole didn't make it home by six o'clock, or seven o'clock, or even by eight o'clock that evening. In fact it was after ten o'clock before a very tired and haggard looking Ole staggered into their house to face the inevitable 'chewing out' he expected from his loving and wonderful wife. Lena of course didn't disappoint him in that regard and after some twenty minutes of shouting back and forth, Lena 'ran down' and Ole had his chance to explain why he was late for supper. Ole said, 'Lena, the first six holes went fine and we were right on schedule, then all of a sudden Sven had a massive and fatal heart attack and from then on for the next twelve holes it was, ... Hit the Ball and Drag Sven - Hit the Ball and Drag Sven.'

26. Ole originally decided to go into the Contracting Business because he had heard it was a business no one ever had any problems. Unfortunately he soon found out this was not true and there could be 'Murphy's Law' days that everything can go wrong and usually does. During the first week of the summer rush, Ole encountered an extremely rough day on one of his Contracts and decided to stop on his way home at Halvors Bar for a 'Relaxer' drink. This particular day was even rougher than usual because the size and complexity of this particular project had really introduced 'Murphy's Law' into the critical path schedule which in turn, had started a 'chain reaction of errors' that left Ole, the primary beneficiary, looking and smelling like he had just climbed out of a live sewer. In fact, Ole smelled so bad that when he got out of his car to go into the Bar, the air that surrounded his body not only turned pale blue from a suffocating pungent odor but immediately attracted swarms of gnats and fruit flies. There was no question in anyone's mind, the 'Trauma' that Ole experienced that day really warranted a couple of stiff slugs of 'Akvavits' to settle him down.

When Ole walked into 'Halvors Bar' and ordered his two double 'Akvavits', no one paid any attention at first, but it wasn't long before the *Air* conditioning system picked up that 'eye-watering odor' and all hell broke loose. When the people lined up along the Bar became aware of the smell, they began to wheeze and cough, and when some of the women began to scream, everyone began stampeding towards the outer corners of the room for fresh air. Finally, Halvor the owner-bartender, came over holding his nose and said, 'Ole, you smell so bad your ruining my business and as sorry as I am to tell you this, I'm going to have to ask you to leave'. Ole said, 'I don't blame you Halvor, and I apologize for my filthy attire and strong odor, but today was probably 'the' roughest day I've ever had in my life on a job and I just had to stop for a 'pick-me-upper' before going home'. By this time Halvor found a clothes pin for his nose so he felt a little more comfortable conversing with Ole, and he said, ' Ole, I've known you a long time and I know you've held many different jobs, but for the life of me, I've never been able to figure out what exactly you do for a living.' Ole straightened up and proudly said, 'Well Halvor, I'm currently a Specialty Sub Contractor that is

'Haz' Licensed to do 'Environmentally Safe Hazardous Waste Cleanup' work but I also have a Sub Specialty 'Haz' License to perform "Elephant Enemas".' When Halvor asked, 'What exactly does that last License entail?' Ole said, 'Halvor, I'll bet you've seen hundreds of Circus Elephant shows in your life and I'll also bet you have never seen any of those Circus Elephants accidentally defecate on the stage during their act'. Halvor thought for a moment and said, 'by golly Ole, you're right. I've never in my life seen an Elephant have an accident on stage during their Act and now that you mention it, I wonder why?' Ole waggled his thumb towards his chest and proudly said, 'Because, I'm the guy that cleans them out before they go on stage, that's why.'

As you can imagine, Halvor was very impressed with the responsibility Ole's job entailed and asked him what tools were required and how he carried out this responsibility. Ole, trying real hard not to brag, answered, 'Actually Halvor, the tools we use don't amount to much. All you need is a fifty-foot length of Fire hose that's been connected to a ten-foot length of two inch Pipe, and a Step Ladder. The most important ingredients for success in this business aren't the Tools; they are Knowledge, Timing and Athletic agility. To perform the actual work in the field, I simply connect the Fire Hose to a High Pressure Fire Plug, set up my stepladder behind the Elephant, raise its tail, ram home the two inch pipe, and holler at Lars, my 'Oiler', to 'Pull the Lever - Full Speed Ahead'. He then opens the Fire Plug full blast, and sets in motion the most ticklish part of my job. I must continue holding on to the pipe with both hands while counting the seconds until the rumbling, earth shaking buildup reaches the roar of a passing F-16 Jet Fighter, then I turn 'er loose and duck for cover.'

Ole choked up with emotion at this point and paused for a moment to regain his composure, then cleared his throat and continued, 'And Halvor, therein lies the problem I have with this job. For some unknown reason, after all my years of experience in this business, I still haven't developed the agility to jump back fast enough to escape that horrendous 'Cleanout Blast', and that in a Nut Shell is the reason I look and smell so bad.' Halvor shook his head slowly in both wonderment and utter disbelief as Ole told his story, and finally said, 'Ole that is absolutely amazing.' Then he paused to adjust the clothespin on his nose and said, 'May I ask you a personal question Ole?' Ole said, 'Sure Halvor, what is it?' Halvor looked Ole right in the eye and said very seriously, 'Ole, why in God's name don't you do something else for a living?' Ole jerked his head back as if he had just been slapped, then he straightened up on his bar stool, wiped his nose, stuck out his chest, and with an exasperated expression of outraged respectability on his face, said loudly, 'What!!! And give up the Contracting Business.'

27. Lena thought Ole was acting strangely when he came home from his last 'Viking Expedition' and decided to take him to a Doctor. Ole reluctantly agreed so they made an appointment to get to the root of the problem with their local Doctor who had never approved of any of Ole's shenanigans from the time they were in grade school together. Well, to make a long story short and after all the tests were completed, the Doctor told Lena that Ole not only had a terribly progressive and ultimately fatal disease commonly known as 'The Saint Vitas Dance' but that he also had picked up an incurable Venereal Disease of some kind. Lena was shocked and tearfully asked the Doctor for his best advice on how to handle the situation. The Doctor thought for a minute while he cleaned his glasses and said, 'If I were you Lena I'd take him as far out in the North Sea as I could and dump him overboard and then if by some slim chance he is able to find his way home, I sure as hell wouldn't sleep with him'.

28. Ole and Lena went to dinner at a fancy restaurant one Saturday night to celebrate Lena's 75th birthday and when the waiter asked Lena what she would like, she said, 'I want something special tonight. I'll have Prime Rib, Mashed Potatoes, and Broccoli'. The waiter said, I'm sorry Madam. We don't have any Broccoli'. Lena said, 'Alright then I'll have a New York Steak, a

Baked Potato and Broccoli.' The waiter said once again. 'I'm sorry Madam. We don't have any Broccoli. Lena studied the menu a third time and said, 'O.K. then, I'll have the Stuffed Alaskan Halibut., Scalloped Potatoes, and Broccoli.' The somewhat exasperated waiter said, 'Madam, how do you spell the TOM in Tomato? Lena said, 'T-O-M'. The waiter said, 'Correct, now how do you spell the POT in Potato? Lena said, p-o-t. The waiter said, 'Correct again, now how do you spell the FRIG in Broccoli?' Lena said, 'There's no FRIGGEN Broccoli'. The waiter said with a sigh, 'Madam, that's what I've been trying to tell you.'

29. As with most people who have lived beyond their 95th birthday, Ole's health began to disintegrate to the point Lena had to put him in a nursing home. Lars went to the nursing home to visit Ole one day and was shocked to see how badly Ole looked and couldn't help but notice how Ole seemed to 'fade out' every so often and slowly begin to lean over to one side until he would almost tip out of his chair. In fact, Lars thought he would probably have fallen over the side of his chair if a nurse hadn't caught him at the last moment and straightened him up again. Then Lars noticed after the nurse left, Ole would begin to lean slowly drift to the other side and the nurse would race back to tip him up again, and so on. This little drama played over and over again all during Lar's visit, and finally Lars said, 'Ole, I want you to tell me the truth. Are you getting good treatment here?' Ole said, 'Lars, this is an exceptionally well-run facility. The food is excellent, the staff is exceptionally well qualified and attentive to all our needs, and the place is kept exceptionally clean. I only have one complaint.' Lars said, 'And what is that Ole?' Ole looked wistfully at Lars and said, 'They won't let me lean over to pass wind.'

30. Lena's health finally reached the point where she too needed to go to a nursing home so she decided to move into the same home with Ole. Everyone who came to visit them always came away feeling very impressed with, not only the quality of the nursing home itself, but how happy all the 'patients' appeared to be. Ole, at age 97, was in a wheelchair when Lena joined him at the ripe old age of 93 with her newly acquired electric wheelchair, complete with mud flaps, Tule Fog lights and a 'cherry red' paint job. They were like two newlyweds again and used to spend many hours out on the front porch after supper listening to the birds sings and watching the beautiful sunsets. Ole would pull his wheelchair up alongside Lena's 'Hotrod' wheelchair on the porch after dinner, lay his hand in her lap, she would lay her hand in his lap, and they would close their eyes and quietly whisper tales of their younger happy bygone days to each other. This went on night after night for many months until one night Lena decided to have a second dish of ice cream and was late for her date with Ole on the front porch after supper. When she got there, much to her chagrin and complete surprise, there sat Ole and another woman with their wheelchairs parked side by side, hands in each other's laps, watching the sunset and mumbling sweet nothings to each other. Lena, as you can imagine, was shocked and angry with Ole and roared up to his wheelchair in her' Hotrod' and demanded, 'Ole, what has that women got that I haven't got?' Ole looked at her sleepily and said, 'She's got Palsy.'

31. Ole and Lena were vacationing at their cabin on a lake in northern Minnesota in the late fall of the year and were caught up in an early winter blizzard that lasted well over a week. This of course nearly ran them out of groceries and Ole became more and more concerned each day the storm continued. Finally, there was a lull in the storm and Ole figured this was the time to cross the lake, which looked frozen over, and buy new supplies at Lars's store. Well, to make a long story short, Ole drafted a long list of supplies and said, 'Lena, I vont yoo to take this grocery list across the lake to Lars Larsen's store and get these tings'. Lena, being the lovely person she was, said, 'Okay Ookey Ole, Jeg vil be gledder too, da valk viII do me gud'. Well, a couple hours later, Lars called Ole on the

telephone and in an aggravated tone of voice said, 'Ole, Jeg vont to know someting. Vy did yu make Lena valk all da vay over here across dat dangerous Lake to my store with a long list of groceries, and din't give her any money to pay for it?'. Ole said, 'I was worried de ice might be thin'.

32. Ole parked his pickup truck filled with cages of live chickens in front of the meat market, reached in the back and picked up a squawking flapping chicken in each hand and proceeded to walk into the store when 'Sven the Svede', who was leaning against a porch post watching Ole, said, 'Hey Ole, If I can guess how many chickens your carrying, can I have one of them?' Ole said, 'Sven, If you can guess how many chickens I'm carrying, you can have both of them'. Sven said, 'Six!!'

33. Ole and Lars went fishing on a lake in Northern Minnesota on a unusually hot day and since they only brought one six pack of beer with them, it wasn't long before it was gone and they were both very thirsty. Ole said, 'Lars, I'm so thirsty I could spit cotton balls.' But just then Ole felt a 'Strike' on his line and pulled in what appeared to be, not a fish but a mud-covered vase. And when he tried to wipe away some of the mud to free his fish hook, low and behold to everyone's amazement out popped a Genie who immediately said, 'Ole, you can have three wishes.' Well, like any sane person, Ole thought he was becoming delirious from thirst but decided to 'play along' and said, 'I don't need three wishes Genie, I only need one and that is you change this lake into a lake of good old fashioned homemade Beer. The Genie waved his wand, 'Zap' he disappeared, and all the water in the lake was turned to Beer. Well, as you can imagine, Ole was ecstatic and gave a war hoop with every coffee cup of beer he dipped from the lake while Lars just kept shaking his head back and forth and saying, 'Boy oh Boy!! Oh boy Ooh boy!! Ole you really done it this time.' Ole finally got a little peeved with Lars and his negative attitude and the 'miracle' in general, so he said sarcastically 'Just what do you mean I've really done it this time?' 'Wull,' Lars said, 'Now we'll have to piss in the boat.'

34. Ole and his Swedish friend Sven went ice fishing in Northern Norway one winter and after they had chopped their holes in the ice, set up their windbreaker huts and began to fish, Ole noticed Sven's earflaps on his cap were still tied up. Ole said, 'Sven, you and I have been fishing this same spot for eight years now and it's always been at least 10 below inside this hut, why is it you don't lower the ear flaps on your cap to protect your ears from frostbite?' Startled by this memory of a very traumatic experience, Sven choked back the emotion that still haunted him, coughed, wiped his nose and said, 'Ole, it's still very hard for me to talk about this but I suppose after eight years it's time I began a healing process of some kind and get on with the rest of my life.' Pausing for a sip of coffee, Sven continued, 'It happened right here the year before you and I started fishing together Ole, and it was a terrible tragedy and the most traumatic experience I've had in my life. Back in those early days I always wore my earflaps down but after that terrible tragedy I swore I'd never wear them down again.' At this point Sven again became very emotional so Ole out of respect paused for a few minutes before asking again softly, 'Tell me what happened on that day so long ago Sven?' After a few more minutes Sven answered in a small quivery voice and said, 'A guy in the next hut stepped outside his hut and shouted as loud as he could, 'Drinks are on the house', and I didn't hear him.'

35. Lena confided to her friend Helga that she had finally figured out after all these years, how to cure her nervous husband Ole of his disgusting habit of constantly chewing his fingernails. Helga said, that is wonderful Lena. How did you do it?' Lena said, 'I hid his false teeth.'

36. Ole and Lena were well into their Retirement years when they used to sit on the front porch in their Rocking Chairs and watch the world go by. One evening Ole began to feel a little amorous

and reached over and gave Lena a little pat on her knee and said, 'Lena, whatever happened to our sex relations?' Lena thought for a minute and said, 'I really don't know Ole. I don't think we even got a Christmas card from them last year.'

37. Ole and Lars went fishing in Canada one summer and came home with only one fish. Ole said, 'The way I've got it figured, that fish cost us over $1000.' Lars studied on that interesting bit of factual data for a minute and replied, 'Well, I'll say one thing for sure. At that price, it's a good thing we didn't catch any more than one fish'.

38. Ole and Lars were sitting at the Bar in 'Halvors Tavern' discussing tough jobs and Lars said, 'For my money, I think an undertaker trying to look sad at a ten thousand dollar funeral would be the toughest'

39. Later that night Ole and Lars were 'staggering' home from celebrating at 'Halvors Tavern' and ended up stumbling along a railroad track. After about a mile Lars said, 'This is the longest flight of stairs I've ever climbed in my life.' And Ole replied, 'That's for sure Lars, but these stairs don't bother me half as much as these low handrails'

40. The telephone rings at the FBI headquarters and the voice says, 'my name is Sven Svensen and I'm calling to report my neighbor, Ole Olsen. He's hiding marijuana in his firewood'. The FBI thanked Sven for his call and said they would look into it. The next day a Swat Team descends on Ole's home and searched the woodshed, and then proceeded with their axes to bust open every stick of wood. Finding no marijuana, they apologized to Ole and leave. Later the evening, Sven calls, 'Ole, did the FBI come and chop your firewood?' To which Ole replied, 'ya sure.' 'Good,' said Sven, 'Now it's your turn to call them. I need my garden spaded.'

41. A large Tour group composed of Swedes, Danes, Finns and Norwegians were on a Cruise when they were all shipwrecked together on a deserted island. By the time they were rescued, the Finns had chopped down all the trees, the Norwegians had built a fishing fleet, the Danes had established cooperatives and the Swedes were still standing around waiting to be introduced.

42. Ole and Lars went ice fishing one winter day and after they had setup their little 'wind breaker' hut and drilled a hole in the ice, a deep voice from above said, 'Deres no fish down der.' Ole looked at Lars and they both blinked, looked all around then skyward, shrugged their shoulders and moved their little hut over ten feet or so, and drilled another hole. Again, the same thing happened, the deep voice from above said, 'Deres no fish down der.' This time Ole looked up at the sky where the voice came from and said, 'Just who are you anyway?' And the booming voice said, 'I'm the Ice Rink Manager.'

43. Ole was temporarily out of work so he volunteered to help his buddy Torvold paint the interior of his home if he would furnish the materials and be given free rein of the house. So the first day Helga, Torvold's wife, went shopping and he was able to paint three rooms, including the bathroom, without interruption. Unfortunately, when Torvald came home from work that night he accidentally made a dirty handprint smudge on the newly painted bathroom wall. The next morning when Ole arrived with his ladder and brushes, Helga answered the door and said, 'Ole, I want you to come into the bathroom with me and I'll show you where my husband put his dirty hand last night'. Ole, taken aback somewhat said, 'Helga, I'm getting a little too old for that sort of thing but I'll be glad to split a beer with you in the kitchen'.

44. Sven, the Swede, walked into a business establishment owned by a Norwegian couple named Ole and Lena, and said he wanted to buy some Swedish Meatballs. Ole looked up from what he was doing, stared at Sven over his glasses for a moment and said, 'You must be Swedish'. Sven, somewhat taken aback said, 'Well yes, now that you mention it, it so happens that I am of Swedish Decent but I take that remark not only as Racist in nature but run a way Racial Profiling at its worst and it ticks me off that you would even ask a question like that in the first place.' Ole chuckled and said, 'Run that by me again?' Sven said 'If f had ordered Spaghetti, would you have asked if I were Italian?' Ole said 'No'. Sven asked again, 'If I had ordered Chow Mien, would you have asked if I were Chinese? Ole said 'No' Sven rose to his full height, stuck out his chest and said, 'Then why in God's name did you ask me if I were a Swede just because 1 asked to buy some Swedish Meatballs?' Ole said, 'This is a Hardware Store.'

45. Ole and Lars rented a fully equipped fishing boat from a local marina and went lake fishing one Sunday and as luck would have it, they had absolutely fantastic 'catch and releases luck'. In fact it was so good Ole turned to Lars and said, 'we've got to 'figger out' a way to mark this fishing hole so we can have this much fun again next year'. Lars studied on that comment until they ran out of bait and had to begin 'dragging up' and said, 'Ole, I've got the answer'. Ole chuckled and said, 'show me' and continued rigging for the trip back to the dock, while Lars sorted through his fishing gear for a small can of red paint and a brush. When he found them, much to Ole's amazement, he painted a red cross on the inside bottom of the boat together with the initials T.I.T.S. (this is the spot). As they motored back to the Dock, Ole kept staring at Lar's creation and finally shaking his head he said to Lars, 'I've seen you do a lot of damn dumb stupid things in my life but, by golly, this one takes the Cake'. Lars said, 'what's so stupid about it? If I remember right, you're the one that said to mark the spot'. Ole shook his head again and with a resigned look on his face and a disgusted tone in his voice, said, 'Don't you get it Lars, how do we know if we'll be able to rent this same boat again next year?'

46. Ole and Lars were eating their brown bag lunches in the park one day and a big dog came up to Ole and licked his hand so Ole gave him part of his sandwich. Lars asked, 'Does your dog bite Ole?' When Ole said 'No' Lars reached over to pet the dog and the dog bit him. Lars said '1 thought you told me your dog didn't bite'. Ole said, 'That's not my dog'.

47. Ole really did have a good dog who was also very smart. When Ole got her as a pup he recognized her superior intelligence right away and registered her at an advanced training school for gifted dogs under the name' Apprentice Swensen'. Well, it goes without saying, Apprentice graduated Cum Laude so as a reward for her straight 'A' Average through school, Ole promoted her to the name' Journeyman Swensen'. The dog of course was very appreciative and really worked hard for the next five or six years to show Ole her appreciation. In fact, she won almost every dog award ever given including several medals for heroism. All this time, Ole got to sit in the 'Crown Jewel Dog Owners Throne' and live high on the hog. Unfortunately, it all came tumbling down when Ole decided to give Journeyman another promotion and he named her 'Superintendent Swensen'. Now all she does is sit on her Ass and Bark.

48. Ole and Lena drove over to Fargo one weekend for a mini-vacation at a fancy new hotel and had a wonderful time until Ole went to the front desk to 'check-out'. Ole was shocked, to put it mildly, with the total amount of their bill and demanded an explanation and correction of the accounting errors' from the clerk at the front desk. Well, to make a long story short, the hotel Manager ended up trying to Referee the shouting match by asking Ole to point out the exact items

in the billing statement that he felt were unfair charges. Ole said, 'that's easy. Look at the first item 'Valet Parking$50.00'. We didn't use Valet Parking. The Hotel Manager said, 'It was there if you wanted it.' Ole said, look at the fifth item. 'Cleaning and Laundry - $50.00'. We didn't send out any Cleaning or Laundry. Again 'It was there if you wanted it.' Ole said, 'And this last item really burns me up - $100.00 for Room Service.' Lena and 1 never had or asked for any Room Service while we were here. The Hotel Manager shrugged his shoulders and said, 'It was there if you wanted it.' Well, as you can imagine, Ole was beside himself with frustration but tactfully resolved the matter by stating quietly, 'OK, I'll pay your bill but I'm deducting $200.00 for kissing my wife'. The Hotel Manager said, 'I never kissed your wife' and Ole said, 'She was there if you wanted to.'

THE END